THE
GOOD HOUSEKEEPING
ILLUSTRATED
COOK BOOK

THE
GOOD HOUSEKEEPING
ILLUSTRATED
COOK BOOK

Zoe Coulson

HEARST BOOKS   NEW YORK

Good Housekeeping Staff

Editor-In-Chief	John Mack Carter
Institute Director	Zoe Coulson
Food Department Director	Mildred Ying
Associate Director	Susan Deborah Goldsmith
Associates	Ellen Connelly
	Joyce A. Kenneally
Assistants	Pamela Madison Berger
	Diane Simone Dixon
	Kristen O'Brien
	Susan Plump
Special Projects Director	Lucy Wing

Designed and produced by Dorling Kindersley, Limited

Managing Editor	Amy Carroll
Managing Art Director	Stuart Jackman
Project Editor	Yvonne McFarlane
Art Editor	Debbie Mackinnon
Contributing Editors	Gill Edden
	Helena Radecka
Editors	Elizabeth Driver
	▉▉▉▉▉er
	▉▉▉▉▉s
	Wendy Hawley
	Isobelle Pover
Assistant designers	Nick Harris
	Gary Marsh

Published by Hearst Books
224 West 57th Street, New York 10019

Library of Congress Cataloging in Publication Data
Main entry under title:

The Good housekeeping illustrated cookbook.

Includes index.
1. Cookery, American. I. Coulson, Zoe. II Good
housekeeping.
TX715.G6237 1980   641.5   79-92727
ISBN 0-87851-037-0

Foreword

Cooking is easier when an expert shows, step-by-step, how to prepare a recipe. We planned this cookbook so that even a beginning cook could successfully use our recipes simply by following the diagrams of the steps along with the recipe itself. In this collection of recipes, we demonstrate all the fundamental cooking techniques, from folding in egg whites, to kneading bread, rolling piecrusts, decorating cakes and cookies, even boning certain cuts of meat and poultry. We've included recipes that are often considered difficult as well as everyday ones.

Since recipe selection and meal planning are easier when a picture shows exactly how the food will look, all of our recipes are shown in the large color picture index at the beginning of the book. You can browse through these pages and select the recipe best suited for your specific occasion. The color pictures also suggest how to garnish and serve the dish. Captions to the pictures provide information on the recipe seasonings, cooking methods used, time needed to prepare the food, number of servings and so on.

For the first time in a cookbook, menu planning is made easier as the pictures are arranged according to the course of the meal, starting with all the appetizers and going through to main dishes, salads, breads and desserts.

Many of these recipes are classics, direct from the pages of Good Housekeeping *Magazine. Others are newly developed for this book. All have had the careful scrutiny of Mildred Ying,* Good Housekeeping's *food editor. She and her staff checked and rechecked these recipes, trying several brands of ingredients, eliminating extra steps, using fewer utensils, confirming the cooking times, making sure they are nutritionally sound and, most importantly, that they tasted as good as they looked.*

Besides Mildred, Ellen Connelly of the food staff helped especially with the planning of the chapters; Lucy Wing helped with checking our how-to drawings and with many hours of proof-reading. Special thanks go to Amy Carroll, Stuart Jackman, Yvonne McFarlane and Debbie Mackinnon of Dorling Kindersley who devoted more than two years of work to the production of this book.

All of us hope that this unique cookbook provides the inspiration for many good-tasting, easily prepared meals to serve your friends and family.

Zoe Coulson, Director
Good Housekeeping Institute

Contents

BEFORE YOU COOK

Before you begin to prepare a recipe for the first time, read it through carefully to make sure that you have allowed enough preparation time. Before actually beginning cooking, assemble and measure all the ingredients and utensils needed for the recipe to be sure you have everything you need. Avoid substituting key ingredients, product forms (such as regular or instant) or package sizes, unless the recipe suggests an alternative. Be cautious, too, about doubling or halving any recipe: although some can be increased successfully, many more cannot. For best results, therefore, make up the recipe as given and, if necessary, repeat it until the required amount is obtained. Seasonings and spices can safely be varied according to personal taste, but it's always a good idea to follow the recipe directions exactly the first time.

Do as much advance preparation as possible before you start mixing and cooking. Measure and mix ingredients carefully, using the correct equipment (pages 10 to 13). Advance preparation of utensils is just as important as assembling ingredients: grease and flour a pan if directed and when a preheated oven is called for, turn it on when called for in the recipe, which will be at least 10 minutes before putting in the food to allow it to preheat to the required temperature. For best results, cook at the temperature specified in the recipe and to be on the safe side, start checking for doneness towards the end of cooking time.

And lastly, get into the habit of cleaning up as you work: this way you will be able to get things prepared faster and will be less likely to make a mistake.

HOW TO USE THIS BOOK
The Color Index pages in this book are organized in menu order, so all you have to do is choose a dish from each course and then turn to the appropriate page and find the recipe.

First, look at the Color Index and find a dish you'd like to prepare. The captions to the photographs will tell you what each recipe contains, how many it will serve, and the page on which it appears in the book.

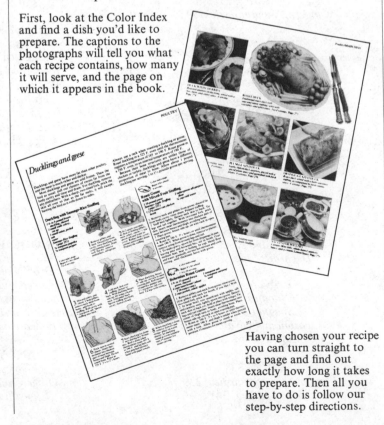

Having chosen your recipe you can turn straight to the page and find out exactly how long it takes to prepare. Then all you have to do is follow our step-by-step directions.

Measuring ingredients

USING THE CORRECT MEASURING EQUIPMENT

Accurate measurements are essential if you want the same good results each time you make a recipe.

For liquids, use a 1-cup liquid measuring cup which is also marked for smaller measurements. Two-cup and 4-cup liquid measuring cups are helpful for measuring larger amounts.

For dry ingredients, use a set of four graduated measuring cups, consisting of ¼-, ⅓-, ½- and 1-cup measures.

A standard set of ¼-, ½-, 1-teaspoon and 1-tablespoon measuring spoons is used for both dry and liquid ingredients.

MEASURING LIQUIDS

Always read the line on a measuring cup at eye level when checking the volume of liquid in a cup.

With the liquid measure on a level surface, slowly pour the liquid into the cup until it reaches the desired line.

If using measuring spoons, pour the liquid just to the top of the spoon without letting it spill over.

MEASURING SUGAR

Lightly spoon sugar into a graduated measuring cup and level off with the straight edge of a knife or spatula.

Brown sugar: Pack the sugar lightly into the cup with the back of a spoon, then level off; it will hold its shape when inverted from the cup.

MEASURING FLOUR

In the recipes in this book all the flours are measured and used straight from the flour package or canister.

Lightly spoon the flour into a graduated measuring cup or spoon; never pack flour down or shake or tap the side of the measuring cup.

Then, quickly level off the surplus flour in the measuring cup with the straight edge of a small kitchen knife.

MEASURING SHORTENING

Liquid shortenings such as salad oil and melted butter or margarine, can be measured in the same way as liquids, left. Measure shortenings such as lard, vegetable shortening, even peanut butter, as shown below.

Pack in the shortening firmly, right to the top of the measuring spoon or graduated cup.

Level off the shortening with the straight edge, not the flat side, of a knife or spatula.

MEASURING BUTTER OR MARGARINE

Each ¼-pound stick of butter or margarine measures ½ cup; the wrapping is usually marked off in table-spoons for measuring smaller amounts.

With a sharp knife just cut off the number of tablespoons needed, following the guidelines on the wrapper.

For butter or margarine not wrapped in this way, measure and level off as for solid shortening.

Choosing saucepans and skillets

RANGE-TOP POTS AND PANS

A good range-top pot or pan should spread heat evenly, be suitable in size and shape for the foods usually cooked, be simple in design, fit range-top or burner size, be durable and easy to clean.

Saucepans: These come with one long handle in sizes ranging from 1 to 5 quarts, usually with covers, to be used on top of the range.

Saucepot: Larger than a saucepan, this has 2 side handles and a cover.

Double boiler: This consists of 2 saucepans, one of which fits inside the other, and a lid. It is ideal for sauces.

Dutch oven: This is a heavy pot with a cover, often used for cooking pot roasts and stews.

HOW TO MEASURE PANS

Be sure your pans are the kind and size specified in the recipe. The size of some cookware is expressed in liquid measurement at its level full capacity.

Measure top inside of bakeware for length, width or diameter; measure perpendicular inside for depth.

Sizes for skillets or frypans and griddles are stated as the top outside dimensions, exclusive of handles.

SKILLETS, OMELET PANS, GRIDDLES

Look for skillets with flat bottoms and comfortable handles.

Skillet or frypan: This comes in sizes ranging from 7 to 12 inches in diameter, with or without a cover.

Omelet pan: Preferably with a non-stick coating, this has sloping sides and no cover.

Griddle: Available round, square or oblong in shape, this has a low rim but no cover. Most often used for pancakes.

MATERIALS FOR SAUCEPANS AND SKILLETS

Aluminum is moderately priced, lightweight, and a good conductor of heat. The heavier the gauge (thickness), the more durable. Aluminum may stain from minerals in water and in foods.

Stainless steel is exceptionally durable, easy to clean, and doesn't react with foods or detergents. Because stainless steel alone is a relatively poor conductor of heat, it is usually combined with other metals to provide more even heat distribution.

Cast iron is heavy to handle, but durable and inexpensive. Cast iron heats slowly and retains heat well. It tends to rust and also to discolor eggs and foods containing acid such as wine or vinegar.

Copper is good looking, very expensive, and an excellent conductor of heat. It should be heavy gauge and lined with another metal.

Glass ceramic's chief advantage is its multi-uses; it can go from freezer to top of range or oven to table.

Finishes and decorations, such as porcelain, acrylic enamel, nonstick coatings, etc., are often applied to cookware to provide color and ease of cleaning, to protect the base metal, and to reduce food sticking and reactions between food and the metal. Utensils that have nonstick finishes may be discolored by high temperatures and grease buildup. Overheating will give a permanent discoloration to a nonstick finish, but stains caused by grease buildup can usually be removed.

COLOR INDEX

Color index contents

APPETIZERS AND FIRST-COURSES
Appetizers 18
First-Course Soups 25

MAIN-COURSES
Soups 26
Eggs 28
Cheese 30
Pasta 32
Vegetables 33
Shellfish 34
Fish 36
Poultry 39
Meat 50
Salads 66

ACCOMPANIMENTS
Vegetables 67
Fruit 72
Rice 73
Pasta 74
Salads 75

BREADS
Yeast Breads 78
Quick Breads 84

DESSERTS
Pies 86
Cakes 90
Desserts 94
Soups 99
Fruit 100
Ice Cream and Sherbet 102

SNACKS AND SANDWICHES
Cookies 104
Candy 106
Sandwiches 108

BEVERAGES
110–112

FULL PAGE COLOR PHOTOGRAPHS
(Following page numbers listed below on left)

144 *Hard-cooked Eggs (recipe page 140), artistically decorated.*

Omelet Fines Herbes (page 146).

Baked Red Snapper with Oyster Stuffing (page 176).

Paella (page 165), Sangria (page 471), Tossed Salad with Lemony-Mustard Dressing (page 318).

208 Left: *Lamb Kabobs (page 228)*; center: *top loin beef steak*; right: *Pork-and-Onion Kabobs (page 213).*

Clockwise from top left: *Chinese Fried Rice (page 341)*; *Moo Goo Gai Pan (page 266)*; *Oriental Anise Beef (page 200)*; *Thin Pork Chops Orientale (page 214)*; *Stir-fried Vegetable Mix (page 299)*; *kiwi fruit (page 307).*

From top: *Herring Salad (page 324)*; *Open Sandwiches (page 458)*; *Danish Cucumber Salad (page 319)*; *platters of sliced cold roast beef, turkey and ham; beer, acquavit, assorted breads.*

From top, left to right: *kalbroulade, pepperoni, ham bologna, olive loaf, headcheese, salami, bologna, blutwurst, krakow, braunschweiger.*

304 *Mixed fresh fruits (pages 301–15).*

Clockwise from left: *Edam, Emmenthaler, Stilton, Port du Salut, cubes of Samsoe, Camembert, rounds of provolone; served with grapes, apples, pears, nectarines, dates, walnuts and wine.*

From top to bottom, left: *corkscrews, bowties, wheels, shells*; center: *spaghetti*; right: *rigatoni, tortellini, ditallini, ridged mostaccioli (pages 328–31).*

Left: *Eggplant Lasagna (page 336)*; right: *Cannelloni (page 335).*

368 *Ice cream parfaits (page 377).*

Clockwise from top: *Strawberries Romanoff (page 304)*; *Individual Strawberry Shortcakes (page 369)*; *strawberries with sugar and cream; Fruit Cream Tarts (page 358).*

Cake decorating ideas (pages 398–9).

Clockwise from top: *Citrus Pinwheels (page 411)*; *Spice Cookies (page 413)*; *Sugar Cookies (page 412)*; *Walnut Clusters (page 407)*; *Truffles (page 420)*; *Marzipan Fruits (page 419).*

16

APPETIZERS

COLD CANAPES (left to right): CAVIAR-EGG ROUNDS; SMOKED SALMON SQUARES; CURRIED-TUNA CANAPES; WATERCRESS CREAM-CHEESE TRIANGLES; TUNA-DILL ROUNDS; BLUE-CHEESE-AND-ASPIC CANAPES; ANCHOVY-CHEESE CIRCLES; ASPARAGUS CANAPES. Pages 115 to 116

PATE DE CAMPAGNE
Ground pork and chicken, cooked with mushrooms, sherry, herbs and bacon. 16 servings; day ahead. Page 122

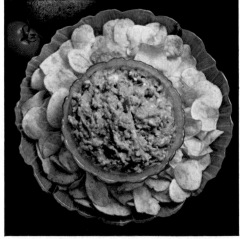

TIDBITS
CHINESE FRIED WALNUTS (left). *Early in day.* **CURRIED ALMONDS** *Early in day.* **CRISP CHEESE TWISTS** Page 114

PORK RILLETTES
Pork roast, cooked with marjoram and thyme, then shredded and served with French bread. 12 servings; early in day. Page 124

GUACAMOLE
Mashed avocado with tomato, onion, garlic, chilies and lemon juice, served with potato chips. 1 hour. Page 124

SPINACH PATE
Chilled loaf of spinach mixture, flavored with basil and cayenne, garnished with Carrot Flowers. 10 servings; day ahead. Page 122

CHICKEN-LIVER PATE
Cooked chicken livers, blended with onion, butter and brandy, then chilled. 12 to 16 servings; 3½ hours. Page 122

RADISH SPREAD (left). *15 minutes.* Page 294. **CHEESE SPREADS** (front, rear and right). Page 124

HOMEMADE PEPPER-HERB CHEESE
Homemade cheese seasoned with herbs and coated with cracked pepper. 5 days ahead. Page 123

GREEN-ONION DIP (left). *15 minutes.* Page 124. **BLUE-CHEESE DIP** (center). *15 minutes.* Page 124. **YOGURT-CHEESE DIP** *15 minutes.* Page 125

BAGNA CAUDA
Hot, creamy, garlic and anchovy dip, served with crisp vegetables. 12 servings; 1½ hours. Page 125

CHILI DIP WITH FRESH VEGETABLES
Chilled fresh vegetables served with a spicy, blended dip; early in day. Page 125

DUCK PATE IN SHERRY ASPIC
Duckling meat, pork, chicken livers, mushrooms and peas baked and topped with gelatin. 10 servings; day ahead. Page 123

PEPPERY DIP WITH VEGETABLES
Mayonnaise-based dip with chili sauce, curry and vinegar, served with cauliflowerets and carrot. Several hours ahead. Page 124

TUNA DIP
Tuna, blended with mayonnaise, anchovies, lemon juice and paprika and served with chips or crackers. Early in day. Page 125

STEAK BITES
Broiled top round steak pieces, served in a mustard-Worcestershire mixture. 20 to 24 servings; 2 hours. Page 119

SWEDISH MEATBALLS
Meatballs cooked in consommé and cream. 40 appetizers; 1 hour. Page 119

TINY HAM-STUFFED TOMATOES
Cherry tomatoes, filled with deviled ham, sour cream and horseradish. 20 appetizers; early in day. Page 126

SAUSAGE-STUFFED MUSHROOMS
Baked mushrooms stuffed with sausage, mozzarella cheese and bread crumbs. 30 appetizers; 1 hour. Page 117

MARINATED ARTICHOKE HEARTS AND MUSHROOMS *Artichoke hearts, mushrooms and pimentos marinated in spicy dressing. 8 servings; early in day. Page 319*

CHICKEN WING APPETIZERS
Chicken wings and green onions cooked in spicy soy sauce; served warm or chilled. 36 appetizers; 1 hour. Page 121

CAPONATA
Italian-style chilled vegetables in tangy dressing. 12 servings; 4 hours. Page 300

CELERY HEARTS VINAIGRETTE
Cooked celery in pimento marinade, served over romaine lettuce. 8 servings; 6 hours. Page 321

NIPPY CARROTS *10 to 12 servings; day ahead.* **PICKLED ONIONS** *16 servings; day ahead.* **HERBED MUSHROOMS** *12 servings; day ahead. All page 126*

SPANAKOPITAS
Phyllo triangles with chopped spinach, cheese and egg filling, baked until golden. 20 servings; 2¼ hours. Page 121

TOSTADA APPETIZERS
Corn tortilla pieces, topped with beef in spicy tomato sauce, with cheese, lettuce and olives. 36 appetizers; 1 hour. Page 118

ANTIPASTO
Platter: Selection of cold meat, fish and cheese on platter. Includes mortadella, ham, salami, sardines and provolone.
In bowls (left to right): MARINATED TUNA AND RED CABBAGE; MARINATED CAULIFLOWERETS; MARINATED EGGPLANT; MARINATED ITALIAN GREEN BEANS. *16 to 18 appetizer servings; early in day.* Page 126

APPETIZER AVOCADOS
Avocado slices with a warm, spicy sauce, garnished with crumbled bacon. 6 servings; 35 minutes. Page 303

HAWAIIAN FRUIT SALAD
Papayas and bananas in lime-flavored syrup, topped with coconut and ginger. 8 servings; 20 minutes. Page 322

STEAMED ASPARAGUS
Tender, cooked asparagus, topped with Hollandaise Sauce. 8 servings; 15 minutes. Page 278

PISSALADIERE
Sliced onions, anchovies, olives, oregano and Swiss cheese, baked on yeast-dough base until golden. 18 servings; 2¼ hours. **Page 117**

HOT APPETIZERS: *Individual Broccoli Quiches. Hot Mushroom Turnovers. Cheesy Shrimp Canapés. Pumpernickel-Muenster Triangles.* **Pages 116 to 118**

SAUSAGE EN CROUTE
Country-style pork sausages, baked in pastry. 32 appetizers; 2½ hours. **Page 121**

GRAVAD LAX
Scandinavian-style fresh salmon, coated with pepper and dill and served chilled, with Mustard Sauce. 12 to 14 servings; 2 to 3 days ahead. **Page 119**

RUMAKI
Marinated chunks of chicken liver and water chestnuts, wrapped in bacon and broiled. 18 appetizers; 1½ hours. **Page 121**

BRIE-IN-BRIOCHE
Whole brie cheese set into a brioche "basket" Served cold with grapes. 24 servings; day ahead. **Page 120**

BROILED GRAPEFRUIT
Halved grapefruits, dotted with brown sugar and butter and broiled until golden. 2 servings; 15 minutes. Page 307

GINGERED MELON WEDGES
Honeydew wedges, sprinkled with confectioners' sugar and ground ginger. 8 servings; 2 hours. Page 310

TORTELLINI IN CREAM SAUCE
Homemade pasta filled with chicken mixture. Served with cream sauce and cheese. 10 servings; 3 hours. Page 335

SCRAMBLED EGGS ARCHDUCHESS
Scrambled eggs with ham, mushrooms and asparagus spears, served on fried bread. 8 servings; 45 minutes. Page 144

STUFFED EGGS and VARIATIONS
Hard-cooked egg yolks, softened with mayonnaise and flavored. 12 halves; 45 minutes. Page 141

EGGS EN GELEE
Hard-cooked eggs garnished with olive and pimento pieces, served chilled in a gelatin mixture. 12 servings; day ahead. Page 141

PICKLED SHRIMP AND CRYSTALLINE ICE BOWL *Marinated shrimp, served in homemade ice bowl. 18 to 20 servings; day ahead. Page 120*

OYSTERS ON THE HALF-SHELL
Freshly-opened oysters served with lemon wedges on bed of crushed ice. 5–6 oysters each serving. Page 161

SHRIMP COCKTAIL WITH TANGY DIP
Chilled fresh-cooked shrimp served on lettuce leaves and topped with cocktail sauce. 6 servings; early in day. Page 164

23

COQUILLES ST. JACQUES
Scallops in a mushroom- and onion-mixture baked in a shell with buttered crumbs and cheese. 8 servings; 50 minutes. Page 163

BACON BROILED SCALLOPS
Bacon slices wrapped around scallops, broiled then seasoned. 8 servings; 20 minutes. Page 163

OYSTERS ROCKEFELLER
Oysters on the half-shell, baked with herbed spinach topping, bacon and grated cheese. 6 servings; 30 minutes. Page 161

QUENELLES IN WINE SAUCE
Poached, ground-fish fillets, served with vermouth sauce and topped with melted cheese. 9 servings; 3 hours. Page 182

FISH MOUSSE
Mixture of poached fish, cream and salad dressing, decorated with olives and pimentos. 8 servings; 6 hours. Page 183

PAN-FRIED OYSTERS
Shucked oysters sprinkled with crushed saltines and fried until golden. 6 servings; 20 minutes Page 161

MUSSELS MARINIERE
Mussels simmered in wine sauce, served garnished with parsley. 4 servings; 1¼ hours. Page 160

BLINI WITH CAVIAR
Tiny buckwheat pancakes, topped with sour cream and caviar. 16 to 24 servings; 55 minutes. Page 118

INDIVIDUAL ASPARAGUS SOUFFLES
Fresh cooked asparagus in a soufflé mixture, baked in ramekins until puffy. 6 servings; 1 hour. Page 149

FRENCH ONION SOUP GRATINEE
Sliced onions cooked in wine and broth; serve garnished with cheese slices on French bread. 4 servings; 45 minutes. Page 130

AVGOLEMONO
Cooked chicken broth and long-grain rice added with eggs and lemon juice, and topped with lemon slices. 6 servings; 30 minutes. Page 130

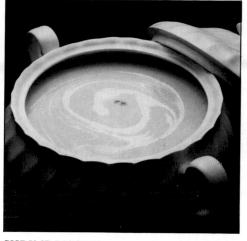

SHRIMP BISQUE
Shrimp, vegetables, white wine, rice, chicken bouillon and spices cooked together with cream added. 10 servings; 1 hour. Page 130

CREAM OF MUSHROOM SOUP
Fresh mushrooms blended with oniony-bouillon mixture and heavy cream added. 8 servings; 45 minutes. Page 131

GAZPACHO
Tomatoes, tomato juice, cucumber, onion, green pepper, and spice blended until finely chopped, chilled. 4 servings; 2½ hours. Page 129

CHILLED CUCUMBER SOUP
Cooked cucumbers, onions, and spices in chicken-broth base, chilled, blended and strained. 6 servings; 4 hours. Page 129

PEA SOUP
Lettuce, onions and seasonings blended with peas and garnished with mint leaves. 10 servings; 45 minutes. Page 130

JELLIED MADRILENE SUPREME
Two cans chilled, canned consommé madrilène broken up and topped with chopped grapes and chopped onion. 6 servings; early in day. Page 129

VICHYSSOISE
Chopped leeks cooked in butter and chicken stock, mixed with cream of potato soup and half-and-half. 4 servings; early in day. Page 129

SEAFOOD GUMBO
Spicy, Creole mixture of onion, shrimp and crab, served with a scoop of rice. 8 servings; 2 hours. **Page 136**

NEW ENGLAND CLAM CHOWDER
Traditional soup of chopped clams and potatoes with a milk base. 4 servings; 30 minutes. **Page 135**

MANHATTAN CLAM CHOWDER
Clams, bacon, potatoes and carrots in a classic herbed tomato base. 8 servings; 1½ hours. **Page 135**

BOUILLABAISSE, AMERICAN STYLE
Bass fillets, littleneck clams and shrimp in a highly seasoned tomato soup. 8 to 10 servings; 1 hour. **Page 136**

SHRIMP CHOWDER
Shrimp, cheese and cubed potatoes combined with milk and garnished with chopped parsley. 8 servings; 1 hour. **Page 136**

FISH CHOWDER
Chunks of flounder fillets, potatoes and onions simmered with herbs in creamy wine sauce. 8 servings; 50 minutes. **Page 135**

CHICKEN SOUP WITH RIVELS
Tiny dumplings added to a rich chicken and vegetable soup. 8 servings; 1½ hours. Page 134

HUNGARIAN GOULASH
Beef stew meat and veal heart cooked with potatoes and onions and seasoned with paprika. 12 servings; 2½ hours. **Page 133**

GERMAN LENTIL SOUP
Lentils, carrots, onions and celery simmered with leftover ham bone and bay leaves. 6 servings; 1½ hours. **Page 132**

NAVY BEAN AND BACON SOUP
Dry navy beans cooked with bacon, celery and tomatoes. 8 servings; 3½ hours. Page 135

SPLIT-PEA SOUP
Leftover ham bone simmered in water with spice bag, split peas, sliced carrots and onion. 6 servings; 1 hour. Page 133

HEARTY BORSCHT
Beets, chunks of beef and shredded cabbage served with a sour-cream topping. 4 servings; early in day. Page 132

CREAMY CHEDDAR-CHEESE SOUP
Shredded cheese stirred into milk and broth mixture, garnished with pumpernickel-bread cubes. 6 servings; 45 minutes. Page 134

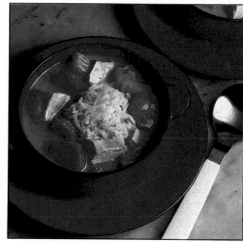

MULLIGATAWNY SOUP
Hearty Indian-style, curry-flavored soup, topped with rice. 6 servings; 1½ hours. Page 134

OLD-FASHIONED BEEF-VEGETABLE SOUP *Chunks of beef and zucchini added to a rich mixture of onion, celery, carrots, cabbage and beans. 10 servings; 1 hour.* Page 132

MINESTRONE
Classic Italian vegetable soup, including kidney beans, zucchini and tomatoes; serve with grated cheese. 8 servings; 2 hours. Page 133

HARD- AND SOFT-COOKED EGGS
Eggs cooked to taste. Solid yolk and firm white or barely-set yolk and creamy white. 1 or 2 eggs per person. Page 140

CREOLE EGGS
Hard-cooked eggs simmered in a spicy tomato-and-green-pepper sauce, spooned over rice. 4 servings; 45 minutes. Page 142

EGGS DIVAN
Stuffed eggs arranged with broccoli spears and topped with a cheese spread, baked. 3 servings; 1 hour. Page 142

SCRAMBLED EGGS
Two eggs, stirred with dash of water or milk, cooked in buttered skillet until set; served here on toast. 2 eggs per person; 5 minutes. Page 144

SHRIMP SCRAMBLE
Shrimp cooked with beaten eggs and served on toasted English muffin halves. 2 servings; 15 minutes. Page 144

FRENCH OMELET
Classic dish of beaten eggs, cooked and folded in half for serving. Serve plain or with a filling. 3 eggs per person; 30 minutes. Page 145

FRIED EGGS
Whole eggs cooked in a little butter and basted until of desired doneness. Two eggs per person; 5 minutes. Page 143

BAKED EGGS
Two eggs in a buttered ramekin, seasoned with salt, pepper and paprika before baking. 2 eggs per person. 30 minutes. Page 143

EGGS MORNAY
Eggs baked for 15 minutes in a mustardy cheese sauce. 4 servings; 40 minutes. Page 143

CLASSIC CHEESE SOUFFLE
Shredded Cheddar cheese and a light white sauce, baked until puffy and golden. 6 servings; 1¼ hours. Page 148

SPINACH SOUFFLE
Puree of chopped spinach and onion in a light white sauce, baked. 6 servings; 1½ hours. Page 149

SALMON PUFF
Canned salmon, stirred into a mustard and Worcestershire-flavored egg mixture before baking. 4 servings; 1¼ hours. Page 149

CHEESE-AND-BACON SOUFFLE
Crumbled fried bacon with cheese and egg-white mixture, baked until golden. 2 servings; 1¼ hours. Page 149

CHICKEN SOUFFLE
Chicken-and-mushroom mixture, baked until puffy and golden brown. 6 servings; 1½ hours. Page 149

PUFFY OMELET
Beaten egg whites folded with beaten yolks, then baked in the oven. Can contain a filling. 2 servings; 30 minutes. Page 146

POACHED EGG
Egg simmered a few minutes in water, drained and served immediately, shown on toast. 2 eggs per person; 5 minutes. Page 142

EGGS BENEDICT
Poached eggs with slices of ham or bacon on English muffin halves, topped with Hollandaise Sauce. 4 servings; 30 minutes. Page 142

SHRIMP CURRY CREPES (top). *1 hour.*
SPINACH CREPES *30 minutes.*
6 servings each. Page 147

29

CLASSIC SWISS FONDUE
Traditional Swiss cheese-wine mixture served hot at the table with bread chunks. 4 servings; 25 minutes. Page 155

CHEDDAR-CHEESE FONDUE
Thick Cheddar cheese variation for serving with French bread chunks. 6 servings; 30 minutes. Page 155

BAKED CHEESE FONDUE
Slices of white bread, topped with American cheese and egg mixture and baked until puffy. 4 servings; 2 hours. Page 155

RACLETTE
Baked cheese from Switzerland, served hot with potatoes, pickles and onions. 4 servings; 20 minutes. Page 154

ITALIAN CHEESE TOAST
Broiled, sliced, Italian bread, topped with mozzarella cheese and an anchovy-caper sauce. 4 servings; 25 minutes. Page 154

WELSH RABBIT
Thick, Cheddar-cheese-sauce topping for warm toast. 6 servings; 20 minutes. Page 154

WELSH RABBIT WITH BEER
American cheese, dry mustard and beer cooked until smooth and served over toast. 4 servings; 20 minutes. Page 154

SWISS-CHEESE-AND-TOMATO BAKE
Baked croutons topped with sliced tomatoes, shredded Swiss Cheese and a mustardy egg mixture. 4 servings; 1¼ hours. Page 154

QUICHE LORRAINE
Classic flan of cheese, bacon, eggs and cream baked in a pie shell. 6 servings; 1½ hours.
Page 156

ITALIAN CHEESE-AND-HAM PIE
Cottage, ricotta and Parmesan cheeses mixed with diced ham and eggs and baked in a two-crust pie. Serve cold and cut into wedges. 10 servings; early in day. Page 157

SWITZERLAND CHEESE-AND-ONION PIE *Chopped onion with Swiss cheese and egg mixture, baked in a piecrust. 6 servings; 1¼ hours.* Page 157

CHEESE-SPINACH-SAUSAGE PIE
Chopped sausage links with spinach, mozzarella and ricotta cheese, baked in a 2-crust pie. Serve hot or cold. 10 servings; 2 hours. Page 156

FRIED CHEESE PATTIES
Crumb-coated, Swiss-cheese mixture served with Spaghetti Sauce. 6 servings; early in day. Page 157

FONDUE BREAD
Yeast dough filled with Muenster cheese, topped with sliced almonds and baked until golden. 8 servings; 2 hours. Page 446

CHEESE PIZZA (left)
Yeast-dough base topped with tomato sauce and mozzarella cheese.
OTHER TOPPINGS (clockwise): *mushrooms, beef, sausage, onion, olives, green pepper, anchovies and pepperoni. 8 servings; 2½ hours.* Page 454

SPAGHETTI WITH FOUR CHEESES
Cooked spaghetti, topped with creamy sauce of mozzarella, fontina, provolone and Parmesan cheeses. 4 servings; 45 minutes. Page 331

BAKED MACARONI AND CHEESE
Elbow macaroni, covered with a thick cheese sauce, topped with buttered bread crumbs and baked. 4 servings; 45 minutes. Page 332

SKILLET MACARONI AND CHEESE
Elbow macaroni, cooked with onion and green pepper, then stirred with cheese and olives. 4 servings; 45 minutes. Page 332

BACON AND EGGS SPAGHETTI
Spaghetti, tossed with crisp bacon and onion, then stirred with beaten eggs and cheese. 4 servings; 30 minutes. Page 331

SPAGHETTI WITH HAM AND PEAS
Quick spaghetti dish, with ham, peas and cheese in a cream sauce. 4 servings; 45 minutes. Page 331

RAVIOLI and JUMBO RAVIOLI
Regular- and large-sized stuffed pasta in Marinara Sauce. 4 servings; 3 hours. Page 333

SPAGHETTI AND MEATBALLS
Small meatballs made of ground beef and bread crumbs in herbed tomato sauce accompany spaghetti. Serve with grated Parmesan cheese. 6 servings; 2¼ hours. Page 331

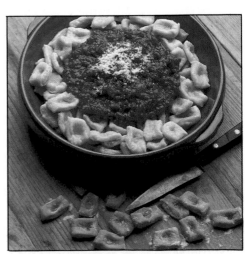

CAVATELLI WITH MEAT SAUCE
Small, homemade pasta, served topped with meat sauce and grated cheese. 4 servings; 4 hours. Page 332

HEARTY MANICOTTI
Manicotti shells, stuffed with cheese mixture, topped with sausage-beef sauce and baked. 8 servings; 2½ hours. Page 334

MANICOTTI
Cheese-stuffed pasta pancakes, baked in a ground veal and tomato sauce. 8 servings; 3 hours. Page 334

CANNELLONI
Squares of pasta, filled with meat, rolled and baked in cheese sauce. 8 servings; 2 hours. Page 335

LASAGNA
Wide noodles, layered with ricotta-cheese mixture, mozzarella and meat sauce, baked. 8 servings; 2½ hours. Page 336

VEAL LASAGNA
Creamy version of classic dish, with cubes of boneless veal baked in a sauce with lasagna noodles. 10 servings; 2½ hours. Page 336

EGGPLANT LASAGNA
Baked layers of noodles, bread-crumbed eggplant slices, tomato sauce and mozzarella cheese. 8 servings; 2¼ hours. Page 336

STUFFED SHELLS
Jumbo macaroni shells, stuffed with a cheese mixture, baked in herbed tomato sauce. 10 servings; 2½ hours. Page 334

PUERTO RICAN BEANS AND RICE
Pink beans cooked with salt pork and green pepper and flavored tomato sauce, served on rice. 6 servings; 3 hours. Page 279

EGGPLANT PARMIGIANA
Layers of sliced eggplant, tomato mixture, Parmesan and mozzarella, baked. 6 servings; 1½ hours. Page 299

33

PAELLA
Classic, Spanish, one-pan meal of seafood, sausage, chicken and saffron rice, served at the table. 8 servings; 2½ hours. **Page 165**

STEAMED CLAMS
In-shell clams steamed open and served with their own broth and melted butter. 6 servings; 1 hour. **Page 162**

CLAM FRITTERS
Chopped clams dipped in batter, fried until golden; served with Tartar Sauce. 4 servings; 45 minutes. **Page 162**

PAN-FRIED CLAMS
Cherrystone clams, dipped in egg and then bread crumbs and fried until golden. 6 servings; 30 minutes. **Page 162**

SCALLOPS BONNE FEMME
Scallops in a creamy wine sauce, topped with parsley and cheese and served with toast points. 4 servings; 40 minutes. **Page 163**

INDIAN SHRIMP CURRY
Fried shrimp in a spicy yogurt mixture, served over rice. 8 servings; 30 minutes. **Page 165**

SHRIMP SCAMPI
Broiled shrimp covered with garlic-flavored butter sauce, garnished with parsley and lemon. 6 servings; 20 minutes. **Page 164**

STIR-FRIED SHRIMP
Tender-fried large shrimp, served over Chinese cabbage, pea pods and straw mushrooms, in a soy- and ginger-flavored sauce. 8 servings; 1½ hours. **Page 165**

BROILED LOBSTER
Whole lobster, split open, brushed with melted butter and broiled. 1 small lobster per serving; 25 minutes. Page 169

LOBSTER THERMIDOR
Cooked lobster meat mixed with creamy sherry sauce. Mixture is returned to shells and broiled with cheese topping until hot. 4 servings; early in day. Page 169

BROILED ROCK LOBSTER TAILS
Broiled lobster tails, served with melted butter or favorite sauce. 1 large tail per serving; 15 minutes. Page 169

PAN-FRIED SOFT-SHELL CRABS
Cooked, whole crabs, served with butter sauce and lemon wedges. 4 servings; 15 minutes. Page 167

CRAB CAKES
Fried patties of cooked crab meat, bread crumbs and spices served with Tartar Sauce. 4 servings; 30 minutes. Page 167

CRAB IMPERIAL
Alaska King crab meat in sherry-egg sauce, baked in a casserole. 8 servings; 1 hour. Page 167

BLUEFISH WITH BUTTERY LEMON SAUCE *Broiled or grilled, pan-dressed fish, basted with lemon sauce during cooking. 8 servings; 20 minutes.* Page 174

BAKED RED SNAPPER WITH OYSTER STUFFING *Whole fish, with chopped oyster, celery and bread-cube stuffing. 8 servings; 1½ hours.* Page 176

35

POACHED SALMON WITH ASPIC
Whole salmon poached in wine and water. Serve with homemade aspic made from cooking liquid and herb mayonnaise. 10 to 12 servings; early in day. Page 176

BROILED SESAME TROUT
Marinated pan-dressed fish, basted with sesame-seed mixture while cooking. 6 servings; 4 hours. Page 174

PAN-FRIED SMELTS
Breaded pan-dressed smelts, fried until golden and served with lime wedges. 6 servings; 1½ hours. Page 175

STRIPED BASS WITH PUNGENT SAUCE
Chinese-style fried fish, served with spicy sauce and stir-fried vegetables. 6 servings; 1½ hours. Page 175

BROILER-BARBECUED FISH DINNER
Seafood-Barbecue Sauce-topped haddock or cod fillets, broiled with mushrooms, cheese and zucchini. 4 servings; 55 minutes. Page 177

FILLETS OF SOLE THERMIDOR
Sole or other white fish fillets poached in milk then broiled in a cheese and sherry sauce until golden. 8 servings; 45 minutes. Page 178

MEDITERRANEAN COD WITH VEGETABLES *Fried fillets, served with mixture of eggplant, onions, peppers and tomatoes. 8 servings; 1½ hours.* Page 178

SHRIMP-STUFFED ROLL-UPS
Sole or other fillets, stuffed with shrimp-and-mushroom mixture, simmered and topped with creamy sauce. 6 servings; 40 minutes. Page 180

BROILED TARRAGON FISH
Flounder or other fillets, broiled with tarragon dressing and served with lemon wedges and parsley. 4 servings; 20 minutes. Page 177

CLAM-STUFFED FILLETS
Flounder, ocean perch or other fillets, stuffed with minced-clam mixture and baked in custard cups. 4 servings; 50 minutes. Page 179

CODFISH STEW
Cod fillets, cooked in seasoned tomato-mixture with potatoes, bacon and onion. 4 servings; 55 minutes. Page 180

POACHED SOLE WITH HOLLANDAISE SAUCE *Sole fillets, simmered in court bouillon, topped with sauce and parsley. 4 servings; 50 minutes.* Page 179

BAKED SOLE WITH LEMON SAUCE
Cooked fillets, covered with thick lemon sauce and garnished with stuffed olives. 8 servings; 30 minutes. Page 179

CREAMED FINNAN HADDIE
Chunks of Finnan haddie simmered in cream sauce, served on toast, garnished with sieved egg yolk. 8 servings; 30 minutes. Page 180

FRIED FISH A LA MARGHERITA
Sole, flounder or other fillets, in herbed tomato sauce. 8 servings; 50 minutes. Page 178

FISH FRY
Batter-coated flounder, turbot or other fillets, fried until golden; serve with Sweet-Sour Sauce. 4 servings; 55 minutes. Page 177

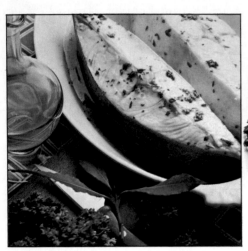

MARINATED SWORDFISH STEAKS
Fish steaks, covered in a tarragon-flavored vinegar marinade and broiled. 6 servings; early in day. Page 182

CHILLED SALMON STEAKS WITH MARINATED CUCUMBER *Cooked steaks served with thin cucumber slices and Green Mayonnaise. 6 servings; 4 hours.* Page 181

HALIBUT STEAK WITH EGGPLANT SAUCE *Broiled, butter-basted fish, served with simmered eggplant sauce. 6 servings; 30 minutes.* Page 181

CODFISH STEAK
Fried steaks accompanied by cooked spinach and mushroom mixture. 4 servings; 40 minutes. Page 182

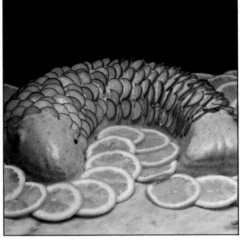

COLD SALMON MOUSSE
Molded canned salmon, mayonnaise, gelatin, flavorings and cream, decorated with radish slices. 6 servings; 4 hours. Page 184

SALMON BURGERS
Seasoned and fried canned, salmon patties, served with Hollandaise Sauce on English muffins. 6 servings; 45 minutes. Page 183

TUNA PIE
Tuna, broccoli, water chestnuts, mushrooms and cheese mixture, topped with pastry and baked. 6 servings; 1½ hours. Page 184

TUNA TETRAZZINI
Cooked spaghetti in cheese sauce, mixed with canned tuna before baking. 8 servings; 1 hour. Page 184

TUNA LOAF WITH CUCUMBER SAUCE
Canned-tuna and saltine mixture, baked in loaf pan and topped with sauce. 8 servings; 1½ hours. Page 183

ROAST TURKEY WITH MOIST BREAD STUFFING AND GIBLET GRAVY *Turkey with homemade stuffing, roasted until golden and served with Giblet Gravy. 12 to 16 servings; 6½ hours. Page 249*

TURKEY MOLE
Traditional Mexican dish of cooked turkey, topped with chocolate-sesame-seed sauce, garnished with avocado. 12 servings; 3 hours. Page 267

TURKEY BREAST WITH GLAZES
Roast turkey breast, brushed with tangy Chutney Glaze towards end of cooking. 12 to 16 servings; day ahead. Page 250

SAUCY TURKEY WINGS
Turkey wings braised in celery sauce until tender. 6 servings; 2½ hours. Page 260

TURKEY ROLL WITH SPINACH STUFFING *Boned turkey breast, cut in half and rolled jelly-roll fashion around stuffing before roasting. 16 servings; 3 hours. Page 251*

TURKEY SAUSAGE KABOBS
Chunks of marinated turkey breast, brown-and-serve sausages, canned pineapple chunks and green onions. 6 servings; 1 hour. Page 263

TURKEY-ROQUEFORT SALAD
*Cooked turkey mixed with Roquefort cheese
and sour cream, served on a canned peach-half.
6 servings; early in day.* Page 269

CHICKEN SALAD
*A simple salad of chicken, celery, green pepper
and onion, coated with a mayonnaise dressing.
6 to 8 servings; early in day.* Page 269

TURKEY IN CHAMPAGNE SAUCE
*Braised turkey meat, in a mushroom, half-and-
half and champagne sauce, served with toast
flowers. 6 servings; 2 hours.* Page 260

TURKEY-TAMALE CASSEROLE
*Mexican-style dish of braised turkey with
kidney beans, chili and herbed cornmeal-batter
topping. 6 servings; 4 hours.* Page 260

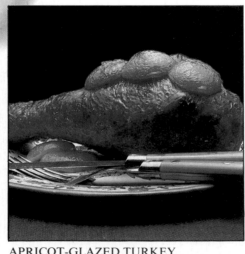

**APRICOT-GLAZED TURKEY
DRUMSTICKS** *Canned apricot halves and
an apricot-preserve glaze on turkey
drumsticks. 4 servings; 2½ hours.* Page 260

**TURKEY BREAST GLACE WITH
SHERRY ASPIC** *Chilled roast turkey breast,
coated with creamy glaze, decoratively garnished. 10 to 15 servings; day ahead.* Page 250

40

CHICKEN CORDON BLEU
Boned chicken breasts, filled with sliced Swiss cheese and cooked ham and simmered in wine sauce. 6 servings; 1¼ hours. Page 257

HERB-ROASTED CAPON
Unstuffed bird, lightly covered with a herbed seasoning and left overnight before roasting. 8 servings; day ahead. Page 251

CHICKEN DINNER WITH SOUR-CREAM GRAVY *Braised chicken with carrots and celery served with gravy and hot rice. 4 servings; 45 minutes. Page 255*

CHICKEN OPORTO
Portuguese dish of boneless chicken breasts, braised in white port with mushrooms and cream. 4 servings; 35 minutes. Page 257

CHICKEN PAPRIKA WITH SPAETZLE
Small, homemade dumplings served with paprika-flavored chicken pieces in a creamy sauce. 6 servings; 45 minutes. Page 254

CHICKEN CURRY, SOUTHERN STYLE
Chicken pieces in a curried sauce with almonds and currants, shown with rice. 4 to 5 servings; 1 hour. Page 255

CHICKEN SEVILLE
Richly-herbed chicken pieces cooked in a vegetable mixture and finished with olives. 6 servings; 1½ hours. Page 256

NUT-STUFFED CHICKEN BREASTS WITH CREAMY GRAVY *Baked chicken breasts stuffed with chopped peanuts. 6 servings; 2 hours. Page 252*

BEER-BATTER CHICKEN
Chicken fried in batter; served here with French fries. 4 servings; 55 minutes. Page 264

ROTISSERIED CHICKEN
Whole chicken, grilled on a spit and basted during cooking with melted butter. Allow ¾ to 1 pound per person. Page 261

FESTIVE CHICKEN WITH ASPARAGUS
Chicken breasts braised with asparagus in cream-of-chicken soup, white wine and blue cheese. 6 servings; 1½ hours. Page 259

CHICKEN CHORIZO
Spicy dish of braised chicken pieces with ham, Spanish sausage and garlic. 6 servings; 1 hour. Page 256

CHICKEN WITH CUCUMBERS
Simmered chicken quarters with cucumber, mushroom and sour cream sauce, topped with cucumber. 4 servings; 1¼ hours. Page 255

SOUR CREAM CHICKEN ENCHILADAS
Fried tortillas, filled with chicken meat, chilies and mushrooms, baked in sour cream and topped with cheese. 6 servings; 1 hour. Page 270

SAVORY CHICKEN
Chicken quarters marinated with garlic, dry mustard and Worcestershire; can be broiled or grilled. 8 servings; 3½ hours. Page 261

CHICKEN CACCIATORE
Classic Italian dish of chicken with onions, tomatoes, green pepper and herbs, in red wine. 4 servings; 1 hour. Page 255

PARTY SHRIMP AND CHICKEN
Chicken breasts braised in a rich sauce of shrimp, tomatoes, port wine and herbs. 6 servings; 45 minutes. Page 258

CHICKEN PERIGORD-STYLE
Boned chicken breasts simmered in a rich, fresh mushroom sauce. 8 servings; 1 hour.
Page 257

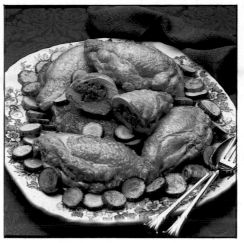

CHICKEN BREASTS WITH SAUSAGE-WALNUT STUFFING *Stuffed chicken breasts simmered in broth, served with sautéed zucchini. 8 servings; 1½ hours. Page 258*

CHICKEN DELHI
Roast spiced chickens, basted during cooking with a yogurt sauce; served over rice. 8 servings; 2½ hours. Page 251

CHICKEN OROBIANCO
Tender chicken breasts teamed with robust pork sausages and cooked with mushrooms and white wine. 8 servings; 1¼ hours. Page 259

CHICKEN WITH ENDIVES
Braised, boned chicken breasts and endives, topped with cheese sauce and buttered crumbs. 4 servings; 45 minutes. Page 257

ROAST CHICKEN WITH SAUSAGE-APPLE STUFFING *Tender roast chicken, stuffed with sausage-apple mixture. 6 servings; 4 hours. Page 251*

CHICKEN AVGOLEMONO
Boneless chicken breasts and sliced zucchini served with egg-yolk and lemon sauce and Orzo-Rice Pilaf. 8 servings; 1 hour. Page 259

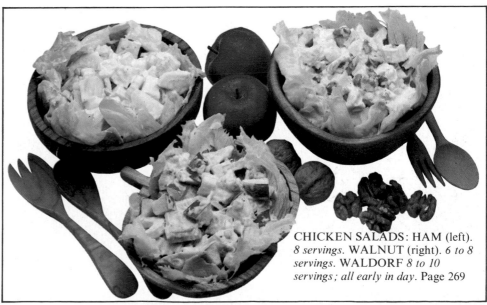

CHICKEN SALADS: HAM (left). *8 servings.* **WALNUT** (right). *6 to 8 servings.* **WALDORF** *8 to 10 servings; all early in day.* Page 269

PAN-FRIED CHICKEN WITH CREAM GRAVY *Chicken pieces shallow-fried in oil until the skin is crisp, served with a milk-based gravy. 4 servings; 1 hour.* Page 263

BAKED CHICKEN *Chicken, dipped first in a flour coating, then melted butter or margarine, and baked. 8 servings; 1 hour.* Page 252

SIMMERED CHICKEN *Stewing chicken in a vegetable seasoned broth, served here with dumplings. 6 servings; 3 hours.* Page 267

COQ AU VIN *Classic French dish of chicken pieces, mushrooms and onions braised in herbs and red wine. 4 servings; 1½ hours.* Page 267

CHICKEN IMPERIAL *Chicken breasts, braised in heavy cream and dry sherry, with mushrooms and minced onion. 8 servings; 1¼ hours.* Page 258

CHEESE AND ANCHOVY BROILED CHICKEN BREASTS *Cheese-topped chicken breasts stuffed with an anchovy mixture. 6 servings; 1 hour.* Page 263

CHICKEN BREASTS WITH ARTICHOKE HEARTS *Baked chicken in a creamy, brandy and lemon sauce, finished with artichoke hearts. 6 servings; 1½ hours.* Page 259

ARROZ CON POLLO *Rice and chicken in a Spanish-style dish with tomatoes, pimentos, olives, sausages and peas. 8 servings; 1¾ hours.* Page 254

CHICKEN KIEV *Boned chicken breast stuffed with chive and parsley butter then deep-fried in a crisp bread-crumb-coating. 6 servings; 3 hours.* Page 265

ROAST DUCKLING MONTMORENCY
Roast quartered duckling, served with a hot cherry and claret sauce. 4 servings; 2½ hours. Page 274

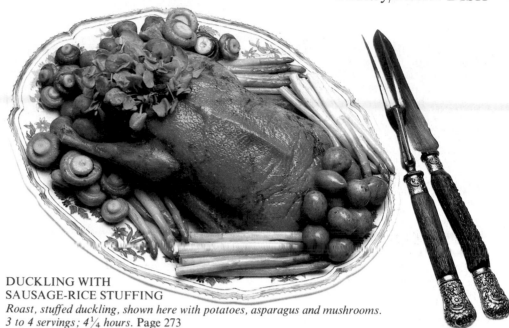

DUCKLING WITH SAUSAGE-RICE STUFFING
Roast, stuffed duckling, shown here with potatoes, asparagus and mushrooms. 3 to 4 servings; 4¼ hours. Page 273

ELEGANT DUCKLING A L'ORANGE
Roast cut-up duckling, served French-style with homemade orange sauce and garnished with orange slices. 4 servings; 2½ hours. Page 274

PLUM-GLAZED DUCKLINGS
Quartered duckling baked with garlic and glazed with a spiced plum sauce. 8 servings; 2¼ hours. Page 276

GLAZES FOR POULTRY
Wine or quince jelly combined with butter and spices make a tasty coating to brush on poultry in last 10 to 20 minutes. Page 276

STUFFINGS FOR POULTRY (from left): CHESTNUT STUFFING
Serve with turkey. 1¼ hours. RICE-RAISIN STUFFING Made with crumbled bacon, raisins, celery and onions. 45 minutes. SAUSAGE-APPLE STUFFING. 45 minutes. All page 253

SAUCES FOR POULTRY:
CURRANT-MINT SAUCE. CRANBERRY-ORANGE SAUCE. LEMON SAUCE.
All made in 10 to 20 minutes. Page 276

SESAME CHUCK STEAK
Chuck blade steak, marinated in sesame-seed mixture, broiled and served with cooked sliced onions. 8 to 10 servings; early in day. Page 198

STANDING RIB ROAST WITH YORKSHIRE PUDDING
Beef rib roast small end, served with individual Yorkshire Puddings and Horseradish Sauce. 14 to 18 servings; 2 to 4 hours. Page 191

NEW ENGLAND "BOILED" DINNER
Simmered boneless fresh beef brisket with cooked vegetables. 14 to 16 servings; 3½ hours. Page 205

CREAMY TOP BLADE STEAKS
Braised steaks served with noodles and topped with dilled sour-cream sauce. 4 to 6 servings; 1¾ hours. Page 200

BARBECUED POT ROAST
Beef chuck 7-bone pot roast braised in a spicy tomato and onion sauce. 10 to 12 servings; 4 hours. Page 195

CALIFORNIA BEEF STEW
Stewed beef chunks, with onions, mushrooms, peas and olives. 6 to 8 servings; 3 hours. Page 203

BRAISED STEAK CAESAR-STYLE
*Beef eye round steaks, braised in
Worcestershire-anchovy sauce and served on
toast. 4 servings; 1¾ hours.* Page 201

LONDON BROIL
*Seasoned flank steak, broiled with halved
tomatoes and mushrooms. 4 servings;
30 minutes.* Page 196

MEAT LOAF (top) *and variation,*
PINEAPPLE MEAT LOAF. *Each 8 servings;
2 hours.* Page 206

**FILETS MIGNONS WITH MUSTARD-
CAPER SAUCE** *Fried beef tenderloin steaks,
served with creamy, vermouth-flavored mustard
and caper sauce. 6 servings; 30 minutes.*
Page 195

**POT ROAST WITH SWEET AND SOUR
CABBAGE** *Braised beef chuck eye roast,
served with cooked red cabbage. 10 servings;
3½ hours.* Page 194

ZITI BAKE
*Baked macaroni, ground beef, ricotta and
Spaghetti Sauce, topped with mozzarella
cheese. 8 servings; 1½ hours.* Page 209

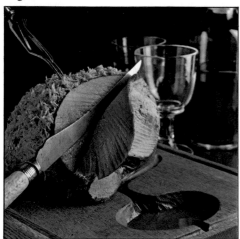

VEGETABLE-TOPPED ROAST BEEF
*Beef round tip roast, topped with shredded
carrots and celery and served with wine gravy.
16 to 18 servings; 3½ hours.* Page 191

CELERY-STUFFED FLANK STEAK
*Flank steak, rolled jelly-roll fashion around
fresh celery stuffing and braised. 6 to 8
servings; 2½ hours.* Page 201

CARBONNADE OF BEEF
*Beef chuck eye steaks cooked in beer with
onions and garlic. 8 servings; 1½ hours.*
Page 199

HAMBURGERS
Pan-broiled, seasoned ground beef patties, served in a bun with catchup. 4 servings; 20 minutes. **Page 205**

MUSHROOM SHERRY POT ROAST
Beef chuck shoulder pot roast, braised with mushrooms and sherry, garnished with mushrooms. 8 to 10 servings; 3 hours. **Page 195**

STEAK DIANE
Rib eye steaks, flamed with brandy and served with a sherry, shallot and chive sauce. 4 servings; 20 minutes. **Page 196**

INDIVIDUAL BEEF WELLINGTONS
Packages of cut-up beef rib eye roast topped with mushrooms and onion baked in pastry. 10-servings; early in day. **Page 192**

LEMON BARBECUED MEAT LOAVES
(top). 6 servings; 1 hour.
COUNTRY MEAT LOAF *8 servings; 2 hours.* **Page 207**

CHILI CON CARNE
Hearty ground beef, kidney bean and chili mixture with accompaniments and bread. 8 to 10 servings; 1½ hours. **Page 209**

MEXICAN-STYLE POT ROAST
Beef chuck arm pot roast, cooked with green and hot peppers, corn and tomato puree. 10 to 12 servings; 2¾ hours. **Page 194**

PRESSURE-COOKED BEEF STEW
Marinated beef chunks, cooked quickly in pressure cooker with salt pork and vegetables. 6 to 8 servings; early in day. **Page 203**

MARINATED PORTERHOUSE STEAK
Beef loin porterhouse steak, marinated in red wine and then broiled. 10 to 12 servings; early in day. **Page 196**

**CUBED STEAKS WITH FRESH
TOMATO SAUCE** *Cooked tomato and green
onion mixture spooned over pan-fried, cubed
beef steaks. 6 to 8 servings; 45 minutes.
Page 198*

ORIENTAL ANISE BEEF
*Boneless chuck shoulder steak, braised with
soy-sauce, anise seed and green onions.
6 to 8 servings; 2¼ hours. Page 200*

DILLED MEATBALLS; *6 servings; 1 hour.*
BURGUNDIED MEATBALLS; *6 servings;
45 minutes.* **MUSHROOM-CHEESE
MEATBALLS**; *8 servings; 1 hour. Page 208*

STEAK MEDICI
*Pan-fried boneless top loin steaks with
mushrooms, in port wine. 4 servings;
25 minutes. Page 197*

TERIYAKI BEEF KABOBS
*Marinated chunks of top round steak broiled
with fresh pineapple chunks. 6 to 8 servings;
4 hours. Page 198*

PEPPER BEEF POT ROAST
*Beef chuck underblade pot roast, braised in
sherry and soy sauce, served with cooked
peppers. 8 to 10 servings; 3 hours. Page 194*

BEEF BOURGUIGNON
*Beef chunks stewed with small white onions,
garlic, carrot and mushrooms in red Burgundy
and brandy. 10 servings; 4½ hours. Page 202*

HERBED SHORT RIBS
*Beef chuck short ribs, baked in a thyme and
tomato sauce. 4 servings; 3 hours. Page 204*

STEAK AND KIDNEY PIE
*Chunks of beef and kidney in a rich wine
gravy, topped with a homemade piecrust and
baked. 8 to 10 servings; 3¾ hours. Page 203*

BARBECUED SHORT RIBS
Precooked beef ribs, grilled with spicy catchup sauce. 6 to 8 servings; day ahead. Page 204

SAUERBRATEN
Marinated bottom round roast, cooked with vegetables and served with gravy. 14 to 16 servings; 2 days ahead. Page 193

SPICY BEEF CHUCK STEAK
Chuck under-blade steak, braised in steak sauce, brown sugar, mustard and lemon juice. 8 to 10 servings; 2 hours. Page 199

DEVILED ROUND STEAK
Breaded beef top round steak, grilled until golden. 10 to 12 servings; 1½ hours. Page 197

WHOLE STUFFED CABBAGE
Cooked cabbage shell, filled with spicy ground-beef and rice mixture and baked with tomato sauce. 6 servings; 3 hours. Page 209

BEEF WITH LEEKS AND CARROTS
Chuck 7-bone steak, braised with leeks and carrots. 6 to 8 servings; 2 hours. Page 199

BEEF STEW
Chunks of meat, carrots, potatoes and peas simmered in bouillon. 8 to 10 servings; 3½ hours. Page 202

BEEF STEAK STROGANOFF
Chuck top blade boneless steaks with onion and mushrooms, served with noodles and sour cream sauce. 1¾ hours. Page 201

COUNTRY POT ROAST
Beef chuck cross rib pot roast braised in tomato juice with vegetables, served with gravy. 20 servings; 5 hours. Page 192

FRUITED POT ROAST
Boneless beef chuck eye roast, braised with apple cider, cloves, dried apricots and prunes. 12 to 14 servings; 4 hours. Page 193

BEEF SHANKS WITH VEGETABLES
Beef shanks, stewed in tomato soup with carrots, onions and lima beans. 8 servings; 4 hours. Page 204

CHATEAUBRIAND
Broiled beef tenderloins, served with ARTICHOKES BEARNAISE *(page 277) and sautéed mushrooms, carrots and celery. 8 servings; 1½ hours.* Page 195

BAKED POT ROAST WITH VEGETABLES *Beef round rump roast, braised in oven with parsnips and lima beans. 8 to 10 servings; 4 hours.* Page 193

SWISS STEAK WITH TOMATO
Chuck arm steak, braised with onions and green pepper in tomato sauce. 8 to 10 servings; 2½ hours. Page 200

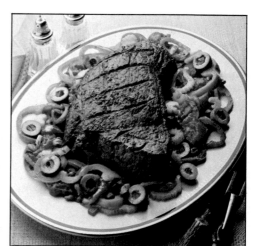

CONTINENTAL BEEF STEAK
Broiled beef top round steak, flavored with herbs; served with peppers, olives, tomatoes and capers. 12 servings; 1 hour. Page 197

ROAST PORK
Baked loin center rib roast, served with pan gravy. 8 servings;
2 hours. **Page 212**

BREADED PORK TENDERLOIN
"Butterflied" tenderloin, flavored and fried.
3 servings; 25 minutes. **Page 213**

PRUNE-STUFFED ROAST PORK
Loin center rib roast stuffed with prunes,
roasted and served with pan gravy. 12 to 14
servings; 3 hours. **Page 212**

BARBECUED SPARERIBS
Precooked pork ribs, grilled over coals and
brushed with chili-flavored sauce. 4 servings;
day ahead. **Page 216**

STUFFED PORK CHOPS WITH APPLE
DRESSING *Loin rib chops stuffed with*
herbed apple mixture and baked in the oven.
6 servings; 2½ hours. **Page 215**

PORK-RIB DINNER
Country style ribs, baked with cabbage,
potatoes, onions and carrots in apple juice.
8 servings; 2½ hours. **Page 216**

BARBECUED PORK IN BUNS
Fried pork loin sirloin cutlets served in toasted
buns, topped with catchup sauce. 6 servings;
20 minutes. **Page 214**

PORK BACK RIBS WITH SAUERKRAUT
Loin back ribs, browned and simmered until
tender with sauerkraut. 6 servings; 2¼ hours.
Page 216

HOCKS AND NAVY-BEAN STEW
Pork hocks, simmered with navy beans, onions and carrots, flavored with a clove-studded onion. 6 servings; 3½ hours. Page 217

BURRITOS
Flour tortillas filled with cooked pork and beef mixture, beans and cheese. 10 servings; 2½ hours. Page 217

STIR-FRIED PORK AND VEGETABLES
(left). 6 servings; 30 minutes. Page 213.
THIN PORK CHOPS ORIENTALE
6 servings; 4½ hours. Page 214

ORANGE PORK CHOPS
Simmered loin rib chops served with spiced orange sauce. 6 servings; 55 minutes. Page 215

PORK ROAST WITH PIQUANTE SAUCE
Pork loin blade roast, baked with a spicy tomato sauce. 10 to 12 servings; 3 hours. Page 213

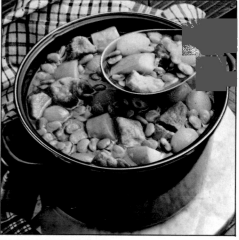

EASY PORK STEW
Pork cubes, baked with onions, lima beans and yellow squash. 10 to 12 servings; 2½ hours. Page 217

PORK-AND-ONION KABOBS
Marinated cubes of shoulder blade roast, grilled with onions. 4 servings; 4½ hours. Page 213

SKILLET-BRAISED PORK CHOPS
Seasoned chops, braised until tender; serve with pan gravy or cook with other seasonings. 4 to 6 servings; 1 hour. Page 214

GRILLED PORK STEAKS WITH PINEAPPLE *Shoulder blade steaks, marinated in pineapple mixture and grilled with pineapple slices. 6 servings; 4 hours. Page 215*

57

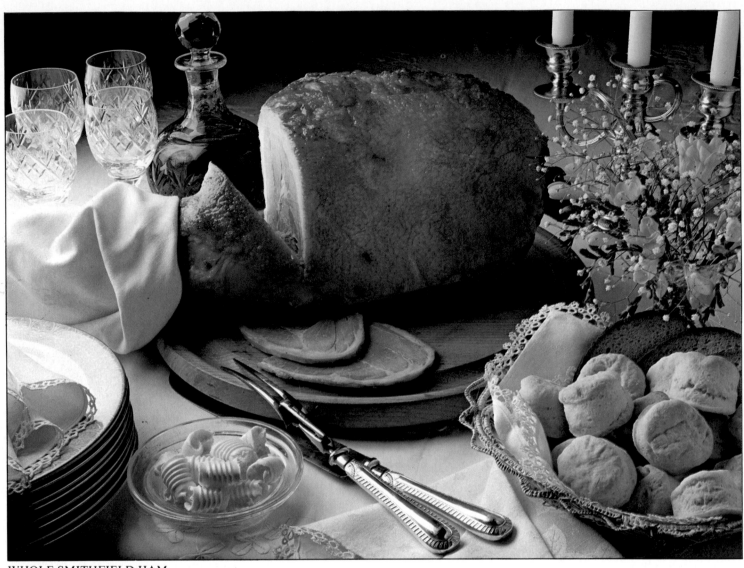

WHOLE SMITHFIELD HAM
*Simmered whole Smithfield ham, brushed with corn syrup and baked in the oven until glazed;
serve whole ham with biscuits and bread for a party, letting each guest help himself.
40 to 60 party servings; day ahead.* Page 221

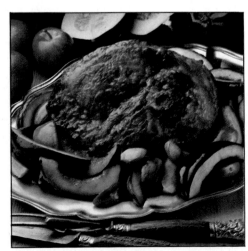

GLAZED HAM PLATTER
*Baked ham, glazed with horseradish and
mustard sauce, served with apples and acorn
squash. 15 to 18 servings; 3 hours.* Page 220

**BARBECUED CANNED HAM AND
PEACHES** *Canned ham, baked with fresh
peaches and homemade barbecue sauce.
10 to 12 servings; 1¾ hours.* Page 220

**SMOKED PORK WITH SWEET
POTATOES** *Pork shoulder roll coated with
brown sugar mixture, baked with canned sweet
potatoes. 8 to 10 servings; 2 hours.* Page 222

**PINEAPPLE-GLAZED BAKED HALF
HAM** *Baked, smoked half ham, with
pineapple and brown sugar glaze. 15 to 20
servings; 2¾ hours.* Page 220

FRUIT-SAUCED HAM SLICES
*Slices of ham, simmered with orange juice,
dried apricots and prunes. 6 servings;
30 minutes.* Page 222

CHOUCROUTE GARNI
*Simmered smoked and fresh pork, onions,
potatoes, bratwurst and sauerkraut served
together. 16 to 20 servings; 3 hours.* Page 222

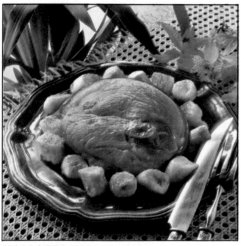

HAM STEAK HAWAIIAN
*Smoked ham center slice and bananas, cooked
in brown sugar and vinegar sauce. 4 to 6
servings; 30 minutes.* Page 221

LEMONY HAM STEAKS
*Ham slices, broiled with a fresh-lemon and
mustard glaze. 6 to 8 servings; 20 minutes.*
Page 222

GLAZED HAM LOAF
*Ground ham, carrot and onion loaf, baked with
pineapple glaze and decorated with pineapple
slices. 4 to 5 servings; 1¾ hours.* Page 223

BAKED PICNIC
*Baked smoked pork shoulder picnic, glazed and
decorated with oranges and cloves.
10 to 16 servings; 3½ hours.* Page 220

COUNTRY HAM STEAK
*Shredded, stir-fried cabbage, baked with
smoked ham and pancake syrup. 6 servings;
1 hour.* Page 222

LEFTOVER HAM IDEAS (from top)
**HAM CASSEROLE; HAM CHEF'S
SALAD; HAM FRUIT SALAD;
GLAZED KABOBS.** Page 223

ROAST LEG OF LAMB
Lamb leg, spread with juniper berries and mustard and roasted with potatoes; served with sauce. 12 to 15 servings; 3 hours. Page 226

LAMB CURRY
Chunks of lamb stew meat, simmered in spicy sauce; served with rice and accompaniments. 6 to 8 servings; 2½ hours. Page 231

LAMB CHOPS WITH VEGETABLE GRAVY *Shoulder blade chops braised with vegetables and wine and served with gravy. 6 servings; 1¾ hours.* Page 229

MARINATED LEG OF LAMB OLE
Leg shank half, marinated in spicy wine and chili sauce, then roasted; serve with gravy. 10 to 12 servings; day ahead. Page 227

BRAISED LAMB NECK SLICES
Lamb-neck slices, simmered in a spicy, prune sauce. 4 servings; 1¼ hours. Page 230

LAMB SHANK STEW
Tomatoes, zucchini chunks and lamb shanks, stewed in bouillon and served with barley or rice. 6 servings; 2½ hours. Page 230

OVEN-BARBECUED LAMB BREAST
Lamb breast pieces, baked with chili sauce, honey and orange slices. 3 to 4 servings; 3½ hours. Page 229

PERSIAN-STYLE LAMB AND ALMONDS *Ground lamb, fried with toasted almonds, mint and lime juice; served on spinach. 4 servings; 25 minutes.* Page 231

ROAST RACK OF LAMB
Lamb rib roast, brushed with apricot glaze during roasting. 4 servings; 2 hours. Page 227

LAMB RIBLETS WITH PINEAPPLE
Lamb riblets in a honey sauce, topped with pineapple chunks and braised in the oven. 6 to 8 servings; 2½ hours. Page 229

ROQUEFORT LAMB CHOPS (top).
8 servings; 1¼ hours.
BROILED GINGERY LAMB CHOPS
6 servings; 30 minutes. Page 228

ROTISSERIED LEG OF LAMB
Boneless leg roast marinated in spicy, wine mixture, then roasted on rotisserie. 16 to 18 servings; day ahead. Page 227

NEAR EAST LAMB STEW (top).
10 to 12 servings; 3 hours. Page 230
LAMB STEW ROSE *6 servings; 3 hours.*
Page 231

LAMB CHOPS A L'ORANGE
Lamb shoulder arm chops, brushed with marmalade and sherry mixture and broiled. 8 servings; 30 minutes. Page 228

LAMB KABOBS
Marinated lamb cubes, eggplant and red pepper, barbecued on a grill. 8 servings; early in day. Page 228

MARINATED BUTTERFLIED LAMB
Boned, half leg of lamb, marinated in wine and garlic and then broiled. 10 to 12 servings; day ahead. Page 226

LAMBURGERS
Broiled, ground-lamb patties, wrapped with bacon slices. 6 servings; 25 minutes. Page 231

LEMON-TARRAGON VEAL ROAST
Boneless veal shoulder, roasted with tarragon and lemon and served with pan gravy. 12 to 14 servings; 3¼ hours. Page 234

SPICY VEAL RUMP ROAST
Veal rump roast, braised with apple juice, onion and pickling spice and garnished with apples. 12 to 14 servings; 3 hours. Page 235

SALTIMBOCCA
Fried cutlets, baked with strips of prosciutto ham and raclette cheese. 4 servings; 40 minutes. Page 236

VEAL STEW MILANESE
Veal chunks, stewed with red wine with tomatoes, carrot, celery and basil, garnished with lemon peel. 6 servings; 2 hours. Page 239

VEAL PICCATA
Thin cutlets, simmered in white wine and lemon juice and topped with lemon slices. 8 servings; 1¼ hours. Page 236

VEAL PAPRIKA
Veal, stewed with onions, paprika and sour cream and served over noodles. 6 to 8 servings; 2½ hours. Page 239

VEAL RIB ROAST MARSALA
Seasoned roast veal, served with Marsala and mushroom gravy. 8 to 10 servings; 3¼ hours. Page 234

VEAL PARMIGIANA
Fried veal cutlets, topped with Marinara Sauce and mozzarella and Parmesan cheeses. 6 servings; 1 hour. Page 236

WIENER SCHNITZEL
Bread-crumbed veal cutlets, fried in butter and garnished with lemon and parsley. 6 servings; 45 minutes. Page 236

SCHNITZEL A LA HOLSTEIN
Wiener Schnitzel topped with a fried egg, anchovy fillets and capers. 6 servings; 45 minutes. Page 236

TOMATO-PAPRIKA VEAL
Braised veal, sliced and served with noodles and creamy tomato-paprika sauce. 12 to 14 servings; 3 hours. Page 235

COUNTRY-STYLE VEAL RUMP ROAST
Boneless roast, braised in mushroom soup with carrots, onion and herbs. 14 to 16 servings; 3¼ hours. Page 234

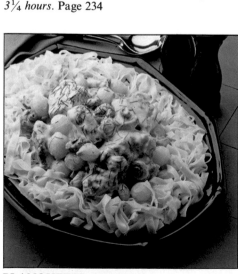

BLANQUETTE DE VEAU
Veal stew meat in a creamy sauce, served over noodles and garnished with dill. 8 to 10 servings; 3 hours. Page 239

VEAL AND PEPPERS
Veal cutlets cooked in butter with red and green peppers and flavorings including basil and oregano. 8 servings; 1 hour. Page 235

VEAL FORESTIER
*Veal rib chops browned in garlic butter, then simmered with vermouth and mushrooms.
6 servings; 45 minutes.* Page 237

VEAL CHOPS WITH AVOCADO (top).
Loin chops baked in rich cream sauce with mushrooms and avocado. 4 servings; 1½ hours. Page 237.

VEAL STEAKS WITH SPAGHETTI
Shoulder arm steaks with herbed tomato sauce served with spaghetti. 4 servings; 1¼ hours. Page 237

BRAISED BREAST OF VEAL AND PEACHES *Veal braised in sherry and soy sauce, then broiled with peaches. 6 servings; 3¼ hours.* Page 238

VEAL STEAK MARSALA
Shoulder blade steaks, braised in wine, until fork-tender. 4 servings; 1¼ hours. Page 237

DEVILED VEAL RIBLETS WITH SAUCY NOODLES *Cooked riblets, dipped in mayonnaise mixture and bread crumbs and broiled. 6 servings; 2 hours.* Page 238

VEAL CHOPS IN TOMATO SAUCE
Top loin chops, braised in tomato and basil sauce and garnished with parsley. 6 servings; 45 minutes. Page 237

HOMEMADE SAUSAGE
Herbed, ground, pork mixture in natural casings, twisted into links and cooked in a skillet. 8 servings; 5 hours. Page 243

"BOILED" FRESH TONGUE
Fresh beef tongue, simmered with onion, mustard seed, peppercorns and cloves. 12 to 14 servings; 3½ hours. Page 241

SWEETBREADS MEUNIERE
Precooked sweetbreads, breaded and broiled until browned, served with buttery lemon juice. 3 to 4 servings; 45 minutes. Page 241

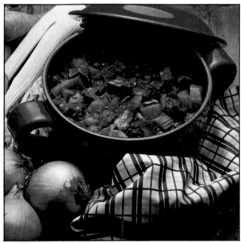

BEEF HEART STEW
Baked stew of heart, canned tomatoes, onions, carrots and celery. 10 servings; 3½ hours. Page 241

PAN-FRIED LIVER AND BACON
Calves' liver, lightly fried in bacon drippings and served with lemon juice and bacon. 4 servings; 20 minutes. Page 240

LAMB KIDNEYS MADEIRA
Kidneys, sprinkled with Madeira and coated with green peppercorns, onion and mustard, then broiled. 4 servings; 1 hour. Page 242

BRAINS AU BEURRE NOIR
Beef brains, cooked gently in butter and served on toasted French bread with caper sauce. 4 servings; 1 hour. Page 241

LIVER JARDINIERE
Beef liver slices, simmered with onions and green pepper, garnished with bacon and tomatoes. 6 to 8 servings; 1¼ hours. Page 240

SAUTEED VEAL KIDNEYS
Veal kidneys, mushrooms and onions, cooked in broth and Madeira, served over toast. 4 to 6 servings; 50 minutes. Page 242

SALADE NICOISE
Classic tuna, egg, anchovy and vegetable salad.
4 servings; early in day. Page 324

CHEF'S SALAD
Chicken, cheese, ham, hard-cooked eggs and
tomatoes on lettuce base. 6 servings;
30 minutes. Page 324

CRAB LOUIS (top). *4 servings; 1 hour.*
PINEAPPLE-CHEESE SALAD *4 servings;*
30 minutes. Page 325

CHUNKY EGG SALAD
Hard-cooked eggs, celery and green pepper,
tossed with mayonnaise mixture and served on
lettuce leaves. 4 servings; 1 hour. Page 325

BUFFET SALAD
Shredded cheese shell, layered with ham,
lettuce and tomatoes and served with mustard
sauce. 6 servings; 2½ hours. Page 325

HAM WITH RICE SALAD
Flavored cooked rice mixed with cooked ham
and green pepper, served chilled on lettuce.
6 servings; 3 hours. Page 325

HERRING SALAD
Rich salad of chopped pickled herring, diced
potatoes and pickled beets in heavy cream.
6 servings; early in day. Page 324

SHRIMP SALAD (left) *and variations. Cooked, shelled shrimp tossed in a*
French-dressing and mayonnaise mixture with celery, walnuts, olives and
onion, served on lettuce. **TUNA SALAD** (center) *and* **SALMON**
SALAD. *4 servings; 1 hour.* Page 325

CAULIFLOWER POLONAISE
Whole, cooked cauliflower, topped with mixture of bread crumbs, chopped egg and lemon juice. 6 servings; 20 minutes. Page 283

BAKED CREAMED SPINACH
Cooked spinach, mixed with a light, creamy sauce and baked. 8 servings; 1 hour. Page 294

RATATOUILLE
Eggplant, peppers, zucchini, onion and tomato, flavored with garlic; serve hot or cold. 8 servings; 45 minutes. Page 298

GREEN BEANS WITH ZUCCHINI (top).
6 servings; 30 minutes. Page 299
STIR-FRIED ZUCCHINI *4 servings; 15 minutes. Page 295*

SUMMER SQUASH MEDLEY
Tender-crisp strips of zucchini and straightneck squash, tossed with butter and lemon. 6 servings; 15 minutes. Page 295

CANDIED SWEET POTATOES (left).
6 servings; 30 minutes. **SHERRIED SWEET POTATOES** *6 servings; 50 minutes. Page 296*

CREAMED ONIONS (left). *8 to 10 servings; 30 minutes. Page 290.* **GLAZED ONIONS** *4 servings; 30 minutes. Page 289*

FRENCH-FRIED ONIONS (left). *6 to 8 servings; 30 minutes.* **PAN-FRIED ONIONS** *4 servings; 15 minutes. Page 290*

BAKED ONIONS
Sliced onions baked in honey and butter until tender and golden brown. 6 to 8 servings; 1 hour. Page 289

67

BOSTON BAKED BEANS
Navy beans, baked with molasses, brown sugar, onions and salt pork. 12 servings; early in day. **Page 278**

BLACKEYE BEANS (left). *Cooked with salt pork. 6 servings; day ahead.* **BEAN RELISH** *Tangy kidney beans and corn. 9 cups; 4½ hours.* **Page 279**

WHOLE GREEN AND WAX BEANS WITH PARSLEY SAUCE *Tender fresh green and wax beans served together in a thick parsley sauce. 8 servings; 30 minutes.* **Page 279**

BRAISED FENNEL
Halved fennel bulbs simmered in bouillon and served with buttery sauce and fennel leaf garnish. 4 servings; 30 minutes. **Page 286**

SPICED CARROTS (top). *12 servings; 45 minutes.* **GLAZED CARROTS** *4 servings; 25 minutes.* **Page 283**

MASHED TURNIPS
Cooked turnips, mashed with butter, seasoned with salt, sugar and pepper. 6 to 8 servings; 40 minutes. **Page 297**

PARSLEY CREAMED PARSNIPS
Cooked, sliced parsnips with a creamy orange-flavored sauce, garnished with chopped parsley. 6 servings; 30 minutes. **Page 290**

HARVARD BEETS
Cooked beets served hot in an onion-vinegar sauce or, if preferred, a piquant orange sauce. 6 servings; 20 minutes. **Page 280**

LIMA BEANS SMITANE (left). *4 servings; 25 minutes.*
ZESTY LIMA BEANS *4 servings; 2 hours.* Both page 280

EGGPLANT WITH CARAWAY SEED
(top). *25 minutes.* SAUTEED EGGPLANT
SLICES *15 minutes; 4 servings each.* Page 285

SUMMER VEGETABLE BOWL
*Corn, onions, green pepper, green beans,
zucchini and celery, garnished with bacon and
tomato. 8 servings; 1 hour.* Page 298

SAUTEED MUSHROOMS (left).
4 servings; 20 minutes. MUSHROOMS IN
SOUR CREAM. *12 first-course servings;
30 minutes.* Both page 288

OKRA VINAIGRETTE
*Chilled tender-crisp okra and chopped pimento
in a vinaigrette sauce. Served on Boston
lettuce. 6 servings; 4½ hours.* Page 289

STIR-FRIED CABBAGE AND ZUCCHINI
*Finely-sliced cabbage and zucchini, stir-fried in
garlic-flavored oil until tender-crisp.
8 servings; 15 minutes.* Page 299

VEGETABLE TRIO
*Carrots, green beans and mushrooms, braised
with thyme butter until tender-crisp.
5 servings; 25 minutes.* Page 298

ENDIVES WITH SWISS CHEESE
*Belgian endives, simmered until tender, then
baked with topping of Swiss cheese and half-
and-half. 6 servings; 1 hour.* Page 286

SAUTEED CARAWAY-CABBAGE
*Coarsely-shredded green cabbage, sautéed in
oil with caraway seed until tender-crisp.
6 servings; 15 minutes.* Page 282

CABBAGE RELISH (left). *3 hours.* RED
CABBAGE AND APPLES (center). *1 hour.*
SKILLET CABBAGE *30 minutes. All 6 to 8
servings.* Page 282

FLAVORED BUTTERS FOR CORN
Serve corn on the cob with butters flavored with chili powder, chives, or dill weed.
Page 284

STIR-FRIED ASPARAGUS
Fresh asparagus cut diagonally and stir-fried, Chinese-style, in salad oil and salt until tender-crisp. 6 servings; 10 minutes. Page 278

LEEKS AU GRATIN
Leeks simmered in water, topped with cheese mixture and broiled until golden. 4 servings; 45 minutes. Page 287

MARINATED PEPPERS (top). *6 servings; early in day.* **HERB SAUTEED GREEN PEPPERS** *4 servings; 15 minutes.* Page 291

VEGETABLE-STUFFED GREEN PEPPERS (left). *4 servings; 15 minutes.* Page 300. **PEPPER-AND-TOMATO SAUTE.** *10 servings; 30 minutes.* Page 299

STIR-FRIED VEGETABLE MIX
Carrots, onion and broccoli stir-fried in hot oil, then simmered with mushrooms until tender-crisp. 6 servings; 25 minutes. Page 299

SAUTEED CUCUMBER RINGS
Peeled cucumber slices with seeds removed, sautéed in butter until tender-crisp. 4 servings; 30 minutes. Page 285

PEAS AMANDINE
Shelled peas, mixed with chopped bacon, minced onion, slivered almonds and heavy cream. 4 servings; 40 minutes. Page 291

CARROTS AND CELERY
Diagonally sliced fresh carrots and celery simmered with light seasonings until tender-crisp. 8 servings; 30 minutes. Page 298

HOT FLUFFY RICE (left). *4 servings;
20 minutes.* **OVEN DINNER RICE**
4 servings; 35 minutes. **Page 338**

RICE PILAF WITH PEAS
*Regular long-grain rice cooked in chicken broth with frozen peas, diced
bacon and finely chopped onion. 12 servings; 40 minutes.* **Page 339**

BAKED SPANISH RICE
*Uncooked long-grain rice baked with onions,
green pepper and tomatoes and topped with
cheese and bacon. 6 servings; 1 hour.* **Page 340**

RICE-AND-MUSHROOM CASSEROLE
*Rice, browned in skillet, then baked with
mushrooms, onions, celery and beef bouillon.
4 servings; 1 hour.* **Page 340**

RED-AND-GREEN RICE
*Hot cooked rice tossed with sliced green
onions, chopped green pepper and pimento.
6 servings; 30 minutes.* **Page 338**

RICE RING
*Cooked rice tossed with parsley and butter and
packed in ring mold; unmold just before
serving. 6 servings; 25 minutes.* **Page 341**

BOILED WILD RICE
*Wild rice, simmered until tender and tossed
with butter or margarine. 6 servings; 1 hour.*
Page 341

PARTY RICE AND NOODLES
*Parboiled or long-grain rice cooked in chicken
broth with onions and mushrooms, then baked
with noodles. 12 servings; 1¼ hours.* **Page 340**

HERBED ORANGE RICE
Long-grain or parboiled rice cooked with orange juice, onion, celery and thyme. 6 servings; 45 minutes. **Page 338**

CURRIED RICE AND ONIONS
Hot cooked rice stirred with half-and-half and seasoned with onions, curry powder and nutmeg. 4 servings; 35 minutes. **Page 339**

CHINESE FRIED RICE
Cooked rice fried with oil, scrambled eggs, crumbled bacon and soy sauce and topped with green onions. 6 servings; 2½ hours. **Page 341**

RISOTTO ALLA MILANESE
Long-grain rice cooked with saffron, minced onion and chicken broth, baked with Parmesan cheese. 6 servings; 45 minutes. **Page 339**

HOMEMADE EGG NOODLES
Homemade pasta dough, cut in strips and cooked until tender. 6 servings; 3½ hours. **Page 330**

NOODLE RING
Cooked egg noodles, tossed with butter and baked in ring mold; serve hot. 6 servings; 45 minutes. **Page 330**

HOMEMADE SPINACH NOODLES
Pasta dough, prepared from blended spinach, flour and eggs, cut into strips and boiled in plenty of water. 8 servings; 3 hours. **Page 330**

FETTUCINI ALFREDO
Medium egg noodles in a creamy mixture of butter, Parmesan and half-and-half. 8 servings; 30 minutes. **Page 330**

CAESAR SALAD
Anchovy fillets, raw egg and Parmesan cheese tossed with romaine lettuce, topped with Garlic Croutons. 6 servings; 30 minutes. **Page 318**

TOSSED SALAD WITH LEMONY-MUSTARD DRESSING *Spinach, Boston lettuce and Belgian endives, coated with fresh dressing. 10 servings; 45 minutes.* **Page 318**

CUCUMBERS IN SOUR CREAM
Thinly sliced cucumbers, with chives or onions in sour cream, served chilled. 6 servings; early in day. **Page 319**

CALIFORNIA SALAD
Avocados and lettuce in zesty, seasoned sauce, garnished with California walnuts. 8 servings; 30 minutes. **Page 318**

TOMATOES VINAIGRETTE
Overlapping tomato slices, sprinkled with oregano-flavored dressing. 6 servings; 2 hours. **Page 319**

POTATO-VEGETABLE SALAD
Overlapping cucumber slices cover a potato-carrot-and-pea-mixture, arranged on Boston lettuce. 8 servings; 1 hour. **Page 320**

COLONEL'S LADY'S SALAD BOWL
Green salad of lettuce, cucumber, celery, onions and peas, tossed with spicy dressing. 12 servings; 20 minutes. **Page 318**

DANISH CUCUMBER SALAD
Thin slices of cucumber in dilled vinegar. 8 servings; 5 hours. **Page 319**

GERMAN HOT-POTATO SALAD
Cooked potatoes and bacon, tossed in a sweet-sour mixture and topped with parsley. 6 servings; 45 minutes. **Page 320**

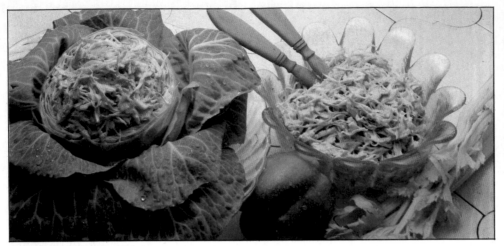

DELUXE COLESLAW
Cabbage, celery, green pepper, carrot and onion, tossed with a creamy dressing. Can be served in Coleslaw Bowl made of cut-out cabbage (above left) or dish. 8 servings; 1½ hours. Page 319

PERFECTION SALAD
Shredded cabbage with celery and pimentos in lemony-vinegar gelatin mixture. 8 servings; 4 hours. Page 323

CRANBERRY-NUT MOLD
Cranberries, celery and walnuts in a wine and lemon-flavored gelatin; served with sour cream dressing. 10 servings; 6 hours. Page 323

BRAISED LEEKS VINAIGRETTE
Cooked leeks marinated in a spiced pimento-oil-vinegar mixture. 8 servings; 6 hours. Page 321

GERMAN SAUERKRAUT SALAD
Grated apple and sauerkraut, marinated an hour ahead. 8 servings; 1½ hours. Page 321

THREE-BEAN SALAD
Green, wax and kidney beans, chilled in an oil and vinegar dressing. 8 servings; early in day. Page 321

TURKISH BEAN SALAD
Cooked dry beans in a herby tomato and ripe olive dressing. 10 servings; 5 hours. Page 321

TOMATO ASPIC
Molded tomato salad, chilled and served with a yogurt-dill dressing. 8 servings; 4 hours. Page 323

WALDORF SALAD
Diced apple, celery, walnut and raisin mixture, tossed with lemony mayonnaise and served on lettuce leaves. 8 servings; 20 minutes. Page 322

ZESTY TANGELO SALAD
Tangelo segments, celery and pimentos, tossed in Italian salad dressing and served on romaine leaves. 6 servings; 40 minutes. Page 315

SALAD DRESSINGS
Salad dressings, flavored with herbs, spices, garlic, cheese and anchovies. 10 to 15 minutes. Page 326

GREEK SALAD
Ripe olives, cucumbers, anchovy fillets, capers, tomatoes, onions and feta cheese with chicory and iceberg lettuce, dressed with olive oil and red wine vinegar. 10 servings; 30 minutes. Page 320

WHITE BREAD
Simple, everyday yeast loaf made using basic breadmaking techniques. 2 loaves; 4 hours. **Page 434**

WHOLE-WHEAT BREAD
Loaves made from whole-wheat- and all-purpose-flour, sweetened with molasses. 2 loaves; 4½ hours. **Page 434**

ROUND RYE BREAD
Caraway seed and buttermilk flavor this rye and all-purpose flour loaf which is baked on a cookie sheet. 2 loaves; 4½ hours. **Page 435**

WHOLE-GRAIN BREAD
Bran, wheat germ, whole-wheat and rye flour dough topped with caraway. 1 loaf; 5 hours. **Page 436**

MARBLED LOAF
Two different doughs, rolled up jelly-roll fashion and then baked. 2 loaves; 4½ hours. **Page 435**

PUMPERNICKEL AND WHOLE-WHEAT BRAID
Braid of dark pumpernickel and honey-sweetened whole-wheat doughs. 1 loaf; 4½ hours. **Page 437**

BRAIDED HERB BREAD
Rosemary flavors a plain dough, which is rolled into pieces and braided. 2 loaves; 4 hours. **Page 437**

CAESAR SALAD
Anchovy fillets, raw egg and Parmesan cheese tossed with romaine lettuce, topped with Garlic Croutons. 6 servings; 30 minutes. **Page 318**

TOSSED SALAD WITH LEMONY-MUSTARD DRESSING *Spinach, Boston lettuce and Belgian endives, coated with fresh dressing. 10 servings; 45 minutes.* **Page 318**

CUCUMBERS IN SOUR CREAM
Thinly sliced cucumbers, with chives or onions in sour cream, served chilled. 6 servings; early in day. **Page 319**

CALIFORNIA SALAD
Avocados and lettuce in zesty, seasoned sauce, garnished with California walnuts. 8 servings; 30 minutes. **Page 318**

TOMATOES VINAIGRETTE
Overlapping tomato slices, sprinkled with oregano-flavored dressing. 6 servings; 2 hours. **Page 319**

POTATO-VEGETABLE SALAD
Overlapping cucumber slices cover a potato-carrot-and-pea-mixture, arranged on Boston lettuce. 8 servings; 1 hour. **Page 320**

COLONEL'S LADY'S SALAD BOWL
Green salad of lettuce, cucumber, celery, onions and peas, tossed with spicy dressing. 12 servings; 20 minutes. **Page 318**

DANISH CUCUMBER SALAD
Thin slices of cucumber in dilled vinegar. 8 servings; 5 hours. **Page 319**

GERMAN HOT-POTATO SALAD
Cooked potatoes and bacon, tossed in a sweet-sour mixture and topped with parsley. 6 servings; 45 minutes. **Page 320**

DELUXE COLESLAW
Cabbage, celery, green pepper, carrot and onion, tossed with a creamy dressing. Can be served in Coleslaw Bowl made of cut-out cabbage (above left) or dish. 8 servings; 1½ hours. Page 319

PERFECTION SALAD
Shredded cabbage with celery and pimentos in lemony-vinegar gelatin mixture. 8 servings; 4 hours. Page 323

CRANBERRY-NUT MOLD
Cranberries, celery and walnuts in a wine and lemon-flavored gelatin; served with sour cream dressing. 10 servings; 6 hours. Page 323

BRAISED LEEKS VINAIGRETTE
Cooked leeks marinated in a spiced pimento-oil-vinegar mixture. 8 servings; 6 hours. Page 321

GERMAN SAUERKRAUT SALAD
Grated apple and sauerkraut, marinated an hour ahead. 8 servings; 1½ hours. Page 321

THREE-BEAN SALAD
Green, wax and kidney beans, chilled in an oil and vinegar dressing. 8 servings; early in day. Page 321

TURKISH BEAN SALAD
Cooked dry beans in a herby tomato and ripe olive dressing. 10 servings; 5 hours. Page 321

TOMATO ASPIC
Molded tomato salad, chilled and served with a yogurt-dill dressing. 8 servings; 4 hours. Page 323

ITALIAN BREAD
Traditional long Italian loaves, topped with an egg-white glaze. 2 loaves; 4 hours. Page 436

SOURDOUGH BREAD
Favorite American bread, using a fermented yeast "starter" to give bread its traditional sour taste. 2 loaves; 4 days. Page 441

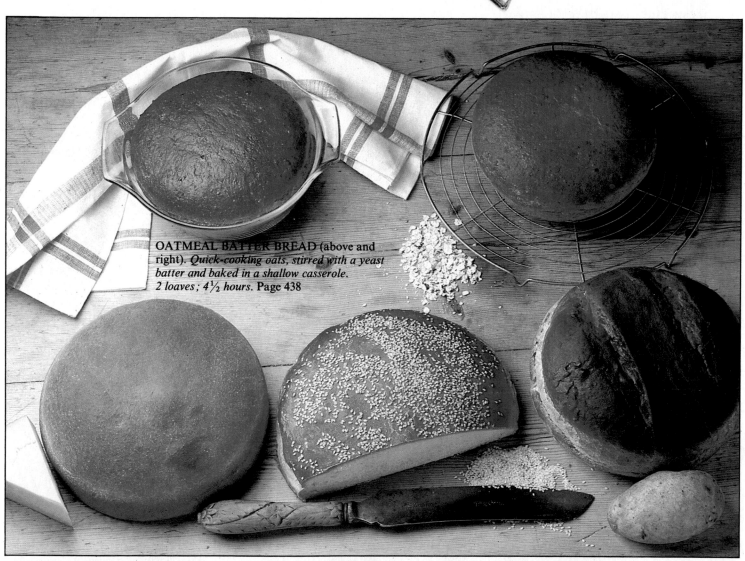

OATMEAL BATTER BREAD (above and right). *Quick-cooking oats, stirred with a yeast batter and baked in a shallow casserole. 2 loaves; 4½ hours. Page 438*

CHEESE CASSEROLE BREAD (left).
All-purpose flour yeast batter, flavored with shredded, sharp Cheddar cheese, baked in a casserole. 1 loaf; 4½ hours. Page 438

SESAME PAN BREAD
Kneaded, white-bread dough, glazed with milk, sprinkled with sesame seeds and baked in cake pans. 2 loaves; 3 hours. Page 438

POTATO BREAD
Mashed potato flavored yeast dough, baked in a shallow casserole until well browned. 2 loaves; 4½ hours. Page 438

DINNER ROLLS *12 to 24 rolls; 3½ hours.*
Pages 439 to 440

VIENNA ROLLS

DOUBLE TWISTS

DINNER BUNS

FAN-TANS

PINWHEELS

CRESCENTS

KNOTS

POSIES

PAN ROLLS

REFRIGERATOR PAN ROLLS
Dough, made ahead and refrigerated, then shaped into balls and let rise before baking. 28–30 rolls; 6 hours. Page 441

PARKER HOUSE ROLLS
Dough from Refrigerator Pan Rolls, cut into circles, dipped in butter, folded and baked. 40 rolls; 6 hours. Page 441

RAISIN BREAD
Sweet loaf, flavored with raisins. 1 loaf;
4½ hours. Page 442

TURTLE BREAD
Novelty bread, easily made from pieces of
sweet dough. 1 turtle, 4½ hours. Page 442

HOT CROSS BUNS
Easter bread flavored with raisins and orange peel and
criss-crossed with sugar icing.
12 buns; 4½ hours. Page 442

KOLACKY
Blueberry, Cherry, Cream-cheese, Lemon,
Orange and Pineapple fillings top a circle of
sweet dough. 1 coffeecake; 4½ hours. Page 443

APRICOT COFFEECAKE
Strips of sweet dough laced across a dried
apricot filling before baking and glazing.
1 coffeecake; 4½ hours. Page 443

CINNAMON ROLLS
Pecan- and raisin-filled dough, rolled jelly-roll
fashion, cut into slices and then baked and
glazed. 15 rolls; 4½ hours. Page 444

FRUITED BRAID
Raisins, candied orange peel and candied citron
flavor a braided dough which is glazed and then
baked. 1 braid; 4½ hours. Page 444

LEMON BUBBLE RING
Rounds of yeast dough, sprinkled with grated
lemon peel, sugar and mace and baked into a
ring in a tube pan. 1 loaf; 4 hours. Page 444

81

APRICOT BUTTERFLY ROLLS *20 rolls; 4½ hours.* Page 445

BRIOCHES *36 brioches; day ahead.* Page 447

CROISSANTS *12 croissants; 8 hours.* Page 448

PARTY DOUGHNUTS *36 doughnuts; 4 hours.* Page 449. JELLY DOUGHNUTS *(right). 36 doughnuts; 4 hours.* Page 449

BABAS AU RHUM *Individual breads, topped with Rum Sauce. 24 babas; 4 hours.* Page 450

DANISH PASTRY *Selection of pastries with choice of Jam, Almond or Cream-Cheese Filling. (From left):* PINWHEEL, FOLDOVER, ENVELOPE, COCKSCOMB. *24 pastries; 5 hours.* Page 451

PITA (POCKET BREAD) *Middle-Eastern style, baked "pocket" bread. 6 breads; 3 hours.* Page 447

WHOLE-WHEAT "SUGAR" BEARS *Shaped sweet dough. 3 bears; 4 hours.* Page 445

CHALLAH *Traditional, Jewish, braided egg bread. 2 loaves; 5½ hours.* Page 453

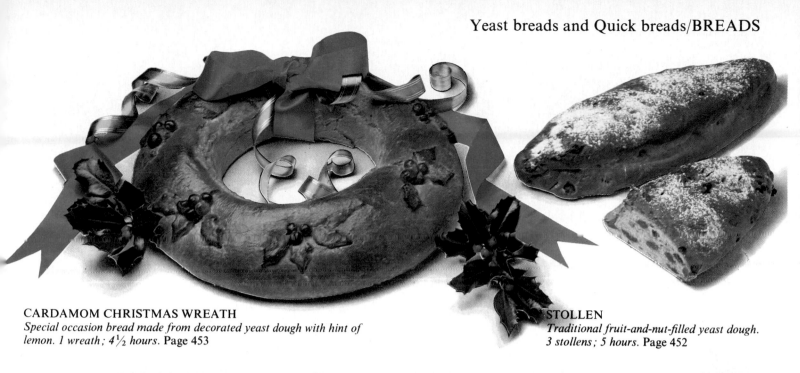

CARDAMOM CHRISTMAS WREATH
Special occasion bread made from decorated yeast dough with hint of lemon. 1 wreath; 4½ hours. Page 453

STOLLEN
Traditional fruit-and-nut-filled yeast dough. 3 stollens; 5 hours. Page 452

ENGLISH MUFFINS
Traditional, cornmeal-coated yeast-dough muffins, browned in a skillet, toasted and served hot. 18 muffins; 3½ hours. Page 446

KULICH
Traditional, Russian Easter bread, made from fruited dough and baked in a coffee can. 3 loaves; 5 hours. Page 452

POPPY-SEED POTICAS
Special yeast dough, filled with poppy seed and walnut mixture and baked. 2 loaves; 6 hours. Page 448

OLD-FASHIONED ROLLS
Yeast dough, shaped into rolls, brushed with melted butter or Egg Glaze and baked until golden. 24 rolls; 3½ hours. Page 439

IRISH SODA BREAD
Traditional, buttermilk-flavored, coarse-textured casserole bread. 1 loaf; 5 hours. Page 429

ZUCCHINI BREAD
Grated zucchini- and chopped-walnut-flavored baked loaf. Serve warm or cold. 2 loaves; 2 hours. Page 429

83

LEMON LOAF
Sweet loaf brushed with lemon juice after baking. 1 loaf; 2 hours. Page 428

CHOCOLATE DATE-NUT LOAF
Pitted dates, walnuts and chocolate pieces in baked loaf. 1 loaf; day ahead. Page 429

NUT BREAD
Chopped California walnuts flavor a traditionally-shaped loaf. 1 loaf; day ahead. Page 428

CORN BREAD
Cornmeal batter, baked and cut into squares for serving. 9 servings; 35 minutes. Page 428

CORN STICKS
Corn Bread batter is used for making these corn sticks. 14 sticks; 35 minutes. Page 428

BUTTERMILK WAFFLES
Buttermilk-flavored batter, baked in waffle baker. 5 waffles; 30 minutes. Page 427

SILVER DOLLAR PANCAKES
Small amounts of pancake batter, cooked on a hot griddle to make tiny pancakes; serve with syrup. 24 pancakes; 30 minutes. Page 427

PANCAKES
Thin batter, cooked in hot skillet until bubbly and golden. 12 pancakes; 30 minutes. Page 426

POTATO PANCAKES
Shredded potato and onion, mixed with egg and flour and fried until golden. 16 pancakes; 1¼ hours. Page 426

PEACH-FILLED COFFEECAKE
12 servings; 1½ hours.
Page 430

CHERRY COFFEECAKE
9 servings; 2 hours.
Page 430

SOUR-CREAM COFFEECAKE
8–10 servings; 2 hours.
Page 430

GIANT POPOVERS
Egg batter, baked in pottery custard cups.
8 popovers; 1½ hours. **Page 427**

BISCUITS and MUFFINS
Quickly made, individual muffins (top left) and biscuits. 12 muffins, 18 biscuits; each 35 minutes. **Pages 423 and 424**

MUFFIN VARIATIONS: WHOLE-WHEAT, BLUEBERRY, ORANGE, BRAN, CORN (clockwise from left).
12–16 muffins; 35–45 minutes. **Page 424**

OLD-FASHIONED DOUGHNUTS AND DOUGHNUT "HOLES" *Deep-fried dough circles and centers, sprinkled with sugar.*
24 doughnuts; 2½ hours. **Page 425**

BEIGNETS
French-style fried dough served with a sweet syrup. 8 servings; 45 minutes. **Page 425**

BOSTON BROWN BREAD
Coffee cans are used to shape this bread flavored with molasses and raisins. 2 loaves; 2½ hours. **Page 429**

POORI (left). *Indian-style fried bread.*
20 poori; 1¾ hours. **ONION THINS**
32 baked crackers; 1½ hours. **Page 431**

85

DEEP-DISH PEACH PIE
Sliced peaches, cinnamon and butter-dotted filling in a piecrust, topped with pastry strips. 10 servings; early in day. **Page 348**

BLACKBERRY PIE
Fresh blackberries in old-fashioned piecrust. 6 servings; 2 hours. Page 346

CHERRY PIE
Pitted tart fresh cherries in scalloped-edged piecrust. 6 servings; 2 hours. Page 346

APPLE PIE
Sliced cooking apples, baked in spicy mixture in piecrust. 6 servings; 2 hours. Page 346

CHOCOLATE CREAM PIE
Rich chocolate mixture, chilled and served here in a baked piecrust, topped with whipped cream. 8 servings; 5½ hours. Page 350

PUMPKIN PIE
Unbaked piecrust, filled with spicy pumpkin mixture, baked and served with Brandy Hard Sauce. 6 servings; early in day. Page 349

PECAN PIE
Traditional baked pie, with pecan halves arranged in single layer on unbaked piecrust; serve cool. 10 servings; early in day. Page 356

PRUNE AND APRICOT PIE
Baked piecrust, filled with prunes, dried apricots and grated peel, garnished with walnuts. 8 servings; early in day. Page 347

LEMON CHIFFON PIE
Light, lemon filling in baked piecrust, garnished with whipped cream and shredded lemon peel. 8 servings; early in day. Page 352

DEEP-DISH PLUM PIE
Fresh plums sprinkled with almond extract, sugar and flour, baked in deep-dish pastry crust, topped with pastry strips. 10 servings; 2 hours. Page 348

FRUIT CREAM TARTS
Homemade cream filling in baked tart shells, topped with a variety of fresh fruits. 12 tarts; early in day. Page 357

RICH BAVARIAN PIE
Baked piecrust, filled with egg-cream mixture flavored with vanilla, served topped with chocolate. 8 servings; early in day. Page 353

RICH BAVARIAN PIE VARIATIONS
Fresh strawberry (left) and coffee variations of Rich Bavarian Pie. 8 servings each; early in day. Page 353

BLUEBERRY COBBLER
Spiced blueberry filling in a deep pie plate topped with crust and baked until golden brown. 6 to 8 servings; 2 hours. Page 346

CHOCOLATE CHIFFON PIE
Chocolate-Wafer Crumb-Crust base, filled with light chocolate-chiffon mixture, served with cream. 8 servings; 4 hours. Page 353

WALNUT TARTS
Egg- and corn-syrup mixture over chopped walnuts in tart shells, baked and topped with cream. 12 tarts; early in day. Page 357

DELUXE APPLE TART
Sliced apples and applesauce baked in sweetened pastry and glazed with apricot mixture. 8 servings; early in day. Page 348

STREUSEL-TOPPED PEAR PIE
Fluted-edged crust, filled with fresh pears and topped with brown sugar, shredded cheese and spices. 8 servings; 2 hours. Page 347

PEACH PIE
Fresh peaches in piecrust, topped with pastry strips. 6 servings; 2 hours. Page 347

ORANGE CHIFFON PIE
Light, creamy orange filling in prepared piecrust, served with whipped cream and orange sections. 8 servings; early in day. Page 352

CUSTARD PIE
Milk custard, baked in piecrust and sprinkled with nutmeg. 6 servings; early in day. Page 349

DOUBLE PEANUT PIE
Creamy peanut butter, peanuts and corn syrup baked in piecrust and garnished with whipped cream. 12 servings; early in day. Page 356

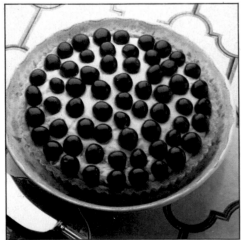

CHERRY CREAM TART
Light, cherry-flavored whipped-cream mixture, served chilled in baked crust, topped with whole cherries. 8 servings; early in day. Page 355

PUMPKIN CHIFFON PIE
Spicy pumpkin filling in graham-cracker and coconut crust, served with whipped cream and coconut. 10 servings; early in day. Page 354

FUDGE-NUT PIE
Chocolate-egg mixture with California walnuts, baked in a piecrust and served with ice cream. 8 servings; early in day. Page 356

COFFEE CORDIAL PIE
Coffee-flavored chiffon mixture in a baked chocolate-wafer crumb crust. 8 servings; 4½ hours. Page 354

RASPBERRY RIBBON PIE
Raspberry mixture layered with cream-cheese mixture and served in baked piecrust. 8 servings; day ahead. Page 354

BLACK BOTTOM PIE
Baked, gingersnap crumb crust, filled with chocolate- and rum-flavored custards. 8 servings; early in day. Page 355

LEMON MERINGUE PIE
Baked piecrust filled with lemon peel and juice mixture, topped with meringue then baked. Serve chilled. 6 servings; 6 hours. Page 351

PEACH MERINGUE TARTS
Sliced peaches, tapioca and lemon juice filling, baked in tart shells, topped with egg whites and baked again. 12 tarts; 3 hours. Page 357

NESSELRODE PIE
Rum-flavored candied fruit filling, served in Graham-cracker crumb crust and garnished with cream. 8 servings; early in day. Page 355

MINCE TARTS
Mincemeat, apples, walnuts and brown sugar in individual tart shells, served warm with Brandy Hard Sauce. 12 tarts; day ahead. Page 357

VANILLA CREAM PIE
Baked crumb crust, filled with vanilla-flavored egg-custard mixture and topped with whipped cream. 8 servings; 5½ hours. Page 350

BANANA CREAM PIE
Baked piecrust filled with vanilla-flavored egg-custard mixture, topped with grated lemon. 8 servings; 5½ hours. Page 350

DEVIL'S FOOD CAKE
Dark-chocolate two-layer cake, topped with Quick Fudge Frosting. 8 to 10 servings; early in day. Page 384

SILVER-WHITE CAKE
White cake, filled and frosted with Mocha Butter-Cream Frosting. 8 servings; early in day. Page 385

SPICY GINGERBREAD
Gingerbread batter, baked and then cooled, topped with whipped cream. 9 servings; early in day. Page 387

GERMAN GOLD POUNDCAKE
Traditional cake baked in loaf or Bundt pan. 16 servings; early in day. Page 386

ORANGE CHIFFON CAKE
Beaten egg whites folded with batter, baked and topped with fluffy orange frosting. 16 servings; early in day. Page 389

DELUXE MARBLE CAKE
Vanilla and chocolate mixtures, cut through to create a design and baked. 10 to 12 servings; early in day. Page 386

SACHERTORTE
Chocolate-cake layers, filled with apricot preserves and glazed with chocolate. 12 servings; 6 hours. Page 394

LANE CAKE
Four-layer white cake with fruit and nut filling and cooked frosting. 16 servings; early in day. Page 387

SUGAR BUSH WALNUT CAKE
Maple-flavored chiffon cake made with finely chopped California walnuts. 12 servings; early in day. Page 389

DARK CHRISTMAS FRUITCAKE
Traditional fruit and nut cake with apple jelly glaze. One 5-pound fruitcake; several weeks ahead. **Page 393**

JELLY ROLL
Jam-filled sponge, rolled and sprinkled with confectioners' sugar. 10 servings; early in day. **Page 391**

MOCHA-CREAM ROLL
Baked cake roll, spread with Mocha-Cream Filling with Chocolate Icing and Sugar Glaze. 10 servings; 2 hours. **Page 391**

HOLIDAY PETITS FOURS
Small sponge cakes with Almond Paste filling iced and decorated. 30 petits fours; early in day. **Page 392**

ANGEL-FOOD CAKE
Favorite cake made fluffy with beaten egg whites; served with berries and ice cream. 12 servings; early in day. **Page 390**

SPICE CAKE
Spicy layers, filled and frosted with Whipped-Cream Frosting. 8 servings; early in day. **Page 387**

FILBERT TORTE
Delicate cake layers, filled and frosted with vanilla flavored, whipped cream and garnished with ground nuts. 12 servings; 3 hours. **Page 395**

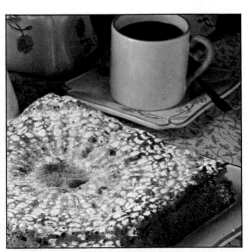

MERRYFIELD APPLE CAKE
Cooking apples, walnuts and raisins baked in a cake and sprinkled with sugar. 18 servings; early in day. **Page 387**

YELLOW CAKE
*Two-layer cake, filled and frosted with
Butter-Cream Frosting. 8 to 10 servings; early
in day.* Page 384

PINEAPPLE-UPSIDE-DOWN CAKE
*Pineapple chunks and cherry, baked with
yellow cake batter and inverted to serve.
12 servings; early in day.* Page 384

COFFEE CLOUD CAKE
*Coffee-flavored sponge batter, baked with
chopped California walnuts. 12 servings; early
in day.* Page 392

BRAZIL-NUT SENSATION FRUITCAKE
*Brazil nuts, dates and maraschino cherries
baked in batter and chilled. One 3-pound
cake; several weeks ahead.* Page 393

CHOCOLATE CHIFFON CAKE
*Cocoa-flavored batter, baked in tube pan and
sprinkled with sugar. 12 servings; early in day.*
Page 389

BLACK FOREST CHERRY TORTE
*Chocolate cake, layered with whipped cream
and tart cherries and richly garnished.
12 servings; 4 hours.* Page 395

BANANA CAKE *Banana-flavored cake
layers, filled and frosted with whipped cream
frosting. 8 to 10 servings; early in day.*
Page 388

FRESH COCONUT CAKE *Filled with
Custard Filling flavored with shredded fresh
coconut. 16 servings; 3 hours.* Page 386

WALNUT-FUDGE CAKE *Light layer
cake, flavored with walnuts and semisweet
chocolate, filled and glazed. 16 servings; early
in day.* Page 388

GOLDEN FRUITCAKE
Candied fruit, raisins and nuts in light batter, baked, then glazed. One 7-pound cake; day ahead. Page 393

DAFFODIL CAKE
Yellow and white cake, baked in tube pan and topped with orange-lemon icing. 12 servings; early in day. Page 390

PARTY CAKE
Three-tiered cake, with Lemon-Butter-Cream Filling and Vanilla-Butter-Cream Frosting, decorated. 62 servings; day ahead. Page 396

CHOCOLATE CAKE *and* **CHOCOLATE CUPCAKES**
The same cocoa butter can be used for 24 individual cupcakes or for a chocolate layer cake (8 to 10 servings). Both are coated with Coffee Cream-Cheese Frosting; early in day. Page 385

SIX-LAYER EGGNOG CAKE
Cake layers, filled with rum-flavored whipped cream and topped with chocolate. 12 servings; 4 hours. Page 394

DELUXE STRAWBERRY SHORTCAKE
Shortcake, sliced in half horizontally, filled and topped with layers of whipped cream and berries. 12 servings; 4 hours. Page 369

STRAWBERRY SOUFFLE
Chilled mixture of strawberries, gelatin, egg whites and cream, prepared in collared soufflé dish. 12 servings; 6 hours. Page 361

POTS DE CREME AU CHOCOLAT
Rich mousse of semisweet chocolate, egg yolks, and half-and-half, chilled and served with whipped cream. 6 servings; 5 hours. Page 362

APPLE STRUDEL
Phyllo pastry filled with apples, raisins, walnuts and spices and baked in the oven. 10 servings; 3 hours. Page 370

FLOATING ISLAND
Vanilla custard topped with soft meringue and decorated with sugar syrup. 4 servings; 1½ hours. Page 365

CREAM PUFF RING
Choux pastry, filled with almond pastry cream and topped with chocolate glaze and strawberries. 10 servings; early in day. Page 367

CREPES SUZETTE
Classic French crêpes, heated at the table in orange sauce and flamed in orange liqueur. 6 servings; early in day. Page 368

DESSERT CREPES WITH ORANGE
SAUCE *Sour cream-filled crêpes, topped with orange sauce. 6 servings; 1 hour.* Page 368

SYLLABUB
Half-and-half beaten until frothy and mixed with lemon juice, Chablis and brandy. 16 servings; 10 minutes. Page 369

CHOCOLATE SOUFFLE
Mixture of chocolate, egg yolks, milk and egg whites, baked. 8 servings; 2 hours. Page 363

INDIVIDUAL CHOCOLATE SOUFFLES
Chocolate and egg mixture, baked until puffy and brown, served with whipped cream and chocolate syrup. 6 servings; 1 hour. Page 363

CREAM PUFFS
Baked pastry shells filled with chilled Vanilla Pastry Cream and topped with confectioners' sugar. 12 servings; early in day. Page 366

SWANS
Choux pastry shapes with vanilla custard filling. 36 pastries; early in day. Page 367

APRICOT-CREAM FLAN
Egg custard in walnut-crumb crust, topped with apricots and melted apple jelly. 8 servings; 5 hours. Page 360

CHOCOLATE CUPS WITH STRAWBERRY CREAM *Handmade chocolate shells, filled with fresh strawberries and cream. 8 servings; 2 hours.* Page 370

BAVARIAN CREAM
A molded mixture of custard and whipped cream, garnished with sliced strawberries and nectarines. 8 servings; early in day. Page 360

SURPRISE ANGEL PECAN PIE
Crustless, pecan-soda-cracker and egg-white pie with whipped cream topping. 8 servings; 4 hours. Page 365

BANANA SOUFFLE
Purée of bananas in nutmeg-and-egg-white-sauce, baked until puffy and brown. Serve with whipped cream. 8 servings; 1 hour. Page 364

CHOCOLATE-CHERRY SOUFFLE
Chocolate, cherry and whipped-cream mixture, chilled in soufflé dish, with cream and cherry topping. 12 servings; early in day. Page 361

ALMOND-CREAM BOMBE
Almond liqueur-soaked cake triangles filled with chocolate-cream mixture. 8 servings; day ahead. Page 375

CHOCOLATE FANCY
Whipped-cream-topped cake, covered with strawberry-cream and chocolate sheet. 16 servings; early in day. Page 374

GALATOBOUREKO (front). *Phyllo with cream filling and syrup topping. 2½ hours.*
BAKLAVA *Phyllo with walnuts and honey. Each 24 servings; 3 hours.* Page 371

STEAMED PUDDING
Traditional Christmas fruit-filled dessert, flamed before serving. 12 servings; 4 hours. Page 375

CREME CARAMEL
Individual, baked vanilla custards served chilled in own syrup. 8 servings; early in day. Page 359

CHOCOLATE-CINNAMON TORTE
Baked cookie circles layered with chocolate cream filling and topped with grated chocolate. 16 servings; day ahead. Page 373

CREME BRULEE
Chilled egg custard, topped with brown sugar and broiled; served cold with sliced fruit. 10 servings; early in day. Page 359

STRAWBERRY MERINGUES
Individual meringues, filled with ice cream and topped with strawberries. 6 servings; early in day. Page 365

FROSTY LIME SOUFFLE
Chilled soufflé flavored with fresh lime juice. 8 servings; early in day. Page 362

ZABAGLIONE
Light, frothy egg-yolk, sugar and Marsala dessert, cooked in double-boiler and served warm. 6 servings; 20 minutes. Page 360

CHOCOLATE ANGEL PIE
Meringue pie shell, filled with rich chocolate and whipped cream filling. 10 servings; early in day. Page 365

ORANGE LIQUEUR SOUFFLE
Soufflé of custard sauce, orange liqueur and egg whites, baked and served hot with bowl of whipped cream. 6 servings; 1¼ hours. Page 364

STRAWBERRY SHORTCAKE
Plain shortcake, split in half and buttered, then filled and garnished with whipped cream and strawberries. 8 servings; 45 minutes. Page 369

SHERRY TRIFLE
Macaroons and sherry-soaked cake, layered with jam, custard, cream, cherry and almond topping. 8 servings; early in day. Page 372

ECLAIRS
Baked choux pastries filled with Vanilla Pastry Cream and topped with a semisweet-chocolate glaze. 10 éclairs; early in day. Page 366

CRANBERRY SOUFFLE
Chilled fresh cranberry soufflé served topped with whole sugared berries. 8 to 10 servings; early in day. **Page 362**

APPLE TURNOVERS (top). *8 filled pastry turnovers; 5 hours.* **Page 372.** **CREAMY RICE PUDDING** *Sweetened rice mixture with cream. 10 servings; 4½ hours.* **Page 341**

CHEESE BLINTZES
Cottage- and cream cheese-filled crêpes, baked until heated and topped with strawberries. 6 servings; early in day. **Page 368**

STRAWBERRY DESSERT OMELET
Baked sweet omelet filled with fresh strawberries and sprinkled with sugar. 4 servings; 30 minutes. **Page 146**

NO-BAKE CHEESECAKE
Creamed cottage cheese-gelatin mixture in unbaked crumb crust, garnished with canned fruit. 10 to 12 servings; early in day. **Page 159**

DELUXE BAKED CHEESECAKE
Filling of cream cheese, sugar and eggs, baked in rich crust, chilled and topped with sour cream. 16 servings; day ahead. **Page 158**

CHOCOLATE CHEESECAKE (top). *16 to 18 servings; early in day.* **CHERRY CHEESECAKE** *12 servings; day ahead.* **Page 158**

DELUXE PEACH-CHEESE PIE
Softened cream cheese in crumb crust, refrigerated and garnished with sliced peaches in apricot glaze. 8 servings; 6 hours. **Page 159**

CREAM-CHEESE RHUBARB PIE
Rhubarb sauce topped with cream cheese and eggs, baked in piecrust with sour cream and almond garnish. 8 servings; 6 hours. **Page 159**

ICED CHERRY SOUP
*Made with canned, tart cherries. 6 servings;
early in day.* Page 137

COLD RASPBERRY SOUP
*Made with frozen raspberries. 6 servings;
early in day.* Page 137

STRAWBERRY SOUP
*Made with fresh strawberries. 3 servings; early
in day.* Page 137

STRAWBERRY-RHUBARB SOUP
*Chilled blend of rhubarb, strawberries and orange sections in sweetened
orange juice, garnished with strawberry slices. 4 servings; 3 hours.*
Page 137

BLENDER BLUEBERRY SOUP
*Blueberries blended with sour cream and
served chilled. 2 servings; 20 minutes.* Page 137

99

CINNAMON APRICOTS IN CREAM
Halved, unpeeled apricots, baked until tender in sugar and cinnamon syrup and finished in heavy cream. 4 servings; 35 minutes. Page 302

STRAWBERRIES ROMANOFF
Fresh strawberries in orange-flavor liqueur, orange juice and brandy, topped with whipped cream. 4 servings; 1½ hours. Page 304

FREEZER STRAWBERRY TOPPING
Sauce of fresh strawberries and orange juice, shown here over pound cake, cheese cake, ice cream and yogurt. 2 days ahead. Page 304

BRANDIED CHERRY SAUCE (left).
30 minutes. Page 305. **BLUEBERRY SAUCE** *20 minutes.* Page 304

STEWED PLUMS (top left). *20 minutes.*
PLUMS IN PORT SAUCE (right).
6 servings; day ahead. **CREAMY PLUM DRESSING** *on fruit; 1¼ hours.* Page 314

PAPAYAS WITH LEMON CREAM
Halved papayas with lemon-flavored, whipped-cream filling, chilled and garnished with lemon slices. 6 servings; 1 hour. Page 312

VERY-BERRY COMPOTE
Strawberries, raspberries and blueberries, topped with ice cream and grated orange peel. 8 to 10 servings; 2½ hours. Page 304

GRAPEFRUIT AMBROSIA
Grapefruit sections, drained and tossed with honey and flaked coconut. 4 servings; 5 minutes. Page 307

STEWED PEACHES (top). *6 servings; 20 minutes.* **BUTTERY BAKED PEACHES** *6 servings; 1 hour.* Page 312

POACHED PEARS IN SAUTERNE (top).
6 servings; 4 hours.
PEARS IN CHOCOLATE SAUCE
2 servings; 30 minutes. Page 313

MINTED GRAPES
Seedless green grapes, marinated in honey, lime juice and chopped mint. 4 servings; early in day. Page 306

BAKED APPLES (top). *Topped with cream. 6 servings; 1 hour.* **APPLESAUCE** *Chunky or smooth. 30 minutes.* Page 301

GINGERED KIWIFRUIT
Sliced kiwifruit and orange sections in ginger syrup, served cold. 4 servings; 2½ hours.
Page 307

BANANA POPS
Banana pieces on wooden ice-cream-bar sticks, rolled in melted chocolate and coconut. 12 pops; 2 hours. Page 303

MARINATED WATERMELON (top).
16 servings; 4 hours. **CANTALOUPE ICE**
5 cups; day ahead. Page 310

RHUBARB SAUCE (top). *20 minutes.*
RHUBARB CRUMBLE *6 servings; 50 minutes.* Page 315

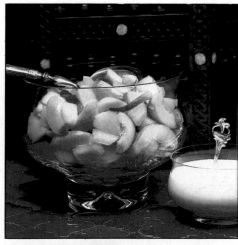

FRESH FRUIT BOWL WITH CARDAMOM DRESSING *Bowl of melons and summer fruit with smooth dressing. 12 servings; 30 minutes.* Page 322

SACRAMENTO FRUIT BOWL
Pineapple, melon, oranges, nectarines, plums, grapes and limes, chilled in anise seed syrup. 10 to 12 servings; early in day. Page 322

HOMEMADE VANILLA ICE CREAM
Egg custard, flavored with vanilla and frozen in ice-cream freezer. Early in day. Page 376

HOMEMADE ICE-CREAM VARIATIONS *Just add flavorings to the basic ice-cream mixture* (left to right): *Spiced Banana; Strawberry; Chocolate; Pistachio; Peach; early in day.* Page 377

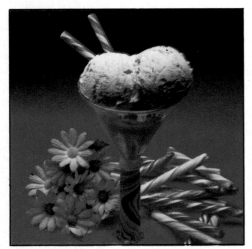

PEPPERMINT-CANDY ICE CREAM
Ice-cream mixture flavored with crushed peppermint candies; 6 hours. Page 377

NESSELRODE ICE-CREAM MOLD
Molded of candied fruit, raisins and walnuts mixed with vanilla ice cream, layered with ladyfingers. 10 servings; day ahead. Page 379

STRAWBERRY ICE MILK
Frozen crushed-strawberry mixture. Early in day. Page 378. *Served here with* REFRIGERATOR COOKIES. Page 411

PINEAPPLE SHERBET
Blended fresh pineapple, sugar, lemon juice and egg whites, frozen until firm. Early in day. Page 380

BAKED ALASKA PIE
Vanilla ice cream and frozen raspberries in a ladyfinger crust, topped with meringue, baked. 12 servings; 5 hours. Page 378

ORANGE MILK SHERBET (left). *Early in day.* Page 380. CANTALOUPE SHERBET *Early in day.* Page 380

102

STRAWBERRY-ORANGE ICE
*Frozen strawberries, fruit juices and liqueur.
Early in day.* Page 381. *Served here with*
CANDIED ORANGE PEEL. Page 311

RAINBOW ICE-CREAM TORTE
*Layered ice creams and sweet cherries in
gingersnap crust. 12 servings; early in day.*
Page 379

**MINTED SHERBET RING WITH
BERRIES** *Lemon sherbet, flavored with crème
de menthe and decorated for serving. 8 to 10
servings; early in day.* Page 380

LEMON ICE IN LEMON CUPS
*Hollowed lemons filled with sweetened fresh
lemon juice mixture, garnished with mint
sprigs. Early in day.* Page 381

WATERMELON ICE
*Blended watermelon chunks, lemon juice and
confectioners' sugar, frozen in freezing
compartment. Early in day.* Page 381

ICE-CREAM BOMBE LES DAMES D'ESCOFFIER
*Molded strawberry and vanilla ice cream with almond brickle-chip center,
decorated with whipped cream and strawberries and served with chocolate
sauce. 12 servings; early in day.* Page 379

COOKIES

FUDGY BROWNIES
24 brownies. **Page 404**

CINNAMON COOKIES
72 cookies. **Page 413**

DOUBLE CHOCOLATE DROPS *48 cookies.*
Page 406

CHRISTMAS WREATHS
54 cookies. **Page 409**

CHOCO-PEANUT DROPS
48 cookies. **Page 407**

OATMEAL COOKIES
48 cookies. **Page 407**

WALNUT CLUSTERS
36 cookies. **Page 407**

RAISIN-ORANGE COOKIES
30 cookies. **Page 407**

SHORTBREAD
14 cookies. **Page 405**

BACKPACKING BARS
12 cookies. **Page 404**

COCONUT MERINGUES
24 cookies. **Page 408**

DANISH ALMOND CAKES
42 cookies. **Page 409**

MARBLED FUDGE BARS
36 cookies. **Page 405**

CHOCOLATE CHIP COOKIES *48 cookies.*
Page 406

GINGERBREAD-MEN COOKIES
24 cookies. **Page 413**

ALMOND LACE ROLLS
30 cookies. Page 407

MADELEINES
30 cookies. Page 409

SOFT MOLASSES COOKIES
30 cookies. Page 406

ALMOND MACAROONS
36 cookies. Page 408

CITRUS PINWHEELS
96 cookies. Page 411

NEAPOLITAN COOKIES
72 cookies. Page 411

FILBERT DROPS
24 cookies. Page 408

LINZER COOKIES
30 cookies. Page 405

LUSCIOUS APRICOT SQUARES
16 cookies. Page 404

TOFFEE BARS
50 cookies. Page 404

PEANUT-BUTTER COOKIES
36 cookies. Page 408

RAISIN-GRANOLA
COOKIES *48 cookies.*
Page 406

CARDAMOM COOKIES
72 cookies. Page 409

ALMOND BUTTER
COOKIES *36 cookies.*
Page 412

SPICE COOKIES
108 cookies. Page 413

PRUNE-RIBBON COOKIES
27 cookies. Page 405

SUGAR COOKIES
72 cookies. Page 412

SPRITZ AND VARIATIONS: RINGLET COOKIES (top). *32 cookies;* **SPRITZ** (center). *108 cookies;* **RASPBERRY THUMB-PRINTS** *72 cookies; 3½ hours.* **Page 410**

CHOCOLATE-DIPPED BUTTER COOKIES *Sour-cream dough, pressed through a tree shaped plate, baked and then glazed. 120 cookies; 4 hours.* **Page 410**

SANDWICH COOKIES *Rolled vanilla cookies with colored frosting. 42 cookies; 3 hours.* **Page 412**

CANDY APPLES *Red Delicious apples, dipped in corn-syrup mixture and left to harden. 8 apples; 2 hours.* Page 302

LOLLIPOPS *Hard candies and corn-syrup mixture, hardened in paper cup molds. 12 lollipops; 3 hours.* **Page 417**

POPCORN BALLS *Popped corn and candied cherries, coated with syrup mixture. 12 balls; 2 hours.* **Page 418**

CHOCOLATE FUDGE *36 pieces; 2½ hours.* Page 415

PEANUT BRITTLE *1 pound; 2 hours.* Page 418

NUTTY BUTTERSCOTCH FUDGE *49 pieces; 1½ hours.* Page 415

MAPLE KISSES *24 pieces; 1½ hours.* Page 415

MOLASSES TAFFY *¾ pound;*
2 hours. Page 416.

MARZIPAN FRUITS *4¼ pounds;*
day ahead. Page 419.

WALNUT CRUNCH
1½ pounds; 3½ hours. Page 418.

DIVINITY
1½ pounds; 1½ hours.
Page 417.

PECAN PENUCHE
2 pounds; 2½ hours.
Page 415.

BONBONS
1 pound; 7 hours.
Page 418.

FONDANT
1 pound; 5 hours.
Page 417

PEPPERMINT PATTIES
64 patties; 3 hours
Page 419.

ORANGE-ALMOND CARAMELS
50 pieces; 1½ hours.
Page 416.

NOUGATS
2¼ pounds; day ahead.
Page 416

CHOCOLATE-DIPPED
FRUIT *and* NUTS *Orange segments,*
peanuts and strawberries covered in melted
chocolate. 1½ hours. Page 420

MELT-AWAY
CHOCOLATE MINTS
Semisweet chocolate squares
flavored with peppermint. 2½ hours. Page 420

TRUFFLES
Sweetened condensed milk and chocolate
rounds, rolled in cocoa. 36 truffles; 2 hours.
Page 420

107

OPEN-FACE STEAK SANDWICHES
Cubed steaks on toasted bread, served with gravy and garnished with watercress. 4 servings; 20 minutes. Page 457

WESTERN SANDWICHES (left). *Ham, green pepper and onion cooked in an omelet and served on toast. 4 sandwiches; 35 minutes. Page 456*

CANADIAN-BACON BUNS *Lightly fried Canadian bacon in toasted hamburger buns. 6 sandwiches; 15 minutes. Page 456*

CURRIED BEEF IN PITA
Curried ground beef, onion, chopped apple, and raisins in pita bread, served with yogurt. 12 sandwiches; 3 hours. Page 457

CROQUE MONSIEUR
Ham, Swiss cheese and mustard on white bread, toasted in the oven until golden. 16 sandwiches; 45 minutes. Page 455

SLOPPY JOES
Ground beef, cooked with onion, green pepper and canned pork and beans, served in long rolls. 6 sandwiches; 30 minutes. Page 456

BARBECUED PORK SANDWICHES
Chunks of pork, cooked with onion and peppers in spicy sauce, served in rolls with lettuce and tomato. 10 sandwiches; 3½ hours. Page 455

MOZZARELLA LOAF
Mozzarella cheese and olives in a long Italian loaf, baked until cheese is melted. 6 servings; 40 minutes. Page 455

REUBEN
Swiss cheese, corned beef and sauerkraut in rye-bread, browned in a skillet. 4 sandwiches; 45 minutes. Page 456

ITALIAN HERO SANDWICHES
Sweet Italian sausages, cooked with onions and peppers and served in hard rolls. 4 sandwiches; 45 minutes. Page 457

TACOS (with CORN TORTILLAS)
Taco shells with chicken or beef filling, served with lettuce, tomato, shredded cheese and hot pepper sauce. 12 sandwiches; 1 hour. Page 456

POOR BOY
Ham, Swiss cheese, cucumber, tomato and dressing in French bread. 6 servings; 20 minutes. Page 457

CLUB SANDWICHES
Layers of toast with crisp bacon, turkey lettuce, tomato and mayonnaise filling. 2 servings; 20 minutes. Page 457

WATERCRESS-WALNUT SANDWICHES (top). *30 minutes.* **KEEP TRIM SANDWICHES: CURRIED SHRIMP** (left) and **CRUNCHY TUNA.** *All page 458*

RIBBON SANDWICHES (top).
50 sandwiches; 3½ hours.
DEVILED HAM PINWHEELS
30 sandwiches; 30 minutes. Page 459

OPEN SANDWICHES
(Top row, left to right) *Egg, caviar and red pepper; shrimp on mayonnaise; Danish Blue, black grapes and walnuts; marinated herring and onion on lettuce.*

(Bottom row, left to right) *Rare roast beef with crumbled fried onion; smoked salmon on lettuce; salami and cucumber twists; cold roast pork with orange twists and crumbled bacon. Page 458*

109

CAFFE ESPRESSO (left). *4 servings; 15 minutes.* CAFE AU LAIT *1 serving; 15 minutes.* Page 467

IRISH COFFEE (left). *1 serving; 15 minutes.* CAFE BRULOT *8 servings; 15 minutes.* Page 467

ICE-CREAM SODAS (back): *Flavored syrups added to milk, ice cream and club soda. 1 serving; 5 minutes.* STRAWBERRY SODA. *1 serving; 5 minutes. All page 469*

CHOCOLATE-ORANGE SODAS (left). *8 servings.* EGG CREAM. *1 serving; both 5 minutes.* Page 469

EGGNOG (top). *38 servings; 2 hours.* Page 470. PARTY ORANGE SODA *16 servings; 15 minutes.* Page 469

ICED COFFEE
Double-strength coffee, poured over ice; serve with cream and sugar, if desired. 15 minutes. Page 467

HEARTY HOT COCOA
Hot cocoa, milk, vanilla and sugar, topped with marshmallow. 6 servings; 15 minutes. Page 468

CHOCOLATE *and* BANANA MILK SHAKES *Chocolate: ice cream, blended with syrup and milk; banana: blended with vanilla ice cream. 2 servings; 10 minutes. Page 469*

MOCHA FLOAT
Chocolate-milk mix, coffee powder and club soda, with ice-cream scoops. 1 serving; 5 minutes. Page 469

FRENCH HOT CHOCOLATE
Rich drink of hot milk and chocolate, beaten with heavy cream. 8 servings; 50 minutes. Page 468

BLACK COW
Chilled root beer topped with scoop of vanilla ice cream. 1 serving; 5 minutes. Page 469

ICED TEA, FAMILY STYLE
Steeped tea, poured over ice cubes and served with sugar and lemon slices. 8 servings; 15 minutes. Page 468

STRAWBERRY SHAKES
Low-calorie, strawberry-and-nonfat-dry-milk-powder shake. 4 servings; 5 minutes. Page 469

SPARKLING STRAWBERRY PUNCH
Strawberries in rosé wine, lemonade and club soda, garnished with orange slices. 36 servings; 10 minutes. Page 471

SANGRIA
Chilled, fruit-filled, Spanish wine-and-soda-water punch. 8 servings; 5 minutes. Page 471

LEMONADE (left). *16 servings; 2 hours.*
EASY-WAY LEMONADE *5 servings; early in day.* Page 470

HOT MULLED WINE
Red wine heated with cinnamon, cloves, orange and lemon slices. 36 servings; 30 minutes. Page 471

WASSAIL BOWL WITH BAKED APPLES
Baked apples in hot, spicy apple cider and juice. 36 servings; 45 minutes. Page 472

FROZEN DAIQUIRIS (left). **FROZEN WHISKEY SOURS** *Both 13 servings; day ahead.* Page 472

WHISKEY-SOUR PUNCH (left). *32 servings; 25 minutes.* **GOLDEN PUNCH** *Non-alcoholic. 20 servings; 10 minutes.* Page 471

GLOGG
Warm alcoholic punch, flamed and topped with almonds. 20 servings; day ahead. Page 471

COCKTAILS (from left): ALEXANDER; MINT JULEP; MARGARITA; OLD-FASHIONED; TOM COLLINS; MANHATTAN; STINGER; MARTINI; BLOODY MARY *and* COMPANY BLOODY MARY. *5 minutes.* Pages 472–3

RECIPES

APPETIZERS

Little nibblers to go with cocktails, dainty canapés to be passed on a tray, colorful appetizers to serve as the first course at dinner, all reflect the skill of the cook and help create an elegant setting for the occasion. The appetizers in this chapter include some to be made ahead, some that are light, crunchy and low in calories and other heartier appetizers for those occasions when the party you are planning is almost a meal.

Tidbits

Crisp Cheese Twists

1¼ cups all-purpose flour
½ cup yellow cornmeal
1 teaspoon salt
1¼ cups shredded Cheddar cheese (5 ounces)
¼ cup shortening
water
grated Parmesan cheese

Color index page 18

Begin 45 mins ahead or early in day

96 appetizers or 24 servings

1. In large bowl, mix flour, cornmeal and salt. With pastry blender or 2 knives used scissor-fashion, cut in Cheddar cheese and shortening until mixture resembles coarse crumbs. With fork, stir in ⅓ cup water. With hands, shape dough into ball. (If mixture is too dry, add more water, a teaspoon at a time, until moist enough to hold together.) Preheat oven to 425°F.
2. Between two 15-inch-long sheets of waxed paper, with rolling pin, roll half of pastry into 12″ by 10″ rectangle. With knife, cut dough into 5″ by ½″ strips. Remove each strip; holding ends, make twist by turning ends in opposite directions. Lay on cookie sheet; press ends to sheet to prevent curling.
3. Bake twists 6 to 8 minutes until golden. When done, sprinkle lightly with Parmesan cheese; cool twists on racks. Repeat with remaining dough.

Cutting the strips: Roll half dough into 12″ by 10″ rectangle, then cut into 5″ by ½″ strips. Repeat.

Making a twist: Hold strip and turn ends in opposite directions to make twist; lay on cookie sheet.

Chinese Fried Walnuts

6 cups water
4 cups California walnuts
½ cup sugar
salad oil
⅛ teaspoon salt

Color index page 18

Begin early in day

4 cups

1. In 3-quart saucepan over high heat, heat water to boiling; add walnuts; reheat to boiling; cook 1 minute. Rinse under running hot water; drain.
2. In large bowl, toss walnuts in sugar.
3. Meanwhile, in electric skillet, heat about 1 inch salad oil to 350°F. With slotted spoon, add about half of walnuts to oil; fry 5 minutes or until golden, stirring often.
4. With slotted spoon, place walnuts in coarse sieve over bowl to drain; sprinkle with salt; toss lightly to keep walnuts from sticking together. Transfer to waxed paper to cool. Fry remaining walnuts. Store in tightly covered container.

Curried Almonds

2 cups blanched whole almonds
1½ tablespoons butter or margarine, melted
1 tablespoon curry powder
2 teaspoons salt

Color index page 18

Begin early in day

2 cups

Preheat oven to 300°F. In 8- or 9-inch cake pan, combine almonds and melted butter. Toast in oven 30 minutes, stirring occasionally. Add curry powder and salt; toss until thoroughly coated. Transfer to waxed paper to cool. Store almonds in tightly covered container.

HOT-PEPPER PECANS: Prepare as above but use **2 cups pecan halves, 1½ tablespoons butter** or margarine, melted, **1 teaspoon salt, 2 teaspoons soy sauce** and **dash hot pepper sauce.** (Makes 2 cups.)

CASHEWS WITH CHILI: Prepare as above but use **2 cups salted cashews, 1½ tablespoons butter** or margarine, melted, **1 tablespoon chili powder** and omit salt. (Makes 2 cups.)

Cold canapés

Curried-Tuna Canapés

Color index page 18

Begin 2 hrs ahead

40 appetizers

Choux paste:
1/4 cup butter or margarine
1/2 cup water
1/8 teaspoon salt
1/2 cup all-purpose flour
2 eggs

Filling:
1 6 1/2- to 7-ounce can tuna
2 hard-cooked eggs
1/2 cup mayonnaise
1/4 cup minced celery
1 tablespoon curry powder
1/4 teaspoon salt
2/3 cup chopped parsley

1 Grease large cookie sheet. Preheat oven to 375°F. Prepare *choux* paste: In 1-quart saucepan over medium heat, heat butter, water and salt until mixture boils. Remove from heat. Add flour all at once. With wooden spoon, vigorously stir until mixture forms a ball and leaves side of pan. Add eggs, one at a time, beating well after each addition, until smooth. Allow mixture to cool slightly; carefully spoon into pastry bag fitted with round tube.

2 Squeeze *choux* paste through pastry bag onto greased cookie sheet to make 20 mounds, each about 2 teaspoonfuls and about 1 inch apart.

3 Bake puffs 20 to 25 minutes, until browned; cool puffs on wire rack.

4 Meanwhile, prepare Filling: In small bowl with fork, stir tuna and its oil until finely flaked; chop hard-cooked eggs.

5 Into flaked tuna, stir mayonnaise, minced celery, chopped hard-cooked eggs, curry powder and salt; cover and chill.

6 When puffs are cool, with sharp knife, cut each puff horizontally in half to make 2 shells.

7 Spoon about 1 rounded teaspoon of mixture into each shell; garnish with chopped parsley.

Caviar-Egg Rounds

Color index page 18

Begin 30 mins ahead

12 appetizers

6 pumpernickel-bread slices
2 hard-cooked eggs
3 pitted ripe olives
mayonnaise
1 tablespoon red caviar

1. Using a 2-inch round cookie cutter, cut 2 circles from each of the bread slices.
2. With sharp knife, cut each hard-cooked egg into 6 thin slices. Cut each olive into 4 slices.
3. Spread a dab of mayonnaise on center of each circle and top with a slice of hard-cooked egg. Garnish with some caviar and a slice of olive.

Tuna-Dill Rounds

Color index page 18

Begin 45 mins ahead

28 appetizers

1 1-pound loaf pumpernickel-bread, sliced
mayonnaise
1 medium cucumber, thinly sliced
1 6 1/2- to 7-ounce can tuna, drained
1/4 cup sour cream
1 teaspoon dill weed
1 teaspoon lemon juice
1/8 teaspoon pepper
1 1/2 teaspoons minced pimento

1. With 2-inch round cutter, cut 2 rounds from each bread slice; spread with some mayonnaise; top with cucumber slice. Chop any leftover cucumber.
2. In small bowl, mix chopped cucumber, 3 tablespoons mayonnaise, tuna and next 4 ingredients. Spoon some mixture on each round; top with some minced pimento.

Watercress Cream-Cheese Triangles

Color index page 18

Begin 15 mins ahead

20 appetizers

1 3-ounce package cream cheese, softened
5 thin white-bread slices, crusts removed
1 bunch watercress, washed and trimmed

Spread cheese on bread slices. Cut each slice into 4 triangles. Top each with 2 sprigs watercress.

Smoked Salmon Squares

Color index page 18

Begin 30 mins ahead

20 appetizers

5 thin white-bread slices
1 3-ounce package cream cheese, softened
3 ounces sliced smoked salmon
strips of peel cut from 2 large lemons

1. Toast bread; trim crusts. Spread bread with cream cheese; cut each slice into quarters.
2. Cut salmon slices to fit on toast; top toast with slices. Garnish with strips of lemon peel.

Anchovy-Cheese Circles

Color index page 18

Begin 15 mins ahead

20 appetizers

10 pumpernickel-bread slices
1 5-ounce jar Old English cheese spread
2 teaspoons horseradish
5 anchovy fillets, cut into strips
5 pimento-stuffed olives, sliced

1. Using 2-inch round cookie cutter, cut 2 circles from each pumpernickel-bread slice.
2. In small bowl, mix cheese spread and horseradish; spread some mixture on each circle. Top with strip of anchovy fillet and olive slice.

Cold canapés

Hot canapés

Blue-Cheese-and-Aspic Canapés

*1 16-ounce can clam-
 tomato juice*
*1 envelope unflavored
 gelatin*
⅓ cup sour cream
*2 tablespoons crumbled
 blue cheese*
*5 thin white-bread
 slices*
*drained capers
 for garnish*

Color index
page 18

Begin 3 hrs
ahead or
early in day

20 appetizers

1 Into 1-quart saucepan,
pour juice; sprinkle over
unflavored gelatin. Cook
the mixture over medium
heat, stirring until the gelatin is completely dissolved.

2 Pour mixture into
15½″ by 10½″ jelly-roll
pan. Refrigerate until the
aspic mixture is completely
set, about 30 minutes.

3 In small bowl, mix sour
cream and crumbled
blue cheese. Trim crusts
from bread slices.

4 Spread sour-cream
mixture on bread; cut
each slice into 4 triangles.
Cut the aspic into
small squares.

5 Pile some aspic on
center of each canapé;
use leftover for salad.
Garnish the canapés with
the drained capers.

Asparagus Canapés

*5 thin white-bread
 slices*
mayonnaise
*1 15-ounce can white
 asparagus spears,
 drained*

*1 whole pimento, cut in
 thin strips*
*1 gherkin, cut in
 20 slices*

Color index
page 18

Begin 20 mins
ahead or
early in day

20 appetizers

1. Trim crusts from bread slices. Spread bread slices
lightly with mayonnaise; cut each slice into quarters.
Cut each asparagus spear in half.
2. On bread squares, arrange asparagus diagonally;
cut asparagus to fit bread if necessary. Arrange 2
pimento strips on each appetizer; garnish with a
gherkin slice.

Individual Broccoli Quiches

*Pastry for 2-Crust Pie
 (page 344)*
*2 tablespoons butter or
 margarine,
 melted*
*½ 10-ounce package
 frozen chopped
 broccoli, thawed*

*¼ pound natural Swiss
 cheese, shredded*
1 cup half-and-half
3 eggs
1 teaspoon salt
⅛ teaspoon pepper

Color index
page 22

Begin 1½ hrs
ahead

36 appetizers

1 Grease and flour thirty-
six 1¾-inch muffin-pan
cups, then prepare pastry.

2 On lightly floured sur-
face with floured roll-
ing pin, roll dough about
⅛ inch thick.

3 Using 3-inch round
fluted cookie cutter, cut
dough into 36 circles, rerolling pastry scraps.

4 Line muffin-pan cups
with pastry circles;
brush pastry lightly with
melted butter; refrigerate
30 minutes. Preheat oven
to 400°F. Drain broccoli
on paper towels.

5 Into each cup, spoon
about 1 teaspoon
broccoli and top with some
cheese. In small bowl with
wire whisk or spoon, mix
well half-and-half, eggs,
salt and pepper.

6 Spoon about 1
tablespoon egg mixture
into each cup. Bake 25
minutes or until knife
inserted in center of quiche
comes out clean. Remove
from hot pan and serve.

INDIVIDUAL SPINACH QUICHES: Prepare as
above but use *½ 10-ounce package frozen chopped
spinach*, thawed, instead of broccoli and *¼
pound Gruyère cheese*, shredded, instead of Swiss
cheese. (Makes 36 appetizers.)

Pissaladière

Color index page 22

Begin 2¼ hrs ahead

36 appetizers or 18 servings

1 package active dry yeast
1 teaspoon salt
about 3 cups all-purpose flour
1 cup water
4 medium onions
3 tablespoons olive oil
½ teaspoon oregano

1 2-ounce can anchovy fillets, drained and chopped
1 7-ounce jar pimento-stuffed olives, drained
¼ pound Swiss cheese

1. In large bowl, combine yeast, salt and 1 cup flour. In 1-quart saucepan over high heat, heat water until very warm (120° to 130°F.).
2. With mixer at low speed, beat water into dry ingredients until just blended. At medium speed, beat 2 minutes, occasionally scraping bowl. Beat in ½ cup flour or enough to make a thick batter; beat 2 minutes more, scraping bowl often. Stir in enough additional flour (about 1 cup) to make a soft dough. Turn onto lightly floured surface; knead until smooth and elastic, about 8 minutes, adding more flour while kneading. Shape dough into ball; place in greased large bowl, turning dough over to grease top. Cover with towel; let rise in warm place (80° to 85°F.), away from draft, until it is doubled in size, about 1 hour.
3. Meanwhile, thinly slice onions. In 10-inch skillet over medium heat, in hot oil, cook onions, stirring, until tender. Remove from heat. Stir in the oregano and the chopped anchovies.
4. Punch down dough; turn onto lightly floured surface. Cover with bowl; let rest 15 minutes. Thinly slice olives; coarsely grate cheese. Preheat oven to 425°F. With lightly floured rolling pin, on greased large cookie sheet, roll dough into 13½″ by 12″ rectangle. Spread onion mixture evenly over dough. Top with olive slices; sprinkle with cheese. Bake 15 to 20 minutes until the piecrust is golden. Cut length-wise into four 13½-inch-long strips, cut each strip crosswise into nine 3″ by 1½″ pieces.

Sausage-stuffed Mushrooms

Color index page 20

Begin 1 hr ahead

30 appetizers

1½ pounds medium mushrooms (about 30)
½ pound pork sausage meat
½ cup shredded mozzarella cheese

¼ cup seasoned bread crumbs
parsley for garnish (optional)

1. Remove stems from mushrooms; chop stems. Set mushrooms and stems aside.
2. In 10-inch skillet over medium heat, cook sausage until well browned. With slotted spoon, remove sausage to paper towels to drain. Spoon off all but 2 tablespoons drippings from skillet.
3. In hot drippings over medium heat, cook mushroom stems until tender, about 10 minutes, stirring frequently. Remove skillet from heat; stir in sausage, cheese and crumbs.
4. Preheat oven to 450°F. Fill mushroom caps with sausage mixture. Place stuffed mushrooms in 15½″ by 10½″ jelly-roll pan. Bake 15 minutes.

Pumpernickel-Muenster Triangles

Color index page 22

Begin 10 mins ahead

16 appetizers

1 8-ounce package Muenster cheese
½ medium onion

4 pumpernickel-bread slices

1. Preheat broiler if manufacturer directs. Cut slices from cheese into halves; cut onion into thin slices and separate into rings.
2. Place two halves of cheese on top of one bread slice; place overlapping onion rings on top of cheese. Repeat with remaining bread, cheese slices and onion rings.
3. Place on cookie sheet and broil for 3 to 5 minutes until cheese is bubbly and light brown.
4. To serve, cut slices neatly into triangles and serve appetizers immediately.

PUMPERNICKEL-CHEDDAR TRIANGLES: Prepare as Pumpernickel-Muenster Triangles (above), but instead of Muenster cheese use *one 8-ounce package sliced Cheddar cheese*.

Cheesy Shrimp Canapés

Color index page 22

Begin 40 mins ahead

20 appetizers

10 white-bread slices
2 tablespoons butter or margarine
½ teaspoon thyme leaves
½ 8-ounce package frozen shelled, deveined shrimp, cooked and chopped

½ cup shredded Swiss cheese (about 2 ounces)
⅓ cup mayonnaise
½ cup fresh bread crumbs
¼ teaspoon salt
fresh dill for garnish

1. Preheat oven to 400°F. Using 2-inch round fluted cookie cutter, cut 2 circles from each white-bread slice (reserve leftover pieces to make fresh bread crumbs later).
2. In 1-quart saucepan over low heat, melt butter or margarine with thyme leaves. With pastry brush, brush bread circles with melted butter mixture; place on small cookie sheet. Bake 10 minutes or until circles are golden.
3. Meanwhile, combine shrimp with remaining ingredients except fresh dill. Shape shrimp mixture into 20 balls.
4. Preheat broiler if manufacturer directs. Lightly press the shrimp balls onto the toasted bread circles. About 7 to 9 inches from source of heat (or at 450°F.), broil shrimp canapés 10 minutes or until they are hot and bubbly.

Cutting out circles: With 2-inch round fluted cookie cutter, cut out 2 circles from each bread slice.

Assembling canapés: Lightly press shrimp balls into toasted circles then broil until hot and bubbly.

Hot canapés

Hearty appetizers

Blini with Caviar

Color index
page 24

Begin 55 mins
ahead

48 Blini or
16 to 24
servings

½ cup buckwheat flour
¼ cup all-purpose flour
1 teaspoon sugar
½ teaspoon baking soda
⅛ teaspoon salt
½ cup milk
1 egg
1 8-ounce container
    sour cream (1 cup)

1 tablespoon butter or
    margarine,
    melted
salad oil
1 2-ounce jar black or
    red salmon or
    lumpfish caviar

1. In small bowl, combine buckwheat flour, all-purpose flour, sugar, baking soda and salt. Stir in milk, egg and 2 tablespoons sour cream until batter is smooth. Add melted butter or margarine; stir until thoroughly blended.
2. Heat griddle or 10-inch skillet over medium heat; lightly brush with salad oil. Pour batter by teaspoonfuls onto hot griddle, making 7 or 8 pancakes at a time. Cook pancakes until tops are slightly set and undersides are golden. With pancake turner, turn pancakes and cook until undersides are firm. Place in single layer on warm large platter; cover and keep warm.
3. Repeat until all batter is used, brushing griddle with more salad oil, if necessary.
4. Spoon remaining sour cream into medium pastry bag with large rosette tube; pipe some sour cream onto each pancake. Top each with some salmon or lumpfish caviar.

VARIATION: Omit buckwheat flour. Use ¾ cup all-purpose flour. Prepare batter and bake as above.

Tostada Appetizers

Color index
page 20

Begin 1 hr
ahead

36 appetizers
or 12 servings

6 corn tortillas
salad oil
¾ pound lean ground
    beef
1 small onion, diced
4 teaspoons chili powder
½ teaspoon salt
½ teaspoon oregano
    leaves

1 8-ounce can tomato
    sauce
¼ pound Cheddar cheese,
    shredded
1½ cups shredded
    iceberg lettuce
¾ cup sliced pitted ripe
    olives

1. With sharp knife, cut each tortilla into 6 wedge-shaped pieces. In 10-inch skillet over medium-high heat, in about ¼ inch hot salad oil, cook tortilla wedges, about a third at a time, 30 seconds. With slotted spoon, turn tortilla "chips;" cook 30 seconds longer or until golden and crisp. Remove; drain on paper towels. Place in single layer on a large platter; keep warm.
2. In 2-quart saucepan over medium-high heat, cook ground beef and onion until meat is browned and onion is tender, stirring occasionally, about 10 minutes. Spoon off excess fat from meat mixture. Stir in chili powder, salt, oregano and half of the tomato sauce; cook 2 minutes. Remove saucepan from heat.
3. Spoon about 1 heaping teaspoon meat mixture on each tortilla chip. Top each with some cheese, lettuce, a half teaspoonful of remaining tomato sauce and some olive slices. Serve immediately.

Hot Mushroom Turnovers

Color index
page 22

Begin early
in day

50 appetizers

3 3-ounce packages
    cream cheese, softened
all-purpose flour
butter or margarine,
    softened
½ pound mushrooms,
    minced
1 large onion, minced
1 teaspoon salt
¼ teaspoon thyme leaves
¼ cup sour cream
1 egg, beaten

1 In medium bowl at medium speed, mix well cream cheese, 1½ cups flour and ½ cup butter, occasionally scraping bowl. Wrap dough; chill 1 hour.

2 In 10-inch skillet over medium heat, in 3 tablespoons butter, cook mushrooms and onion until tender.

3 Stir in salt, thyme leaves and 2 tablespoons flour until blended; stir in sour cream.

4 On floured surface, thinly roll out half of dough; with cookie cutter, cut twenty 2¾-inch circles. Roll scraps into ball; chill.

5 On one half of each circle, put a teaspoonful of mushroom mixture. Brush edges with beaten egg.

6 Fold dough over filling; with fork, press edges together; prick tops; place on ungreased cookie sheets. Repeat with remaining dough and filling.

7 Brush turnovers with egg. Cover; chill. *About 25 minutes before serving:* Preheat oven to 450°F. Bake turnovers 12 minutes or until golden.

Steak Bites

Color index page 19

Begin 2 hrs ahead

48 appetizers or 20 to 24 servings

1 2-pound beef top round steak, cut 1 inch thick
seasoned meat tenderizer
½ cup dry red wine
1 garlic clove, crushed
2 tablespoons butter
1½ teaspoons dry mustard

1 teaspoon Worcestershire
¼ teaspoon salt
⅛ teaspoon hot pepper sauce
parsley sprigs for garnish

1. Prepare steak with meat tenderizer as label directs. In 13″ by 9″ baking dish, mix wine and garlic. Add steak; cover; refrigerate 1½ hours, turning once.
2. Preheat broiler if manufacturer directs. Place steak on rack in broiling pan, reserving marinade. About 5 inches from source of heat (or at 450°F.), broil steak 10 minutes. Turn; broil 8 minutes more for rare or until of desired doneness.
3. Meanwhile, in 1-quart saucepan over low heat, melt butter. Stir in mustard, Worcestershire, salt, hot pepper sauce and 2 tablespoons marinade. Cook until heated through.
4. When steak is done, place on carving board; cut into 1-inch cubes. Place steak with juices in chafing dish. Pour butter mixture over cubes. Garnish with parsley. Serve with cocktail picks.

OTHER BEEF CUTS: Instead of beef top round steak, use *one 2-pound top quality beef chuck under blade steak boneless*, cut 1 inch thick. Or, omit meat tenderizer and use one 2-pound beef loin or loin top sirloin steak boneless, cut 1 inch thick.

Swedish Meatballs

Color index page 19

Begin 1 hr ahead

40 appetizers

1 pound ground beef
1½ cups seasoned dried bread crumbs
½ cup dry sherry
½ teaspoon ground mace
½ teaspoon salt
⅛ teaspoon pepper
1¼ cups heavy or whipping cream

all-purpose flour
2 tablespoons salad oil
2 tablespoons butter or margarine
1 10½-ounce can condensed beef consommé
1 bay leaf

1. In large bowl, combine first 6 ingredients with ¾ cup cream; shape into 40 small meatballs. On waxed paper, in about ¼ cup flour, coat meatballs.
2. In 12-inch skillet over medium-high heat, in hot oil, brown meatballs well. Drain on paper towels. Wipe skillet clean.
3. In same skillet over medium heat, melt butter or margarine. Stir in 1 tablespoon flour until well blended and smooth. Gradually stir in undiluted consommé and ½ cup cream; heat to boiling, stirring constantly. Add meatballs and bay leaf; simmer, covered, 15 minutes or until meatballs are tender. Discard bay leaf. Serve Swedish Meatballs in chafing dish to keep hot.

TO FREEZE AHEAD: Up to 1 month before serving: Prepare recipe as above but place in freezer-safe container. Freeze. *To serve:* In 3-quart saucepan over medium heat, heat meatballs with *¾ cup water* until hot, stirring often.

Gravad Lax

Color index page 22

Begin 2 to 3 days ahead

12 to 14 servings

2 tablespoons salt
4 teaspoons sugar
1 teaspoon peppercorns, coarsely crushed
1½ pounds center-cut fresh salmon, scaled, with skin on and bones removed

1 tablespoon brandy (optional)
½ bunch fresh dill
Mustard Sauce (below)
fresh dill and lemon wedges for garnish

1 In cup, combine salt, sugar and peppercorns; rub into all sides of fish; sprinkle with brandy.

2 Place ⅓ of dill in shallow *glass* baking dish; put 1 piece of fish, skin side down, on dill.

3 Top with another ⅓ of dill; add another piece of fish, skin side up, and top with remaining dill.

4 Cover salmon with plastic wrap; set plate (larger than salmon) on it. Place 2 heavy cans of food on top. Refrigerate 24 to 36 hours. *Early on day of serving:* Prepare sauce.

5 *Just before serving:* Scrape dill and seasonings from salmon. Place salmon, skin side down, on serving board.

6 Garnish with fresh dill and lemon wedges. Slice salmon thinly on the slant, away from the skin. Serve with Mustard Sauce.

MUSTARD SAUCE: *Early in day:* In blender container, blend *½ cup prepared mustard, ½ cup salad oil, ⅓ cup sugar, ¼ cup white vinegar, 1 teaspoon sour cream* and *⅛ teaspoon salt* till smooth, about 1 minute. Chill, covered. Stir in *¼ cup chopped dill* just before serving. (Makes 1¼ cups.)

Hearty appetizers

Pickled Shrimp and Crystalline Ice Bowl

Color index page 23

Begin day ahead

18 to 20 servings

Crystalline Ice Bowl (below) (optional)
3 pounds large shrimp in shell
6 cups boiling water
1 celery stalk
1 bay leaf
¼ teaspoon peppercorns
salt
1 cup salad oil

⅔ cup lemon juice
½ cup vinegar
3 tablespoons pickling spice, tied in cheese-cloth bag
2 teaspoons sugar
2 sprigs fresh dill

1. Prepare Crystalline Ice Bowl.
2. Shell and devein shrimp, leaving tails on.
3. To boiling water in 4-quart saucepan over low heat, add shrimp, celery, bay leaf, peppercorns, 1 tablespoon salt. Simmer 3 minutes or until shrimp turns pink. Drain.
4. In large bowl, stir remaining ingredients; stir in 5 teaspoons salt. Add shrimp and toss well. Marinate in refrigerator overnight, tossing occasionally.
5. *To serve:* Drain the shrimp well and serve them in the Crystalline Ice Bowl.

MAKING A CRYSTALLINE ICE BOWL

Cover bottom of 3-quart freezersafe bowl with *ice cubes*. Set a 1½-quart freezersafe bowl in center of larger bowl on top of ice cubes.

(Place can of frozen juice in small bowl to keep it from floating later.) Fill space between large and small bowls halfway up with ice cubes. Carefully tuck *dill sprigs*, *lemon slices*, *bay leaf* and *pickling spice* between ice cubes against larger bowl.

Place in freezer. Pour *cold water* between bowls to about 2 inches from bottom; freeze. Pour in another inch ice water; let freeze. Repeat until ice is ½ inch below rim of large bowl.

Remove weight from small bowl; fill with warm, not hot, water for about 1 minute; lift small bowl. Dip large bowl in warm water for about 1 minute; unmold Crystalline Ice Bowl and use immediately.

Brie-in-Brioche

Color index page 22

Begin day ahead

24 servings

¾ cup sugar
¾ teaspoon salt
3 packages active dry yeast
about 5½ cups all-purpose flour
1 cup butter or margarine
¾ cup milk
7 eggs

2 teaspoons water
1 2¼-pound wheel Brie (7 to 8 inches in diameter), at room temperature
grapes for garnish

1. In large bowl, combine sugar, salt, yeast and 2 cups flour. In 1-quart saucepan over low heat, heat butter and milk until very warm (120° to 130°F.). (Butter does not need to melt completely.)
2. With mixer at low speed, beat liquid into dry ingredients until just blended. Increase speed to medium; beat 2 minutes, occasionally scraping bowl. Gradually beat in 6 eggs and 1½ cups flour to make a thick batter; continue beating 2 minutes, occasionally scraping bowl. With wooden spoon, stir in 1½ cups flour to make a very soft dough; beat with spoon 5 minutes.
3. Place dough in large, greased bowl. Cover with towel; let rise in warm place (80° to 85°F.), away from draft, until doubled, about 1 hour. Stir down dough; cover bowl tightly with foil or plastic wrap and refrigerate overnight.
4. *Early in day:* Punch down dough; turn onto lightly floured surface; cover with bowl; let rest 15 minutes. Grease 10″ by 2″ springform pan. Shape dough into a smooth ball; place in pan. Cover with towel; let rise in warm place until doubled in size, about 1 hour.
5. Preheat oven to 325°F. In cup, combine water with remaining 1 egg. Brush dough with egg mixture. Bake 45 minutes or until brioche sounds hollow when tapped with fingers. Remove brioche from pan to wire rack to cool.
6. *To serve:* With serrated knife, slice off top of brioche, 2 inches from bottom; set aside. Place Brie on bottom half of brioche; with knife, make outline of Brie in brioche; remove Brie. With spoon, remove enough center of brioche to make a basket (reserve center for bread crumbs another day). Set Brie in basket; arrange on large platter. Lean top on Brie. Garnish platter with grapes.
7. Cut brioche with Brie into wedges. Serve with fork and knife or brioche may be eaten out of hand, letting each person help himself.

Marking basket: Place Brie on brioche; with knife, mark outline on brioche.

Cutting out basket: Remove brioche within outline to make basket.

Spanakopitas

Color index page 20

Begin 2¼ hrs ahead

42 appetizers or 20 servings

2 tablespoons olive oil
1 small onion, diced
1 10-ounce package frozen chopped spinach, thawed and squeezed dry
1 egg

⅓ cup grated Parmesan cheese
⅛ teaspoon pepper
about ⅓ pound phyllo (strudel leaves)
½ cup butter or margarine, melted

1 In 2-quart saucepan over medium heat, in hot oil, cook onion until tender, stirring occasionally. Remove from heat; stir in spinach, egg, cheese and pepper.

2 With knife, cut phyllo lengthwise into 2-inch-wide strips. Place strips on waxed paper then cover with slightly damp towel.

3 Brush top of one strip of phyllo with melted butter; place 1 teaspoonful spinach mixture at short end of strip.

4 Fold one corner of strip diagonally over filling so the short edge meets the long edge, forming a right angle.

5 Continue folding over at right angles until you reach the end of the strip to form a triangular-shape package. Repeat with remaining phyllo strips and spinach filling.

6 Preheat oven to 425°F. Place packages, seam side down, in 15½" by 10½" jelly-roll pan; brush with butter. Bake triangles 15 minutes or until golden brown. Serve hot.

TIROPITAS: In small bowl with fork, crumble ¼ *pound feta cheese*; stir in *½ cup ricotta cheese*, *2 tablespoons chopped parsley*, *1 egg* and *¼ teaspoon pepper*. Prepare phyllo strips as above; cut; brush with melted butter; fill with cheese mixture; bake.

Sausage en Croûte

Color index page 22

Begin 2½ hrs ahead

32 appetizers

8 country-style pork sausage links, each about 4 inches long
water

½ cup butter
2 cups all-purpose flour
½ teaspoon salt
2 eggs

1. In covered 10-inch skillet over medium heat, simmer sausages and ¼ cup water 5 minutes; uncover; cook sausages until browned, turning often; refrigerate until cold.
2. In medium bowl with pastry blender, cut butter into flour and salt until mixture resembles coarse crumbs. In 1-cup measure, beat eggs; add water to measure ⅔ cup. Sprinkle 6 tablespoons egg mixture into flour mixture, mixing with fork until moist; shape into ball. Preheat oven to 425°F.
3. On floured surface, roll dough into 20″ by 10″ rectangle; cut into eight 5-inch squares. Brush each square with some egg mixture; place a sausage along one edge; roll up; seal ends; place seam side down on greased cookie sheet. Bake 20 minutes or until golden. Cut each roll into 4 slices.

Chicken-Wing Appetizers

Color index page 20

Begin 1 hr or day ahead

36 appetizers or 18 servings

18 chicken wings (about 3 pounds)
2 tablespoons salad oil
3 green onions, cut into 3-inch pieces
½ cup soy sauce
⅓ cup medium or dry sherry

¼ cup catchup
2 tablespoons sugar
¼ teaspoon ground ginger
3 star anise (optional)
1 large head iceberg lettuce, shredded

1. Cut wing tips off at joint (use tips in soup another day); cut each wing in half at joint.
2. In 5-quart Dutch oven over high heat, in hot oil, cook wings and two-thirds green-onion pieces, stirring constantly, about 7 minutes. Reduce heat to medium; add soy sauce and remaining ingredients except lettuce; stir to blend well. Cover and cook about 25 minutes, stirring occasionally.
3. Uncover and cook 10 minutes longer, stirring frequently, until almost all liquid is absorbed and chicken is tender. Serve warm on bed of lettuce or cover and refrigerate to serve cold later. Garnish with remaining green-onion pieces.

Rumaki

Color index page 22

Begin 1½ hrs ahead or early in day

18 appetizers

½ pound chicken livers
about 9 bacon slices, halved crosswise
1 8½-ounce can water chestnuts, drained

½ cup soy sauce
½ teaspoon curry powder
¼ teaspoon ground ginger

1. Prepare rumaki: Cut livers into chunks. Wrap each bacon piece around a water chestnut and chunk of liver; secure with toothpick.
2. In medium bowl, stir soy sauce, curry powder and ginger. Add rumaki and toss. Cover and chill at least 1 hour, tossing occasionally.
3. *At serving time:* Preheat broiler if manufacturer directs. Drain rumaki and broil, turning frequently, until liver is cooked, about 10 minutes.

Pâtés

Pâté de Campagne

Color index
page 18

Begin day
or up to
1 wk ahead

16 servings

2 tablespoons salad oil
*¼ pound mushrooms,
chopped*
½ cup chopped onion
*1 small garlic clove,
minced*
¼ cup medium sherry
1½ teaspoons salt
*½ teaspoon cracked
pepper*
½ teaspoon thyme leaves
*⅛ teaspoon ground
nutmeg*

½ pound ground pork
*½ pound ground chicken
(about 1 whole
medium chicken
breast)*
¼ pound ground pork fat
*¼ cup shelled pistachio
nuts*
*2 tablespoons chopped
parsley*
1 egg
*1 8-ounce package sliced
bacon*

1 In 3-quart saucepan over medium heat, in hot oil, cook mushrooms, onion and garlic until tender, stirring often.

2 Add sherry, salt, pepper, thyme and nutmeg; heat to boiling. Reduce heat; simmer 5 minutes, stirring often. Remove saucepan from the heat.

3 Stir in pork, chicken, pork fat, pistachios, parsley and egg. With spoon, beat the mixture until thoroughly mixed.

4 Line bottom and sides of 8½″ by 4½″ loaf pan with bacon, letting slices hang over sides of pan. Reserve some bacon slices for top of loaf.

5 Spoon mixture into loaf pan, packing it down firmly. Fold bacon over, then top with reserved bacon slices. Bake in 350°F. oven 1¼ hours. Cover; chill overnight.

6 *To serve:* Dip pan in 2 inches hot water for 15 seconds; lift from water. Run metal spatula between pâté and sides of pan; invert onto platter. Cut pâté into slices.

Chicken Liver Pâté

Color index
page 18

Begin 3½ hrs
or up to
3 days ahead

2¼ cups or
12 to 16
servings

*¾ cup butter or
margarine*
1 pound chicken livers
1 medium onion, minced

2 tablespoons brandy
¼ teaspoon salt
⅛ teaspoon pepper

1. In 10-inch skillet over medium-high heat, in ¼ cup hot butter, cook chicken livers with onion until chicken livers are tender but still pink inside, about 5 minutes, stirring often.
2. In covered blender container at low speed, blend mixture until smooth, stopping blender occasionally and scraping sides with rubber spatula.
3. Meanwhile, in same skillet over low heat, melt remaining butter; add to chicken-liver mixture with brandy, salt and pepper; blend well. Spoon into small bowl; cover; refrigerate.

COUNTRY LIVER PATE: Prepare livers as in step 1, above; substitute *⅓ cup minced green onions* for onion and add *½ pound mushrooms* and *1 medium garlic clove,* minced. Stir in *½ cup dry white wine* and *⅛ teaspoon hot pepper sauce*; cover and simmer 5 minutes. Prepare as in steps 2 and 3, but omit brandy and pepper; increase salt to 1 teaspoon. (Makes 3 cups or 16 to 20 servings.)

Spinach Pâté

Color index
page 18

Begin day
ahead

10 servings

*3 10-ounce packages
frozen chopped
spinach, thawed*
*¼ cup butter or
margarine*
*1 bunch green
onions, thinly sliced
(1 cup)*
*2 large carrots, coarsely
shredded*
1 cup half-and-half

1¾ teaspoons salt
1 teaspoon basil
*⅛ teaspoon cayenne
pepper*
4 eggs
*watercress sprigs or
Carrot Flowers (page
327) for garnish*

1. Place spinach in colander in sink; using back of wooden spoon, press spinach to remove moisture. With hands, squeeze spinach to remove any remaining moisture. With knife, finely chop spinach.
2. Grease well 8½″ by 4½″ loaf pan; line bottom of pan with foil. In 2-quart saucepan over medium heat, in hot butter or margarine, cook onions and carrots until tender, about 5 minutes, stirring frequently. Stir in spinach, half-and-half, salt, basil and cayenne pepper; heat to boiling. Remove saucepan from heat; stir in eggs. Spoon mixture into loaf pan, spreading evenly; cover with foil.
3. Place loaf pan in 13″ by 9″ baking pan. Fill baking pan with hot water to come 1 inch up sides of loaf pan. Bake in 375°F. oven for 1¼ hours or until knife inserted in center through foil comes out clean. Cool in pan on wire rack 15 minutes. Place 2 heavy cans on top to weigh down pâté. Refrigerate overnight.
4. *About 15 minutes before serving:* Remove cans and foil from top of pâté. With metal spatula, loosen pâté from pan. Invert platter over pan; then invert platter and pan together and lift pan off. Remove foil; cut pâté into 10 slices. Garnish platter with watercress or Carrot Flowers.

Duck Pâté in Sherry Aspic

1 4- to 5-pound frozen
duckling, thawed
½ pound lean pork
dry sherry
¼ pound large
mushrooms
3 tablespoons butter or
margarine
¾ pound chicken livers
2 green onions, sliced
¼ pound pork fat, diced
1 teaspoon salt

½ teaspoon pepper
⅓ cup frozen peas,
thawed
2 10½-ounce cans
condensed beef broth
3 packages unflavored
gelatin

Color index page 19

Begin day or up to
3 days ahead

10 servings

1 Remove skin, fat and bones from duckling; discard skin and fat; reserve bones for soup another day. Dice duckling meat and lean pork. In medium bowl, combine duckling, pork and 3 tablespoons sherry. Cover with plastic wrap; refrigerate 2 hours. Reserve 1 mushroom; chop remainder.

2 In 12-inch skillet over medium heat, in hot butter, cook livers, green onions and mushrooms until livers are firm, about 10 minutes.

3 In covered blender container, blend chicken-liver mixture, pork fat, salt and pepper until smooth, stopping occasionally to scrape sides of container with rubber spatula.

4 Spread ⅓ of liver mixture in 8½" by 4½" loaf pan; sprinkle with ⅓ of peas; top with ⅓ of duckling mixture. Repeat layering twice more. Press down firmly.

5 Place loaf pan in 13" by 9" baking pan. Add water to 1 inch up side of loaf pan. Bake in 350°F. oven 1¾ hours. Cover with foil; place 2 heavy cans on top. Chill overnight.

6 *4 hours before serving:* In 2-quart saucepan over undiluted beef broth and ½ cup sherry, sprinkle gelatin. Over low heat, cook, stirring, until the gelatin is dissolved.

7 Pour ⅛ inch gelatin mixture in bottom of 9" by 5" loaf pan; refrigerate 20 minutes until set. Cut reserved mushroom in ¼-inch-thick slices.

8 Arrange mushroom slices on gelatin in loaf pan. Top with ⅛ inch gelatin; refrigerate 20 minutes until set. Remove cans and foil from pâté.

9 Remove pâté from pan and place on top of gelatin; pour remaining gelatin mixture around pâté. Cover and refrigerate 2 hours until set.

10 Moisten large platter. Dip point of knife in warm water; with point, loosen gelatin. Dip pan in warm water; turn out pâté onto platter.

Spreads

Color index page 19

Begin 5 days ahead

2 cups

Homemade Pepper-Herb Cheese

2 pints half-and-half
2 tablespoons
buttermilk
muslin cloth
1 teaspoon salt
1 teaspoon herb or Italian
seasoning

double layer cheesecloth
2 tablespoons cracked
black pepper
crackers or
melba toast

1 In 2-quart saucepan over medium-low heat, heat half-and-half to lukewarm (90° to 100°F.); stir in buttermilk. Pour into medium bowl.

2 Cover bowl; let stand in warm place (80° to 85°F.) 24 to 48 hours until mixture is yogurt-like (soft curd). Line a colander with muslin cloth and place it in the sink.

3 Pour soft curd into colander; let drain 10 minutes. Place colander on a wire rack in a large saucepot; cover saucepot with plastic wrap and refrigerate 18 to 24 hours.

4 Into medium bowl, spoon curd from muslin cloth; stir in salt and herb seasoning. Discard liquid (whey) in pot; wash pot.

5 Line 2-cup molded plastic fresh-produce basket with double layer of dampened cheesecloth, leaving 2-inch overhang. Spoon curd into container and fold the cheesecloth ends over the edges.

6 Place on wire rack in saucepot; cover with plastic wrap. Refrigerate 18 to 24 hours. Carefully unmold cheese onto serving dish; pat pepper evenly over cheese. Serve with crackers.

Spreads

Dips

Pork Rillettes

Color index
page 18

Begin early
in day
or up to
3 days ahead

2 cups
spread or
12 servings

3 pounds pork shoulder
  blade (Boston) roast
  boneless
1 cup water
2 teaspoons salt
1½ teaspoons coarsely
  ground black pepper
1 teaspoon marjoram
  leaves

½ teaspoon thyme
  leaves
1 bay leaf
1 garlic clove, crushed
toasted French-bread
  slices or
  crackers

1. With sharp knife, cut pork into ½-inch cubes.
2. In 5-quart Dutch oven, combine pork cubes with remaining ingredients except toasted French bread; over high heat, heat to boiling. Reduce heat to low; cover and simmer until meat is very tender and falls apart when tested with a fork, about 2½ hours, stirring occasionally.
3. When meat is done, uncover Dutch oven and over low heat, cook meat until all liquid has evaporated, stirring often. Discard bay leaf.
4. With 2 forks, pull meat into shreds. Spoon mixture into 2-cup covered crock; pack down well. Refrigerate. Use chilled mixture on toasted French-bread slices or crackers.

CHEESE SPREADS

Prepare any or all of the spreads below. Pack each mixture into a container; cover and refrigerate overnight to develop the flavor.

NUTTY BLUE: In medium bowl, mix well *four 4-ounce packages blue cheese*, crumbled (about 4 cups), *1 cup pistachio nuts*, chopped, and *⅓ cup milk*. (Makes 2 cups; Color index, page 18.)

ANCHOVY-OLIVE: In medium bowl with spoon, stir *one 8-ounce package Neufchâtel cheese*, softened, *12 medium pimento-stuffed olives*, minced, and *4 teaspoons anchovy paste* until well mixed. (Makes about 1½ cups.)

PEPPERY MONTEREY: In large bowl with spoon, mix well *1 pound natural Monterey (Jack) cheese*, finely shredded (about 5 cups), *½ cup mayonnaise, 2 teaspoons cracked black pepper* and *¼ teaspoon salt*. (Makes about 2 cups; Color index, page 18.)

HAM-AND-SWISS: In large bowl with spoon, mix well *½ pound cooked ham*, minced, *½ pound natural Swiss cheese*, finely shredded (about 2½ cups), *1 cup sour cream, ¼ cup chopped parsley, 1 tablespoon prepared mustard with onion bits* and *¾ teaspoon salt*. (Makes about 2½ cups; Color index, page 18.)

CHEDDAR-BEER: In large bowl with spoon, mix well *1 pound Cheddar cheese*, finely shredded (about 4 cups), *¾ cup beer* or white wine and *½ teaspoon salt*. (Makes about 2½ cups.)

LONGHORN-PIMENTO: In large bowl with spoon, stir *one 10-ounce package longhorn cheese*, finely shredded (about 3½ cups), *one 4-ounce can pimentos*, drained and diced, *¼ cup milk, 1 teaspoon Worcestershire* and *¾ teaspoon salt* until well mixed. (Makes about 1⅔ cups.)

Guacamole

Color index
page 18

Begin 1 hr
ahead

2 cups dip

1 medium tomato
2 medium avocados
2 tablespoons lemon
  juice
1¼ teaspoons salt
½ small onion, minced
1 small garlic clove,
  minced
1 4-ounce can chopped
  mild green chilies,
  drained
fresh coriander leaves
  (optional)
potato chips or fresh
  vegetables

1 Peel and dice tomato. Then, cut each avocado in half lengthwise; remove seed; peel.

2 In bowl, mash avocado with lemon juice. Stir in salt, tomato, onion, garlic and chilies.

3 Spoon into medium bowl. Garnish with coriander if desired. Serve with potato chips.

Peppery Dip with Vegetables

Color index
page 19

Begin several
hrs ahead

1 cup dip

1 cup mayonnaise
2 tablespoons grated
  onion
2 teaspoons tarragon
  vinegar
2 teaspoons chopped
  chives
2 teaspoons chili
  sauce

½ teaspoon curry
  powder
½ teaspoon salt
¼ teaspoon pepper
⅛ teaspoon ground
  thyme
raw cauliflowerets
carrot sticks

In small bowl, stir all ingredients except the cauliflowerets and carrots; cover; refrigerate. Spoon into bowl; set on plate; surround with vegetables.

Blue-Cheese Dip

Color index
page 19

Begin 15 mins
ahead

1⅔ cups dip

1 cup sour cream
⅓ cup milk
4 ounces blue cheese

3 dashes hot pepper sauce
½ teaspoon
  Worcestershire

In small bowl with spoon, mix well all ingredients; cover with plastic wrap and refrigerate dip until ready to serve.

Green-Onion Dip

Color index
page 19

Begin 15 mins
ahead

1 cup dip

1 cup sour cream
1 envelope beef-flavor
  bouillon
¼ cup thinly sliced green
  onion

1 teaspoon
  Worcestershire
potato or corn
  chips

In a small bowl with spoon, mix first 4 ingredients; cover and refrigerate dip. Serve with chips.

Yogurt-Cheese Dip

Color index page 19

Begin 15 mins ahead

1½ cups dip

1 8-ounce package cream cheese, softened
½ cup plain yogurt
¾ teaspoon salt
⅛ teaspoon dill weed
fresh vegetables

In small bowl with mixer at medium speed, beat cream cheese just until smooth and fluffy. Gradually beat in next 3 ingredients until smooth and thoroughly blended. Spoon into serving bowl; serve with fresh vegetables.

Tuna Dip

Color index page 19

Begin early in day

2 cups dip

1 6½- to 7-ounce can tuna, packed in water, drained
1 cup mayonnaise
1 2-ounce can anchovy fillets, drained
2 tablespoons lemon juice
¼ teaspoon salt
⅛ teaspoon cracked black pepper
⅛ teaspoon paprika
1 tablespoon capers, drained (optional)
potato chips, corn chips, crackers or vegetables

1. In blender container at high speed, blend tuna with next 6 ingredients until smooth; pour dip into a bowl; sprinkle with capers. Cover and refrigerate.
2. *To serve:* Surround Tuna Dip with chips, crackers or vegetables.

Chili Dip with Fresh Vegetables

Color index page 19

Begin early in day

2½ cups dip

1 medium bunch celery
3 medium zucchini
1 bunch broccoli
1 pound large mushrooms
1 28-ounce can tomatoes, drained
1 small onion
¼ cup lightly packed parsley
¼ cup mild green chilies
1 medium garlic clove
1 tablespoon white vinegar
1 teaspoon oregano leaves
½ teaspoon salt

1. Separate celery into stalks and cut zucchini into sticks. Cut broccoli into flowerets and cut each mushroom in half. Wrap vegetables separately in plastic wrap; refrigerate.
2. Prepare dip: In blender container at low speed, blend remaining ingredients until smooth. Pour dip into small bowl; cover; refrigerate.
3. *About 15 minutes before serving:* Into a basket lined with foil place dip; surround with vegetables.

Preparing the vegetables: Cut zucchini and celery into sticks; cut broccoli into flowerets and cut mushrooms in half.

Serving the dip: Line large basket with foil; arrange vegetables and dip in basket. Let each person help himself.

Bagna Cauda

Color index page 19

Begin 1½ hrs ahead

2 cups dip or 12 servings

1 medium head romaine lettuce
1 medium bunch celery, separated into stalks
3 medium red peppers, cut into wedges
3 medium green peppers, cut into wedges
1 medium bunch broccoli, cut into flowerets
3 medium zucchini, cut into long wedges
1 pound large mushrooms, each cut into quarters
1 bunch green onions
1 pint cherry tomatoes

Hot Creamy Dip:
2 cups heavy cream
3 tablespoons butter
1 garlic clove, minced
1 2-ounce can anchovy fillets, drained and mashed
1 teaspoon salt
1 teaspoon thyme leaves
1 teaspoon oregano leaves
⅛ teaspoon pepper
breadsticks

1 Line a large basket with 13″ by 9″ baking dish. Arrange in basket first 9 ingredients. Cover; refrigerate.

2 In 2-quart saucepan over medium-high heat, heat cream to boiling; cook, stirring, until reduced to about 1⅓ cups. Remove from heat.

3 In 1-quart saucepan over medium heat, in hot butter, cook garlic 1 minute. Stir in next 5 ingredients. Cook, stirring, until smooth.

4 Remove from heat; with wire whisk, gradually stir in cream until mixture is smooth.

5 Pour into 1-quart candle-warmer dish. Serve with prepared vegetables in basket accompanied by breadsticks.

Antipasto

Vegetables

Antipasto can be eaten either as an appetizer or as a main course. For a main dish, serve it with wine and plenty of fresh, crusty bread.

Antipasto

Color index page 21

Begin early in day or day ahead

16 to 18 appetizer servings or 6 main-dish servings

Marinated Italian Green Beans (below)
Marinated Eggplant (below)
Marinated Tuna and Red Cabbage (below)
Marinated Cauliflowerets (below)
lettuce leaves
1 8-ounce can sardines in tomato sauce

½ 6- or 8-ounce package sliced cooked ham
1 4-ounce package sliced mortadella
½ 8-ounce package sliced salami or 2 4-ounce packages sliced pepperoni
½ 8-ounce package sliced provolone

1. Prepare Marinated Italian Green Beans, Marinated Eggplant, Marinated Tuna and Red Cabbage and Marinated Cauliflowerets.
2. *About 30 minutes before serving:* Line a tray with lettuce leaves and on them arrange the sardines, ham, mortadella, salami and provolone. Arrange the vegetables in decorative bowls and serve alongside the tray. Let each guest help himself.

MARINATED ITALIAN GREEN BEANS: *Up to 5 hours before serving or day ahead:* Prepare *one 9-ounce package frozen Italian green beans* as label directs; drain. In large bowl, combine green beans, *½ cup chopped onion, ¼ cup olive oil, ¼ cup cider vinegar, 2 tablespoons sugar* and *¾ teaspoon salt.* Cover and refrigerate at least 4 hours, stirring the mixture occasionally.

MARINATED EGGPLANT: *Up to 2 hours before serving or day ahead:* In 10-inch skillet over medium heat, heat *¼ cup olive oil* until hot. Add *½ medium eggplant,* cut into bite-size pieces, *1 medium red pepper,* cut into thin strips, *½ small garlic clove,* minced, *¼ cup chopped onion, 2 tablespoons water, 1 teaspoon salt, ½ teaspoon sugar* and *½ teaspoon thyme leaves;* cook about 15 minutes or until vegetables are tender, stirring occasionally. Spoon mixture into medium bowl; cover and refrigerate until well chilled.

MARINATED TUNA AND RED CABBAGE: *Up to 2 hours before serving or day ahead:* Into medium bowl, spoon *one 3½-ounce can tuna* and its oil. With fork, flake tuna into small pieces. Add *1 cup chopped red cabbage, 1 tablespoon capers, 1½ teaspoons wine vinegar, ⅛ teaspoon salt* and *⅛ teaspoon cracked pepper* and mix well. Cover and refrigerate at least 1½ hours to ensure that the flavors are well blended.

MARINATED CAULIFLOWERETS: *Early in day or day ahead:* In large bowl, mix well *1 medium head cauliflower,* cut into bite-size cauliflowerets, *⅓ cup olive oil, ¼ cup cider vinegar, 1½ teaspoons sugar, 2 teaspoons chopped parsley, ¾ teaspoon salt, ¼ teaspoon basil* and *⅛ teaspoon pepper.* Cover; refrigerate, stirring occasionally.

Tiny Ham-stuffed Tomatoes

Color index page 20

Begin early in day

20 appetizers

1 pint cherry tomatoes
2 2¼-ounce cans deviled ham
2 tablespoons sour cream

2 tablespoons horseradish
parsley for garnish

1. Thinly slice tops from cherry tomatoes; remove pulp; drain shells upside down on paper towels.
2. In small bowl, combine ham, sour cream and horseradish; fill the tomato shells with the ham mixture. Refrigerate.
3. *To serve:* Garnish tomatoes with parsley.

Herbed Mushrooms

Color index page 20

Begin day or up to 3 days ahead

12 servings

1 pound small mushrooms
⅓ cup cider vinegar
2 tablespoons salad oil
1½ teaspoons fines herbes

1½ teaspoons sugar
1 teaspoon salt
1 4-ounce jar diced pimentos, drained

Trim tough ends of mushroom stems; rinse; pat dry. In large bowl, gently mix mushrooms with remaining ingredients. Cover and refrigerate, stirring occasionally. Serve with toothpicks.

Nippy Carrots

Color index page 20

Begin day or several days ahead

10 to 12 servings

1 pound medium carrots
3 tablespoons salad oil
3 garlic cloves, minced
1 tablespoon chopped onion

¼ cup vinegar
1 tablespoon mixed pickling spice
1½ teaspoons salt
½ teaspoon dry mustard
⅛ teaspoon pepper
1 onion, thinly sliced

1. Cut carrots diagonally into thin slices. In 12-inch skillet over medium heat, in hot oil, cook garlic and chopped onion until tender, about 5 minutes; add carrots and vinegar. Loosely tie pickling spice in a square of cheesecloth; add to carrots with salt, dry mustard and pepper.
2. Simmer, covered, 5 minutes until carrots are crunchy and crisp; discard spice bag. Pour mixture into shallow dish; top with sliced onion. Cover and refrigerate, tossing occasionally.

Pickled Onions

Color index page 20

Begin day or up to 1 wk ahead

16 servings

3½ pounds small white onions
2 tablespoons mixed pickling spice
1 teaspoon crushed red pepper

4 cups cider or red wine vinegar
1 cup sugar
1 cup water
1 tablespoon salt

1. Peel onions, leaving a little of the root end to help hold shape during cooking. Tie pickling spice and red pepper in cheesecloth.
2. In 4-quart saucepan over high heat, heat spice bag, vinegar, sugar, water, salt and onions to boiling. Reduce heat to low; cover; simmer 10 minutes. Discard spice bag. Carefully ladle onions and liquid into large bowl; cover with plastic wrap; refrigerate.
3. *To serve:* Drain onions thoroughly.

Cheese and fruit tasting

This is an easy, casual and conversation-making way to entertain friends before dinner; it is also appropriate for mid-afternoon gatherings and luncheon and dinner desserts. Here are some hints on setting up the cheese and fruit tasting.

SELECTING CHEESE

Cheese is classified according to texture. (For further information about cheese, see page 150.) For tasting, choose any variety except the hard-grating ones such as Parmesan or soft and unripened cheeses like ricotta.

Select at least three cheeses with different flavors, textures, colors and shapes. For example, a soft, mild-flavored Bel Paese and a hard longhorn Cheddar contrast nicely in flavor with a blue cheese such as Stilton, and pungent, nutty-flavored aged Samsoe. Gjetöst contributes a rectangular shape, sweet flavor and golden-brown color to the cheese board, Edam, with its red wax coating, adds a bright splash of color.

Allow a total of at least a quarter pound of cheese per person (remember that any leftovers will keep well). Buy slightly more of a hard cheese for the sake of appearance, as hard cheeses are smaller in proportion to weight than soft cheeses. For full flavor, remove cheese from the refrigerator about 1 hour before serving and serve it at room temperature.

SELECTING FRUIT

Seasonal varieties of fruit include peaches, nectarines, sweet cherries, figs, grapes, apricots, pineapple, strawberries, plums and melons. For added interest, try some of the more unusual fruits such as papaya and mangoes. Dried fruits such as prunes and raisins, and nuts, also team nicely with cheese and fresh fruits.

SETTING THE TABLE

Arrange cheese simply on a wooden cheese board or scratch-resistant tray or platter, put the fresh fruit in a basket or bowl, and place unsalted crackers or breadsticks in a basket. Set out napkins, small knives and plates for your guests.

Let guests help themselves to cheese and fruit or, for faster self-service, cut cheeses and fruits into bite-size cubes, slices or wedges and arrange them decoratively on platters or trays.

Wine is the appropriate pre-dinner drink to serve with cheese and fruit; choose from appetizer, white or red table wines, or champagne or other sparkling wines. Sweet dessert wines can be offered if the tasting serves as dessert. Serve the wine at the correct temperature: chilled, for appetizer, white table and sparkling wines, room temperature for red table wine; and have glasses on trays on the table or nearby. For further information about choosing wines, see page 474.

SERVING CHEESE WITH FRUIT

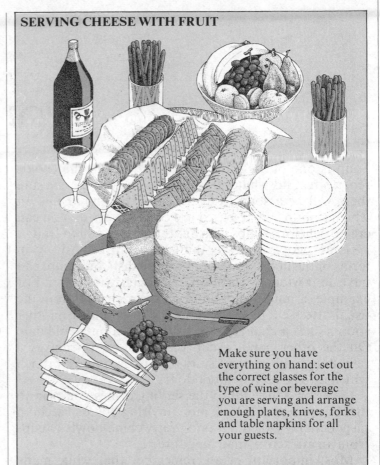

Make sure you have everything on hand: set out the correct glasses for the type of wine or beverage you are serving and arrange enough plates, knives, forks and table napkins for all your guests.

SOME CHEESE AND FRUIT COMBINATIONS

Brie, Monterey (Jack) and Feta with tangerines, strawberries and dried prunes.

Liederkranz, Gouda and Danish blue with cantaloupe chunks, peaches and small apples.

Gloucester, Gorgonzola and Gruyère with cherries, dried figs, nectarines and unsalted cashews.

Colby, Gjetöst, Emmenthaler and Roquefort with apricots, pineapple and plums.

Cheddar, Provolone and Camembert with pineapple, grapes, pears and walnuts.

Jarlsberg, Port du Salut and Stilton with kiwi fruit, apples, bananas and fresh figs.

SOUPS

Soup is one of the most versatile dishes in the cook's repertoire, and whatever the occasion, you can be sure there will be a soup to fit the bill. The ingredients on which a soup can be based are equally varied. You can create delicious soups with anything from fish to fruit.

Some people tend to think of soup exclusively in terms of the first course, or as a main dish, but soups can have a far wider application, particularly in winter. For example, a mug of hot soup makes a change from the usual after-school snack; and hot bouillon or another soup makes a change from coffee or tea on a cold day. On the other hand, a cup of ice-cold soup makes a refreshing and unusual start to a mid-summer brunch which is to be served out of doors.

Give some thought to the serving dishes you plan to use. Soups not only look more inviting but also seem to taste better if ladled out into pretty china bowls or cups from an attractive, matching tureen.

Most important of all, remember that while many soups may be equally good served hot or cold, none benefit from being served lukewarm. For hot soup the dishes should be warmed beforehand if possible, and if you are planning to serve soup cold, make sure that the bowls as well as the soup have been thoroughly chilled.

STOCK SUBSTITUTES

Cans and cubes have virtually done away with the need for regular stock-making in today's kitchen, and it would be hard to go back to the days when a stock pot bubbled permanently on the stove. Cubes and envelopes of chicken-, beef-, or vegetable-flavor bouillon, jars of condensed bouillon or stock base, and canned, ready-to-use or condensed broth are time-saving substitutes for stock, to add to or be turned into soup in a moment.

One easy way of adding a personal touch to instant broth is to boost its flavor with fresh vegetables. Use whatever you have at hand – a small onion, 1 or 2 carrots, a chunk of parsnip, a few lettuce leaves and a celery stalk, all finely chopped. Make up the bouillon cubes with water as directed on the label. Add 1 or 2 parsley sprigs, a piece of bay leaf and 2 or 3 black peppercorns, and the chopped vegetables. Cook gently with the lid on for 10 to 15 minutes. Add more water if necessary, and puree the soup in a blender or strain through a sieve, if a smooth consistency is desired.

THICKENING SOUPS

Some soups thicken naturally as their ingredients cook: beans and potatoes, for example, can be left as they are, or rubbed through a sieve or food mill, or put through an electric blender or food processor for a smoother texture. But for soups which are not to be pureed, a thickener can be used. This usually takes the form of flour or cornstarch, or eggs. In both cases, it is a good idea to add the thickener with the pan off the heat to avoid the danger of lumping.

Use flour for soups which are to be served hot. Cornstarch, which gives a lighter, subtler texture is better for cold ones. In a small bowl, blend the flour (or cornstarch) to a smooth, thin paste with a few table-spoons cold water. Stir this into the soup, heat to boiling, and simmer, stirring frequently, until it has thickened and any taste of uncooked flour disappears.

If using eggs as a thickener, beat whole ones or yolks together before adding a few tablespoons of the hot soup. When thoroughly blended, pour the mixture into the pan, stirring vigorously. The soup may still be hot enough for the egg mixture to thicken it without further heating, but if not, return the pan to a very low heat and stir constantly until thickened. Do not let the soup boil.

STORING SOUPS

For short-term storage, keep the soup in a covered container in the refrigerator for up to 2 or 3 days. It can also be stored in the freezer. But if you plan to freeze it for more than a week or so keep the following tips in mind. Seasonings are affected by freezing – some become stronger while others lose their potency, so it is always a good idea to keep seasonings mild and leave final adjustments until after thawing. Some ingredients, such as potatoes, do not freeze well and should always be cooked separately and added to the soup after thawing. Soup thickened with flour is likely to separate when frozen over a long period of time.

To freeze soup, chill it thoroughly, then pour it into a rigid freezer container, leaving the usual 1/2-inch head-space per pint to allow for expansion, seal tightly, and label. Soups can be stored in the freezer for up to 3 months. Soups can either be reheated gently from their frozen state or first thawed in the refrigerator, then reheated. Be sure you reheat the soup gradually.

First-course soups

A first-course soup should stimulate the appetite without satisfying it, creating enthusiasm for what is to follow. For this reason, the soup course should always be planned along with the other dishes in the menu. Avoid repeating flavors, textures, even colors if possible. Gazpacho is scarcely the best prelude to a main dish dressed with tomato sauce, though its sharp, refreshing flavor may be just the right note on which to start a dinner party centered around a rich, creamy main course. On the other hand, if the main dish is a simple roast or salad, start with a rich cream soup.

Remember that many cold soups, including the famous vichyssoise, are also delicious hot and if the weather changes unexpectedly, you can act accordingly. Leave final seasoning adjustments until you have decided how the soup is to be served, for the balance of flavors alters noticeably depending on whether it is to be served hot or chilled; chilling often reduces flavor intensity.

Chilled Cucumber Soup

Color index page 25

Begin 4 hrs ahead

6 servings or 5¼ cups

¼ cup butter or margarine
4 cups chopped peeled cucumbers
1 cup chopped green onions

¼ cup all-purpose flour
4 cups chicken broth
salt and pepper
½ cup half-and-half
cucumber slices for garnish

1 In 12-inch skillet over medium-high heat, in butter, cook cucumbers and onions. Blend flour well into the pan juices.

2 Gradually add broth, stirring; cook until mixture thickens and begins to boil. Add salt and pepper to taste.

3 Cover; simmer over low heat 10 minutes, stirring occasionally. Refrigerate until chilled.

4 In covered blender container at medium speed, blend some of mixture until smooth.

5 Strain blended mixture through sieve into bowl; discard seeds. Repeat with rest of mixture.

6 Stir in half-and-half. Pour into chilled individual bowls; garnish with cucumber slices.

Gazpacho

Color index page 25

Begin 2½ hrs or up to 1 wk ahead

4 servings

3 cups tomato juice
3 tablespoons olive or salad oil
3 large tomatoes, peeled and seeded
1 cucumber, peeled and seeded
1 small onion, cut up

1 small green pepper, cut up
1 small garlic clove
1 teaspoon sugar
¾ teaspoon salt
½ teaspoon hot pepper sauce

In covered blender container at high speed, blend all ingredients, one-third at a time, until finely chopped. Pour into large bowl; cover and chill.

FROZEN GAZPACHO: In covered blender container at high speed, blend *3 medium tomatoes,* peeled and seeded, *1 small onion,* cut up, *1 small red pepper,* cut up, *1 small garlic clove, 1 cup tomato juice, 2 teaspoons sugar, ½ teaspoon salt, 1½ teaspoons Worcestershire* and *¼ teaspoon hot pepper sauce* until pureed. Pour into 9″ by 9″ metal baking pan. Cover; freeze 2 hours until frozen but soft, stirring occasionally. Cut *1 medium cucumber* into spears. Blend gazpacho smooth and slushy. Serve with cucumber spears.

Vichyssoise

Color index page 25

Begin early in day

4 servings or 3½ cups

2 tablespoons butter
½ cup chopped leeks (white part only)
½ teaspoon chicken stock base
⅔ cup water

1 10½-ounce can condensed cream of potato soup
1 cup half-and-half
½ cup milk
chopped chives

1. In 10-inch skillet over medium heat, in hot butter, cook leeks 5 minutes; add chicken stock base and water; heat to boiling. Reduce heat to low; cover and simmer 10 minutes.
2. Stir in undiluted soup, half-and-half, milk; chill.
3. *Just before serving:* In covered blender container at low speed, blend soup smooth. Top with chives.

Jellied Madrilène Suprême

Color index page 25

Begin early in day

6 servings or 3¼ cups

2 13-ounce cans consommé madrilène
2 tablespoons chopped seedless green grapes

2 tablespoons chopped onion

1. Chill cans of consommé madrilène.
2. *Just before serving:* In medium bowl, with fork, break up madrilène. Top with grapes and onion.

First-course soups

Avgolemono

Color index page 25

Begin 30 mins ahead

6 servings or 5½ cups

3 13 ¾-ounce cans chicken broth
¼ cup regular long-grain rice

4 eggs
3 tablespoons lemon juice
lemon slices (optional)

1. In 3-quart saucepan over high heat, heat broth and rice to boiling. Reduce heat to low; cover and simmer 15 minutes or until rice is tender.
2. In small bowl with wire whisk or hand beater, beat eggs and lemon juice together until frothy.
3. Into egg mixture, stir small amount of hot broth; pour egg mixture into broth, stirring. Cook over low heat, stirring, until soup is hot (do not boil).
4. Serve topped with lemon slices, if you wish.

Pea Soup

Color index page 25

Begin 45 mins ahead

10 servings or 5 cups

¼ cup butter
4 cups shredded lettuce
½ large onion, chopped
1 tablespoon all-purpose flour
1 teaspoon sugar
¼ teaspoon ground coriander

3 13¾-ounce cans chicken broth
2 10-ounce packages frozen peas
1 cup milk
mint leaves for garnish (optional)

1. In 3-quart saucepan over medium heat, in hot butter, cook lettuce and onion until tender, stirring often. Add flour, sugar and coriander. Slowly stir in broth; add peas, reserving a few for garnish; cook, covered, 15 minutes.
2. In covered blender container, blend mixture, a cup at a time; return it to the pan. Add milk; reheat. Garnish with reserved peas and mint, if you wish.

Shrimp Bisque

Color index page 25

Begin 1 hr ahead

10 servings or 8½ cups

3 tablespoons olive oil
1½ pounds medium shrimp, shelled and deveined (reserve shells)
¼ cup butter
1 large onion, diced
1 carrot, chopped
1 celery stalk, chopped
2½ cups water

1 cup dry white wine
¼ cup regular long-grain rice
1 bay leaf
1 teaspoon salt
¼ teaspoon cayenne
3 chicken-flavor bouillon cubes
1 16-ounce can tomatoes
2 cups heavy cream

1. In 4-quart Dutch oven over medium-high heat, in hot olive oil, cook shrimp shells until pink, stirring constantly with slotted spoon. Discard shells, leaving flavored oil in Dutch oven.
2. Add shrimp to oil and cook, over medium-high heat, stirring frequently, until shrimp turn pink, about 3 minutes; spoon into bowl.
3. Reduce heat to medium; add butter, onion, carrot and celery; cook, stirring occasionally, until tender.
4. Stir in next 7 ingredients and heat to boiling. Reduce heat to low; cover and simmer 15 minutes or until rice is tender. Remove Dutch oven from heat.
5. Discard bay leaf. Drain juice of tomatoes into rice mixture. Remove seed from tomatoes; stir tomatoes into rice mixture and add cooked shrimp.
6. In covered blender container at high speed, blend one half of mixture at a time until smooth.
7. Return shrimp mixture to Dutch oven; stir in cream. Over medium heat, heat just to boiling.

French Onion Soup Gratinée

Color index page 25

Begin 45 mins ahead

4 servings or 6 cups

¼ cup butter or margarine
3 large onions, sliced (about 4 cups)
1 teaspoon sugar
1 tablespoon all-purpose flour
2½ cups water
½ cup red cooking wine
2 10½-ounce cans condensed beef broth
1 long loaf French bread
1 8-ounce package Swiss cheese slices

1 In 4-quart saucepan over medium heat, in hot butter, cook onions and sugar for 10 minutes.

2 Stir in flour until well blended with the onions and the pan juices.

3 Add water, wine and undiluted beef broth; heat to boiling. Reduce heat to low; cover and simmer 10 minutes.

4 Cut four 1-inch-thick slices of bread from loaf; save remaining bread to eat with soup. Toast the bread slices in 325°F. oven just until lightly browned, about 10 minutes.

5 Ladle soup into four 12-ounce oven-safe bowls and place 1 slice toasted bread on surface of soup in each bowl.

6 Fold Swiss cheese slices and fit onto toasted bread slices in soup.

7 Place soup bowls in jelly-roll pan for easier handling. Bake in 425°F. oven 10 minutes or just until cheese is melted.

Cream of Mushroom Soup

Color index page 25

Begin 45 mins ahead

8 servings or 7 cups

1 pound mushrooms
½ cup butter or margarine
1 teaspoon lemon juice
1 small onion, sliced
⅓ cup all-purpose flour
3½ cups water
3 chicken-flavor bouillon cubes or envelopes
1 teaspoon salt
¼ teaspoon pepper
1 cup heavy or whipping cream

1 Trim tough stem ends of mushrooms; remove stems; set aside. With knife, slice mushroom caps thinly.

2 In 4-quart saucepan over medium-high heat, in hot butter or margarine, cook sliced mushrooms and lemon juice until mushrooms are just tender, stirring.

3 Reduce heat to medium-low; with slotted spoon, remove mushrooms to bowl. In saucepan in remaining butter, cook onion and stems; cook until onion is tender.

4 Stir in flour until blended; cook 1 minute, stirring the mixture constantly.

5 Gradually stir in water and bouillon; cook, stirring constantly, until mixture is thickened.

6 Into blender container, ladle half of mixture; cover and at high speed, blend until smooth. Repeat with other half.

7 Return mixture to saucepan; stir in salt, pepper, cream and mushroom slices; reheat just until soup is boiling.

GARNISHES FOR SOUPS

A well-chosen garnish such as a sprinkling of finely chopped parsley or chives, a slice of lemon or a few paper-thin slices of cucumber can turn an otherwise ordinary soup into something quite special. For a more decorative effect, swirl a tablespoon of cream lightly into each bowl to marbleize the surface. Grated cheese should be served separately so that each person can help himself.

CHOPPED HARD-COOKED EGG

LEMON SLICES

MEATBALLS

CROUTONS

SLICED CAULIFLOWERETS

CARROT AND CELERY STICKS

WHIPPED OR SOUR CREAM

GRATED CHEESE

BACON BITS

SLICED ALMONDS

Croutons can be passed around in a separate bowl to be added to each portion of soup at the very last moment. You can use any light or dark bread slices for making croutons.

Trim off the crusts and cut the bread into small even-sized cubes.

Fry cubes in salad oil, a mixture of butter and oil or bacon drippings until crisp and golden, stirring constantly while frying.

Main-dish soups

A main-dish soup makes a first-class informal lunch or family supper. It is substantial and filling with crusty hot bread and butter as an accompaniment. Serve a tossed salad or fresh vegetable relishes to complete the menu.

The flavors of fish, meat and chicken soups can be enhanced by adding a small amount of red table wine or cooking wine or a lemon slice and gently reheating for a minute or two to bring out the flavor. Make sure not to cook the soup for too long after adding the red wine or lemon slice, or the flavor will be lost.

Small portions of these substantial soups can also be served as a first course before a light main dish.

Hearty Borscht

Color index page 27

Begin early in day or day ahead

4 servings or 8 cups

3 cups hot water
1 pound beef brisket, cut into 1-inch chunks
2 medium carrots, sliced
1 medium onion, sliced
1 stalk celery, cut into chunks
1 bay leaf
3 medium beets

salt
½ 6-ounce can tomato paste
1½ teaspoons sugar
½ small head cabbage, shredded
1 tablespoon cider vinegar
½ cup sour cream

1 To 5-quart saucepot or Dutch oven over medium-low heat add water, beef, carrots, onion, celery, bay leaf, 2 sliced beets and 1½ teaspoons salt.

2 Cover and simmer 2 hours. Shred remaining beet and, with tomato paste, sugar and 1 teaspoon salt, stir into soup.

3 Cover again and simmer 20 minutes. Remove pan from heat and discard bay leaf. Chill.

4 About 20 minutes before serving: Remove hardened fat from surface of chilled soup.

5 Over medium heat, heat soup to boiling. Add cabbage; cook 15 minutes. Stir in vinegar.

6 Serve in large soup plates or wide bowls, each portion garnished with some sour cream.

German Lentil Soup

Color index page 26

Begin 1½ hrs ahead

6 servings or 11 cups

4 bacon slices, diced
2 medium onions, sliced
2 medium carrots, sliced
1 cup sliced celery
1 ham bone
1 16-ounce package lentils

½ teaspoon pepper
½ teaspoon thyme leaves
2 bay leaves
8 cups hot water
salt
2 tablespoons lemon juice

1. In 5-quart Dutch oven or large saucepot over medium-high heat, fry bacon until lightly browned; push to side of pan.
2. Add onions, carrots and celery and over medium heat, cook until onions are tender, about 5 minutes.
3. Add ham bone, lentils, pepper, thyme, bay leaves, hot water and 2 teaspoons salt.
4. Cover; simmer over low heat 1 hour or until lentils are tender. Discard bay leaves.
5. Remove ham bone to cutting board and cut off any meat; cut into small pieces.
6. Stir meat, lemon juice and salt to taste into soup.

Old-fashioned Beef -Vegetable Soup

Color index page 27

Begin 1 hr ahead

10 servings or 16 cups

¼ cup salad oil
1 small onion, diced
3 celery stalks, sliced
2 medium carrots, sliced
½ small head cabbage, shredded
1 medium zucchini, cut into ½-inch chunks
1½ pounds beef for stew, cut into ½-inch chunks

6 medium potatoes
1 28-ounce can tomatoes
6 cups water
1 16-ounce can cut green beans, drained
1 8-ounce can baby lima beans, drained
4 teaspoons salt
½ teaspoon pepper
½ teaspoon basil

1. In 8-quart Dutch oven or saucepot over high heat, in very hot salad oil, cook onion, celery, carrots, cabbage and zucchini until vegetables are lightly browned, stirring frequently. With slotted spoon, remove vegetables to medium bowl; set aside.
2. In same Dutch oven over high heat, in remaining oil, cook beef chunks, stirring frequently, until meat is well browned on all sides.
3. Meanwhile, peel potatoes; shred 1 potato and cut remaining 5 potatoes into 1-inch cubes. To meat chunks add reserved vegetable mixture, potatoes, tomatoes with their liquid and remaining ingredients; heat to boiling. Reduce heat to low; cover and simmer 25 to 30 minutes or just until beef chunks and medium potatoes are fork-tender.

Split-Pea Soup

Color index page 27

Begin 1 hr ahead

6 servings or 7 cups

1 ham bone (left over from whole or half ham, preferably with enough meat left to make 1½ cups)
1 16-ounce package split peas
2 carrots, thinly sliced
1 medium onion, chopped
7 cups water
¼ teaspoon whole allspice
¼ teaspoon peppercorns
1 bay leaf
salt

1 In 5-quart Dutch oven over medium heat, heat bone, split peas, carrots, onion and water to boiling.

2 Tie allspice, peppercorns and bay leaf in piece of cheesecloth. Add to bone mixture.

3 Reduce heat to low; cover; simmer 1 hour. Discard spice bag; add salt if necessary.

4 Remove bone to cutting board. Cut off meat and discard bone.

5 Cut meat into bite-size chunks and return to soup for serving.

SOUP ACCOMPANIMENTS

Crisp accompaniments contrast pleasantly with any soup. Choose from a selection of the following: hot crusty bread or toast with garlic, herb or onion butter; plain or seasoned bread sticks or melba toast; cheese, rye, wheat or oyster crackers; potato or corn chips and saltines or soda crackers.

Making melba toast: Cut unsliced loaf of bread into ⅛-inch-thick slices. If you like, remove crusts, then cut slices diagonally into triangles. Place on cookie sheet; bake 15 minutes or until golden, crisp and curled, turning once.

Minestrone

Color index page 27

Begin 2 hrs ahead

8 servings or 16 cups

⅓ cup olive or salad oil
¼ cup butter or margarine
1 large onion, diced
2 large carrots, diced
2 stalks celery, diced
2 medium potatoes, diced
½ pound green beans, cut into 1-inch pieces
6 cups water
¼ small head cabbage, shredded
1 16-ounce can tomatoes
½ 10-ounce bag fresh spinach, coarsely shredded

2 medium zucchini, diced
6 beef-flavor bouillon cubes or envelopes, or 2 tablespoons beef-flavor stock base
1 teaspoon salt
1 16- to 20-ounce can white kidney (cannellini) beans, drained
1 16- to 20-ounce can red kidney beans, drained
½ cup grated Parmesan or Romano cheese

1. In 8-quart Dutch oven or large saucepot over medium heat, in hot oil and butter or margarine, cook onion, carrots, celery, potatoes and green beans until vegetables are lightly browned, about 20 minutes, stirring occasionally .
2. Add water, cabbage, tomatoes with their liquid, spinach, zucchini, bouillon cubes and salt. Over high heat, heat to boiling, stirring to break up tomatoes.
3. Reduce heat to low; cover; simmer 40 minutes or until all the vegetables are very tender, stirring occasionally; do not overcook.
3. Stir in beans; cook 15 minutes longer or just until the soup is slightly thickened.
5. To serve: Ladle soup into bowls and pass cheese separately to sprinkle over each individual serving.

Hungarian Goulash

Color index page 26

Begin 2½ hrs ahead

12 servings or 15 cups

3 tablespoons lard or shortening
1½ cups fresh or frozen chopped onions
1 small green pepper, cut into ½-inch chunks
1 large garlic clove, crushed
6 cups water
1½ pounds beef stew meat, cut into ¾-inch cubes

1 veal heart (about 12 ounces) cut into ¾-inch cubes
2 tablespoons paprika
4 teaspoons salt
¼ teaspoon crushed red pepper
¼ teaspoon caraway seed
1½ pounds potatoes, peeled and cut into ¾-inch cubes
1 16-ounce can tomatoes

1. In 5-quart Dutch oven over medium-low heat, in hot lard or shortening, cook onions, green pepper and garlic just until onion is tender, about 10 minutes, stirring occasionally.
2. Add water, beef, heart, paprika, salt, red pepper and caraway seed; heat to boiling. Reduce heat to low; cover and simmer 1½ hours or just until meat is fork-tender.
3. Add potatoes; cover and cook 10 minutes longer or until potatoes are tender.
4. Drain liquid from tomatoes and add to mixture in Dutch oven. With small knife, coarsely chop tomatoes; stir into mixture.
5. Cook soup just until heated through.
6. Ladle into warm soup plates and serve at once.

Main-dish soups

Mulligatawny Soup

Color index
page 27

Begin 1½ hrs
ahead

6 servings or
8 cups

5 bacon slices, diced
1 2½-pound broiler-
fryer
4 cups chicken broth
2 carrots, sliced
2 stalks celery, chopped
1 apple, chopped
1 tablespoon curry
powder
6 peppercorns, crushed
2 whole cloves
1 bay leaf
3 tablespoons all-
purpose flour
⅓ cup water
1 cup half-and-half
1½ cups hot cooked rice

1 In 5-quart Dutch oven over medium-high heat, fry bacon until crisp. Cut up chicken into serving pieces; add the chicken portions to pan and brown well on all sides.

2 Remove chicken pieces and bacon from pan. Drain on paper towels. Pour off any fat in pan.

3 Return chicken and bacon to pan; add the next 8 ingredients. Heat mixture just to boiling.

4 Cover; simmer over low heat, 30 minutes, or until the chicken is fork-tender.

5 Cut meat from bones. Return to soup; discard bones, cloves, bay leaf. In cup, with spoon, blend flour with water.

6 Gradually add flour mixture to simmering soup, stirring. Add half-and-half; do not boil.

7 To serve: Ladle soup into warmed bowls. Spoon a mound of hot rice into each of the bowls.

Chicken Soup with Rivels

Color index
page 26

Begin 1½ hrs
ahead

8 servings or
12 cups

1 3½- to 4-pound
broiler-fryer
1 large onion, chopped
6 cups hot water
3 cups sliced carrots
¼ teaspoon pepper
salt

1 cup all-purpose
flour
1 egg
1 to 2 tablespoons
milk
1 cup chopped celery
with leaves

1. In 8-quart Dutch oven or large saucepot over high heat, heat chicken, onion, water, carrots, pepper and 1 tablespoon salt to boiling. Reduce heat to low; cover and simmer 45 minutes or until chicken is fork-tender.
2. Remove chicken to cutting board; allow to cool.
3. Meanwhile, prepare the rivels: In medium bowl with fork, stir flour, egg, ½ teaspoon salt and approximately 1 tablespoon milk, to make a crumbly but moist mixture.
4. With spoon, sprinkle rivels into simmering soup. Add celery; cook 20 minutes or until tender.
5. Cut chicken meat from bones into small chunks; stir into soup; reheat.

Making the rivels:
Combine rivel ingredients to make a crumbly but still moist mixture.

Adding rivels to soup:
With a spoon, carefully sprinkle rivels into the simmering soup.

Creamy Cheddar-Cheese Soup

Color index
page 27

Begin 45 mins
ahead

6 servings or
8 cups

¼ cup butter or
margarine
1 medium onion, chopped
¼ cup all-purpose
flour
3 cups chicken broth
3 cups milk

1 pound Cheddar cheese,
shredded (about
4 cups)
3 pumpernickel-bread
slices, toasted
and cut into cubes

1. In 3-quart saucepan over medium-high heat, in hot butter or margarine, cook onion until tender, about 5 minutes. Stir in flour and cook until flour has blended with onion mixture.
2. Add chicken broth; cook, stirring constantly, until mixture is slightly thickened. Add milk and heat just to boiling, stirring constantly.
3. In covered blender container at medium speed, blend about ¼ of milk mixture at a time until smooth. Return to saucepan and, over medium heat, heat just to boiling; remove from heat.
4. With wire whisk or slotted spoon, stir in cheese until melted. If cheese does not melt completely, cook over very low heat about 1 minute, stirring the soup constantly.
5. Serve soup garnished with pumpernickel cubes.

Fruit soups

Although usually thought of as desserts, fruit soups also make an unusual and refreshing first course for a summer meal. Most of them are purees sweetened and diluted with wine, fruit juice or simply iced water. They can be made in a matter of minutes, using a blender.

Strawberry-Rhubarb Soup

1 pint strawberries
1 pound rhubarb
1¼ cups orange juice
about ½ cup sugar
¼ cup chopped orange sections

Color index page 99

Begin 3 hrs ahead

4 servings or 4¼ cups

1 Hull and slice strawberries and set aside 4 of the best slices.

2 Trim rhubarb, discarding any tough fibers. Cut stalks into bite-size chunks.

3 In 3-quart saucepan over medium heat, heat fruit and orange juice to boiling. Simmer about 10 minutes.

4 Remove pan from heat. Stir in sugar to taste. Allow to cool.

5 In covered blender container at low speed, blend soup, half at a time.

6 Pour soup into a bowl and fold in orange sections. Refrigerate, covered.

7 Serve soup in chilled bowls, each garnished with a strawberry slice.

Strawberry Soup

1 pint strawberries
½ cup white wine
1 teaspoon grated lemon peel
½ cup sugar
2 tablespoons lemon juice

Color index page 99

Begin early in day

3 servings or 2⅔ cups

1. Hull strawberries. Slice 3 berries; set aside.
2. In covered blender container at medium speed, blend whole berries and remaining ingredients until smooth. Cover and refrigerate until well chilled.
3. Serve soup in chilled soup bowls or cups, garnished with reserved sliced strawberries.

Blender Blueberry Soup

⅓ cup sour cream
1 10-ounce package frozen blueberries, partially thawed
2 tablespoons sugar
lemon slices for garnish

Color index page 99

Begin 20 mins ahead

2 servings or 1¾ cups

1. In covered blender container at low speed, blend sour cream, blueberries and sugar until smooth. (Or, press blueberries through food mill; mix puree with sour cream and sugar until smooth).
2. Serve soup garnished with lemon slices.

Cold Raspberry Soup

4 10-ounce packages frozen raspberries, thawed
2 cups port
4 short cinnamon sticks
2 teaspoons cornstarch
½ cup water

Color index page 99

Begin early in day

6 servings or 6 cups

1. In 3-quart saucepan over medium heat, heat raspberries, port and cinnamon sticks to boiling. Reduce heat to low and simmer 10 minutes.
2. In measuring cup, mix cornstarch with water. Slowly stir into soup; cook until thickened, stirring. Cover and refrigerate.
3. *To serve:* Remove cinnamon sticks.

Iced Cherry Soup

2 16-ounce cans pitted tart cherries
water
½ cup sugar
½ teaspoon anise seed, crushed
2 tablespoons lemon juice
3 tablespoons cornstarch
½ teaspoon red food color
sour cream for garnish
mint leaves for garnish

Color index page 99

Begin early in day

6 servings or 6 cups

1. Drain cherries, reserving liquid; add water to cherry liquid to make 5 cups. In 3-quart saucepan over medium heat, heat cherries, liquid, sugar, anise seed and lemon juice to boiling. Reduce heat to low and simmer, covered, 30 minutes.
2. In covered blender container, blend mixture until smooth, one half at a time. Return mixture to pan.
3. Blend cornstarch with ½ cup water; stir into mixture; heat to boiling, stirring constantly. Stir in food color; cover and refrigerate.
4. *To serve:* Garnish soup with sour cream and mint.

EGGS

The egg is a remarkable culinary ingredient, never out of season, economical, and treasured by all the great cuisines of the world. Cooked in the shell or cracked open into a pan, it makes a near-perfect convenience food. In one form or another, eggs can be served at any meal, in any guise, savory or sweet. Whole eggs can be used to bind and leaven, to provide elasticity to puffs and batters, or for coating foods to enhance them with a rich, golden glaze. Egg yolks thicken sauces and custards and emulsify with oil to make salad dressings; egg whites can be beaten to moist, glossy, stiff peaks to raise soufflés and angel-food and chiffon cakes.

No matter what the method, eggs should always be cooked at moderate to low temperatures. They will become dry or rubbery if the heat is too high or even if they are cooked too long at a low temperature. Saucepans made of stainless steel, glass, porcelain, enamel or any metal with a non-stick finish are all suitable for cooking eggs. When eggs are cooked in water in aluminum pans, the metal sometimes darkens; this is not harmful to either the pan or the eggs.

CHOOSING EGGS

A white egg may look more wholesome and inviting than a brown egg or vice versa, depending on personal preference, but the color of the shell is of no culinary significance. It is dictated by the breed of hen that laid it. What is important for the cook is that the egg be fresh. For good appearance, eggs which are to be eaten soft-cooked, fried or poached should be as fresh as possible. For cooking or baking with other ingredients they can be older; in fact, older whites will beat to greater volume and if hard-cooked, older eggs shell more cleanly.

Eggs are sold by grade and size according to United States Department of Agriculture standards. The grading refers to their appearance, not their quality; all have the same food value. Grade AA eggs have firm, high yolks and thick whites. These are the ideal eggs to serve where their appearance is important – poached, fried or cooked in the shell. Grade A eggs, which have slightly thinner whites, are all-purpose eggs, equally good cooked whole and used in recipes. The whites of Grade B eggs are less thick and the yolks may be somewhat flattened and enlarged; they are good for use in recipes. Eggs range in size from Jumbo, Extra Large and Large to Medium and Small. They are classed in accordance with minimum weights per dozen. The Good Housekeeping recipes in this book all use Large eggs.

When buying eggs, check that none are cracked. A cracked egg may contain bacteria that will cause food poisoning. If you do find an egg that is cracked, use it in a recipe that calls for thorough cooking of the egg.

FRESH OR STALE?

If you suspect that an egg is no longer fresh, break it into a saucer and sniff it. A fresh egg, when opened, will smell clean and faintly sweet, if at all, whereas the offensive smell of a bad egg is unmistakable. You can tell a lot by appearance, too. The white should be translucent, thick and firmly shaped, the yolk smooth and well rounded. If the yolk is flat and the white runs thinly all over the saucer, the egg is past its best. Any spots of blood on the egg yolk have probably been caused by the rupture of a blood vessel during the formation of the egg and will not affect its quality or flavor. Remove the spot with the tip of a spoon if you like. Stringy white fibers, or chalazae, are often found in the white of a fresh egg. These are quite normal, and their role is to hold the yolk in place in the center of the egg. As the egg gets older, the chalazae tend to disappear, thus allowing the egg yolk to move about freely inside the shell.

STORING EGGS

Eggs keep fresh for up to a month if stored in the refrigerator, either in their boxes, or with large ends up in the egg section to keep the yolks centered. Egg shells are porous so they should be kept well away from strong-smelling foods such as cheese and onions. For recipes using beaten egg whites, the eggs should be separated when cold and the whites allowed to come to room temperature so they will beat to a higher volume. Eggs which are to be fried or poached will always keep their shape better if they are still chilled.

Leftover eggs or separated yolks and whites can be stored safely for a few days in the refrigerator in a tightly covered container. They can also be frozen. Leftover whole yolks can be cooked by being placed in a strainer and lowered into a small saucepan with enough simmering water to cover. Leftover whites can be hard-cooked by being baked in a well-greased shallow baking dish in a 325°F. oven for approximately 10 minutes.

SEPARATING EGGS

It is easier to separate eggs if they are firm and chilled. To avoid ruining a bowlful of whites with a broken yolk or stale egg, crack each egg open separately over a small bowl or cup. Give it a sharp tap against the side of the bowl and follow the half-shell method shown below. Drop the yolk into another bowl. Take care not to puncture the yolk on the sharp edge of the shell. Remove any trace of egg yolk from a bowl of whites with a spoon or piece of paper towel moistened in cold water.

Half-shell method: Gently pull the cracked shell apart with the thumbs so that some of the white drops down into the bowl. Transfer the yolk carefully back and forth from one half-shell to the other until it is quite free of white.

Removing a piece of eggshell: Use a spoon or piece of moistened paper towel to remove any shell in the whites.

BEATING EGGS

Whole eggs, egg yolks and egg whites are beaten for use in many recipes. Recipes describe well-beaten whole eggs or egg yolks as "thick and lemon colored" or "fluffy and lemon colored." It usually takes just a few minutes' beating with a fork, whisk, egg beater or mixer for eggs to become well beaten.

Egg whites reach their highest volume if beaten at room temperature, so carefully separate them from the yolks well ahead of time; even a tiny bit of yolk present in the whites will greatly reduce their foaming action. Egg whites increase many times in volume when beaten, so follow the recipe directions for bowl size. The bowl and beaters must be perfectly clean since even the slightest bit of fat will prevent the whites from beating to their fullest volume.

If using an electric mixer, turn it to high speed, beating the whites to the correct consistency called for in the recipe; if beating by hand, use an egg beater or a wire whisk and work steadily. Once the whites are foamy, recipes sometimes call for a little cream of tartar to

increase the stability of the foam. Other recipes call for the addition of sugar after the whites are beaten into soft peaks – for example, angel-food cakes. Because sugar retards the foaming action it should be added in small amounts at a time. For recipes that call for "foamy" or "frothy" egg whites, beat until the mixture is foamy but still unstable; it will separate easily back into a liquid form. For recipes that call for "soft peaks," beat the whites until they are moist and shiny and form soft peaks when the beaters or whisk are raised. For "stiff peaks," beat the whites until moist and glossy and they form stiff straight peaks when the beaters or whisk are raised; they should be stable but not dry. Be careful not to overbeat egg whites or they will become stiff and dry, having lost their elasticity, and will almost certainly collapse as soon as heat is applied.

FOLDING IN EGG WHITES

Stiffly beaten egg whites should be prepared and combined with the basic mixture at the very last moment, just before they are baked or set with gelatin, depending on the recipe. "Folding," rather than stirring or mixing, incorporates the egg whites as lightly as possible so that the little bubbles of air that have already been beaten in to them will not break down.

Folding in the whites:
With a rubber spatula or spoon, cut straight down through the center, across the bottom and up the side of the bowl.

Give the bowl a quarter turn and repeat the folding action as lightly as possible until the egg whites are evenly dispersed throughout, taking care not to overwork the mixture.

USING EGGS AS A THICKENER

Eggs, particularly the yolks, are often used to thicken and enrich sauces. The success of thickening with eggs depends on cooking the mixture below boiling point until the desired consistency is reached. Too high heat or heat applied too long will curdle the mixture. Some recipes specify the cooking of custards and sauces over just simmering water in a double boiler and custards are set in a pan of water to bake to better control the temperature. To help prevent curdled sauces, first stir a little of the hot mixture into the eggs to raise their temperature before adding them to the mixture; cook over low heat, stirring constantly, just until the sauce reaches the consistency required for the recipe.

Hard- and soft-cooked eggs

Hard-cooked eggs are easy and quick as a main dish or are excellent for salads and appetizers. Contrary to shelled-egg cooking, eggs in the shell should be cooked over high heat just until the water boils then removed and left to stand for the doneness desired. Never boil eggs. If eggs are boiled or overcooked, the yolks will become hard or may turn an unattractive greenish-gray.

A classic soft-cooked egg has a barely set yolk and a completely opaque white that is still soft and creamy. Cook as shown right, letting the eggs stand for 2 to 3 minutes for medium-soft eggs. If you have more than 6 eggs in the pan, let these stand a shorter time after boiling. If you prefer slightly firmer eggs, just let them stand in the pan of water off the heat for about one more minute. Soft-cooked eggs that are not served in the shell should be plunged into cold water as soon as cooking is complete. If they are to be served warm, remove the shell as soon as it is cool enough to handle; for serving cold, leave the eggs in cold water for about 8 minutes, then carefully peel away the shell.

Hard-cooked eggs, prepared using the method shown right, should be removed from the heat once the water starts to boil, and left to stand for 15 minutes. If a large number of eggs are to be cooked at once, a frying basket can be used to lift them in and out of the water simultaneously. As soon as the eggs are done, put the pan under running cold water and leave until they are cold. This not only stops the eggs overcooking, but also makes them easier to peel. Very fresh eggs are hard to peel because they contain a very small air space at their large end. It is a good idea, then, to buy your eggs several days ahead, since storage allows the air space at the large end of the egg to expand, making later peeling easier.

SHELLING A HARD-COOKED EGG

Store shelled eggs in a tightly covered container in the refrigerator and use as soon as possible. Shelling eggs is easy if you follow the method shown here.

Color index page 28

1 to 2 eggs per person

Hard- or Soft-cooked Eggs

1 Put the *eggs* in a pan roomy enough to hold them without crowding, with *cold water* to cover by at least 1 inch.

2 Over high heat, heat water and eggs until just fully boiling.

3 Remove saucepan from heat, cover tightly and let stand 15 minutes for hard-cooked, 2 minutes for medium soft-cooked.

4 Pour off the hot water and run cold water over eggs to stop cooking and make peeling easier if eggs are to be peeled for immediate use.

Cracking the shell: Gently tap the shell against a flat surface, taking care not to damage the egg.

Removing the shell: Under running cold water, gently peel off pieces of shell, beginning at the large end. Take great care, especially with fresh eggs, not to peel the white away with the shell accidentally.

EGG GARNISHES

Hard-cooked eggs make attractive, easy garnishes. Yolks may be pressed through a fine strainer and sprinkled over soups, rice dishes and vegetables. Egg whites cut into shapes with small cutters make a pretty decoration, particularly for appetizers, snacks and canapés.

Whole hard-cooked eggs, sliced or cut in wedges, will add the finishing touch to salads and other cold dishes. When slicing hard-cooked eggs, make sure your knife is very sharp and cut carefully to avoid crumbling the yolk. Egg slicers and wedgers are useful for cutting uniform shapes.

Sieving the yolks: Using back of a spoon, firmly press yolks through a fine strainer.

Making decorative shapes: Cut egg whites into fancy shapes with small canapé cutters.

Stuffed Eggs

Color index
page 23

Begin 45 mins
ahead

12 stuffed
halves

6 hard-cooked
  eggs
¼ cup mayonnaise

¼ teaspoon salt
⅛ teaspoon pepper

1 Shell eggs and with small, sharp knife, slice them in half lengthwise.

2 Gently remove yolks and place them in a small bowl. With fork, finely mash yolks.

3 Add mayonnaise, salt and pepper. Mix until smoothly blended.

4 With spoon, pile yolk mixture into egg white centers. Cover eggs and refrigerate until you are ready to serve.

STUFFED-EGG VARIATIONS

Color index
page 23

Stir one of these into above egg-yolk mixture:

BACON: Add *2½ tablespoons crumbled, crisp-fried bacon.*

MEXICAN STYLE: Increase salt to ½ teaspoon; add *⅓ cup drained, chopped tomatoes* and *1 teaspoon chili powder.*

SHRIMP SALAD: Add *2 tablespoons chopped cooked shrimp* and *2 tablespoons minced celery.*

CUCUMBER-DILL: Add *¼ cup minced cucumber, 1 teaspoon dillweed* and *1 teaspoon cider vinegar.*

HAM-OLIVE: Use only 2 tablespoons mayonnaise in egg-yolk mixture and omit salt; add *one 2¼-ounce can deviled ham* and *3 tablespoons chopped ripe olives.*

TUNA: Add *3 tablespoons flaked tuna* and *2 teaspoons lemon juice.*

PIZZA: Use only 2 tablespoons mayonnaise; add *1 teaspoon oregano leaves, ⅛ teaspoon garlic powder* and *2 tablespoons catchup.*

ANCHOVY: Add *½ 2-ounce can anchovies,* minced.

RADISH: Add *3 tablespoons minced radishes.*

CAPERS: Add *2 teaspoons minced capers.*

OLIVE: Add *6 pimento-stuffed olives,* minced, and *2 tablespoons prepared mustard.*

Eggs en Gelée

Color index
page 23

Begin day
ahead

12 first-
course
servings

12 hard-cooked eggs,
  shelled
**French or Italian
  dressing**
**1 envelope unflavored
  gelatin**
⅓ cup cold water
**1 10½-ounce can
  condensed beef
  consommé, undiluted**
2 canned pimentos
10 pitted ripe olives

1 Halve eggs lengthwise; remove yolks and add dressing just to moisten. Stuff mixture into egg whites and smooth the tops with a knife.

2 Press halves together, removing any of the excess stuffing mixture.

3 Place each egg in muffin-size foil baking cup. Arrange cups close together in shallow baking pan.

4 In 2-quart saucepan, sprinkle gelatin on water. Stir in consommé. Over high heat, heat to boiling, stirring until gelatin dissolves. Cool.

5 With star aspic cutter, cut 12 stars from pimentos. Cut each olive into 6 thin slivers.

6 Arrange pimento stars and olive slivers on eggs in attractive design.

7 Spoon gelatin mixture over each egg until cup is almost full. Refrigerate decorated eggs until set.

141

Hard- and soft-cooked eggs | Poached eggs

Eggs Divan

Color index
page 28

Begin 1 hr
ahead

3 servings

*6 hard-cooked eggs,
cooled and
shelled*
¼ cup mayonnaise
*1 tablespoon
instant minced
onion*
¼ teaspoon salt

*1 10-ounce package
frozen broccoli
spears*
*1 8-ounce jar
pasteurized process
cheese spread*

1 Halve eggs lengthwise and remove yolks. In small bowl combine yolks, mayonnaise, onion and salt. Spoon stuffing into egg white centers.

2 Cook broccoli in boiling salted water as label directs; drain well. Preheat oven to 400°F.

3 In 12″ by 8″ greased baking dish, arrange the broccoli spears in 3 separate rows. Place stuffed eggs in between.

4 Spoon cheese spread generously over broccoli. Bake dish in oven 10 minutes or until cheese spread is hot and bubbling slightly on the top.

Creole Eggs

Color index
page 28

Begin 45
mins ahead

4 servings

*¼ cup butter or
margarine*
*1 large onion,
chopped*
*1 medium green
pepper, seeded
and chopped*
*1 garlic clove,
minced*
1 teaspoon salt
⅛ teaspoon rosemary

⅛ teaspoon paprika
*1 16- or 17-ounce can
tomatoes*
*8 hard-cooked eggs,
cooled, shelled
and halved
lengthwise*
*2 cups hot cooked
rice*

1. In 10-inch skillet over medium heat, in melted butter or margarine, cook onion, pepper, garlic, salt, rosemary and paprika until onion and pepper are soft, about 5 minutes, stirring occasionally.
2. Add tomatoes with their liquid and eggs; simmer gently, covered, 10 minutes until thoroughly heated.
3. To serve: Spoon egg mixture over rice.

Poached eggs

Eggs which are to be poached in simmering liquid should be as fresh and cold as possible. If an egg is stale, the white will not set neatly around the yolk, but will start to separate from it and coagulate in ragged shreds as soon as it hits the liquid.

If you are poaching more than 3 or 4 eggs at a time, it is easier to cook them in batches so that you can keep track of them and lift them out of the pan in the same order as they went in. Eggs may be poached in a variety of simmering (not boiling) liquids including milk, soup, tomato juice, vegetable cocktail juice and broth.

Poached Eggs

Color index
page 29

2 eggs
per person

1 Lightly grease a saucepan or deep skillet. Pour in *1½ inches water;* over high heat, heat to boiling and reduce the heat to low, simmering.

2 Break the egg into a saucer and gently slip it into the simmering water. Repeat with other eggs; cook 3 to 5 minutes until of desired firmness.

3 Remove the cooked eggs from the liquid with a slotted spoon.

4 Drain eggs in spoon thoroughly over paper towels and serve at once.

Eggs Benedict

Color index
page 29

Begin 30
mins ahead

4 servings

*Hollandaise Sauce
(page 463)*
4 eggs
2 English muffins

butter or margarine
*4 slices Canadian bacon
or cooked ham*

1. Prepare Hollandaise Sauce; keep warm.
2. Poach 4 eggs until of desired doneness. Keep eggs warm. Preheat broiler if manufacturer directs.
3. Split muffins; spread each half lightly with butter or margarine. Place, buttered side up, on broiling pan, with bacon or cooked ham alongside. Broil until muffin halves are toasted and bacon or ham is heated through.
4. On heated platter, place bacon or ham slice on each muffin half; top each with a poached egg. Generously spoon Hollandaise Sauce over eggs.

Baked eggs

Baked eggs look most attractive served in ramekins, cocottes or casseroles. Once again, timing is of the essence, and it is important not to overcook the eggs – the yolks should be soft and the whites just set.

Baked Eggs

Color index
page 28

Begin 30 mins
ahead

2 eggs
per person

1 Preheat oven to 325°F. For each serving, generously butter an ovenproof ramekin.

2 Break *2 eggs* into each buttered ramekin and sprinkle with *salt, pepper* and a pinch of *paprika*.

3 Arrange ramekins on cookie sheet, bake 15 to 20 minutes or just until egg whites are opaque and yolks are softly set.

4 Garnish eggs if you like, and serve the ramekins at once on small plates.

BAKED EGG VARIATIONS

Add *a little cream* to the bottom of the ramekins before adding the eggs and stir in *cooked ham, chopped sautéed mushrooms,* or *cooked asparagus*.

Eggs Mornay

Color index
page 28

Begin 40 mins
ahead

4 servings

2 tablespoons butter or margarine	*dash hot pepper sauce*
2 tablespoons all-purpose flour	*2 cups milk*
1 teaspoon salt	*¼ cup grated Parmesan cheese*
½ teaspoon dry mustard	*8 eggs*
⅛ teaspoon pepper	

1. In 2-quart saucepan over medium heat, into hot butter or margarine, stir flour, salt, mustard, pepper and hot pepper sauce. Gradually stir in milk; cook, stirring constantly, until mixture is thickened. Stir in cheese until melted. Preheat oven to 400°F.
2. Pour half of sauce into 4 buttered 10-ounce custard cups or individual baking dishes. Break 2 eggs into each dish over sauce; spoon remaining sauce over eggs leaving yolks partially uncovered. Bake eggs 15 minutes, or until of desired doneness.

Fried eggs

Always cook fried eggs over low heat, or the whites will be crisp and toughened around the edges before the yolks are barely hot and not cooked through.

The skillet should be large enough for the eggs to stay separate so they can be turned easily if desired; once the whites have joined together you will have to separate them by cutting. Use only a minimum of fat (1 tablespoon for a small skillet, up to 3 tablespoons for a medium-sized skillet), or the eggs will be too greasy. Use butter, margarine or bacon drippings.

To serve an egg "sunny side up" cook on one side only. If serving an egg "once over easy" turn it over after frying the bottom and cook the yolk until slightly set.

Fried Eggs

Color index
page 28

2 eggs per
person

1 In a skillet over medium heat, heat the *butter* or margarine just until it is melted and hot.

2 One at a time, break the *eggs* into a saucer or cup and slip them into skillet. Reduce heat to low.

3 Cook the eggs, basting yolks with butter from the skillet until the whites are cooked through and opaque, and the yolks are of desired firmness.

4 Or, as soon as the whites are firm enough, turn eggs with a pancake turner and cook other side until yolk is of desired firmness.

5 Remove eggs from pan; season with *salt* and *pepper,* and serve at once.

Scrambled eggs

Scrambled eggs must be cooked slowly if they are to stay creamy and, for the best results, the eggs should be at room temperature. By mixing 2 tablespoons milk, cream or water with every 2 eggs you can slow the cooking and make them fluffier and more tender. Eggs should not be stirred too often: frequent stirring breaks them into small pieces and they become dry and crumbly.

The size of the skillet you choose is important, too – the egg mixture should not be more than 1 inch deep, otherwise the portion that cooks at the beginning will have toughened before the remaining mixture has had a chance to thicken. The skillet should be made from a material that conducts heat evenly.

Scrambled Eggs

Color index
page 28

2 eggs
per person

1 Break **2 eggs** into bowl, add **2 tablespoons liquid** and sprinkle with **salt** and **pepper.** With a fork beat slightly just until mixed.

2 In 9-inch skillet over medium heat, melt **1 tablespoon butter** or margarine, tilting the skillet to coat both the base and side thoroughly

3 Pour in the egg mixture and as it begins to set, with spatula, stir slightly so thin, uncooked egg flows to bottom.

4 Cook the egg mixture gently until set but still very moist; remove from heat. Eggs will continue to cook from pan heat.

5 Pile eggs onto warmed plate, or hot buttered toast and serve the dish immediately.

Shrimp Scramble

Color index
page 28

Begin 15
mins ahead

2 servings

4 eggs
2 tablespoons milk
1 4½-ounce can shrimp
½ teaspoon salt
⅛ teaspoon pepper
¼ teaspoon prepared
  mustard
2 English muffins,
  split
butter or margarine

1 In medium bowl with fork, beat eggs and milk. Drain shrimp and stir into eggs with salt, pepper and mustard. Toast muffins; butter and keep warm.

2 In 10-inch skillet, over medium heat, melt 1 tablespoon butter. Add egg mixture; cook, stirring lightly with fork.

3 When eggs are set and creamy, spoon over toasted muffin halves. Serve immediately.

Scrambled Eggs Archduchess

Color index
page 2 3

Begin 45
mins ahead

4 main-dish
or
8 appetizer
servings

butter or margarine	*6 eggs*
4 white-bread slices	*3 tablespoons milk*
1 10½-ounce can	*¼ teaspoon paprika*
asparagus spears	*½ teaspoon salt*
¼ cup sliced	*½ cup diced cooked*
mushrooms	*ham*

1. In 10-inch skillet over low heat, melt 2 tablespoons butter; cook 2 bread slices at a time in butter until golden on both sides; remove slices to platter; keep warm.
2. In 1-quart saucepan over medium heat, heat asparagus spears; drain and keep warm.
3. In same skillet, melt 1 tablespoon butter; add mushrooms and cook 3 minutes or until tender; spoon into small bowl.
4. In medium bowl with wire whisk, beat eggs, milk, paprika and salt.
5. In same skillet over low heat, melt ¼ cup butter; add egg mixture and cook, stirring, until mixture begins to thicken. Stir in ham and mushrooms; cook until eggs are nearly set, stirring.
6. To serve: Spoon egg mixture over bread slices; top with asparagus spears.

SCRAMBLED EGG VARIATIONS: When the eggs are partially cooked, stir in *chopped parsley or chives, minced cooked ham, shredded Cheddar or Swiss cheese, or cooked sliced mushrooms.*

See descriptions, page 16

Omelets

A French omelet should be shiny and delicately browned on the outside, moist and creamy in the center. You can serve it plain or with any one of the fillings on page 146. The puffy omelet, a cross between an omelet and a soufflé, is finished by baking in the oven. It, too, can be eaten plain or with fillings for a main dish, or it can be served with a sweet filling and eaten as a dessert. The eggs for a puffy omelet are separated, and the yolks mixed into the beaten whites.

Remember that the eggs should always be cooked over moderate to low heat. With practice, you can turn out a perfect omelet every time. Timing is important; have any fillings warm and get the plate ready before you start cooking the eggs. An individual omelet should not take more than a few minutes.

Always coat the pan lightly with butter or margarine to prevent sticking, and make sure the egg mixture is not more than ¼ inch deep in the pan. It is not necessary to turn the omelet over, but the edge should be raised with a spatula and the pan shaken gently to keep the uncooked mixture moving freely. When the omelet is almost set but still moist on the surface, increase the heat slightly to brown the bottom. Have a warmed plate handy to receive the folded omelet: an omelet should never wait. Add your choice of filling, if desired, and serve the omelet without delay.

THE OMELET PAN

An omelet can be made in any good skillet with a flared side and an easy-to-grip, heat-resistant handle. Easiest to use are those made from aluminum, copper or stainless steel (combined with aluminum, copper or carbon steel) because they conduct and distribute heat well. A nonstick coating in the pan is especially helpful for omelet making and enables you to reduce the amount of butter necessary for cooking the eggs.

OMELET PAN

Pan size is important. Too thin an omelet will cook too quickly and be tough; too thick an omelet will not completely "set" and will split and ooze when you attempt to fold it. A 7- or 8-inch top diameter (5- or 6-inch base diameter) pan is the size for a 3-egg omelet.

French Omelet

3 eggs
1 tablespoon cold
*   water*
¼ teaspoon salt
⅛ teaspoon pepper
1 tablespoon butter
*   or margarine*

Color index page 28
Begin 30 mins ahead
1 main-dish serving

1 Break the eggs into a small bowl. Add the water, salt and pepper.

2 Beat the eggs vigorously with a wire whisk or fork – just enough to mix the egg yolks and whites.

3 In a 7-inch omelet pan or skillet over medium heat, melt butter or margarine; tilt the skillet so that the butter coats the entire surface of the pan.

4 Pour in eggs all at once. Let them set around edge. Shake pan occasionally to keep omelet moving freely over the bottom of the pan.

5 With a metal spatula lift edge as it sets, tilting skillet to allow uncooked egg mixture to run under omelet.

6 Continue to shake pan for a few seconds longer until you can feel the omelet sliding freely over the pan surface.

7 When omelet is set but still moist on the surface, increase heat slightly to brown bottom. Remove pan from heat.

8 Tilt pan away from you and using the spatula, lift the edge of the omelet and quickly fold in half.

9 Slide omelet on to a warm plate, garnish if you wish. Serve the hot omelet immediately.

See descriptions, page 16

Omelets

FILLING OMELETS

While omelets can be served plain folded in half, you can vary them with a filling. If you want to add the filling before removing the omelet from the pan, follow the method below. Or you can spoon the filling between the halves immediately after sliding the omelet out on the plate.

Adding a filling: Spread the prepared filling over one half of the cooked omelet with a spatula.

Folding the omelet: Gently fold the other half over the filling.

FILLINGS AND FLAVORINGS

About 15 minutes before serving, prepare any of the following as fillings for two 3-egg omelets.

 COOKED HAM: In a small skillet over medium heat, melt *1 tablespoon butter* or margarine. Add *¾ cup cooked ham,* cut into thin strips, and cook until hot, stirring frequently to prevent burning. Sprinkle with *⅛ teaspoon seasoned pepper.*

 FINES HERBES: Add *4 teaspoons mixed dried herbs* or *¼ cup finely chopped fresh herbs* to the beaten eggs before cooking. Parsley, chives and tarragon are all suitable for a fines herbes omelet.

 CHEESE: Sprinkle each omelet with *half of ⅓ cup shredded Cheddar cheese,* or a mixture of Parmesan and Swiss cheese, just before folding.

 ASPARAGUS: Cook *half 10-ounce package frozen cut-up asparagus* as label directs; drain. In 1-quart saucepan over low heat, heat *1½ teaspoons butter* or margarine; blend in *1 teaspoon all-purpose flour;* slowly stir in *¼ cup milk, ¼ teaspoon seasoned salt* and *⅛ teaspoon pepper* and cook, stirring until thickened. Stir in asparagus.

 CREOLE SAUCE: In a small skillet over medium-high heat, heat *1 tablespoon salad oil.* Add *6 tablespoons each chopped green pepper* and *chopped celery,* and *2 tablespoons chopped onion;* cook until tender, about 5 minutes, stirring occasionally. Add *2 medium tomatoes,* peeled and chopped, *¼ teaspoon oregano leaves* and *¼ teaspoon salt.* Mix well and simmer, covered, for 10 minutes, stirring often.

 COOKED SHRIMP: In 1-quart saucepan, prepare *one ¾-ounce package white sauce mix* as label directs; when smooth, stir in *½ cup diced cooked shrimp, 1 teaspoon lemon juice, 1½ teaspoons chopped parsley* and *dash Worcestershire;* heat.

Puffy Omelet

Color index page 29

Begin 30 mins ahead

2 main-dish servings

*4 eggs, separated
¼ teaspoon cream of tartar*

*¼ teaspoon salt
¼ cup cold water
2 tablespoons butter*

1 In large bowl with mixer at high speed, beat egg whites until foamy. Add cream of tartar; beat until whites form stiff peaks. Preheat oven to 350°F.

2 In small bowl with mixer at high speed, beat yolks with salt and water until light and fluffy then carefully fold into beaten egg whites.

3 In ovensafe 10-inch skillet, over medium heat, melt butter. Add egg mixture; cook until golden on the underside of the omelet, about 3 minutes.

4 Place skillet in the oven and bake omelet for 10 minutes, or until surface is golden and springs back when pressed lightly with the tip of a finger.

5 Run spatula around side of skillet to loosen omelet and make a slit part way across center.

6 With a spatula, fold the omelet in half. Slide the omelet onto a warm plate and serve immediately.

Color index page 98

STRAWBERRY DESSERT OMELET: Prepare Puffy Omelet (above), but add *2 tablespoons sugar* to yolk mixture. Toss *2 cups sliced strawberries* with *1 tablespoon sugar;* fill baked omelet; fold. Sprinkle with *confectioners' sugar.* (Makes 4 servings.)

PEACH DESSERT OMELET: Prepare Dessert Omelet as above but omit berries. Heat *one 17-ounce can cling-peach slices,* drained, *2 tablespoons brandy* and *¼ teaspoon almond extract;* fill omelet; fold. Sprinkle with a little *confectioners' sugar.* (Makes 4 servings.)

Crêpes

Crêpe batter should be made up at least 2 hours in advance to give flour time to absorb the liquid.

Special crêpe pans have a diameter of 7 to 9 inches with sloping sides to allow a crêpe to slip out without tearing. Below is an easy method for turning crêpes using a second skillet; if using only one pan, turn the crêpe with a pancake turner.

Crêpes can also be made ahead. Wrap in foil; freeze for up to 2 months. Thaw at room temperature 1 hour.

Crêpes

Begin 2½ hrs ahead

12 crêpes

melted butter	*½ teaspoon salt*
1½ cups milk	*3 eggs*
⅔ cup all-purpose flour	

1 In medium bowl with wire whisk, beat 2 tablespoons butter and remaining ingredients till smooth. Cover; refrigerate batter at least 2 hours.

2 Brush bottoms of 7-inch crêpe pan and 10-inch skillet with melted butter; over medium heat, heat both pans.

3 Pour scant ¼ cup batter into crêpe pan; tip to coat bottom; cook 2 minutes till top is set, underside just browned.

4 With metal spatula, lift edge of crêpe all around. Shake pan gently so crêpe will come loose.

5 Invert crêpe into hot skillet; cook other side 30 seconds. Meanwhile, start cooking another crêpe in crêpe pan.

6 Slip cooked crêpe onto waxed paper. Stack crêpes one on top of another to keep warm.

Spinach Crêpes

Color index page 29

Begin 30 mins ahead

6 main-dish servings

2 10-ounce packages frozen chopped spinach	*⅛ teaspoon pepper*
¼ cup butter	*2 cups half-and-half*
¼ cup all-purpose flour	*1 cup shredded Swiss cheese*
1 teaspoon salt	*Crêpes (left)*

1. In 2-quart saucepan, cook the spinach as labels direct, drain thoroughly.
2. Meanwhile, in 3-quart saucepan over low heat, melt butter; stir in flour, salt and pepper until blended. Over medium heat, gradually stir in half-and-half; cook, stirring constantly, until thickened.
3. Add cooked spinach and cheese; cook, stirring, until cheese melts. Spoon about ¼ cup spinach and cheese mixture into center of each crêpe and roll up.

Shrimp Curry Crêpes

Color index page 29

Begin 1 hr ahead

6 main-dish servings

water	*4 teaspoons curry powder*
2 12-ounce packages frozen, shelled and deveined shrimp	*¼ cup all-purpose flour*
	1 chicken-flavor bouillon cube
¼ cup butter	*¼ teaspoon thyme leaves*
½ cup chopped onion	*½ cup heavy cream*
½ cup diced celery	*½ teaspoon salt*
1½ cups peeled, cored and diced cooking apples	*Crêpes (left)*

1. In 4-quart saucepan over high heat, heat 2 inches water to boiling. Add shrimp and reheat to boiling. Reduce heat to low; cook 1 minute until shrimp are tender and pink; drain; cool; cut into ½-inch pieces.
2. Meanwhile, in 3-quart saucepan over medium heat, melt butter. Add onion and celery; cook until tender, stirring, about 10 minutes. Add apple and curry powder; cook 5 minutes. Over low heat, stir in flour until blended. Gradually stir in 1 cup water, bouillon and thyme. Cook, stirring, until thickened.
3. In covered blender container at high speed, blend mixture until smooth. Return to saucepan; stir in shrimp, cream and salt; heat through. Spoon about ¼ cup mixture onto each crêpe and roll up.

FILLING A CREPE

Spoon about ¼ cup of filling mixture across the center of each crêpe.

Fold one edge of the crêpe over the filling and roll up carefully. Arrange the finished crêpes, seam side down, on a warmed serving dish and keep hot in the oven while filling remainder.

Soufflés

A soufflé consists of a thick sauce of flour, butter, milk and egg yolks, folded into stiffly beaten egg whites. Always cook the flour and butter first before adding any liquid so that a smooth sauce is formed; then boil for a minute to get rid of the raw taste of uncooked flour.

Let the egg whites warm to room temperature in a covered bowl so they will beat to a greater volume. Fold the sauce gently into the egg whites, taking care not to stir the whites or they will lose their volume. Pour the mixture into a soufflé dish (prepared by greasing the base only, or the mixture will not rise as high as it could).

Bake soufflés on a rack positioned slightly below the center of the oven so that the mixture itself is centered; remove any other racks above it – your soufflé may rise higher than you expect. When done, a soufflé should be golden brown and puffy. It should be served as soon as it is ready, but in an emergency it can be left in an oven which has been turned off, for about 10 minutes only.

TESTING A SOUFFLE
To test the soufflé for doneness after the baking time specified in recipe, gently insert a table knife into the center of the soufflé; if it comes out clean the soufflé is done. Do not open the oven door before the end of the baking time; cold air could cause the soufflé to fall.

SOUFFLE DISHES
Traditional soufflé dishes are round, of medium depth with straight sides and are usually made of porcelain, earthenware or glass, but soufflés can also be baked in straight-sided ovensafe casseroles. If your soufflé is to look tall and impressive, there should always be enough uncooked egg mixture to fill the dish about three-quarters full so that it puffs up well above the rim as it rises during cooking time.

SOUFFLE DISHES

SERVING THE SOUFFLE
Using a large serving spoon reach down to the base of the dish. Each portion should include a piece of the crisp crust and some of the lighter center. Take a large spoonful at a time so that you do not damage the texture of the rest of the soufflé in the dish.

Classic Cheese Soufflé

¹⁄₄ cup butter or margarine
¹⁄₄ cup all-purpose flour
1 teaspoon salt
¹⁄₈ teaspoon cayenne pepper
1¹⁄₂ cups milk
2 4-ounce packages shredded Cheddar cheese (2 cups)
6 eggs, separated

Color index page 29

Begin 1¼ hrs ahead

6 servings

1 In 2-quart saucepan over medium heat, melt butter or margarine; stir in flour, salt and cayenne pepper until smooth.

2 Slowly stir in milk and cook, stirring constantly just until sauce is smooth and thickened.

3 Add cheese and heat, stirring, just until the cheese melts. Remove pan from the heat. Preheat oven to 325°F.

4 In small bowl with fork, beat egg yolks slightly. Beat in small amount of the hot sauce to prevent lumping when added to saucepan.

5 Slowly pour warm egg mixture into hot sauce in pan, stirring rapidly to prevent eggs lumping.

6 In large bowl with mixer at high speed, beat egg whites just until stiff peaks form. Lightly grease bottom only of a 2-quart soufflé dish.

7 With rubber spatula, gently fold cheese sauce into beaten egg whites.

8 Pour mixture gently into prepared dish. For "top hat" effect, with spoon, make a 1-inch deep circle in top of cheese mixture, 1 inch from side.

9 Bake soufflé in center of oven for 1 hour or until puffy and golden brown. Serve immediately.

Chicken Soufflé

Color index
page 29

Begin 1½ hrs
ahead

6 servings

¼ cup butter
½ cup chopped
  mushrooms
3 tablespoons chopped
  onion
2 tablespoons all-
  purpose flour

1 cup milk
1 chicken-flavor bouillon
  cube
5 eggs, separated
2 cups finely chopped,
  cooked chicken
½ teaspoon salt

1. Grease bottom of 2-quart soufflé dish. In 2-quart saucepan over medium heat, in hot butter, cook mushrooms and onion until tender. Stir in flour until smooth. Reduce heat to low; add milk and bouillon cube; cook, stirring, until thickened.
2. In small bowl with fork, beat egg yolks slightly; beat in small amount of hot sauce; slowly stir egg mixture back into sauce. Cook over low heat, stirring, until thickened. Remove from heat; stir in chicken. Preheat oven to 325°F.
3. In large bowl, with mixer at high speed, beat egg whites and salt until stiff peaks form. Gently fold chicken mixture into egg whites. Pour into soufflé dish. Bake 1 hour or until puffy and golden brown.

Cheese-and-Bacon Soufflé

Color index
page 29

Begin 1¼ hrs
ahead

2 servings

3 tablespoons butter
2 tablespoons all-
  purpose flour
½ teaspoon salt
1 cup evaporated milk

1 cup shredded Cheddar
  cheese
3 eggs, separated
¼ cup crumbled, fried
  bacon pieces

1. Grease bottom of 1½-quart soufflé dish. In 1-quart saucepan over medium heat, into hot butter, stir flour and salt until smooth. Gradually stir in undiluted milk; cook, stirring, until thickened. Stir in cheese until melted.
2. In small bowl, with fork, beat egg yolks slightly. Stir in small amount of cheese sauce; slowly stir egg mixture back into sauce, stirring to prevent lumping. Cook over low heat, stirring. Set aside.
3. Preheat oven to 350°F. In large bowl, with mixer at high speed, beat egg whites until stiff; gently fold in bacon and cheese mixture. Pour into dish; bake 40 to 50 minutes or until golden.

Individual Asparagus Soufflés

Color index
page 24

Begin 1 hr
ahead

6 first-course
servings

¼ cup butter
¼ cup all-purpose flour
1 teaspoon salt
1½ cups milk

½ pound asparagus,
  cooked, drained and
  cut into small chunks
6 eggs, separated

1. In 2-quart saucepan over medium heat, into hot butter, stir flour and salt until blended. Gradually stir in milk and cook, stirring, until sauce is thickened. Add asparagus; remove from heat.
2. In small bowl with fork, beat egg yolks slightly; beat in small amount of hot asparagus sauce; slowly stir egg mixture back into sauce; set aside.
3. Preheat oven to 325°F. In large bowl with mixer at high speed, beat egg whites until stiff; gently fold in asparagus sauce; spoon into 6 greased 10-ounce ramekins placed in a shallow baking pan for easier handling. Bake 30 minutes or until puffy.

Salmon Puff

Color index
page 29

Begin 1¼ hrs
ahead

4 servings

1 16-ounce can salmon
3 tablespoons butter or
  margarine
3 tablespoons all-purpose
  flour
1 teaspoon salt
½ teaspoon dry mustard

½ teaspoon
  Worcestershire
1 cup milk
4 eggs, separated

1. Grease bottom of 1½-quart soufflé dish. In medium bowl, flake undrained salmon. In 2-quart saucepan over medium heat, into hot butter or margarine, stir flour, salt, mustard and Worcestershire. Gradually stir in milk and cook, stirring constantly until mixture is thickened; cool about 10 minutes.
2. In small bowl, with fork, beat egg yolks slightly. Into yolks, stir small amount of hot sauce; stirring rapidly to prevent lumping, slowly pour egg mixture back into sauce. Cook, stirring, until mixture is thickened. Stir in salmon. Preheat oven to 375°F.
3. In large bowl with mixer at high speed, beat egg whites until stiff peaks form. With rubber spatula, gently fold salmon mixture into beaten whites. Pour into dish and bake 40 to 45 minutes or until puffy and golden. Serve at once.

Spinach Soufflé

Color index
page 29

Begin 1½ hrs
ahead

6 servings

⅓ cup chopped onion
2 10-ounce packages
  frozen chopped spinach
  or 2 10-ounce bags
  fresh spinach
¼ cup butter or
  margarine

¼ cup all-purpose flour
salt
⅛ teaspoon cayenne
  pepper
1½ cups milk
6 eggs, separated

1. Grease the bottom of a 2-quart soufflé dish.
2. If using frozen spinach, add onion to spinach and cook as labels direct; drain. Or, prepare and cook fresh spinach: Wash spinach well under running cold water; trim off tough ribs and stems. In 5-quart saucepot over medium heat, heat to boiling ¼ inch water and 1 teaspoon salt. Add spinach and onion and return to boiling; cover and cook 3 minutes. Drain spinach mixture well.
3. Puree either frozen or fresh spinach mixture with food mill or blender or rub through a coarse strainer with the back of a spoon.
4. In 2-quart saucepan over medium heat, into hot butter or margarine, stir flour, salt and cayenne until smooth. Slowly stir in milk; cook, stirring, until sauce is smooth and thickened.
5. In small bowl with fork, beat egg yolks slightly. Into egg yolks, beat small amount of the hot sauce; slowly pour egg mixture into sauce, stirring rapidly. Cook over low heat (do not boil), stirring, until thickened. Remove from heat and stir in spinach mixture. Set aside. Preheat oven to 325°F.
6. In large bowl with mixer at high speed, beat egg whites until stiff peaks form. With rubber spatula, gently fold spinach mixture into egg whites; pour into soufflé dish. Bake 1 hour or until soufflé is puffy and golden brown.

CHEESE

Cheese is among the most versatile of foods – it may be served as a snack, main dish or as a separate course, in sandwiches, salads and dips, as well as in the preparation of all kinds of dishes, from soups and sauces to desserts. Cheese is a concentrated food, containing most of the nutrients of milk, and protein of the same high quality as that in meat, fish and eggs.

CHOOSING CHEESE

Your choice of cheese will depend on how you plan to use it: whether it is to be eaten as is, in sandwiches, or as part of a cheese board, or in cooked dishes. Almost any cheese is suitable for eating with bread or on crackers. There are so many varieties to choose from that the only way you will get to know them is to experiment and taste as many kinds as possible.

Cheese falls into two main types: natural cheese and pasteurized process cheese products. Natural cheese is made directly from milk. Some is ripened (aged) to develop a characteristic flavor and texture and may be labeled to indicate the degree of ripening with terms such as "mild" and "sharp", while some natural cheese is unripened. Different methods of making natural cheese account for the varying characteristics. Cheeses produced by the same method are grouped as a "family", and although textures and sharpness vary, the flavors within a "family" are basically similar. There are nine such basic cheese "families": Cheddar, Dutch, Provolone, Swiss, Blue, Parmesan, Fresh, Surface-ripened and Whey.

Natural cheeses may also be classified by texture or consistency: hard-grating, such as Parmesan; hard, such as Cheddar and Swiss; semisoft, such as Brick and Bel Paese; soft, such as Brie and Limburger, and soft, unripened, such as cottage and ricotta.

Pasteurized process cheese is made by grinding and blending one or more natural cheeses of varying strengths, then heating or "pasteurizing" with an emulsifier to stop further ripening and produce cheese of uniform, consistent flavor and texture. When milk solids are added, the cheese becomes pasteurized process cheese food and is softer and easier to spread. Pasteurized process cheese spreads are similar, but ingredients are added to make them still more moist, soft and spreadable, ideal for on sandwiches.

SERVING CHEESE

Cheese should always be removed from the refrigerator and left unwrapped for at least 30 minutes, preferably an hour, before serving, to allow it to come to room temperature and develop its full flavor. The only exceptions are fresh cheeses such as cottage, cream and Neufchâtel, which should be eaten chilled, straight from the refrigerator. Some cheeses, such as Camembert, are at their best when they are almost runny; let them soften at room temperature for an hour or two before serving.

Cheese is appropriate served at any time of day, from breakfast to supper, as a between-meal snack, or as the *pièce de résistance* of a cheese and wine party or a fondue supper. In many countries a cheese course is also often served at formal dinners.

Wine is the perfect accompaniment to cheese, and if you are serving it after a meal, accompany it with the wine you had with the main course or with a dessert wine. Cider, beer, coffee, tea, even a glass of milk, may also be drunk with cheese, and if cheese and bread are the main course of an informal supper, you may like to accompany it with a bowl of thick, hot soup.

CUTTING CHEESE

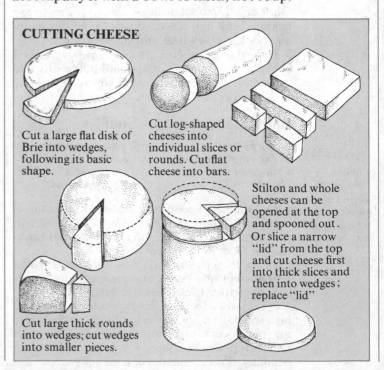

Cut a large flat disk of Brie into wedges, following its basic shape.

Cut log-shaped cheeses into individual slices or rounds. Cut flat cheese into bars.

Cut large thick rounds into wedges; cut wedges into smaller pieces.

Stilton and whole cheeses can be opened at the top and spooned out. Or slice a narrow "lid" from the top and cut cheese first into thick slices and then into wedges; replace "lid"

STORING CHEESE

The harder the cheese, the longer it will keep without deteriorating. Natural cheeses should be stored in the refrigerator, tightly wrapped to prevent them drying out. Leave the original wrapping intact, or if this is not suitable, rewrap the cheese closely in waxed paper or foil to keep air out. After cutting off a piece, rewrap the cut surface carefully. Unopened hard and wax-coated cheeses such as Cheddar, Edam and Swiss, may be stored in the refrigerator for 3 to 6 months. Once they have been opened, they will keep for 3 to 4 weeks, only 2 weeks if bought ready-sliced. Soft cheeses have a much shorter storage life: cream cheese and Neufchâtel, 2 weeks, cottage and ricotta, no more than 5 days. Soft ripe cheeses, such as Brie or Camembert which are in their prime, should be used immediately.

Even when correctly stored, the surface of a hard cheese may turn moldy. Should this happen, simply cut off the affected piece or scrape the surface clean. Mold is harmless and neither the cheese's quality nor its flavor will be affected.

Grated Parmesan, Romano and American cheese food may be stored at room temperature unless otherwise directed on the label, and most pasteurized process cheese products need not be refrigerated until they have been opened. Once they have been opened, however, they must be stored in the refrigerator. Follow instructions on the label or seal tightly in plastic wrap or bags, in foil, or in covered containers. Some products in glass jars will keep indefinitely at room temperature. Opened jars should also be tightly covered and stored in the refrigerator. The only exceptions are cheese products in squeeze packs and aerosol cans, which must never be refrigerated.

Leftover cheese which is too dry and hard to eat should be grated and placed in the refrigerator in a screwtop jar. It will come in useful for cooking and garnishing, and can be kept for 2 to 3 weeks.

FREEZING CHEESE

Most cheeses can be frozen provided they are sealed in foil or other moistureproof wrapping to prevent them drying out. A small cheese such as Camembert may be frozen in its original package. Some hard and semihard cheeses can be stored safely for up to 3 months, if frozen in small (½ - pound) packages or cut into 1-inch-thick slices before freezer-wrapping. Cheese which has been cut into small cubes should be used within 3 weeks and uncreamed (dry) cottage cheese should only be kept in the freezer for 1 or 2 weeks. Freezing is not recommended for creamed cottage cheese.

COOKING WITH CHEESE

When cooking with cheese, the important thing to remember is that excessive heat and prolonged cooking turns it stringy and leathery. High heat may also cause a mixture of cheese, eggs and milk to curdle. When making a sauce, stir in the cheese toward the end of cooking time and continue cooking and stirring over low heat just long enough to melt the cheese and blend it smoothly with other ingredients. A cheese topping should be broiled several inches away from the source of heat, and for baked dishes, the oven temperature should be kept down to low or moderate (325° to 350°F.). Similarly, when topping a baked casserole with cheese, add the topping during the last few minutes of baking time and remove the casserole from the oven just as soon as the cheese has melted and is bubbling and golden on top.

Cheese melts quickly and evenly and blends readily with other ingredients if it is first shredded or grated. You will find it easier to grate when it is chilled. Pasteurized process cheese products should be diced before use and soft unripened cheeses, such as Neufchâtel or cream cheese, are best if first allowed to soften at room temperature.

Allow 4 ounces for every cup of shredded or cubed cheese called for in the recipe, 3 ounces per cup if it is very hard-grating cheese such as Parmesan.

THE CHEESE BOARD

Choose cheese for your cheese board with special care. Try to offer at least three different kinds, varying in flavor from mild to sharp and in texture from soft or creamy to firm. Pick cheeses of different colors and shapes, and serve wedges, bars and chunks of different sizes. A whole cheese – a red cannonball of Edam or a wheel of Camembert – will add a dramatic touch to your cheese board.

Arrange the cheese in groups by flavor – mild, medium and strong. If you are serving a very strong, ripe cheese, it may be advisable to keep it on a separate board to avoid mixing flavors and aromas. Make sure that cheeses are in their prime – Brie and Camembert, for example, should not be served when either over- or under-ripe. Provide sharp, thin knives for cutting firm cheeses into portions and butter knives for soft cheeses such as Port du Salut or cream cheese.

Fruit makes a pleasant accompaniment to the cheese board. Arrange a variety of ripe fresh fruit – pears, apples, grapes – in a bowl or basket. Arrange a basketful of crusty French or Italian bread cut into slices or chunks, and some thin, crisp, unsalted crackers. These enhance cheese flavors without competing with them and, in addition, provide interesting texture contrast. For informal serving after dinner or for snacks, crisp Norwegian flat-bread, melba toast, sesame-seed crackers, graham crackers and other breads are nice choices with cheese. Thin-sliced dark rye or pumpernickel bread also goes well with full-flavored cheeses such as a sharp Cheddar or a Camembert.

American cheeses

CHEESE	CHARACTERISTICS	USE
Blue	A semisoft, ripened blue cheese, piquant in flavor. Look for cylinders and cut portions of slightly crumbly white cheese with blue-green markings.	Use in appetizers, dips, salads, salad dressings, sandwiches and snacks.
Brick	A semisoft, ripened cheese, mild to moderately sharp in flavor. Look for loaves, bricks and slices of creamy, yellow cheese with small holes.	Use in appetizers, sandwiches and snacks.
Cheddar	A hard, ripened cheese, mild to very sharp in flavor, depending on age. Look for wheels, cylindrical loaves, wedges, slices and cubes of smooth, white to yellow-orange cheese. **Coon, Longhorn, Colby** and **Tillamook** are all forms of Cheddar.	Use in appetizers, sandwiches and snacks and grated in cooking.
Cottage Cheese	A soft, unripened cheese, lumpy in appearance, mildly acidic in flavor. Look for cartons of small- or large-curd cheese, creamed or uncreamed. Also available with added flavorings. Eat fresh.	Use in salads, sandwiches and snacks, cheesecakes and in cooking.
Cream Cheese	A soft, unripened cheese, rich, full but mildly acidic in flavor. Sold foil-wrapped. Eat fresh.	Use in appetizers, sandwiches, cheesecakes and frostings.
Liederkranz	A soft, ripened cheese, robust in flavor. Look for small, foil-wrapped loaves of smooth, creamy yellow cheese with a russet surface.	Use in appetizers, salads, snacks, with fruit.
Monterey (Jack)	A semisoft, ripened cheese, mild in flavor. Look for wheels and slices of creamy white, open-textured cheese.	Use in sandwiches, snacks and in cooking.
Neufchâtel	A soft, unripened cheese, mild, slightly acid, resembling cream cheese in flavor. Look for foil-wrapped bars.	Use in dips, spreads, salads, sandwiches, snacks and cheesecakes.
Swiss	A firm, ripened cheese, sweet and nutlike in flavor. Look for segments, pieces and slices of light yellow cheese with large round holes.	Use in salads, sandwiches and in cooking.

European cheeses

CHEESE	CHARACTERISTICS	USE
Bel Paese	A semisoft, ripened Italian cheese, usually mild in flavor. Look for creamy white segments and small wheels with a grayish or brownish crust.	Use in appetizers, snacks, sandwiches and as dessert.
Brie	A soft, ripened French cheese, mild to pungent in flavor. Look for thin medium wheels and wedges with a creamy interior and chalky (edible) crust.	Use in appetizers, snacks and as dessert.
Caerphilly	A semihard ripened English cheese mild in flavor. Look for wheels, wedges and oblongs of smooth white cheese.	Use in salads, sandwiches and snacks.
Camembert	A soft, ripened French cheese, mild to pungent in flavor. Look for small wheels or wedges with creamy interior and thin chalky (edible) crust.	Use in appetizers, snacks and as dessert.
Cheshire	A hard, ripened cheese, mild yet mellow in flavor. Look for wheels, wedges and oblongs of crumbly orange cheese.	Use in salads, sandwiches and snacks.
Danish Blue	A semisoft ripened Danish blue cheese, sharp and slightly salty in flavor. Look for prepacked chunks and wedges of slightly crumbly white cheese, marbled with blue mold.	Use in salads, sandwiches and snacks.
Edam	A hard, ripened Dutch cheese, mild and nutlike in flavor. Look for red, wax-coated balls, oblongs and cut pieces with a yellow interior.	Use in appetizers, salads, sandwiches, snacks and as dessert.
Emmenthaler	A firm, ripened Swiss cheese, sweet and nutlike in flavor. Look for wheels and slices with a light yellow interior.	Use in salads, sandwiches, snacks, in cooking and as dessert.
Feta	A semisoft, ripened Greek cheese, salty and sharp in flavor. Look for flaky white cheese packed in brine.	Use in appetizers, salads, snacks and in cooking.
Fontina	A semisoft to hard, ripened Italian cheese, nutty in flavor. Look for wheels and cut pieces of medium-yellow cheese with some small holes.	Use in appetizers, snacks, in cooking and as dessert.

CHEESE	CHARACTERISTICS	USE	CHEESE	CHARACTERISTICS	USE
Gloucester (Double Gloucester)	A hard, ripened cheese, mellow or tangy in flavor. Look for wheels and wedges of close-textured cheese.	Use in salads, snacks and sandwiches.	Petit Suisse	A soft, unripened French cream cheese, mild in flavor. Look for small cylinders.	Use in sandwiches, with fruit and in desserts.
Gorgonzola	A semisoft, ripened, blue-veined Italian cheese, piquant in flavor. Look for wheels and wedges with a clay-colored outer crust and a white interior marbled with blue-green mold.	Use in salads, sandwiches and snacks.	Port du Salut	A semisoft, ripened French cheese, mellow to robust in flavor. Look for wheels and wedges with a yellow interior and orange rind.	Use in appetizers, snacks, with fruit and as dessert.
Gouda	A hard, ripened Dutch cheese, mild to mellow in flavor. Look for flattened balls with yellow-orange interior, yellow or red wax coating.	Use in appetizers, salads, sandwiches, snacks and as dessert.	Provolone	A hard, ripened Italian cheese, mild to sharp and smoky in flavor. Look for pear, ball or sausage shapes and slices.	Use in appetizers, salads, sandwiches, snacks, for grating and as dessert.
Gjetöst	A firm, unripened Norwegian whey cheese, sweet in flavor. Look for golden-brown cubes and rectangles.	Use in appetizers, snacks and as dessert.	Raclette	A semifirm, ripened Swiss cheese, varying according to whether served hot or cold. Look for wheels and cut pieces with a cream interior with tiny holes and a thin brownish rind.	Use in snacks and in cooking.
Gruyère	A hard, ripened Swiss cheese, sweetish and nutty in flavor. Look for light yellow wheels and wedges.	Use in salads, sandwiches, snacks, in cooking and as dessert.	Ricotta	A soft, unripened Italian whey cheese, sweetish in flavor. Look for cartons and cans.	Use in appetizers, salads, snacks, in cooking and desserts.
Jarlsberg	A firm, ripened Norwegian cheese, resembling *Emmenthaler* in flavor. Look for wheels, segments and slices with a light yellow interior and large holes.	Use in salads, sandwiches, snacks, in cooking and as dessert.	Romano	A very hard, ripened Italian cheese, sharp and piquant, resembling *Parmesan*.	Use in cooking or sprinkle on pasta or salads.
Limburger	A soft, ripened German cheese, strong in flavor and aroma. Look for rectangles with an orange-yellow rind and a creamy white interior.	Use in appetizers, sandwiches, snacks and as dessert.	Roquefort	A semisoft, ripened French blue cheese, sharp in flavor. Look for cylinders and wedges with a white interior marbled with mold.	Use in appetizers, dips, sandwiches, snacks and as dessert.
Mozzarella	A firm, unripened Italian cheese, mild in flavor. Look for cut pieces; also available shredded.	Use in appetizers, salads, sandwiches and in cooking (especially in pizzas).	Samsoe	A firm, ripened Danish cheese, with a nutty flavor. Look for yellow wheels and wedges with small holes.	Use in appetizers, sandwiches, snacks and as dessert.
Muenster (Münster)	A semisoft, ripened French cheese, mild to mellow. Look for small wheels, segments and slices with a yellow-tan surface and white interior with many holes.	Use in appetizers, sandwiches and snacks.	Sapsago	A hard, ripened clover-flavored light green Swiss cheese, pungent in flavor. Look for small cones; also sold grated.	Use in cooking or sprinkle on pasta or salads.
Parmesan	A very hard, ripened Italian cheese, sharp to piquant in flavor. Look for creamy white or yellow wedges or cylinders; also sold grated.	Use in cooking or sprinkle on pasta and salads.	Stilton	A semisoft, ripened blue cheese, piquant but not harsh in flavor. Look for slightly crumbly, blue-veined wedges, oblongs and wheels.	Use in appetizers, salads, snacks and as dessert.
			Wensleydale	A semihard cheese, mild and creamy in flavor. Look for small cylinders, wedges and oblongs of off-white to creamy-yellow flaky cheese.	Use in salads, sandwiches and snacks.

Simple main dishes

Welsh Rabbit with Beer

Color index page 30

Begin 20 mins ahead

4 servings

4 white or rye bread slices
1 pound American cheese
¾ cup beer
1 teaspoon dry mustard
½ teaspoon Worcestershire
¼ teaspoon salt

1 Toast bread slices in electric toaster or under broiler and keep warm until required.

2 With shredder or knife, coarsely shred or cut the cheese into slivers.

3 In 2-quart saucepan over low heat, or chafing dish over boiling water, mix cheese with beer.

4 Add mustard, Worcestershire and salt; cook, stirring until the mixture is smooth.

5 Pour the hot cheese mixture over the warm toast and serve at once.

Welsh Rabbit

Color index page 30

Begin 20 mins ahead

6 servings

¼ cup butter or margarine
½ cup all-purpose flour
½ teaspoon salt
⅛ teaspoon dry mustard
⅛ teaspoon cayenne pepper

2 cups milk
1 teaspoon Worcestershire
2 cups shredded sharp Cheddar cheese
toasted white or rye bread slices

1. In 2-quart saucepan over low heat, melt butter or margarine. Stir in flour, salt, mustard and cayenne until blended. Add milk and Worcestershire; cook, stirring, until thickened.
2. Add cheese and cook, stirring, just until cheese is melted and well blended. Pour hot cheese mixture over the warm toast and serve immediately.

Italian Cheese Toast

Color index page 30

Begin 25 mins ahead

4 servings

1¼ cups half-and-half
½ 2-ounce can anchovy fillets, drained and chopped
1 tablespoon olive or salad oil
1 teaspoon cornstarch
½ teaspoon paprika

1 tablespoon capers
1 12-inch loaf Italian bread
1 8-ounce package mozzarella cheese, thinly sliced
1 tablespoon chopped parsley

1. In 2-quart saucepan, combine first 5 ingredients. Over medium heat, cook mixture, stirring constantly, until boiling; boil 1 minute. Reduce heat to low; stir in capers; cover; keep warm.
2. Meanwhile, preheat broiler if manufacturer directs. From Italian bread, diagonally cut eight 1-inch-thick slices (serve remaining bread another day, if you like).
3. In each of four 16-ounce broiler-safe cook-and-serve casseroles, place 2 slices bread in one layer. (For easier handling, place casseroles in 15½″ by 10½″ jelly-roll pan.) Toast bread 1 to 2 minutes on each side until golden.
4. Remove jelly-roll pan from broiler. Arrange cheese slices, overlapping slightly, on top of bread; broil until cheese is just melted.
5. Spoon cream mixture evenly over cheese. Garnish with parsley. Serve immediately.

Raclette

Color index page 30

Begin 20 mins ahead

4 servings

1 pound Raclette cheese
freshly ground pepper or paprika

hot cooked potatoes, dill pickles, cocktail onions (optional)

1. Preheat oven to 375°F. With sharp knife, cut rind from cheese; cut cheese into thin slices. In shallow baking dish, place one-half of cheese slices, overlapping them slightly.
2. Bake in oven until cheese is just melted and smooth, about 4 to 6 minutes; remove from oven. Place hot dish on serving plate or wooden serving board (to make serving easy while at the same time keeping the cheese hot).
3. Sprinkle cheese with pepper or paprika. Let each person help himself to a serving of Raclette; eat as is or over hot boiled potatoes; accompany with dill pickles and cocktail onions, if you like. Repeat the process with the rest of the cheese.

Swiss-Cheese-and-Tomato Bake

Color index page 30

Begin 1¼ hrs ahead

4 servings

4 cups croutons
2 medium tomatoes, thinly sliced
½ pound natural Swiss cheese, shredded (2 cups)

2 eggs
1½ cups milk
¾ teaspoon salt
½ teaspoon paprika
½ teaspoon dry mustard

1. Preheat oven to 350°F. Arrange croutons in 9-inch pie plate. Top croutons with tomato slices; sprinkle with shredded Swiss cheese.
2. In small bowl with fork or wire whisk, beat remaining ingredients; pour over cheese.
3. Bake 40 minutes or until puffy and browned. Serve immediately.

Fondues

Classic Swiss Fondue

Color index page 30

Begin 25 mins ahead

4 servings

1 garlic clove, halved
1½ cups dry white wine
1 tablespoon kirsch,
brandy or lemon juice
1 pound natural Swiss
cheese
3 tablespoons all-purpose
flour
⅛ teaspoon pepper
⅛ teaspoon ground nutmeg
French bread

1 Rub inside of fondue pot or saucepan with halved garlic clove; discard garlic.

2 Pour wine into fondue pot; over low heat, heat until hot but not boiling. Stir in kirsch, brandy or lemon juice.

3 Meanwhile, shred cheese and toss in medium bowl with flour until well mixed.

4 Add cheese to wine by handfuls, stirring constantly with wooden spoon until cheese is melted. Stir in pepper and ground nutmeg.

5 Cut bread into chunks for dipping, keeping fondue hot on table-top burner or fondue stand.

6 Let each person spear one chunk of bread at a time on a long-handled fondue fork and dip into the fondue.

Cheddar-Cheese Fondue

Color index page 30

Begin 30 mins ahead

6 servings

2 cups half-and-half
1 tablespoon Worcestershire
2 teaspoons dry mustard
1 garlic clove, halved
1½ pounds mild or sharp Cheddar cheese, shredded (about 6 cups)
3 tablespoons all-purpose flour
salt
chunks of crusty French bread or cooked, shelled and deveined shrimp or cooked ham chunks

1. In fondue pot or saucepan (aluminum saucepan may turn mixture dark but it will not alter taste) over low heat, heat half-and-half, Worcestershire, mustard and garlic, stirring, until hot but not boiling. Discard garlic.
2. Meanwhile, in medium bowl, toss Cheddar cheese with flour until well mixed.
3. Into hot mixture with fork or wire whisk, gradually stir cheese. Cook over low heat, stirring constantly, until cheese is melted and mixture is smooth and bubbling. Add salt to taste. (If made in saucepan, pour into fondue pot for serving. Keep hot over low heat on fondue stand.)
4. Let each person spear chunks of French bread, shrimp or cooked ham chunks on long-handled fondue fork and dip in fondue.

Baked Cheese Fondue

Color index page 30

Begin 2 hrs ahead

4 servings

4 white bread slices
butter or margarine, softened
1 cup shredded or slivered American cheese
4 eggs
2 cups milk
1 teaspoon salt
½ teaspoon dry mustard

1. Spread bread lightly with butter or margarine; cut into 1-inch squares.
2. In greased 1½-quart casserole, arrange half of squares; top with half of cheese; repeat.
3. In medium bowl with wire whisk or hand beater, beat eggs with rest of ingredients; pour over cheese.
4. Set casserole in shallow baking pan on oven rack; fill pan with enough hot water to come halfway up side of casserole.
5. Bake in 350°F. oven 1 hour and 25 minutes or until puffed and golden. Serve at once.

Layering ingredients: In greased casserole, alternate layers of white bread and shredded or slivered cheese.

Baking the fondue: Set casserole in pan on rack; add hot water to pan to come halfway up casserole. Bake in 350°F. oven.

155

Quiches, pies and patties

Quiche Lorraine

*pastry for 1 piecrust
(page 344)*
*1 tablespoon butter,
softened*
12 bacon slices
4 eggs
*2 cups heavy or whipping
cream*
¾ teaspoon salt
*⅛ teaspoon ground
nutmeg*
*¼ pound natural Swiss
cheese, shredded
(1 cup)*

Color index
page 31

Begin 1½ hrs
ahead

6 servings

1 Prepare and roll out pastry; line one 9-inch pie plate. Spread crust evenly with softened butter; chill well.

2 In 10-inch skillet over medium heat, fry bacon slices until crisp and brown.

3 Drain bacon on paper towels and crumble. Preheat oven to 425°F.

4 Spread crumbled bacon pieces in prepared piecrust.

5 With wire whisk, beat eggs, cream, salt and nutmeg. Stir in cheese.

6 Pour egg mixture into crust. Bake 15 minutes; turn oven control to 325°F.; bake 35 minutes.

7 Quiche is cooked when knife inserted in center comes out clean. Let stand 10 minutes before serving.

SWISS CHEESE QUICHE: Prepare piecrust as above. Omit bacon. Prepare cheese mixture as above, omitting nutmeg; pour into piecrust. Bake as for Quiche Lorraine, above.

CRAB QUICHE: Prepare piecrust and cream mixture as for Quiche Lorraine; set both aside. In 1-quart saucepan over medium heat, melt *3 tablespoons butter* or margarine; add *2 tablespoons minced green onions;* cook until tender, about 5 minutes. Into cream mixture, stir green onion mixture, *two 6-ounce packages frozen snow crab,* thawed and well drained, *2 tablespoons dry vermouth, ¼ teaspoon salt* and *⅛ teaspoon cayenne pepper.* Pour into piecrust and bake as for Quiche Lorraine, left.

MUSHROOM QUICHE: Prepare piecrust and cream mixture as for Swiss Cheese Quiche; set both aside. In 10-inch skillet over medium-high heat, melt *¼ cup butter* or margarine; add *½ pound mushrooms,* very thinly sliced, *2 tablespoons minced green onions, ¼ teaspoon salt* and *⅛ teaspoon pepper;* cook until vegetables are tender, about 5 minutes, stirring often. Into cream mixture stir mushroom mixture. Pour into piecrust and bake as for Quiche Lorraine, left. *To reheat if made ahead:* Cover quiche with foil. Bake in 325°F. oven 40 minutes or until heated through.

Cheese-Spinach-Sausage Pie

*1 pound sweet Italian
  sausage links, chopped*
6 eggs
*2 10-ounce packages
  frozen chopped
  spinach, thawed and
  well drained*
*1 16-ounce package
  mozzarella cheese,
  shredded*

⅔ cup ricotta cheese
½ teaspoon salt
⅛ teaspoon pepper
*⅛ teaspoon garlic
  powder*
*pastry for 2-crust 9-inch
  pie (page 344)*
1 tablespoon water

Color index
page 31

Begin 2 hrs
ahead

10 servings

1. In 10-inch skillet over medium heat, cook sausages until well browned, about 10 minutes, stirring frequently. Spoon off fat from sausages.
2. Reserve 1 egg yolk. In large bowl, combine remaining eggs with sausage and next 6 ingredients.
3. Prepare pastry; divide into 2 pieces, one slightly larger than the other; shape each piece into a ball. On lightly floured surface with lightly floured rolling pin, roll larger ball into a circle, ⅛ inch thick and 2 inches larger all around than 9-inch pie plate; line pie plate with pastry. Spoon mixture onto pastry.
4. On lightly floured surface with lightly floured rolling pin, roll remaining ball into 10-inch circle. With knife, cut out small circle in center of pastry. Place pastry over filling. With kitchen shears, trim pastry, leaving ½-inch overhang; fold overhang under and press gently all around rim to make stand-up edge. With knife, cut slits in pastry top.
5. In small bowl, combine reserved egg yolk with water; brush top of pie. Reroll pastry scraps; with knife, cut to make decorative design and place on top of pie; brush design with egg-yolk mixture.
6. Bake in 375°F. oven for 1¼ hours or until pie is golden. Let stand 10 minutes; then cut into wedges.
To serve cold: Early in day or day ahead, prepare recipe as above; refrigerate pie, uncovered, until well chilled. Cover with plastic wrap or foil and refrigerate; pie should be used within 2 days.

Color index
page 31

Begin 1¼ hrs
ahead

6 servings

Switzerland Cheese-and-Onion Pie

*pastry for one 9-inch
    piecrust, well chilled
    (page 344)*
butter or margarine
*1 large onion, chopped
    (about 1 cup)*
*1 tablespoon all-purpose
    flour*

*½ pound natural Swiss
    cheese, shredded
    (2 cups)*
3 eggs
1 cup half-and-half
1 teaspoon salt

1. Prepare and roll out pastry; line one 9-inch pie plate. Spread piecrust with 1 tablespoon butter or margarine; chill well.
2. In small skillet over medium heat, in 2 tablespoons melted butter or margarine, cook chopped onion until tender, about 5 minutes, stirring occasionally; spread evenly in piecrust. Meanwhile, preheat oven to 400°F.
3. In medium bowl, toss well flour with cheese; sprinkle over onion in piecrust.
4. In same bowl with wire whisk or hand beater, beat eggs with half-and-half and salt; pour over shredded Swiss cheese.
5. Bake 10 minutes. Turn oven control to 325°F. and bake 30 to 35 minutes longer until knife inserted in center comes out clean. Let pie stand 10 minutes, then cut into wedges.

Color index
page 31

Begin early
in day

10 servings

Italian Cheese-and-Ham Pie

*1 16-ounce container
    creamed cottage
    cheese (2 cups)*
*1 15- or 16-ounce
    container ricotta
    cheese (2 cups)*
*2 cups diced cooked ham
    (¾ pound)*
*⅔ cup grated Parmesan
    cheese*

3 eggs
*2 teaspoons Italian
    seasoning*
½ teaspoon salt
¼ teaspoon pepper
*pastry for two 2-crust
    9-inch pies (page 344)*
*1 egg yolk, slightly
    beaten*

1. In medium bowl, mix well creamed cottage cheese and next 7 ingredients; set aside.
2. Prepare pastry as recipe directs. With hands, shape ⅔ of pastry into large ball; shape remaining pastry into another ball.
3. On lightly floured surface with lightly floured rolling pin, roll large ball into 16-inch circle, about ⅛ inch thick. Fold circle into fourths and carefully lift into 10-inch springform pan; unfold. With fingers, lightly press pastry into bottom and sides of pan; trim edges of pastry to make it even with rim of pan. Brush pastry with some beaten egg yolk.
4. Spoon cheese mixture into pastry-lined pan; fold edges of pastry over filling; brush pastry with some beaten egg yolk. Preheat oven to 375°F.
5. Roll remaining pastry ball into a 10-inch circle. With knife, cut design in pastry. Place pastry circle over filling in pan, pressing lightly around edges to seal; brush top with remaining egg yolk.
6. Bake pie 1 hour or until knife inserted in center comes out clean. Cool pie in refrigerator until serving time.
7. To serve: Carefully remove sides of springform pan. With a sharp knife, cut pie into wedges.

Fried Cheese Patties

Color index
page 31

Begin early
in day or
day ahead

6 servings

*⅓ cup butter
    or margarine*
*1 teaspoon prepared
    mustard*
½ teaspoon salt
*¼ teaspoon cracked
    pepper*
all-purpose flour
2 cups milk
*½ pound Swiss,
    Gruyère or Jarlsberg
    cheese, shredded
    (2 cups)*

1 tablespoon grated onion
2 egg yolks
2 eggs
*¾ cup dried bread
    crumbs*
*2½ cups Spaghetti Sauce
    (page 337)*
½ cup salad oil
*parsley sprigs for
    garnish (optional)*

1 In 2-quart saucepan over medium heat, into hot butter or margarine, stir mustard, salt, pepper and ⅔ cup flour until blended. Slowly stir in milk; cook, stirring constantly, until thickened. Stir in cheese and onion until mixture is smooth. In measuring cup with fork, lightly beat together egg yolks.

2 Stir small amount of hot sauce into yolks. Slowly pour egg mixture back into sauce, stirring until thickened. Cover. Refrigerate 6 hours.

3 In pie plate with fork, beat 2 eggs. Sprinkle ⅓ cup flour on sheet of waxed paper and bread crumbs on another.

4 To form patties: Shape mixture into eighteen ½-inch-thick patties. Coat each patty with flour; dip each patty in beaten egg, then roll in bread crumbs. Refrigerate 1 hour.

5 *About 20 minutes before serving:* In 10-inch skillet over medium heat, in hot oil, brown 6 cheese patties about 2 minutes on each side. Meanwhile, heat sauce.

6 Remove patties to paper towels to drain; keep warm in 300°F. oven Repeat to cook all patties. Serve with sauce; garnish with parsley, if you like.

Cheese desserts

Whether it is a simple dish of fresh pears and Roquefort or a glorious cheesecake, a cheese dessert is an elegant finale to any dinner.

Some especially good cheese and fruit combinations are: apple or melon slices with Cheddar or Provolone; strawberries or grapes with cream cheese or Colby; bananas or figs with Stilton or Port du Salut; fresh pineapple chunks or seedless raisins with Brie or Neufchâtel; red or purple plums with Camembert.

Baked or unbaked cheesecakes and cheese pies may be hearty and rich or fluffy and light. Store leftovers, closely wrapped, in the refrigerator and serve within a day or two.

Deluxe Baked Cheesecake

3/4 cup butter or
margarine,
softened
all-purpose flour
sugar
3 egg yolks
grated peel of
2 lemons
5 8-ounce packages
cream cheese
5 eggs

1/4 cup heavy or whipping
cream
1 tablespoon grated
orange peel
1/4 teaspoon salt
1 cup sour cream for
garnish

Color index page 98
Begin day ahead
16 servings

1 In small bowl with mixer at low speed, beat butter, 1 1/4 cups flour, 1/4 cup sugar, 1 egg yolk and half of lemon peel until dough is well mixed.

2 Refrigerate, covered, for 1 hour. Preheat oven to 400°F. Press 1/3 of dough into bottom of 10-inch springform pan. Bake 8 minutes; allow to cool.

3 Turn oven to 475°F. In large bowl with mixer at medium speed, beat cream cheese just until smooth; slowly beat in 1 3/4 cups sugar until smooth.

4 With mixer at low speed, beat in 3 tablespoons flour and remaining ingredients except sour cream. At high speed, beat 5 minutes.

5 Press rest of dough around side of springform pan to within 1 inch of top; do not bake dough.

6 Pour cheese mixture into pan; bake 12 minutes. Turn oven to 300°F.; bake 35 minutes. Turn off oven; leave in oven 30 minutes. Remove; cool in pan on rack. Chill.

7 To serve: Remove side of pan. With large spatula, loosen cake from pan; slide onto serving plate. Spread top of cheesecake with sour cream to garnish.

Color index page 98
Begin early in day or up to 1 wk ahead
16 to 18 servings

Chocolate Cheesecake

3/4 cup butter
all-purpose flour
sugar
3 egg yolks
5 8-ounce packages
cream cheese
5 eggs

1/4 cup milk
1/4 teaspoon salt
1 8-ounce package
semisweet-chocolate
squares, melted
whipped cream for
garnish (optional)

1. In small bowl with mixer at low speed, beat butter, 1 1/4 cups flour, 1/4 cup sugar and 1 egg yolk until dough is well mixed; cover; refrigerate 1 hour.
2. Preheat oven to 400°F. Press 1/3 of dough into bottom of 10-inch springform pan; reserve remaining dough in refrigerator. Bake bottom crust 8 minutes; cool. Turn oven control to 475°F.
3. Meanwhile, in large bowl with mixer at medium speed, beat cream cheese just until smooth. Reduce speed to low; gradually beat in 1 3/4 cups sugar, 3 tablespoons flour and rest of ingredients except cream until blended. At high speed, beat 5 minutes.
4. Press reserved dough around side of pan to within 1 inch of top; do not bake. Pour cheese mixture into pan; bake 12 minutes. Turn oven control to 300°F.; bake 50 minutes. Turn off oven; leave in oven 30 minutes. Cool in pan on rack 30 minutes. Refrigerate, covered; serve within 1 week, garnished with whipped cream, if you like.

Color index page 98
Begin day ahead or up to 3 days ahead
12 servings

Cherry Cheesecake

1 cup graham-cracker
crumbs
1/2 cup finely chopped
California walnuts
1/3 cup butter, melted
sugar
3 8-ounce packages
cream cheese

6 eggs
2 cups sour cream
2 tablespoons cornstarch
1 tablespoon lemon juice
2 teaspoons vanilla
extract
Cherry Topping (below)

1. Preheat oven to 350°F. In medium bowl with fork, mix first 3 ingredients and 1/4 cup sugar. Press mixture firmly on bottom and around side of 9″ by 3″ springform pan to within 1 1/2 inches of top.
2. In large bowl with mixer at medium speed, beat cream cheese until smooth; slowly beat in 1 1/2 cups sugar. With mixer at low speed, beat in eggs and remaining ingredients except Cherry Topping. At medium speed, beat 3 minutes.
3. Pour mixture into pan; bake 1 hour or until lightly browned. Turn off oven; leave in oven 30 minutes. Remove; cool in pan on rack. Cover; chill.
4. To serve: Remove side of pan. With large spatula, loosen cake from pan bottom; slide onto plate. Spoon Cherry Topping evenly over cheesecake.

CHERRY TOPPING: In bowl with spoon, mix *one 21-ounce can cherry-pie filling* with *1 tablespoon grated lemon peel* and *1/2 teaspoon lemon juice.*

No-bake Cheesecake

2 eggs, separated
1 cup milk
2 envelopes unflavored
    gelatin
1 cup sugar
1/4 teaspoon salt
1 teaspoon grated lemon
    peel
3 cups creamed cottage
    cheese
1 tablespoon lemon
    juice
1 teaspoon vanilla
    extract

mixture for Unbaked
    Crumb Crust
    (page 345)
1 cup heavy or whipping
    cream
chopped nuts or canned
    fruit for garnish

Color index page 98
Begin early in day
or day ahead
10 to 12 servings

1 In small bowl, beat egg yolks with milk until mixed; in 2-quart saucepan, stir gelatin with sugar and salt.

2 Stir yolk mixture into gelatin mixture. Cook over medium heat, stirring, until mixture thickens and coats spoon.

3 Remove from heat; add lemon peel; cool. Into large bowl, press cottage cheese through sieve; add lemon juice and vanilla.

4 Add gelatin mixture. Chill about 30 minutes, stirring, until mixture mounds when dropped from spoon.

5 Meanwhile, press half of crust mixture in bottom of 9-inch springform pan.

6 In small bowl with mixer at high speed, beat egg whites just until stiff peaks form; spoon onto gelatin mixture.

7 Beat cream until soft peaks form; spoon onto egg whites; fold egg whites and cream into gelatin mixture.

8 Pour gelatin mixture into prepared spring-form pan.

9 Sprinkle top with remaining crumb mixture and refrigerate until firm.

10 To serve: Remove side of pan and with spatula, loosen cake from bottom. Slide onto plate. Garnish with fruit or nuts

---

Color index page 98
Begin 6 hrs ahead or early in day
8 servings

Cream-Cheese Rhubarb Pie

4 cups rhubarb, cut in
    1-inch pieces
3 tablespoons cornstarch
1/4 teaspoon salt
sugar
1 9-inch unbaked
    piecrust (page 344)

1 8-ounce package cream
    cheese
2 eggs
1 cup sour cream
almonds for garnish

1. In 2-quart saucepan over medium heat, cook rhubarb, cornstarch, salt and 1 cup sugar, stirring often, until mixture boils and thickens. Meanwhile preheat oven to 425°F.
2. Pour rhubarb mixture into piecrust. Bake 10 minutes; remove from oven.
3. Meanwhile, in small bowl with mixer at medium speed, beat cream cheese, eggs and 1/2 cup sugar until smooth; pour over rhubarb mixture.
4. Turn oven control to 350°F. Bake pie 30 to 35 minutes until set; cool on wire rack; chill.
5. To serve: Spread sour cream on top of pie. Garnish pie with almonds.

Color index page 98
Begin 6 hrs ahead or early in day
8 servings

Deluxe Cheese Pie

mixture for Unbaked
    Crumb Crust
    (page 345)
1 1/2 8-ounce packages
    cream cheese, softened

2 eggs
1/2 cup sugar
1/2 teaspoon vanilla
    extract
1 cup sour cream

1. Preheat oven to 350°F. Grease well 8-inch pie plate. Prepare crumb crust and gently press to bottom and side of pie plate.
2. In small bowl with mixer at low speed, beat cheese with eggs, sugar and vanilla just until mixed. Beat at high speed just until smooth; pour into prepared crumb crust.
3. Bake 35 minutes or until set. Spread pie with sour cream and cool on wire rack. Refrigerate, covered, until required.

PINEAPPLE-CHEESE PIE: Prepare as above but omit sour cream; cool pie. Meanwhile, prepare Pineapple Glaze: In 1-quart saucepan, stir *1 cup canned crushed pineapple,* undrained, with *1 teaspoon cornstarch.* Cook over low heat, stirring constantly, until thickened and clear; stir in *1 tablespoon lemon juice;* cool. Spread on top of cooled pie.

PEACH-CHEESE PIE: Prepare as above but omit sour cream; cool pie. Meanwhile, drain well *one 29-ounce can sliced cling peaches;* place peach slices on paper towels, patting dry; chill until pie is cool. Arrange peaches in overlapping rows on top of pie. In 1-quart saucepan, heat *1/4 cup apricot preserves* with *1 teaspoon lemon juice* until preserves melt; use to brush over peach slices.

159

SHELLFISH

Shellfish fall into two main categories, mollusks such as oysters, clams, mussels and scallops, and crustaceans – lobsters, crabs and shrimp. Shellfish are particularly rich in minerals; they contain high-quality protein, are a good source of vitamins and are low in calories.

Fresh, uncooked shellfish should be bought live. Mollusks should be tightly closed. If the shells are slightly parted, a sharp tap should be enough to make them snap shut again. Shucked mollusks should be plump and shiny, free of odor and with little or no liquor (surrounding liquid). Crustaceans survive longer out of water but their movements become slow and languid. Crabs and lobsters should be lively; when picked up, the lobster tails should curl under, not hang down. The amount of shellfish to buy depends on whether or not it has been shelled or shucked. Where we give recommended amounts for individual servings of each shellfish, these should be used only as a guide. If in doubt, especially with crabs, discuss the number to buy with your marketman.

Store fresh shellfish loosely wrapped in the refrigerator and cook them within 1 day.

Mussels

Mussels are sold fresh in the shells. Buy them from a reliable fish market or gather them fresh only when in season in your particular area. (They could be toxic if eaten out of season.)

Mussels must be alive when cooked, the shells unbroken and tightly closed, or they should close if touched. Rinse thoroughly under running cold water to remove all sand. Discard any that remain open. Scrub clean with a stiff metal brush, scraping off any loose barnacles with a knife. With shears, clip off beards.

To steam mussels, place them in a large pot in a small amount of boiling water. Tightly cover pot and simmer over medium heat 5 to 10 minutes until all the shells open up. Discard any unopened shells.

Clipping off beards: Use kitchen shears to cut off any beards.

Color index page 24

Begin 1¼ hrs ahead

4 servings

Mussels Marinière

3 pounds mussels (about 5 to 6 dozen)	½ cup dry white wine
butter or margarine	¼ teaspoon salt
3 shallots, minced	⅛ teaspoon pepper
1 garlic clove, minced	1 tablespoon chopped parsley

1. Discard any mussels that remain open when tapped with fingers. Clean and remove beards.
2. In 5-quart saucepot or Dutch oven over medium-high heat, in 2 tablespoons hot butter or margarine, cook shallots and garlic 1 minute, stirring. Add wine and mussels; sprinkle mussels with salt and pepper. Cover and simmer 6 to 8 minutes until shells open, stirring occasionally.
3. With slotted spoon, remove mussels to bowl. (Discard any that remain unopened.) Without disturbing sediment in bottom of saucepot, pour stock into 1½-quart saucepan; heat.
4. Meanwhile, discard halves of mussel shells to which meat is not attached. Arrange mussels in shells, open side up, in soup plates. Into hot stock, stir 1 tablespoon butter or margarine; pour over mussels; sprinkle servings with parsley.

Cooking mussels: Simmer 6 to 8 minutes until shells open; remove to bowl.

Arranging shells in plates: Place mussels in half-shells, open side up.

SCALING FISH

Place fish on a board or in sink, grip the fish firmly by the tail and scrape scales off with the dull edge of a knife, a vegetable peeler or fish scaler, holding the knife almost at right angles to the body of the fish and working from the tail toward the head. Pay particular attention to the area around the fins and near the base of the head. Turn the fish over and remove scales from the other side working from tail to head in the same way. Rinse the fish thoroughly with cold water after scaling.

Scaling a fish: Lay the fish on a board and with one hand, hold it firmly by the tail. With a knife in the other hand, beginning at the tail and working toward the head, scrape off the scales. Turn the fish and repeat on the other side.

CLEANING FISH

With a sharp knife, slit the belly of the fish open from the vent (anal opening) to the head. Remove entrails and rinse the cavity clean. Often small fish are cooked with only the entrails removed or with entrails and head removed. Give the fish a final rinse with cold water making sure it is thoroughly clean inside and out and blot it dry with paper towels. It is now ready for cooking whole, cutting into steaks or filleting.

REMOVING HEAD AND FINS

With sharp knife, cut around pelvic fins; remove and discard. Next, cut off head above collarbone, together with pectoral fins. Cut off the tail.

Or, if fish is large with strong backbone, cut down each side of head to bone, lay fish on its back at edge of counter and bend head back until bone snaps. Cut through any remaining flesh to free head.

To remove dorsal fin, make deep incision on each side of fin. Rip fin out, with root bones, by pulling sharply in direction of head. Remove remaining fins in same way. Never trim them off as this leaves root bones.

FILLETING FISH

Fillets are removed in one piece from each side of the backbone of a fish. A knife with a sharp blade is essential for filleting fish. When filleting, there is no need to remove the head and tail. If the fillets are to be skinned, there is no need to remove the scales.

With sharp knife, cut through fish along the backbone from tail to just behind head, cutting right down to the bone.

Holding the blade almost flat and parallel with the body of the fish, cut the flesh away from the backbone to the tail, allowing the knife to run over the rib bones. Cut with clean, even strokes, being careful not to cut into the flesh.

Lift the fillet off in one piece. Turn the fish over and remove the other fillet.

SKINNING A FILLET

If you wish, you may skin the fillet; place it, skin side down, on a cutting board. Use the tip of your knife to loosen enough skin at the tail end to give you a good grip; be careful not to cut through the skin. Holding down the tail end of the skin securely with one hand, and with the knife held almost flat in the other hand, cut the flesh of the fish free from the skin.

Grasping the tail end of the skin with one hand, with the knife held almost flat, cut the flesh free with the other.

FISH GLOSSARY

Court bouillon: Seasoned liquid in which fish may be poached. Usually a mixture of lightly salted water and white wine (or white wine vinegar), with seasonings such as onion, celery, carrot and herbs and spices – parsley, bay leaves, whole peppercorns and cloves. If available, some fish bones and trimmings may also be included. Before poaching fish, these ingredients are often simmered together in a covered pan for 20 to 30 minutes to extract their flavor.

Drawn fish: A whole fish with entrails removed but which is not boned.

Dressed fish: A fish that has been scaled and had entrails removed; it usually also has the head, tail and fins removed. Smaller fish prepared in this manner are described as pan-dressed.

Fillets: Sides of fish cut lengthwise from the backbone, so that they are boneless and ready for cooking. They are usually skinned. Butterfly fillets are whole fish split lengthwise down the front so that the backbone can be removed, and opened out flat, the two sides held together by the skin and a little uncut flesh.

Butterflying a fillet: Cut fish lengthwise down front; remove backbone and open out flat.

Steaks: Crosscut sections of a large dressed fish, usually cut at least ¾ inch thick from the thickest part of the fish.

Cutting steaks: After scaling and cleaning a large fish, cut off the head and fins; then, with sharp knife, starting at the head end, cut crosswise sections into steaks about ¾ to 1 inch thick.

Portions and sticks: Fish cut into uniform pieces. Usually sold breaded, partially cooked and frozen. Cook as package label directs.

CHOOSING CANNED FISH

Look for a dependable brand name and the variety that suits your needs. Most varieties of canned fish come in several forms, ranging from the kinds which are best for dishes such as party salads where color and texture play an important part, to varieties, often cheaper, which are more suitable for sandwich fillings and cooked dishes, where appearance is less important.

Salmon: Salmon is usually packed in 3¾-ounce, 7¾-ounce and 15½- and 16-ounce cans. There are several varieties available, differing slightly in color, texture and flavor. *Sockeye, Red* and *Blueback* are all the same species, deep salmon-pink in color, firm in texture and rich in oil. They break into medium flakes and are ideal for dishes such as salads and party casseroles in which firmness and good color are important. *King* and *Chinook* are rich in oil and break into large flakes but are rather softer in texture than Sockeye. Use them for salads. *Medium Red, Coho* and *Silver* are large-flaked and can be used in most recipes. Nearly half of all the canned salmon sold is *Pink*. It is small-flaked and goes well in entrees, soups and sandwiches. *Chum* and *Keta* are large-flaked and coarse-textured. Use them for casseroles and other cooked dishes where their lighter color is not important.

Tuna: Canned tuna comes packed in oil or water, solid- or fancy-pack, chunk-style and flaked or grated, in cans weighing 3¼ or 3½ ounces, 6½ or 7 ounces and 12½ or 13 ounces. Use the solid-pack for cold plates and party salads, chunks for salads and casseroles, and the flaked for appetizers and sandwich fillings. *Albacore* is the only white-meat canned tuna. It usually comes solid-pack or chunk-style and is more expensive than other tunas. *Yellowfin,* a light-meat variety, accounts for most of the available canned tuna and comes in chunk-, solid- or flake-style. *Skipjack* and *Bluefin* are also light-meat tunas available in chunk-, solid- and flake-style.

Mackerel: Like sardines, mackerel are not usually boned before canning since the bones soften during the canning process. Salted mackerel are available in 8-ounce cans, plain mackerel in 15-ounce cans.

Sardines: Sardines belong to the herring family and are usually sold canned in a variety of oils and sauces. The canning process softens the bones so that they can be eaten whole. Serve them as appetizers or as fillings in sandwiches Sardines are usually sold in cans weighing 3¾, 4⅜, 5½, 8 and 15 ounces.

Anchovies: These tiny members of the herring family are sold cured, canned or bottled in oil or brine. They usually come in the form of flat fillets but the fillets may also be rolled up and the rolls stuffed with capers. Anchovies are usually sold in 2-ounce cans.

COOKING FISH

Fish needs very little cooking – just long enough to coagulate the protein and bring out its flavor; it is ready as soon as the flesh has lost its translucent appearance and turned opaque and milky right through. Test for doneness by inserting a fork deep into the thickest part and gently parting the flesh which should come up in thick flakes or layers. With a whole fish or steak the flesh should come away cleanly from the backbone.

Most kinds of fish, either fresh or frozen, can be prepared in any one of the following ways, and, provided you allow extra cooking time, many can be cooked from the frozen state.

BROILED OR GRILLED FISH

Steaks, fillets and pan-dressed whole fish, about 1 inch thick, are best for broiling. Thinner pieces tend to dry out too quickly, while thicker ones may brown on the surface before they are cooked through. Brush generously with melted butter or margarine, oil or sauce before and during broiling. Thicker pieces (pan-dressed fish or steaks) should be turned once halfway through broiling. Broiled fish will take 10 to 15 minutes.

PAN-FRIED FISH

Fillets, thin steaks and pan-dressed whole fish can all be pan-fried successfully. Fish is usually breaded before frying (see Breading Fish, below right). Fry over medium-high heat in about ⅛ inch of heated fat – vegetable shortening or oil is best because of its high smoking point. Turn the fish once halfway through frying. Fish cooked in this manner will be cooked in 8 to 10 minutes, depending on thickness.

OVEN-FRIED FISH

Individual portions of fish are first breaded (see Breading Fish), then oven-fried or baked in preheated 450°F. oven. Place the breaded fish in a well-greased baking pan (to simulate deep-fat frying), drizzle a little salad oil, melted butter or margarine over the fish if liked, and bake for 10 to 15 minutes, or until fish flakes easily with a fork. No turning or basting is necessary in this method of cooking; the breading of the fish prevents any of the flavorful juices escaping.

DEEP-FRIED FISH

Bread-crumb- or batter-coated fillets, steaks and pan-dressed fish may all be fried successfully in deep fat. Bread the fish and put on a rack to dry for a few minutes. Meanwhile, heat 2 inches of vegetable shortening or oil in a deep, heavy saucepan or deep-fryer to 350°F. Gently lower fish into saucepan with pancake turner, or arrange fish in fry basket in a single layer and carefully lower basket into hot fat. Fry fish until golden and cooked through, usually 3 to 5 minutes. Drain the fish thoroughly on paper towels.

BAKED FISH

Whole dressed fish, fillets or steaks, may all be baked in a preheated 350°F. oven. There is no need to turn them while baking. To prevent fish drying out while it is in the oven, brush with melted butter, margarine or oil, or cover with a sauce. A 3-pound dressed fish takes 30 to 35 minutes; steaks, fillets, 12 to 15 minutes. Stuffed fish will need an additional 20 to 30 minutes' baking. Fish cooked from the frozen state will take slightly longer.

POACHED FISH

Fish fillets, steaks and whole dressed fish cook quickly in simmering liquid in a covered skillet or pan. Lightly salted water, milk, a mixture of water and white wine, or a well-seasoned *court bouillon* are all suitable. After poaching the fish, some of this liquid may be strained and used to make a sauce for the fish. Fillets and steaks will be ready in 5 to 10 minutes. Thicker, dressed fish will take longer. Do not allow the poaching liquid to boil at any point as this will cause fish to be tough textured or might even cause the flesh to break up.

STEAMED FISH

Fish fillets, steaks and pan-dressed fish may all be steamed. Use a steam cooker or a deep pan with a rack and a tightly fitting cover. Pour water into pan to below level of steam cooker liner or rack; heat to boiling. Put fish in greased, shallow baking dish; place on rack; cover pan and simmer until fish flakes when tested with a fork. Fillets and steaks will take 5 to 10 minutes, thicker whole fish will need several minutes longer.

BREADING FISH

If fish is frozen, thaw it before breading. First pat the fish dry with paper towels. Then dip in milk or egg beaten with a little milk, allowing excess to drain off, and coat with fine dried bread crumbs, cornflake crumbs, cornmeal or flour. For a slightly more substantial coating, dust the fish with seasoned flour before dipping it in egg and coating it with crumbs. Let the coated fish dry on a rack a few minutes before following recipes for pan-frying, oven-frying or deep-frying.

Dip fish in milk or egg beaten with a little milk. (For a thicker coating, first dust fish with seasoned flour.)

Coat fish with fine dried bread crumbs, cornflake crumbs, cornmeal or flour. Allow fish to dry on rack before frying.

Whole fish

Broiled Sesame Trout

Color index
page 36

Begin 4 hrs
ahead

6 servings

*6 serving-size rainbow
trout or other locally
available fish,
pan-dressed*
½ cup lemon juice
4 teaspoons salt
¼ teaspoon pepper
¼ cup sesame seed
*¾ cup butter or
margarine*

1 With sharp knife, make 3 light slashes on each side of fish, without cutting flesh too deep.

2 In 13″ by 9″ baking pan, mix lemon juice, salt and pepper. Add fish and turn over to coat with marinade. Cover; refrigerate at least 3 hours, turning occasionally.

3 In 1-quart saucepan over medium heat, toast sesame seed until golden, stirring and shaking pan occasionally. Add butter or margarine and heat until melted.

4 Place fish on rack in broiling pan. Drain marinade from baking pan into sesame seed mixture. Preheat broiler if manufacturer directs.

5 Broil fish about 5 minutes on each side, basting frequently with sesame seed mixture.

6 Test fish for doneness with a fork. Trout are cooked when their flesh flakes easily.

7 With pancake turners, lift fish carefully onto warm platter and spoon hot juices over it.

Bluefish with Buttery Lemon Sauce

Color index
page 35

Begin 20 mins
ahead

8 servings

1 cup butter or margarine
⅓ cup lemon juice
¼ cup chopped parsley
*1 tablespoon grated
lemon peel*
1 tablespoon salt
1 teaspoon sugar
¼ teaspoon pepper
*8 1-pound bluefish,
pan-dressed*

1. Preheat broiler if manufacturer directs. In 1-quart saucepan over high heat, melt butter or margarine; stir in lemon juice, parsley, lemon peel, salt, sugar and pepper.
2. Place fish on rack in broiling pan and brush with butter mixture. Cook about 5 minutes, then turn and cook 5 minutes more or until fish flakes easily when tested with a fork. During cooking, brush bluefish frequently with butter mixture.

GRILLED BLUEFISH: Prepare outdoor grill for barbecuing as manufacturer directs. Place *bluefish* in folding wire grill and cook over hot coals, brushing frequently with the *butter mixture* during cooking.

CARVING A WHOLE FISH

The directions below are for a whole, unstuffed fish. If the fish is stuffed, remove and serve stuffing after cutting top of fish and before removing bones to serve lower portion.

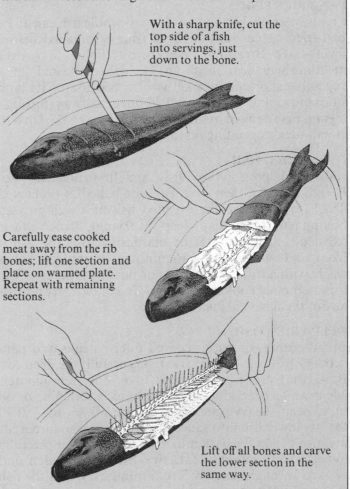

With a sharp knife, cut the top side of a fish into servings, just down to the bone.

Carefully ease cooked meat away from the rib bones; lift one section and place on warmed plate. Repeat with remaining sections.

Lift off all bones and carve the lower section in the same way.

Pan-fried Smelts

Color index
page 36

Begin 1½ hrs
ahead

6 servings

½ *cup all-purpose flour*
1 teaspoon salt
¼ *teaspoon pepper*
2 eggs
2 tablespoons water
½ *cup dried bread*
  crumbs
2 pounds smelts,
  pan-dressed
½ *cup salad oil*
2 tablespoons butter or
  margarine
lime or lemon wedges for
  garnish

1 On waxed paper, combine flour, salt and pepper. In pie plate with fork, beat eggs with water. Onto second sheet of waxed paper, pour bread crumbs.

2 Using tongs, coat fish one by one. Dip each first in flour mixture.

3 Then dip each fish in egg mixture, then coat well in bread crumbs.

4 Place coated fish on a rack over another sheet of waxed paper. Let dry 30 minutes.

5 In 12-inch skillet over medium heat, heat oil and butter or margarine. Fry the fish a few at a time, turning them after they have fried for 2 minutes.

6 Still over medium heat, fry smelts 2 minutes longer on other side or just until the flesh flakes easily when tested with a fork.

7 With pancake turner, lift cooked smelts onto warm platter and keep hot until all fish are cooked. Garnish with lime or lemon wedges.

Striped Bass with Pungent Sauce

Color index
page 36

Begin 1½ hrs
ahead

6 servings

1 3½-pound whole
  striped bass or sea
  bass, dressed, with
  head and tail on
1 tablespoon dry sherry
salt
salad oil
cornstarch
1 small carrot, cut into
  3-inch-long
  matchstick-thin strips
1 stalk celery, cut into
  3-inch-long
  matchstick-thin strips

¾ *cup sugar*
½ *cup white wine*
  vinegar
½ *cup catchup*
2 tablespoons sweet
  pickle relish
2 teaspoons soy
  sauce
1¼ cups water
2 medium lemons,
  sliced, for garnish

1. Rinse fish under running cold water; pat dry. With sharp knife, cut fish crosswise into two pieces; score 3 crosswise slashes about ½ inch deep on both sides of each piece to help fish cook more evenly and reduce cooking time.

2. In small bowl, mix sherry and 1 teaspoon salt. With hand, rub mixture inside and outside of fish. Place fish on platter; cover; refrigerate 30 minutes.

3. In 6-quart Dutch oven or saucepot, over medium-high heat, heat about 1 inch salad oil to 350°F. on deep-fat thermometer.

4. Meanwhile, again pat fish dry; on waxed paper, coat fish inside and out with ⅓ cup cornstarch. Carefully slip 1 piece of fish into hot oil; cook 8 minutes or until underside is golden and fish flakes easily when tested with fork.

5. Turn fish over to brown other side, about 8 minutes. Drain on paper towels 1 minute; place on warm platter; keep warm. Repeat with second piece. Reassemble pieces to make a whole fish.

6. Meanwhile, in 2-quart saucepan over high heat, in 1 tablespoon hot oil, stir-fry (stirring quickly and constantly) carrot, celery and ½ teaspoon salt, 2 minutes or until vegetables are tender-crisp. Spoon into small bowl; set aside.

7. In same saucepan over medium-low heat, heat sugar, vinegar, catchup, pickle relish, soy sauce, water and 3 tablespoons cornstarch to boiling, stirring frequently with wire whisk. Continue cooking for 2 minutes, stirring frequently. Pour sauce over and around fish; sprinkle with carrot mixture; garnish with lemon.

Scoring fish pieces: With a sharp knife, make 3 crosswise slashes ½ inch deep on both sides of fish.

Reassembling fried fish: After frying, on warm platter, reassemble pieces to make whole fish.

Whole fish

Color index page 35
Begin 1½ hrs ahead
8 servings

Baked Red Snapper with Oyster Stuffing

1 4- to 4½-pound red snapper, dressed
salt
salad oil
1 cup water
¾ cup minced celery
¼ cup chopped onion
1 8-ounce container shucked oysters

3 cups day-old bread cubes
¼ cup butter or margarine, melted
1 teaspoon poultry seasoning
¼ teaspoon pepper

1 Sprinkle inside and outside of fish with salt; brush one side with oil. Brush large shallow roasting pan with oil; place fish, oiled side down, in pan.

2 Make stuffing: In 2-quart saucepan over high heat, in boiling water, cook celery and onion until tender; drain, reserving liquid. Put onion and celery in large bowl. Into 1-cup measuring cup, drain liquid from oysters; add celery liquid to make ½ cup. Cut up oysters; add to celery and onion. Stir in bread cubes, butter, poultry seasoning, pepper and celery-oyster liquid.

3 With spoon, lightly fill cavity with oyster stuffing mixture.

4 Skewer cavity closed with toothpicks. Brush other side of fish with salad oil.

5 Bake in 350°F. oven 1 hour 10 minutes brushing fish occasionally with salad oil; with 2 pancake turners, lift fish to warm platter. Remove toothpicks.

6 To serve: Cut top side of fish into squares just down to bone. Serve squares with some of stuffing. Lift off all bones and repeat with other side of fish.

Poached Salmon with Aspic

8 cups water
2 cups white table wine
4 carrots, sliced
2 medium onions, cut into thin wedges
2 stalks celery, sliced
4 teaspoons salt
1 teaspoon thyme leaves
½ teaspoon peppercorns
1 bay leaf
1 5- to 6-pound whole salmon, dressed, with head and tail on
3 envelopes unflavored gelatin

2 medium lemons, thinly sliced, for garnish
parsley or watercress sprigs for garnish
Herb Mayonnaise (page 185)

Color index page 36
Begin early in day or day ahead
10 to 12 servings

1 In 26-inch fish poacher over high heat, heat first 9 ingredients to boiling. (The poacher will require 2 heating units.)

2 Meanwhile, rinse salmon under running cold water. Cut head off salmon if you wish and add to poaching liquid.

3 Place salmon on poaching rack; lower into liquid. Cover; simmer 30 minutes or until fish flakes when tested with fork.

4 Remove rack from poacher and with 2 pancake turners, place salmon on large platter. Cover; chill well.

5 Meanwhile, ladle poaching liquid into cheesecloth-lined sieve over a large bowl; discard all vegetables.

6 Into 2-quart saucepan, measure 4 cups strained poaching liquid; refrigerate until cool.

7 Sprinkle gelatin over liquid; over medium heat, cook, stirring, until dissolved. Pour into 13″ by 9″ baking pan; cover; refrigerate until aspic is set.

8 *To serve:* With small knife or kitchen shears, carefully cut skin around top half of salmon; remove and discard skin.

9 Cut aspic into small cubes; sprinkle around salmon. Garnish with lemon slices and parsley. Serve salmon with Herb Mayonnaise.

176

Fish fillets

Broiled Tarragon Fish

Color index page 37

Begin 20 mins ahead

4 servings

¼ cup salad oil
1 tablespoon lemon juice
½ teaspoon tarragon
½ teaspoon salt
⅛ teaspoon pepper
1 16-ounce package frozen flounder, Greenland turbot, sole, whiting or other fish fillets, partially thawed

1 lemon, cut into 4 wedges, for garnish
parsley sprigs for garnish

1 Preheat broiler if manufacturer directs. In small bowl with fork, mix salad oil, lemon juice, tarragon, salt and pepper.

2 Place flounder fillets in broiling pan and broil, basting generously with oil mixture occasionally.

3 Broil 5 to 8 minutes until fish flakes easily when tested with a fork.

4 Lift fillets onto warm plate and garnish with lemon wedges and parsley.

Broiler-barbecued Fish Dinner

Color index page 36

Begin 55 mins ahead

4 servings

Seafood Barbecue Sauce (below right)
¼ pound large mushrooms
4 small zucchini
melted butter
salt and pepper

grated Parmesan cheese
1 16-ounce package frozen haddock or cod fillets, partially thawed

1. Prepare sauce. Grease broiling-pan rack. Remove mushroom stems (save for use another day). Place mushroom caps on rack. Halve zucchini lengthwise; place, cut side up, beside mushrooms.
2. Preheat broiler if manufacturer directs. Brush mushrooms and zucchini generously with melted butter or margarine; sprinkle lightly with salt and pepper. Sprinkle zucchini lightly with cheese. Cut fillets crosswise into 4 chunks and place on rack. Spoon barbecue sauce over fish.
3. Broil 10 to 12 minutes until fish flakes easily when tested with a fork and zucchini is tender; baste mushrooms occasionally with melted butter.

Fish Fry

Color index page 37

Begin 55 mins ahead

4 servings

1 16-ounce package frozen flounder, sole or Greenland turbot or other fillets, partially thawed
Sweet-Sour Sauce (below)
salad oil
¾ cup all-purpose flour
⅔ cup water
1 teaspoon double-acting baking powder
1 teaspoon salt

1 Place unopened package of frozen fish in large pan; add enough cold water just to cover package. Let stand until flounder fillets are partially thawed, about 30 minutes. While fish is thawing in water, prepare Sweet-Sour Sauce. Keep sauce warm until needed.

2 Separate flounder fillets; pat dry with paper towels. In 12-inch skillet over medium heat, heat about 1 inch oil to 370°F. on deep-fat thermometer.

3 In medium bowl, mix flour, water, baking powder and salt, then using tongs, coat fillets with flour mixture.

4 Fry fish fillets in hot salad oil until golden, about 4 to 8 minutes, carefully turning fillets once.

5 When cooked, remove fillets to drain well on paper towels. Serve fillets with hot Sweet-Sour Sauce spooned over.

SWEET-SOUR SAUCE: In 1-quart saucepan with spoon, stir *2 tablespoons sugar, 1 tablespoon cornstarch* and *½ teaspoon chili powder* until well mixed; stir in *⅔ cup water, 3 tablespoons catchup* and *1 tablespoon cider vinegar* until smooth. Over medium-high heat, cook until mixture is thickened and boils, stirring constantly; cook 1 minute longer, stirring constantly. Remove from heat; stir in *¼ cup chopped sweet pickle* or pickle relish.

SEAFOOD BARBECUE SAUCE: In 2-quart saucepan over medium heat, simmer *2 small onions,* sliced, *½ cup catchup, ⅓ cup salad oil, 2 tablespoons diced celery, 2 teaspoons dry mustard, 1 teaspoon salt, 2 teaspoons Worcestershire, 2 teaspoons lemon juice* and *¼ teaspoon pepper* for 10 minutes, stirring frequently, until vegetables are tender.

Fish fillets

Fried Fish à la Margherita

2 16-ounce packages
  frozen sole, flounder or
  ocean perch fillets
1 15-ounce can tomato
  sauce
2 tablespoons finely
  chopped parsley

1 teaspoon oregano
  leaves
¼ cup olive or salad oil
¼ cup butter or
  margarine
parsley sprigs for
  garnish (optional)

Color index
page 37
Begin 50 mins
ahead
8 servings

1. Place unopened packages of frozen fish in large pan; add cold water to cover packages. Let stand until fillets are partially thawed, about 30 minutes. Carefully separate fillets; pat dry with paper towels.
2. In medium bowl, stir tomato sauce, parsley and oregano leaves until well mixed; set aside.
3. In 12-inch skillet over medium-high heat, in hot oil and butter or margarine, cook fillets 2 or 3 minutes on each side until fish flakes easily when tested with a fork.
4. Pour sauce over fish; cook 2 minutes, occasionally basting fish with sauce. Serve fish with sauce from skillet. Garnish with parsley, if you like.

Mediterranean Cod with Vegetables

2 16-ounce packages
  frozen cod or other
  fillets
⅔ cup salad oil
3 garlic cloves, slivered
1 medium eggplant, cut
  up
3 medium onions, cut into
  wedges
2 green peppers, cut up
¼ teaspoon pepper

¾ cup water
salt
1 egg
2½ cups fresh bread
  crumbs (5 white
  bread slices)
2 tablespoons chopped
  fresh dill or
  1 tablespoon dill weed
3 medium tomatoes, cut
  into wedges

Color index
page 36
Begin 1½ hrs
ahead
8 servings

1. Place unopened packages of frozen fish in large pan; add cold water to cover packages. Let stand until fillets are partially thawed, about 30 minutes.
2. In 12-inch skillet over medium-high heat, in ⅓ cup hot salad oil, cook garlic until golden; with slotted spoon, discard garlic. Add eggplant and onions; cook until vegetables are browned, stirring frequently, about 5 minutes. Stir in green peppers, pepper, water and 1½ teaspoons salt; cover and cook 5 minutes longer, stirring occasionally. Remove cover; continue cooking until all the water has evaporated. Spoon vegetables into medium bowl; keep warm.
3. Meanwhile, bread fish: Cut each package of cod fillets crosswise into 4 pieces; sprinkle with 1 teaspoon salt. In pie plate with fork, beat egg. On waxed paper, combine bread crumbs and dill. Dip fish in egg; coat with bread-crumb mixture.
4. In same skillet over medium-high heat, heat remaining ⅓ cup salad oil; cook fish 10 minutes or until it flakes easily when tested with fork, turning fish once. Remove fish to warm large platter; keep warm while vegetables are heated.
5. Return vegetables to skillet; add tomatoes and cook, stirring frequently, until tomatoes are heated through. Remove vegetables to warm platter and arrange mixture next to fish.

Fillets of Sole Thermidor

5 tablespoons butter
8 sole or other fillets
  (about 2 pounds)
2 teaspoons salt
½ teaspoon seasoned salt
⅛ teaspoon pepper
1¼ cups milk
3 tablespoons all-purpose
  flour
1 cup grated Cheddar
  cheese
3 tablespoons sherry
  (optional)
paprika

Color index
page 36
Begin 45 mins
ahead
8 servings

1 Preheat oven to 350°F. In 1-quart saucepan, melt 2 tablespoons butter; brush over sole fillets. Sprinkle with salt, seasoned salt and pepper.

2 Roll up each fillet and place, seam side down, in 9" by 9" baking dish.

3 Pour ½ cup milk over fillets; bake in oven 25 minutes or until fish flakes easily when tested with fork.

4 Meanwhile, in 2-quart saucepan over medium heat, melt remaining butter. Stir in flour; gradually add remaining milk; cook, stirring, until thickened.

5 Reduce heat; stir in cheese and sherry. Preheat broiler if manufacturer directs.

6 Spoon liquid from cooked fish. Stir ¼ cup liquid into cheese sauce. (If not using sherry use extra 3 tablespoons liquid.)

7 Pour cheese sauce over fish; sprinkle with paprika. Broil about 1 minute, just until cheese sauce is slightly golden.

Baked Sole with Lemon Sauce

Color index
page 37

Begin 30 mins
ahead

8 servings

*2 16-ounce packages
frozen sole, ocean
perch, flounder or
other fillets, thawed
1 teaspoon salt
¼ teaspoon pepper
3 tablespoons butter or
margarine*

*2 egg yolks
1 tablespoon water
1 tablespoon all-purpose
flour
¾ cup chicken broth
2 tablespoons lemon juice
4 stuffed olives, sliced, for
garnish*

1. Preheat oven to 350°F. Grease a large, shallow baking dish; arrange fillets in dish. Sprinkle fillets with salt and pepper; dot with 2 tablespoons butter or margarine. Bake 10 minutes or until fish flakes easily when tested with a fork.
2. Meanwhile, prepare sauce: In cup, mix egg yolks with water; set aside. In heavy 1-quart saucepan over medium heat, into 1 tablespoon hot butter or margarine, stir flour until well blended. Gradually stir in chicken broth and lemon juice and cook, stirring, until mixture is thickened; remove saucepan from heat.
3. Into egg yolks, stir small amount of hot sauce; slowly pour egg mixture back into the sauce, stirring rapidly to prevent lumping. Cook, stirring, until thickened (do not boil). Spoon off any liquid from fish. Pour sauce over fish and garnish with olives.

Clam-stuffed Fillets

Color index
page 37

Begin 50 mins
ahead

4 servings

*1 8-ounce can minced
clams
¼ cup butter or
margarine
⅓ cup chopped celery
¼ cup chopped onion
salt*

*3 cups white bread cubes
1 egg
⅛ teaspoon thyme leaves
1 pound flounder, ocean
perch or Greenland
turbot fillets
parsley sprigs for garnish*

1. Grease four 6-ounce custard cups. Drain clams, reserving 2 tablespoons clam liquid; set aside. In 2-quart saucepan over medium heat, in hot butter, cook celery, onion and ½ teaspoon salt until celery is tender, about 5 minutes. Stir in clams, reserved liquid, bread, egg, thyme. Preheat oven to 350°F.
2. Pat fish fillets dry with paper towels and sprinkle with ¼ teaspoon salt. Line custard cups with fillets, cutting fillets to fit if necessary. Spoon ½ cup clam mixture into center of each fillet-lined custard cup.
3. Place cups in 9-inch cake pan for easier handling. Bake 20 to 25 minutes until fish flakes easily when tested with a fork and stuffing is heated. To serve: Remove from cups; garnish.

Lining custard cups:
Add fillets to cups, cutting to fit if necessary.

Removing fillets: Use 2 spoons to gently lift fillets onto warm platter.

Poached Sole with Hollandaise Sauce

Color index
page 37

Begin 50 mins
ahead

4 servings

*Court bouillon:
1 carrot, sliced
1 stalk celery, sliced
1 small onion, sliced
1 lemon, thinly
sliced
4 peppercorns
2 bay leaves
2 parsley sprigs
1 teaspoon salt
2 cups water*

*1 16-ounce package
frozen sole fillets,
partially thawed
Hollandaise Sauce
(page 463)
chopped parsley for
garnish
lemon wedges
for garnish*

1 To make *court bouillon*: In 12-inch skillet over high heat, heat carrot, celery, onion, lemon, peppercorns, bay leaves, parsley sprigs, salt and water to boiling.

2 Cover, reduce heat and simmer 10 minutes. With a slotted spoon, remove the vegetables and spices; discard.

3 With serrated knife, cut fish into serving-size portions. Place fish portions in *court bouillon*.

4 Cover skillet and simmer fish over low heat 10 to 12 minutes, or until fish flakes easily when tested with a fork. Meanwhile, prepare Hollandaise Sauce.

5 With slotted pancake turner, carefully remove fish pieces and arrange on warm platter. Discard *court bouillon*.

6 To serve: Spoon Hollandaise Sauce over fish. Garnish platter with chopped parsley and lemon wedges.

Fish fillets

Shrimp-stuffed Roll-ups

Color index
page 37

Begin 40 mins
ahead

6 servings

¼ cup butter or
  margarine
1 cup shelled, deveined
  and chopped shrimp
1 cup chopped
  mushrooms
¼ cup dried bread
  crumbs
½ teaspoon dill weed
salt
6 sole or other fillets
  (about 2 pounds)
1 cup dry white wine
½ cup water
2 tablespoons cornstarch
½ cup half-and-half
1 egg

1 In 10-inch skillet over medium heat, in butter, cook shrimp and mushrooms until shrimp turn pink. Stir in crumbs, dill and ½ teaspoon salt.

2 Spoon shrimp mixture onto center of each fillet; roll up. Secure with toothpicks.

3 In cleaned skillet over high heat, heat to boiling fillets, wine, water and 1½ teaspoons salt.

4 Reduce heat to low; cover; simmer 12 to 15 minutes. With slotted spoon, remove fillets to warm platter. Remove toothpicks; keep fish warm until needed.

5 In small bowl, blend cornstarch and half-and-half; stir into fish liquid. Cook over medium heat, stirring, just until boiling and thickened.

6 In small bowl, beat egg slightly; stir a little hot sauce into beaten egg; pour mixture back into sauce, stirring rapidly.

7 Cook, stirring, until thick, but do not boil. Spoon some sauce over fillets and pass remainder separately in sauce boat.

Codfish Stew

Color index
page 37

Begin 55 mins
ahead

4 servings

1 16-ounce package
  frozen cod fillets
3 bacon slices
1 medium onion
1 16-ounce can whole
  white potatoes
1 16-ounce can tomatoes
¼ cup catchup
1 teaspoon
  Worcestershire
¼ teaspoon seasoned
  pepper
⅛ teaspoon thyme
  leaves

1. Place unopened package of frozen fish into large pan; add cold water to cover package. Let stand until fish fillets are partially thawed, about 20 minutes. Cut fillets into bite-size chunks; set aside.
2. Cut bacon into 1-inch pieces; thinly slice onion. Drain potatoes; cut each potato in half.
3. In 2-quart saucepan over medium heat, cook bacon until just limp; add onion and cook until onion is browned. Stir in potatoes, tomatoes with their liquid, catchup, Worcestershire, pepper and thyme; cook 5 minutes, stirring occasionally.
4. Add fish; cook about 10 minutes longer or until fish flakes easily when tested with a fork, stirring fish mixture often.

Creamed Finnan Haddie

Color index
page 37

Begin 30 mins
ahead (Finnan
haddie)
1½ hrs ahead
(smoked cod)

8 servings

2 pounds Finnan haddie
  or smoked cod fillets,
  cut in large pieces
3 tablespoons butter or
  margarine
4 teaspoons all-purpose
  flour
2 cups milk
1 cup heavy or whipping
  cream
4 hard-cooked eggs
parsley for garnish
Holland rusks or toast
  points (optional)

1. If using smoked cod: In large, shallow pan, place fillets and cover with cold water. Soak 1 hour, then drain thoroughly.
2. In 12-inch skillet over medium heat, into hot butter or margarine, stir flour until blended. Gradually stir in milk and cream and cook, stirring, until the flour mixture is slightly thickened and comes to a boil.
3. Add fish pieces; cover. Simmer 15 minutes or until fish flakes easily when tested with a fork.
4. Reserve 2 hard-cooked egg yolks for garnish; chop whites and other 2 egg yolks.
5. In the sauce, with fork, coarsely flake fish. Stir in chopped eggs and pour into warm dish.
6. Through coarse sieve, press reserved egg yolks over top. Garnish with parsley. Serve creamed fish on Holland rusks or toast points.

Flaking the fish: After poaching in sauce, flake fish coarsely with fork.

Garnishing: Press yolks through coarse sieve over Creamed Finnan Haddie.

Fish steaks

Halibut Steak with Eggplant Sauce

Color index page 38
Begin 30 mins ahead
6 servings

1 large green pepper
1 large onion
1 1-pound eggplant
⅓ cup salad oil
2 8-ounce cans tomato sauce
½ cup dry white wine
1 garlic clove, minced
1 bay leaf
¼ cup butter
2 tablespoons lemon juice
½ teaspoon salt
¼ teaspoon pepper
1 2-pound halibut steak

1 With sharp knife, cut green pepper into ½-inch strips and thinly slice onion. With vegetable peeler, peel eggplant; cut eggplant into ½-inch cubes.

2 In 12-inch skillet over medium heat, in hot oil, cook green pepper and onion until tender; then add cubed eggplant.

3 Add tomato sauce, wine, garlic and bay leaf; simmer 15 minutes.

4 Meanwhile, grease broiling pan rack. Preheat broiler if manufacturer directs.

5 In 1-quart saucepan over low heat, melt butter with lemon juice, salt and pepper.

6 Place halibut steak on rack and brush generously with butter mixture. Broil 5 minutes; turn; lightly brush again with butter mixture.

7 Broil 5 minutes longer or just until fish flakes easily when tested with a fork. Serve halibut steak with hot eggplant sauce.

Chilled Salmon Steaks with Marinated Cucumber

Color index page 38
Begin 4 hrs ahead
6 servings

4 cups water
salt
6 salmon steaks, about ½ inch thick (2 pounds)
2 large cucumbers, thinly sliced
½ cup white vinegar
2 tablespoons sugar
¼ teaspoon pepper
1 small onion, thinly sliced
romaine leaves and lemon wedges for garnish
Green Mayonnaise Dressing (page 185)

1 In 12-inch skillet over high heat, heat to boiling water and 2 tablespoons salt. Add 3 salmon steaks. Reheat to boiling.

2 Reduce heat to low; cover; simmer 5 to 8 minutes or until fish flakes. Grease 15½" by 10½" jelly-roll pan.

3 Remove each steak and drain over paper towels. Repeat with remaining steaks; place steaks in pan; cover; refrigerate.

4 Meanwhile, in medium bowl, toss cucumbers and 1 tablespoon salt. Let stand 30 minutes; drain in colander; press out liquid.

5 Discard liquid and return cucumbers to bowl; add vinegar, sugar, pepper and onion and mix well. Cover and refrigerate.

6 On each plate arrange salmon on romaine leaf with cucumbers and lemon. Pass Green Mayonnaise Dressing separately.

181

Fish steaks

Ground fillets

Color index page 38

Begin early in day

6 servings

Marinated Swordfish Steaks

2 1½-pound swordfish or
halibut steaks
⅓ cup salad oil
⅓ cup tarragon or cider
vinegar
2 bay leaves
2 tablespoons chopped
parsley

2 teaspoons salt
1 teaspoon
Worcestershire
¼ teaspoon tarragon or
¾ teaspoon chopped
fresh tarragon
¼ teaspoon pepper
1 lime

1. Place the swordfish or halibut steaks in a large shallow dish.
2. In a measuring cup, combine oil, vinegar, bay leaves, parsley, salt, Worcestershire, tarragon and pepper for marinade; pour over fish. Cover the dish and refrigerate, turning the fish occasionally to coat in marinade.
3. *About 25 minutes before serving:* Preheat broiler if manufacturer directs.
4. Place fish steaks in broiling pan reserving marinade, and broil 15 minutes or until the fish flakes easily when tested with a fork. Baste swordfish or halibut steaks occasionally with marinade.
5. Meanwhile, cut lime into 6 wedges. With a pancake turner, carefully lift swordfish or halibut steaks to warm platter. Serve with lime.

Color index page 38

Begin 40 mins ahead

4 servings

Codfish Steak

1 10-ounce bag spinach
½ cup butter or
margarine
1 1-pound cod, halibut or
hake steak
½ teaspoon salt

½ pound mushrooms,
sliced
2 tablespoons lemon
juice
lemon wedges for
garnish

1. Wash spinach well; drain in colander; pat dry with paper towels.
2. In 12-inch skillet over medium-high heat, in hot butter or margarine, place fish steak; sprinkle the steak with salt and cook until fish flakes easily when tested with a fork, about 10 minutes, turning once with a pancake turner. Remove fish to warm large platter and keep warm.
3. To drippings in skillet, add sliced mushrooms and lemon juice; cook until mushrooms are tender, about 5 minutes. With slotted spoon, spoon mushrooms into small bowl.
4. To remaining drippings in skillet, add spinach; cook 2 to 3 minutes until just tender, stirring occasionally. Stir in cooked mushrooms; heat mixture thoroughly
5. With slotted spoon, arrange spinach and mushroom mixture around fish; then pour liquid on fish and vegetable mixture. Garnish the platter with lemon wedges.

Quenelles in Wine Sauce

Quenelles:
2 pounds flounder fillets,
or 2 16-ounce
packages frozen
flounder or other
fillets, thawed, cut into
chunks
¼ cup butter or
margarine
water
1 cup all-purpose flour
3 eggs, beaten
¼ teaspoon pepper
⅛ teaspoon ground
nutmeg
salt
1 cup heavy cream

Wine Sauce:
3 tablespoons all-purpose
flour
2 tablespoons butter or
margarine, softened
½ cup dry vermouth
1 teaspoon lemon juice
¼ teaspoon salt
⅛ teaspoon pepper
1 cup shredded Swiss
cheese

Color index page 24

Begin 3 hrs ahead

9 appetizer or

6 main-dish servings

1 Prepare quenelles: Pat fish dry with paper towels pressing out liquid. With food grinder, using fine cutting disk, grind fish into paste.

2 In 3-quart saucepan over medium heat, heat butter and 1 cup water to boiling. Remove from heat; add flour and beat until mixture forms ball.

3 Beat in eggs until thoroughly blended. Stir in fish, pepper, nutmeg and 1½ teaspoons salt. Refrigerate mixture about 1½ hours.

4 Stir in 2 tablespoons cream. In deep 12-inch skillet over medium heat, boil 8 cups water and 1 tablespoon salt. Reduce heat to very low.

5 Divide half quenelle mixture into 9 equal portions. Using 2 spoons, shape portions into ovals.

6 Gently drop shaped quenelles into simmering water in skillet.

7 Cook, uncovered, 15 minutes until quenelles roll easily; drain on paper towels. Repeat. (Reserve 2 cups water.)

8 Arrange cooked and drained quenelles in 13" by 9" baking dish; keep quenelles warm.

9 Prepare sauce: In 2-quart saucepan over high heat, heat reserved poaching water to boiling. Boil 15 minutes to reduce by half. In small bowl, blend flour and butter; stir into liquid. Over medium heat, cook, stirring, until slightly thickened. Add vermouth, lemon juice, salt and remaining cream. Cook, stirring, about 5 minutes until thickened. Preheat oven to 475°F.

10 Spoon sauce over quenelles; sprinkle with cheese. Bake 5 to 8 minutes until cheese melts.

Canned fish

Fish Mousse

2½ cups water
2 envelopes unflavored
  gelatin
1 small onion, sliced
2 teaspoons salt
½ teaspoon peppercorns
½ teaspoon basil
1 16-ounce package
  frozen flounder,
  pollock, sole or cod
  fillets
½ cup salad dressing or
  mayonnaise
1 tablespoon lemon juice

¼ teaspoon hot pepper
  sauce
½ cup heavy or whipping
  cream
pitted olives and
  pimentos for garnish
lettuce leaves
lemon wedges

Color index page 24
Begin 6 hrs or day ahead
8 appetizer or
4 main-dish servings

1 In 12-inch skillet, into water, sprinkle gelatin. Cook over low heat, stirring, until gelatin is dissolved.

2 Add onion, salt, peppercorns and basil; heat to boiling. Reduce heat to low; cover and simmer 5 minutes.

3 Add frozen fish fillets to skillet; heat to boiling. Reduce heat; simmer 15 minutes until fish flakes easily. With slotted spoon, remove fish from liquid.

4 Strain liquid into 4-cup measure, discarding onion and peppercorns. If needed add water to make 2¼ cups liquid. Add fish; cover; refrigerate until thickened.

5 In covered blender container, at medium speed, blend until smooth fish mixture, salad dressing, lemon juice and hot pepper sauce.

6 Pour mixture into large bowl. Whip cream; fold into mixture. Pour into 5-cup fish-shaped mold; refrigerate until set, about 4 hours.

7 To serve: Unmold mousse by dipping mold into hot water for a few seconds.

8 Place flat platter over mold; invert both together and lift off mold. With sharp knife, finely slice olives and pimentos.

9 Arrange lettuce leaves and lemon wedges around fish mousse and garnish with sliced pitted olives and pimentos.

Color index page 38
Begin 1½ hrs ahead
8 servings

Tuna Loaf with Cucumber Sauce

Tuna Loaf:
18 saltine crackers, finely
  crushed
1 cup finely chopped
  celery
3 6½- or 7-ounce cans
  tuna, drained
2 tablespoons grated
  onion
¼ teaspoon pepper
¾ teaspoon salt
1 cup milk
3 eggs, slightly beaten

Cucumber Sauce:
2 medium cucumbers,
  peeled, seeded and
  chopped
water
2½ tablespoons butter or
  margarine
2½ tablespoons all-
  purpose flour
1 teaspoon salt
1½ teaspoons grated
  lemon peel
1 teaspoon lemon juice
2 egg yolks
chopped parsley and
  cucumber slices for
  garnish

1. Preheat oven to 350°F. In large bowl, combine milk, eggs and crackers; let stand 5 minutes, stirring often. Stir in celery, tuna, onion, pepper and salt.
2. Pour tuna mixture into well-greased 10" by 5" by 3" loaf pan. Bake tuna loaf for 1 hour or until knife inserted in center comes out clean. Cool slightly.
3. *About 15 minutes before serving:* Prepare Cucumber Sauce: In 2-quart saucepan, simmer cucumbers in 1 cup water until tender-crisp. Drain; add water to liquid to make 1¾ cups; set aside. In same saucepan, over medium heat, melt butter or margarine; add flour; stir until smooth. Slowly add reserved liquid; cook, stirring, until thickened. Add salt, lemon peel, juice and cooked cucumber; cook just until boiling. In small bowl, beat egg yolks slightly; stir in some hot liquid; slowly add mixture to pan; cook, stirring, until thickened (do not boil).
4. Loosen loaf from pan; invert onto platter; pour on some sauce; garnish. Pass remaining sauce.

Color index page 38
Begin 45 mins ahead
6 servings

Salmon Burgers

3 eggs
1 16-ounce can salmon,
  drained
2½ cups fresh bread
  crumbs (about 5
  slices)
⅔ cup chopped celery
⅓ cup chopped green
  onions

3 tablespoons salad
  oil
3 English muffins, split
  and toasted
1⅓ cups Hollandaise
  Sauce (page 463)

1. In large bowl with fork, beat eggs slightly. Add salmon, crumbs, celery and green onions and mix well. Shape mixture firmly into 6 patties.
2. In 12-inch skillet over medium heat, in hot oil, fry patties, turning once, 10 minutes until browned.
3. Top each muffin with a patty; spoon on sauce.

Canned fish

Tuna Pie

Color index
page 38

Begin 1½ hrs
ahead

6 servings

*1 10-ounce package
frozen broccoli spears,
thawed*
*1 8- to 8½-ounce can
water chestnuts,
drained*
*¼ cup butter or
margarine*
*¼ cup all-purpose
flour*
1 teaspoon salt
½ teaspoon paprika

2¼ cups milk
*½ cup shredded Swiss
cheese*
*½ pound mushrooms,
sliced*
*1 12½- to 13-ounce can
tuna, drained*
*pastry for 1-crust 9-inch
pie (page 344)*
1 egg yolk
1 teaspoon water

1. Cut broccoli into 2-inch pieces; cut water chestnuts into ¼-inch slices; set aside.
2. In 3-quart saucepan over low heat, melt butter or margarine; stir in flour, salt and paprika until blended. Gradually stir in milk and cook, stirring constantly, until mixture is thickened and smooth.
3. With rubber spatula, gently stir in broccoli, water chestnuts, cheese, mushrooms and tuna; spoon mixture into 2-quart casserole.
4. Prepare pastry. On lightly floured surface with lightly floured rolling pin, roll pastry to a circle ⅛ inch thick and about 1 inch larger all around than casserole. Place pastry loosely over tuna mixture.
5. Preheat oven to 375°F. With kitchen shears, trim pastry edge, leaving 1-inch overhang; fold overhang under and press gently all around casserole rim to make a high stand-up edge. With sharp knife, cut slits in pastry top to allow steam to escape.
6. Reroll pastry trimmings. With leaf-shaped cookie cutter, cut several leaves. With tip of small knife, score several lines on leaves to resemble veins. Arrange the scored leaves in attractive pattern in the center top of pie.
7. In small bowl, mix well egg yolk with water. Brush pastry with egg-yolk mixture. Bake 30 to 35 minutes or until crust is golden and mixture is heated.

Tuna Tetrazzini

Color index
page 38

Begin 1 hr
ahead

8 servings

*1 8-ounce package
spaghetti, broken in
pieces*
*2 2½-ounce cans sliced
mushrooms*
¼ cup all-purpose flour
*¼ cup butter or
margarine*
1¼ cups milk

¼ cup medium sherry
*½ pound pasteurized
process cheese, cubed
(2 cups)*
½ teaspoon seasoned salt
*¼ teaspoon ground
nutmeg*
*2 6½- or 7-ounce cans
tuna, drained*

1. Cook spaghetti as label directs; drain and set aside. Drain mushrooms, reserving ⅓ cup liquid. Preheat oven to 350°F.
2. For sauce, in 2-quart saucepan over low heat, stir flour into hot butter or margarine, until blended. Gradually stir in milk, sherry and mushroom liquid and cook, stirring, until thickened. Stir in cheese, seasoned salt and nutmeg until cheese melts.
3. Stir spaghetti, tuna and mushrooms into sauce. Pour mixture into 2½-quart, shallow baking dish. Bake in oven 20 minutes or until light golden.

Cold Salmon Mousse

Color index
page 38

Begin 4 hrs
or day ahead

6 main-dish
servings

*1 envelope unflavored
gelatin*
water
salad oil
*1 cup heavy or
whipping cream*
*1 15½-ounce can
salmon, drained and
flaked*
½ cup mayonnaise
½ teaspoon salt

*¾ teaspoon dill weed or 2
teaspoons chopped
fresh dill*
½ teaspoon paprika
*½ teaspoon hot pepper
sauce*
1 bunch radishes
2 peppercorns
*2 medium lemons, thinly
sliced, for garnish*

1. In small bowl, mix gelatin with ¼ cup cold water. Let gelatin stand 5 minutes to soften. Add ½ cup *very hot* tap water to gelatin mixture and stir until gelatin is completely dissolved, about 3 minutes. Cover and refrigerate until slightly chilled.
2. With pastry brush, lightly brush 5½-cup fish or other favorite mold with salad oil.
3. In small bowl with mixer at medium speed, beat cream until stiff peaks form. In large bowl with mixer at medium-high speed, beat salmon, mayonnaise, salt, dill weed, paprika, hot pepper sauce and gelatin mixture until smooth, scraping bowl often with rubber spatula. Fold in cream. Spoon salmon mixture into mold; cover and refrigerate until set, about 3 hours.
4. *To serve:* Thinly slice radishes; cut slices in half. Unmold mousse onto large platter. Decorate head of fish with peppercorns for eyes. Carefully press radish slices overlapping slightly, about ⅛ inch deep, into mousse in rows to resemble scales, making sure that rounded end of each radish extends at a slight angle. Garnish platter with lemon slices.

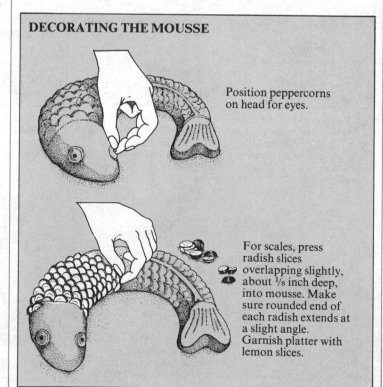

DECORATING THE MOUSSE

Position peppercorns
on head for eyes.

For scales, press
radish slices
overlapping slightly,
about ⅛ inch deep,
into mousse. Make
sure rounded end of
each radish extends at
a slight angle.
Garnish platter with
lemon slices.

Cooking on a rotisserie: This is also a form of roasting. As with other dry-heat methods, low to moderate temperatures should be used. Meat cuts should be as uniform in shape and thickness as possible. Insert the spit through center of the roast lengthwise, fastening the meat securely so that it does not slip. Test for balance by rotating the spit in the palms of your hands. Insert the meat thermometer (see page 188). If it does not stay securely in position, after the approximate roasting time, stop the rotisserie, insert the thermometer and read the temperature. Following manufacturer's directions, cook the meat to the desired degree of doneness. Meat cooked on a rotisserie is self-basting,but it may be basted occasionally for added flavor and color. Sweet basting sauces should not be applied until the last half-hour of cooking.

Broiling or grilling: Steaks and chops should be at least ¾ inch thick, ham slices at least ½ inch thick. Trim excess fat from meat and slash the edge of fat at 2-inch intervals so it won't curl during broiling. Preheat broiler if manufacturer directs, or prepare coals. Rub the broiling pan rack with a piece of fat trimmed from the meat. Place the meat on the rack, then place the pan in the broiler. Steaks, chops and patties ¾ to 1 inch thick should be 2 to 3 inches from the heat; cuts 1 to 2 inches thick should be 3 to 5 inches from the heat. Broil meat until top is browned (lightly browned for cured and smoked pork). Season top if desired (ham and bacon will not need seasoning) and with tongs, turn meat. Broil until of desired degree of doneness; cut slit near bone and check color to test doneness.

Pan-broiling: The meat cut should be no more than 1 inch thick and it will take about half as long as if broiled in broiler. Place meat in an unheated heavy skillet or on a griddle. Most meats have enough fat to prevent sticking. However, if meat is very lean, pan may first be brushed lightly with fat or rubbed with a piece of fat trimmed from the meat. Over medium-low to medium heat, cook meat slowly, turning occasionally. Pour off fat as it accumulates so that meat does not fry. Brown meat on both sides.

Pan-frying: In a skillet, over medium to medium-high heat, using a little hot salad oil or other fat if necessary, brown the meat on both sides. (Add a little salad oil only if cut is low in fat, such as liver, or if meat is coated with flour or bread crumbs.) Season, if desired, and continue cooking over medium-low to medium heat, turning occasionally, until done. Do not cover, or crispness will be lost. Serve meat at once.

Braising: In a large, heavy skillet or Dutch oven over medium-high heat in a little hot salad oil or fat melted from meat, brown the meat on all sides; spoon off drippings. Season meat and add a little liquid if needed. Less tender cuts require liquid; tender ones, such as pork

chops, may not. Cover the pan tightly to keep in the steam and simmer the meat over low heat or in a preheated 325°F. to 350°F. oven until fork-tender.

Cooking in liquid: Large cuts: In a large, heavy saucepot, over medium-high heat, brown meat on all sides to develop flavor and color. (Corned beef and other cured meats are not browned.) Add hot or cold liquid to cover the meat; season, if desired. Over high heat, heat liquid to boiling; reduce heat to low, cover pan and simmer (don't boil) until the meat is fork-tender. Add any vegetables just long enough before meat is done to cook them. If meat is to be served cold, chill it in the cooking liquid in the refrigerator to improve juiciness and flavor and reduce shrinkage.

Stewing: For a browned stew, in a heavy saucepan over medium-high heat, in a little hot salad oil, brown the pieces of meat on all sides, a few at a time, removing them as they brown. Meat may be coated with flour before browning. When all pieces are browned, return meat to the pan. For a light stew, omit flouring and browning. Add hot or cold liquid just to cover the meat. Season, if desired; cover and simmer (don't boil) until the meat is fork-tender. Add any vegetables just long enough before meat is done to cook them. When done, remove both meat and vegetables to a warm dish and keep hot: if desired, thicken the remaining liquid to make a gravy or sauce. Serve the gravy over the meat and vegetables or pass it in a gravy boat.

TENDERIZING MEAT

Meat tenderizers: These are derivatives of natural food-tenderizing agents found in some tropical fruits which soften meat tissue only while meat is cooking. Be sure to follow directions on the label: don't use more and don't leave it on longer than the label recommends, or meat surface might become mushy. Also, don't use it on naturally tender cuts, such as sirloin steak, or on beef tendered with papain.

Mechanical methods: Grinding makes meat tender, as does "cubing," which breaks down the connective tissue by machine. Pounding meat, as directed in some recipes, achieves the same results.

Beef "tendered with papain": This is a scientific commercial process that utilizes protein derivatives from such fruits as papaya (papain). The tendering develops only as the beef cooks, making it possible to cook more beef cuts by dry heat, and shortening cooking time for those cuts that must be cooked by moist heat.

Aging: This improves the tenderness of some beef cuts. At the storage plant, beef is hung for a specified time, in rooms with controlled temperature and humidity.

Marinating: Soaking meat, particularly in acid mixtures such as lemon juice or vinegar, tenderizes meat and adds flavor. Often herbs and spices are included in marinades.

Beef

USING A MEAT THERMOMETER

For meats that are roasted in an open pan, insert the thermometer so that its point is centered in the thickest part of the meat. Make sure that it is not resting on bone or in fat, or it will not register the correct temperature. If necessary, pierce the meat with a skewer first to make insertion of the thermometer easier.

When roasting frozen meat, insert thermometer about halfway through the roasting period, when meat is partially thawed (check first with a skewer).

For rotisserie cooking, the dial type of thermometer is recommended. Insert it at a slight angle or through the end of the roast halfway between the spit and the surface of the meat, making sure that its point is not resting on bone or fat, or touching the spit.

Use a meat thermometer to test for doneness accurately. Some dial types, left, have short stems for rotisserie cooking.

MAKING GRAVY

Remove the cooked meat and any vegetables to a warmed platter; keep warm while making gravy.

For roasts: Into 2-quart saucepan, measure ¼ cup fat from roasting pan (or use butter or margarine). Pour 1 cup water or bouillon into the roasting pan; stir to loosen the brown bits in the bottom of the pan. Into fat in saucepan over medium heat, stir ¼ cup all-purpose flour; cook, stirring constantly until brown. Slowly stir in liquid from the roasting pan; add 1 cup water and heat to boiling, stirring until thickened. If you like, add bottled sauce for gravy to make a rich color; add salt and pepper to taste. (Makes 2 cups.)

For pan-fried meat: In skillet over medium heat, in ¼ cup hot drippings (or butter or margarine), cook ¼ cup all-purpose flour until brown. Gradually stir in 2 cups water, milk or bouillon; heat to boiling, stirring until thickened. If you like, add bottled sauce for gravy to make a rich brown color; add salt and pepper to taste. (Makes 2 cups.)

For pot roasts and braised meat: Spoon fat from pan liquid; measure liquid and heat. For each cup liquid, in cup, blend 2 tablespoons all-purpose flour with ¼ cup water; stir into simmering liquid and cook, stirring, until thickened. Season if needed.

For stews: Thicken gravy as for pot roasts but use only 1 tablespoon flour for each cup liquid.

POPULAR BEEF CUTS

Beef rib roast small end: Also known as standing rib roast; suitable for roasting.

Beef rib eye roast: Also known as Delmonico pot-roast or Delmonico roast or regular roll roast; suitable for roasting.

Beef round tip roast cap off: Also known as full trimmed tip roast. Bone and cap muscle are removed. If of high quality it can be roasted, otherwise it should be braised.

Beef bottom round roast: Also known as beef bottom round pot roast; suitable for braising, or roasting, if high quality

Beef chuck eye roast boneless: Also known as chuck roll; suitable for braising, or roasting, if high quality.

Beef chuck short ribs: Also known as barbecue and braising ribs; suitable for braised dishes or cooking in liquid.

DORLING KINDERSLEY

Adapted from *The Meat Board Meat Book* by Barbara Bloch, copyright © 1977 by National Live Stock & Meat Board and The Benjamin Company, Inc., published by McGraw-Hill. Used by permission.

Beef chuck arm pot roast: Also known as round bone pot roast; suitable for pot roasts and other braised dishes.

Beef flank steak: Also known as London broil or plank steak, it is suitable for braising, but can be broiled, if high quality.

Beef top loin steak: Popular names include Shell, club, strip and Delmonico steak; suitable for broiling, pan-broiling and pan-frying.

Beef chuck shoulder pot roast boneless: Also known as shoulder or English roast; suitable for pot roasts and other braised dishes.

Beef chuck under blade steak: Also known as bottom chuck steak; suitable for braising, or broiling, pan-broiling and pan-frying, if high quality.

Beef porterhouse steak: Contains tenderloin of at least 1¼ inches diameter; suitable for broiling, pan-broiling and pan-frying.

Beef round rump roast boneless: Usually found tied; suitable for braised dishes but may be roasted, if high quality.

Beef chuck blade steak: Also known as blade steak or blade cut; suitable for braising or broiling or pan-broiling, if high quality.

Beef pin bone sirloin steak: Otherwise known as sirloin steak; suitable for broiling, pan-broiling and pan-frying.

Beef chuck 7-bone steak: Also known as center chuck steak; suitable for braising.

Beef rib eye steak: Also known as Delmonico and fillet steak; suitable for broiling, pan-broiling and pan-frying.

Beef bottom rump round roast: Also known as round tip roast, it is an irregular, thick cut suitable for braising, roasting, if high quality.

Beef shank cross cuts: Also known as center beef shank; suitable for braising.

Beef top round steak: Suitable for braising or broiling, pan-broiling and pan-frying, if high quality.

Beef

From succulent steaks and tender, juicy roasts to hearty hamburgers and spicy meat loaves, beef provides us with a greater variety of cuts and more ways of cooking than any other meat.

BUYING BEEF

Beef should be a uniform bright color, varying from light to deep red. The texture of the meat should be fine rather than coarse, firm and slightly moist, and the bones should be red and porous. The color of the fat varies with age, feed and breed of the animal, and cannot be taken as a guide to quality.

Some beef, usually cuts such as roasts and some steaks, is aged to increase its tenderness. Always check if the meat you are buying has been aged so you will know whether or not to tenderize it. Beef may also be pretendered with papain. If this has been done, the label on the package will carry special cooking directions and it is important that you follow these.

TESTING FOR DONENESS

Roast and broiled beef may be cooked rare, medium or well done according to taste. Rare beef cooked to an internal temperature of 140°F. is reddish-pink inside with an abundance of clear red juice of a lighter color. Medium beef is cooked to 160°F. Beef is well done when the meat thermometer reads 170°F. and is a uniform brown color throughout, with clear, golden juices. Cooked braised or simmered beef should be fork-tender.

The table below is intended as a guide for roasting beef; times are for roasting meat straight from the refrigerator.

TIMETABLE FOR ROASTING BEEF				
Weight *(in pounds)*	Approximate cooking time* *(in hours)*			Oven Temperature
	Rare 140°F.**	Medium 160°F.**	Well done 170°F.**	
Rib roast 4 to 6	1¾ to 2½	2¼ to 3½	2¾ to 4	325°F.
6 to 8	2¼ to 3	2¾ to 3½	3¼ to 4¼	325°F.
Rib eye roast 4 to 6	1¼ to 1¾	1¼ to 2	1½ to 2¼	350°F.
Tenderloin (whole) 4 to 6	45 to 60 mins			425°F.
Tenderloin (half) 2 to 3	45 to 50 mins			425°F.
Rump roast boneless 4 to 6		1¾ to 2½		325°F.
Tip roast 3½ to 4		2 to 2¼		325°F.
6 to 8		3 to 4		325°F.

*Remove meat from oven when internal temperature is 5 to 10 degrees below desired doneness as meat continues cooking
**Temperature on meat thermometer

CARVING BEEF

Rib roast of beef: Place the beef on a cutting board or warm platter with the large end down and the ribs to your left. Insert carving fork, tines down, between the top and second rib of the roast. With the carving knife, carefully cut across the meat toward the rib bone, making a slice about ¼ inch thick.

Remove knife and, with tip, cut down along side of rib bone to release meat; place the slice on a warm dinner plate.

Continue cutting slices, removing each rib bone as it is exposed.

Boneless roast: Place the roast on a board or warm platter. Cut away any strings (or, if the roast starts to fall apart, leave one or two in place to help the roast hold its shape). Using a fork to anchor the meat, start cutting crosswise across the fibers (grain) of the meat into slices ¼ to ½ inch thick.

Steak or arm or blade pot roast: With the roast on a cutting board and using a fork to anchor the meat, cut between muscles and around bones. Carve one section at a time, turning to cut across the grain of the meat. Cut the pieces into slices of desired thickness. Repeat with remaining sections of meat.

Tender roasts

Standing Rib Roast with Yorkshire Pudding

Color index page 50

Begin 2 to 4 hrs ahead

14 to 18 servings

1 2- to 3-rib beef rib roast small end (4 to 6 pounds)
salt and pepper
2 eggs
1 cup milk
½ teaspoon salt
1 cup all-purpose flour
Horseradish Sauce (page 463)

1 Place roast on rib bones in open roasting pan. Sprinkle with salt, pepper.

2 Insert meat thermometer into thickest part, making sure it is in center of roast and not resting on bone or fat.

3 Roast in 325°F. oven until internal temperature reaches 140°F. for rare (1¾ to 2½ hours); 160°F. for medium (2¼ to 3½ hours); 170°F. for well done (2¾ to 4 hours). When roast is done, allow it to stand at room temperature 15 minutes for easier carving. About 5 minutes before end of roasting time, prepare Yorkshire Pudding.

4 In medium bowl with wire whisk, beat eggs until foamy; beat in milk and ½ teaspoon salt; gradually beat in flour until batter is smooth.

5 When roast is done, spoon off 2 tablespoons drippings and divide into twelve 3-inch muffin cups; tilt to coat evenly; turn oven to 400°F.

6 Heat muffin pan in oven 5 minutes; pour 2½ tablespoons batter in each greased muffin cup. Bake 30 minutes.

7 Loosen Yorkshire Pudding; transfer to platter and serve immediately with roast and Horseradish Sauce.

STANDING RIB ROAST AU JUS: Prepare Standing Rib Roast. After removing roast from pan, spoon off fat from meat juices in pan; use 2 tablespoons fat for Yorkshire Pudding; discard remaining fat. Into meat juices in pan, pour a little *water* (about ⅓ to ½ cup). Over medium-high heat, heat mixture to simmering, stirring and scraping until browned bits are dissolved; strain mixture. Serve over slices of meat.

Vegetable-topped Roast Beef

Color index page 51

Begin 3½ hrs ahead

16 to 18 servings

1 4½-pound beef round tip roast cap off
2 tablespoons prepared mustard
¼ teaspoon pepper
salt
1 cup shredded carrots
½ cup minced celery leaves
1 teaspoon thyme leaves
1 cup water
⅓ cup dry red wine

1. Place round tip roast on a small wire rack in a medium open roasting pan. Spread the top of roast with the mustard; sprinkle with pepper and 1 teaspoon salt. On waxed paper, combine the shredded carrots, celery leaves and thyme. Reserve ¼ cup of the vegetable mixture. With hands, evenly press the remaining vegetable mixture on top of the mustard and seasoning on roast.
2. Insert meat thermometer into the center of the beef roast. Roast in 325°F. oven for 1 hour. Cover the roast beef loosely with a tent of folded foil, leaving the thermometer uncovered and continue roasting until the thermometer reaches 160°F. for medium (about 2 hours) or until of desired doneness.
3. When roast is done, place on warm large platter or carving board; sprinkle top with reserved vegetable mixture; keep warm.
4. Remove the wire rack from the roasting pan. Spoon off any fat from the pan; discard the fat. Into the pan, pour the water and the dry red wine; add ¼ teaspoon salt; stir until the brown bits on the bottom of the pan are loosened.
5. Over medium-high heat, heat the mixture to boiling, stirring constantly and scraping until the brown bits are dissolved.
6. To serve: Slice the roast beef. Spoon the gravy over individual portions.

Coating meat: Spread on mustard and sprinkle with salt and pepper; then evenly press vegetable mixture on top of roast.

Making foil tent: To prevent topping burning, cover roast loosely with tent of folded foil; leave thermometer uncovered.

Tender roasts

Individual Beef Wellingtons

1 pound medium mushrooms
¼ cup butter or margarine
1 medium onion, minced
3 cups fresh bread crumbs
½ teaspoon pepper
¼ teaspoon thyme leaves
salt
pastry for 4 2-crust pies (page 344)
1 4-pound beef rib eye roast

2 eggs, separated
water
curly endive for garnish
preserved or fresh kumquats for garnish (optional)

Color index page 52
Begin early in day
10 servings

1 Remove stems from 10 mushrooms; set mushrooms aside. Mince remaining mushrooms and the extra stems.

2 In 12-inch skillet over medium heat, in hot butter, cook minced mushrooms and onion 5 minutes, until all liquid is evaporated.

3 Stir in bread crumbs, pepper, thyme and 1½ teaspoons salt; cool. Prepare pastry; divide into 5 equal pieces.

4 Trim fat off roast; cut meat in half lengthwise; slice each half crosswise into 5 equal pieces. Dry with paper towels.

5 On floured surface with floured stockinette-covered rolling pin, roll 1 piece pastry to 14" by 11"; cut 2 rectangles 6½" by 10"; reserve scraps.

6 Place ⅓ cup of mushroom mixture in center of pastry rectangle. Top with piece of meat.

7 Sprinkle meat lightly with salt; top with 1 whole mushroom. In bowl with fork, beat egg whites with 2 teaspoons water; brush pastry edges.

8 Fold pastry over meat and mushroom; overlap edges; press to seal; place on cookie sheet. Refrigerate while preparing remainder.

9 Roll out pastry scraps; with sharp knife, cut into designs. Brush backs with egg white; arrange on pastry. Refrigerate.

10 *About 35 minutes before serving:* Preheat oven to 400°F. In cup, beat egg yolks with 2 teaspoons water; brush over pastry. Bake 25 minutes for rare, 27 minutes for medium-doneness. With pancake turner, place Wellingtons on warm platter. Garnish the platter with curly endive and, if you wish, preserved or fresh kumquats. These may be either sliced or left whole, if you prefer. Serve immediately.

Less tender roasts and pot roasts

Color index page 54
Begin 5 hrs ahead
20 servings

Country Pot Roast

2 garlic cloves
1 5-pound beef chuck cross rib pot roast boneless or bottom rump round roast
¼ cup all-purpose flour
¼ cup salad oil
1 cup tomato juice
2 medium carrots, sliced

2 medium onions, cut up
1 cup thinly sliced celery
1 tablespoon salt
1 teaspoon oregano leaves
¼ teaspoon pepper
celery leaves or parsley sprigs for garnish

1 Crush garlic; rub onto roast. On waxed paper, coat meat with flour.

2 In 8-quart Dutch oven over high heat, in hot salad oil, cook pot roast until it is evenly browned on all sides.

3 Add tomato juice and remaining ingredients except celery leaves; heat to boiling. Reduce the heat to low.

4 Cover Dutch oven and simmer for 4 hours or until the meat is fork-tender, turning it occasionally. Transfer the meat to a warm platter.

5 Fill blender three-fourths full with liquid and vegetables; cover; blend at high speed; pour into large bowl; repeat until all is blended.

6 Return the blended mixture to the Dutch oven; heat to boiling. Garnish the roast with celery leaves and serve with the hot gravy.

Sauerbraten

3 medium onions,
 sliced
3 medium carrots,
 sliced
2½ cups dry red wine
2 cups water
¼ cup red wine vinegar
2 large celery stalks,
 sliced
2 bay leaves
6 peppercorns
¼ teaspoon mustard
 seed
1 5-pound beef bottom
 round roast
2 tablespoons all-purpose
 flour

¼ teaspoon cracked
 black pepper
salt
¼ cup salad oil
 or shortening
⅓ cup fine gingersnap
 crumbs
½ cup sour cream

Color index page 54

Begin 2 to 3 days ahead

14 to 16 servings

1 In 3-quart saucepan over medium heat, heat 2 onions, 1 carrot and next 7 ingredients to boiling. Reduce heat to low; cover saucepan; simmer 10 minutes.

2 Pour into large bowl, cover and cool. Add roast, turning to coat. Cover and refrigerate 2 to 3 days, turning the meat each day.

3 *About 4 hours before serving:* Remove meat; dry with paper towels; coat with flour, pepper and 1 teaspoon salt. Strain marinade, reserving liquid.

4 In 8-quart Dutch oven over medium-high heat, in hot oil, cook meat until browned, 15 to 20 minutes. Remove meat; pour off all but 1 tablespoon of the drippings.

5 In drippings over medium heat, cook rest of vegetables 3 minutes, stirring. Add the meat.

6 Add marinade; heat to boiling. Reduce heat to low; cover; simmer 3½ hours, turn occasionally.

7 Remove meat to warm platter; keep warm. Spoon off and discard the fat from gravy.

8 Add cookie crumbs and 1 teaspoon salt. Over medium-high heat, stir until mixture thickens.

9 With a wire whisk, blend in sour cream. Cook, stirring, until heated through (do not boil).

10 Spoon some of the sour-cream gravy over the meat and pass remaining gravy separately.

Color index page 55

Begin 4 hrs ahead

8 to 10 servings

Baked Pot Roast with Vegetables

1 3-pound beef round
 rump roast
 boneless
1 large onion, sliced
1 garlic clove,
 crushed
2 tablespoons
 Worcestershire
4 teaspoons salt
1 teaspoon sugar

¼ teaspoon cracked
 black pepper
2 cups water
4 medium parsnips,
 cut into chunks
1 24-ounce bag frozen
 lima beans
parsley sprigs for garnish
 (optional)

1. In 5-quart Dutch oven, place beef round rump roast. Add onion, garlic, Worcestershire, salt, sugar, pepper and water. Cover and bake in 350°F. oven for 2 hours.
2. Add the parsnip chunks and the lima beans to the Dutch oven and continue baking 1 to 1½ hours more until the vegetables and the meat are fork-tender, turning the meat occasionally.
3. Transfer the meat to a warm platter. Remove the strings and discard them.
4. With slotted spoon, arrange vegetables around meat. With large spoon, skim fat from the liquid in Dutch oven. Serve liquid over meat and vegetables. Garnish with parsley if you like.

Color index page 55

Begin 4 hrs ahead

12 to 14 servings

Fruited Pot Roast

2 tablespoons shortening
 or salad oil
1 4-pound beef chuck eye
 roast boneless
2 medium onions, sliced
1 cup apple cider or juice
2 tablespoons brown
 sugar
2 teaspoons salt

1 teaspoon seasoned
 pepper
¼ teaspoon ground
 cloves
1½ cups dried apricots
1½ cups pitted prunes
2 tablespoons all-purpose
 flour (optional)
¼ cup water (optional)

1. In 5-quart Dutch oven over medium-high heat, in hot shortening, cook chuck roast until well browned on all sides.
2. Add onions, apple cider, brown sugar, salt, seasoned pepper and cloves; heat to boiling. Reduce heat to low; cover and simmer 3½ hours or until meat is almost fork-tender, turning meat occasionally and adding more cider during cooking if necessary.
3. Add the apricots and the pitted prunes to the mixture in the Dutch oven. Continue cooking 20 minutes or until the meat is fork-tender. Place the meat on a warm platter.
4. Spoon the fat from liquid in the Dutch oven. If you like, blend flour and water until smooth; gradually stir into the pan liquid and cook over medium heat, stirring constantly, until the mixture is thickened. Serve sauce with the meat.

Less tender roasts and pot roasts

Pot Roast with Sweet and Sour Cabbage

Color index page 51

Begin 3½ hrs ahead

10 servings

2 tablespoons salad oil
1 3-pound beef chuck eye roast boneless, cut 2 inches thick
2 medium onions, sliced
½ cup red wine vinegar
5 teaspoons salt
4 teaspoons light brown sugar

1 teaspoon caraway seed
½ teaspoon cracked black pepper
water
1 medium head red cabbage
2 tablespoons all-purpose flour

1. In 8-quart Dutch oven over medium-high heat, in hot oil, cook roast until well browned on all sides. Stir in onions, vinegar, salt, sugar, caraway seed, pepper and ¼ cup water; heat to boiling. Reduce heat to low; cover and simmer 2½ hours or until meat is fork-tender, turning meat occasionally. Meanwhile, coarsely shred cabbage; discard any tough ribs; set aside.
2. When meat is done, remove meat to large platter; keep warm. Skim off fat from liquid in Dutch oven. Add cabbage; over medium-high heat, heat to boiling. Reduce heat to low; cover and simmer 30 minutes or until cabbage is tender, stirring often.
3. In cup, stir flour and ¼ cup water until blended. Gradually stir flour mixture into cabbage in Dutch oven. Cook over medium heat, stirring gently, until mixture is thickened. Spoon cabbage around meat.

Pepper Beef Pot Roast

Color index page 53

Begin 3 hrs ahead

8 to 10 servings

2 tablespoons salad oil
3 large sweet red and/or green peppers, cut in ½-inch strips
1 3-pound beef chuck underblade pot roast, cut 1½ inches thick

1 medium onion, thinly sliced
¼ cup dry sherry
2 tablespoons soy sauce
water
1 tablespoon cornstarch
1 teaspoon sugar

1. In 8-quart Dutch oven over medium-high heat, in hot oil, cook pepper strips, stirring constantly with slotted spoon until tender-crisp, about 3 minutes. Remove peppers to medium bowl; cover; chill.
2. In oil remaining in Dutch oven, over medium-high heat, cook roast until browned on both sides. Add onion, sherry, soy sauce and 2 tablespoons water; heat to boiling. Reduce heat to low; cover and simmer 2 to 2½ hours until meat is fork-tender, adding more water, if necessary, and turning meat occasionally.
3. Place roast on warm large platter; keep warm. Pour pan liquid into 2-cup measure (set pan aside); let stand a few seconds until fat separates from meat juices. Skim 1 tablespoon fat from juices; return to Dutch oven. Spoon off and discard excess fat; add water to juices if necessary, to make 1½ cups.
4. Into fat in Dutch oven, stir cornstarch and sugar until blended; gradually stir in pan juices. Cook over medium heat, stirring, until thickened. Return peppers to Dutch oven; heat through.
5. To serve, spoon peppers around roast and pour remaining sauce on top of roast.

Mexican-style Pot Roast

Color index page 52

Begin 2¾ hrs ahead

10 to 12 servings

1 tablespoon salad oil
3 medium garlic cloves, each cut in half
1 3-pound beef chuck arm pot roast, cut 1½ inches thick
4 medium, hot red or hot green peppers, diced
2 medium onions, diced
1 16-ounce can tomato puree

¼ cup red wine vinegar
1 tablespoon sugar
1 tablespoon salt
1 teaspoon oregano leaves
4 medium green peppers, each cut into quarters
2 10-ounce packages frozen whole-kernel corn

1 In 8-quart Dutch oven over medium-high heat, in hot salad oil, cook the halved garlic cloves until lightly browned; discard garlic cloves.

2 Add beef chuck arm pot roast and cook until well browned on all sides. Remove the meat to a plate and set aside.

3 In same Dutch oven in drippings over medium heat, cook hot peppers and onions 10 minutes or until tender, stirring frequently.

4 Return meat to Dutch oven; add tomato puree, vinegar, sugar, salt and oregano; over high heat, heat to boiling. Reduce heat to low; cover and simmer 1 hour.

5 Add the quartered green peppers; cover and simmer 1 hour longer or until the meat is fork-tender. Carefully skim off the fat from juices remaining in Dutch oven.

6 Add the corn to the meat mixture; over high heat, heat to boiling. Reduce heat to low; cover and simmer 5 minutes or until the kernels of corn are tender.

Tenderloin

Barbecued Pot Roast

Color index
page 50

Begin 4 hrs
ahead

10 to 12
servings

2 tablespoons salad oil
1 5-pound beef chuck 7-
bone (center cut) pot
roast, cut 2½ inches
thick
2 medium onions, sliced
1 garlic clove, minced
1 8-ounce can tomato
sauce
1 6-ounce can tomato
paste

⅔ cup packed light
brown sugar
½ cup cider vinegar
1 tablespoon salt
2 tablespoons
Worcestershire
1 teaspoon dry mustard
¼ teaspoon pepper
2 bay leaves
parsley sprigs for garnish

1. In 8-quart Dutch oven over medium-high heat, in hot salad oil, cook pot roast until well browned on both sides. Remove meat to platter.
2. In same Dutch oven over medium heat, in drippings, cook onions and garlic until lightly browned, about 5 minutes, stirring occasionally. Spoon off drippings from Dutch oven. Stir in tomato sauce and remaining ingredients except parsley. Return meat to Dutch oven. Over high heat, heat to boiling. Reduce heat to low; cover and simmer 3¼ hours or until meat is fork-tender, turning meat once.
3. To serve: Place meat on platter. Skim fat from liquid; discard bay leaves; spoon liquid into gravy boat. Garnish roast with parsley.

Mushroom Sherry Pot Roast

Color index
page 52

Begin 3 hrs
ahead

8 to 10
servings

1 tablespoon salad oil
1 2¾-pound beef
chuck shoulder
pot roast boneless,
cut 1½ inches thick
¾ pound mushrooms
⅓ cup dry sherry
water

1 teaspoon salt
1 bay leaf
1 tablespoon butter or
margarine
1 tablespoon all-purpose
flour
parsley sprigs for garnish

1. In 12-inch skillet over medium-high heat, in hot oil, cook roast until well browned on both sides. Reserve 6 large mushrooms for garnish; remove stems. Dice stems and remaining mushrooms.
2. Add diced mushrooms, sherry, ⅓ cup water, salt and bay leaf to skillet; heat to boiling. Reduce heat to low; cover and simmer 2 hours until meat is fork-tender, turning once.
3. *About 15 minutes before meat is done:* Flute reserved mushroom caps: Hold mushroom, top up. Beginning at center-top of mushroom and rotating cap, cut curved slit from center of cap to outside edge. Space several curved slits around cap. Cut second set of slits parallel to the first to make thin wedges. Lift out wedges; add to skillet.
4. In small skillet over medium-low heat, in hot butter, cook mushroom caps, turning once, until golden brown, about 5 minutes; keep warm.
5. When roast is done, place on warm platter; keep warm. In cup, blend flour and 2 tablespoons water. Gradually stir into liquid in skillet; cook, stirring, until slightly thickened; discard bay leaf.
6. To serve, pour some gravy over roast. Garnish with fluted mushrooms and parsley. Pass remaining gravy in gravy boat.

Filets Mignons
with Mustard-Caper Sauce

Color index
page 51

Begin 30 mins
ahead

6 servings

3 tablespoons butter
6 loin tenderloin steaks,
each cut 1½ inches
thick
½ cup dry vermouth
2 tablespoons chopped
green onions
½ cup water
½ cup heavy or whipping
cream

2 tablespoons capers
2½ teaspoons prepared
mustard
1 teaspoon salt
½ teaspoon coarsely
ground black pepper
1 beef-flavor bouillon
cube or envelope
watercress for garnish

1. In 12-inch skillet over medium-high heat, in hot butter, cook steaks until underside is browned, about 4 minutes; turn and cook about 5 minutes longer for rare. Remove steaks to warm platter and keep warm.
2. Reduce heat to medium. To drippings in skillet add vermouth and green onions; cook about 2 minutes, stirring to loosen brown bits on bottom of skillet. Stir in water, heavy cream, capers, prepared mustard, salt, coarsely ground black pepper and bouillon cube; heat sauce to boiling.
3. To serve: Garnish platter with watercress. Pass sauce in gravy boat.

Châteaubriand

Color index
page 55

Begin 1½ hrs
ahead

8 servings

8 large artichokes
2 2-pound beef
loin tenderloin
roasts

1 tablespoon salt
Béarnaise Sauce
(page 463)

1. Prepare artichokes (page 277), but cut off two-thirds of tops, leaving 1-inch bottoms. Cook bottoms; cool slightly; with spoon, scoop out and discard fuzzy "chokes." Return the artichokes to cooking liquid and keep them warm.
2. Preheat the broiler if manufacturer directs. Sprinkle roasts with salt. Place both pieces of meat on rack in the broiling pan; broil 30 minutes for rare or until of the desired doneness, turning once.
3. Prepare Béarnaise Sauce.
4. To serve: With slotted spoon, remove artichoke bottoms from cooking liquid; drain on paper towels; spoon some Béarnaise Sauce into center of each. Slice meat thickly. Arrange meat slices on center of warm large platter and surround them with the stuffed artichokes.

Serving Châteaubriand:
Slice the meat and arrange on warm platter with the stuffed artichokes.

195

Tender steaks

London Broil

**1 1½-pound high-
  quality beef flank
  steak
seasoned salt
seasoned pepper
2 medium tomatoes
bottled Italian
  dressing
6 large mushrooms**

Color index
page 51

Begin 30 mins
ahead

4 servings

1 Preheat broiler if
manufacturer directs.
With sharp knife, score
both sides of the
steak; place on rack in
broiling pan.

2 Sprinkle steak with 1
teaspoon seasoned salt,
⅛ teaspoon seasoned pep-
per. Cut tomatoes in half.

3 Brush tomatoes with
Italian dressing and
arrange, cut side up,
around steak; broil 5
minutes. Meanwhile, wash
and slice mushrooms.

4 With tongs, turn steak;
sprinkle with 1 tea-
spoon seasoned salt, ⅛
teaspoon seasoned pepper.

5 Arrange mushroom
slices in overlapping
rows on broiler rack; brush
with Italian dressing.

6 Broil the steak 5
minutes more for rare
or 6 minutes for medium.
To check the doneness,
with a knife, make a small
cut in the center of meat.

7 With knife in slanting
position, carve thin
slices across width of
steak. Serve slices with
broiled vegetables. Spoon
drippings over, if you like.

Marinated Porterhouse Steak

**1 4-pound beef loin
  porterhouse or pin bone
  sirloin steak, cut about
  1½ inches thick
½ cup red Burgundy**

**1 tablespoon seasoned
  salt
¼ teaspoon seasoned
  pepper**

Color index
page 52

Begin early in
day or
day ahead

10 to 12
servings

1. In large, shallow baking dish, place steak. For
marinade, pour wine over steak. Cover and refrigerate at least 4 hours or overnight, turning meat
occasionally.
2. *About 40 minutes before serving:* Preheat broiler if
manufacturer directs. With tongs, place steak on
greased rack in broiling pan; reserve marinade.
Sprinkle steak with seasoned salt and pepper.
3. Broil steak 30 minutes for rare or until of desired
doneness, basting occasionally with marinade and
turning once.

ZESTY MARINADE: Prepare as above, but in step
1, omit wine; substitute mixture of ⅓ *cup bottled
steak sauce, 3 tablespoons lemon juice, 2 tablespoons
salad oil and 1½ teaspoons sugar.* In step 2, omit
seasoned salt and seasoned pepper; sprinkle steak
with ½ *teaspoon salt* and ¼ *teaspoon pepper.*

Steak Diane

Color index
page 52

Begin 20 mins
ahead

4 servings

**4 beef rib eye steaks,
  each cut about ½ inch
  thick
salt
pepper
4 tablespoons butter or
  margarine**

**¼ cup brandy
2 small shallots, minced
3 tablespoons chopped
  chives
½ cup dry sherry**

1. On cutting board, with meat mallet, edge of plate
or the dull edge of French knife, pound the steaks
until about ¼ inch thick, turning occasionally.
Sprinkle each of the steaks with salt and pepper.
2. In chafing dish over high heat, in 1 tablespoon hot
butter or margarine, cook one steak just until both
sides are browned.
3. Pour 1 tablespoon brandy over steak and with
match set aflame. When the flaming stops, stir in ¼
each of shallots and chives; cook, stirring constantly, until the shallots are tender, about 1 minute.
Add 2 tablespoons sherry; heat through.
4. Place the steak on a warm dinner plate and pour
sherry mixture over it. Keep warm. Repeat with
remaining steaks.

Pounding steaks: Use a
meat mallet to pound
steaks to ¼ inch thick.

Flaming steaks: Pour over
brandy then use long
match to set steaks aflame.

Deviled Round Steak

Color index
page 54

Begin 1½ hrs
ahead

12 to 14
servings

1 4-pound beef top round steak, cut 1½ inches thick	1 teaspoon dry mustard
6 tablespoons butter or margarine, softened	½ teaspoon curry powder
1 tablespoon Worcestershire	¼ teaspoon salt
	¼ teaspoon pepper
	1 cup dried bread crumbs

1. Prepare outdoor grill for barbecuing. Meanwhile, trim any excess fat from the round steak. In small bowl, mix the butter or margarine with the Worcestershire, dry mustard, curry powder, salt and pepper; set mixture aside.
2. Place steak on grill over medium coals; grill 35 minutes for rare or until of the desired doneness, turning occasionally.
3. Remove the steak from the grill. With narrow metal spatula, spread one side of steak with ½ of butter mixture and pat on ½ of bread crumbs. Repeat with remaining butter mixture and bread crumbs on other side of steak.
4. Return steak to grill; continue grilling 5 minutes longer or until crumbs are golden, turning once.

TO BROIL IN OVEN: About 1 hour before serving, preheat broiler if manufacturer directs. Place steak on rack in broiling pan. About 3 to 5 inches from source of heat, broil steak 35 minutes for rare or until of desired doneness, turning once. Remove steak from broiler and season on both sides as above with butter mixture and bread crumbs. Return steak to broiler; broil 3 to 5 minutes on each side or until crumbs are golden.

Continental Beef Steak

Color index
page 55

Begin 1 hr
ahead

12 to 14
servings

1 4-pound beef top round steak, cut about 1½ inches thick	1½ cups thinly sliced celery
unseasoned instant meat tenderizer	2 14½-ounce cans sliced baby tomatoes, drained
½ teaspoon oregano	1 10-ounce jar colossal stuffed olives, drained and halved
¼ teaspoon seasoned pepper	2 tablespoons capers, drained
1 garlic clove, minced	
3 large green or red peppers	
3 tablespoons salad oil	

1. Preheat broiler if manufacturer directs. With sharp knife, lightly score both sides of steak. Use meat tenderizer as label directs; sprinkle both sides of steak with oregano, seasoned pepper and minced garlic. Place steak on greased rack in broiling pan; broil 35 minutes for rare or until of desired doneness, turning once.
2. Meanwhile, slice the green peppers crosswise into rings; discard the seeds.
3. In 12-inch skillet over medium-high heat, in hot salad oil, cook peppers and celery 10 minutes or until tender-crisp. Add tomatoes, olives and capers; heat through.
4. Place steak on warm large platter; with slotted spoon, spoon vegetables around it.

Steak Medici

Color index
page 53

Begin 25 mins
ahead

4 servings

4 tablespoons butter or margarine
4 beef top loin steaks boneless, each cut ¾ inch thick
½ pound mushrooms, cut into ¼-inch slices
¾ teaspoon salt or seasoned salt
¼ cup red port wine
chopped parsley for garnish

1. In 12-inch skillet over medium-high heat, in 2 tablespoons hot butter, brown steaks on both sides. Use tongs to turn them.

2. Cook until of the desired doneness, about 3 minutes per side for rare. Remove the steaks to a large warm platter and keep warm.

3. In same skillet over medium heat, melt the remaining butter.

4. Add the sliced mushrooms together with the salt and cook, stirring, until the mushrooms are just tender.

5. Stir in wine, scraping to loosen brown bits from bottom of skillet.

6. Pour mushroom and wine mixture over steaks; garnish steaks with chopped parsley and serve immediately.

Tender steaks

Sesame Chuck Steak

½ cup salad oil
⅓ cup sesame seed
4 medium onions
½ cup soy sauce
¼ cup lemon juice
1 tablespoon sugar
¼ teaspoon cracked
    black pepper
2 garlic cloves,
    crushed
1 2½-pound beef chuck
    blade steak,
    cut 1 inch thick
watercress sprigs for
    garnish

Color index
page 50

Begin early
in day or
day ahead

8 to 10
servings

1 In 10-inch skillet over medium-high heat, in hot salad oil, cook sesame seed until golden, stirring. Slice onions thickly.

2 In 13″ by 9″ baking dish, mix sesame-seed-oil mixture and onions. Add next 5 ingredients.

3 Trim excess fat from steak; add meat to marinade; turn to coat; cover; chill at least 8 hours, turning occasionally.

4 45 minutes before serving: Preheat broiler if manufacturer directs. Place steak on rack in broiling pan. Drain onions; set aside; reserve marinade.

5 Broil steak 25 minutes for rare or as desired, brushing frequently with the marinade. Turn steak once.

6 In 10-inch skillet over medium heat, cook onions and remaining marinade until tender, stirring occasionally.

7 To serve, arrange the steak and sliced onions on a heated large platter. Garnish with sprigs of watercress.

Cubed Steaks with Fresh Tomato Sauce

Color index
page 53

Begin 45 mins
ahead

6 to 8
servings

¼ cup salad oil
2 pounds beef or veal
    cubed steaks
6 medium tomatoes
¼ cup chopped green
    onions

2 tablespoons sugar
2 teaspoons salt
2 teaspoons basil
2 tablespoons
    cornstarch
cold water

1. In 10- or 12-inch skillet over medium-high heat, in hot salad oil, cook steaks, a few at a time, 2 or 3 minutes on each side or until of desired doneness; place on warm platter and keep warm. Chop 3 tomatoes and slice the rest.

2. Reduce heat to medium; to same skillet, add ¼ cup water, chopped tomatoes, green onions, sugar, salt and basil. Blend cornstarch and ¼ cup water until smooth; gradually stir into tomato mixture and cook, stirring, until thickened. Add sliced tomatoes; cook until heated through. Spoon tomato mixture over steaks.

Teriyaki Beef Kabobs

Color index
page 53

Begin 4 hrs
ahead or
early in day

6 to 8
servings

1 2-pound beef top round
    steak, cut about 1 inch
    thick
¼ cup packed light
    brown sugar
¼ cup soy sauce
2 tablespoons lemon
    juice
1 tablespoon salad oil

¼ teaspoon ground
    ginger
1 garlic clove,
    minced
1 small pineapple,
    cut into 1-inch
    chunks

1. Trim any excess fat from steak and cut meat into 1-inch chunks.

2. Prepare marinade: Combine brown sugar, soy sauce, lemon juice, oil, ginger and garlic; stir in beef chunks. Cover and refrigerate at least 3 hours, stirring meat often.

3. About 30 minutes before serving: Preheat broiler if manufacturer directs. Thread meat and pineapple chunks alternately on 12-inch metal skewers. (Pineapple quickly tenderizes meat, so thread skewers just before broiling; if done earlier, meat becomes mushy.)

4. Broil 15 minutes until rare or of desired doneness, basting occasionally with marinade and turning once. To check doneness make slit in center of meat.

Marinating beef: Stir meat into marinade; cover; refrigerate 3 hours, stirring mixture often.

Threading skewers: Just before broiling, thread meat and pineapple alternately on skewers.

Less tender steaks

Carbonnade of Beef

Color index
page 51

Begin 1½ hrs
ahead

8 servings

*2 beef chuck eye steaks
boneless, each cut
1 inch thick
(about 2¾ pounds)*
*4 tablespoons butter or
margarine*
*2 large onions,
sliced*
*1 small garlic clove,
minced*
*1 beef-flavor bouillon
cube or envelope*

*½ teaspoon salt or
seasoned salt*
*¼ teaspoon thyme
leaves*
*⅛ teaspoon cracked
black pepper*
*½ 12-ounce can beer
(¾ cup)*
*1 tablespoon all-purpose
flour*

1 On cutting board, cut each chuck eye steak crosswise into 4 pieces.

2 In 12-inch skillet over medium-high heat, in 2 tablespoons hot butter, cook the steak pieces, a few at a time, until they are browned on all sides. Remove to a platter.

3 Reduce heat to medium. In same skillet, melt remaining butter. Stir in onions and garlic; cook, stirring, until onions are tender, about 10 minutes.

4 Stir in bouillon, salt, thyme leaves, pepper and ½ cup beer, scraping to loosen brown bits from bottom of skillet. Return steaks to skillet; heat to boiling.

5 Reduce heat to low; cover and simmer 50 minutes or until the steaks are fork-tender, turning once. Arrange on a warm platter and keep warm.

6 Prepare the gravy: Carefully skim off the fat in the skillet. In a small cup with a spoon, combine flour and remaining ¼ cup beer; stir until well blended. Gradually stir into the liquid in the skillet and cook over medium heat, stirring constantly until the gravy is smooth and thickened. Spoon some of the gravy over the steaks on the platter. Pour the remaining gravy in the skillet into a gravy boat to pass it separately when serving the steaks.

Spicy Beef Chuck Steak

Color index
page 54

Begin 2 hrs
ahead

8 to 10
servings

1 tablespoon salad oil
*1 beef chuck underblade
steak (about 3 pounds),
cut 1 inch thick*
*½ cup bottled steak
sauce*
¼ cup water

*3 tablespoons brown
sugar*
*2 tablespoons prepared
mustard*
1 teaspoon lemon juice
parsley sprigs for garnish

1. In 12-inch skillet over medium-high heat, in hot salad oil, cook chuck steak until well browned on both sides.
2. Meanwhile, in cup, combine steak sauce, water, brown sugar, mustard and lemon juice until blended. Pour mixture over steak; heat to boiling. Reduce heat to low; cover and simmer steak 1½ hours or until fork-tender, turning steak once.
3. To serve, with 2 pancake turners, remove steak to warm large platter; garnish with parsley. With a spoon, skim fat from liquid in skillet and discard. Pour liquid over steak or serve separately.

BEEF STEAK CREOLE: Prepare as in step 1, above, but use 8-quart Dutch oven and in step 2, omit steak sauce, water, brown sugar, prepared mustard and lemon juice. Remove meat from Dutch oven and into hot fat, stir *¼ cup all-purpose flour*, stirring constantly until flour is dark brown (mixture will be thick). Add *2 large celery stalks*, diced, *1 medium green pepper*, diced and *1 medium onion*, diced; cook over medium heat until vegetables are tender, about 10 minutes. Add *one 16-ounce can stewed tomatoes, 1 tablespoon sugar, 2½ teaspoons salt* and *½ teaspoon hot pepper sauce*. Add meat and cook.

Beef with Leeks and Carrots

Color index
page 54

Begin 2 hrs
ahead

6 to 8
servings

*1 tablespoon salad
oil*
*1 beef chuck
7-bone steak
cut 1 inch thick
(about 2½ pounds)*
*1 beef-flavor bouillon
cube or envelope*
1 bay leaf
½ teaspoon salt

*¼ teaspoon thyme
leaves*
*⅛ teaspoon pepper
water*
3 large leeks
6 large carrots
*1 tablespoon all-purpose
flour*

1. In 8-quart Dutch oven over medium-high heat, in hot salad oil, cook chuck steak until well browned on both sides. Add bouillon, bay leaf, salt, thyme, pepper and 1 cup water; heat to boiling. Reduce heat to low; cover and simmer steak 1¼ hours or until almost fork-tender.
2. Meanwhile, cut off roots and discard tough outer green leaves from leeks. Cut leeks lengthwise in half; rinse under running cold water to remove sand. Cut leeks crosswise into 2-inch pieces. Thinly slice carrots.
3. Place leeks and carrots in liquid around steak. Cover and cook 20 minutes longer or until steak and vegetables are fork-tender; discard bay leaf. In cup, combine flour and ¼ cup water until blended. Stir flour mixture into hot liquid in pan. Cook over medium heat, stirring until slightly thickened.

Less tender steaks

Swiss Steak with Tomato

Color index
page 55

Begin 2½ hrs
ahead

8 to 10
servings

*1 2½- to 3-pound beef
chuck arm steak
boneless, cut about 1
inch thick*
*2 tablespoons all-purpose
flour*
3 tablespoons salad oil
*2 large onions, thinly
sliced*
*1 small green pepper,
diced*
*1 8-ounce can tomato
sauce*

*1 small garlic clove,
minced*
1 teaspoon salt
¼ teaspoon pepper
1 bay leaf
*hot mashed potatoes,
buttered cooked
noodles or cooked
rice (optional)*
*celery leaves for
garnish (optional)*

1 Cut off any excess fat from arm steak. On cutting board, coat meat on one side with half of flour.

2 With a meat mallet, pound the meat well. Turn meat over and repeat the flouring and pounding with the mallet on the other side.

3 In 12-inch skillet over medium-high heat, in hot salad oil, cook meat until well browned on both sides. Remove meat.

4 To drippings in skillet, add onions and green pepper and cook, stirring frequently, until onions are lightly browned, about 5 minutes.

5 Add tomato sauce, next 4 ingredients and meat; heat to boiling. Reduce heat to low; cover and simmer about 2 hours or until meat is fork-tender, turning meat once.

6 To serve, place meat on warm platter. Discard bay leaf; spoon fat from liquid in skillet. Serve meat and liquid with mashed potatoes. If you like, garnish with celery leaves.

Oriental Anise Beef

Color index
page 53

Begin 2¼ hrs
ahead

6 to 8 servings

1 bunch green onions
½ cup dry sherry
¼ cup soy sauce
1 tablespoon sugar
*2 teaspoons anise
seed*
*½ teaspoon ground
ginger*

water
*1 beef chuck shoulder
steak boneless, cut 1½
inches thick (about 2
pounds)*
2 teaspoons cornstarch
hot cooked rice

1. Cut off roots from onions; cut onions into 1-inch pieces. In 10-inch skillet, place half of the onion pieces; stir in sherry, soy sauce, sugar, anise seed, ground ginger and ¼ cup water. Add the steak. Over high heat, heat to boiling. Reduce heat to low; cover and simmer steak 1¾ hours or until fork-tender, turning steak once.
2. When steak is done, remove to platter; keep warm. In cup, combine ¼ cup water and cornstarch until blended. Gradually stir cornstarch mixture into liquid in skillet. Cook over medium heat, stirring constantly, until thickened. Stir in remaining half of onion pieces. Spoon sauce over steak. Cut steak into thin slices to serve. Serve with rice.

Creamy Top Blade Steaks

Color index
page 50

Begin 1¾ hrs
ahead

4 to 6 servings

1 tablespoon salad oil
*4 beef chuck top blade
steaks boneless, each
cut 1 inch thick (about
1½ pounds)*
⅓ cup water
*1 beef-flavor bouillon
cube or envelope*

½ teaspoon salt
⅛ teaspoon pepper
*¾ 8-ounce package
medium egg noodles*
*1 8-ounce container sour
cream*
½ teaspoon dill weed
watercress for garnish

1. In 12-inch skillet over medium-high heat, in hot oil, cook steaks until well browned on both sides. Stir in water, bouillon, salt and pepper; heat to boiling. Reduce heat to low; cover and simmer steaks 1¼ hours or until fork-tender, turning steaks with tongs once during cooking.
2. Prepare noodles as label directs.
3. When steaks are done, remove to warm large platter. Drain noodles; place on platter; keep warm. Stir sour cream and dill into hot liquid in skillet. Cook, stirring, until slightly thickened (do not boil). Spoon some sauce over steaks; pass remainder in sauceboat. Garnish platter with watercress.

Serving steaks: Spoon some sauce over meat and noodles. Pass remainder separately. Garnish platter with watercress.

Braised Steak Caesar-style

Color index
page 51

Begin 1¾ hrs
ahead

4 servings

⅓ cup olive or salad oil	1 tablespoon
2 garlic cloves, sliced	Worcestershire
4 diagonal slices French	1 teaspoon lemon juice
bread, each cut ½ inch	¼ teaspoon dry mustard
thick	water
4 beef eye round steaks,	1 tablespoon all-purpose
each cut 1 inch thick	flour
(about 1½ pounds)	chopped parsley for
1 2-ounce can anchovy	garnish
fillets, drained	

1. In 10-inch skillet over medium heat, in hot oil, brown garlic; discard garlic. Spoon all but 1 tablespoon oil into a small bowl.

2. In remaining oil, cook bread until golden on both sides, adding a little more garlic-flavored oil if needed. Remove bread to platter.

3. In same skillet over medium-high heat, heat remaining garlic-flavored oil. Add steaks; cook until well browned on both sides. Meanwhile, mince enough anchovies to make 1 tablespoon.

4. When steaks are browned, stir in minced anchovies, Worcestershire, lemon juice, mustard and ⅓ cup water; heat to boiling. Reduce heat to low; cover and simmer steaks 1¼ hours or until fork-tender, turning once.

5. Place 1 steak on each piece of toast; keep warm. In cup, blend flour and ¼ cup water. Stir into hot liquid in skillet. Cook over medium heat, stirring until thickened. Spoon some sauce over steaks; pass remainder in sauceboat. Garnish with parsley and remaining anchovies.

Beef Steak Stroganoff

Color index
page 54

Begin 1¾ hrs
ahead

4 to 6 servings

1 tablespoon butter	1 8-ounce package wide
4 beef chuck top blade	egg noodles
steaks boneless, each	1 tablespoon all-purpose
cut 1 inch thick (about	flour
1½ pounds)	½ cup sour cream
1 medium onion, sliced	1 tablespoon chopped
1 teaspoon salt	parsley for garnish
⅛ teaspoon pepper	(optional)
water	
2 4- or 4½-ounce cans	
whole mushrooms	

1. In 12-inch skillet over medium-high heat, in hot butter, cook steaks and onion until meat is well browned on both sides, about 10 minutes. Add salt, pepper, ¼ cup water and liquid from mushrooms; heat to boiling. Reduce heat to low; cover and simmer 1¼ hours or until steaks are fork-tender. Add mushrooms; heat through.

2. About 20 minutes before steaks are done, prepare noodles as label directs; drain. Spoon noodles onto warm platter.

3. Remove steaks and mushrooms to platter with noodles; keep warm. In cup stir flour and ¼ cup water until blended. Gradually stir into liquid in skillet. Cook over medium heat until sauce is thickened, stirring. Stir in sour cream; heat through (do not boil). Spoon sauce over steaks and noodles. Sprinkle with parsley if you like.

Celery-stuffed Flank Steak

Color index
page 51

Begin 2½ hrs
ahead

6 to 8 servings

1 2-pound beef flank	⅛ teaspoon thyme leaves,
steak	crushed
pepper	water
1 cup fresh bread crumbs	all-purpose flour
¾ cup diced celery	1 tablespoon cornstarch
1 small onion, minced	¼ teaspoon ground
butter or margarine	ginger
½ teaspoon salt	

1. With a large sharp knife, score the steak to make a diamond pattern on both sides; sprinkle the steak with pepper.

2. In medium bowl, combine bread crumbs, celery, onion, 1 tablespoon melted butter or margarine, salt, thyme, ⅛ teaspoon pepper and 2 tablespoons water; spread evenly on one side of steak, leaving a 1-inch border. Roll steak from a long side, jelly-roll fashion; secure with toothpicks or string. On waxed paper, coat meat lightly with flour.

3. In 5-quart Dutch oven over medium-high heat, in 2 tablespoons hot butter or margarine, cook the meat until well browned on all sides. Add 1 cup water; heat to boiling. Reduce heat to low; cover and simmer 2 hours or until meat is fork-tender, stirring liquid and adding water, if necessary. Place meat on warm platter: remove toothpicks or string and keep meat warm.

4. In cup, blend cornstarch and ginger with 2 tablespoons cold water until smooth; stir into hot liquid in Dutch oven and cook over medium heat, stirring constantly, until mixture is thickened. Stir in more water, if necessary. Serve gravy separately in sauceboat, to eat with steak.

Scoring steak: Use a sharp knife to score both sides of the flank steak in a diamond pattern.

Stuffing steak: Spread stuffing then roll up from long side jelly-roll fashion. Secure with toothpicks.

Serving steak: Cut the steak into slices and serve with gravy passed separately in sauceboat.

Stew meat

Beef Stew

2½ pounds beef for stew
⅓ cup all-purpose flour
⅓ cup salad oil
1 large onion, chopped
1 garlic clove, minced
3 cups water
4 beef-bouillon cubes
1 teaspoon salt
½ teaspoon
    Worcestershire
¼ teaspoon pepper
5 medium potatoes,
    cut in chunks
1 16-ounce bag carrots,
    cut in chunks
1 10-ounce package
    frozen peas

Color index
page 54

Begin 3½ hrs
ahead

8 to 10
servings

1 Cut meat into 1½-inch chunks. On waxed paper, coat stew meat with flour; reserve leftover flour. In 6-quart Dutch oven over medium-high heat, heat oil.

2 Brown meat all over in oil, a few pieces at a time; remove pieces as they brown. Reduce heat to medium.

3 To drippings in pan, add onion and garlic; cook 3 minutes, stirring, until onion is almost tender. Stir in reserved flour.

4 Gradually add water, bouillon, salt, Worcestershire, pepper; cook, stirring, until mixture is slightly thickened.

5 Add meat; heat to boiling, stirring. Reduce heat to low; cover; simmer 2½ hours until almost tender, stirring occasionally.

6 Add potato and carrot chunks; over medium heat, heat to boiling. Reduce heat to low; cover and simmer 20 minutes.

7 Stir in frozen peas; cover and simmer 5 to 10 minutes or until all the vegetables are tender. Serve immediately.

Beef Bourguignon

1 8-ounce package sliced
    bacon, cut into 1-inch
    pieces
20 small white onions
3 pounds beef for stew,
    cut into 2-inch chunks
all-purpose flour
1 large carrot,
    chopped
1 large onion,
    chopped
¼ cup brandy

2 garlic cloves,
    crushed
2 teaspoons salt
½ teaspoon thyme
    leaves, crushed
¼ teaspoon pepper
1 bay leaf
3 cups red Burgundy
butter or margarine
1 pound mushrooms,
    sliced

Color index
page 53

Begin 4½ hrs
ahead

10 servings

1. In 6-quart Dutch oven over medium-high heat, cook the bacon pieces until browned. With a slotted spoon, remove the bacon to paper towels to drain; set aside.

2. Discard all but 3 tablespoons drippings. In drippings in Dutch oven, cook small white onions until lightly browned, stirring occasionally. With slotted spoon, remove the onions and place in a small bowl; set aside.

3. Meanwhile, on waxed paper, coat meat chunks with 3 tablespoons flour. In drippings in Dutch oven over medium-high heat, cook meat, several pieces at a time, until well browned on all sides, removing pieces as they brown.

4. To drippings in the Dutch oven, add the chopped carrot and onion and cook over medium heat, stirring frequently, until tender, about 5 minutes. Return the beef to Dutch oven; pour brandy over all and set aflame with match. When flaming stops, add reserved bacon, garlic, salt, thyme leaves, pepper, bay leaf and Burgundy. Cover and bake in 325°F. oven 3½ hours or until fork-tender.

5. About 1 hour before meat is done, in 10-inch skillet over medium heat, in 2 tablespoons hot butter or margarine, cook mushrooms until golden brown, about 7 minutes.

6. Meanwhile, in small bowl with spoon, mix 2 tablespoons softened butter or margarine and 2 tablespoons flour until smooth.

7. Remove Dutch oven from oven. Into hot liquid in Dutch oven, add flour mixture, ½ teaspoon at a time, stirring after each addition, until blended. Add reserved onions and mushrooms to Dutch oven. Cover and bake until onions are fork-tender. Serve immediately.

Flaming beef: Pour brandy over beef, carrot and onion and immediately set aflame with a long match.

Thickening sauce: Stir in flour mixture, ½ teaspoon at a time, until blended; return to oven.

Color index page 50

Begin 3 hrs ahead

6 to 8 servings

California Beef Stew

3 bacon slices, diced
2 pounds beef for stew,
 cut in 1½-inch chunks
water
1 cup dry red wine
1 beef-flavor bouillon
 cube
2 garlic cloves, minced
½ small onion, minced
2 teaspoons salt

¼ teaspoon thyme leaves
1 strip orange peel
18 small white onions
¾ pound small
 mushrooms
2 tablespoons cornstarch
1 10-ounce package
 frozen peas
½ cup pitted ripe olives,
 drained

1. In 6-quart Dutch oven over medium-high heat, fry bacon until crisp; push bacon to side of pan.
2. To drippings in pan, add stew meat and cook until well browned. Stir in 1 cup water, wine and next 6 ingredients; heat to boiling. Reduce heat to low; cover and simmer 2½ hours or until meat is fork-tender, stirring occasionally.
3. Meanwhile, in covered, 2-quart saucepan over high heat, in about 1 inch boiling salted water, cook onions 10 minutes; add mushrooms; cook 5 more minutes; drain.
4. Blend cornstarch and 3 tablespoons water; stir into stew; cook over medium heat, stirring, until thickened. Add onions, mushrooms, frozen peas and olives; cover; cook 10 minutes or until peas are fork-tender. Serve immediately.

Color index page 52

Begin early in day

6 to 8 servings

Pressure-cooked Beef Stew

½ cup red table wine
2 tablespoons salad oil
2 pounds beef for stew,
 cut into 1½-inch chunks
¼ pound lean salt pork,
 cut into ½-inch cubes
1 16-ounce can tomatoes
1 large onion, minced
1 large carrot, minced
1 celery stalk, minced

½ garlic clove, minced
1 bay leaf
1½ teaspoons salt
1 teaspoon thyme leaves
3 parsley sprigs
12 stuffed olives, halved
1 3-ounce can whole
 mushrooms, drained
hot cooked noodles
 (optional)

1. Prepare marinade: In large bowl, combine wine and salad oil. Add beef chunks and turn over to coat with marinade. Cover and refrigerate at least 4 hours, turning often.
2. *About 30 minutes before serving:* Drain meat, discard marinade. In 4-quart pressure cooker over medium-high heat, fry salt pork until golden; add beef and cook until well browned. Add tomatoes and their liquid and remaining ingredients except mushrooms. Cover and bring cooker to 15 pounds pressure as manufacturer directs; cook 20 minutes. Remove cooker from heat and reduce pressure quickly as manufacturer directs before uncovering. Add mushrooms and heat. Discard parsley and bay leaf. Serve over noodles if you like.

Steak and Kidney Pie

1 beef kidney (about 1
 pound)
2½ pounds beef for stew,
 cut into 1-inch chunks
¼ cup all-purpose
 flour
salad oil
1 large onion, chopped
½ cup dry red wine or
 beer
water
2 beef-flavor bouillon
 cubes or envelopes
2 teaspoons
 Worcestershire

¼ teaspoon pepper
pastry for 9-inch
 Unbaked Piecrust
 (page 344)
1 egg yolk

Color index page 53

Begin 3¾ hrs ahead

8 to 10 servings

1 Wash kidney; remove membrane and hard white parts and with sharp knife, cut into 1-inch chunks.

2 On waxed paper, coat kidney and beef chunks with flour. In 5-quart Dutch oven over medium-high heat, heat 3 table-spoons oil.

3 Cook kidney and beef chunks, several pieces at a time, until well brown-ed. Remove pieces as they brown and add more oil, as needed.

4 Reduce heat to medium; add onion to drippings. Cook until onion is almost tender, about 3 minutes, stirring occasionally.

5 Stir in wine, ½ cup water, bouillon, Worcestershire and pep-per, stirring to dissolve bouillon cubes.

6 Add meat and heat to boiling; reduce heat to low. Cover and simmer 2 hours or until meat is fork-tender.

7 Spoon mixture into 2-quart round shallow casserole. Preheat oven to 400°F. Prepare pastry; roll into circle 1 inch larger than casserole.

8 Fit crust loosely over meat mixture; trim back pastry overhang to about 1 inch and make a fluted edge.

9 Beat egg yolk with 1 teaspoon water. Brush pastry with egg-yolk mix-ture. With point of knife, make slits in crust.

10 Bake pie 40 minutes until browned and bubbly. Cover loosely with foil if crust browns too quickly.

Short ribs and shanks

Herbed Short Ribs

Color index
page 53

Begin 3 hrs
ahead

4 servings

all-purpose flour
3 pounds beef chuck short
ribs
2 tablespoons salad oil
or shortening
water
1 small onion,
chopped
2 tablespoons catchup
2 teaspoons salt
¼ teaspoon pepper
¼ teaspoon thyme leaves,
crushed

1 In ¼ cup flour on waxed paper, with tongs, coat the chuck short ribs well on all sides.

2 In 12-inch skillet with ovensafe handle over medium-high heat, in hot oil or shortening, cook meat until well browned on all sides.

3 Add ½ cup water, onion, catchup, salt, pepper and thyme to meat in the skillet.

4 Cover skillet. Bake in 350°F. oven 2½ hours or until meat is fork-tender, stirring once or twice during cooking.

5 With slotted spoon, remove meat to warm platter; keep warm while making gravy.

6 Spoon off all but 3 tablespoons drippings from skillet, leaving browned bits in pan; over medium heat, stir in 2 tablespoons flour.

7 Gradually stir in 1¼ cups water and cook, stirring constantly, until mixture is smooth and thickened. Spoon gravy over the meat.

Barbecued Short Ribs

Color index
page 54

Begin early
in day or
day ahead

6 to 8 servings

5 pounds beef chuck
short ribs
water
1½ cups catchup
½ cup white vinegar
⅓ cup packed brown
sugar
1 tablespoon
Worcestershire

2 teaspoons grated lime
peel
1½ teaspoons dry
mustard
¾ teaspoon garlic
salt
¼ teaspoon pepper

1. In 8-quart Dutch oven, cover beef short ribs with water; over high heat, heat to boiling. Reduce heat to low; cover and simmer 2 hours or until ribs are fork-tender. Remove ribs to platter; cover and refrigerate.

2. *About 1 hour before serving:* Prepare outdoor grill for barbecuing. Meanwhile, in small bowl combine catchup and remaining ingredients. Place cooked ribs on grill over medium coals; cook 20 to 25 minutes until heated through, brushing occasionally with catchup mixture and turning often.

Precooking ribs: Simmer ribs 2 hours until fork-tender. Remove to platter; cover and refrigerate.

Grilling ribs: Heat through ribs, brushing with catchup mixture and turning often.

TO BROIL IN OVEN: Precook ribs as above. About 40 minutes before serving, preheat broiler if manufacturer directs. Prepare catchup mixture as above. Place ribs on rack in broiling pan; broil ribs 20 to 25 minutes until heated through, brushing with catchup mixture occasionally and turning ribs once.

Beef Shanks with Vegetables

Color index
page 55

Begin 4 hrs
ahead

8 servings

3 tablespoons salad oil
8 beef shank cross cuts,
each cut about 1 inch
thick
2 10¾-ounce cans
condensed tomato soup
water
¼ cup sugar

1 tablespoon salt
¼ teaspoon pepper
10 large carrots, cut
crosswise in half
6 small onions, cut in half
1 10-ounce package
frozen lima beans

1. In 8-quart Dutch oven over medium-high heat, in hot oil, cook shanks until well browned.

2. Add undiluted soup, 2 cups water, sugar, salt and pepper; heat to boiling. Reduce heat to low; cover and simmer 2¼ hours, stirring occasionally.

3. Add carrots and continue cooking 40 minutes. Add onions and cook 30 minutes. Stir in beans and simmer 10 minutes more until meat and vegetables are tender. Serve immediately.

Brisket

Ground beef

New England "Boiled" Dinner

Color index page 50

Begin 3½ hrs ahead

14 to 16 servings

1 4- to 5-pound beef brisket flat half boneless
1 garlic clove
1 bay leaf
½ teaspoon peppercorns
water
1 medium rutabaga
1 medium head cabbage
16 medium carrots
16 small red potatoes

1 In 8-quart Dutch oven, place beef, garlic, bay leaf, peppercorns and enough water to cover meat. Over high heat, heat to boiling.

2 Reduce heat to low; cover; simmer 3 to 3½ hours until meat is fork-tender. Remove meat with slotted spoon and keep it warm.

3 Cut rutabaga and cabbage into wedges and add with remaining vegetables to liquid in Dutch oven.

4 Over high heat, heat to boiling. Reduce heat to low; cover and simmer about 30 minutes or until the vegetables are fork-tender.

5 To serve, slice beef and arrange on warm large platter with rutabaga, cabbage, carrots and small red potatoes.

CORNED BEEF AND CABBAGE: Prepare as above but, for meat, use *one 4- to 5-pound corned beef brisket flat half boneless* and, for the vegetables, use only *1 large head cabbage*, cut into thin wedges; cook 3 to 3½ hours or until the meat is fork-tender. Add the cabbage wedges 15 minutes before the end of cooking time.

OTHER VEGETABLES: Substitute the vegetables in the recipe above with a selection of the following: 1 10-ounce container Brussels sprouts, 1 pound whole green beans, 8 small white onions, 4 medium parsnips, cut in 2-inch chunks, and 4 medium turnips, cut in halves.

When beef is ground from a specific cut, it may carry the name of the cut, as "ground beef round." Beef ground from less tender cuts, is labeled "ground beef." Labels may also indicate proportion of fat to lean.

Ground beef—approximately 75% lean, the least expensive kind, is suitable for hamburgers, meat sauces and any dish during the preparation of which you will have an opportunity to spoon off excess fat.

Lean ground beef—approximately 80% lean, makes good, lean hamburgers, meat loaves, meatballs and any dishes which contain other ingredients such as bread crumbs or noodles to absorb fat as it cooks out.

Extra-lean ground beef—approximately 85% lean, is recommended in dishes for fat-controlled diets, where it is important to eliminate as much fat as possible.

Hamburgers

Color index page 52

Begin 20 mins ahead

4 servings

1 pound lean ground beef
2 tablespoons minced onion
1 teaspoon salt
¼ teaspoon pepper
catchup , mustard or relish

plain or toasted hamburger buns, toasted split English muffins, toasted white bread slices (optional)

1 With spoon, mix well ground beef, onion, salt and pepper.

2 Shape mixture gently into 4 patties, each about 1 inch thick.

3 Over medium heat, heat skillet until very hot. Cook patties 3 to 4 minutes each side, turning them once.

4 Serve Hamburgers plain or with one of the suggested toppings, in buns, if you like.

BROILED HAMBURGERS: Preheat broiler if manufacturer directs. Prepare ground-beef mixture as above; shape into thick patties; arrange on rack in broiling pan. Broil about 2 inches from heat source, about 8 minutes, turning once. If you like, during last few minutes, top with one of the following: *Cheddar cheese slice* or catchup, chili or soy sauce.

Ground beef

HAMBURGER SERVING IDEAS

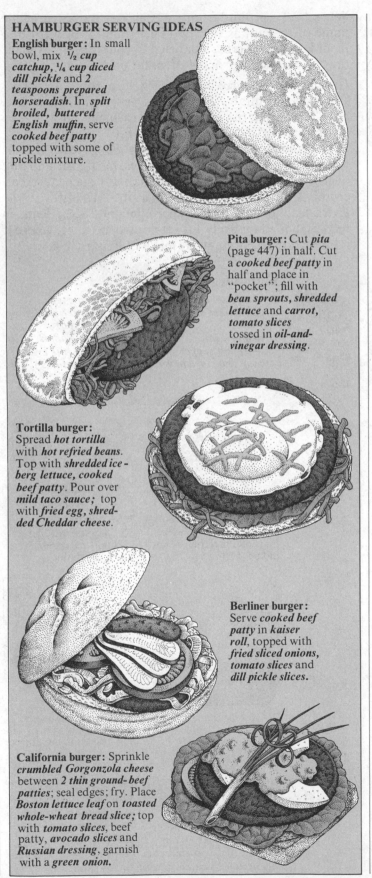

English burger: In small bowl, mix *½ cup catchup*, *¼ cup diced dill pickle* and *2 teaspoons prepared horseradish*. In *split broiled, buttered English muffin*, serve *cooked beef patty* topped with some of pickle mixture.

Pita burger: Cut *pita* (page 447) in half. Cut a *cooked beef patty* in half and place in "pocket"; fill with *bean sprouts, shredded lettuce* and *carrot, tomato slices* tossed in *oil-and-vinegar dressing*.

Tortilla burger: Spread *hot tortilla* with *hot refried beans*. Top with *shredded iceberg lettuce, cooked beef patty*. Pour over *mild taco sauce*; top with *fried egg, shredded Cheddar cheese*.

Berliner burger: Serve *cooked beef patty* in *kaiser roll*, topped with *fried sliced onions, tomato slices* and *dill pickle slices*.

California burger: Sprinkle *crumbled Gorgonzola cheese* between *2 thin ground-beef patties*; seal edges; fry. Place *Boston lettuce leaf* on *toasted whole-wheat bread slice*; top with *tomato slices*, beef patty, *avocado slices* and *Russian dressing*, garnish with a *green onion*.

Meat Loaf

2 pounds lean ground beef
2 cups fresh white or whole-wheat bread crumbs (about 4 bread slices)
½ cup milk
½ cup minced onion
2 eggs
2 teaspoons salt
¼ teaspoon pepper

Color index page 51

Begin 2 hrs ahead

8 servings

1 In large bowl, mix well lean ground beef, fresh bread crumbs and remaining ingredients.

2 Spoon mixture into 9" by 5" loaf pan; with spoon, level top. Bake in 350°F. oven 1½ hours.

3 Let meat loaf stand 5 minutes at room temperature; pour off and discard drippings.

4 With spatula, loosen meat loaf from pan; invert onto warm platter and remove loaf pan.

FLAVORED MEAT LOAVES

 GERMAN-STYLE MEAT LOAF: Drain *one 8-ounce can sauerkraut*, reserving liquid. Prepare Meat Loaf as above but omit milk and substitute *2 cups caraway-rye bread crumbs* for bread crumbs; add sauerkraut. To liquid, add *water* to make ½ cup; add to mixture.

 MONTEREY MEAT LOAF: Prepare Meat Loaf as above but add *½ teaspoon oregano* to mixture. In loaf pan, spread half of mixture; from *one 8-ounce package pasteurized process Monterey (Jack) cheese slices*, arrange 2½ cheese slices on meat. Top with remaining mixture. Bake loaf as directed but during last 10 minutes, remove from oven; repeat cheese layer; top cheese with *1 medium tomato*, peeled and sliced. Finish baking the loaf. With 2 pancake turners, lift meat loaf, top side up, to warm platter.

 PINEAPPLE MEAT LOAF: Prepare Meat Loaf as above but omit milk and add juice drained from *one 8¼-ounce can sliced pineapple*. In shallow baking pan, shape mixture into 11" by 5" oval loaf; top with pineapple slices. Bake 1 hour.

 CURRIED MEAT LOAF: Prepare Meat Loaf as above but add *1 cup shredded peeled apples*, *½ cup minced celery* and *1 tablespoon curry powder* to mixture.

FILLED MEAT LOAF: Prepare meat-loaf mixture as left but spread half of mixture in loaf pan; top with *one of the following fillings:* 4 or 5 whole medium mushrooms; ¼ pound mushrooms, minced; 1 10-ounce package frozen chopped spinach, thawed and drained; 1 cup shredded mozzarella or scamorze cheese; 4 hard-cooked eggs; 2 frankfurters or ¼ pound knackwurst, cut lengthwise into fourths; 4 or 5 pasteurized process cheese slices (overlap slightly). Add remaining meat mixture. Bake as directed.

SPINACH-CHEESE MEAT LOAF: Prepare Meat Loaf as left but omit milk; add *one 8-ounce container creamed cottage cheese*; set aside. In medium bowl, combine *one 10-ounce package frozen chopped spinach*, thawed and drained, *¼ cup minced onion*, *½ teaspoon salt*, *⅛ teaspoon ground nutmeg* and *1 egg*. In 10" by 6" baking dish, spread half of meat mixture; top with spinach mixture, then with remaining meat mixture; level top. Bake 1½ hours. (Makes 10 servings.)

MEAT LOAF ADDITIONS: Prepare Meat Loaf, opposite, but add *one or more of the following:* 1 garlic clove, minced, ½ teaspoon caraway seed, ½ teaspoon oregano, 1 tablespoon chili powder.

Lemon Barbecued Meat Loaves

Color index
page 52

Begin 1 hr
ahead

6 servings

1½ pounds lean ground beef	⅓ cup packed brown sugar
2 cups fresh bread crumbs (about 4 bread slices)	1 teaspoon dry mustard
¼ cup lemon juice	¼ teaspoon ground allspice
¼ cup minced onion	¼ teaspoon ground cloves
1 egg	
2 teaspoons seasoned salt	6 thin lemon slices
½ cup catchup	

1. Preheat oven to 350°F. Grease 13" by 9" baking pan. In large bowl, mix well the ground beef, fresh bread crumbs, lemon juice, minced onion, egg and seasoned salt. Shape the mixture into 6 individual loaves; place in baking pan. Bake 15 minutes.

2. Meanwhile, prepare the sauce: In small bowl, combine the catchup, brown sugar, mustard, allspice and ground cloves. Mix well. Spoon the sauce over the loaves in the baking pan and top each one with a lemon slice; bake 30 minutes longer, basting occasionally with sauce from the baking pan. Serve sauce over the meat loaves.

Shaping loaves: With hands, shape the meat mixture into 6 loaves.

Adding sauce: Spoon over sauce then top each loaf with a lemon slice.

Country Meat Loaf

Color index
page 52

Begin 2 hrs
or day ahead

8 servings

2 tablespoons salad oil	¼ teaspoon cracked black pepper
1 medium onion, chopped	1 egg
1 celery stalk, finely chopped	1 8-ounce can tomato sauce
3 white or whole-wheat bread slices	1 tablespoon light brown sugar
2 pounds lean ground beef	1 tablespoon cider vinegar
1 medium carrot, finely shredded	1 tablespoon prepared mustard
1½ teaspoons salt	

1 In 2-quart saucepan over medium heat, to the hot salad oil, add the chopped onion and celery. Cook about 10 minutes, stirring occasionally with a slotted spoon.

2 Into large bowl, tear bread slices into small pieces; add onion and celery mixture.

3 To the bread and onion mixture add the lean ground beef, shredded carrot, salt, pepper, egg and one half of the can of tomato sauce. Stir thoroughly to mix.

4 In 12" by 8" baking dish, with hands, shape ground beef mixture into 8" by 4" loaf; set aside.

5 In cup with spoon, combine the light brown sugar, cider vinegar, prepared mustard and remaining tomato sauce. Mix thoroughly.

6 Spoon sauce over meat loaf in baking dish. Bake in 350°F. oven 1½ hours. Serve meat loaf warm; or cover and refrigerate to serve cold.

Ground beef

Dilled Meatballs

Color index page 53

Begin 1 hr ahead

16 to 18 appetizer or 6 main-dish servings

1½ pounds lean ground beef
¾ cup quick-cooking oats, uncooked
1 egg
1 teaspoon salt
¼ teaspoon pepper
dill weed
2 tablespoons salad oil
1 cup water
1 beef-flavor bouillon cube or envelope
1 cup sour cream

1 In large bowl with spoon, mix beef, oats, egg, salt, pepper and ½ teaspoon dill weed.

2 With hands, form the ground-beef mixture into evenly shaped 1-inch meatballs.

3 In 12-inch skillet over medium-high heat, in hot oil, cook meatballs, a few at a time. Turn with a spoon until well browned on all sides.

4 With a slotted spoon, remove the meatballs to a large bowl as they brown. When all are browned, pour off any remaining oil in the skillet.

5 Return meatballs to skillet. Stir in water and bouillon. Over medium heat, heat to boiling.

6 Reduce heat to low; cover the skillet and simmer 15 minutes, stirring the meatballs and liquid frequently.

7 Stir in sour cream and 2 teaspoons dill weed to the meatballs and liquid; heat through (but be careful not to boil).

Mushroom-Cheese Meatballs

Color index page 53

Begin 1 hr ahead

16 to 18 appetizer or 8 main-dish servings

salad oil
¼ cup finely chopped onion
¼ cup finely chopped green pepper
1½ pounds lean ground beef
1 egg
¾ teaspoon salt
¼ teaspoon cracked black pepper
½ pound mushrooms, sliced
2 tablespoons all-purpose flour
2 cups water
1 8-ounce package pasteurized process cheese spread, sliced
2 tablespoons cooking or dry sherry

1. In 12-inch skillet over medium-high heat, in 2 tablespoons hot salad oil, cook onion and green pepper until tender, about 5 minutes.
2. In large bowl, mix well onion mixture, ground beef, egg, salt and pepper. Shape mixture into 1-inch round meatballs.
3. In same skillet over medium-high heat, in 3 more tablespoons hot salad oil, cook meatballs, a few at a time, until well browned on all sides, removing meatballs to large bowl as they brown. Pour off all but 2 tablespoons drippings from skillet.
4. In drippings remaining in skillet over medium heat, cook sliced mushrooms until tender, about 5 minutes.
5. In small bowl, blend flour with water. Return meatballs to skillet; stir in flour mixture and cheese; heat to boiling. Reduce heat to low; cover and simmer 15 minutes, stirring occasionally. Add sherry; heat through.

Burgundied Meatballs

Color index page 53

Begin 45 mins ahead

10 to 12 appetizer or 6 main-dish servings

1 pound lean ground beef
¾ cup dried bread crumbs
¾ cup milk
1 egg
1 small onion, minced
½ teaspoon salt
¼ cup salad oil
2 tablespoons all-purpose flour
1 cup water
1 cup red Burgundy
1 beef-flavor bouillon cube
¾ teaspoon sugar

1. In large bowl, mix well first 6 ingredients; shape mixture into 1-inch meatballs.
2. In 12-inch skillet over medium-high heat, in hot salad oil, cook meatballs, a few at a time, until well browned on all sides. With slotted spoon, remove them to plate as they brown.
3. Into drippings remaining in skillet over medium heat, stir flour until blended. Gradually stir in water, Burgundy, bouillon and sugar and cook, stirring constantly, until mixture is thickened. Add meatballs; heat to boiling. Reduce heat to low; cover and simmer 15 minutes.

TO DO AHEAD: Up to 1 month ahead, prepare meatballs as in steps 1 and 2 above; place in freezer-safe container or freezer-weight plastic bag with metal tie or zip top. Freeze. *Day before serving*, thaw meatballs overnight in refrigerator. About 20 minutes before serving, prepare sauce as above but use *2 tablespoons salad oil* instead of drippings. Return meatballs to sauce in skillet and heat through.

See descriptions, page 16

Color index page 51
Begin 1½ hrs ahead
8 servings

Ziti Bake

Spaghetti Sauce
(page 337)
1 16-ounce package
ziti macaroni
1 pound lean ground
beef
1 15-ounce container
ricotta cheese
½ cup grated Parmesan
cheese

¼ cup finely chopped
parsley
1 egg, slightly beaten
¾ teaspoon salt
¼ teaspoon pepper
1 8-ounce package
mozzarella or
scamorze cheese,
shredded

1. Prepare Spaghetti Sauce.
2. Meanwhile, in 8-quart Dutch oven, prepare ziti macaroni as label directs; drain. Set aside.
3. In same Dutch oven over medium-high heat, cook ground beef until well browned, about 10 minutes, stirring occasionally. Preheat oven to 350°F.
4. Remove Dutch oven from heat; stir in ricotta, next 5 ingredients and half of Spaghetti Sauce until well mixed. Add ziti and toss gently to coat well.
5. Spoon mixture into 13" by 9" baking pan; pour remaining Spaghetti Sauce evenly over ziti mixture; sprinkle with mozzarella cheese. Bake 20 minutes or until hot and bubbly.

Color index page 52
Begin 1½ hrs ahead
8 to 10 servings

Chili con Carne

1 tablespoon salad oil
2 pounds lean ground
beef
1 cup coarsely chopped
onions
¼ cup diced green
pepper
2 large garlic cloves,
minced

2 16-ounce cans tomatoes
or 4 cups chopped,
peeled fresh tomatoes
¼ to ⅓ cup chili powder
1½ teaspoons salt
2 16- or 17-ounce cans
red kidney or pinto
beans
Accompaniments (below)

1. In 5-quart Dutch oven over medium-high heat, in hot salad oil, cook ground beef, onions, green pepper and garlic until onion is tender, about 10 minutes, stirring frequently.
2. Add tomatoes and their liquid, chili powder and salt; heat to boiling. Reduce heat to low; cover and simmer 1 hour, stirring occasionally.
3. Stir in beans and their liquid; heat. Serve in soup bowls with a choice of accompaniments.

ACCOMPANIMENTS: Shredded mild Cheddar or Monterey (Jack) cheese, shredded iceberg lettuce, diced avocados, minced onions, chopped green pepper, chunks of French bread, saltine crackers, hot Corn Tortillas (page 431), tortilla or corn chips.

TEXAS-STYLE CHILI: For ground beef, substitute *1 2-pound beef chuck underblade steak boneless*, cut into ½-inch cubes. Cook as in steps 1 and 2 above, but simmer 1½ hours or until fork-tender. Omit beans, serve as above. (Makes 6 to 8 servings.)

See descriptions, page 16

Whole Stuffed Cabbage

1 28-ounce can tomatoes
1 6-ounce can tomato
paste
1 tablespoon brown
sugar
½ teaspoon
Worcestershire
⅛ teaspoon ground
allspice
salt
1 medium head green
cabbage

1 pound ground beef
1 medium onion, diced
1 garlic clove, minced
½ teaspoon pepper
1 cup cooked rice
2½ cups water

Color index page 54
Begin 3 hrs ahead
6 servings

1 In 3-quart saucepan, combine tomatoes and their liquid, the tomato paste, brown sugar, Worcestershire, allspice and ½ teaspoon salt. Mix together thoroughly. Over high heat, heat to boiling, stirring constantly; reduce heat to low, cover the saucepan and simmer 20 minutes, stirring the mixture occasionally.

2 Discard tough outer leaves from cabbage. Carefully remove 2 large leaves and reserve. With sharp knife, cut out stem and center of cabbage, leaving a 1-inch-thick shell.

3 Discard the stem from the cabbage; with sharp knife, evenly dice cut-out cabbage center.

4 In 5-quart Dutch oven over medium-high heat, cook beef, onion, garlic, pepper, 1 teaspoon salt and 1 cup diced cabbage about 15 minutes.

5 Stir in rice and 1 cup tomato mixture. Remove from heat. Carefully spoon off any excess fat from surface of the mixture.

6 Fill cabbage shell with beef mixture; cover opening with the large reserved leaves.

7 With string, tie cabbage securely to hold leaves firmly in position.

8 Into same Dutch oven, stir water, scraping pan to loosen brown bits at the bottom. Add the remaining diced cabbage and the tomato mixture; mix well.

9 Place cabbage, stem end down, in sauce. Over high heat, heat to boiling. Reduce heat to low; cover; simmer 2 hours, basting occasionally with sauce.

10 To serve, place cabbage, stem end down, on deep, warm platter; discard string. Spoon over sauce and cut the cabbage in wedges. Serve immediately.

Pork

POPULAR FRESH PORK CUTS

Pork shoulder arm picnic: Also known as picnic, this is suitable for baking and roasting.

Pork leg whole: Also known as fresh ham, this cut contains the hind leg bone and is suitable for roasting.

Pork shoulder arm roast: Also known as pork arm roast, this has the shank removed and is suitable for roasting.

Pork loin rib chops: Also known as center cut pork chops, they are suitable for roasting, baking and broiling.

Pork loin center rib roast: Also known as center cut pork roast, it contains the loin eye muscle and rib bones.

Pork loin chops: Also known as loin end chops, they are suitable for braising, and pan-frying.

Pork loin tenderloin and slices: Very tender roast and slices are suitable for braising and baking.

Pork loin sirloin chops: Also known as sirloin pork chops, they are suitable for braising and broiling.

Pork loin sirloin cutlets: Boneless tender slices cut from sirloin end of loin are suitable for braising and broiling.

Pork loin blade roast: Also known as 5- or 7-rib roast and rib end roast, this is suitable for roasting.

Pork shoulder blade roast: Also known as Boston butt roast or pork butt, this is the top portion of the shoulder and is suitable for roasting.

Pork shoulder blade steak: This is suitable for braising and broiling.

Pork shoulder blade roast boneless: It is usually tied with string or placed inside elastic netting. Suitable for roasting.

Pork loin country style ribs (Country ribs): These contain either rib bones or backbones and can be baked, braised or cooked in liquid.

Pork spareribs: These long rib bones with a thin covering of meat are suitable for baking and broiling.

Adapted from The Meat Board Meat Book, © *National Live Stock & Meat Board.*

POPULAR SMOKED PORK CUTS

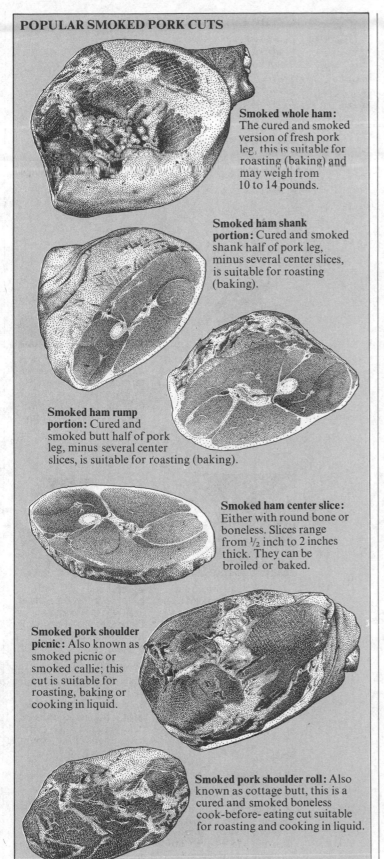

Smoked whole ham: The cured and smoked version of fresh pork leg, this is suitable for roasting (baking) and may weigh from 10 to 14 pounds.

Smoked ham shank portion: Cured and smoked shank half of pork leg, minus several center slices, is suitable for roasting (baking).

Smoked ham rump portion: Cured and smoked butt half of pork leg, minus several center slices, is suitable for roasting (baking).

Smoked ham center slice: Either with round bone or boneless. Slices range from ½ inch to 2 inches thick. They can be broiled or baked.

Smoked pork shoulder picnic: Also known as smoked picnic or smoked callie; this cut is suitable for roasting, baking or cooking in liquid.

Smoked pork shoulder roll: Also known as cottage butt, this is a cured and smoked boneless cook-before- eating cut suitable for roasting and cooking in liquid.

Unlike beef, cuts of fresh pork vary little in tenderness and most can be successfully cooked by one of the dry heat methods, roasting, broiling, pan-broiling and frying (see pages 186–87). See pages 218–19 for information on smoked pork.

BUYING FRESH PORK

Choose meat that has a high proportion of lean to fat and bone. The fat should be solid and white, the lean firm and fine-textured, grayish pink to light red.

TESTING FOR DONENESS

Pork is always cooked well-done and should be a uniform light gray color throughout. When the meat is broiled, pan-broiled or pan-fried, make a small slit in the center of the meat or near the bone to check the color. For roast pork, use a meat thermometer. It should register 170°F. Braised pork and pork cooked in liquid should be fork-tender.

TIMETABLE FOR ROASTING FRESH PORK *				
Type of cut	**Weight** *(in pounds)*	**Meat thermometer reading**	**Approximate cooking time**** *(in hours)*	**Oven temperature**
Loin roasts center rib				
or loin	3 to 5	170°F.	1½ to 2½	325°F.
loin half	5 to 7	170°F.	2¾ to 4	325°F.
loin blade				
or sirloin	3 to 4	170°F.	2 to 2¾	325°F.
top loin, bone-				
less (double)	3 to 5	170°F.	1¾ to 2¾	325°F.
Crown roast	4 to 6	170°F.	2¼ to 3½	325°F.
Shoulder arm picnic				
bone-in	5 to 8	170°F.	2½ to 4	325°F.
boneless	3 to 5	170°F.	1¾ to 2¾	325°F.
Shoulder blade (Boston) roast	4 to 6	170°F.	2¾ to 4	325°F.
Shoulder arm roast	4 to 6	170°F.	2¾ to 4	325°F.
Leg (fresh ham)				
half bone-in	5 to 8	170°F.	2¾ to 4¾	325°F.
whole boneless	10 to 14	170°F.	4 to 5½	325°F.
whole bone-in	12 to 16	170°F.	4½ to 5¾	325°F.
Tenderloin	½ to 1		¾ to 1	325°F.

* Meat at refrigerator temperature
** Remove meat from oven when internal temperature is 5 to 10 degrees below desired doneness as meat continues cooking

CARVING LOIN ROAST

After roasting, cut backbone from ribs and discard. Place roast on cutting board with rib side facing you. Anchor meat with a fork, cut closely along each side of every rib; one slice will contain the rib, next one will be boneless.

Roast pork

Roast Pork

*1 3-pound pork loin
center rib roast*
salt
pepper
*butter or margarine
(optional)*
*water or chicken
broth*
*¼ cup all-purpose
flour or 2 tablespoons
cornstarch*

Color index
page 56

Begin 2 hrs
ahead

8 servings

1 Place roast, fat side up, on rib bones in open roasting pan. Sprinkle meat lightly with salt and pepper.

2 Insert meat thermometer into center of roast. Roast in 325°F. oven 1½ to 1¾ hours, until thermometer reaches 170°F. Remove roast to platter.

3 Into 2-cup measure, pour pan drippings (set pan aside). Let stand a few seconds until fat separates from meat juice.

4 Skim ¼ cup fat from the drippings into 1-quart saucepan. (Add butter or margarine, if necessary, to make ¼ cup.)

5 Add ½ cup water to roasting pan; stir until brown bits are loosened; add to meat juice in cup and add enough water or chicken broth to make 2 cups liquid. Into fat in saucepan over medium heat, blend flour or cornstarch, 1 teaspoon salt and ¼ teaspoon pepper. Gradually stir in meat-juice mixture and cook, stirring constantly, until gravy is thickened. Pour into gravy boat to serve hot with roast.

6 To carve, cut away back bone; discard. Cut along each side of rib bone. Alternate slices will contain rib bone.

Prune-stuffed Roast Pork

*½ 12-ounce package
pitted prunes*
1 cup boiling water
*1 4½- to 5-pound pork
loin center rib roast*
¼ teaspoon pepper
salt
ground ginger
*3 tablespoons all-purpose
flour*
½ cup half-and-half
*1 teaspoon red currant
jelly*

Color index
page 56

Begin 3 hrs
ahead

12 to 14
servings

1 In medium bowl, soak the prunes in boiling water for 30 minutes.

2 Drain the prunes thoroughly and pat them dry on paper towels.

3 With a long, narrow, sharp knife, pierce through center of roast from one end to the other, twisting the knife slightly as you cut to form a long slit in the meat.

4 Pack prunes into slit with the handle of a wooden spoon or fingers.

5 Sprinkle roast with pepper, 1 teaspoon salt and 1 teaspoon ginger. Place the roast, fat side up, in a shallow open roasting pan.

6 Insert meat thermometer, being careful not to touch bone or stuffing. Roast in 325°F. oven 2 to 2½ hours until thermometer reaches 170°F.

7 When done, place meat on heated platter and make gravy: Pour drippings into 2-cup measure; let stand a few seconds until fat separates. Return 3 tablespoons of fat to pan; spoon off any remaining fat. Over low heat, stir in flour. Add enough water to drippings to make 1 cup; stir into flour mixture, scraping to loosen brown bits. Stir in half-and-half, jelly, ¼ teaspoon ginger and salt to taste; cook until gravy is thickened. Pass gravy separately.

Hocks and stew meat

Hocks and Navy-Bean Stew

Color index
page 57

Begin 3½ hrs
ahead

12 cups or
6 servings

4 fresh pork hocks
2 tablespoons salt
¼ teaspoon pepper
2 garlic cloves, crushed
1 bay leaf
water
3 cups dry navy beans
    (1½ 16-ounce
    packages)
4 whole cloves
1 pound small white
    onions (about 12)
1 pound carrots, cut in
    chunks
2 tablespoons lemon
    juice

1 In 8-quart saucepot over high heat, heat to boiling first 5 ingredients and 5 cups water. Reduce heat to low; cover; simmer 1½ hours, skimming off fat.

2 Meanwhile, rinse navy beans in running cold water, discarding any small stones or discolored or shriveled pieces.

3 In 4-quart saucepan over high heat, in 9 cups boiling water, heat beans to boiling; boil 2 minutes. Remove from heat; cover; soak 1 hour; drain thoroughly.

4 Add beans to hocks; simmer 30 minutes more. Stick cloves into 1 onion. Add all onions and carrots to saucepot; over high heat, heat to boiling.

5 Reduce heat to low; cover; simmer 1 hour until meat and vegetables are fork-tender. Add lemon juice in last ¼ hour. Discard bay leaf, cloves.

6 Remove hocks to cutting board and discard skin and bones.

7 Cut meat in bite-size pieces; return to pot. Reheat before serving.

Easy Pork Stew

Color index
page 57

Begin 2½ hrs
ahead

10 to 12
servings

¼ cup all-purpose flour
salt
¼ teaspoon pepper
¼ teaspoon ground
    ginger
3 pounds pork cubes
¼ cup salad oil
¾ cup water
½ cup cooking sherry

½ teaspoon sugar
1¼ pounds tiny white
    onions
2 10-ounce packages
    frozen lima beans,
    thawed
1½ pounds yellow
    straight-neck squash,
    cut in 1½-inch chunks

1. On waxed paper, mix flour, 1 tablespoon salt, pepper and ginger; toss pork with mixture to coat.
2. In 6-quart Dutch oven with ovensafe handles over medium-high heat, in hot oil, brown pork well, pushing cubes aside as they brown. Spoon off any excess fat. Add water, sherry, sugar and onions. Heat to boiling, stirring to loosen brown bits. Cover; bake in 350°F. oven 1 hour, stirring occasionally.
3. Add lima beans, squash and 2 teaspoons salt. Continue baking 45 minutes or until squash is tender-crisp, stirring occasionally. Skim off fat.

Burritos

Color index
page 57

Begin 2½ hrs
ahead

10 servings

salad oil
1 pound beef for stew, cut
    into ½-inch chunks
½ pound pork pieces, cut
    into ½-inch chunks
1 cup chopped onions
1 garlic clove, minced
salt
water

4½ cups all-purpose flour
½ cup lard or shortening
1 15½-ounce can refried
    beans
¼ cup shredded longhorn
    or Cheddar cheese
1 4-ounce can diced green
    chilies

1. In 10-inch skillet over medium-high heat; in 2 tablespoons hot salad oil, cook beef and pork chunks until browned; add onion, garlic, 1 teaspoon salt and 1½ cups water; heat to boiling. Reduce heat to low; cover and simmer 2 hours or until meat is fork-tender and begins to fall apart. Meanwhile, prepare Flour Tortillas.
2. In bowl, mix 4 cups flour with 2 teaspoons salt; cut in lard until blended. Add 1 cup warm water; mix well. Turn dough onto floured surface; knead until smooth, about 3 minutes, adding more flour if needed.
3. Divide dough into 10 pieces; cover. On floured surface with rolling pin, roll one dough piece into 10-inch circle. In ungreased 12-inch skillet over medium-high heat, cook tortilla 1 minute until brown specks appear; turn, cook 30 seconds. Place between sheets of foil; keep warm. Repeat with rest of pieces.
4. About 5 minutes before meat mixture is done, in 2-quart saucepan over medium heat, in 1 tablespoon hot oil, heat refried beans and cheese until hot and cheese is melted, stirring occasionally.
5. When meat is done, add chilies and, with spoon, gently flake meat. Continue cooking until mixture is thickened and all liquid has evaporated.
6. In center of each tortilla, spread about 2 tablespoons bean mixture in a thin layer. Spoon on about 2 tablespoons meat mixture. Fold tortilla over filling to make a "package." Eat sandwich-style.

217

Smoked pork

A wide and varied choice of smoked pork products is available, ranging from large holiday hams to economical, everyday cuts—smoked hocks, spareribs and bacon. Half and whole hams should be stored in the refrigerator for no more than a week before use; ham steaks for 3 to 4 days; sliced boiled ham and prosciutto for up to 3 days; and bacon for 5 to 7 days.

SMOKED HAMS AND PICNICS

Both hams and picnics are usually sold fully cooked and ready-to-serve. Flavor and texture are improved by heating them to an internal temperature of 140°F. or as label directs. Some cook-before-eating hams are sold; cook hams to an internal temperature of 160°F., picnics to 170°F.

Fully cooked hams include the following:

Bone-in ham or its two halves—butt half and shank half. If sold as portions, several center slices probably would have been removed.

Partially boned hams are either shankless or semi-boneless. In the latter case, both shank bone and aitchbone will have been removed, leaving only the leg.

Boneless hams, known as "rolled", "shaped" or "formed" hams, are sold whole, weighing 7 to 14 pounds, in halves, quarters, pieces and slices or steaks.

Canned hams are always boneless and fully cooked, and may be smoked or unsmoked. Some are also flavored.

Boiled ham is sold sliced by the pound or prepackaged.

Prosciutto is an Italian-style pressed ham, deep red in color, with a strong flavor. It is sold in paper-thin slices.

Cook-before-eating hams are usually sold bone-in. They include the "country" hams—"Smithfield", "Tennessee", "Kentucky" and "Virginia". Country hams are usually heavily cured and smoked, and require soaking and precooking unless label directs otherwise.

Smoked picnics are sold whole and usually fully cooked. When sold boneless they are called pork shoulder roll.

COOKING HAMS AND PICNICS

Roasting: Roast a fully cooked ham or picnic according to timetable. A cook-before-eating ham should be cooked to an internal temperature of 160°F., a picnic to 170°F. Plan to have the meat ready about 15 minutes before it is to be served so it can "set" for easier carving. To decorate a ham, score surface lightly in a diamond pattern and stud each diamond with a clove before it goes into the oven. If meat is to be glazed, plan to start glazing it about 30 minutes before the end of cooking

Cooking in liquid: Place picnic in a large saucepot and cover with water. Over high heat, heat to boiling. Reduce heat to low; cover and simmer until meat is tender, 3½ to 4 hours. Drain.

Glazing after simmering: Place picnic on rack in roasting pan and bake in preheated 400°F. oven for 15 to 30 minutes, brushing 2 or 3 times with glaze.

TIMETABLE FOR ROASTING SMOKED PORK*				
Type of cut	Weight *(in pounds)*	Meat thermometer reading	Approximate cooking time** *(in hours)*	Oven temperature
Fully cooked				
Smoked ham whole	10 to 14	140°F.	2½ to 3½	325°F.
half or portion	5 to 7	140°F.	1½ to 2	325°F.
Boneless smoked ham whole	7 to 10	140°F.	2½ to 3	325°F.
	10 to 12	140°F.	3 to 3½	325°F.
	12 to 14	140°F.	3½ to 4	325°F.
half	5 to 7	140°F.	2 to 2¼	325°F.
portion	3 to 4	140°F.	1½ to 1¾	325°F.
Semi-boneless smoked ham whole	10 to 12	140°F.	3 to 3½	325°F.
half	4 to 6	140°F.	1¾ to 2½	325°F.
Canned ham	1½ to 3	140°F.	1 to 1½	325°F.
	3 to 7	140°F.	1½ to 2	325°F.
	7 to 10	140°F.	2 to 2½	325°F.
	10 to 13	140°F.	2½ to 3	325°F.
Smoked shoulder arm picnic	5 to 8	140°F.	2 to 3¼	325°F.
Smoked shoulder roll (butt)	2 to 4	170°F.	1¼ to 2¼	325°F.
Canadian-style bacon	2 to 4	160°F.	1¼ to 2¼	325°F.
Cook before eating				
Smoked ham whole	10 to 14	160°F.	3 to 4¼	325°F.
	5 to 7	160°F.	1¾ to 2½	325°F.
half or portion	3 to 4	160°F.	1¾ to 2¼	325°F.
Smoked shoulder arm picnic	5 to 8	170°F.	2½ to 4	325°F.

*Meat at refrigerator temperature
**Remove meat from oven when internal temperature is 5 to 10 degrees below desired doneness as meat continues cooking

SMOKED SHOULDER ROLLS

Roasting: Before roasting remove any casing then follow directions for hams; internal temperature should be 170°F. A 2- to 4-pound shoulder roll will take 1¼ to 2¼ hours. If desired, glaze as for hams.

Cooking in liquid: Cook and glaze as for picnics. A 2- to 4-pound shoulder roll takes 1½ to 2 hours to simmer. Then, place roll in baking dish; glaze.

HAM SLICES

Center-cut slices usually are cut from fully cooked ham. Ham slices 1 to 2 inches thick may be baked, broiled or braised. Slices 1 inch thick may also be pan-broiled. Broil or pan-broil slices ½ to ¾ inch thick.

Broiling: Slash fat around edge of ham slice in several places to prevent curling. Place slice on rack in broiling pan and broil 2 to 3 inches from heat until browned on both sides, turning once. Ham slices 1 inch thick will take 16 to 20 minutes; slices ½ inch thick are done in 10 to 12 minutes

Pan-broiling: Rub surface of skillet with a piece of fat trimmed from edge of ham slice. Slash fat around edge of ham slice in several places to prevent curling. In skillet over medium heat, cook ham slice until well browned on both sides, turning occasionally and pouring off fat as it accumulates in pan.

Braising: Over medium heat, rub bottom of heavy skillet or Dutch oven with a piece of fat trimmed from edge of ham slice. Add ham and cook until well browned on both sides. Add a little liquid; reduce heat to low; cover tightly and cook until ham is tender.

BACON

Bacon is sold in slices, varying in thickness according to whether it is thin-sliced, regular-sliced or thick-sliced, or in pieces, with the rind left on (slab bacon), for slicing as needed. The flavor depends on the curing and smoking process used, and the bacon may be lean or fat, depending on the cut from which it comes. Sliced bacon may be baked, broiled, pan-broiled, or pan-fried.

Baking: Arrange bacon slices on rack in open roasting pan, overlapping lean edge of each slice with fat edge of the next. Bake in a preheated 400°F. oven until browned and crisp, 10 to 12 minutes.

Broiling: Separate bacon slices carefully so they do not tear and place on rack in broiling pan. Broil 3 inches from heat for 3 to 4 minutes until browned; turn and brown other side, taking care not to burn bacon. Drain on paper towels.

Pan-frying: In a cold, heavy skillet lay the number of slices required in one piece without separating them. (A 10-inch skillet will hold one 8-ounce package of bacon slices at one time.) Over medium heat, cook bacon 5 to 8 minutes, separating slices with tongs so they lie flat in the pan and turning them occasionally to brown them evenly on both sides. When browned, remove from pan and drain on paper towels.

CANADIAN-STYLE BACON

Canadian-style bacon is the large rib-eye muscle of the pork loin, cured and smoked. It is boneless and usually lean, and is sold in 2- to 4-pound pieces or sliced. Roast large pieces. Broil, pan-broil or pan-fry slices until lightly browned on both sides, turning occasionally.

SMOKED PORK LOIN AND CHOPS

A smoked pork loin should be roasted. Chops up to ½ inch thick may be pan-broiled or pan-fried; if cut thicker, they should be broiled or baked.

CARVING HAM

Whole ham: Place on cutting board or warm platter, fat side up, with shank to your right. Using a fork to anchor meat, cut a few slices from thin side; steady ham on this surface.

Starting at shank end, slicing down to bone, cut out small wedge of meat. Continue cutting down to bone in slices ¼ inch thick until you reach aitchbone at other end.

Starting at shank end, release meat slices by cutting along leg bone. For more servings, turn ham to its original position and cut slices to bone.

Rump half ham: Place ham on its cut surface. Using a fork to anchor meat, cut down along aitchbone to remove chunky boneless piece of meat.

Place piece on its freshly cut surface and cut uniform slices about ¼ inch thick down to board.

Hold remaining piece, slice across, then cut along bone to free each slice.

Smoked ham and picnics

Pineapple-glazed Baked Half Ham

Color index
page 59

Begin 2¾ hrs
ahead

15 to 20
servings

*1 5-to 7-pound fully
cooked smoked rump or
shank half ham
1 8-ounce can crushed
pineapple, well drained*

*½ cup packed brown
sugar*

1. Place ham on rack in open roasting pan. Insert meat thermometer into center of meat, being careful not to allow it to touch bone or fat. Bake in 325°F. oven 1 to 1½ hours.
2. Meanwhile, in bowl, combine crushed pineapple with the brown sugar.
3. Remove ham from oven; carefully cut off any tough outer skin from it and discard. With spoon, evenly pat the prepared pineapple mixture on ham. Bake 30 minutes longer or until meat thermometer reaches 140°F.

Removing skin: Before adding glaze cut off any tough outer skin from the ham; discard skin.

Adding the glaze: Use a spoon to pat the prepared pineapple mixture onto the ham.

Baked Picnic

Color index
page 59

Begin 3½ hrs
ahead

10 to 16
servings

*1 5- to 8-pound fully
cooked smoked pork
shoulder arm picnic
½ cup orange
marmalade*

*1½ teaspoons prepared
mustard
1 small orange
whole cloves*

1. Place picnic on rack in open roasting pan. Insert meat thermometer from top center of the thickest part, making sure pointed end is in center of picnic and not resting on bone or fat.
2. Bake at 325°F. 1½ to 2¾ hours; remove picnic from oven and, with sharp knife, cut skin and excess fat from picnic, leaving thin fat covering.
3. Meanwhile, prepare orange glaze: In 1-quart saucepan over low heat, heat orange marmalade and mustard until marmalade is melted.
4. With a pastry brush, brush half of the prepared orange glaze evenly over the picnic. Return the picnic to the oven and bake 20 minutes longer until the internal temperature reaches 140°F.
5. Remove picnic from oven; remove meat thermometer. Cut oranges into very thin slices and halve them; arrange in rows over picnic overlapping them slightly and fastening with cloves. Brush remaining warm glaze over orange slices.
6. Return the picnic to the oven and bake 10 minutes more until the orange slices are heated through. Allow the Baked Picnic to cool slightly to serve warm or serve cold later.

Barbecued Canned Ham and Peaches

Color index
page 58

Begin 1¾ hrs
ahead

10 to 12
servings

*1 3-pound canned ham
½ cup sugar
½ cup chili sauce
1 tablespoon lemon juice
2 teaspoons
Worcestershire*

*½ teaspoon chili powder
½ cup water
5 medium peaches,
peeled and
halved*

1. Remove any gelatin from ham. Place ham in 12″ by 8″ baking dish; insert meat thermometer into center of ham. Bake in 325°F. oven 1¼ hours.
2. Meanwhile, in 2-quart saucepan over medium heat, heat to boiling sugar, chili sauce, lemon juice, Worcestershire, chili powder and water, stirring occasionally. Remove sauce from heat; add peaches and gently stir to coat well.
3. Spoon peaches into baking dish and pour remaining sauce over ham. Bake ham and peaches about 20 minutes more, basting occasionally with sauce, until thermometer reaches 140°F. Place ham on warm platter; arrange peaches around it.

Glazed Ham Platter

Color index
page 58

Begin 3 hrs
ahead

15 to 18
servings

*1 5- to 6-pound fully
cooked smoked semi-
boneless half ham
½ cup pineapple
preserves
½ cup apple jelly
2 tablespoons prepared
horseradish
2 tablespoons prepared
mustard
1 cup packed light brown
sugar
½ cup maple-flavor syrup*

*¼ teaspoon ground
cinnamon
⅛ teaspoon ground
allspice
water
3 medium acorn squash,
cut into ¾-inch wedges
butter or margarine
3 large red cooking
apples, cut into ½-inch
wedges*

1. Place ham on rack in open roasting pan. Insert meat thermometer, avoiding bone or fat. Bake ham in 325°F. oven 1 to 1½ hours.
2. Meanwhile, make glaze: In 1-quart saucepan over low heat, combine pineapple preserves, apple jelly, horseradish and mustard until jelly melts. Brush over ham and bake ham 30 minutes longer until thermometer reads 140°F, brushing often with glaze.
3. Meanwhile, in 1-quart saucepan combine sugar, syrup, cinnamon and allspice; set aside. In 12-inch skillet over medium heat, heat ½ inch water and squash to boiling. Reduce heat to low; cover; simmer about 10 minutes until squash is fork-tender; drain. To squash in skillet add ¼ cup butter and half sugar mixture. Over medium heat, cook until butter and sugar melt and squash is glazed, stirring gently; keep warm.
4. In another 12-inch skillet over medium-high heat, in ¼ cup hot butter, cook apples until tender, about 5 minutes, stirring. Add remaining sugar mixture and continue cooking until sugar is melted and apples are glazed, stirring gently with rubber spatula. Place ham on warm large platter; arrange squash and apples around ham. Pour any remaining glaze over squash and apples.

Ham slices

Whole Smithfield Ham

Color index page 58

Begin day ahead

40 to 60 appetizer servings

1 10- to 12-pound cook-before-eating Smithfield ham or country ham
water
dark corn syrup
little hot biscuits or assorted sliced breads

1 Place the ham, skin side down, in saucepot large enough to hold the whole ham; add enough water to cover the ham completely. Allow to stand at room temperature for at least 12 hours or overnight.

2 *About 5 hours before serving:* Discard water; scrub ham; rinse. Again cover ham with water. Over high heat, heat to boiling.

3 Reduce heat to low; cover; simmer 20 minutes per pound until bone on small end feels loose. Preheat oven to 325°F.

4 Remove ham to rack in open roasting pan; discard water. Cool ham 20 minutes. Remove skin; trim fat leaving about ¼ inch fat.

5 Brush ham with dark corn syrup. Bake 15 minutes or until ham is evenly glazed.

6 Place ham on cutting board. Wrap small end in napkin to grasp. Set out biscuits and breads. Let each guest cut ham.

LEFTOVER SMITHFIELD HAM

CHICKEN SOUP: Add minced ham to chicken soup.

SEASONING: Add small chunks of ham to vegetables as they are cooking.

APPETIZER: Put slices of ham on melon wedges.

Ham Steak Hawaiian

Color index page 59

Begin 30 mins ahead

4 to 6 servings

½ cup packed light or dark brown sugar
¼ cup butter or margarine
¼ cup red or white wine vinegar
1 smoked ham center slice, cut ½ to ¾ inch thick (about 1½ pounds)
4 firm medium bananas

1 In 12-inch skillet over medium heat, heat brown sugar, butter or margarine and vinegar until sugar is melted, stirring frequently.

2 Add ham slice to sugar mixture; cook 5 minutes on each side or until heated through.

3 With pancake turner, arrange ham on heated platter; keep warm.

4 Remove skillet from heat. Cut bananas into 1½-inch chunks. Add bananas to the sugar mixture in the skillet.

5 Cook over medium heat, basting bananas with sauce until bananas are heated through, about 5 minutes.

6 With spoon, carefully spoon banana chunks onto platter to surround ham slice. Spoon sauce remaining in skillet over ham and banana mixture. Serve Ham Steak Hawaiian immediately.

221

Ham slices

Lemony Ham Steaks

Color index
page 59

Begin 20 mins
ahead

6 to 8 servings

¾ cup packed light
  brown sugar
3 tablespoons prepared
  mustard
1½ tablespoons lemon
  juice
¾ teaspoon grated
  lemon peel

1 lemon, thinly sliced
2 smoked ham boneless
  center slices, each
  cut about ¾ inch thick
  (about 1 pound each)

1. Preheat broiler if manufacturer directs. Make glaze: In small bowl, combine first 4 ingredients. Cut lemon slices in half; set aside.
2. Place ham slices in large broiling pan. Broil 2 minutes, brush with some of glaze and broil 5 minutes more. Turn and broil 2 or 3 minutes.
3. Arrange lemon slices on steaks; brush with rest of glaze; broil 5 minutes more or until glaze is bubbling and steaks are heated through.

Fruit-sauced Ham Slices

Color index
page 59

Begin 30 mins
ahead

6 servings

6 smoked ham boneless
  center slices, each
  about ½ inch thick
1 cup pitted dried prunes
1 cup dried apricots

1¾ cups orange juice
¼ cup sugar
1 tablespoon cornstarch
2 tablespoons water

1. Trim piece of fat from ham slice; slash edges of ham slices. In 12-inch skillet over medium-high heat, heat piece of fat until lightly browned, rubbing fat on bottom of skillet to grease it; discard piece of fat. Cook ham slices, a few at a time, until lightly browned on both sides, removing the slices as they brown.
2. Into skillet, stir prunes, apricots, orange juice and sugar. Return ham to skillet, overlapping slices to fit; spoon some juice over slices; heat to boiling. Reduce heat to low; cover; simmer 20 minutes or until apricots are tender. Place ham slices on warm platter; keep warm.
3. In cup, blend cornstarch and water until smooth; stir into hot mixture in skillet and cook over medium heat, stirring constantly, until mixture is thickened and boils. Serve fruit sauce with ham.

Country Ham Steak

Color index
page 59

Begin 1 hr
ahead

6 servings

¼ cup butter
1 small head cabbage
  (about 1½ pounds),
  coarsely shredded
½ teaspoon salt

1 smoked ham center
  slice, cut about
  1 inch thick
2 tablespoons pancake
  syrup

1. Preheat oven to 350°F. In 12-inch skillet over medium-high heat, in hot butter, cook the coarsely shredded cabbage and salt, stirring quickly and frequently, until cabbage is tender-crisp, about 5 minutes. Spoon cabbage evenly into 13" by 9" baking dish.
2. Place ham slice on top of cabbage; drizzle syrup over ham and cabbage.
3. Bake in oven 30 minutes or until ham is heated through, stirring cabbage occasionally so that it does not stick. Serve immediately.

Smoked shoulder rolls

Choucroute Garni

Color index
page 59

Begin 3 hrs
ahead

16 to 20
servings

1 2- to 2½-pound smoked
  pork shoulder roll
1 2- to 2½-pound pork
  shoulder blade
  (Boston) roast
  boneless
2 cups dry white wine
1 13¾-ounce can chicken
  broth

8 juniper berries or 2
  tablespoons gin
6 medium onions, halved
8 medium potatoes,
  halved
6 fresh bratwurst or
  frankfurters
4 cups well-drained
  sauerkraut

1. In 10- to 12-quart saucepot, heat to boiling smoked pork shoulder roll (remove any casing), pork shoulder blade roast, wine, canned chicken broth and juniper berries or gin. Reduce heat to low; cover and simmer 1½ hours.
2. Add remaining ingredients in layers: first the onions, then potatoes, bratwurst and sauerkraut; cover tightly and simmer for 35 to 40 minutes until the meat and vegetables are fork-tender.
3. With slotted spoon, place the sauerkraut, bratwurst, potatoes and onions on warm large platter. Slice the shoulder blade roast and smoked pork roll and arrange on the same platter. Drain fat from the pan liquid; discard the juniper berries. Serve liquid over meat and vegetables and pass the remainder separately in a gravy boat.

Serving Choucroute Garni:
Spoon some pan liquid over meat and vegetables. Pass rest in gravy boat.

Smoked Pork with Sweet Potatoes

Color index
page 58

Begin 2 hrs
ahead

8 to 10
servings

1 2½- to 3-pound smoked
  pork shoulder roll
1 cup packed light brown
  sugar
½ teaspoon ground
  nutmeg

3 tablespoons water
2 17-ounce cans
  vacuum-packed
  sweet potatoes

1. Remove any casing from smoked shoulder roll. Place meat in open roasting pan. Insert meat thermometer into center of meat. Roast in 325°F. oven 30 minutes.
2. Meanwhile, in small bowl, blend the light brown sugar, ground nutmeg and water.
3. Remove roasting pan from oven; place the sweet potatoes in one layer around meat; brush meat and potatoes with brown-sugar mixture. Roast about 1 hour longer or until meat thermometer reaches 170°F., brushing occasionally with the pan liquid. Place the meat and potatoes on warm platter; spoon pan liquid over all. Serve immediately.

Glazes and leftover ham

GLAZES

ORANGE-MINCEMEAT: In covered blender container at low speed, blend *½ cup drained mincemeat* and *¼ cup orange marmalade* until glaze is smooth. (Makes about ¾ cup.)

CURRY-ORANGE: In small bowl with fork, stir *⅔ cup light corn syrup, 1 tablespoon curry powder* and *1 tablespoon grated orange peel* until blended. (Makes about ⅔ cup.)

TOMATO-ONION: In 1-quart saucepan over medium heat, in *1 tablespoon butter* or margarine, cook *2 tablespoons minced onion* until tender, about 3 minutes, stirring occasionally. Stir in *one 8-ounce can tomato sauce, 2 tablespoons dark brown sugar* and *1 teaspoon Worcestershire*; heat to boiling. Reduce heat to low; simmer 5 minutes or until glaze is slightly thickened. (Makes about 1 cup.)

LEFTOVER HAM

GLAZED KABOBS: Alternately skewer *chunks of ham* with *thick wedges of apple*, brush with *orange marmalade* diluted with *lemon juice*; broil, until kabobs are glazed.

HAM DIP: Combine *finely chopped ham* with *sour cream, mayonnaise, Worcestershire* and *salt*; mix until of spoonable consistency; use as dip.

HAM AND SWISS SPREAD: Combine *ground ham* with *shredded Swiss cheese* and *softened cream cheese*, thinned with *milk* and seasoned with *⅛ teaspoon hot pepper sauce*; use as sandwich filling.

CREAMED VEGETABLES WITH HAM: Stir *bits of ham* or matchstick-size strips of ham into *creamed potatoes*, cauliflower or leeks; eat as a main dish.

HAM CHEF'S SALAD: Arrange *chunks or slivers of ham, tomato slices, olives, cucumber sticks* and *sliced radishes* over *macaroni* or *potato salad*.

HAM PATTIES: Combine *ground ham* with an *egg* and add *bread crumbs, ⅛ teaspoon ground sage* and *⅛ teaspoon pepper*; shape into small patties and fry in *butter*; serve in buns as a main dish if you like.

HAM FRUIT SALAD: Combine *diced ham* with *chopped walnuts* or almonds and *sliced celery*, moistened with *mayonnaise*; fill a halved *avocado*, cantaloupe or papaya.

HAM AND WATERCRESS SOUP: Heat homemade or canned *chicken broth* to boiling; add *sliced mushrooms, slivered pieces of ham* and *watercress*; reheat to boiling; serve as first course.

HAM CASSEROLE: Combine *kidney beans* or canned pork and beans, *catchup, brown sugar, mustard* and *diced green pepper* with *chunks of ham*; bake until mixture is bubbly.

MINCED HAM TOPPINGS: Serve *minced ham* over scrambled eggs, cooked vegetables, tossed salads, potato salads, bean or vegetable soup.

Glazed Ham Loaf

Color index page 59

Begin 1¾ hrs ahead

4 or 5 servings

1 pound ground smoked ham
1 large carrot, grated
1 small onion, minced
1 cup fresh bread crumbs
2 eggs
2 tablespoons chopped parsley
2 teaspoons prepared mustard

1 8-ounce can pineapple slices in juice
2 tablespoons light brown sugar
2 teaspoons cornstarch
1 tablespoon butter or margarine
1 tablespoon lemon juice

1 In medium bowl with fork, mix well first 7 ingredients. Grease 11" by 7" baking pan.

2 In pan, shape ham mixture into 7" by 3" loaf. Bake in 350°F. oven 30 minutes. Into 1-quart saucepan, drain the pineapple juice and reserve the pineapple slices.

3 Into pineapple juice, stir brown sugar and cornstarch until completely smooth. Over medium heat, stir the mixture until thickened and boiling.

4 Remove from heat; stir in butter or margarine and lemon juice until well blended.

5 Remove ham loaf from oven; with a pastry brush, carefully brush the meat loaf all over with the pineapple and lemon juice glaze.

6 Overlap pineapple slices on top. Bake 30 minutes longer, brushing occasionally with glaze. Let loaf stand 5 minutes for easier slicing.

223

Lamb

POPULAR LAMB CUTS

Lamb leg whole: Also known as leg roast, sirloin on. Contains sirloin section with hip bone and shank portion with round bone; outside covered with fell. This is suitable for roasting.

Lamb leg shank half: Lower half of leg and round leg bone. Heavily muscled, with fat and fell covering, this is suitable for roasting.

Lamb shank: Also known as lamb trotter, cut from the arm, it is suitable for braising and cooking in liquid.

Lamb shoulder neck slices: Also known as lamb neck and lamb for stew bone-in, they are suitable for braising.

Lamb rib roast: Also known as rack roast and rib rack, it contains rib bones, backbone and thick, meaty rib eye muscle and is suitable for roasting.

Lamb breast riblets: Cuts are long and narrow and are suitable for braising or cooking in liquid.

Lamb shoulder blade chop: Also known as blade cut chop, this is suitable for braising, broiling and pan-frying.

Lamb rib chop: Also known as rack lamb chop, this is suitable for broiling, pan-broiling and pan-frying.

Lamb loin chop: Contains part of backbone; this is suitable for broiling and pan-broiling.

Lamb leg sirloin chop: Cut from sirloin section of leg, this can be broiled, pan-broiled or pan-fried.

Lamb breast: Contains the ribs; also known as breast of lamb. Oblong in shape, with layers of fat within the lean, it is suitable for braising or roasting.

Lamb shoulder arm chop: Also known as arm cut and round bone chop, this is suitable for braising, broiling and pan-broiling.

LAMB

Lamb is a tender, lean meat with a delicate yet distinctive flavor which is enhanced by seasonings and flavorings of all kinds, ranging from garlic and herbs and spices to fruit and nuts.

BUYING LAMB

The meat of high-quality lamb is pink to light red in color, firm and fine-textured, with red, porous bones. The color of the fat cannot be taken as a guide to quality because it varies according to the animal's age, breed and feed; the fat should not be too thick in relation to lean meat.

The thin, papery skin that surrounds chops, steaks and roasts should feel fresh, moist and pliable, not dry or wrinkled, This skin, known as the "fell," should be left on roasts to help them hold their shape during cooking. However, if it has not been removed from steaks and chops when you buy them, pull it off yourself before you cook them. When buying rib roasts, ask the meatman to loosen the backbone from the ribs to make carving easier.

Some lamb cuts, such as rib crown roast, are expensive and are suitable only for special occasions, but there are a number of lamb cuts which are excellent value for everyday budget meals. These include riblets and shanks, which are very economical. If planning to serve kabobs, the cubes can be cut from any thick, solid piece of boneless lamb. You can cut the cubes at home from an unrolled boneless shoulder roast.

COOKING LAMB

Most lamb cuts are tender enough to be cooked by one of the dry heat methods, roasting, broiling, pan-broiling or pan-frying (see pages 186–87), but lamb is also delicious braised or cooked in liquid.

Whichever method you choose, it is always important to remember to keep temperatures low to moderate so that the meat will not cook too quickly and will be as tender, juicy and flavorful as possible.

TESTING FOR DONENESS

Roast lamb can be served rare, medium or well done. For rare lamb, the thermometer should read 140°F. and the meat will be reddish inside. For medium lamb, the thermometer should read 160°F. and the meat will be brownish-pink with a tinge of red. For well-done lamb, the thermometer should register 170°F. and there will be no sign of pink in the meat. Remember to let lamb stand 15 minutes when you take it out of the oven. This will make for much easier carving.

To test broiled, pan-broiled and pan-fried lamb for doneness, make a small slit in the center of the meat or near the bone and check the color. Braised lamb or lamb cooked in liquid should be fork-tender.

TIMETABLE FOR ROASTING LAMB *				
Weight (in pounds)	Approximate cooking time** (in hours)			Oven temperature
	Rare 140°F.	Medium 160°F.	Well done 170°F.	
Leg whole				
5	1¾	2	2½	325°F.
7	2¼	3	3½	325°F.
9	3	3¾	4½	325°F.
Leg shank half				
3 to 4	1¼ to 1¾	1½ to 2	1¾ to 2¼	325°F.
Leg sirloin half				
3 to 4	1 to 1¼	1¼ to 1¾	1½ to 2	325°F.
Leg roast boneless				
3	1¼	1½	1¾	325°F.
5	2	2½	3	325°F.
7	3	3½	4	325°F.
Rib roast (rack)				
1½ to 2	¾	1	1¼	375°F.
2 to 3	1	1¼	1½	375°F.
Shoulder roast square cut whole				
4 to 6		1¾ to 2½	2 to 3	325°F.
Shoulder roast boneless				
3½ to 5	1¾ to 2½	2 to 3	2⅓ to 3¼	325°F.

*Meat at refrigerator temperature.
**Remove meat from oven when internal temperature is 5 to 10 degrees below desired doneness as meat continues cooking.

CARVING A LEG OF LAMB

Place leg of lamb on cutting board or warm platter with leg or shank bone to your right. Using a fork to anchor meat, and holding knife in a slanting position almost parallel to the surface of lamb, make a ¼-inch-thick slice about a third of the way along the leg toward the shank end. Remove slice.

Cut next slice ¼ inch farther toward the large end and cut parallel to the bone. Continue cutting slices until you reach the bone.

After removing the top slices, turn leg slightly and carve the sides in long slender slices.

Lamb roasts

Roast Leg of Lamb

Color index page 60

Begin 3 hrs ahead

12 to 15 servings

3 juniper berries
2 teaspoons dry mustard
¼ teaspoon pepper
salt
water
1 5-pound lamb leg whole
12 small potatoes, peeled
¼ cup gin (optional)
½ cup red currant jelly
2 tablespoons cornstarch

1 Crush juniper with mustard, pepper, 2 teaspoons salt and 2 teaspoons water. Spread on lamb.

2 Place lamb, fat side up, on rack in open roasting pan. Insert meat thermometer into center of thickest part of meat, taking care not to touch bone. Roast 1⅔ to 2½ hours in 325°F. oven, until meat thermometer reaches 140°F. for rare or 160°F. for medium or 170°F. for well done. Meanwhile, cut potatoes into 1-inch-thick slices. About 45 minutes before meat is done, sprinkle the potato slices with 1 teaspoon salt.

3 Put potatoes on rack around meat; cook until fork-tender, brushing with drippings. Place potatoes, meat on platter.

4 Pour pan liquid into 2-cup measure; let stand until fat separates; spoon fat from liquid; discard.

5 Add 1¼ cups water to pan; cook over medium heat, stirring to loosen bits; add to liquid in cup with gin. Add water to make 1¾ cups.

6 In 2-quart saucepan over medium heat, heat measured liquid and jelly to boiling, stirring constantly until the jelly is melted.

7 Blend cornstarch, ¼ teaspoon salt and ¼ cup water; stir into liquid in pan until thickened. Carve lamb. Serve sauce separately.

Marinated Butterflied Lamb

Color index page 61

Begin day ahead

10 to 12 servings

1 4-pound lamb leg shank half
1 tablespoon peppercorns
⅓ cup Burgundy
3 tablespoons olive oil
1½ teaspoons salt
1½ teaspoons oregano, crushed
1 large garlic clove, slivered
parsley sprigs for garnish

1. Butterfly leg of lamb (see below).
2. On cutting board, between double thickness of waxed paper, with meat mallet or clean hammer, pound peppercorns until coarsely cracked.
3. For marinade, in 12″ by 8″ baking dish, combine peppercorns and next 5 ingredients. Add butterflied lamb; turn over to coat evenly. Cover with plastic wrap; refrigerate at least 12 hours, turning meat occasionally.
4. *About 45 minutes before serving:* Preheat broiler if manufacturer directs. Drain lamb, reserving marinade. Place lamb on rack in broiling pan. Broil about 5 inches from source of heat (or at 450°F.) for 10 minutes, occasionally basting with marinade. Turn and broil 15 minutes longer for rare or until meat is of desired doneness. Place on carving board; garnish lamb with sprigs of parsley.

BUTTERFLYING A LAMB LEG SHANK HALF

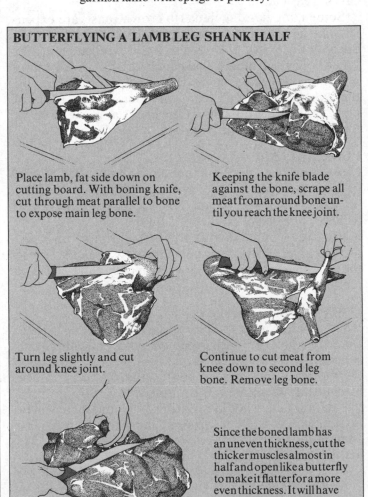

Place lamb, fat side down on cutting board. With boning knife, cut through meat parallel to bone to expose main leg bone.

Keeping the knife blade against the bone, scrape all meat from around bone until you reach the knee joint.

Turn leg slightly and cut around knee joint.

Continue to cut meat from knee down to second leg bone. Remove leg bone.

Since the boned lamb has an uneven thickness, cut the thicker muscles almost in half and open like a butterfly to make it flatter for a more even thickness. It will have an irregular shape. Trim excess fat from meat.

Marinated Leg of Lamb Olé

Color index page 60

Begin day ahead

10 to 12 servings

salt
¹/₂ cup orange juice
¹/₂ cup dry red wine
¹/₂ cup chili sauce
2 tablespoons salad oil
1 small onion, minced
1 garlic clove, minced
2 tablespoons sugar

2 teaspoons chili powder
1 teaspoon basil
1 4-pound lamb leg shank half
water
3 tablespoons all-purpose flour

1. In large shallow pan, for marinade, mix 2 teaspoons salt and remaining ingredients except leg of lamb, water and flour. Add lamb and turn over to coat with marinade. Cover with plastic wrap and refrigerate at least 12 hours, turning lamb occasionally.

2. *About 3¹/₂ hours before serving:* Place lamb, fat side up, on rack in open roasting pan; reserve marinade. Insert meat thermometer into center of meat, being careful thermometer does not touch bone. Roast in 325°F. oven about 1²/₃ hours or until meat thermometer reaches 140°F. for rare, 160°F. for medium or 170°F. for well done, basting occasionally with marinade. Place meat on warm platter; let rest 15 minutes.

3. Meanwhile, make gravy: Pour pan liquid into a 4-cup measure or medium bowl (set pan aside); let stand a few minutes until fat separates from meat liquid. Skim 3 tablespoons fat from liquid into 2-quart saucepan; skim remaining fat and discard. Add 1¹/₂ cups water to roasting pan; cook over medium heat, stirring until brown bits are loosened; add mixture and reserved marinade to liquid in cup. (Add more water if needed to make 2¹/₂ cups.) Over medium heat, into hot fat in saucepan, stir flour and ¹/₄ teaspoon salt until blended; gradually stir in liquid mixture and cook, stirring, until thickened. Serve gravy with lamb.

Rotisseried Leg of Lamb

Color index page 61

Begin day ahead

16 to 18 servings

¹/₂ cup salad oil
¹/₂ cup white wine
¹/₂ cup red wine vinegar
1 garlic clove, crushed
2 teaspoons salt
¹/₂ teaspoon rubbed sage

¹/₂ teaspoon ground ginger
¹/₄ teaspoon pepper
1 5-pound lamb leg roast boneless
Mint Sauce (page 243)

1. In large, shallow dish, for marinade mix well all ingredients except lamb and Mint Sauce. Add lamb; coat well with marinade. Cover and refrigerate, turning lamb occasionally.

2. *About 3 hours before serving:* Place lamb on rotisserie skewer as manufacturer directs; reserve marinade. Insert meat thermometer into center of lamb, being careful thermometer does not touch skewer or heating element or oven as it turns. Roast on rotisserie about 2 to 3 hours until meat thermometer reaches 140°F. for rare, 160°F. for medium or 170°F. for well done, brushing frequently with marinade. Meanwhile prepare Mint Sauce.

3. Remove skewer and strings. Let meat stand 15 minutes for easier carving. Serve with Mint Sauce.

Roast Rack of Lamb

Color index page 61

Begin 2 hrs ahead

4 servings

³/₄ teaspoon garlic salt
¹/₄ teaspoon salt
¹/₈ teaspoon pepper
1 8-rib lamb rib roast (about 2¹/₂ pounds)
¹/₄ cup apricot preserves
2 teaspoons lemon juice

1 Preheat oven to 375°F. Combine garlic salt, salt and pepper; rub into meat. Place lamb on rib bones in roasting pan.

2 Insert meat thermometer. Roast 1 hour or until thermometer reaches 140°F. for rare, 160°F. for medium or 170°F. for well-done meat.

3 Meanwhile, in 1-quart saucepan over medium heat, heat apricot preserves and lemon juice until preserves are melted.

4 During last 30 minutes of roasting, brush lamb with apricot mixture occasionally.

5 Remove roast to cutting board; let stand 10 minutes for easier carving; with sharp knife, cut backbone from ribs; discard.

6 To serve, anchor meat with fork and carve between every rib bone, allowing 2 ribs for each individual serving.

227

Lamb cubes

Lamb Kabobs

Color index
page 61

Begin early
in day or
day ahead

8 servings

2 tablespoons butter
1/2 cup chopped onion
1 small green pepper,
 diced
1 celery stalk, diced
1 garlic clove, minced
1 8-ounce can
 tomatoes
1 6-ounce can tomato
 paste
1/4 cup water
2 tablespoons light brown
 sugar
1 1/2 teaspoons vinegar

1/2 teaspoon salt
1/2 teaspoon hot pepper
 sauce
1/4 teaspoon cracked
 pepper
1 medium eggplant
2 medium red peppers
2 pounds lamb cubes for
 kabobs

1 In 2-quart saucepan over medium heat, in hot butter, cook onion, green pepper, celery and garlic 10 minutes or until vegetables are tender.

2 Add tomatoes and their liquid and next 7 ingredients; heat to boiling. Reduce heat to low; simmer 5 minutes. Spoon mixture into large bowl; chill.

3 Cut eggplant lengthwise in half, then crosswise into 1-inch-thick slices. Cut red peppers into 2-inch pieces.

4 When tomato mixture is cool, add lamb, eggplant and red peppers; mix well; cover; chill 4 hours or overnight, stirring.

5 About 1 hour before serving: Prepare outdoor grill for barbecuing. On four 18-inch skewers, thread lamb alternately with vegetables. Spoon marinade into pan; cover.

6 Place skewers on grill over medium coals; cook 30 minutes or until lamb is of desired doneness, turning often. Heat marinade on same grill to serve with lamb.

Chops

Lamb Chops à l'Orange

Color index
page 61

Begin 30 mins
ahead

8 servings

1 10-ounce jar orange
 marmalade
2 tablespoons butter or
 margarine
1 tablespoon dry
 sherry
1 garlic clove, minced

1 1/2 teaspoons salt
8 lamb shoulder arm
 chops, each cut
 about 1 inch
 thick

1. Preheat broiler if manufacturer directs. In 1-quart saucepan over low heat, heat all ingredients except chops until marmalade melts, stirring.

2. Place chops on rack in broiling pan; broil 10 to 15 minutes until of desired doneness, turning once and brushing occasionally with marmalade mixture.

Roquefort Lamb Chops

Color index
page 61

Begin 1 1/4 hrs
ahead

8 servings

1/4 pound Roquefort
 cheese
1 teaspoon salt
1 teaspoon
 Worcestershire
1/8 teaspoon pepper
8 lamb 2-rib rib chops,
 each cut about
 2 1/2 inches thick
1 10 1/2-ounce can
 condensed consommé,
 undiluted

1 Preheat oven to 325°F. Stir and mash Roquefort, salt, Worcestershire and pepper until mixed.

2 Trim chops, leaving thin layer of fat; over fat sides, to within about 1 inch of both ends, spread some Roquefort mixture.

3 Set chops on bones in 12" by 8" baking dish; add consommé. Bake 50 minutes or until of desired doneness, basting.

Broiled Gingery Lamb Chops

Color index
page 61

Begin 30 mins
ahead

6 servings

2 tablespoons salad
 oil
1 1/2 teaspoons ground
 ginger
1/2 teaspoon salt
1/2 teaspoon garlic
 powder

6 lamb loin chops, each
 cut about 1 inch thick
 or 6 lamb leg sirloin
 chops, each cut about
 1/2 inch thick
1 pound mushrooms,
 stems removed

1. Preheat broiler if manufacturer directs. Combine oil, ginger, salt and garlic powder.

2. Place chops on greased rack in broiling pan; brush one side with some oil mixture. Broil 5 minutes; turn chops and arrange mushroom caps around chops; brush both with remaining oil mixture; broil until of desired doneness. Serve chops immediately.

Breasts and riblets

Lamb Chops with Vegetable Gravy

Color index page 60

Begin 1¾ hrs ahead

6 servings

*6 lamb shoulder blade
  chops, each cut
  ¾ inch thick*
*¼ teaspoon pepper
salt*
*3 tablespoons all-purpose
  flour*
¼ cup salad oil
3 medium carrots, sliced
1 large onion, diced
*1 large celery stalk,
  sliced*
1 garlic clove, minced
½ cup dry red wine

*2 tomatoes, peeled,
  seeded and diced*
*1 beef-flavor bouillon
  cube or envelope*
1 bay leaf
*½ teaspoon thyme
  leaves*
*¼ teaspoon ground
  allspice*
*celery leaves for
  garnish*

1 On waxed paper,
sprinkle lamb chops
with pepper and 1 tea-
spoon salt; using tongs,
coat well with flour.

2 In 12-inch skillet over
medium-high heat, in
hot oil, cook chops, half at
a time, until browned on
both sides, removing chops
to a platter as they brown.

3 In skillet over medium
heat, in drippings, cook
carrots, onion, celery and
garlic 5 minutes, stirring
occasionally. Add wine,
next 5 ingredients and 1
teaspoon salt. Add chops.

4 Heat to boiling.
Reduce heat to low;
cover; simmer 50 minutes
or until chops are tender,
turning once; remove to
platter. Discard bay leaf
and any bones.

5 Spoon mixture into
blender container; skim
fat from top. Cover; blend
at medium speed until mixture is smooth.

6 Pour gravy into same
skillet; over medium
heat, heat to boiling;
spoon over chops. Garnish
with celery leaves.

Oven-barbecued Lamb Breast

Color index page 60

Begin 3½ hrs ahead

3 or 4 servings

1 3-pound lamb breast
3 medium oranges
½ cup chili sauce
2 tablespoons honey
1 teaspoon salt
*1 teaspoon
  Worcestershire*
*¼ teaspoon cracked
  black pepper*

1 Cut lamb breast into
serving-size portions.
Grate 1 tablespoon peel
and squeeze ¼ cup juice
from 1 orange.

2 In small bowl, mix well
orange peel, juice, chili
sauce and remaining in-
gredients; set aside.

3 Place lamb in open
roasting pan; pour
chili-sauce mixture over
lamb portions.

4 Bake in 325°F. oven
2½ to 3 hours until
fork-tender, basting with
sauce occasionally.
Meanwhile, slice rest of
oranges crosswise.

5 During last 15 minutes
of cooking time, add
orange slices to lamb to
heat through.

Lamb Riblets with Pineapple

Color index page 61

Begin 2½ hrs ahead

6 to 8 servings

*1 16-ounce can pineapple
  chunks*
¼ cup honey
*3 tablespoons white wine
  vinegar*
1 tablespoon salt
1 teaspoon Worcestershire

*¼ teaspoon ground
  ginger*
6 pounds lamb riblets

1. In 17¼" by 11½" roasting pan, mix liquid drained
from pineapple with honey, vinegar, salt,
Worcestershire and ginger. (Reserve pineapple.)
2. Add riblets; cover pan tightly with foil and bake in
325°F. oven 2 hours or until riblets are fork-tender.
During last 10 minutes, add pineapple chunks.
3. Place riblets and pineapple on warm platter.

Shanks and neck slices

Stew meat

Lamb Shank Stew

Color index
page 60

Begin 2½ hrs
ahead

6 servings

12 medium tomatoes
   (about 4 pounds)
6 lamb shanks (about 6
   pounds)
all-purpose flour
¼ cup salad oil
1 cup chopped onions
2 carrots, sliced
1 garlic clove, minced
¼ cup dry vermouth
2 chicken-flavor bouillon
   cubes or envelopes

4 teaspoons sugar
1 tablespoon salt
2 teaspoons rosemary
½ teaspoon pepper
3 medium zucchini, cut
   into 1½-inch chunks
⅓ cup water
1 tablespoon grated
   lemon peel
3 cups hot cooked barley
   or rice

1. Peel 6 tomatoes; cut into quarters; set aside. Cut remaining tomatoes into wedges; cover and refrigerate. On waxed paper, coat lamb shanks with 2 tablespoons flour.

2. In 8-quart Dutch oven over medium-high heat, in hot salad oil, cook shanks, a few at a time, until well browned on all sides, removing the lamb shanks as they brown.

3. To oil remaining in Dutch oven, add onions, carrots and garlic; cook until lightly browned, about 10 minutes, stirring occasionally. Return meat to Dutch oven; add quartered tomatoes, vermouth, bouillon, sugar, salt, rosemary and pepper; heat to boiling. Reduce heat to low; cover and simmer 1¼ hours or until meat is almost tender, stirring mixture occasionally.

4. Add zucchini; cover and simmer 15 minutes or until zucchini is tender. In cup with fork, mix water and 3 tablespoons flour until smooth; gradually stir into hot liquid in Dutch oven and cook, stirring constantly, until slightly thickened. Add tomato wedges; heat through. Sprinkle stew with lemon peel; serve with hot cooked barley or rice.

Braised Lamb Neck Slices

Color index
page 60

Begin 1¼ hrs
ahead

4 servings

2 pounds lamb neck
   slices, each cut
   ¾ inch thick
3 tablespoons all-purpose
   flour
1 tablespoon salad oil
1 cup water
1 cup pitted prunes

2 tablespoons sugar
2 tablespoons cider
   vinegar
1¼ teaspoons salt
¼ teaspoon ground
   cinnamon
¼ teaspoon ground
   allspice

1. On waxed paper, coat lamb neck slices with flour. In 12-inch skillet over medium-high heat, in hot salad oil, cook slices until well browned, turning once. Skim off fat from skillet.

2. Add water; heat to boiling. Reduce heat to low; cover and simmer 45 minutes. Turn neck slices and stir in prunes; cover and simmer 10 minutes. Add sugar and remaining ingredients. Cover and simmer 5 minutes longer or until meat is fork-tender. Serve slices and pan liquid in warm deep platter.

CARAWAY LAMB NECK SLICES: Prepare as above but omit prunes and remaining ingredients. Increase water to 1½ cups; add *1 teaspoon caraway seed* and *1 beef-flavor bouillon cube or envelope* with water. Cook 1 hour or until meat is fork-tender.

Near-East Lamb Stew

Color index
page 61

Begin 3 hrs
ahead

10 to 12
servings

3 pounds lamb for stew,
   cut into 1½-inch
   chunks
¼ cup all-purpose
   flour
¼ cup salad or
   olive oil
1 cup water
2 medium onions, diced
2 garlic cloves, minced
2 tablespoons seasoned
   salt

½ teaspoon seasoned
   pepper
½ teaspoon thyme
   leaves
4 medium tomatoes
2 green peppers
1 medium eggplant
hot cooked rice for
   10 servings

1 On waxed paper, coat chunks of lamb stew meat thoroughly with the flour.

2 In 6-quart Dutch oven over medium-high heat, in hot salad oil, cook lamb, several pieces at a time, until browned on all sides, removing pieces as they brown.

3 Return meat to Dutch oven; stir in water, onions, minced garlic, seasoned salt, seasoned pepper and thyme. Heat to boiling; reduce to low; cover; simmer 2 hours.

4 Peel tomatoes and cut into wedges; cut green peppers and eggplant into even-sized chunks.

5 Add tomato wedges, green pepper and eggplant chunks to Dutch oven and cook 30 minutes longer, stirring the stew occasionally.

6 When the meat and all the vegetables are fork-tender, remove Dutch oven from heat and serve the meat and vegetables over hot cooked rice.

Ground lamb

Lamb Curry

Color index page 60

Begin 2½ hrs ahead

6 to 8 servings

2 pounds lamb for stew, cut into 1-inch chunks
¼ cup all-purpose flour
salad oil
2 medium onions, sliced
1 garlic clove, minced
1 to 3 tablespoons curry powder
2 teaspoons salt
¼ teaspoon ground cinnamon
¼ teaspoon ground cloves
⅛ teaspoon coarsely ground pepper
1 beef-flavor bouillon cube or envelope
1 cup water
½ cup tomato juice
hot cooked rice for 6 servings
Curry Accompaniments (below)

1. On waxed paper, coat lamb pieces with flour. In 12-inch skillet over medium-high heat, in 2 tablespoons hot salad oil, cook lamb until well browned, removing pieces as they brown and adding more oil if necessary.

2. Into drippings in skillet, stir the sliced onions, minced garlic and curry powder; cook over medium heat until onions are tender, about 5 minutes, stirring frequently.

3. Return meat to skillet; add salt, cinnamon, cloves, pepper, bouillon and water; heat to boiling. Reduce heat to low; cover and simmer 2 hours or until meat is fork-tender, stirring occasionally. Stir in tomato juice; heat through.

4. Serve on a bed of hot cooked rice; pass a selection of Curry Accompaniments.

CURRY ACCOMPANIMENTS: In separate small bowls, place two or more of these accompaniments, to be sprinkled over individual servings of Lamb Curry: chutney, raisins, tomato wedges, salted almonds or peanuts, chopped parsley, pineapple chunks, banana slices, fried onion rings, crisp bacon bits, currant jelly, chopped hard-cooked eggs, sweet or sour pickles, flaked coconut, sliced avocado, finely shredded orange peel.

Lamb Stew Rosé

Color index page 61

Begin 3 hrs ahead

6 servings

1 tablespoon salad oil
2 pounds lamb for stew, cut into 1½-inch chunks
1 cup rosé
2 garlic cloves, minced
1½ teaspoons salt
¼ teaspoon pepper
¼ teaspoon rosemary, crushed
1 pint cherry tomatoes
1 3-ounce jar almond- or pimento-stuffed olives, drained
hot cooked buttered rice for 6 servings

1. In 12-inch skillet over medium-high heat, in hot salad oil, cook lamb stew meat, half at a time, until meat is well browned on all sides, removing pieces as they brown.

2. Return all browned meat to skillet. Stir in rosé, minced garlic, salt, pepper and crushed rosemary; heat to boiling. Reduce heat to low; cover and simmer about 2½ hours until the meat is fork-tender, stirring occasionally.

3. Add tomatoes and olives; heat 5 minutes. Serve with hot cooked rice.

Persian-style Lamb with Almonds

Color index page 60

Begin 25 mins ahead

4 servings

1 tablespoon salad oil
½ cup slivered almonds
1 pound ground lamb
1½ cups chopped onions
1 beef-flavor bouillon cube
¼ teaspoon salt
½ teaspoon garlic salt
¼ teaspoon pepper
1 tablespoon lime or lemon juice
1 teaspoon dried mint
spinach leaves
1 medium tomato, cut into wedges

1 In 10-inch skillet over medium heat, in hot salad oil, cook slivered almonds, stirring, until golden brown. Remove almonds to plate.

2 Over medium-high heat, in oil remaining in skillet, cook ground lamb and next 5 ingredients, stirring, until meat is browned, about 10 minutes.

3 To lamb, add almonds, lime juice and mint. Stir mixture to blend well.

4 Line platter with spinach leaves; spoon meat mixture onto spinach leaves and garnish with tomato wedges.

Lamburgers

Color index page 61

Begin 25 mins ahead

6 servings

6 ground lamb patties
1 teaspoon salt
¼ teaspoon pepper
6 bacon slices

1. Preheat broiler if manufacturer directs. Sprinkle lamb patties with salt and pepper. Wrap edge of each patty with bacon slice, securing with toothpick. Place patties on greased rack in broiling pan; broil 5 minutes.

2. With pancake turner, turn patties. Broil 5 minutes longer or until patties are of desired doneness. To serve, remove and discard toothpicks. Arrange lamb patties on large warm platter.

Veal

POPULAR VEAL CUTS

Veal rib roast: Contains ribs, rib eye muscle, feather-bones and part of chine bone. It is suitable for roasting.

Veal leg rump roast boneless: A boneless roast also known as rolled rump roast or rump of veal boneless. It can be braised or roasted.

Veal leg rump roast: Also known as veal rump roast or rump of veal. It can be braised or roasted.

Veal shoulder blade steak: Also known as shoulder veal chops, this cut can be braised or pan-fried.

Veal cutlets: Very lean, boneless slices from leg. They are suitable for braising or pan- frying.

Veal breast: Also known as breast-of-veal, it contains lower ribs. Quite lean with some layering of fat; it is suitable for braising or roasting.

Veal breast riblets: Also known as veal riblets. They contain rib bones and can be braised or cooked in liquid.

Veal shoulder roast boneless: The shoulder cut with bones removed, rolled and tied. It is suitable for braising or roasting.

Veal loin chops: These contain tenderloin and are suitable for braising or pan-frying.

Veal top loin chops: Veal loin chops with tenderloin removed; can be braised or pan-fried.

Veal rib chops: Contain rib eye muscle but not tenderloin. They can be braised or pan-fried.

Veal stew meat: Pieces may come from shoulder, shank or round and are suitable for braising or cooking in liquid.

Veal is the most delicate of all meats, with a subtle flavor and texture. This almost bland flavor makes it perfect for seasoning with herbs and other, more distinctively flavored, ingredients. Because veal comes from young animals only, it is always very lean, with no marbling and only a thin external layer of fat. It also has a comparatively large amount of connective tissue. Like beef, better grades of veal carry federal grade stamps.

BUYING VEAL

The lean of good-quality veal is firm and fine-textured, ranging in color from creamy white to the palest pink. Avoid veal which is flabby or brightly colored. Any visible fat should also be pale, almost white, and bones should be soft and very red.

COOKING VEAL

Because of its lack of fat and the large proportion of connective tissue in the meat, veal calls for careful, thorough cooking at low to moderate temperatures. Otherwise, it can easily toughen and become dry. For the same reason, veal should never be broiled.

TESTING FOR DONENESS

Roast veal to an internal temperature of 170°F. (Use a meat thermometer to avoid guesswork.) The exterior will be reddish-brown, the interior a uniform creamy white. To test pan-fried veal for doneness, make a small slit in the center of the meat or near the bone to check that the color is creamy white throughout. Braised veal and veal cooked in liquid should be tender when pierced with a fork.

CUTTING VEAL FOR SCALOPPINE

Scaloppine, sometimes called "escalopes" or "scallops" are thin, boneless slices of veal cut from leg round roast or loin. With boning knife, separate roast into muscles, removing bone, membrane and any fat. With knife in a slanting position, cut thin-as-possible slices across width of each muscle. Place the veal between sheets of waxed paper and with a meat mallet or the dull edge of a French knife, pound them to ⅛ to 1/16 inch thickness. The scaloppine can then be pan-fried, stuffed, rolled and braised, or they can be used in recipes for cutlets on pages 235 to 236.

Cutting scaloppine: With knife in slanting position, slice meat across grain into ¼ inch slices.

Pounding veal: On cutting board with meat mallet, pound veal slices between sheets of waxed paper to ⅛ inch thickness.

TIMETABLE FOR ROASTING VEAL*				
Type of cut	Weight *(in pounds)*	Meat thermometer reading	Approximate cooking time** *(in hours)*	Oven temperature
Leg rump or round roast	5 to 8	170°F.	2 to 3¼	325°F.
Loin roast	4 to 6	170°F.	2 to 3	325°F.
Rib roast	3 to 5	170°F.	1¾ to 3	325°F.
Shoulder roast boneless	4 to 6	170°F.	2¾ to 4	325°F.

* *Meat at refrigerator temperature*
** *Remove meat from oven when internal temperature is 5 to 10 degrees below desired doneness, as meat continues cooking*

CARVING VEAL

Rib roast: Remove backbone, leaving as little meat on it as possible, before bringing roast to table. Place roast on platter with rib side facing you. Insert a fork in top of roast to anchor meat, then cut closely alongside of each rib. One slice will contain a rib, the next will be boneless.

Boneless roast: Place meat on board or warm platter as it was roasted. Remove all strings (or leave one or two in place if roast starts to fall apart). Using a fork to anchor meat, start cutting right side of roast into slices ¼ to ½ inch thick.

Leg round roast: Place roast on cut surface. Anchor with fork and cut along aitchbone to remove boneless piece of meat; place piece on its cut surface and cut into ¼-inch-thick slices.

Anchoring remaining half, slice across meat until knife strikes aitchbone; cut down along bone to release each slice.

Veal roasts

Lemon-tarragon Veal Roast

2 teaspoons salt
2 teaspoons grated lemon
*   peel*
1 teaspoon tarragon
*   leaves*
1 4-pound veal shoulder
*   roast boneless*
water
¼ cup all-purpose
*   flour*
1 beef-flavor bouillon
*   cube or envelope*

Color index
page 62

Begin 3¼ hrs
ahead

12 to 14
servings

1 In small bowl with a spoon, stir together salt, grated lemon peel and tarragon leaves.

2 With tip of sharp knife, make about 2 dozen slits, about 2½ inches deep, over top and sides of veal shoulder roast, taking care not to cut string.

3 Into each slit in the meat, with spoon, insert some of salt mixture.

4 Sprinkle any remaining salt mixture over the veal roast.

5 Place meat on rack in open roasting pan; insert meat thermometer into center of thickest part of meat. Roast in 325°F. oven 2¾ hours or until temperature is 170°F.

6 Place veal on warm platter; let stand 15 minutes for easier carving. With knife, carefully remove strings.

7 Meanwhile, prepare the gravy: Spoon off any fat from drippings in roasting pan. Add 1½ cups water to drippings; stir to loosen brown bits at the bottom of the pan. In cup, blend flour with ½ cup water until smooth; gradually stir into liquid in roasting pan. Stir in the bouillon cube or envelope. Cook over medium heat, stirring constantly until the gravy is smooth and thickened; serve over the meat.

Veal Rib Roast Marsala

Color index
page 62

Begin 3¼ hrs
ahead

8 to 10
servings

1 4-pound veal rib roast
1 teaspoon salt
¼ teaspoon pepper
¼ teaspoon thyme leaves,
*   crushed*
1 bay leaf, finely
*   crumbled*

1¼ cups water
¼ pound mushrooms,
*   thinly sliced*
1 shallot, minced
2 tablespoons all-purpose
*   flour*
¼ cup dry Marsala

1. In shallow roasting pan, place roast on rib bones. In small bowl or cup, combine salt, pepper, thyme and bay leaf; rub over meat.

2. Insert meat thermometer into center of thickest part of roast. Roast in 325°F. oven 2½ hours or until meat thermometer reaches 170°F. Cut off backbone and discard. Place meat on warm platter.

3. For gravy, into 2-quart saucepan, spoon 2 tablespoons fat from drippings in roasting pan; spoon off any remaining fat from drippings and discard. Into roasting pan over medium heat, stir water and cook, stirring to loosen brown bits at the bottom of the roasting pan.

4. In hot fat, in saucepan over medium heat, cook mushrooms and shallot until mushrooms are tender. Stir in flour until blended. Gradually stir in water mixture and Marsala and cook, stirring, until thickened; boil 1 minute; serve with meat.

Seasoning the meat: Combine salt, pepper, thyme and bay leaf and rub over meat.

Removing backbone: When meat is done, cut off backbone and discard.

Country-style Veal Rump Roast

Color index
page 63

Begin 3¼ hrs
ahead

14 to 16
servings

1 4-pound veal leg rump
*   roast boneless*
3 medium carrots, diced
1 medium onion, chopped
⅔ cup water
1 10 ¾-ounce can
*   condensed cream of*
*   mushroom soup*

1 teaspoon salt
¼ teaspoon coarsely
*   ground black pepper*
¼ teaspoon marjoram
*   leaves*
1 bay leaf

1. In 8-quart Dutch oven over medium-high heat, cook veal leg rump roast until well browned on all sides. Push roast to one side of Dutch oven; add carrots and onion; cook, stirring occasionally, about 5 minutes. Skim off any excess fat.

2. Add water, undiluted soup, salt, pepper, marjoram leaves and bay leaf; heat to boiling, stirring constantly. Reduce heat to low; cover and simmer 2½ to 3 hours until meat is fork-tender, stirring.

3. To serve, place meat on warm platter; discard bay leaf. Pour pan liquid into gravy boat.

Cutlets

Spicy Veal Rump Roast

Color index page 62

Begin 3 hrs ahead

12 to 14 servings

2 tablespoons salad oil
1 5-pound veal leg rump roast
1 tablespoon mixed pickling spice
1 medium onion, diced
1 teaspoon curry powder
1¾ cups apple juice
2½ teaspoons salt

¼ teaspoon pepper
5 small red cooking apples
⅓ cup water
3 tablespoons all-purpose flour
celery leaves for garnish

1. In 8-quart Dutch oven over medium-high heat, in hot salad oil, cook veal roast until well browned on all sides.

2. Meanwhile, cut a double-thickness of cheesecloth, 5 inches square. On it, place pickling spice. Pull corners up to form small bag; tie securely with color-fast or undyed cotton string.

3. When veal is browned, remove to platter. In drippings in Dutch oven, cook onion and curry, stirring occasionally, until onion is tender, about 5 minutes. Stir in apple juice, salt, pepper and spice bag; return veal to Dutch oven; heat to boiling. Reduce heat to low; cover and simmer 2½ hours or until veal is fork-tender, turning veal occasionally.

4. About 10 minutes before veal is done, core and cut apples into thick wedges. When veal is done, place on platter; keep warm. Discard spice bag from liquid in Dutch oven; add apples.

5. In cup, stir water and flour until blended. Gradually stir into liquid in Dutch oven; cook over medium heat, stirring constantly, until mixture is thickened and apples are tender.

6. To serve, with slotted spoon, spoon apples around meat; garnish with celery leaves. Pour gravy into gravy boat and pass with meat.

Tomato-paprika Veal

Color index page 63

Begin 3 hrs ahead

12 to 14 servings

2 tablespoons salad oil or shortening
1 5-pound veal leg rump roast
1 cup chopped onions
1 cup tomato juice
2 tablespoons paprika
2 teaspoons salt

¼ teaspoon crushed red pepper
2 tablespoons cornstarch
¼ cup water
½ cup sour cream
hot cooked noodles or mashed potatoes

1. In 5-quart Dutch oven over medium-high heat, in hot salad oil, cook rump roast until well browned on all sides; remove meat.

2. In drippings, over medium heat, cook onion until tender, about 5 minutes. Stir in tomato juice, paprika, salt and red pepper; return meat to Dutch oven and heat to boiling. Reduce heat to low; cover and simmer 2½ hours or until meat is fork-tender, turning meat occasionally. Place meat on warm platter; keep warm.

3. For sauce, in cup, blend cornstarch with water until smooth; gradually stir into hot mixture in Dutch oven and cook, stirring constantly, until sauce is thickened. Stir in sour cream until blended; heat (do not boil). Serve sauce over sliced veal and hot cooked noodles or mashed potatoes.

Veal and Peppers

Color index page 63

Begin 1 hr ahead

8 servings

⅓ cup olive or salad oil
2 garlic cloves, sliced
2 medium onions, sliced
3 green peppers, sliced
3 red peppers, sliced
2 tablespoons red wine vinegar
1 teaspoon basil
½ teaspoon oregano leaves
salt and pepper
8 veal cutlets, each cut about ¼ inch thick
⅓ cup all-purpose flour
butter or margarine

1 In 12-inch skillet over medium-high heat, in hot oil, cook garlic until browned; discard. Add the sliced onions and peppers; cook 2 minutes, stirring.

2 Stir in vinegar, basil, oregano, 2 teaspoons salt and ¼ teaspoon pepper. Reduce heat to medium; cover; cook about 10 minutes.

3 With slotted spoon, remove vegetables to medium bowl; keep warm.

4 With meat mallet, pound cutlets until ⅛ inch thick; sprinkle with 1 teaspoon salt and ¼ teaspoon pepper.

5 On waxed paper, coat cutlets with flour. In same skillet over medium-high heat, melt 3 tablespoons butter.

6 Cook meat, a few pieces at a time, until lightly browned on both sides, adding more butter if necessary.

7 When all of veal is cooked, arrange the meat with the peppers and onions on warm platter or serve in skillet.

Cutlets

Wiener Schnitzel

Color index
page 63

Begin 45 mins
ahead

6 servings

*6 large veal cutlets,
each cut about
1/4 inch thick*
2 eggs
1 1/4 teaspoons salt
*1/2 teaspoon coarsely
ground pepper*
*1/3 cup all-purpose
flour*
*1 1/2 cups dried bread
crumbs*
*1/2 cup butter or
margarine*

*2 lemons, each cut into 8
wedges*
*3 tablespoons chopped
parsley*
*6 anchovy fillets, drained
(optional)*
*capers, well drained
(optional)*

1 On cutting board with
meat mallet, pound veal
cutlets to about 1/8 inch
thickness, turning once.

2 In pie plate, beat eggs,
salt and pepper. On
waxed paper, place flour;
on another sheet, place the
bread crumbs.

3 Coat veal in flour, then
dip in eggs, then coat
well with bread crumbs.

4 In 12-inch skillet over
medium heat, in 1/4 cup
hot butter, cook meat, a
few pieces at a time, 3 or 4
minutes on each side till
brown adding butter as
needed. Remove to platter.

5 Garnish veal with
lemon and parsley.
Serve with anchovies and
capers if desired.

A LA HOLSTEIN: Prepare veal cutlets as in the
Wiener Schnitzel recipe, above, but serve each one
topped with a *fried egg*.

Saltimbocca

Color index
page 62

Begin 40 mins
ahead

4 servings

*4 veal cutlets, each cut
about 1/4 inch thick*
1/4 cup butter
1/4 cup medium sherry

*1/4 pound thinly sliced
prosciutto, cut in thin
strips*
1/2 pound raclette

1. Preheat oven to 350°F. With meat mallet, pound
cutlets until about 1/8 inch thick, turning once. In 12-
inch skillet over medium-high heat, in hot butter,
cook cutlets until lightly browned on both sides.
Place in 12" by 8" baking dish.
2. To drippings in skillet, add sherry and stir to
loosen brown bits; pour over meat. Arrange prosciutto strips over veal. Bake 5 minutes. Remove
from oven; coarsely shred cheese and sprinkle over.
Bake 4 to 5 minutes more until cheese is melted.

Veal Piccata

Color index
page 62

Begin 1 1/4 hrs
ahead

8 servings

*2 pounds veal cutlets,
each cut 1/4 inch thick*
salt and pepper
1/3 cup all-purpose flour
1/3 cup olive oil
2 tablespoons butter

1 cup water
1/2 cup dry white wine
*1 chicken-flavor bouillon
cube or envelope*
2 medium lemons
parsley sprigs

1. With meat mallet, pound cutlets to 1/8 inch
thickness. On waxed paper, sprinkle with 1 teaspoon
salt and 1/4 teaspoon pepper; coat with flour.
2. In 12-inch skillet over medium-high heat, in hot
olive oil and butter, cook veal, a few pieces at a time,
until lightly browned on both sides, removing pieces
as they brown and adding more oil if necessary.
3. Reduce heat to low. Into drippings in skillet, stir
water, wine, bouillon and 1/2 teaspoon salt, scraping
to loosen brown bits. Return veal to skillet; cover
and simmer 15 minutes until cutlets are fork-tender.
Cut 1 lemon in half; squeeze to remove juice; thinly
slice the other. Overlap cooked cutlets on large
platter; keep warm. Stir lemon juice into liquid in
skillet. Over high heat, heat to boiling. Spoon liquid
over cutlets; garnish with lemon slices and parsley.

Veal Parmigiana

Color index
page 62

Begin 1 hr
ahead

6 servings

*2 cups Marinara Sauce
(page 337)*
1 cup dried bread crumbs
1 teaspoon salt
1/8 teaspoon pepper
2 eggs
*6 veal cutlets, each cut
about 1/4 inch thick*

*3 tablespoons butter or
margarine*
*1 8-ounce package
mozzarella cheese, cut
into 6 slices*
*1/4 cup grated Parmesan
cheese*

1. Prepare Marinara Sauce.
2. On waxed paper, mix bread crumbs, salt and
pepper. In pie plate, beat eggs lightly. Dip cutlets in
egg, then bread crumbs; repeat to coat each twice.
3. In 12-inch skillet over medium-high heat, in hot
butter, fry cutlets, a few at a time, until browned on
both sides, about 10 minutes. Arrange cutlets in
skillet; spoon some sauce over each cutlet; top each
with slice of mozzarella; sprinkle with Parmesan.
Reduce heat to low; cover and cook until cheese is
melted, about 5 minutes.

Chops and steaks

Veal Forestier

Color index page 64

Begin 45 mins ahead

6 servings

6 veal rib chops, each cut ½ inch thick
¼ cup all-purpose flour
butter or margarine
1 garlic clove, halved
½ pound mushrooms, thinly sliced
½ cup dry vermouth
1 teaspoon salt
⅛ teaspoon pepper

1. On waxed paper, coat chops lightly with flour. In 12-inch skillet over medium-high heat, in 2 tablespoons hot butter, cook garlic until brown; discard garlic. In butter remaining in skillet, cook chops, half at a time until well browned on both sides, removing chops as they brown to platter and adding a little more butter if needed.
2. Reduce heat to low. In same skillet, melt 2 tablespoons more butter; cook mushrooms until just tender. Stir in vermouth, salt and pepper, scraping to loosen brown bits. Return chops to skillet; cover; simmer 15 minutes until chops are fork-tender.
3. To serve, arrange chops on warm platter; pour mushroom mixture in skillet over chops.

Veal Chops with Avocado

Color index page 64

Begin 1½ hrs ahead

4 servings

4 veal loin chops, each cut about ¾ inch thick
2 tablespoons butter
¼ pound mushrooms, sliced
¼ cup minced onion
2 tablespoons medium sherry
1 teaspoon salt
dash hot pepper sauce
1 small ripe avocado
2 teaspoons cornstarch
½ cup heavy or whipping cream
1 teaspoon chopped fresh dill

1. Preheat oven to 350°F. Slash fat on edge of chops. In 10-inch skillet with ovensafe handle, over medium heat, in hot butter, cook mushrooms and onion until tender, about 5 minutes.
2. Arrange chops in skillet. Add sherry, salt and hot pepper sauce; heat to boiling. Cover and bake 1 hour or until meat is fork-tender.
3. Cut avocado in half; remove seed and skin. Slice avocado and arrange over chops. Bake, uncovered, 10 minutes or until avocado is heated through. Place chops on warm platter.
4. Blend cornstarch and 1 tablespoon cream until smooth; stir in remaining cream. Gradually stir into hot liquid in skillet and cook over medium heat, stirring until thickened. Stir in dill. Serve chops immediately with sauce.

Slashing fat: Cut through fat on edge of chops in several places.

Adding avocado: Arrange avocado slices over veal chops in skillet.

Veal Chops in Tomato Sauce

Color index page 64

Begin 45 mins ahead

6 servings

6 veal top loin chops, each cut ½ inch thick
¼ cup all-purpose flour
butter or margarine
3 medium tomatoes (about 1 pound), peeled, seeded and cubed
¼ cup water
1 chicken-flavor bouillon cube or envelope
1 teaspoon basil
½ teaspoon sugar
1 tablespoon chopped parsley

1. On waxed paper, coat loin chops lightly with flour. In 12-inch skillet over medium-high heat, in 3 tablespoons hot butter, cook chops until well browned on both sides, removing chops as they brown and adding a little more butter if needed.
2. Reduce heat to low. In same skillet, melt 2 tablespoons more butter. Stir in tomatoes, water, bouillon cube, basil and sugar, scraping to loosen brown bits. Return chops to skillet; over high heat, heat to boiling. Reduce heat to low; cover and simmer 15 minutes or until meat is fork-tender.
3. To serve, arrange chops on warm platter; pour tomato sauce over chops; sprinkle with parsley.

Veal Steaks with Spaghetti

Color index page 64

Begin 1¼ hrs ahead

4 servings

2 veal shoulder arm steaks, each cut about 1 inch thick
2 tablespoons all-purpose flour
2 tablespoons olive oil
1 8-ounce can stewed tomatoes
1 6-ounce can tomato paste
1½ teaspoons seasoned salt
1 teaspoon sugar
¼ teaspoon seasoned pepper
¼ teaspoon oregano, crumbled
1 8-ounce package spaghetti, cooked

1. On waxed paper, coat veal steaks with flour. In 12-inch skillet over medium-high heat, in hot oil, cook meat until well browned on both sides.
2. Add remaining ingredients except spaghetti; heat to boiling. Reduce heat to low; cover and simmer 1 hour or until steaks are fork-tender, turning once. Serve with spaghetti.

Veal Steak Marsala

Color index page 64

Begin 1¼ hrs ahead

4 servings

4 veal shoulder blade steaks, each cut ¾ inch thick
¾ teaspoon salt
¼ teaspoon pepper
2 tablespoons all-purpose flour
butter or margarine
½ cup dry Marsala
½ cup water
chopped parsley for garnish

1. On waxed paper, sprinkle veal steaks lightly with salt and pepper; coat well with flour.
2. In 12-inch skillet over medium-high heat, in 3 tablespoons hot butter, cook steaks until well browned on both sides, adding more butter if needed. Remove steaks to platter; keep warm.
3. Reduce heat to low. Stir wine and water into drippings, scraping to loosen brown bits. Return veal to skillet; cover; simmer 45 minutes or until veal is fork-tender. Arrange on warm platter; pour liquid in skillet over steaks. Garnish with parsley.

Breast and riblets

Deviled Veal Riblets with Saucy Noodles

Color index page 64

Begin 2 hrs ahead

6 servings

1 13¾-ounce can chicken broth
1 carrot, cut up
1 celery stalk, cut up
1 small onion, cut up
¼ teaspoon pepper salt
5 pounds veal breast riblets
⅓ cup mayonnaise
¼ cup dry mustard
4 garlic cloves, minced

2 tablespoons milk
¾ cup dried bread crumbs
¼ cup butter or margarine, melted
Saucy Noodles (right)
1 small tomato, cut into wedges for garnish

1 At high speed, blend broth, carrot, celery, onion, pepper and 2 teaspoons salt until vegetables are finely chopped.

2 In 6-quart Dutch oven over high heat, heat to boiling veal breast riblets and blended vegetable-broth mixture.

3 Reduce heat to low; cover; simmer 1 hour, occasionally turning riblets. Remove riblets; let cool about 15 minutes. Reserve meat juice in Dutch oven.

4 Preheat broiler if manufacturer directs. In 10" by 6" baking dish, combine mayonnaise, mustard, garlic, milk, and 1 teaspoon salt.

5 Dip riblets into mayonnaise mixture; on waxed paper, coat with bread crumbs. Place on rack in broiling pan; drizzle with half of butter. Broil 15 minutes.

6 Turn riblets; drizzle with remaining butter. Broil 15 minutes more. Prepare Saucy Noodles; arrange with riblets on platter; garnish with tomato wedges.

SAUCY NOODLES: Prepare *one 8-ounce package broad egg noodles* as label directs; drain. Meanwhile, pour reserved meat juice into small bowl; let stand a few seconds until fat separates from meat juice. Skim 3 tablespoons fat from meat juice into same Dutch oven; skim off and discard any remaining fat. Into fat in Dutch oven over medium heat, stir *3 tablespoons all-purpose flour* until blended; gradually stir in 1½ cups meat juice; cook, stirring constantly, until mixture is thickened. Add hot noodles and *2 tablespoons chopped parsley*; gently stir noodles to coat well.

Braised Breast of Veal and Peaches

Color index page 64

Begin 3¼ hrs ahead

6 servings

1 4-pound veal breast
1 garlic clove, cut in thin slivers
½ cup dry sherry
2 tablespoons soy sauce
½ cup packed dark brown sugar

4 teaspoons prepared mustard
1 29-ounce can cling-peach halves, well drained
thin slices French or Italian bread

1. With tip of sharp knife, make 1-inch-long slits on fatty side of veal breast and insert garlic.
2. Place meat, fat side up, in 13" by 9" baking pan; pour on sherry and soy sauce. Cover pan tightly with foil and bake in 325°F. oven 2½ to 3 hours until meat is fork-tender.
3. Preheat broiler if manufacturer directs. Remove meat from oven. Spoon pan drippings into gravy boat; let stand until fat separates. Spoon off fat and discard. Keep pan drippings warm.
4. In small bowl, blend brown sugar and mustard until smooth. Arrange peach halves, cut sides up, around meat. Spread brown-sugar mixture on top of meat and peaches. Broil 3 to 5 minutes until brown-sugar mixture melts and peaches are hot. Serve meat with French bread and pan drippings.

Inserting garlic: With a sharp knife, make slits on fatty side of breast and insert garlic.

Adding brown-sugar mixture: Spread mixture over top of meat and cut sides of peaches.

VEAL BREAST WITH PLUM GLAZE: Prepare as steps 1 and 2 above; remove from oven and omit steps 3 and 4. In covered blender container, blend *one 17-ounce bottle chutney, 4 large plums*, peeled and cut up, and *¼ teaspoon salt* until smooth; place in same bowl. Turn oven control to broil. Place veal breast, bone side up, on rack in broiling pan; brush with some mixture. Broil 10 to 15 minutes until glaze is lightly browned. Turn veal over and baste; broil 10 to 15 minutes longer.

Stew meat

Blanquette de Veau

Color index
page 63

Begin 3 hrs
ahead

8 to 10
servings

1 stalk celery, diced
1 carrot, diced
2 whole cloves
1 bay leaf
2½ pounds veal for stew,
cut into 1½-inch
chunks
½ cup dry vermouth or
other dry white wine
2 teaspoons salt
1 pound small white
onions

1 pound small
mushrooms
4 egg yolks
½ cup heavy or whipping
cream
hot cooked egg noodles
or rice, or mashed or
boiled potatoes
chopped dill or parsley
for garnish

1 Prepare bouquet garni:
Cut double-thickness of
cheesecloth into 8-inch
square. On it, place first 4
ingredients; pull up
corners and tie securely
with undyed cotton string.

2 In 5-quart Dutch oven
over medium-high heat,
heat to boiling bouquet
garni, veal, vermouth
and salt. Reduce heat to
low; cover and simmer
1½ hours.

3 Add onions and mush-
rooms. Over high heat,
heat to boiling. Reduce
heat to low; cover and simmer 30 minutes or until
fork-tender. Discard the
bouquet garni.

4 In small bowl with wire
whisk, mix egg yolks
and cream; stir in about
½ cup hot broth from
Dutch oven.

5 Slowly pour egg-yolk
mixture into stew, stir-
ring rapidly to prevent
lumping. Cook, stirring,
until mixture is thickened
(do not boil).

6 Serve stew over hot
cooked egg noodles,
rice, or mashed or boiled
potatoes. Garnish with a
sprinkling of chopped
dill or parsley.

Veal Paprika

Color index
page 62

Begin 2½ hrs
ahead

6 to 8 servings

3 tablespoons butter or
margarine
2 pounds veal for stew,
cut into 1-inch chunks
2 large onions, diced
1 tablespoon paprika
1¾ teaspoons salt
water

1 8-ounce package
medium egg noodles
1 tablespoon all-purpose
flour
½ cup sour cream
chopped parsley for
garnish

1. In 5-quart Dutch oven over medium-high heat, in
hot butter or margarine, cook veal stew meat,
several pieces at a time, until well browned on all
sides, removing pieces as they brown.
2. Reduce heat to medium; add onions and paprika
to drippings in Dutch oven and cook until onions
are tender, about 10 minutes, stirring occasionally.
3. Return meat to Dutch oven; add salt and ½ cup
water; heat to boiling. Reduce heat to low; cover
Dutch oven and simmer 1¼ hours or until meat is
fork-tender.
4. Meanwhile, cook noodles as label directs; drain.
5. In cup, blend flour and 2 tablespoons water until
smooth; gradually stir into hot liquid in Dutch oven
and cook over medium heat, stirring constantly,
until mixture is thickened. Stir in sour cream; heat
(do not boil). Serve over noodles. Garnish with
chopped parsley.

Veal Stew Milanese

Color index
page 62

Begin 2 hrs
ahead

6 servings

¼ cup olive or salad
oil
2 pounds veal for stew,
cut into 1¼-inch
chunks
1 large onion, diced
1 large carrot, diced
1 large stalk celery,
diced
1 garlic clove,
minced
⅓ cup white chianti or
other dry white wine
1 16-ounce can tomatoes

2 teaspoons salt
½ teaspoon basil
¼ teaspoon coarsely
ground black pepper
1 bay leaf
1 chicken-flavor bouillon
cube or envelope
Risotto alla Milanese
(page 339)
(optional)
1 tablespoon chopped
parsley
1½ teaspoons grated
lemon peel

1. In 5-quart Dutch oven over medium-high heat, in
2 tablespoons hot oil, cook veal, ⅓ at a time, until
well browned on all sides, removing pieces with
slotted spoon as they brown and adding more oil if
necessary.
2. In same Dutch oven over medium heat, in
drippings, cook onion, carrot, celery and garlic until
lightly browned, about 5 minutes, stirring occasionally. With spoon, stir in wine, tomatoes with
their liquid, and next 5 ingredients, breaking up
tomatoes into small pieces.
3. Return veal to Dutch oven; heat to boiling.
Reduce heat to low; cover and simmer 1¼ hours or
until veal is fork-tender, stirring occasionally.
4. Meanwhile, prepare the Risotto alla Milanese, if
desired; keep warm.
5. To serve, spoon veal into serving dish; discard bay
leaf. Sprinkle with parsley and lemon peel. Serve
with risotto.

Variety meat

Variety meats are highly nutritious, are generally economical, and contain little or no fat or gristle, so there is little waste. However, they are highly perishable and should be cooked, or at least precooked, as soon as possible after purchase. Sweetbreads, brains and tripe are especially perishable.

Liver: Veal, calves' and lamb liver are the most delicate; beef and pork liver have the strongest flavor; beef liver is the least tender. Before cooking, remove any membrane from the liver. Veal and lamb liver may be broiled, pan-broiled or pan-fried. Pork and beef liver are best braised. Allow 1 pound for 4 servings.

Sweetbreads, a great delicacy, are tender and subtly flavored. They are the thymus gland of veal, calf or young beef. If not to be used immediately, they should be precooked. Sweetbreads should be soaked and peeled before cooking; then broiled, braised or cooked in liquid. If cooked in water, the membrane may be removed after cooking.

Tongue may be purchased fresh, smoked, corned or pickled, also canned. A less tender meat, it needs long, slow cooking in liquid. Smoked or pickled tongue may also need soaking for several hours before cooking. To prepare cooked tongue for serving, see recipes. One beef tongue makes 12 to 16 servings; 1 veal tongue, 3 to 6 servings; 1 pork tongue, 2 to 4 servings; 1 lamb tongue, 2 to 3 servings.

Brains: Beef, veal, lamb and pork brains are tender and delicately flavored. They should be soaked and peeled before cooking, then broiled, braised or cooked in liquid. If cooked in water, membrane may be removed after cooking. If they are not to be served immediately, they should be precooked; reheat in a sauce or pan-fry. Allow 1 pound for 4 servings.

Kidneys: Veal, lamb and pork kidneys are tender enough to be broiled. Beef kidneys are less tender, more strongly flavored, and should be braised or cooked in liquid. To prepare kidneys for cooking, remove membranes and hard white part. One beef kidney makes 4 to 6 servings; 1 veal kidney, 3 to 4 servings; 1 pork kidney, 1 to 2 servings; 1 lamb kidney, ½ to 1 serving.

Heart is a firm-textured meat, with little waste. A less tender meat, it should be braised, cooked in liquid or ground and used in recipes. To trim heart, see Beef Heart Stew, page 241. One beef heart makes 10 to 12 servings; 1 pork or veal heart, 2 to 3 servings; 1 lamb heart, 1 serving.

Tripe: Plain, honeycomb and pocket tripe, all from beef, are sold fresh, pickled or canned. Honeycomb is considered the best. Fresh tripe is sold partially cooked and requires about 1½ hours further cooking in salted water, tightly covered, to make it tender. Pickled tripe is sold thoroughly cooked and need only be soaked before use. Allow 1 pound for 4 servings.

Color index page 65

Begin 20 mins ahead

4 servings

Pan-fried Liver and Bacon

1 8-ounce package bacon slices
1 pound calves' liver, sliced about ¼ inch thick
2 tablespoons all-purpose flour
¼ teaspoon salt
4 lemon wedges (optional)
chopped parsley for garnish

1 In 10-inch skillet over medium heat, fry bacon until crisp; drain on paper towels; keep warm. Pour off all but 2 tablespoons fat from skillet.

2 Trim any membrane from edges of liver slices. On waxed paper, coat liver with flour.

3 Over medium heat, in hot fat, cook liver 4 minutes, turning once, until crisp and brown on outside, delicate pink inside.

4 Sprinkle with salt; squeeze over a little lemon juice. Place liver and bacon on warm platter; garnish with parsley.

Color index page 65

Begin 1¼ hrs ahead

6 to 8 servings

Liver Jardinière

2 pounds beef liver, sliced about ¼ inch thick
3 tablespoons all-purpose flour
1 8-ounce package bacon slices
3 medium onions, thinly sliced
3 large green peppers, thinly sliced
2 teaspoons salt
¼ teaspoon pepper
1 16-ounce can tomatoes

1. On waxed paper, lightly coat liver slices with flour. In 12-inch skillet over medium heat, fry bacon until crisp; drain on paper towels; crumble; set aside. Pour off drippings and reserve.

2. Over medium heat, in ¼ cup bacon drippings, fry liver, a few pieces at a time, until lightly browned on both sides. Remove from pan.

3. Meanwhile, to skillet, add 2 or 3 tablespoons more bacon drippings, onions, next 3 ingredients and brown lightly. Add juice from tomatoes (reserve tomatoes); place liver on top; cover; cook over low heat 25 minutes or until liver is tender. During last minutes, add tomatoes to heat through. To serve, sprinkle bacon on top.

Sweetbreads Meunière

Color index
page 65

Begin 45 mins
ahead

3 to 4
servings

1 pound veal sweetbreads
hot water
salt
lemon juice
vinegar (optional)
¼ teaspoon ground
ginger (optional)

½ cup butter or
margarine
⅓ cup dried bread
crumbs
chopped parsley for
garnish

1. Wash sweetbreads. Precook: In 3-quart saucepan, place sweetbreads with hot water to cover. For each 4 cups water, add 1 teaspoon salt and 1 tablespoon lemon juice or vinegar. If you like, add ginger. Over high heat, heat to boiling. Reduce heat to low; cover tightly; simmer 20 minutes; drain. Place in cold water; remove membrane. Cut out veins and connective tissue. Halve sweetbreads lengthwise.
2. Meanwhile, preheat broiler if manufacturer directs. In 1-quart saucepan over low heat, melt butter. Place bread crumbs on waxed paper. Dip sweetbreads in butter, then in bread crumbs; reserve leftover butter. Place sweetbreads on greased rack in broiling pan and broil 8 to 10 minutes until lightly browned, turning once. Place on warm platter.
3. Reheat butter; stir in 2 tablespoons lemon juice; pour over sweetbreads. Garnish with parsley.

"Boiled" Fresh Tongue

Color index
page 65

Begin 3½ hrs
ahead

12 to 14
servings

1 3½-pound fresh beef
tongue
1 medium onion, sliced
2 tablespoons salt
½ teaspoon mustard
seed
½ teaspoon peppercorns

5 whole cloves
1 bay leaf
hot water
Creamy Cucumber Sauce
or Spicy Cranberry
Sauce (page 243)

1. In 8-quart Dutch oven over high heat, heat to boiling first 7 ingredients and enough hot water to cover. Reduce heat to low; cover and simmer 3 hours or until meat is fork-tender.
2. Plunge tongue into cold water and remove skin, bones and gristle as shown below. Serve hot or cold with sauce. To serve cold, cover and refrigerate in cooking liquid to cool (it will be juicier).

REMOVING SKIN, BONES AND GRISTLE FROM "BOILED" TONGUE

Slit skin on underside from thick end to tip; loosen skin all around thick end. Grasp skin at thick end and pull it off.

With sharp knife, carefully trim all bones and gristle from thick end of tongue. Cut tongue into thin slices.

Brains au Beurre Noir

Color index
page 65

Begin 1 hr
ahead

4 servings

2 beef brains, halved
(about 1½ pounds)
water
salt
lemon juice or white
vinegar
2 tablespoons all-purpose
flour
6 tablespoons butter or
margarine

4 French bread slices,
toasted
2 tablespoons chopped
parsley
1 teaspoon capers,
drained

1. Wash brains. Precook: In 3-quart saucepan or Dutch oven, place brains with water to cover. For each 4 cups water, add 1 teaspoon salt and 1 tablespoon lemon juice or vinegar; over high heat, heat to boiling. Reduce heat to low; cover and simmer 20 minutes; drain. Cover with cold water to cool quickly; drain. Carefully remove membrane, being careful to keep brains in one piece. Pat dry with paper towels.
2. On waxed paper, coat brains with flour.
3. In 10-inch skillet over medium heat, in hot butter, cook brains until lightly browned on all sides, turning with pancake turner. Carefully place each brain on a French bread slice on warm platter. Sprinkle with parsley; keep warm.
4. Into drippings in skillet, stir 1 tablespoon white vinegar and capers; pour over brains.

LAMB BRAINS: Use *4 lamb brains* (about 1 pound), instead of beef; do not halve.

Beef Heart Stew

Color index
page 65

Begin 3½ hrs
ahead

10 servings

1 beef heart
1 29-ounce can tomatoes
2 medium onions,
chopped
1 tablespoon salt
1 teaspoon basil
½ teaspoon thyme
leaves

¼ teaspoon pepper
2 bay leaves
1 garlic clove, minced
3 medium carrots, cut
into ½-inch pieces
3 celery stalks, cut into
½-inch pieces

1. With kitchen shears, split heart open; remove fat and white tubes; wash heart. With sharp knife, cut meat into 1-inch chunks.
2. In 5-quart Dutch oven over high heat, heat meat, tomatoes, onions, salt, basil, thyme, pepper, bay leaves and garlic to boiling. Cover and bake in 350°F. oven 1½ hours.
3. Add carrots and celery pieces and bake 1 hour.

Cutting open heart: Use kitchen shears to split heart open.

Removing fat and tubes: Cut away all fat and white tubes, leaving only meat.

Variety meat

Color index page 65

Begin 50 mins ahead

4 to 6 servings

Sautéed Veal Kidneys

2 veal kidneys	*½ cup chicken broth*
3 tablespoons butter	*2 tablespoons Madeira*
¼ pound mushrooms, sliced	*¼ teaspoon salt*
	toast points
2 green onions, sliced	*chopped parsley*

1. Cut kidneys into 1-inch chunks, removing membrane and hard white parts.

2. In 10-inch skillet over medium-high heat, in hot butter, cook mushrooms and onions until tender, about 5 minutes. With slotted spoon, remove from skillet; set aside. In drippings in skillet, cook kidneys until lightly browned, about 3 minutes, stirring kidneys occasionally.

3. Add mushroom mixture, chicken broth, Madeira and salt; heat to boiling. Reduce heat to low; cover and simmer 30 minutes or until kidneys are fork-tender. Serve with toast points. Garnish mixture with chopped parsley.

Color index page 65

Begin 1 hr ahead

4 servings

Lamb Kidneys Madeira

8 lamb kidneys	*1 teaspoon Worcestershire*
2 tablespoons Madeira	
1 teaspoon drained green peppercorns	*½ teaspoon dry mustard*
⅓ cup butter or margarine, softened	*¼ teaspoon garlic salt*
	toast points
¼ cup minced onion	
3 tablespoons chopped parsley	

1. Remove membranes from kidneys. Firmly grasp kidney. With knife, begin splitting kidney lengthwise, cutting about two-thirds of way down into kidney, exposing thin white veins; repeat on other side of white piece. Insert knife under each vein; cut vein loose. (Be careful not to cut kidney into pieces.) Discard white piece and veins. Wash kidney.

2. Spread kidney open and place, cut side up, on greased rack of broiling pan. Repeat with remaining kidneys. Sprinkle over Madeira.

3. Preheat broiler if manufacturer directs. In small bowl with pestle, crush peppercorns. Add butter and remaining ingredients except toast points; mix well. Spoon mixture over kidneys.

4. Broil kidneys about 6 minutes for rare, 8 minutes for medium and 10 minutes for well done. Serve with toast; spoon pan drippings over kidneys.

Splitting kidney: With knife next to white piece, split kidney lengthwise.

Adding Madeira: Arrange kidneys on greased rack and sprinkle over Madeira.

Sausage

The many different types of sausages available, both fresh and cooked, make a useful and popular standby for quick meals, snacks and sandwiches. Sausage is meat that is ground and seasoned. It is grouped according to the way it is made. Varieties include:

Fresh sausage: Usually made of pork, sometimes beef. Refrigerate and use within 2 or 3 days.

Uncooked smoked sausage: Refrigerate and use as above. Includes kielbasa and mettwurst.

Cooked sausage: Made from fresh, not cured, meat; is ready-to-serve. Unsliced pieces may be refrigerated for 4 to 6 days before use. Sliced pieces should be eaten within 2 to 3 days. Blood sausage and liverwurst are examples.

Cooked, smoked sausage: Made of fresh meat, smoked, and fully cooked. Refrigerate and eat within 4 to 5 days. If sliced, use within 2 or 3 days. See below on how to serve hot. Frankfurters and some salami are types.

Dry and semi-dry sausages: Smoked or unsmoked, these are ready-to-eat. Refrigerate and use within 2 to 3 weeks. They include salami, pepperoni and cervelat.

Cooked meat specialities: Include a variety of ready-to-serve meat products. Most are presliced and packaged; some are spreadable. Use within 2 or 3 days.

COOKING FRESH AND UNCOOKED SMOKED SAUSAGE

Make sure that sausage links or patties are cooked thoroughly; turn links with tongs during cooking so that you avoid piercing the casings.

Pan-frying: Place links in cold skillet with 2 to 4 tablespoons water; cover tightly and, over low heat, cook 5 to 8 minutes, depending on size. Remove cover of skillet and cook the links until they are browned, turning them occasionally. Cook sausage patties in a skillet over medium heat until they are browned, turning them frequently with pancake turner.

Broiling: Place sausage links on rack in a broiling pan and broil until well done, turning and brushing them occasionally either with sauce or with butter or margarine. Uncooked bratwurst and bockwurst should be placed in a pan of water, heated to boiling and left to stand about 10 minutes before broiling. Drain them thoroughly before broiling as above.

Baking: Place links or patties on rack in open roasting pan and bake in preheated 400°F. oven 20 to 30 minutes, depending on size.

HEATING COOKED SMOKED-SAUSAGE LINKS

Cooked smoked-sausage links may be heated through in simmering water; pan-fried over medium heat in 1 or 2 tablespoons hot salad oil, butter or margarine until browned on all sides; or brushed with melted fat, placed on rack in broiling pan and broiled 3 inches from heat until links are evenly browned on all sides.

Homemade Sausages

**2 pounds pork shoulder
  blade roast boneless,
  cut into 1-inch cubes**
¼ cup chopped parsley
2½ teaspoons salt
1 teaspoon rubbed sage
½ teaspoon pepper
**2 yards natural sausage
  casing**
water

Color index page 65

Begin 5 hrs ahead

2 pounds or 8 main-dish servings

1 With food grinder, using coarse cutting disk, grind cubed pork into large bowl.

2 Add chopped parsley, salt, rubbed sage and pepper; mix well. Refrigerate mixture until well chilled, about 3½ hours.

3 Rinse casing in several changes of warm water; slip one end of casing over faucet and run warm water through it.

4 Cover casing with warm water and let soak 30 minutes until it is supple.

5 Remove cutting disk from meat grinder and attach sausage horn as manufacturer directs.

6 Place some of meat mixture in grinder and grind just until meat reaches the end of the sausage horn.

7 Slip entire length of sausage casing onto horn, allowing 2 inches to extend over end; tie end of casing in knot.

8 To fill casing, gradually grind meat mixture into casing, pulling casing gently to fill evenly. Do not overfill casing.

9 Twist casing at 5-inch intervals or at desired lengths to form links, pressing meat away from twists. With kitchen shears, cut into links. Cover; refrigerate.

10 To cook: In covered 12-inch skillet over low heat, in ¼ cup simmering water, cook links 5 minutes; uncover; brown over medium heat 20 minutes.

Sausage Patties: *About 1 hour before serving:* Prepare the meat mixture as for Homemade Sausages, above, but in step 2 do not refrigerate; shape the meat mixture into patties. In 12-inch skillet over medium-low heat, cook the patties about 25 minutes or until they are browned and well done. Carefully turn the patties occasionally with pancake turner to ensure they cook and brown evenly. (Makes 8 main-dish servings.)

Sauces for meat

Begin 1½ hrs ahead

1 cup or 6 servings

Mint Sauce

2 bunches mint
¼ cup cider vinegar
4 teaspoons sugar

**2 tablespoons boiling
  water**

1. Rinse mint well in cold water; drain thoroughly. Trim any tough stems. On cutting board, finely chop mint to make 1 cup.
2. In small bowl, combine mint with remaining ingredients. Let stand 1 hour to blend flavors. Serve with roast or broiled lamb.

Begin 15 mins ahead

1⅔ cups

Spicy Cranberry Sauce

**1 16-ounce can whole-
  cranberry sauce**
2 tablespoons butter
**1 tablespoon light brown
  sugar**
1 tablespoon horseradish

½ teaspoon dry mustard
**¼ teaspoon ground
  allspice**

In 2-quart saucepan over medium heat, heat to boiling all ingredients, stirring occasionally. Reduce heat and simmer about 5 minutes. Serve with sliced tongue, roast pork or baked ham.

Begin 10 mins ahead

1½ cups

Raisin Sauce

½ cup water
**½ cup dark seedless
  raisins**
⅓ cup currant jelly
**½ teaspoon grated
  orange peel**
⅛ teaspoon salt

**⅛ teaspoon ground
  allspice**
1 tablespoon cornstarch
⅓ cup orange juice

In 1-quart saucepan over medium-high heat, heat to boiling water, raisins, jelly, orange peel, salt and allspice. In cup, blend cornstarch with orange juice; stir into raisin mixture and cook, stirring, until thickened and clear. Serve with baked ham, sliced tongue or roast pork.

Begin 15 mins ahead or early in day

1½ cups

Creamy Cucumber Sauce

**1 medium cucumber,
  peeled and seeded**
1 cup sour cream

1 teaspoon grated onion
½ teaspoon salt

Onto waxed paper shred cucumber; pat dry. In medium bowl, stir cucumber and remaining ingredients until blended. Cover and refrigerate. Serve with sliced tongue, roast beef or baked ham.

POULTRY

Poultry, which includes turkey, chicken, duckling, goose and Rock Cornish hens, is plentiful fresh or frozen the year around – and in a form to meet the needs of every cook. Birds range from 1-pound Rock Cornish game hens to massive turkeys weighing 24 pounds and more. There is also a wide choice of "parts" – halves, quarters, breasts, legs, thighs and drumsticks – and boneless roasts. In the case of long-roasting turkeys, some need little watching since they are sold prebasted, injected with fat or broth to keep them moist.

Holidays and festivals are traditionally celebrated with a roast bird, but poultry is equally at home fried or baked at family meals, or combined with other flavors to make excitingly different dishes for more formal occasions. When it comes to cooking, then, there are few meats to match poultry for versatility. Poultry is also one of the most economical sources of high-quality protein and, serving for serving, chicken and turkey are actually lower in calories than most other meats.

CHOOSING POULTRY
When choosing poultry, you will find many items carry helpful information on the label or wrapper. Poultry processors as well as supermarkets label products to indicate the quality; sometimes cooking directions are also included. A United States Department of Agriculture circular mark proves that the bird has been inspected for wholesomeness and has met rigid federal standards. Birds of the highest quality of meatiness and appearance also have a shield-shaped label stating that they are USDA "Grade A". The age of the bird may also be indicated; age determines its tenderness. Young poultry has tender meat and can successfully be broiled, barbecued, fried or roasted. Older or "mature" birds are more richly flavored, but the meat is less tender and should be tenderized by braising or simmering in liquid. Choose a whole bird with a plump, well-rounded breast and clear skin free of blemishes and bruising. (Skin color may vary from white to yellow according to what the bird was fed and is not an indication of quality.)

STORING UNCOOKED POULTRY
Store uncooked fresh poultry in its plastic wrap in the refrigerator and use within 2 or 3 days. If wrapped in meat market paper, unwrap it, place it on a platter and cover loosely with waxed paper before refrigerating. Wrap and refrigerate giblets separately. Frozen unstuffed poultry should be kept in the freezer just until time to thaw and roast. Remember that commercially stuffed frozen poultry should always be kept strictly according to label directions.

THAWING FROZEN POULTRY
Frozen poultry is best thawed gradually in the refrigerator, but to speed up the process if you are in a hurry, use the cold water method.

Refrigerator method: Place the bird, in its plastic wrap, on a tray in the refrigerator. The exact thawing time will depend on the size of the bird and the temperature of the refrigerator, but it can be estimated as follows:

REFRIGERATOR METHOD FOR THAWING POULTRY			
Weight *(in pounds)*	Thawing time *(in hours)*	Weight *(in pounds)*	Thawing time *(in days)*
1 to 2	12	6 to 12	1½ to 2
2 to 4	12 to 24	12 to 20	2 to 3
4 to 6	24 to 36	20 to 24	3 to 3½

Cold water method: Place bird in its original plastic wrap in a large pan or in the sink and cover with cold water. Change the water regularly as its temperature drops until bird thaws. Small chickens and Rock Cornish hens will thaw within about 1 hour, 4- to 12-pound birds in 3 to 6 hours. A 12- to 20-pound turkey will take 6 to 8 hours to thaw and a 24-pounder should be ready for cooking within approximately 10 hours.

STORING AND FREEZING COOKED POULTRY
Cooked poultry should stand at room temperature no more than about 1½ hours after cooking. Store loosely wrapped in the refrigerator and use within 2 or 3 days. Store stuffing and gravy separately in covered containers. Gravy should be reheated to boiling and poured into a warmed gravy boat just before serving.

Before freezing cooked poultry, cool and separate the meat, stuffing and gravy. Freezer-wrapped cooked poultry will retain its quality for about 2 months. Stuffing and gravy should always be used within 1 month of freezing.

TYPES OF POULTRY

Geese (4 to 14 pounds) look deceptively large, so allow 1 to 1½ pounds per serving.

Whole turkeys (4 to over 24 pounds) are plump, tender birds; allow about 1 pound per serving for birds up to 12 pounds, ¾ pound per serving for larger ones.

Hens, stewing chickens or fowls (2½ to 8 pounds) are mature birds needing long, slow cooking to make them tender.

Ducklings (3 to 7 pounds) have a low proportion of meat to bone. Allow at least 1 pound duckling per serving.

Roasting chickens (3½ to 6 pounds) are meaty, tender birds equally good either oven-roasted or rotisserie-cooked.

Capons (6 to 8 pounds) are neutered male chickens noted for their tenderness, with a large proportion of white meat to dark. They are an excellent choice for roasting for a dinner party.

Broiler-fryers (1½ to 4 pounds) are all-purpose birds which may be broiled, fried, roasted, braised or stewed. They can be bought whole or cut up.

Rock Cornish hens are a breed of tiny chicken. A small one makes 1 portion, a larger one will serve 2 people.

OTHER WAYS OF BUYING POULTRY

Turkey breasts are sold whole. They are sometimes sliced into cutlets or steaks for recipes or made into roasts (below).

Chicken leg

Chicken breasts are sold whole or halved.

Chicken wing

Turkey roasts are boneless pieces of white and dark meat in natural proportions, or white or dark meat only. Smoked turkey comes cured, thoroughly smoked and cooked. Just heat and eat.

CUTTING UP A TURKEY

With turkey breast side up, cutting close to leg, cut through skin between leg and breast. Bend leg back until hip joint cracks.

Remove leg from body by cutting through hip joint. Repeat with other leg.

Separate thighs from drumsticks by holding a leg in both hands and bending to crack joint. Cut through joint.

Remove wings by bending them back and cutting through joint at breast. Cut tips from wings at joints.

Place carcass on one side; with poultry shears, cutting from leg joint, cut through to backbone and along backbone to neck. Turn and cut along other side to remove breast. Backbone will remain intact.

Hold breast, skin side down, and bend it back to crack the breastbone. With poultry shears, cut along each side of breastbone.

CUTTING UP A CHICKEN

Place chicken, breast side up, on cutting board. Pull one leg away from body and slice through skin between leg and breast.

Lift chicken and bend back leg until hip joint cracks. Remove leg from body by cutting close to body through hip joint. Repeat with other leg.

To separate drumstick from thigh, hold leg in both hands and bend to crack joint. Cut through joint.

Remove each wing by bending it back and cutting through joint.

Place carcass on one side. Cutting from leg joint with poultry shears or kitchen shears, cut to backbone and along backbone to neck. Turn carcass and cut along other side to remove breast. Backbone will remain intact.

Divide breast lengthwise in two by holding it, skin side down, and bending it back to snap the breastbone.

With knife, cut breast in half along breastbone, leaving breastbone on one half of breast.

HALVING A CHICKEN

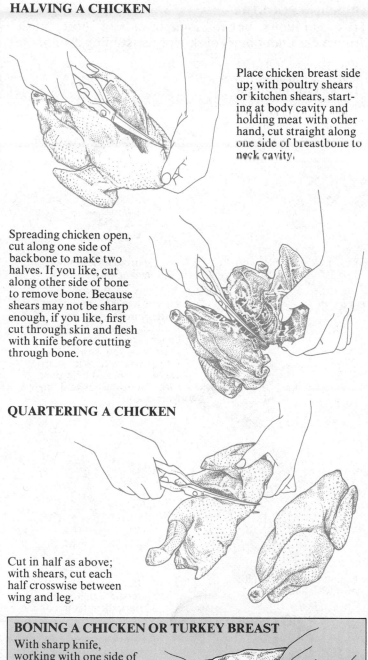

Place chicken breast side up; with poultry shears or kitchen shears, starting at body cavity and holding meat with other hand, cut straight along one side of breastbone to neck cavity.

Spreading chicken open, cut along one side of backbone to make two halves. If you like, cut along other side of bone to remove bone. Because shears may not be sharp enough, if you like, first cut through skin and flesh with knife before cutting through bone.

QUARTERING A CHICKEN

Cut in half as above; with shears, cut each half crosswise between wing and leg.

BONING A CHICKEN OR TURKEY BREAST

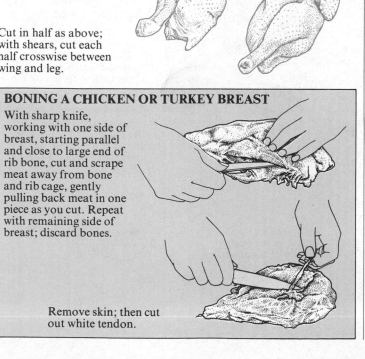

With sharp knife, working with one side of breast, starting parallel and close to large end of rib bone, cut and scrape meat away from bone and rib cage, gently pulling back meat in one piece as you cut. Repeat with remaining side of breast; discard bones.

Remove skin; then cut out white tendon.

QUARTERING A DUCKLING

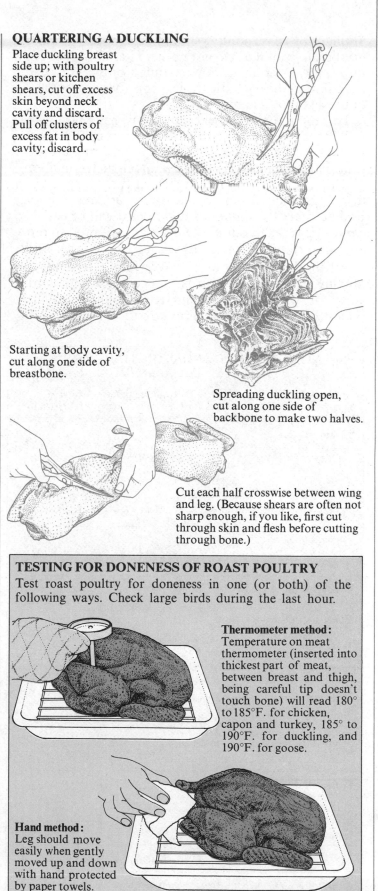

Place duckling breast side up; with poultry shears or kitchen shears, cut off excess skin beyond neck cavity and discard. Pull off clusters of excess fat in body cavity; discard.

Starting at body cavity, cut along one side of breastbone.

Spreading duckling open, cut along one side of backbone to make two halves.

Cut each half crosswise between wing and leg. (Because shears are often not sharp enough, if you like, first cut through skin and flesh before cutting through bone.)

TESTING FOR DONENESS OF ROAST POULTRY

Test roast poultry for doneness in one (or both) of the following ways. Check large birds during the last hour.

Thermometer method: Temperature on meat thermometer (inserted into thickest part of meat, between breast and thigh, being careful tip doesn't touch bone) will read 180° to 185°F. for chicken, capon and turkey, 185° to 190°F. for duckling, and 190°F. for goose.

Hand method: Leg should move easily when gently moved up and down with hand protected by paper towels.

Roast poultry

Stuffing for roast poultry should be spooned in loosely just before cooking. Do not bother to stuff the neck of a bird under 4 pounds. For unstuffed birds, skewer the neck skin to the back; tie the legs together across the tail or use a stuffing clamp.

To keep the breast meat moist, cover the bird with a foil "tent" during the last hour of roasting. Never partially roast any poultry one day and complete it the next: bacteria are likely to grow under such conditions. Unless you are roasting a prebasted turkey, spoon pan drippings, melted butter, margarine or salad oil over bird at intervals while roasting. A bird will be easier to carve if it is taken out of the oven and allowed to rest – about 30 minutes for a turkey, less for smaller birds.

When the meal is over, cover and refrigerate the stuffing, gravy and meat separately and use within a day or so. Or, wrap separately and freeze poultry meat up to 3 months, the stuffing and gravy up to 1 month.

· TIMETABLE FOR ROASTING POULTRY

Ready-to-cook weight *(in pounds)*	Oven temperature	Cooking time *(in hours)*	Internal temperature
Turkey, stuffed			
8 to 12	325°F.	3½ to 4	180 to 185°F.
12 to 16	325°F.	4 to 4½	
16 to 20	325°F.	4½ to 5	
20 to 24	325°F.	5 to 6	
Turkey, unstuffed: allow about ½ hour less			180 to 185°F.
Capon, stuffed			
5 to 6	325°F.	2½ to 3	180 to 185°F.
6 to 8	325°F.	3 to 4	
Capon, unstuffed: allow about ½ hour less			180 to 185°F.
Chicken, stuffed or unstuffed			
2 to 2½	325°F.	1½	180 to 185°F.
2½ to 3	325°F.	2	
3 to 4	325°F.	2½	
4 to 6	325°F.	2½ to 3½	
Rock Cornish hen, stuffed or unstuffed*			
1 to 2	350°F.	1 to 1½	
Whole duckling, stuffed or unstuffed			
3½ to 5½	325°F.	2 to 2½	185 to 190°F.
Goose, stuffed			
9 to 11	350°F.	3¼ to 4	190°F.
11 to 13	350°F.	4 to 4½	
Goose, unstuffed: allow about ½ hour less			190°F.

*Bird is too small to use meat thermometer. Test for doneness by moving legs up and down and pinching with fingers protected with paper towels. Leg will move easily and feel soft.

TRUSSING POULTRY

Truss as follows, but for some brands of turkey push drumsticks under band of skin or use stuffing clamp.

With bird breast side up, fold neck skin under turkey. Lift wings up toward neck, then fold under back of bird so they balance bird and keep neck skin in place.

Fasten skin to back with 1 or 2 skewers, if necessary.

Tie drumsticks and tail together with string.

CARVING

Place roasted bird on warm platter or cutting board 15 to 30 minutes to allow it to "set" for easier carving. Place bird directly in front of you with breast of bird at your left. With sharp carving knife and long-tined fork, cut drumstick and thigh from body.

Disjoint it by bending it down with hand.

Remove drumstick to a separate plate and slice dark meat from bone.

Insert fork securely into upper part of wing; make a long deep cut above wing joint through breast to bird's frame.

From halfway up breast, carve downward with a straight motion; when knife reaches slice made across from wing, poultry slices will fall free. Carve enough thin slices for serving. Carve more as needed.

Roast Turkey with Moist Bread Stuffing

*1 12- to 16-pound frozen
   ready-to-stuff
   prebasted turkey,
   thawed*
*Moist Bread Stuffing
   (page 253)*
salad oil
Giblet Gravy (below)

Color index page 39
Begin 6½ hrs ahead
12 to 16 servings

1 Remove giblets and neck from inside turkey and reserve for gravy. Rinse bird with running cold water; drain well.

2 Spoon some stuffing lightly into neck cavity (do not pack). Fold neck skin over and fasten to back with 1 or 2 skewers.

3 With bird breast side up, lift wings up toward neck, then fold under back of bird so they stay flat and keep neck skin in place.

4 Spoon remaining stuffing lightly into body cavity. Close by folding skin lightly over opening; skewer closed.

5 Depending on brand of bird, with string, tie legs to tail; or push drumsticks under band of skin or use stuffing clamp.

6 On rack in open roasting pan, place bird breast side up. Brush skin lightly with salad oil.

7 Insert meat thermometer into meat between breast and thigh, being careful that pointed end does not touch bone.

8 Roast at 325°F. 4 to 4½ hours, covering with a "tent" of foil when bird turns golden. Check doneness during last 30 minutes.

9 Toward end of roasting, remove foil; coat bird with drippings. Bird is done when thermometer reads 180° to 185°F.

Giblet Gravy

*reserved giblets
   and neck*
1 celery stalk, cut up
*½ cup chopped
   onion*
salt
water
turkey pan drippings
*6 tablespoons all-purpose
   flour*

Begin 2 hrs ahead
5 cups

1 While turkey is roasting, in 3-quart saucepan over high heat, heat to boiling giblets, neck, celery, onion, 1 teaspoon salt and water to cover.

2 Reduce heat to low; cover; simmer 1 hour until giblets are tender. Drain, reserving broth; discard celery and onion. Chop neck meat and giblets.

3 When turkey is done, remove rack from pan; pour pan drippings into a 4-cup measure; let drippings stand until fat separates from meat juice.

4 Skim ⅓ cup fat from drippings into 2-quart saucepan; skim off and discard any fat remaining on surface of drippings.

5 Add reserved broth to roasting pan; stir until brown bits are loosened.

6 Add liquid to meat juice in cup to make 4 cups (add water if necessary).

7 Into fat in saucepan over medium heat, stir flour and 2 teaspoons salt.

8 Gradually stir in meat-juice mixture; cook, stirring until thickened.

9 Add reserved chopped giblets and neck meat; cook until heated through.

Roast turkey and chicken

Color index page 39
Begin day ahead
12 to 16 servings

Turkey Breast with Glazes

1 6- to 7-pound frozen   *melted butter or*
* turkey breast,*   *margarine*
* thawed*   *Glaze (below)*

1. Thaw turkey breast overnight in refrigerator. Remove the wrapping.
2. *About 3½ hours before serving*: Place on rack in open roasting pan. Insert meat thermometer into center of roast. Roast in 325°F. oven 3 to 3½ hours or until internal temperature reaches 180° to 185°F., basting occasionally with melted butter or margarine or pan drippings.
3. Meanwhile, prepare one of glazes, below. During last 20 minutes of roasting time, lightly brush turkey roast several times with glaze.

GLAZES FOR TURKEY BREAST

APPLE-JELLY: In 1-quart saucepan over low heat, stir *1 cup apple jelly* with *½ teaspoon salt* until melted. (Makes 1 cup.)

APRICOT: In 1-quart saucepan over low heat, stir *1 cup apricot preserves* and *½ cup chopped dried apricots* until blended. (Makes 1 cup.)

CHUTNEY: In cup, over *¼ cup golden raisins*, pour *½ cup boiling water* and set aside 15 to 20 minutes to "plump"; drain. In 1-quart saucepan over low heat, stir raisins, *½ cup chutney* and *½ cup red currant jelly* until blended and jelly is melted. (Makes 1 cup.)

TANGY-CATCHUP: In 1-quart saucepan over medium heat, heat *¼ cup grape jelly*, *⅔ cup catchup* and *½ teaspoon bottled sauce for gravy* until blended and jelly is melted. (Makes 1 cup.)

Sherry Aspic

2 10½-ounce cans   *2 envelopes unflavored*
* condensed beef broth*   *gelatin*
½ cup dry sherry

1. In 2-quart saucepan, combine undiluted broth and sherry. Sprinkle gelatin evenly over mixture.
2. Over medium heat, cook mixture until gelatin is completely dissolved, stirring constantly.
3. Pour into 13″ by 9″ baking pan. Cover and refrigerate until Sherry Aspic is set.

Turkey Breast Glacé with Sherry Aspic

1 6-pound turkey breast
Sherry Aspic (below left)
1 cup heavy cream
1 cup water
3 tablespoons white wine
¼ teaspoon tarragon
1 chicken bouillon cube
1 envelope unflavored
* gelatin*
Garnish: *2 cherry*
tomatoes, 1 large green
onion, 2 large pitted ripe
olives, 3 carrot slices

Color index page 40
Begin day ahead
12 to 15 servings

1 Roast turkey as label directs; cover; refrigerate until well chilled. Meanwhile, prepare Sherry Aspic. For cream mixture: In 2-quart saucepan, combine next 5 ingredients.

2 Sprinkle gelatin over mixture; over medium heat, stir until gelatin dissolves. Cover; chill until consistency of unbeaten egg whites.

3 On rack over waxed paper in shallow baking pan, place chilled turkey breast. Quickly spoon some cream mixture evenly over breast to coat thinly. Refrigerate to set.

4 Repeat coating several times until all the cream mixture has been used. If mixture becomes too thick set pan in bowl of hot water and stir until of sauce-like consistency.

5 Meanwhile, for garnish, cut cherry tomatoes into quarters but do not cut through; with spoon, carefully scoop out seeds and pulp.

6 Dip green onion into very hot water for a few seconds; drain; cut lengthwise into thin strips.

7 Cut olives into thin wedges. With canapé cutter, cut slices of carrot into flower shapes.

8 Arrange garnish vegetables on slightly set cream mixture. Refrigerate turkey breast until serving time.

9 To serve: With 2 pancake turners, lift turkey onto large platter.

10 Cut aspic into ½-inch cubes. Arrange cubes around turkey.

Turkey Roll with Spinach Stuffing

Color index
page 39

Begin 3 hrs
ahead

16 servings

*Spinach Stuffing
(page 253)*
*1 6-pound turkey breast,
boned, halved and
skinned (reserve
skin)*
1 teaspoon salt
*¼ cup butter or
margarine, melted*

**Gravy: *2 cups water,
2 tablespoons all-purpose
flour, ½ teaspoon salt,
⅛ teaspoon pepper***

1 Prepare stuffing. Place each half-breast, cut side up, on board. Starting at long side, cut horizontally in half, but not all the way through; open out meat like a butterfly.

2 Spread meat open. With meat mallet or dull edge of French knife, pound until about 10″ by 9″ and ¼ inch thick.

3 Sprinkle with half of salt then cover with half of stuffing. Starting at narrow end, roll up jelly-roll fashion. Place one piece of skin on top of roll.

4 Tie roll with string. Repeat steps 2–4 with remaining half-breast.

5 Place rolls, skin side up, on rack in roasting pan. Brush with butter. Insert meat thermometer in center of one roll.

6 Roast at 325°F. until thermometer reads 185°F., about 1¾ hours; remove the strings.

7 Make gravy: Pour drippings into 4-cup measure; let stand until fat separates. Pour 2 tablespoons fat into 1-quart saucepan; skim off and discard remaining fat. Add water to roasting pan; stir to loosen brown bits; add to meat juice in cup. Into fat in saucepan, over medium heat, stir flour, salt, pepper and meat-juice; cook, stirring until the gravy is thick.

Roast Chicken with Sausage-Apple Stuffing

Color index
page 43

Begin 4 hrs
ahead

6 servings

*Sausage-Apple Stuffing
(page 253)*
*1 5- to 5½-pound
roasting chicken*

*salad oil, butter or
margarine*

1. Prepare the stuffing. Remove giblets and neck from inside bird. Rinse bird with running cold water and drain well. Spoon some stuffing lightly into neck cavity. Fold neck skin over stuffing. With bird breast side up, lift wings up toward neck, then fold under back of bird to balance it.
2. Spoon remaining stuffing into body cavity; fold skin over opening; rub bird with salad oil. Bake any leftover stuffing in covered, greased small casserole during last 30 minutes of roasting chicken.
3. Insert meat thermometer into thickest part of meat between breast and thigh (do not touch bone). Place chicken, breast side up, on rack in open roasting pan. Roast, uncovered, in 325°F. oven 2½ to 3 hours.
4. When chicken turns golden cover loosely with a "tent" of folded foil. Remove foil during last hour of roasting time. Brush bird generously with pan drippings, oil or melted butter. Chicken is done when thermometer reads 180° to 185°F. Start checking for doneness during the last 30 minutes.

Herb-roasted Capon

Color index
page 41

Begin day
ahead

8 servings

1 6- to 8-pound capon
¼ cup salt
1 teaspoon parsley flakes
¾ teaspoon thyme leaves

½ teaspoon rubbed sage
*⅛ teaspoon cracked
pepper*
salad oil

1. Prepare capon as for Roast Chicken (above) but do not stuff. Mix salt and next 4 ingredients and rub over outside and in body cavity. Cover and refrigerate at least 12 hours or overnight.
2. Brush skin with oil, roast, uncovered, in 325°F. oven 3 to 4 hours, basting frequently.

Chicken Delhi

Color index
page 43

Begin 2½ hrs
ahead

8 servings

*2 3-pound broiler-
fryers*
*1½ teaspoons ground
ginger*
*⅛ teaspoon ground
coriander*
⅛ teaspoon pepper
3 tablespoons butter

1 cup minced onions
1 cup plain yogurt
1 cup half-and-half
1 tablespoon turmeric
1½ teaspoons salt
*about 6 cups hot cooked
rice*

1. Remove giblets and neck from chickens. (Use giblets and neck for broth, if you like.) Rinse and drain chicken well. With string, tie legs and tail of each chicken together. Combine ginger, coriander and pepper; rub into birds and place in open roasting pan.
2. In 2-quart saucepan over medium heat, melt butter; stir in next 5 ingredients; pour over birds. Roast in 325°F. oven about 2 hours or until fork-tender, basting frequently.
3. Lift chickens to warm platter; remove strings. Spoon pan sauce over rice; serve with chicken.

Baked chicken

Baking chicken is the same cooking technique as roasting chicken – the whole bird or parts are baked, uncovered, with uniform heat. However, the oven temperature is usually higher for baking than for roasting. Sometimes chicken pieces are marinated in a sauce before baking, then, during cooking, the remaining marinade is spooned over the pieces. Among the many good tasting sauces to use for marinating are barbecue sauce, French, Italian or other favorite salad dressing, red or white wine, or one of the marinade recipes from page 262. Stuffed chicken breasts can also be baked and are equally good cooked in a marinade.

Baked Chicken

Color index page 44

Begin 1 hr ahead

8 servings

½ cup butter or margarine
½ cup all-purpose flour
2 teaspoons salt

2 teaspoons paprika
¼ teaspoon pepper
2 3-pound broiler-fryers, each cut into quarters

1 In a large roasting pan in 425°F. oven, melt the butter or margarine.

2 Meanwhile, in pie plate, combine flour, salt, paprika and pepper. Coat the chicken quarters evenly with the mixture.

3 In roasting pan, place the chicken pieces, skin side down, in melted butter. Bake 30 minutes.

4 Turn the chicken pieces and bake 15 minutes more until pieces are fork-tender.

Chicken Sauterne

Color index page 46

Begin early in day or day ahead

4 servings

¾ cup sauterne
2 tablespoons salad oil
2 tablespoons chopped parsley
2 tablespoons chopped green onions

2 teaspoons salt
¼ teaspoon paprika
2 2-pound broiler-fryers, each cut in half

1. In 13″ by 9″ baking dish, for marinade, mix all ingredients except chicken. Add chicken; coat with marinade. Cover and refrigerate at least 4 hours.
2. *About 1 hour before serving:* Preheat oven to 375°F. Place chicken, skin side down, in marinade. Bake 25 minutes, basting occasionally; turn; bake 25 minutes more or until fork-tender, basting occasionally. Pour drippings into cup; spoon off fat; discard. Serve remaining liquid over chicken.

Nut-stuffed Chicken Breasts with Creamy Gravy

Color index page 41

Begin 2 hrs ahead

6 servings

⅓ cup finely chopped salted peanuts
¼ cup minced parsley
salt
6 medium whole chicken breasts, each skinned, boned and cut in half
butter or margarine
½ teaspoon paprika

2 tablespoons all-purpose flour
1 chicken-flavor bouillon cube or envelope or 1 teaspoon chicken-flavor stock base
1¼ cups milk
parsley for garnish

1. In small bowl, combine peanuts, minced parsley and ½ teaspoon salt; set aside.
2. With meat mallet or dull edge of French knife, pound each chicken piece until ¼ inch thick.
3. To stuff chicken breasts: Overlap two pieces about 1 inch; sprinkle with a generous tablespoonful of peanut mixture to within ½ inch of edges; fold the two long sides slightly toward the middle; roll chicken breast in the opposite direction, jelly-roll fashion; fasten seam with two toothpicks.
4. Repeat this process with each of the remaining pieces of chicken breast.
5. In 13″ by 9″ baking dish, melt ½ cup butter or margarine in 400°F. oven; stir in paprika and 1 teaspoon salt until well mixed. Arrange stuffed chicken breasts, seam side down, in baking dish; brush with butter mixture in pan. Bake 40 minutes or until chicken is fork-tender, basting occasionally with pan drippings.
6. Spoon 3 tablespoons pan drippings into 1-quart saucepan. Over medium heat, into drippings, stir flour, bouillon and ½ teaspoon salt until blended. Gradually stir in milk; cook, stirring constantly, until mixture is thickened.
7. Discard toothpicks from stuffed chicken breasts; arrange on warm platter.
8. To serve: Garnish with finely chopped parsley Pour gravy into gravy boat; pass separately.

Folding the edges: Fold long sides of chicken toward middle.

Rolling the chicken breast: Roll each stuffed breast up, jelly-roll fashion.

Stuffings

When stuffing whole birds, prepare stuffing just before roasting. You will need ¾ to 1 cup stuffing per pound of bird. Stuffing expands during cooking, so pack it lightly into the bird. If you wish, bake extra stuffing in a covered, greased casserole along with the bird during the last 30 to 45 minutes of roasting time.

Moist Bread Stuffing

Begin 30 mins ahead

10 cups

1 cup butter or margarine	2 teaspoons poultry seasoning
2 cups diced celery	½ teaspoon pepper
1½ cups chopped onions	18 cups white bread cubes
¼ cup minced parsley	3 eggs, slightly beaten
2¼ teaspoons salt	

1. In 8-quart Dutch oven over medium heat, in hot butter or margarine, cook celery and onions until tender, about 10 minutes.
2. Add parsley, salt, poultry seasoning and pepper; stir well until thoroughly mixed.
3. Stir in bread cubes and eggs; mix together well.

Mixed-Fruit Stuffing

Begin 45 mins ahead

8 cups

1 12-ounce package mixed dried fruit, cut in pieces	1 cup sugar
water	5 cups lightly packed, day-old bread cubes
1 medium onion, minced	1 teaspoon salt
1 16-ounce package cranberries	½ teaspoon ground allspice

1. If prunes have pits, remove and discard. In 2-quart saucepan over high heat, heat 2 cups water, fruit and onion to boiling. Reduce heat to low; simmer 15 minutes or until fruit is tender; pour mixture into large bowl.
2. In same pan over medium heat, heat ¼ cup water, cranberries and sugar to boiling. Reduce heat to low; simmer 7 minutes or until berries pop, stirring occasionally. Drain liquid from berries. Pour berries into fruit mixture.
3. Add remaining ingredients; toss lightly.

Chestnut Stuffing

Color index page 49

Begin 1¼ hrs ahead

11 cups

1½ pounds chestnuts	1 teaspoon thyme leaves
water	1 teaspoon marjoram
1 cup butter	½ teaspoon seasoned pepper
1½ cups diced celery	8 cups fresh bread crumbs
1 cup chopped onions	
2 teaspoons salt	

1. With tip of sharp knife, mark an "X" in flat side of each chestnut. In 3-quart saucepan, cover chestnuts with water.
2. Over high heat, heat to boiling; cook 1 minute. Remove pan from heat. With slotted spoon remove 3 or 4 chestnuts at a time; remove shells and skins. Coarsely chop chestnuts; set aside.
3. In 6-quart Dutch oven over medium heat, in hot butter, cook celery and next 5 ingredients about 10 minutes or until vegetables are tender.
4. Remove pan from heat. Stir in chestnuts and bread crumbs; mix all ingredients together well.

Rice-Raisin Stuffing

Color index page 49

Begin 45 mins ahead

14 cups

2½ cups long-grain rice	¾ cup butter
1 8-ounce package sliced bacon	4 cups diced celery
¾ cup dark seedless raisins	2 cups diced onions
	1 tablespoon salt
⅓ cup boiling water	½ teaspoon pepper

1. Prepare rice as label directs. Meanwhile, in 12-inch skillet over medium-low heat, cook bacon; drain on paper towels; crumble into pieces. In bowl, combine raisins with water.
2. In 8-quart Dutch oven over medium heat, in hot butter, cook celery, onions, salt and pepper 10 minutes, stirring often.
3. Remove celery mixture from heat; stir in rice, bacon pieces and seedless raisins.

Sausage-Rice Stuffing

Begin 25 mins ahead

3 cups

¾ cup regular long-grain rice	1 green onion, thinly sliced
½ pound sweet Italian sausage links, casings removed	⅛ teaspoon pepper

1. Prepare rice as label directs; meanwhile, in 10-inch skillet over medium heat, cook sausage until well browned, breaking apart with fork. Drain.
2. Toss rice with sausage, onion and pepper.

Sausage-Apple Stuffing

Color index page 49

Begin 45 mins ahead

6¼ cups

1 pound pork-sausage meat	4 cups fresh bread crumbs
3 large apples, peeled, cored and chopped	2 eggs
1 large onion, chopped	1½ teaspoons salt
1 cup chopped celery	1 teaspoon poultry seasoning

1. In 4-quart saucepan over medium heat, cook sausage meat until browned, breaking apart with fork. Remove meat to medium bowl.
2. Pour off drippings but return ¼ cup to pan. In drippings over medium heat, cook apples, onion and celery until celery is tender, about 10 minutes.
3. Remove from heat. Add sausage meat and remaining ingredients. Stir until well mixed.

Spinach Stuffing

Begin 30 mins ahead

3½ cups

1 10-ounce package frozen chopped spinach, thawed	½ 15-ounce container ricotta cheese (1 cup)
½ cup butter or margarine	1 egg
¼ pound mushrooms, thinly sliced	1 tablespoon minced parsley
1 cup diced celery	1 teaspoon salt
½ cup chopped onion	½ teaspoon poultry seasoning
3 cups fresh bread crumbs	⅛ teaspoon pepper

1. Squeeze spinach dry with paper towels.
2. In 4-quart saucepan over medium heat, in hot butter or margarine, cook mushrooms, celery and onion until tender, about 5 minutes, stirring occasionally; remove from heat.
3. Add remaining ingredients and spinach; mix well.

Braised chicken

Braising usually involves two cooking techniques. First, most recipes call for cooking the food in hot fat until well browned on all sides. Next, flavorings and a small quantity of liquid, such as water, chicken broth, tomato juice or wine, are added. The skillet is then tightly covered and the poultry simmered over low heat until it is fork-tender. Sometimes, the covered skillet is transferred to the oven to complete cooking (be sure the handle of the skillet is ovensafe). Whatever the method. braising is a *slow - cooking method* and should never be hurried.

Select the pan for braising according to the recipe and the shape and size of the poultry. For poultry pieces a deep, heavy skillet with a close-fitting lid will often do well. For larger quantities a Dutch oven is more suitable. Select a pan large enough to hold the bird, its liquid and other ingredients comfortably.

Only a small quantity of liquid is used for braising, usually ½ to 1 cup. During long braising times, therefore, it is best to check the liquid occasionally during cooking, adding a few tablespoons more liquid if it has evaporated too much.

Arroz con Pollo

Color index
page 44

Begin 1¾ hrs
ahead

8 servings

¼ cup salad oil
1 4- to 5-pound roasting chicken, cut up
1 cup chopped onion
1¼ cups water
1 16-ounce can tomatoes
1 4-ounce jar diced pimentos
1 2-ounce jar pimento-stuffed olives
2 cups regular long-grain rice
1 tablespoon salt
¼ teaspoon pepper

2 chicken-flavor bouillon cubes or envelopes or 2 teaspoons chicken-flavor stock base
½ pound fresh pork-sausage links, cut into ½-inch pieces
1 10-ounce package frozen peas, thawed

1 In 8-quart Dutch oven over medium-high heat, in hot oil, brown chicken, a few pieces at a time; set aside. In drippings, over medium heat, cook onion until it is tender.

2 Add chicken, water, tomatoes, pimentos and olives and all their liquids and remaining ingredients except peas; heat to boiling.

3 Reduce heat to low. Cover Dutch oven and simmer chicken mixture 30 minutes or until chicken is almost fork-tender, occasionally lifting rice with fork.

4 Add thawed peas to Dutch oven and cook 10 minutes more. (If mixture seems dry when peas are added, cook covered; if it seems moist, cook uncovered.)

Chicken Paprika with Spaetzle

Color index
page 41

Begin 45 mins
ahead

6 servings

1 2½- to 3-pound broiler-fryer, cut up
⅓ cup all-purpose flour
2 tablespoons salad oil
2 medium onions, thinly sliced
2 teaspoons salt

1 tablespoon paprika
⅛ teaspoon pepper
1½ cups water
1 chicken-flavor bouillon cube or envelope
Spaetzle (below)
½ cup sour cream

1. Coat chicken with flour; reserve remaining flour. In 12-inch skillet over medium-high heat, in hot salad oil, cook chicken until browned on all sides, about 7 to 10 minutes. Remove chicken.
2. To oil in skillet, add remaining flour and onions; cook, stirring constantly, for 2 minutes. Stir in salt, paprika, pepper, water and bouillon. Return chicken to skillet; cover and reduce heat to medium; simmer 25 minutes or until chicken is fork-tender, turning once.
3. Meanwhile, prepare the Spaetzle. With tongs, remove chicken to large platter. Spoon fat from gravy in pan; stir in sour cream until blended.
4. To serve: Add Spaetzle and heat through: spoon around chicken.

SPAETZLE: In 6-quart Dutch oven over high heat, heat *4 quarts water* and *1 teaspoon salt* to boiling. Meanwhile, in medium bowl with wire whisk or spoon, beat *2 cups all-purpose flour, ½ cup water, 3 eggs* and *½ teaspoon salt* until smooth. Reduce heat to medium. Over boiling water with rubber spatula, press batter through colander or spaetzle maker. Stir water gently so spaetzle will not stick together. Boil 5 minutes or until tender but firm *(al dente)*; drain.

Making spaetzle with a colander: Press batter through colander if you have no spaetzle maker.

Cooking the spaetzle: While cooking, stir water gently to keep spaetzle from sticking.

Chicken Oporto

Color index page 41

Begin 35 mins ahead

4 servings

½ cup butter
½ pound mushrooms, thinly sliced
¼ cup all-purpose flour
2 teaspoons salt
¼ teaspoon pepper
¼ teaspoon ground nutmeg

4 medium whole chicken breasts, skinned and boned
1½ cups heavy or whipping cream
⅓ cup white port wine

1. In 12-inch skillet over medium-high heat, in hot butter, cook mushrooms 5 minutes. With slotted spoon, remove to small bowl; set aside.
2. On waxed paper, combine flour, salt, pepper and nutmeg; use to coat chicken breasts. In same skillet in remaining butter, over medium-high heat, cook the chicken breasts until browned on all sides.
3. Stir in cream, port and mushrooms; heat to boiling. Reduce heat to low; cover and simmer 15 minutes or until chicken is fork-tender.

Chicken with Endives

Color index page 43

Begin 45 mins ahead

4 servings

4 medium whole chicken breasts, skinned and boned
water
butter or margarine
1 teaspoon salt
4 small Belgian endives, trimmed
2 tablespoons lemon juice

2 tablespoons drained bottled capers
½ cup fresh bread crumbs
1 tablespoon all-purpose flour
¼ pound natural Swiss cheese, shredded (about 1 cup)

1. Tuck under edges of chicken breasts for a more attractive shape. In 10-inch skillet over medium-low heat, heat ½ cup water and 2 tablespoons butter until melted. Arrange chicken in skillet; sprinkle with salt and place 1 endive on each breast; sprinkle endives with lemon juice.
2. Cover skillet; simmer 25 minutes or until chicken and endives are fork-tender. Remove endive-topped chicken to platter. Sprinkle with capers.
3. Meanwhile, in small skillet over medium heat, heat 2 tablespoons butter and bread crumbs until crumbs are browned, stirring frequently; set aside.
4. In cup, blend flour and 2 tablespoons water until smooth; gradually stir into hot liquid in skillet (there should be about ⅔ cup liquid left in skillet) and cook over medium heat, stirring constantly, until mixture is thickened. Remove from heat; stir in cheese until melted; pour over chicken; top with bread crumbs.

Adding the endives: Sprinkle with salt and put an endive on each breast.

Serving the chicken: Pour melted cheese sauce over and top with bread crumbs.

Chicken Cordon Bleu

Color index page 41

Begin 1¼ hrs ahead

6 servings

6 medium whole chicken breasts, skinned and boned
1 8-ounce package Swiss cheese slices
1 8-ounce package sliced cooked ham
3 tablespoons all-purpose flour
1 teaspoon paprika

6 tablespoons butter or margarine
½ cup dry white wine
1 chicken-flavor bouillon cube or envelope or 1 teaspoon chicken-flavor stock base
1 tablespoon cornstarch
1 cup heavy or whipping cream

1. Spread chicken breasts flat; fold cheese and ham slices to fit on top; fold breasts over filling and fasten edges with toothpicks.
2. On waxed paper, mix flour and paprika; use mixture to coat chicken pieces.
3. In 12-inch skillet over medium heat, in hot butter or margarine, cook chicken until browned on all sides. Add wine and bouillon. Reduce heat to low; cover and simmer 30 minutes or until fork-tender; remove the toothpicks.
4. In cup, blend cornstarch and cream until smooth; gradually stir into skillet. Cook, stirring constantly, until thickened; serve over chicken.

Assembling the chicken and filling: Fold chicken breasts over the cheese and ham slices and fasten securely with toothpicks.

Frying the chicken: In 12-inch skillet over medium heat, in hot butter or margarine, brown chicken on all sides.

Chicken Périgord-Style

Color index page 43

Begin 1 hr ahead

8 servings

½ cup butter or margarine
8 whole chicken breasts, skinned and boned
½ pound mushrooms, sliced

⅓ cup all-purpose flour
¼ teaspoon salt
1 13¾-ounce can chicken broth
2 tablespoons half-and-half

1. In 12-inch skillet or 6-quart Dutch oven over medium-high heat, in 6 tablespoons hot butter or margarine, cook chicken, a few pieces at a time, until browned on all sides. Set chicken aside.
2. In drippings over medium heat, in remaining 2 tablespoons butter, cook mushrooms until golden, about 5 minutes. With slotted spoon, remove mushrooms to small bowl.
3. Into drippings, over medium heat, stir flour and salt until blended. Gradually stir in chicken broth and half-and-half and cook, stirring constantly, until mixture is thickened.
4. Place chicken and mushrooms in sauce. Reduce heat to low; cover and simmer 25 minutes.

Braised chicken

Chicken Breasts with Sausage-Walnut Stuffing

*1 pound sweet Italian
  sausage links, casings
  removed*
*½ cup chopped
  California walnuts*
⅓ cup chopped celery
¼ cup chopped onion
*½ cup fresh bread
  crumbs*
1 egg
*8 small whole chicken
  breasts, boned*
¼ cup all-purpose flour
½ teaspoon paprika
2 tablespoons salad oil

*2 chicken-flavor bouillon
  cubes or envelopes*
1½ cups water
*2 tablespoons butter or
  margarine*
4 medium zucchini, sliced
salt and pepper
1 tablespoon cornstarch
*2 tablespoons white table
  wine*

Color index page 43
Begin 1½ hrs ahead
8 servings

1 In 8-quart Dutch oven
over medium-high heat,
cook sausage, nuts, celery
and onion until meat is
browned, stirring often.

2 Add fresh bread
crumbs and egg; stir
until well mixed. Set mixture aside until needed.

3 Place each breast, skin
side up, on cutting
board. With meat mallet
or dull edge of French
knife, pound breast to
¼-inch thickness.

4 Top half of each breast
with a scant ½ cup of
sausage mixture. Fold
other half over filling and
fasten edges of breast with
toothpicks.

5 On waxed paper, mix
flour and paprika. Coat
breasts with mixture. In
same Dutch oven over
medium heat, in hot oil,
brown breasts.

6 Add bouillon and
water. Reduce heat to
low; cover and simmer 30
minutes or until chicken is
fork-tender.

7 Meanwhile, in 12-inch
skillet, in melted butter,
cook zucchini, stirring
frequently, until tender.
Sprinkle with salt and
pepper to taste.

8 ...sfer zucchini to
...serving dish;
arra... ...hicken on top.
Ren... ...e toothpicks.

9 In cup, blend the corn-
starch with wine. Stir
into liquid in Dutch oven
and cook until thickened.

10 Pour into gravy boat
and serve with
chicken and zucchini.

Color index page 44
Begin 1¼ hrs ahead
8 servings

Chicken Imperial

*4 large whole chicken
  breasts, halved and
  skinned*
all-purpose flour
*½ cup butter or
  margarine*
*1 pound small
  mushrooms,
  quartered*

*1 tablespoon minced
  onion*
*1 cup heavy or whipping
  cream*
¼ cup dry sherry
1½ teaspoons salt
⅛ teaspoon pepper
2 tablespoons water

1. On waxed paper, coat chicken breasts with ¼
cup flour. In 12-inch skillet over medium heat, in
hot butter or margarine, cook chicken, a few pieces
at a time, until lightly browned on all sides. Set
chicken breasts aside.

2. In drippings in skillet over medium heat, cook
mushrooms and onion 5 minutes, stirring frequently. Stir in cream, sherry, salt and pepper and
stir to blend well. Return chicken to skillet.

3. Reduce heat to low; cover skillet and simmer
20 minutes or until chicken is fork-tender. Remove
chicken to warm platter.

4. In cup, blend 1 tablespoon flour with water.
Gradually add to pan liquid, stirring constantly,
and cook until mixture is thickened.

5. To serve: Spoon sauce over chicken.

Color index page 42
Begin 45 mins ahead
6 servings

Party Shrimp and Chicken

*¼ cup butter or
  margarine*
1 cup chopped onion
*1 small garlic clove,
  minced*
*3 medium whole chicken
  breasts, halved*
2 teaspoons salt
½ teaspoon pepper
*1 8-ounce can tomato
  sauce*

¼ cup port wine
1 teaspoon basil
*¼ cup chopped
  parsley*
*1 16-ounce package
  frozen, shelled
  and deveined
  shrimp*

1. In 12-inch skillet over medium heat, in hot butter
or margarine, cook onion and garlic until tender,
about 5 minutes. With slotted spoon, remove mixture to small bowl.

2. Rub chicken breasts with salt and pepper. In
butter remaining in skillet, cook chicken breasts
until golden on all sides.

3. Stir in tomato sauce, wine, basil, 3 tablespoons
parsley and reserved onion mixture; heat to boiling.
Reduce heat to low; cover and simmer 10 minutes or
until chicken is tender.

4. Add frozen shrimp; over high heat, heat to
boiling. Reduce heat to low; simmer 2 or 3 minutes
until shrimp is just pink and tender, stirring often.
Skim off fat, if you like.

5. To serve: Spoon mixture into deep dish; sprinkle
lightly with the remaining chopped parsley.

Chicken Orobianco

Color index
page 43

Begin 1¼ hrs
ahead

8 servings

¼ cup olive oil
2 garlic cloves, quartered
4 medium whole chicken
breasts, halved
2 pounds hot Italian
sausage links or pork-
sausage links
2 cups Orobianco or light
muscat

½ pound mushrooms,
sliced
1 teaspoon salt
toast points
2 tablespoons cornstarch
¼ cup water

1. In 12-inch skillet over medium heat, in hot oil, cook garlic until golden; with slotted spoon, remove garlic; discard. In drippings in skillet over medium-high heat, cook chicken and sausages, a few pieces at a time, until browned. Spoon off all but 2 tablespoons drippings. Return chicken and sausage to skillet. Stir in Orobianco, sliced mushrooms and salt; heat mixture to boiling.
2. Reduce heat to low; cover skillet and simmer 30 minutes or until chicken is fork-tender, basting occasionally with liquid in skillet. On warm platter, arrange toast points; with tongs, place chicken and sausage on toast; keep warm.
3. In cup, blend cornstarch and water; gradually stir into hot liquid and cook over medium heat, stirring constantly, until mixture is thickened.
4. To serve: Spoon some of sauce over chicken. Pass remaining sauce in gravy boat.

Chicken Avgolemono

Color index
page 43

Begin 1 hr
ahead

8 servings

Orzo-Rice Pilaf (below)
2 tablespoons butter
2 garlic cloves, sliced
4 large whole chicken
breasts, boned and halved
water
2 medium zucchini, sliced
5 egg yolks

1 tablespoon cornstarch
2 teaspoons salt
⅛ teaspoon cayenne
pepper
1 chicken-flavor bouillon
cube or envelope
5 tablespoons lemon juice

1. Prepare Orzo-Rice Pilaf. In 12-inch skillet over medium-high heat, in hot butter, cook garlic until brown; discard garlic. In same skillet, in remaining butter, cook chicken breasts until browned on all sides. Add ½ cup water; heat to boiling. Reduce heat to low; cover; simmer 10 minutes. Add zucchini; cook 10 minutes longer or until chicken and zucchini are tender.
2. Meanwhile, in 1-quart heavy saucepan with wire whisk, beat egg yolks, cornstarch, salt and cayenne pepper until blended; stir in 1½ cups water and chicken bouillon. Over medium-low heat, heat mixture, stirring until thickened (do not boil), about 10 minutes. Stir in lemon juice.
3. Arrange chicken mixture on warm platter; spoon on sauce. Serve with Orzo-Rice Pilaf.

ORZO-RICE PILAF: In 2-quart saucepan over medium-high heat, melt *½ cup butter* or margarine. Add *1 cup orzo* (rice-shaped pasta); cook until golden, stirring often, about 10 minutes. Stir in *4 cups water, 1 cup regular long-grain rice* and *3 chicken-flavor bouillon cubes;* heat to boiling. Reduce heat to low; cover and simmer 30 minutes or until liquid is absorbed and orzo and rice are tender.

Festive Chicken with Asparagus

Color index
page 42

Begin 1½ hrs
ahead

6 servings

3 medium whole
chicken breasts,
halved
2 tablespoons all-
purpose flour
3 tablespoons salad
oil
¼ cup dry white wine

¼ cup blue cheese,
crumbled (1 ounce)
1 10¾-ounce can
condensed cream of
chicken soup
½ teaspoon salt
¼ teaspoon pepper
1 pound asparagus

1. On waxed paper, coat chicken breasts with flour. Preheat oven to 375°F. In 12-inch skillet over medium-high heat, in hot salad oil, cook chicken pieces until lightly browned on all sides.
2. Meanwhile, in shallow, 3-quart casserole, mix well wine, blue cheese, undiluted cream of chicken soup, salt and pepper. Arrange chicken in soup mixture and spoon some mixture over chicken to coat it. Bake in oven 30 minutes.
3. Meanwhile, prepare asparagus: Hold base of asparagus stalk firmly and bend stalk; end will break off at spot where it becomes too tough to eat. Discard ends; trim scales if stalks are gritty. Cut each asparagus spear crosswise in half; rinse under running cold water; drain.
4. Remove casserole from oven and arrange asparagus between chicken pieces. Cover casserole tightly with foil or lid and bake 30 minutes longer or until chicken is fork-tender and asparagus is tender-crisp. Serve in casserole.

Chicken Breasts with Artichoke Hearts

Color index
page 44

Begin 1½ hrs
ahead

6 servings

3 medium whole
chicken breasts,
halved
all-purpose flour
2 tablespoons salad oil
2 tablespoons butter or
margarine
1 teaspoon salt
⅛ teaspoon white
pepper
3 tablespoons brandy
2 teaspoons lemon juice

1½ cups water
2 chicken-flavor bouillon
cubes or envelopes
or 1 teaspoon
chicken-flavor
stock base
1 cup sour cream
2 9-ounce packages
frozen artichoke
hearts, thawed and
well drained

1. On waxed paper, coat chicken breasts with ¼ cup flour. In 12-inch skillet over medium-high heat, in hot salad oil, cook chicken until lightly browned on all sides. Place chicken in 12″ by 9″ baking dish; set aside. Preheat oven to 350°F.
2. In 2-quart saucepan over low heat, in melted butter or margarine, stir 2 tablespoons flour with salt and pepper until smooth. Gradually stir in brandy, lemon juice, water and chicken bouillon; cook, stirring constantly, until thickened and smooth. With wire whisk, gradually blend in sour cream; pour mixture over chicken.
3. Cover baking dish tightly with foil and bake chicken 45 minutes.
4. Remove foil from baking dish and add artichoke hearts. Cover and return to oven; continue baking 15 minutes longer or until chicken and artichoke hearts are fork-tender.

Braised turkey

Turkey in Champagne Sauce with Toast Flowers

Color index
page 40

Begin 2 hrs
ahead

6 servings

1 tablespoon salad oil
2 2- to 2½-pound turkey
legs (thigh and
drumstick)
4 cups water
1 large onion, thinly
sliced
1¾ teaspoons salt
½ teaspoon pepper
⅓ cup all-purpose flour

1½ cups half-and-half
3 tablespoons butter or
margarine
½ pound mushrooms,
sliced
1 split dry champagne
(about 6 ounces)
⅓ cup minced parsley
Toast Flowers (below)

1. In 12-inch skillet over medium-high heat, in hot salad oil, cook turkey legs until well browned on all sides. Add water, onion, salt and pepper; heat to boiling. Reduce heat to low; cover and simmer 1½ hours or until turkey is fork-tender.
2. Remove turkey from skillet; cool slightly until easy to handle. Cut turkey meat into 1-inch pieces; discard skin and bones. Meanwhile, over high heat, cook turkey broth in skillet until it reduces to about 1½ cups.
3. In small bowl with spoon, blend flour with ½ cup half-and-half; gradually stir into broth until smooth; stir in remaining half-and-half. Cook, stirring, until cream sauce boils and is thickened.
4. In 10-inch skillet over medium heat, in hot butter or margarine, cook mushrooms until tender; gently stir into cream sauce with turkey meat, champagne and ¼ cup parsley; heat.
5. To serve: Spoon turkey mixture into chafing dish if you like. Garnish with remaining parsley and serve with Toast Flowers.

TOAST FLOWERS: Preheat oven to 450°F. Using a 3- to 4-inch flower-shaped cookie cutter, cut "flowers" from *18 white bread slices.* Place on cookie sheet. Bake flowers 3 to 5 minutes until golden.

Apricot-glazed Turkey Drumsticks

Color index
page 40

Begin 2½ hrs
ahead

4 servings

4 turkey drumsticks
(about 4 pounds)
2 celery stalks, halved
1 medium onion, halved
1 tablespoon salt
½ teaspoon peppercorns,
crushed

hot water
¾ cup apricot preserves
1 8¾-ounce can apricot
halves, drained, for
garnish

1. In 8-quart saucepot, place turkey, celery, onion, salt and peppercorns and add hot water to cover; over high heat, heat mixture to boiling. Reduce heat to medium-low; cover and simmer 1½ hours or until drumsticks are fork-tender.
2. Meanwhile, in 1-quart saucepan over medium heat, melt apricot preserves. Preheat oven to 400°F.
3. Remove turkey from broth; drain well. (Strain; cover and refrigerate broth for soup another day.) With hands protected by paper towels, pull tendons from ends of turkey drumsticks.
4. Place turkey in open roasting pan; brush with apricot preserves; top with drained apricot halves and brush them with preserves.
5. Bake in oven 10 minutes to glaze turkey.

Turkey-Tamale Casserole

Color index
page 40

Begin 4 hrs
ahead

6 servings

salad oil
1 1-pound frozen
turkey thigh,
thawed
water
½ cup chopped
onion
½ cup chopped celery
1 16-ounce can
tomatoes
1 15½- or 16-ounce
can red kidney
beans
2 teaspoons chili
powder
1 teaspoon salt

¼ teaspoon pepper
Tamale Topping:
¾ cup cornmeal
¼ cup all-purpose
flour
1½ teaspoons double-
acting baking
powder
½ teaspoon salt
½ teaspoon ground
sage
1 egg
½ cup milk
2 tablespoons salad oil

1. In 10-inch skillet over medium-high heat, in 2 tablespoons hot salad oil, cook turkey thigh until well browned. Add ½ cup water; heat to boiling. Reduce heat to low; cover and simmer 2½ hours, until turkey is fork-tender, adding more water if needed.
2. Remove turkey from skillet; cool slightly until easy to handle. Remove meat from bones; cut meat in ½-inch pieces. (Refrigerate broth for use in soup another day.)
3. In 3-quart saucepan over medium heat, in 2 tablespoons hot salad oil, cook onion and celery until tender, about 5 minutes, stirring occasionally. Add turkey, tomatoes and their liquid, kidney beans and their liquid, chili powder, salt and pepper; heat to boiling, stirring occasionally.
4. Spoon hot turkey mixture into 2-quart casserole. Preheat oven to 400°F.
5. Meanwhile, prepare Tamale Topping: In medium bowl with fork, combine cornmeal, flour, baking powder, salt and sage.
6. In small bowl with fork, stir together egg, milk and salad oil until well mixed; stir into flour mixture just until batter is mixed.
7. Pour batter over hot turkey mixture in casserole; bake 20 minutes or until toothpick inserted in center of Tamale Topping comes out clean. Serve piping hot at table in casserole.

Saucy Turkey Wings

Color index
page 39

Begin 2½ hrs
ahead

6 servings

4 pounds turkey wings
2 tablespoons salad oil
1 10½-ounce can
condensed cream of
celery soup

1 teaspoon salt
½ teaspoon paprika
¼ teaspoon pepper

1. Separate wings at joints. (Use wing tips for soup, if you like.)
2. In 12-inch skillet over medium-high heat, in hot salad oil, cook turkey, a few pieces at a time, until browned on all sides; arrange in 15½″ by 10½″ roasting pan.
3. In small bowl, combine undiluted soup, salt, paprika and pepper; spoon soup mixture over turkey. Cover roasting pan and bake in 350°F. oven 2¼ hours or until turkey wings are fork-tender.

Broiled chicken

The tender meat of most chicken and turkey makes it very suitable for broiling in the broiler or on the rotisserie. Outdoor grilling is the same cooking technique as broiling.

Unless the manufacturer's directions state otherwise, always preheat the broiler. For easier cleaning, line the broiler pan with foil and brush the rack with salad oil ahead of time.

The exact distance from the source of heat will depend on the thickness of the piece of meat, but generally, the rack should be between 7 and 9 inches away; adjust the distance if this is not close enough.

Rotisseried Chicken

Color index
page 42

Allow
¾–1 pound
uncooked
chicken
per serving

1 Remove giblets; rinse and drain chicken well. Skewer neck skin to back and tie wings to body.

2 Insert spit through body lengthwise and tighten holding prongs. Fix bird firmly.

3 Carefully tie first the bird's tail and then its drumsticks to the spit.

4 If cooking 2 birds, mount them on the spit in opposite directions to balance evenly. Turn spit slowly to test balance.

5 Following manufacturer's directions, cook, basting occasionally with *melted butter*. If using sauce, baste during last 20 minutes of cooking time.

6 To test for doneness, insert meat thermometer in thigh, next to body, avoiding bone. Bird is done when it reads 180° to 185°F.

Savory Chicken

Color index
page 42

Begin 3½ hrs
ahead

8 servings

20 medium garlic cloves	4 teaspoons dry mustard
1½ cups tarragon vinegar	2½ teaspoons salt
¼ cup sugar	2 3- to 3½-pound broiler-fryers, quartered
2 tablespoons salad oil	
2 tablespoons Worcestershire	

1. Into 13″ by 9″ baking dish, with garlic press, crush garlic cloves. Stir in next 6 ingredients.
2. Add chicken pieces; turn pieces to coat them evenly in marinade. Cover; refrigerate at least 2 hours, turning chicken often.
3. *About 1¼ hours before serving:* Prepare outdoor grill for barbecuing. Place chicken on grill over medium coals; cook 35 minutes or until chicken is fork-tender, turning chicken frequently and basting occasionally with remaining marinade.

TO BROIL IN OVEN: Marinate chicken as above. About 50 minutes before serving, preheat broiler if manufacturer directs. Place chicken, skin side down, in broiling pan. Broil 40 minutes or until chicken is fork-tender, turning once and basting occasionally with remaining marinade.

Tandoori Chicken

Color index
page 46

Begin day
ahead

4 servings

1 medium onion, diced	1 teaspoon sugar
1 garlic clove	½ teaspoon ground cumin
3 tablespoons salad oil	½ teaspoon turmeric
2 tablespoons lemon juice	¼ teaspoon ground cardamom
1 tablespoon minced, peeled ginger root or ¾ teaspoon ground ginger	¼ teaspoon cayenne pepper
2 teaspoons salt	¼ cup plain yogurt
1½ teaspoons ground coriander	1 3-pound broiler-fryer, quartered

1. In blender container, place all ingredients except yogurt and chicken. Cover blender; at high speed, blend until mixture is pureed. Pour mixture into 12″ by 8″ baking dish; stir in yogurt.
2. With sharp knife, make 3 diagonal slashes in each chicken-breast half; do not cut all the way through to the bone. Make 2 diagonal slashes in each thigh. Make several small cuts in each drumstick. Add chicken to yogurt mixture. Cover; refrigerate at least 12 hours, turning chicken occasionally.
3. *About 1¼ hours before serving:* Prepare outdoor grill for barbecuing. When grill is ready, place chicken on grill over low coals. Cook 35 minutes or until chicken is fork-tender, turning chicken frequently and basting often with some yogurt mixture.

TO BROIL IN OVEN: Marinate chicken as above. About 50 minutes before serving, preheat broiler if manufacturer directs. Place chicken, skin side down, in broiling pan. Baste with some yogurt mixture. About 7 to 9 inches from source of heat (or at 450°F.), broil chicken 25 minutes or until browned. Turn; baste with remaining mixture; broil 15 minutes longer or until chicken is fork-tender.

Broiled turkey and chicken

Color index
page 45

Begin 50 mins
ahead

4 servings

Broiled Lemon-Chicken

½ cup butter or
margarine
¼ cup lemon juice
1½ teaspoons salt
1 teaspoon sugar
¼ teaspoon pepper
1 2½- or 3-pound
broiler-fryer,
quartered
4 medium tomatoes
2 teaspoons grated lemon
peel (optional)
2 teaspoons chopped
parsley (optional)

1 Preheat broiler if
manufacturer directs. In
1-quart saucepan over low
heat, heat butter or
margarine, lemon juice,
salt, sugar and pepper
until butter is melted.

2 Place chicken, skin side
down, on large broiling
pan; broil 20 minutes.

3 Baste with butter
mixture frequently to
moisten and add flavor to
chicken pieces.

4 Meanwhile, cut
tomatoes into 6
wedges about ¾ way
through, gently spreading
tomato wedges apart.

5 Turn chicken pieces.
Arrange tomatoes on
same broiling pan.

6 Broil 15 to 20 minutes
more until chicken is
fork-tender, basting
chicken and tomatoes with
butter mixture frequently.

7 Transfer to warm
platter and sprinkle
chicken with grated lemon
peel and chopped parsley
to garnish, if desired.

Color index
page 46

Begin early
in day

4 servings

Chicken Marinated in Chili Sauce

1 12-ounce bottle chili
sauce
½ cup red wine
vinegar
1 tablespoon
horseradish

1 garlic clove,
quartered
1 teaspoon salt
1 3-pound broiler-fryer,
cut up

1. In 13″ by 9″ baking dish, mix all ingredients
except chicken. Place chicken in marinade; cover
and refrigerate chicken at least 2 hours, turning the
pieces occasionally.
2. *About 45 minutes before serving:* Preheat broiler
if manufacturer directs. Place chicken on rack in
broiling pan; broil 35 minutes or until fork-tender,
basting the chicken pieces with marinade and turning occasionally with tongs.

Coating with marinade:
Turn chicken occasionally
in marinade to coat the
pieces evenly.

Broiling chicken: Place
chicken on rack in broiling
pan and baste occasionally
with marinade.

OUTDOOR BARBECUE VARIATION: *About 1
hour and 10 minutes before serving:* Prepare grill
for outdoor barbecuing. Place chicken on grill
over medium coals; grill 35 minutes or until
chicken is fork-tender. Baste chicken with
marinade and turn occasionally.

MARINADES

Enhance and vary the flavor of broiled chicken by marinating it first. Refrigerate the bird in the marinade for at least 2
hours, turning it occasionally to make sure it is completely
coated. If there is any leftover marinade it can be used to
baste the chicken during the cooking time.

LIME MARINADE: In 13″ by 9″ baking dish,
mix *1 tablespoon grated lime peel, ½ cup lime*
juice, 3 tablespoons salad oil, 4 teaspoons salt and
¼ teaspoon cracked pepper. Use to marinate
chicken or other poultry and for basting poultry
while grilling or broiling. (Makes about ⅔ cup or
enough marinade for one broiler-fryer.)

GREEN ONION-SOY MARINADE: In 13″ by
9″ baking dish, mix *½ cup thinly sliced green*
onions, ½ cup soy sauce, 2 tablespoons light brown
sugar, 2 tablespoons dry sherry, ½ teaspoon salt
and *½ teaspoon ground ginger.* Use to marinate
chicken or other poultry and for basting poultry
while grilling or broiling. (Makes about 1 cup or
enough marinade for one broiler-fryer.)

Fried chicken

Color index page 44
Begin 1 hr ahead
6 servings

Cheese and Anchovy Broiled Chicken Breasts

1 2-ounce can anchovy fillets
2 tablespoons minced onion
1 teaspoon lemon juice
3 large whole chicken breasts, halved
1 8-ounce package mozzarella cheese, cut into 12 slices

1. Drain 1 tablespoon oil from can of anchovy fillets into 1-quart saucepan; discard all the remaining oil; mince anchovies.
2. Over medium heat, in hot anchovy oil, cook onion and anchovies about 5 minutes or until paste forms; stir in lemon juice. Remove from heat and let paste cool slightly.
3. Preheat broiler if manufacturer directs. Lift skin from each half-breast to make a small pocket; rub 1 teaspoon anchovy mixture on meat.
4. Place chicken, skin side down, on rack in broiling pan, 7 to 9 inches from source of heat (or at 450°F.); broil 20 minutes. Turn; broil 15 minutes more or until tender. Top half-breasts with cheese. Broil 5 minutes or until cheese is bubbly.

Stuffing the breast: Rub some anchovy mixture on the meat under skin.

Adding the cheese: 5 minutes before end of cooking, top with cheese.

Color index page 39
Begin 1 hr ahead
6 servings

Turkey-Sausage Kabobs

⅓ cup soy sauce
⅓ cup cooking sherry
3 tablespoons sugar
3 tablespoons salad oil
1 5- to 6-pound frozen turkey breast, slightly thawed
1 8-ounce package brown-and-serve sausages
1 8-ounce can pineapple chunks, drained
4 green onions, cut into 1½-inch pieces

1. In medium bowl, mix first 4 ingredients. With sharp knife, cut one side of turkey breast into 1-inch chunks (about 1 pound meat); use remaining turkey in other recipes. Add turkey chunks to bowl; toss lightly. Refrigerate 30 minutes. Cut each sausage crosswise in half.
2. Preheat broiler if manufacturer directs. On six 14-inch metal skewers, alternately thread turkey, sausages, pineapple and green onions. Broil 10 to 12 minutes until turkey is tender, basting frequently with marinade and turning once.

Fried chicken will be juicier if first coated with flour, crushed cereal flakes or dried bread crumbs. An easy way of coating is to shake the chicken one piece at a time in a bag of flour or crumbs. Let the coated pieces dry on wire racks about 15 minutes before frying.

Chicken pieces can also be fried successfully in the oven. This method involves less handling than pan-frying, so the coating is less likely to be dislodged.

Chicken which is stir-fried is cooked quickly over very high heat in only a small amount of oil. Depending on the ingredients, at the end of cooking time you will have tender-crisp vegetables and succulent pieces of chicken.

Pan-fried Chicken with Cream Gravy

¼ cup all-purpose flour
1 2½- to 3-pound broiler-fryer, cut up
¼ cup salad oil
salt and pepper
Cream Gravy:
¼ cup all-purpose flour
2½ cups milk
1 tablespoon chopped parsley
1 tablespoon dry or medium sherry (optional)
salt and pepper

Color index page 44
Begin 1 hr ahead
4 servings

1 Put the flour on a sheet of waxed paper and coat chicken on all sides.

2 In 12-inch skillet over medium-high heat, brown chicken on all sides in hot oil, turning frequently. Sprinkle chicken lightly with salt and pepper.

3 Reduce heat to medium-low. Cover; cook until fork-tender, about 25 minutes, removing cover for last few minutes to crisp skin. Transfer to warm platter.

4 Make gravy: Pour off all but ¼ cup drippings from skillet; blend in flour. Over medium heat, cook, stirring and scraping bits loose from skillet, until golden.

5 Gradually stir in milk and cook, stirring constantly, until mixture is smooth and thickened.

6 Stir in parsley and sherry, if used, and season to taste with salt and freshly ground pepper.

7 Serve chicken with some gravy poured over it, accompanied by remainder in a gravy boat.

Fried chicken

Beer-Batter Chicken

Color index
page 41

Begin 55 mins
ahead

4 servings

⅔ cup all-purpose
   flour
1 teaspoon salt
½ teaspoon double-
   acting baking powder

⅓ cup beer
1 egg
salad oil
1 3-pound broiler-fryer,
   cut up

1. In bowl with fork, mix first 3 ingredients. In
another bowl, beat together beer, egg and 2
teaspoons salad oil; stir liquid into flour mixture.
2. Coat half of chicken pieces with batter.
3. Meanwhile, in 12-inch skillet over medium
heat, heat ½ inch salad oil to 370°F.
4. Fry chicken pieces until browned and tender,
about 20 minutes, turning once. Drain on paper
towels. Repeat with remaining chicken.

Crunchy Drumsticks

Color index
page 46

Begin early
in day or
day ahead

8 servings

1 cup orange juice
1 tablespoon salad oil
1 tablespoon salt
¼ teaspoon pepper
3 pounds chicken
   drumsticks (about 1
   large or 2 small
   drumsticks per person)
1¼ cups quick-cooking
   oats, uncooked
¼ cup butter or
   margarine

1 In 13" by 9" baking
dish, mix first 4
ingredients; add chicken,
turning to coat well.
Cover; refrigerate at least
4 hours, turning often.

2 About 1 hour before
serving: On waxed
paper, coat chicken
drumsticks with oats.

3 Line jelly-roll pan with
foil; add butter and
melt in 400°F. oven.
Remove from oven; tilt to
spread butter evenly.

4 Arrange drumsticks in
one layer in pan,
turning to coat with butter.

5 Bake 40 to 50 minutes
until drumsticks are
fork-tender, turning once.

Oven-fried Chicken

Color index
page 45

Begin 1¼ hrs
ahead

4 servings

¼ cup butter or
   margarine
¾ cup cracker meal
1 teaspoon salt

⅛ teaspoon pepper
1 2½- to 3-pound
   broiler-fryer, cut up

1. In 13" by 9" baking dish, melt butter or margarine in 400°F. oven. On waxed paper, mix cracker meal, salt and pepper. Remove dish from oven.
2. With tongs, roll chicken in melted butter or
margarine, then coat with crumbs on all sides;
place in dish. Bake 40 to 50 minutes.

CORN-CRISPED: Preheat oven to 400°F. Prepare as above but omit butter or margarine; pour
⅓ cup undiluted evaporated milk in pie plate and
substitute ¾ cup corn-flake crumbs for cracker
meal; use to coat chicken.

ITALIAN-SEASONED: Prepare as above but
substitute ¾ cup Italian-seasoned bread crumbs for
cracker meal; omit salt and pepper.

Lemon Chicken on Spinach Leaves

Color index
page 46

Begin 45 mins
ahead

6 servings

3 large whole chicken
   breasts, halved
1 cup chicken broth
⅓ cup sugar
⅓ cup lemon juice
2 tablespoons water

1 tablespoon dry sherry
1½ teaspoons soy sauce
cornstarch
½ 10-ounce bag spinach
1 teaspoon salt
½ cup salad oil

1. Working with one half-breast at a time place it
skin side up; with tip of sharp knife starting parallel
and close to large end of rib bone, cut and scrape
meat away from bone and rib cage, gently pulling
back meat in one piece as you cut. Discard bones;
remove skin and white tendon.
2. In 1-quart saucepan, mix well chicken broth,
sugar, lemon juice, water, sherry, soy sauce and
2 tablespoons cornstarch. Cook over medium heat
until sauce is smooth and thickened, stirring constantly. Keep warm.
3. Shred spinach coarsely and arrange on platter.
4. Sprinkle chicken with salt. Coat chicken with
about ⅓ cup cornstarch. In 12-inch skillet over
medium-high heat in hot salad oil, cook chicken
until lightly browned and fork-tender, about 10
minutes. Arrange chicken on spinach and pour
some sauce over chicken; pour remaining sauce into
gravy boat and pass separately.

Boning half-breast: Cut
and scrape meat away
from bone in one piece.

Shredding spinach: Shred
spinach coarsely and
arrange on platter.

Chicken Kiev

¾ *cup butter or*
  margarine, softened
1 *tablespoon chopped*
  parsley
1 *tablespoon chopped*
  chives
⅛ *teaspoon pepper*
salt
6 *medium whole*
  chicken breasts,
  skinned and boned
¼ *cup all-purpose*
  flour

1 *egg*
1 *tablespoon water*
  about ¾ *cup dried*
  bread crumbs
  salad oil

Color index page 44
Begin 3 hrs ahead
6 servings

1 In small bowl, combine butter, parsley, chives, pepper and ½ teaspoon salt. On waxed paper, pat to 4½" by 3"; freeze.

2 With smooth side of meat mallet or dull edge of French knife, pound each chicken breast until ¼ inch thick.

3 Cut firm butter mixture into six ¾" by 3" strips. Place one strip lengthwise in center of one side of a chicken breast.

4 Roll up, bringing wider edge of breast over butter to enclose strip.

5 Secure with toothpicks. Repeat with remaining chicken breasts.

6 On waxed paper, mix flour and 1 teaspoon salt. In pie plate, mix egg and water. Place crumbs on another sheet of paper. Coat rolls with flour, egg, then crumbs.

7 On cookie sheet, place chicken rolls in a single layer. Cover lightly with waxed paper; refrigerate 1 to 2 hours to allow crumbs to dry out.

8 In 4-quart saucepan, heat 3 inches oil to 300°F. on deep-fat thermometer. Lower in 2 breasts.

9 Fry 15 minutes or until browned and firm when pressed with back of fork. Do not pierce. Drain.

10 Remove toothpicks and keep rolls warm in oven while frying remaining chicken breasts.

Color index page 46
Begin 2½ hrs ahead
6 servings

Crispy Chicken Rolls

3 *large whole chicken*
  breasts, skinned, boned
  and halved
1¼ *cups cooked, shelled*
  and deveined shrimp,
  chopped
¾ *cup butter or*
  margarine, softened
salt

¼ *cup chopped green*
  onions
salad oil
1 *cup all-purpose*
  flour
1¼ *teaspoons double-*
  acting baking
  powder
¾ *cup water*

1 With mallet or dull edge of French knife, pound chicken pieces to about ¼ inch thickness.

2 In medium bowl, combine shrimp with butter or margarine, 1½ teaspoons salt and green onions. Spoon mixture on to centers of breasts leaving ½ inch edge all around.

3 Starting at one of the narrow ends, roll up each chicken piece, jelly-roll fashion. Fasten with toothpicks. Cover and refrigerate 15 minutes.

4 Meanwhile, in 5-quart Dutch oven over medium-high heat, heat 1 inch oil to 370°F. In medium bowl with wire whisk, blend flour, baking powder, 1 teaspoon salt and water.

5 With tongs, roll 3 chicken rolls, one at a time, into flour mixture making sure all the sides are coated evenly.

6 To fry chicken rolls: Lower into hot salad oil and fry until golden, 10 to 15 minutes, turning occasionally. With a slotted spoon, remove rolls from oil and allow them to drain on paper towels. Keep warm. Repeat with remaining rolls. Using a fork to hold chicken rolls steady, remove toothpicks. Place rolls on a warm serving platter. Serve immediately so that the chicken rolls are hot and retain their crispness.

265

Stir-fried chicken

Stir-fried Chicken

Color index
page 45

Begin 45 mins
ahead

4 servings

2 large whole chicken
  breasts, skinned, boned
  and halved
2 tablespoons salad oil
1 cup thinly sliced celery
1 medium green pepper,
  cut in thin strips
1 small onion, sliced
1 teaspoon salt
¼ teaspoon ground
  ginger
1 16-ounce can bean
  sprouts, drained

1 5-ounce can water
  chestnuts, drained and
  sliced
1 envelope chicken-flavor
  bouillon or 1 teaspoon
  chicken-flavor stock
  base
½ cup water
2 teaspoons cornstarch
2 tablespoons soy sauce
3 cups hot cooked rice
  (optional)
¾ cup almonds, toasted

1 On cutting board, slice chicken crosswise into ¼-inch-wide strips. In 12-inch skillet over high heat, heat salad oil.

2 Cook celery, pepper, onion, salt and ginger, stirring quickly and frequently (stir-frying) until vegetables are tender-crisp, about 3 minutes.

3 With slotted spoon, remove vegetables to a warm plate; keep warm. To oil left in skillet, add chicken and stir-fry until chicken turns white, about 3 to 5 minutes.

4 Return vegetables to skillet. Add bean sprouts, water chestnuts, chicken bouillon or stock base and water.

5 In cup, blend cornstarch smoothly with soy sauce. Gradually stir into hot mixture in skillet and cook, stirring constantly, until thickened.

6 Spoon stir-fried chicken and vegetables over hot cooked rice. Sprinkle toasted almonds over the top and serve immediately.

Moo Goo Gai Pan

Color index
page 45

Begin 35 mins
ahead

4 servings

2 large whole chicken
  breasts, skinned,
  boned and halved
1 tablespoon cornstarch
2 tablespoons dry sherry
¾ teaspoon minced,
  peeled ginger root
⅛ teaspoon monosodium
  glutamate
salt

⅓ cup salad oil
¾ cup California
  walnuts
1 15-ounce can Chinese
  straw mushrooms,
  drained
1 8½-ounce can sliced
  bamboo shoots,
  drained (about 1 cup)
¼ pound snow peas

1. With sharp knife, slice across width of chicken breasts to make very thin pieces. In medium bowl, mix well chicken, cornstarch, sherry, ginger, monosodium glutamate and 1½ teaspoons salt.
2. In 12-inch skillet over medium-high heat, in hot oil, cook walnuts about 3 minutes until lightly browned, stirring constantly. Spoon walnuts onto paper towels to drain, leaving oil in skillet.
3. In hot oil in skillet, stir-fry (stirring quickly and frequently) mushrooms, bamboo shoots, snow peas and ½ teaspoon salt until snow peas are tender-crisp, about 3 to 5 minutes. Spoon vegetables into a medium bowl, leaving oil in skillet.
4. In remaining oil, stir-fry chicken mixture 5 minutes or until chicken is tender; stir in vegetables. Spoon onto warm platter; sprinkle with walnuts.

Chicken with Orange Peel Szechuan Style

Color index
page 45

Begin 1 hr
ahead

4 servings

1 large orange
2 large whole chicken
  breasts, skinned and
  boned
1 tablespoon soy sauce
1 tablespoon dry sherry
4 green onions, cut in
  2-inch pieces
¼ teaspoon crushed red
  pepper

1 teaspoon minced,
  peeled ginger root or
  ¼ teaspoon ground
  ginger
2½ teaspoons
  cornstarch
½ teaspoon sugar
½ teaspoon salt
½ cup orange juice
¼ cup salad oil

1. With vegetable peeler, cut peel from orange into 1½-inch-wide pieces, being careful not to cut into white membrane. Cut pieces into 1½-inch-long strips. On small cookie sheet, let peels dry slightly in 200°F. oven 30 minutes.
2. Cut chicken into 1½-inch pieces. In medium bowl, mix well chicken, soy sauce, sherry, green onions, red pepper and ginger. In small bowl, mix well cornstarch, sugar, salt and orange juice. Cover and refrigerate both.
3. *About 15 minutes before serving:* In 10-inch skillet over medium heat, in hot oil, with slotted spoon, stir-fry (stirring quickly and frequently) peels until crisp and edges are slightly browned, about 2 minutes; drain on paper towels.
4. In oil remaining in skillet, over high heat, stir-fry chicken mixture until chicken loses pink color and is tender, about 4 minutes. Stir orange-juice mixture, then add to chicken and stir-fry until mixture is slightly thickened and coats chicken.
5. Spoon onto warm platter; sprinkle with peels.

Simmered chicken and turkey

Whole mature or young birds or poultry parts can be simmered or stewed in a large pan with seasonings and enough water to cover. Cook over low heat (do not boil). Cool and use meat in other recipes, if you like.

Simmered Chicken

Color index
page 44

Begin 3 hrs
ahead

6 servings

1 4½- to 5-pound stewing
chicken, cut up
1 medium onion studded
with 3 whole cloves
3 celery tops
1 carrot, sliced
2 bay leaves
1 tablespoon salt
3 cups hot water

1 In 8-quart saucepot over high heat, heat to boiling chicken, neck and giblets and remaining ingredients; reduce heat.

2 Cover; simmer 2 to 2½ hours. Discard onion, celery and bay leaves. Put chicken into serving dish or, to use later, follow step 3.

3 Place pot in cold water in sink 30 minutes. Stir broth often. Change water when warm. Refrigerate; use within 3 days.

Begin 3 hrs
ahead

6 servings

SIMMERED CHICKEN WITH DUMPLINGS:
Prepare Simmered Chicken (above). In large bowl with fork, stir *1⅓ cups all-purpose flour, 2 teaspoons double-acting baking powder, 1 teaspoon chopped parsley* and *½ teaspoon salt* until mixed. In cup, combine *⅔ cup milk* with *2 tablespoons salad oil;* slowly stir into flour until soft dough forms. Drop by heaping tablespoons onto chicken. Cook uncovered 10 minutes; cover and cook 10 minutes more. With slotted spoon, remove dumplings. Spoon chicken into serving dish; top with dumplings.

Cooking dumplings: Spoon dough onto simmering chicken and broth.

Serving dumplings: Spoon them over hot chicken pieces in serving dish.

Coq au Vin

Color index
page 44

Begin 1½ hrs
ahead

4 servings

½ pound salt pork, diced
1 3- to 3½-pound broiler-
fryer, cut up
½ pound small
mushrooms
½ pound small white
onions
¼ cup minced shallots
1 garlic clove, minced
1 cup dry red wine

¾ cup water
½ teaspoon thyme leaves
⅛ teaspoon pepper
1 bay leaf
4 parsley sprigs
2 tablespoons butter,
softened
2 tablespoons all-purpose
flour

1. In 8-quart Dutch oven over medium heat, cook salt pork until golden and crisp, stirring often. With slotted spoon, remove pork to paper towels to drain. In drippings, cook chicken until browned, about 20 minutes. Remove to medium bowl.
2. Spoon off all but about ¼ cup fat from Dutch oven; add mushrooms, onions, shallots and garlic. Cook until just wilted, about 5 minutes, stirring occasionally. Stir in wine, water, thyme, pepper, bay leaf and parsley. Place chicken and salt pork over vegetables. Over high heat, heat to boiling. Reduce heat to low; cover; simmer 20 minutes or until chicken is fork-tender.
3. Meanwhile, in cup, blend butter and flour.
4. Remove chicken and vegetables to platter; discard bay leaf and parsley. Blend flour mixture into pan juices. Heat to boiling, stirring. Spoon over chicken.

Turkey Molé

Color index
page 39

Begin 3 hrs
ahead

12 to 15
servings

1 6-pound turkey breast
4 cups water
3 tablespoons sesame
seed
2 tablespoons lard
1 medium onion, diced
1 garlic clove, minced
1 square semisweet
chocolate
⅓ cup golden raisins
¼ cup slivered blanched
almonds
1 10-ounce can mild red
enchilada sauce

2 ready-to-eat taco
shells, crumbled
1 slice white bread,
crumbled
1 teaspoon salt
¼ teaspoon ground
cinnamon
¼ teaspoon ground
coriander
¼ teaspoon anise seed,
crushed
⅛ teaspoon ground cloves
⅛ teaspoon pepper
1 medium avocado

1. In 8-quart Dutch oven over medium heat, simmer turkey and water about 1½ hours or until tender. Drain and reserve 1¾ cups broth. Slice meat and arrange on warm platter; keep warm.
2. Meanwhile, in 12-inch skillet over medium-high heat, cook sesame seed until lightly browned; remove to paper towel. In same skillet, in hot lard, cook onion and garlic until tender; stir in chocolate. Heat until chocolate melts. In covered blender container, blend 1 tablespoon toasted sesame seed, chocolate mixture and remaining ingredients except avocado until smooth.
3. Return mixture to skillet and stir in reserved broth. Over medium heat, heat to boiling, stirring constantly. Spoon some sauce on turkey; sprinkle with remaining sesame seed.
4. Peel, seed and slice avocado; use to garnish turkey. Pass remaining sauce separately.

Simmered chicken

Chicken Tetrazzini

2 2½- to 3-pound broiler-
 fryers
2 small onions
¼ teaspoon pepper
salt
water
1 16-ounce package
 spaghetti
½ cup butter
½ pound mushrooms,
 sliced
1 tablespoon lemon juice
½ cup all-purpose flour

¼ teaspoon ground
 nutmeg
paprika
½ cup dry sherry
 (optional)
1 cup half-and-half
1 3-ounce jar grated
 Parmesan cheese

Color index page 45
Begin 2 hrs ahead
8 servings

1 In 8-quart saucepot,
 place chickens, 1 onion,
pepper and 1 tablespoon
salt. Cover with water.
Over high heat, heat to
boiling. Reduce heat to
low; cover and simmer
chickens 30 minutes or
until fork-tender. Remove
chickens to large bowl.

2 Strain chicken broth,
 reserving 3½ cups (4
cups if sherry is not used).
Store the remaining broth
to use another day.

3 When chickens are
 cool, remove meat in
large pieces and discard
bones and skin. Cut
chicken in large chunks;
set aside.

4 After preparing
 spaghetti as label
directs, drain in a colander.
Spread it out evenly
in a greased 13″ by 9″
baking dish.

5 Chop remaining onion.
 In 4-quart saucepan
over medium heat, in 2
tablespoons hot butter,
cook onion, mushrooms
and lemon juice 5 minutes.
Remove to medium bowl.

6 In same saucepan, melt
 remaining butter.
When hot, stir in flour,
1 tablespoon salt, nutmeg
and ½ teaspoon paprika
until mixture is smooth.

7 Gradually stir in sherry
 and reserved chicken
broth and cook, stirring,
until liquid is thickened.

8 Add half-and-half,
 chicken chunks and
mushroom mixture and
over low heat, cook,
stirring, just until mixture
is heated through.

9 Spoon chicken mixture
 over spaghetti in
baking dish. Sprinkle
with grated Parmesan
cheese and add a
little paprika.

10 Bake in 350°F. oven
 30 minutes or until
spaghetti and chicken
mixture are thoroughly
heated and surface is
golden and bubbly.

Color index page 46
Begin 2½ hrs ahead
8 servings

Chicken Pot Pie

2 2½-pound broiler-
 fryers, cut up
½ teaspoon pepper
½ teaspoon marjoram
 leaves
2 bay leaves
water
salt
2 large carrots, sliced
1 large celery stalk,
 sliced
¾ pound small white
 onions

all-purpose flour
1¾ cups half-and-half
1 10-ounce package
 frozen baby lima
 beans, thawed
½ pound small
 mushrooms, each cut
 in half
pastry for 2-crust pie
 (page 344)
1 egg yolk

1. In 5-quart Dutch oven over high heat, heat first 4
ingredients, 4 cups water and 1 tablespoon salt to
boiling. Reduce heat to low; cover and simmer 35
minutes or until chicken is fork-tender.
2. When chicken is done, reserve 1 cup broth. (Use
remaining broth in soup another day.) Cool chicken
slightly; remove and discard bones and skin; cut
meat into 1-inch pieces.
3. In 3-quart saucepan over high heat, heat carrots,
celery, onions and reserved 1 cup broth to boiling.
Reduce heat to low; cover and simmer 10 minutes or
until vegetables are almost tender. Remove from
heat. Remove vegetables to small bowl, leaving
broth in saucepan.
4. In small bowl with fork, blend ⅓ cup flour with
¾ cup half-and-half; gradually stir into broth in
saucepan until smooth; stir in remaining half-and-
half. Over low heat, cook, stirring constantly, until
sauce is thickened.
5. Stir in chicken, cooked vegetables, lima beans,
mushrooms and 1¾ teaspoons salt. Spoon chicken
mixture into 13″ by 9″ baking dish. Preheat oven to
350°F. Prepare pastry.
6. On lightly floured surface with lightly floured
rolling pin, roll dough into 14″ by 10″ rectangle.
With knife, cut out small circle in center of pastry.
Place pastry loosely over filling. With kitchen
shears, trim edge, leaving 1-inch overhang; fold
overhang under; make a high stand-up edge.
7. In small bowl, mix well egg yolk with 1 teaspoon
water. Brush pastry with egg-yolk mixture. Bake 1
hour or until crust is golden and mixture is hot.

Covering the pie: Place
pastry over filling; with
kitchen shears, trim edge.

Shaping pie edge: Fold
overhang under and press
to make stand-up edge.

Cooked turkey and chicken meat

Chicken or Turkey Salad

Color index page 40

Begin early in day

6 to 8 servings

2/3 cup mayonnaise
2 tablespoons cider vinegar
1 teaspoon salt
4 to 5 cups cut-up, cooked chicken or turkey
1 cup sliced celery
1 cup minced green pepper
2 teaspoons grated onion
romaine or iceberg lettuce leaves

1 In large bowl with fork, combine mayonnaise, vinegar and salt.

2 Add chicken and remaining ingredients except romaine; toss well. Cover and refrigerate.

3 To serve: On chilled platter, arrange romaine leaves. Lightly pile salad on it.

HAM AND CHICKEN SALAD: Prepare as above but substitute *2 cups cooked ham chunks* for 2 cups of the chicken. Add *1 cup fresh or drained, canned pineapple chunks* to mixture. (Makes 8 servings.)

CHICKEN-WALDORF SALAD: Prepare as above but before refrigerating, add *2 cups diced unpeeled red apples* and *2/3 cup chopped California walnuts* or pecans to mixture. (Makes 8 to 10 servings.)

TOASTED-WALNUT-CHICKEN SALAD: In 1-quart saucepan over medium heat, in *2 teaspoons hot butter* or margarine, cook *1/2 cup chopped California walnuts* and *1/8 teaspoon salt* 3 to 4 minutes until crisp. Cool toasted walnuts; add to chicken mixture. (Makes 6 to 8 servings.)

Variations color index page 43

Turkey-Roquefort Salad

Color index page 40

Begin early in day

6 servings

1 8-ounce container sour cream (1 cup)
1 3-ounce wedge or 2 1 1/4-ounce wedges Roquefort cheese, or 1 4-ounce package blue cheese, crumbled

1 teaspoon salt
3 cups cut-up, cooked turkey or chicken
lettuce leaves or chicory
1 29-ounce can cling-peach halves, drained

1. In medium bowl with wire whisk or fork, mix sour cream with Roquefort and salt until well blended. Gently stir in turkey until well coated; cover and refrigerate turkey mixture.
2. To serve: Arrange lettuce leaves or chicory and 6 peach halves on chilled serving plate. Gently stir turkey mixture and spoon over peach halves, dividing equally among halves. (Refrigerate remaining peach halves to use another day.)

Chicken à la King

Color index page 45

Begin 40 mins ahead

8 servings

6 tablespoons butter
1/2 pound mushrooms, sliced
1/4 cup diced green pepper
6 tablespoons all-purpose flour
3 cups half-and-half
4 cups cubed, cooked chicken or turkey
1 4-ounce jar diced pimentos, drained
2 egg yolks
2 tablespoons medium sherry
1 teaspoon salt
8 patty shells, warmed

1 In 10-inch skillet over medium heat, in hot butter, cook mushrooms and green pepper 5 minutes or until tender.

2 Stir in flour until blended. Gradually stir in half-and-half and cook, stirring constantly, until thickened.

3 Add chicken and pimentos. Heat to boiling, stirring often. Reduce heat to low. Cover and cook 5 minutes.

4 In cup, stir yolks until mixed. Stir in a little hot sauce; slowly pour mixture back into sauce, stirring rapidly to prevent lumping. Cook, stirring, until thickened.

5 Stir in sherry and salt and spoon the chicken mixture into patty shells.

Creamy Chicken Hash

Color index page 46

Begin 25 mins ahead

4 servings

2 tablespoons butter
1 small onion, diced
1 tablespoon all-purpose flour
1 teaspoon salt

3/4 cup half-and-half
2 cups cubed, cooked potatoes
2 cups cubed, cooked chicken or turkey

1. In 10-inch skillet over medium heat, in hot butter, cook onion until tender, about 5 minutes. Stir in flour and salt; gradually stir in half-and-half and cook, stirring, until thickened.
2. Stir in potatoes and chicken. Cover; simmer over low heat 10 minutes until heated through.

Cooked chicken meat

Sour Cream Chicken Enchiladas

Color index
page 42

Begin 1 hr
ahead

6 servings

3½ cups sour cream
3 5-ounce cans boned
  chicken, cut up
  (about 2 cups)
2 4-ounce cans
  mushroom stems and
  pieces, drained
1 4-ounce can green
  chilies, drained
⅓ cup onion flakes

1 teaspoon chili powder
½ teaspoon salt
½ teaspoon garlic powder
¼ teaspoon pepper
  salad oil
12 Corn Tortillas
  (page 431)
⅓ pound Cheddar
  cheese, shredded

1. In 13" by 9" baking pan, spread 1 cup sour cream. In 2-quart saucepan with fork, flake chicken; add ½ cup sour cream, mushrooms and next 6 ingredients. Cook over low heat, stirring occasionally, just until heated through.
2. In 8-inch skillet over medium-high heat, in about ½ inch hot oil, fry 1 tortilla, a few seconds on each side, until it softens. For an enchilada, along center of tortilla, spread ¼ cup chicken mixture; fold sides over filling and place, seam side down, in sour cream in pan. Repeat.
3. Preheat oven to 450°F. Spread enchiladas with remaining sour cream, then sprinkle with cheese. Bake 8 minutes or until cheese is melted.

Chicken Croquettes

Color index
page 46

Begin early
in day or
day ahead

4 servings

2½ cups ground, cooked
  chicken or turkey
1 cup Thick White Sauce
  (page 461)
2 tablespoons chopped
  parsley
1 tablespoon minced
  onion
½ teaspoon lemon juice
⅛ teaspoon rubbed sage

salt
1 egg
1 tablespoon water
¼ cup all-purpose flour
½ cup dried bread
  crumbs
salad oil
Mushroom Sauce
  (page 462) or Cheese
  Sauce (page 461)

1. In medium bowl, blend well first 6 ingredients. Add salt to taste. Cover; chill several hours.
2. *About 30 minutes before serving:* Shape chilled mixture into 8 cones. In shallow dish with fork, beat egg with water. Place flour and bread crumbs on separate sheets of waxed paper. Coat each croquette first in flour, then in egg, then in crumbs.
3. In 4-quart saucepan over medium heat, heat 1 inch oil to 370°F. Fry croquettes until golden brown, turning frequently. Drain on paper towels; serve with Mushroom or Cheese Sauce.

Forming the croquettes: With hands, shape chicken mixture into cones.

Coating the cones: Coat croquettes first in flour, then egg, then crumbs.

Chicken livers

Chicken Livers Sauté

Color index
page 47

Begin 30 mins
ahead

6 servings

6 tablespoons butter or
  margarine
1½ pounds chicken livers
1 small onion, coarsely
  chopped
¼ cup all-purpose flour
2 cups water
¼ cup dry or medium
  sherry
1½ teaspoons salt
toast or toasted split
  English muffins

1 In 10-inch skillet over medium heat, in butter, cook livers and onion about 10 minutes, stirring.

2 With slotted spoon, place cooked livers and onion in bowl.

3 Into drippings in skillet, add flour; with spoon, stir together until well blended.

4 Stir in water; cook over medium heat, stirring, until thickened.

5 Stir in liver mixture, sherry and salt; heat. Serve on toast.

Chicken Livers Aloha

Color index
page 47

Begin 30 mins
ahead

4 servings

¼ cup butter or
  margarine
1 cup chopped celery
½ cup chopped onion
1 medium green pepper,
  sliced
1½ pounds chicken livers
1 15½-ounce can
  pineapple chunks,
  drained

2 tablespoons brown
  sugar
1 tablespoon cornstarch
1¾ teaspoons salt
¾ cup water
2 tablespoons cider
  vinegar
3 cups hot cooked rice

1. In 12-inch skillet over medium-high heat, in hot butter, cook celery, onion and green pepper until tender-crisp, about 5 minutes. Add livers; cook 10 minutes, stirring; add pineapple.
2. In small bowl, mix sugar, cornstarch and salt. Stir in water and vinegar until smooth. Stir into chicken livers; cook, stirring, until thickened. Serve with rice.

Ducklings and geese

Ducklings and geese have more fat than other poultry, and the meat is much richer and darker.

Most ducklings and geese are sold frozen. Thaw the bird as usual; pull out clusters of excess fat from the body cavity and rinse and drain. For duckling, remove any pinfeathers. With a sharp, two-tined fork, prick the skin all over so that as the fat melts, it will escape, basting the bird as it rolls down its sides.

Always use a rack when roasting a duckling or goose. Roast duckling in a 325°F. oven until the thermometer registers a temperature of 185° to 190°F. Roast goose in a 350°F. oven, to an internal temperature of 190°F.

Because their bone structures are unlike those of chicken or turkey, ducklings and geese have a different proportion of meat to bone. Allow about 1 pound duckling per serving, 1 to 1½ pounds goose per serving.

Duckling with Sausage-Rice Stuffing

1 4- to 5-pound frozen
duckling, thawed
1 small stalk celery,
cut up
1 small onion, peeled
salt
water
Sausage-Rice Stuffing
(page 253)
¼ teaspoon paprika
⅛ teaspoon pepper

Color index page 49
Begin 4¼ hrs ahead
3 to 4 servings

1 Remove giblets and neck. Discard fat from cavity; rinse duckling with cold running water; drain well. Pat dry; remove pinfeathers; refrigerate.

2 In 2-quart saucepan, heat to boiling giblets, neck, celery, onion, ½ teaspoon salt and water to cover. Reduce heat; cover; simmer until tender; drain. Prepare the stuffing.

3 Discard celery and onion. Chop giblets; remove neck meat from bone; add both to stuffing. Rub cavity with ½ teaspoon salt. Spoon stuffing into neck.

4 Fold neck skin over stuffing; skewer to back. With duckling breast side up, lift wings toward neck; fold under back. Spoon stuffing into body cavity; skewer closed.

5 Place duckling, breast side up, on rack in open roasting pan. Rub mixture of paprika, pepper and 1½ teaspoons salt over bird. Tie legs with string.

6 Prick skin in several places. Insert thermometer into thickest part of meat between breast and thigh. Do not touch bone. Roast at 325°F. 2¼ to 2½ hours.

7 Start checking for doneness during last 30 minutes. Bird is done when thermometer reads 185°F. to 190°F. and leg feels soft when pinched (protect hand with paper towel).

8 When duckling is done, remove skewers and strings; place on warm platter; let duckling stand at room temperature 15 minutes for easier carving.

Color index page 48
Begin 4 hrs ahead
8 servings

Roast Goose with Mixed-Fruit Stuffing

1 10-pound goose
Mixed-Fruit Stuffing
(page 253)
1 13¾-ounce can chicken
broth

2 tablespoons all-purpose
flour
¼ cup cold water

1. Remove neck and giblets from goose; discard fat from body cavity; rinse; drain. Prepare stuffing.
2. Stuff bird lightly. Skewer neck skin to back. Tie legs and tail together. With two-tined fork, prick skin. Insert meat thermometer into thickest part of meat between breast and thigh, avoiding bone.
3. Place goose, breast side up, on wire rack in open roasting pan.
4. Roast at 350°F. 3 hours or until thermometer reads 190°F. When goose is done, remove to platter; remove string from around legs and tail.
5. To make gravy, spoon fat from drippings in pan, leaving juice and browned bits; stir in broth. Over medium heat, heat to boiling. In cup, blend flour and water; gradually stir into hot mixture and cook, stirring, until thickened. Serve with goose.

Color index page 48
Begin 4¼ hrs ahead
8 to 10 servings

Bohemian Roast Goose

1 9- to 11-pound frozen
goose, thawed
4 cups sauerkraut (about
2 16-ounce cans)
2 cups peeled, cubed apples

1 teaspoon salt
½ teaspoon caraway
seed

1. Remove giblets and neck from goose; rinse goose. (Use giblets and neck for broth, if you like.) With two-tined fork, prick skin.
2. In large bowl, toss sauerkraut with apples, salt and caraway seed; lightly spoon into goose. Skewer neck skin to back (or, hold in place with wings). Tie legs and tail together. Insert meat thermometer into center of thigh next to body, avoiding bone. Place, breast side up, on rack in open roasting pan.
3. Roast at 350°F. 3¼ to 4 hours or until thermometer reads 190°F. and thigh is tender when pierced with a fork. Allow goose to stand at room temperature 15 minutes for easier carving.

Ducklings

Shanghai Duckling with Leeks

Begin 2½ hrs ahead

4 servings

8 medium leeks
1 4½- to 5-pound frozen duckling, thawed
½ cup dry sherry
½ cup soy sauce
½ teaspoon sugar
¼ teaspoon ground ginger
1¼ cups water
3 small carrots, each cut lengthwise into 4 strips

1 Prepare leeks: Trim roots and discard tough leaves; cut each crosswise in half. Rinse halves with running cold water to remove sand. Cover and refrigerate root halves; cut remaining halves crosswise into ½-inch slices and place in 6-quart cook-and-serve Dutch oven.

2 Remove giblets and neck from bird; trim as much fatty skin from around neck and body cavity as possible. Rinse duckling, giblets and neck with cold water.

3 Place duckling, breast side down, on leeks in Dutch oven and tuck giblets and neck around it.

4 Add sherry, soy sauce, sugar, ginger and water. Over high heat, heat to boiling. Reduce heat to low; cover and simmer for 30 minutes.

5 With large spoon, turn duckling over; cover; cook 1 hour more, spooning pan liquid over duckling to baste occasionally.

6 Skim and discard fat from pan liquid, then place carrot strips and reserved leeks around duckling; increase heat to high and heat mixture to boiling.

7 Reduce heat to low; cover; cook 20 minutes more or until bird and vegetables are fork-tender, basting occasionally with pan liquid. Serve at once.

Elegant Duckling à l'Orange

Begin 2½ hrs ahead

4 servings

1 4- to 5-pound frozen duckling, thawed
⅛ teaspoon pepper salt
2 oranges
water
2 teaspoons cornstarch
¼ cup sugar
1 chicken-flavor bouillon cube
2 tablespoons brandy

1. Remove giblets and neck from duckling. Rinse bird under running cold water; pat dry.
2. Remove excess fat from inside of cavity; cut off and discard neck skin. Cut duckling into quarters; sprinkle with pepper and 1 teaspoon salt.
3. Place pieces, skin side down, on rack in 13″ by 9″ open roasting pan. Roast at 350°F. 1 hour; turn; roast 45 minutes more or until thickest part of drumstick feels soft when pinched with fingers protected with paper towels.
4. *About 30 minutes before duckling is done, prepare sauce:* Into 1-cup measuring cup, squeeze juice from 1 orange; add water to make 1 cup. Stir in cornstarch and ¼ teaspoon salt until cornstarch is completely dissolved; set aside.
5. In 2-quart saucepan over medium heat, heat sugar until melted and a light caramel color, stirring constantly with wooden spoon. Remove from heat and let cool 10 minutes. Add orange-juice mixture and bouillon (sugar will harden). Return to heat; cook 5 minutes more or until reduced by half and sugar is completely dissolved, stirring constantly. Stir in brandy; keep warm.
6. Slice remaining orange. Arrange duckling pieces on warm platter and pour on orange sauce. Garnish the duckling with orange slices.

Roast Duckling Montmorency

Begin 2½ hrs ahead

4 servings

1 4- to 5-pound fresh or thawed frozen duckling, quartered
1 teaspoon salt
¼ teaspoon pepper
1 17-ounce can pitted dark sweet cherries, drained
½ cup claret
2 tablespoons currant jelly
1 teaspoon cornstarch
¼ cup water
1 tablespoon butter or margarine

1. With two-tined fork, prick skin of duckling in several places; sprinkle with salt and pepper. Place duckling, skin side up, on rack in open roasting pan. Roast in 350°F. oven 1¾ to 2 hours or until duckling pieces are fork-tender.
2. Meanwhile, in medium bowl, stir cherries with claret; set aside.
3. Place duckling on warm platter; keep warm. Remove rack; pour all fat from roasting pan.
4. Into roasting pan over medium heat, drain wine from cherries; scrape to loosen browned bits from pan. Pour mixture into 1-quart saucepan; add jelly. In cup, blend cornstarch and water until smooth; gradually stir into wine mixture; cook over medium heat, stirring, until smooth and slightly thickened.
5. Add cherries and butter; heat, stirring, until cherries are hot and butter is melted and blended. Serve duckling with hot cherry sauce.

Peking Duck

5 quarts boiling water
*1 5-pound fresh or
    thawed frozen
    duckling, cleaned and
    with giblets and fat
    removed*
1 tablespoon salt
*1 tablespoon dry or
    cooking sherry*
Thin Pancakes (right)
*¼ cup maple-flavored
    syrup*
*½ cup canned hoisin
    sauce*
*4 green onions, cut into
    2-inch pieces*

Color index page 48
Begin day ahead
4 main-dish servings.

1 Pour boiling water slowly, in a fine stream, over both sides of duckling, so its skin becomes almost white; drain thoroughly.

2 With paper towels, gently pat skin and body cavity dry. Then rub body cavity with salt and sherry.

3 On large wire rack across top of a medium open roasting pan, place duckling, breast side down. Refrigerate, uncovered, until early in evening. Make Thin Pancakes.

4 *Early in evening:* Generously brush duckling skin with maple syrup; refrigerate, breast side up, uncovered, until needed next day.

5 *Next day, about 5 hours before serving:* Transfer duckling, rack and pan to 175°F. oven; roast 1½ hours. Turn oven control to 325°F.; roast duckling, breast side down, 1½ hours, then breast side up, 1 to 1½ hours, until skin is crisp. 15 minutes before duckling is done, heat Thin Pancakes.

To serve: Place hoisin sauce in small bowl, and green onions on a small plate. When duckling is done, thinly slice duckling skin and meat into about 2" by 1" pieces; arrange on warm plate. Pass duckling, hoisin sauce and green onions along with heated Thin Pancakes. Let each person assemble his portion as shown (right).

Thin Pancakes

*2½ cups all-purpose
    flour*
½ teaspoon salt
*1 cup boiling water
    salad oil*

1. In large bowl, combine flour and salt; gradually add water, blending with fork, until mixture is size of peas. Press into a ball; on lightly floured surface, knead to a soft, smooth dough, about 5 minutes.
2. Shape into a roll 16 inches long; cut crosswise, into 16 slices. Cover slices with damp cloth.
3. Place 2 slices on lightly floured surface; with fingers, flatten each into 3-inch circle. Brush tops generously with oil; place one on top of another with oiled tops together. With lightly floured rolling pin, roll from center to form 8-inch circle, turning it over several times to roll evenly.
4. In ungreased 8-inch skillet over medium heat, cook each side of circle 2 to 3 minutes or until light brown; remove to 8-inch pie plate and with fingers, carefully separate its 2 warm layers, making 2 thin pancakes. Stack these, one on top of the other, browned side up; cover with foil.
5. Repeat, making 16 pancakes in all. Wrap pie plate and refrigerate until required.
6. *To reheat pancakes:* In large saucepot, in ¾ inch water, place 3 inverted 6-ounce custard cups. Remove wrap from pie plate; place plate on top of custard cups. Cover saucepot; over medium heat, heat water to boiling. Reduce heat to low; simmer 10 minutes or until pancakes are soft and hot.

Forming the pancake: Place oiled sides of two 3-inch circles together then roll to 8-inch circle.

Separating pancakes: Separate the warm layers of each cooked pancake, making 2 thin pancakes.

ASSEMBLING A PORTION

Each person assembles 1 or 2 pieces of duckling, a dab of hoisin sauce and a piece of green onion on the center of each soft, hot pancake.

The pancake is then rolled or folded over twice into a neat package. Eat sandwich-style.

Ducklings

Sauces for poultry

Plum-glazed Ducklings

Color index
page 49

Begin 2¼ hrs
ahead

8 servings

**2 4- to 5-pound fresh or
thawed frozen
ducklings, quartered**
garlic salt
**¼ cup butter or
margarine**
1 medium onion, chopped
**1 17-ounce can purple
plums**
**½ cup packed light
brown sugar**
⅓ cup chili sauce
¼ cup soy sauce
¼ cup lemon juice
1 teaspoon salt
**1 teaspoon ground
ginger**
**2 teaspoons prepared
mustard**
**1 teaspoon
Worcestershire**

1. With two-tined fork, prick skin of ducklings in several places; sprinkle with garlic salt.
2. Place ducklings, skin side up, on racks in 2 open roasting pans. Roast in 350°F. oven 2 hours or until ducklings are tender.
3. Meanwhile, in 2-quart saucepan over medium heat, in hot butter or margarine, cook onion, stirring occasionally, 5 minutes or until tender.
4. Into blender container, drain liquid from plums; pit plums and add to container. Add onion mixture, brown sugar and remaining ingredients. Cover and blend at high speed until smooth.
5. Pour plum mixture into saucepan. Over medium heat, simmer plum mixture 25 minutes, stirring the mixture occasionally.
6. When ducklings are done, remove pans from oven; turn oven control to 400°F. Remove ducklings and racks from pans; pour off fat; discard. Return racks and ducklings to pans and brush with some of sauce. Roast ducklings 15 minutes longer, brushing occasionally with sauce. Serve ducklings with remaining plum sauce.

GLAZES FOR POULTRY

Allow about ½ cup glaze for 4- to 10-pound birds; for larger birds, double the recipe. During the last 10 to 20 minutes of roasting time, brush the bird several times with one of these glazes.

QUINCE: In 1-quart saucepan over low heat, stir *½ cup quince jelly, 1 tablespoon butter or margarine, 1 teaspoon ground cinnamon* and *½ teaspoon ground cloves* until blended. (Makes ½ cup.)

WINE-JELLY: In 1-quart saucepan over low heat, stir *½ cup wine jelly* with *¼ teaspoon salt* until blended. (Makes ½ cup.)

NUTTY: In 1-quart saucepan over medium heat, melt *½ cup apple jelly;* stir in *½ cup orange juice* and *½ cup chopped California walnuts.* (Makes 1⅓ cups.)

HONEY-BARBECUE: In small bowl, mix *½ cup honey, 1 tablespoon soy sauce* and *½ teaspoon ground ginger,* until well blended. (Makes ½ cup.)

ORANGE-WALNUT: In 1-quart saucepan over medium heat, heat *1 cup orange marmalade, ½ cup finely chopped California walnuts, 3 tablespoons lemon juice, 1 tablespoon instant minced onion* and *2½ teaspoons salt* until marmalade is melted. (Makes 1⅔ cups.)

Either sweet or savory sauces go well with all types of poultry, particularly with roast birds. Provide 1 cup of sauce for every 4 to 5 servings of poultry.

Cranberry-Orange Sauce

Begin 20 mins
ahead

3 cups

2 tablespoons cornstarch
**1 teaspoon grated lemon
peel**
**½ teaspoon ground
cloves**
¼ teaspoon salt
1½ cups orange juice
1 teaspoon lemon juice
**1 16-ounce can whole-
cranberry sauce**

1. In 2-quart saucepan, combine cornstarch with lemon peel, cloves and salt; stir in orange and lemon juice until smooth.
2. Over high heat, cook, stirring constantly, until sauce is smooth and thickened.
3. Stir in cranberry sauce and heat through, stirring occasionally. Serve hot or cold.

Lemon Sauce

Begin 10 mins
ahead

1 cup

¼ cup sugar
¼ cup lemon juice
4 teaspoons cornstarch
**1 tablespoon grated
lemon peel**
½ teaspoon salt
**⅛ teaspoon ground
ginger**
1 drop yellow food color
1 cup water

1. In 1-quart saucepan, mix well first 7 ingredients; stir in water to blend smoothly.
2. Cook over medium heat, stirring constantly, until mixture is slightly thickened. Serve hot.

Watercress Sauce

Begin 20 mins
ahead

2 cups

**1 13¾-ounce can chicken
broth (about 1¾ cups)**
**3 tablespoons all-purpose
flour**
⅓ cup cold water
**2½ cups coarsely
chopped watercress**
½ teaspoon salt
⅛ teaspoon pepper

1. In 1½-quart saucepan over high heat, heat chicken broth to boiling.
2. Meanwhile, in cup with fork, blend flour and water until smooth. Reduce heat to medium; gradually stir mixture into hot broth.
3. Cook, stirring constantly, until sauce is smooth and thickened. Stir in remaining ingredients; simmer 2 minutes. Serve hot with hot poultry.

Currant-Mint Sauce

Begin 10 mins
ahead

1 cup

**1 10-ounce jar red
currant jelly (1 cup)**
**2 tablespoons shredded
orange peel**
**2 tablespoons chopped
mint leaves**

In small bowl with fork, stir all ingredients until well mixed. Serve with roast chicken or turkey.

Curried Pineapple Sauce

Begin 15 mins
ahead

1 cup

**1 8¼-ounce can crushed
pineapple**
2 tablespoons butter
1 teaspoon curry powder

In 1-quart saucepan over medium-high heat, heat to boiling all ingredients, stirring occasionally. Reduce heat to low; cover; simmer 5 minutes. Serve hot.

VEGETABLES

Vegetables are becoming an increasingly important part of our diet. They are a good source of vitamins and minerals and many are high in fiber. Furthermore, most vegetables are low in calories. Canned, frozen and dried vegetables assure a year-round supply of varieties.

Whatever the method, keep cooking to a minimum. When boiling vegetables, use as little water as possible, then save the nutrient-rich liquid for use in stocks and sauces. Serve vegetables as accompaniments to main dishes or in stews and casseroles.

The servings specified in the recipes in this chapter are accompaniment servings unless otherwise indicated. Directions for buying and using individual vegetables are given in the following pages.

Artichokes

Also known as French or globe artichokes.

Season: All year. Best supplies of artichokes are in March, April and May.

Look for: Compact, plump heads, heavy in relation to their size, with tightly closed, thick green leaves. Size is not an indication of quality. Avoid over-mature ones with hard-tipped, blemished or spreading leaves.

To store: Refrigerate in a plastic bag with a few drops of water. Use within a few days.

To prepare: Cut off stem and top, trim thorny tips of leaves and pull loose leaves from around bottom of artichoke as shown right.

To cook: In large saucepot over medium heat, in 1 inch boiling, salted water, place artichokes on their stem ends. Add a few lemon slices, heat to boiling, cover saucepot, reduce heat to low and cook about 30 minutes or until leaf can be pulled out easily.

Seasonings: Cook with bay leaf, garlic, oregano.

To serve: Serve artichokes as hot or cold appetizer or salad, and in recipes. Eat with melted butter, Lemon Butter, Hollandaise or Bearnaise Sauce (all on page 463). Allow 1 artichoke per person.

Preparing artichokes: With sharp knife, cut stem from artichoke and 1 inch straight across the top.

With scissors, trim thorny tips of leaves; brush cut edges with lemon juice to prevent discoloration. Pull loose leaves from around bottom.

Eating artichokes: Pull out a leaf and dip base in melted butter or sauce on side of plate; pull through teeth, scraping out pulp. Discard leaves on plate.

Cut out fuzzy "choke" in center of artichoke; cut solid heart into chunks and dip in sauce.

ARTICHOKES BEARNAISE

With spoon, scoop out choke from *cooked artichoke*. Fill center with *Bearnaise Sauce* (page 463). Serve warm. (Color index, page 55.)

VEGETABLES
Asparagus

Season: March to July; sometimes in fall.
Look for: Straight stalks with closed, compact tips, good green color almost entire length (the white area at the end is tough and must be discarded).
To store: Refrigerate in crisper or wrapped in plastic bags. Use within 1 to 2 days.
To prepare: See below.
To cook: In large skillet over medium heat, in ½ inch boiling, salted water, heat stalks to boiling; reduce heat to low; cover and simmer until tender-crisp; whole asparagus take about 5 minutes, cut-up stalks about 3 to 5 minutes. Or, steam or stir-fry or use in recipes for soups, main dishes, salads, appetizers.
Seasonings: Cook with allspice, mustard, coriander, lemon, seasoned salt and pepper.
To serve: Eat hot or cold, with or without sauce.

Preparing asparagus:
Hold base of stalk firmly and bend stalk; break off end where it is too tough to eat; discard end.

With sharp knife, trim scales if stalks are gritty.

Steamed Asparagus

Color index page 21

Begin 15 mins ahead

8 first-course servings or 4 accompaniment servings

water	*Hollandaise Sauce*
1 pound asparagus	*(page 463) or Lemon*
salt	*Butter (page 463)*

1. In asparagus steamer or 3-quart saucepan with rack, heat ½ inch water to boiling.
2. Add asparagus. Cover; steam asparagus 8 to 10 minutes until tender.
3. Salt to taste. Serve with Hollandaise Sauce or Lemon Butter.

STEAMED CUT ASPARAGUS: Cut asparagus diagonally into 2-inch pieces and steam as above, cooking 6 to 8 minutes until tender-crisp.

Stir-fried Asparagus

Color index page 70

Begin 10 mins ahead

6 servings

1½ pounds asparagus	*½ teaspoon salt*
2 tablespoons salad oil	

1. Cut asparagus diagonally into 3-inch pieces.
2. In 10-inch skillet or 5-quart Dutch oven over high heat, in very hot salad oil, cook asparagus, stirring quickly and frequently (stir-frying) until well coated. Sprinkle with salt; continue stir-frying about 3 minutes more or until tender-crisp.

Beans, dry

LARGE LIMA BEANS

BLACKEYE BEANS

GARBANZO BEANS

KIDNEY BEANS

LENTILS

Season: All year.
Look for: Packages.
To store: Keep in packages or in covered containers.
To prepare: Rinse well; discard any stones or shriveled beans. Dry beans and whole peas require soaking before cooking, split peas and lentils do not. *Overnight soaking:* Cover each cup beans or whole peas with 3 cups water; let stand 12 hours or overnight. *Quicker soaking:* Add beans or whole peas to boiling water, allowing 3 cups water for each cup beans or whole peas. Over high heat, heat to boiling; boil 2 minutes. Remove from heat; cover and leave for 1 hour; then cook in same water.
To cook: After soaking, add 1 teaspoon salt for each cup dry beans or peas. Over medium-low heat, simmer, covered, until tender following timetable below. One cup dry beans or peas yields 2 to 2½ cups cooked.
Seasonings: Cook with onion, garlic or bay leaf.
To serve: Serve hot; serve cold in salads; use in recipes.

1 CUP SOAKED	COOKING TIMES
Black beans	2 hours
Blackeye beans (peas or cowpeas)	25 to 30 minutes
Garbanzo beans (chick-peas)	2 to 2¼ hours
Great Northern beans	1 to 1½ hours
Kidney beans	1½ hours
Lentils (*no soaking required*)	25 to 30 minutes
Large lima beans	1 hour
Pea beans (navy beans)	1½ hours
Peas, split (*no soaking required*)	45 minutes
Peas, whole	1 hour
Pink beans	2 hours
Pinto beans	2 hours
Red beans	2 hours
Soy beans	1½ hours

Boston Baked Beans

Color index page 68

Begin early in day or day ahead

12 servings

2 16-ounce packages dry	*1 tablespoon dry mustard*
pea (navy) beans	*1 teaspoon pepper*
water	*1 large onion, studded*
4 teaspoons salt	*with 4 whole cloves*
¾ cup dark molasses	*1 8-ounce piece salt pork,*
½ cup packed dark	*with rind slashed*
brown sugar	

1. Soak beans in water in 5-quart Dutch oven following quick soak method above; heat to boiling. Reduce heat to low; add salt; cover; simmer 1 hour.
2. Stir in molasses and next 3 ingredients. Tuck onion and salt pork into beans. Cover; bake in 250°F. oven 7 hours, adding more water if needed to keep beans moist but not too wet. Discard cloves.

Beans, green and wax

Blackeye Beans

Color index
page 68

Begin day
ahead

6 servings

1 16-ounce package dry
   blackeye beans
water

¼ pound salt pork, sliced
   or cut into chunks
salt and pepper

1. Soak beans in water to cover overnight.
2. *About 2 hours before serving:* Drain beans. In 5-quart Dutch oven over medium-high heat, heat beans, salt pork and 2 quarts water to boiling. Reduce heat to low; cover and simmer 1¼ hours or until beans are tender, stirring occasionally. Season to taste with salt and pepper.

Bean Relish

Color index
page 68

Begin 4½ hrs
or up to
1 wk ahead

9 cups relish

6 cups cooked dry red
   kidney or red beans
2 12-ounce cans
   vacuum-packed corn
1½ cups cider vinegar
1 cup sugar
3 medium onions, sliced

2 teaspoons salt
2 teaspoons mustard seed
1 teaspoon cracked
   pepper
1 cup water
3 tablespoons cornstarch

1. In large bowl, combine the red kidney or red beans, corn and its liquid; set aside.
2. In 2-quart saucepan over medium heat, heat vinegar, sugar, onions, salt, mustard seed and cracked pepper to boiling. Cover and cook until onions are tender, about 5 minutes.
3. Meanwhile, combine water and cornstarch until blended. Gradually add cornstarch mixture to vinegar mixture and cook, stirring constantly, until mixture boils. Boil 1 minute; remove from heat. Pour vinegar and cornstarch mixture over bean mixture and stir to mix well.
4. Cover and refrigerate about 4 hours or overnight, stirring occasionally.

Puerto Rican Beans and Rice

Color index
page 33

Begin 3 hrs
ahead

6 main-dish
servings

1 16-ounce package dry
   pink beans
6 cups water
2 teaspoons salt
½ cup diced salt pork
1 large onion, diced
1 large green pepper,
   diced

1 8-ounce can tomato
   sauce
½ teaspoon oregano
   leaves
¼ teaspoon garlic
   powder
¼ teaspoon pepper
4 cups hot cooked rice

1. Rinse beans under running cold water and discard any stones or shriveled beans. In 5-quart Dutch oven over medium-high heat, heat beans and water to boiling; boil 2 minutes. Remove from heat; cover and let stand 1 hour.
2. Do not drain beans; add salt. Over high heat, heat beans to boiling. Reduce heat to low; cover Dutch oven and simmer 40 minutes, stirring occasionally.
3. Meanwhile, in 10-inch skillet over medium heat, cook salt pork until well browned, about 10 minutes. Add onion and green pepper; cook until tender, stirring occasionally. Stir onion mixture, tomato sauce, oregano leaves, garlic powder and pepper into beans; cook 40 to 50 minutes until beans are tender and mixture is thickened. Serve spooned over the hot cooked rice.

Season: All year.
Look for: Crisp tender beans without scars. Well-shaped pods with small seeds are most desirable. Length is unimportant.
To store: Refrigerate in crisper or plastic bags; use within 1 or 2 days.
To prepare: See below.
To cook: In saucepan over medium heat, in 1 inch boiling, salted water, heat beans to boiling. Reduce heat to low; cover and simmer whole or cut-up beans 10 minutes, French-cut beans 5 minutes, or until tender-crisp. Beans are also good used in recipes for stews, pot roasts, main dishes and cold salads.
Seasonings: Cook with chili powder, chives, dill, lemon, mustard, onion, sage, parsley, seasoned salt and seasoned pepper, or try adding a few tablespoons of bacon or ham drippings.
To serve: Eat hot, with or without sauce.

Preparing beans: Rinse beans in cold water, then snap off ends; the string will come off with the stem end.

Leave whole, or snap or cut into bite-size pieces.

Whole Green and Wax Beans with Parsley Sauce

Color index
page 68

Begin 30 mins
ahead

8 servings

water
1 pound green beans
1 pound wax beans
2 tablespoons butter or
   margarine
2 tablespoons all-purpose
   flour

1½ teaspoons salt
⅛ teaspoon pepper
1 cup chicken broth
2 egg yolks
½ cup milk
1 cup chopped parsley

1. In 12-inch skillet over medium heat, in 1 inch boiling water, heat beans to boiling; reduce heat to low; cover and simmer 10 minutes or until tender-crisp. Drain.
2. Meanwhile, prepare sauce: In 2-quart saucepan over medium heat, into hot butter, stir flour, salt and pepper until blended. Gradually stir in chicken broth; cook, stirring constantly, until sauce is thickened. Reduce heat to low.
3. In small bowl, beat egg yolks with milk; stir in small amount of hot sauce. Slowly pour egg mixture into sauce stirring rapidly to prevent lumping; cook, stirring constantly, until thickened (do not boil). Stir in the beans and the chopped parsley.

Beans, lima

Season: All year. Best supplies of lima beans are in August and September.

Look for: Well-filled, tender, green pods. Avoid dried, spotty or yellowing, wilted ones. Shelled lima beans should be plump, with green to greenish-white skins.

To store: Refrigerate in crisper or in plastic bags. Use within 1 to 2 days.

To prepare: See below.

To cook: In saucepan over medium heat, in 1 inch boiling, salted water, heat beans to boiling. Reduce heat to low; cover and simmer 20 to 30 minutes until beans are tender. Lima beans may also be added to stews, pot roasts and soups.

Seasonings: Cook with garlic, onion, parsley.

To serve: Eat hot or cold, with or without sauce. Good topped with White or Cheese Sauce (page 461) or Mushroom Sauce (page 462).

Preparing lima beans: Snap off one end of pod and open to remove beans.

Or, with knife, cut off thin strip from the inner edge of the pod and push out beans

Lima Beans Smitane

Color index page 68

Begin 25 mins ahead

4 servings

1½ pounds lima beans, shelled, or 1 10-ounce package frozen baby lima beans
1 pimento, diced
½ cup sour cream
3 tablespoons chopped chives
¼ teaspoon garlic salt
¼ teaspoon salt
¼ teaspoon pepper

1. Cook shelled lima beans as above, or cook frozen beans as label directs; drain.
2. Lightly toss beans, pimento, sour cream, chives, garlic salt, salt and pepper.

Zesty Lima Beans

Color index page 68

Begin 2 hrs ahead

4 servings

1 10-ounce package frozen lima beans
½ cup sliced canned water chestnuts
¼ cup Italian dressing
¾ teaspoon dill weed

1. Cook lima beans as label directs; drain.
2. Add chestnuts, Italian dressing and dill weed to lima beans and toss to combine well. Cover mixture and refrigerate to chill.

Beets

Season: All year. Best supplies of beets are from June to November.

Look for: Smooth, firm, rich red beets of uniform size, with no ridges, blemishes or soft spots, and with fresh green tops, if any.

To store: Cut off stems and tops. Refrigerate tops and beets in crisper or plastic bags. Use beets within a week or so, preferably sooner. Use tops as soon as possible (see Lettuce and other greens, page 288).

To prepare: See below.

To cook: In saucepan over medium heat, in 1 inch boiling, salted water, heat whole beets to boiling. Reduce heat to low. Cover and simmer 30 minutes to 1 hour until fork-tender (depending on maturity and size of beets). Drain and peel (see below). Or, peel beets before cooking, slice or dice, and cook over medium heat 15 to 20 minutes until tender. Or, use in soups and salads.

Seasonings: Cook with allspice, celery seed, cloves, dill, nutmeg, orange, lemon.

To serve: Serve hot or cold, with or without sauce.

Preparing beets: Cut off stem ends. Scrub raw beets under running cold water being careful not to damage the skins.

Peeling cooked beets: First cool beets in cold water, then remove skins with a sharp knife.

Harvard Beets

Color index page 68

Begin 20 mins ahead

6 servings

¼ cup sugar
1 tablespoon cornstarch
½ teaspoon salt
⅓ cup vinegar
1 tablespoon butter or margarine
1 teaspoon minced onion
3 cups cooked, sliced beets or 2 16-ounce cans sliced beets, drained

1. In 1-quart saucepan, combine sugar, cornstarch and salt; slowly stir in vinegar; add butter or margarine and minced onion; over medium heat, cook until thickened, stirring constantly.
2. Reduce heat to low; add beets and cook just until heated through, stirring occasionally.

BEETS IN ORANGE SAUCE: Prepare as above but use *½ cup orange juice* instead of vinegar and *1 teaspoon grated orange peel* instead of onion.

Broccoli

Season: All year. Lowest supplies in June, July, August.
Look for: Tender, firm stalks and tightly closed, dark-green flowerets.
To store: Refrigerate in crisper or plastic bag. Use within 1 or 2 days.
To prepare: See below.
To cook: In skillet over medium heat, in 1 inch boiling, salted water, heat broccoli to boiling. Reduce heat to low; cover and simmer about 10 minutes until tender-crisp. Or, use in poultry dishes, casseroles, soups.
Seasonings: Cook broccoli with coriander, dill, mustard, nutmeg, oregano.
To serve: Eat hot, with or without sauce.

Preparing broccoli:
Remove any large leaves and cut off any woody stalk ends. Split stalks lengthwise 2 or 3 times to speed cooking. Rinse well.

Stir-fried Broccoli

Color index page 72

Begin 15 mins ahead

4 to 6 servings

3 tablespoons salad oil
1 bunch broccoli, cut in 2″ by ½″ pieces
¼ cup water
½ teaspoon salt
¼ teaspoon sugar

1. In 12-inch skillet or 5-quart Dutch oven over high heat, in very hot oil, cook broccoli, stirring quickly and frequently (stir-frying) until well coated.
2. Add water, salt and sugar. Reduce heat to medium-high; cover and cook 2 minutes; uncover and stir-fry 5 to 6 minutes more until tender-crisp.

Swiss-Cheese Broccoli

Color index page 72

Begin 1 hr ahead

8 servings

water
1 pound broccoli, coarsely chopped
salt
3 tablespoons butter
2 tablespoons all-purpose flour
3 tablespoons chopped onion
1¼ cups milk
2 cups shredded natural Swiss cheese
2 eggs, beaten

1. Grease a 10″ by 6″ baking dish. In 2-quart saucepan over high heat, in 1 inch boiling water, heat broccoli and ½ teaspoon salt to boiling; cover and cook 10 minutes; drain; set aside.
2. Meanwhile, in 2-quart saucepan over medium heat, melt butter; stir in flour and 1½ teaspoons salt until smooth. Add onion and cook 1 minute. Preheat oven to 325°F. Slowly stir in milk; cook, stirring constantly, until mixture thickens and begins to boil; remove from heat.
3. Stir in cheese and broccoli until cheese melts slightly; stir in eggs. Pour into baking dish; bake 30 minutes or until firm to the touch.

Brussels sprouts

Season: September to May.
Look for: Firm, fresh, bright green sprouts with tight-fitting outer leaves free from black spots. Puffy or soft sprouts are usually poor in quality.
To store: Refrigerate in crisper or wrapped in plastic bag. Use within 1 or 2 days.
To prepare: See below.
To cook: In saucepan over medium heat, in 1 inch boiling, salted water, heat sprouts to boiling. Reduce heat to low; cover and simmer about 10 minutes or until tender-crisp. Or, bake or use in recipes.
Seasonings: Cook Brussels sprouts with caraway, dill, mustard, ground nutmeg.
To serve: Eat hot, with or without sauce. Often served combined with carrots, squash or chestnuts.

Preparing Brussels sprouts:
Remove any yellow leaves and trim the stems.

With a sharp knife, cut an X into stem end to speed cooking time. Rinse sprouts.

Baked Brussels Sprouts

Color index page 71

Begin 1 hr ahead

4 to 6 servings

½ cup dried bread crumbs
2 tablespoons butter or margarine, melted
¼ teaspoon cracked pepper
1 teaspoon salt
2 10-ounce packages frozen Brussels sprouts, partially thawed and drained

1. Preheat oven to 350°F. In 2-quart casserole, stir all the ingredients, except Brussels sprouts, until thoroughly blended.
2. Add Brussels sprouts; toss to mix well; cover and bake 45 minutes until sprouts are tender-crisp.

Sweet-and-Sour Brussels Sprouts

Color index page 71

Begin 30 mins ahead

8 to 10 servings

½ 8-ounce package sliced bacon, diced
3 10-ounce containers Brussels sprouts or 3 10-ounce packages frozen Brussels sprouts, thawed
½ medium onion, minced
2 tablespoons cider vinegar
1 tablespoon sugar
¾ teaspoon salt
¼ teaspoon dry mustard
⅛ teaspoon pepper

1. In 5-quart Dutch oven or 4-quart saucepan over medium-low heat, cook diced bacon until browned. With slotted spoon, remove the bacon pieces to drain on paper towels.
2. In same Dutch oven, in bacon drippings, cook Brussels sprouts with onion, vinegar, sugar, salt, mustard and pepper until tender-crisp, about 10 minutes, stirring occasionally.
3. Stir bacon into Brussels sprouts mixture.

281

Cabbage

SAVOY CABBAGE

GREEN CABBAGE

Season: All year.

Look for: Firm heads, heavy for their size, with fresh, crisp leaves. Most popular green varieties include Danish, pointed and domestic. Savoy-type cabbage has crinkled green leaves, loosely formed heads. Red varieties have distinctive reddish-purple color.

To store: Refrigerate cabbage in crisper or wrapped in plastic bag. Use within 1 or 2 weeks.

To prepare: See below.

To cook: In saucepan over medium heat, in 1 inch boiling, salted water, heat cabbage to boiling. Reduce heat; cover and simmer 10 to 15 minutes for wedges, 3 to 10 minutes for shredded cabbage. Or, steam, stir-fry or cook in recipes.

Seasonings: Cook with allspice, caraway seed, cloves, curry, mustard, tarragon.

To serve: Eat cabbage raw in salads or serve hot, with or without seasonings.

Preparing cabbage: Discard any wilted or discolored outer leaves. Rinse in cold water.

With a large sharp knife, cut the cabbage in half and then into quarters.

Cut core off each wedge, leaving just enough to retain shape of wedge.

Or, shred the cabbage, using a large sharp knife or shredder; discard core.

Skillet Cabbage

Color index page 69

Begin 30 mins ahead

6 to 8 servings

8 bacon slices, *diced*
½ cup minced onion

1 medium cabbage, shredded
2 teaspoons salt

1. In 12-inch skillet over medium heat, fry diced bacon together with the minced onion until onion is tender, about 5 minutes.
2. Add shredded cabbage and salt and cook mixture, stirring occasionally with slotted spoon, until cabbage is tender, about 10 minutes.

Red Cabbage and Apples

Color index page 69

Begin 1 hr ahead

8 servings

¼ cup butter or margarine
2 medium cooking apples, peeled, cored and thinly sliced
1 medium onion, diced
1 medium head red cabbage, shredded (about 8 cups)

1 cup water
½ cup red wine vinegar
⅓ cup sugar
1½ teaspoons salt
⅛ teaspoon pepper
1 bay leaf

1. In 4-quart saucepan over medium heat, in hot butter or margarine, cook apples and onion until tender, about 10 minutes.
2. Add cabbage, water, red wine vinegar, sugar, salt, pepper and bay leaf; heat mixture to boiling. Reduce heat to low; cover and simmer 40 minutes or until cabbage is very tender, stirring occasionally.
3. To serve, discard bay leaf.

Sautéed Caraway-Cabbage

Color index page 69

Begin 15 mins ahead

6 servings

1 small green cabbage
3 tablespoons salad oil

1 teaspoon caraway seed
1 teaspoon salt

1. With knife, coarsely shred cabbage.
2. In 5-quart Dutch oven over high heat, in hot salad oil, cook cabbage, caraway seed and salt, stirring quickly and frequently (stir-frying) until cabbage is tender-crisp, about 10 minutes.

Cabbage Relish

Color index page 69

Begin 3 hrs ahead

6 to 8 servings

¾ cup white vinegar
¾ cup water
2 teaspoons salt
⅓ cup sugar
1 tablespoon mustard seed
6 cups shredded green cabbage

1 cup cut-up green pepper (¾-inch cubes)
2 4-ounce cans pimentos, cut into ¾-inch cubes
1 red onion, thinly sliced

1. In 3-quart saucepan, combine vinegar with water, salt, sugar and mustard seed. Over high heat, heat this marinade to boiling. Reduce heat to low; simmer 5 minutes; cool until warm.
2. In large bowl, combine cabbage, green pepper, pimentos, onion; pour marinade over vegetables, then toss to coat well.
3. Refrigerate relish, covered, 2 hours, tossing occasionally. Toss again before serving. Eat chilled, with cold sliced ham or pork.

Cucumbers

Season: All year. Best supplies from May to August.
Look for: Firm, well-shaped cucumbers with good, green color. Overmature ones are dull or yellow and look overgrown and puffy. Smaller varieties of cucumber are ideal for pickling.
To store: Refrigerate; use within 3 to 5 days.
To prepare: Rinse in cold water. Trim ends and cut cucumber into desired shapes. It is not necessary to peel cucumber unless called for in recipe.
To cook: Halve cucumber lengthwise. In saucepan over medium heat, in 1 inch boiling, salted water, heat cucumber to boiling. Reduce heat to low; cover and simmer 5 to 10 minutes, until tender-crisp. Or use in recipes for pickles or cold soup.
Seasonings: Sprinkle pepper, dill, tarragon, parsley or chives over sliced fresh cucumber.
To serve: Eat raw, in salads, or as cooked vegetable.

Sautéed Cucumber Rings

Color index
page 70

Begin 30 mins
ahead

4 servings

3 medium cucumbers
2 tablespoons butter
½ teaspoon salt
⅛ teaspoon pepper

1. Peel cucumbers. Cut each cucumber crosswise into thirds; with spoon, remove seeds. Cut cucumbers crosswise into ¼-inch-thick slices to form rings.
2. In 12-inch skillet over medium-high heat, melt butter; add cucumber rings, salt and pepper; cook 10 minutes or until cucumbers are just tender-crisp, stirring occasionally.

CUCUMBER GARNISHES

Slices: Score unpeeled cucumber lengthwise with sharp-tined fork; cut crosswise into very thin slices

Wedges: Cut peeled or unpeeled cucumber in half lengthwise then crosswise; cut quarters lengthwise into thick or thin wedges.

Twists: Slice unpeeled cucumber crosswise in thin slices. Cut each slice from center to edge. Twist cut edges in opposite directions.

Eggplant

Season: All year.
Look for: Firm, heavy eggplant free from blemishes with a uniformly dark, rich purple color and a bright green cap. Avoid wrinkled or flabby eggplant which are usually bitter-tasting.
To store: Refrigerate. Use within 1 or 2 days.
To prepare: See below.
To cook: In large saucepan over medium heat, in 1 inch boiling, salted water, heat eggplant to boiling. Reduce heat to low; cover and simmer about 5 minutes or until tender. Or, sauté or use in recipes for main dishes or with other vegetables.
Seasonings: Cook with oregano, sage, garlic.
To serve: Eat as cooked vegetable.

Preparing eggplant: With knife, trim stem end and slice or cut unpeeled eggplant into desired shape just before cooking; eggplant discolors quickly.

Eggplant with Caraway Seed

Color index
page 69

Begin 25 mins
ahead

4 servings

2 tablespoons salad oil
¾ cup chopped bacon slices
1 medium onion, sliced
1 teaspoon caraway seed
2 teaspoons vinegar
¾ teaspoon salt
1 small eggplant, cubed

1. In 10-inch skillet over medium-high heat, in hot salad oil, cook all ingredients but eggplant 5 minutes or until bacon and onion are light brown.
2. Reduce heat to medium; add eggplant and cook, covered, 5 to 7 minutes until eggplant is tender, stirring occasionally.

Sautéed Eggplant Slices

Color index
page 69

Begin 15 mins
ahead

4 servings

1 medium eggplant (about 1 pound)
⅓ cup olive or salad oil
2 tablespoons butter or margarine
¾ cup water
1 teaspoon salt
⅛ teaspoon pepper
chopped parsley

1. With knife, cut eggplant crosswise into ½-inch-thick slices; cut each slice in half. In 12-inch skillet over medium-high heat, in hot oil and butter or margarine, cook eggplant, stirring constantly, until well coated with oil mixture.
2. Add water, salt and pepper; cook, stirring frequently, until eggplant slices are tender, about 5 minutes more. To serve, garnish with parsley.

Endives, Belgian

Also known as French endives.

Season: September to June.

Look for: Small, compact endives with white leaves edged with pale green. Avoid any with wilted outer leaves. (For curly endives, see Lettuce and other greens, page 288.)

To store: Refrigerate in crisper or wrapped in plastic bags. Use within 1 or 2 days.

To prepare: See below.

To cook: In saucepan over medium heat, in ½ inch boiling, salted water, heat endives to boiling. Reduce heat to low; cover and simmer about 15 minutes, until endives are tender-crisp.

Seasonings: Cook with lemon, ground nutmeg.

To serve: Eat raw, with dressing as salad or appetizer. Or serve hot as vegetable.

Preparing endives: Rinse in cold water, then with a small sharp knife, cut root ends from endives.

With hands, remove any wilted or bruised outer leaves.

Endives with Swiss Cheese

Color index page 69

Begin 1 hr ahead·

6 servings

water	¼ cup butter or
12 small Belgian endives	margarine
salt	pepper
½ pound natural Swiss	⅓ cup half-and-half
cheese, shredded	

1. In 4-quart saucepan over medium heat, in 1 inch boiling water, heat endives and 1 teaspoon salt to boiling. Reduce heat to low; cover and simmer 10 minutes; drain. Preheat oven to 350°F.

2. Arrange 6 endives in metal 12″ by 8″ baking dish; sprinkle with half of cheese and dot with half of butter or margarine; sprinkle lightly with salt and pepper. Repeat.

3. Pour half-and-half over all. Bake 10 to 15 minutes until cheese is melted.

4. Turn heat control to broil; place baking dish under broiler for about 3 minutes until the cheese is golden brown and bubbling.

Fennel

Also known as anise, sweet anise or finocchio.

Season: October to March.

Look for: Well-shaped white bulbs with green, feather-like leaves.

To store: Refrigerate fennel in crisper or wrapped in plastic bags. Use within 3 to 5 days.

To prepare: See below.

To cook: In saucepan over medium heat, in ½ inch boiling, salted water, heat cut-up fennel to boiling. Reduce heat to low; cover and simmer 10 to 20 minutes or until tender. Or use in recipes for tomato sauce or fish soups. Flavor is pungent, so use sparingly as seasoning.

To serve: Serve raw as a snack or use in salads as celery. Use cooked pieces as vegetable with melted butter or margarine and lemon juice.

Preparing fennel: Rinse in cold water. Cut off root ends and leaves from bulb.

Cut bulb lengthwise in half then slice into sticks or pieces.

Braised Fennel

Color index page 68

Begin 30 mins ahead

4 servings

2 large bunches fennel	2 tablespoons butter or
1¾ cups water	margarine, softened
2 chicken-flavor bouillon	1 tablespoon all-purpose
cubes or envelopes	flour

1. With knife, cut top off each bulb of fennel just below leaves, leaving stalks and bulb about 6 inches long. Cut bulb lengthwise in half. Chop enough fennel leaves to measure 2 tablespoons; set aside. Refrigerate leftover leaves for garnish another day.

2. In 12-inch skillet over medium heat, heat fennel, water and bouillon to boiling. Reduce heat to low; cover and simmer 15 minutes or until fennel bulbs are tender.

3. Meanwhile, in small bowl with spoon, blend butter or margarine and flour until smooth. With slotted pancake turner, remove fennel to serving dish; keep warm. With wire whisk, stir butter mixture into liquid remaining in skillet. Over medium heat, cook, stirring, until mixture is slightly thickened and boils. Spoon sauce over fennel. Garnish with chopped fennel leaves.

Kohlrabi

Season: May to November. Best supplies of kohlrabi are in June and July.
Look for: Small or medium-size bulbs with fresh tops and tender rind.
To store: Cut off tops and discard. Refrigerate and use within 2 or 3 days.
To prepare: See below.
To cook: In a saucepan over medium heat, in 1 inch boiling, salted water, heat cut-up kohlrabi to boiling. Reduce heat to low; cover and simmer 15 to 30 minutes or until kohlrabi is tender.
Seasonings: Cook with mustard, tarragon.
To serve: Eat peeled raw strips as snack or appetizer. Use cooked pieces as a vegetable; use in recipes.

Preparing kohlrabi: Rinse in cold water, then with a small sharp knife, peel kohlrabi thinly and slice or cut up.

Cheesy Kohlrabi

Color index page 71

Begin 45 mins ahead

6 servings

water
8 medium kohlrabi, peeled and sliced into ¼-inch slices
1 teaspoon salt
3 tablespoons butter
¼ cup all-purpose flour
1 10½-ounce can condensed chicken broth

¼ cup shredded American cheese
⅛ teaspoon ground allspice
2 tablespoons chopped parsley for garnish

1. In 2-quart saucepan over medium heat, in 1 inch boiling water, heat kohlrabi and salt to boiling. Reduce heat to low; cover and simmer 30 minutes or until tender; drain.
2. Meanwhile, in 3-quart saucepan over low heat, into hot butter, stir flour until smooth. Gradually add undiluted chicken broth and cook, stirring constantly, until mixture is thickened.
3. Remove from heat and stir in cheese until melted and smooth. Add kohlrabi and cook until heated through. Sprinkle the mixture with allspice, then garnish with the chopped parsley.

Leeks

Season: All year. Best supplies September to November.
Look for: Leeks with white bulb base and fresh green tops, usually trimmed.
To store: Refrigerate, wrapped. Use within 3 to 5 days.
To prepare: See below.
To cook: In saucepan over medium heat, in 1 inch boiling, salted water, heat leeks to boiling. Reduce heat to low; cover and simmer 10 to 15 minutes or until tender; drain. Or use in recipes for soups or main dishes.
Seasonings: Cook with ginger, rosemary or sage.
To serve: Eat raw, finely shredded, in salads. Or use leeks as cooked vegetable.

Preparing leeks: Cut off roots and trim leaf end. Cut leeks crosswise in half, then cut root ends lengthwise in half.

Rinse under running cold water to remove sand. Use halved or cut up.

To cook a large amount, tie leeks loosely with string into bundles; cook 30 minutes; when done, remove strings.

Leeks au Gratin

Color index page 70

Begin 45 mins ahead

4 servings

8 medium leeks
3 tablespoons butter
3 tablespoons all-purpose flour
½ teaspoon dry mustard

½ teaspoon salt
1 cup milk
1 cup shredded Cheddar cheese
1 cup fresh bread crumbs

1. Cook leeks; place in broilersafe 9″ by 9″ baking pan. Preheat broiler if manufacturer directs.
2. In 1-quart saucepan over low heat, melt butter; stir in flour, mustard and salt till smooth. Gradually stir in milk; cook, stirring, until thickened; stir in cheese till melted; pour mixture over leeks.
3. Sprinkle with crumbs. Broil to brown crumbs.

Lettuce and other greens

ROMAINE

ICEBERG

CHICORY

Season: All year.
Look for: Clean, crisp, tender leaves, free from decay or dirt. Crisphead varieties of lettuce (including Iceberg) have solid heads and are heavy for their size. Butterhead lettuces (including Boston and Bibb) have soft leaves with lighter-color inside leaves; Cos or Romaine lettuce have crisp coarse leaves with heavy midribs; looseleaf lettuces (including Bunching) have soft textured leaves, and are available either in long bunches or loose. Stem lettuce (Celtuce) has an enlarged stem (leaves are peeled and stem is eaten fresh or in Chinese recipes). Other greens include beet or turnip tops, cilantro (Mexican or Chinese parsley), Swiss chard, dandelion, Belgian endive (see page 286), escarole, kale, collards, leafy broccoli, mustard greens, parsley, rape, sorrel, chicory (curly endive), rapini, spinach (see page 294) and watercress. All these other greens should have fresh tender green leaves and be free from excessive sand or dirt; injured, dried or yellow leaves and coarse stems usually indicate poor quality and may cause waste.
To store: All greens which are to be served raw should be refrigerated in a crisper or plastic bag. Use Crisphead lettuce within 3 to 5 days. Use looser, leafier kinds of lettuce and other greens within 1 or 2 days.
To prepare: See pages 316 to 317.
To cook: In deep skillet or Dutch oven over medium heat, in ¼ inch boiling, salted water, cook tender leafy greens 1 to 3 minutes, until wilted, stirring occasionally; cook other greens 5 to 10 minutes or until tender-crisp. Lettuce is also good stir-fried, braised or used in recipes for vegetable dishes, soups and "wilted" salads.
Seasonings: Cook with allspice, bacon drippings, lemon, onion, nutmeg, vinegar.
To serve: Eat lettuce and other greens fresh in salads with dressings; use as cooked vegetable; in sandwiches or to garnish salads and main dishes.

288

Mushrooms

Season: All year.
Look for: Firm, plump, cream-colored mushrooms with short, clean-cut stems and caps that are either closed around the stems or slightly open, and with pink or light-tan gills. Buy only cultivated mushrooms. Wild varieties may be poisonous.
To store: Refrigerate, covered. Use within 1 or 2 days.
To prepare: See below.
To cook: Brush with melted butter or margarine and broil 4 to 5 minutes until fork-tender, or sauté (below) or use in recipes for soups and main dishes.
Seasonings: Cook with garlic, lemon, onion, nutmeg.
To serve: Eat raw in salads or serve hot as a vegetable.

Preparing mushrooms: Do not peel or soak; rinse in cold water; drain well. Pat dry with paper towels. Cut thin slice from stem.

Leave whole; or cut mushrooms in thin slices parallel to the stem; or cook as recipe directs.

Sautéed Mushrooms

Color index page 69

Begin 20 mins ahead

4 servings

¼ cup butter or margarine
2 tablespoons minced onion
1 pound mushrooms, sliced

1 teaspoon lemon juice
½ teaspoon salt
⅛ teaspoon pepper
4 white bread slices, toasted and buttered

1. In 10-inch skillet over medium heat, in hot butter or margarine, cook onion until tender, about 5 minutes. Add mushrooms; cook, covered, stirring occasionally, about 10 minutes.
2. Stir in lemon juice, salt and pepper. Serve mixture on hot buttered toast, or as is.

MUSHROOMS IN CREAM: Prepare as for Sautéed Mushrooms but omit lemon juice and stir in *2 tablespoons dry sherry* and *⅓ cup half-and-half*.

Mushrooms in Sour Cream

Color index page 69

Begin 30 mins ahead

12 servings

½ cup butter or margarine
2 pounds mushrooms, sliced
½ cup minced green onions

1 teaspoon salt
½ teaspoon pepper
½ cup sour cream

1. In 12-inch skillet over medium-high heat, melt butter. Add mushrooms, green onions, salt and pepper and cook, stirring frequently, until mushrooms are tender, about 10 minutes.
2. Stir in sour cream; heat through (do not boil). Spoon mushroom mixture into medium bowl. Serve warm or refrigerate to serve cold later.

Okra

Season: All year. Best supplies from May to October.
Look for: Young, tender green pods 4 to 8 inches long.
To store: Refrigerate. Use within 1 to 2 days.
To prepare: See below.
To cook: In saucepan over medium heat, in 1 inch boiling, salted water, heat okra to boiling. Reduce heat to low; cover and simmer whole okra 5 to 10 minutes or cut-up okra 3 to 5 minutes. Use in recipes.
Seasonings: Cook with cayenne or onions.
To serve: Eat okra as a cooked vegetable, hot or cold.

Preparing okra: Wash in cold water. Cut off stems. Leave okra whole or cut into pieces.

Okra Vinaigrette

Color index page 69

Begin 4½ hrs or day ahead

6 servings

water
2 pounds okra
salt
½ cup olive or salad oil
⅓ cup white vinegar
½ teaspoon dry mustard
½ teaspoon thyme leaves

¼ teaspoon sugar
⅛ teaspoon pepper
1 large garlic clove, crushed
¼ cup chopped pimento
Boston lettuce leaves

1 In 12-inch skillet over medium heat, in 1 inch boiling water, heat okra and ½ teaspoon salt to boiling. Cover and cook 5 minutes or until tender.

2 In large bowl with fork, mix well 1¼ teaspoons salt with oil and remaining ingredients except pimento and Boston lettuce.

3 Add okra and pimento; toss to coat mixture thoroughly. Cover and refrigerate at least 4 hours or overnight, tossing occasionally.

4 *Just before serving:* Line 6 individual salad plates with Boston lettuce leaves, then arrange chilled okra mixture on top of lettuce.

Onions

Season: All year.
Look for: Clean, firm onions, with dry, brittle, papery skins. Avoid onions which have begun sprouting.
To store: Store in refrigerator or cool room temperature (60°F. or below) in container allowing good circulation of air. Keep dry. Onions may be stored several months.
To prepare: See below.
To cook: In saucepan over medium heat, in 1 inch boiling, salted water, heat whole onions to boiling. Reduce heat to low; cover and simmer 15 to 20 minutes until tender. Or, use in recipes.
Seasonings: Cook with cloves, dill, nutmeg or paprika.
To serve: Eat raw in sandwiches and salads. Or serve hot or cold, with or without sauce.

Preparing onions: With a small sharp knife, cut off stem and roots; pull off dry, outer skin.

Slice, chop or dice. To dice: Cut onion in half; place half on cut side; cut lengthwise into ¼-inch slices; hold together and cut crosswise into ¼-inch slices.

Baked Onions

Color index page 67

Begin 1 hr ahead

6 to 8 servings

⅓ cup honey
¼ cup butter

½ teaspoon salt
6 large onions, sliced

1. Preheat oven to 425°F. In 1-quart saucepan over medium heat, heat honey, butter and salt.
2. In greased 13″ by 9″ baking dish, arrange onions; pour honey-butter mixture evenly over onions. Bake 45 minutes or until onions are fork-tender and golden brown in color.

Glazed Onions

Color index page 67

Begin 30 mins ahead

4 servings

water
1½ pounds medium onions
⅓ cup sugar

2 tablespoons butter or margarine
¼ teaspoon salt

1. In 2-quart saucepan over medium heat, in 1 inch boiling water, heat onions to boiling. Reduce heat to low; cover and simmer 15 to 20 minutes; drain.
2. In 10-inch skillet over low heat, stir sugar, butter, 2 teaspoons water and salt until mixed.
3. Add onions; cook until golden and glazed, about 5 minutes, stirring occasionally.

Onions

Pan-fried Onions

Color index page 67

Begin 15 mins ahead

4 servings

¼ cup butter or margarine
4 to 5 medium onions, thinly sliced

1 teaspoon salt
¼ teaspoon thyme leaves
⅛ teaspoon pepper

1. In 10-inch skillet over medium heat, in hot butter, cook onions, covered, 5 minutes.
2. Add salt, thyme and pepper; cook, uncovered, until onions are tender, about 8 minutes, stirring onion mixture occasionally.

French-fried Onions

Color index page 67

Begin 30 mins ahead

6 to 8 servings

3 large onions, sliced ¼ inch thick
salad oil

½ cup milk
1 cup all-purpose flour
½ teaspoon salt

1. Separate onion slices into rings. In electric skillet, heat ¾ inch salad oil to 370°F.
2. In small dish, place milk. In small bowl, stir flour and salt until mixed. Dip rings in milk, then in flour mixture. Repeat to coat twice.
3. In hot salad oil, cook onions 3 minutes or until lightly browned. Drain thoroughly on paper towels. Serve immediately.

Creamed Onions

Color index page 67

Begin 30 mins ahead

8 to 10 servings

water
salt
2 pounds small white onions
6 tablespoons butter or margarine

3 tablespoons all-purpose flour
1½ cups milk
paprika

1. In 2-quart saucepan over medium heat, in 1 inch boiling, salted water, heat onions to boiling. Reduce heat to low; cover and simmer 10 to 15 minutes or until the onions are tender.
2. Meanwhile, in 1-quart saucepan over medium heat, melt butter; stir in flour until smooth; slowly stir in milk and ¼ teaspoon salt and cook, stirring constantly, until thickened.
3. Drain onions and place in serving dish; pour on sauce and sprinkle lightly with paprika.

GREEN ONIONS, SCALLIONS AND SHALLOTS

SHALLOT

GREEN ONION

Green onions, shoots of any onion harvested before the bulb forms, are available all year. Eat fresh or use in recipes. *Scallions* technically are shoots of white onions only; in a few places in the United States, the word scallion is used to mean green onions. *Shallots* have distinctive bulbs made up of cloves like garlic. Green shallots are available in summer; dry bulbs are available year round. Use in recipes.

Parsnips

Season: All year.
Look for: Smooth, firm, well-shaped parsnips of medium size. Avoid any large, coarse roots or ones with gray or soft spots.
To store: Refrigerate. Use within 2 weeks.
To prepare: See below.
To cook: In saucepan over medium heat, in 1 inch boiling, salted water, heat parsnips to boiling. Reduce heat to low; cover and simmer 20 to 30 minutes for whole vegetables, 8 to 15 minutes for cut-up parsnips or until tender. Use in recipes for soups, stews, pot roasts. Or, mash and season as potatoes.
Seasonings: Serve parsnips with cinnamon, ginger, orange or tarragon.
To serve: Eat as cooked vegetable. Serve with Hollandaise Sauce or White Sauce (page 461).

Preparing parsnips: Scrub the parsnips in cold water; cut off stem ends and tails.

Remove skin of parsnips with a vegetable peeler.

Leave parsnips whole; or halve, slice or cut them into quarters as shown, right.

Parsley Creamed Parsnips

Color index page 68

Begin 30 mins ahead

6 servings

1 pound parsnips
1 cup water
salt
2 tablespoons all-purpose flour

½ cup milk
⅛ teaspoon pepper
1 teaspoon grated orange peel
chopped parsley

1. Peel parsnips, then slice in ⅛-inch slices. In 2-quart saucepan over medium heat, heat parsnips, water and ½ teaspoon salt to boiling. Reduce heat to low; cover and simmer about 10 minutes until parsnips are fork-tender. Drain parsnips, reserving ½ cup liquid.
2. In 1-quart saucepan over medium heat, stir flour with milk until well mixed. Add reserved liquid, pepper and ½ teaspoon salt; cook, stirring constantly, until thickened and smooth. Stir in grated orange peel. Stir sauce with parsnips. Sprinkle mixture lightly with chopped parsley.

Peas

Season: All year. Best supplies January to August.
Look for: Fresh, young pods, light-green in color, slightly velvety to the touch and well filled with well-developed peas. Pods with immature peas are usually flat, dark green, wilted; overmature pods are swollen, light, wrinkled and yellowish, flecked with gray.
To store: Refrigerate in pods. Use within 2 days.
To prepare: See below.
To cook: In saucepan over medium heat, in 1 inch boiling, salted water, heat peas to boiling. Reduce heat to low; cover and simmer 5 to 8 minutes, until tender.
Seasonings: Cook with chives, lettuce leaves, marjoram, mint, nutmeg, oregano, onion, savory, rosemary, tarragon, thyme.
To serve: Eat as cooked vegetable.

Preparing peas: Press pods between thumb and forefinger to open; push peas out with thumb. Rinse peas in colander under running cold water. Discard pods.

Color index page 70

Begin 40 mins ahead

4 servings

Peas Amandine

2 pounds peas
water
salt
⅔ cup chopped bacon
   slices

¼ cup minced onion
½ cup slivered almonds
½ cup heavy or whipping
   cream

1. Shell peas (yield should be about 1⅔ cups).
2. In 2-quart saucepan over medium heat, in 1 inch boiling water, heat peas and 2 teaspoons salt to boiling. Reduce heat to low; cover pan and simmer 5 minutes; drain.
3. In 10-inch skillet over medium heat, fry bacon and onion until light brown. Add peas, almonds and 1 teaspoon salt; heat through. Stir in cream. Serve in individual dishes.

SNOW PEAS

Snow peas, also known as Chinese peas, are in season from May to September. Look for delicate fresh green, thin pea pods. Refrigerate and use within a day or two. To prepare, just rinse in cold water, carefully stem and string the pods (do not shell). Cook as for ordinary peas and eat pod and all, as a cooked vegetable or in recipes for Chinese dishes.

Peppers

Season: All year.
Look for: Peppers that are firm, shiny and thick-fleshed, medium to dark green. When mature, peppers turn red. Pimentos are a mild, sweet pepper.
To store: Refrigerate. Use within 3 to 5 days.
To prepare: See below.
To cook: Cook in recipes for main dishes or casseroles and as a seasoning for meat, in Creole, Spanish and Italian dishes. For stuffed peppers, parboil before stuffing: In large saucepan over high heat, in boiling water to cover, cook peppers 3 to 5 minutes; drain.
To serve: Eat fresh in salads; as cooked vegetable.

Preparing peppers: Rinse in cold water. Cut around stem; remove core, seeds and white membrane.

Use whole, to stuff. Or, cut into rings, strips or halves, dice or slivers.

Herb Sautéed Green Peppers

Color index page 70

Begin 15 mins ahead

4 servings

2 tablespoons butter
3 large green peppers, cut
   into ½-inch strips

1½ teaspoons marjoram
½ teaspoon salt

In 12-inch skillet over medium heat, in hot butter, cook all ingredients until peppers are tender, about 10 minutes, stirring occasionally.

Marinated Peppers

Color index page 70

Begin early in day or day ahead

6 servings

6 large green peppers
⅓ cup mayonnaise
¼ cup white wine vinegar

2 teaspoons sugar
1 teaspoon salt
¼ teaspoon white pepper

1. Preheat oven to 450°F. On cookie sheet, place peppers; bake 15 minutes or until skin puckers. Peel skin while warm; core; cut into ¼-inch strips.
2. In medium bowl, combine remaining ingredients until smooth. Add pepper strips; toss until strips are well coated; cover and refrigerate.
3. *To serve:* Drain sauce from pepper strips.

CHILI PEPPERS

Chili peppers, the hot varieties of pepper, are smaller than sweet peppers and can be red, green or yellow. Use in salads, main dishes; prepare with care, washing hands after handling.

Potatoes

Season: All year.

Look for: Smooth, well-shaped, firm potatoes free of blemishes or sprouts.

To store: Store in dark, dry place at coolest room temperature (don't refrigerate) for about 1 week.

To prepare: See below.

To cook: Boiled potatoes: In saucepan over high heat, heat potatoes and enough salted water to cover to boiling. Reduce heat to low; cover and simmer new potatoes 15 to 20 minutes, general-purpose potatoes about 30 minutes, or until tender. Potatoes are also good baked or fried or used in recipes.

Seasonings: Sprinkle cooked potato with basil, caraway seed, celery seed, chives, dill, onion, thyme.

To serve: Eat as cooked vegetable in recipes for main dishes, casseroles; or eat in hot or cold salads.

Preparing potatoes:
Scrub in cold water. Remove skin with vegetable peeler. Use quickly to avoid discoloration and loss of food value. When possible, cook without peeling to save nutrients.

Baked Potatoes

Color index
page 71

Begin 1 hr
ahead

6 servings

*6 medium baking
   potatoes, unpeeled
shortening or salad oil*

Toppings: *sour cream,
butter or margarine,
shredded Cheddar cheese*

Preheat oven to 450°F. Wash and dry potatoes; rub with shortening. If you like a steamed texture, wrap potatoes in foil. Place in shallow pan. Bake 45 minutes or until fork-tender. Serve with choice of toppings. If desired, slash top.

Mashed Potatoes

Color index
page 71

Begin 50 mins
ahead

6 servings

*6 medium potatoes,
   peeled*
salt
water

*¼ cup butter or
   margarine*
¼ teaspoon pepper
¼ to ½ cup hot milk

1. In 3-quart saucepan over high heat, heat potatoes, 1 teaspoon salt and water to cover to boiling. Reduce heat to low; cover potatoes and simmer 30 minutes or until fork tender; drain.

2. In large bowl with mixer at low speed, beat potatoes, butter, 1 teaspoon salt and pepper until fluffy. Beating at medium speed, slowly add milk until mixture is moist; continue beating 2 minutes or until mixture is smooth.

French-fried Potatoes

Color index
page 71

Begin 30 mins
ahead

8 servings

salad oil   *salt*
8 medium potatoes

1. In deep-fat fryer, heat about 2 inches oil to 400°F.
2. Meanwhile, peel potatoes; cut potatoes into ¼-inch slices; cut slices into ¼-inch lengthwise strips. Or, use crinkle cutter to cut strips. Rinse in cold water; drain; dry well with paper towels.
3. Cover bottom of fryer basket with even layer of potatoes; gently lower into hot oil and fry 5 minutes or until golden brown; drain on paper towels. Repeat with remaining potatoes. Sprinkle lightly with salt to taste; serve immediately.

Cutting potato strips: Cut ¼-inch-thick slices; cut slices into ¼-inch strips.

Using crinkle cutter: Cut slices or strips with cutter for special effect.

Pan-roasted Potatoes

Color index
page 71

Begin 1¼ hrs
ahead

6 servings

*6 medium potatoes,
   peeled*
1 teaspoon salt
water

*paprika, parsley or
   thyme leaves*

1. In 3-quart saucepan over high heat, heat potatoes, salt and water to cover potatoes to boiling. Reduce heat to low; cover and simmer 10 minutes.
2. Drain potatoes; arrange around beef or pork roast in roasting pan; turn to coat with drippings in pan. Bake 40 to 60 minutes at 325°F. along with roast, turning occasionally, just until tender and evenly browned all over.
3. To serve: Sprinkle potatoes with paprika, parsley or thyme. Arrange around roast on platter.

VARIATION: When not roasting with meat, boil potatoes as above. Meanwhile, preheat oven to 400°F. In shallow baking pan, melt *½ cup butter* or margarine. Add boiled potatoes to melted butter or margarine, turning to coat evenly. Bake, turning often, 40 minutes or until tender.

Home-fried Potatoes

Color index
page 71

Begin 25 mins
ahead

4 servings

*3 tablespoons bacon
   drippings*
*4 medium potatoes,
   cooked, peeled and
   thinly sliced*

salt and pepper
paprika

In 10-inch skillet over medium-high heat, in hot drippings, fry potato slices 10 minutes or until browned, occasionally turning with pancake turner. Sprinkle with salt, pepper and paprika to taste.

Pumpkin

Hash Brown Potatoes

Color index page 71

Begin 45 mins ahead

6 servings

½ cup butter
5 or 6 medium potatoes,
peeled and finely diced
or coarsely shredded
(about 6 cups)

1 teaspoon salt
½ teaspoon paprika
(optional)
¼ teaspoon pepper

1. In 10-inch skillet (preferably with a non-stick finish) over medium heat, in hot butter, cook potatoes, covered, 10 minutes.
2. Uncover and sprinkle potatoes with salt, paprika and pepper.
3. Continue cooking 15 minutes or until the potatoes are tender and brown, occasionally turning with a pancake turner.

Potatoes au Gratin

Color index page 71

Begin 55 mins ahead

6 servings

3 tablespoons butter or
margarine
5 or 6 medium potatoes,
peeled and thinly sliced
(about 6 cups)
1½ teaspoons salt

1 4-ounce package
shredded Cheddar
cheese (1 cup)
½ cup fresh bread
crumbs

1. Preheat oven to 425°F. In 12″ by 8″ baking pan in oven, melt butter. Remove from oven. Add potatoes and salt; toss together and arrange potatoes in even layer in baking pan.
2. Sprinkle with cheese and bread crumbs. Cover with foil. Bake 20 minutes; uncover and bake 15 minutes more or until potatoes are tender.

Potatoes Anna

Color index page 71

Begin 1½ hrs ahead

4 servings

2 tablespoons butter or
margarine
1 teaspoon salt

3 large potatoes, peeled
(about 4 cups)

1. In 1-quart saucepan over low heat, melt butter with salt. Preheat oven to 425°F.
2. With knife, slice potatoes about ¼ inch thick.
3. In greased 8-inch pie plate, arrange potato slices, overlapping them; drizzle butter mixture on top. Cover plate tightly with foil; bake 20 minutes.
4. Uncover and bake about 55 minutes more or until potatoes are very tender and crusty.
5. Let stand at room temperature 5 minutes. With metal spatula, carefully loosen potatoes from pie plate. Place inverted plate over potatoes; holding both plates, invert and unmold. Cut into wedges.

Adding butter mixture: Slowly pour melted butter mixture over sliced potatoes to cover evenly.

Serving potatoes: Carefully loosen cooked sliced potatoes from plate; invert onto serving plate.

Season: October.
Look for: Firm, bright pumpkins, free from blemishes.
To store: Store in cool, dry place. Use within 1 month.
To prepare: See below.
To cook: In a saucepan over medium heat, in 1 inch boiling, salted water, heat cut-up pumpkin to boiling. Reduce heat to low; cover and simmer 25 to 30 minutes or until tender, depending on size of chunks. Drain; cool slightly. Remove peel.
Seasonings: Cook with allspice, cinnamon, cloves, ginger, nutmeg.
To serve: Eat hot as vegetable or in pies or bread.

Preparing pumpkin: With large knife, halve or quarter pumpkin.

With a spoon, scoop out the seeds and stringy portions.

Cut the pumpkin flesh into large chunks.

Honeyed Pumpkin

Color index page 72

Begin 45 mins ahead

4 servings

1 4-pound pumpkin
4 cups water
1 teaspoon salt
2 tablespoons butter or
margarine

2 tablespoons honey
½ teaspoon ground
allspice (optional)

1. With sharp knife, cut pumpkin into quarters. Remove seeds and stringy portions.
2. In 4-quart saucepan over high heat, heat pumpkin, water and salt to boiling; reduce heat to low; cover and simmer 25 to 30 minutes until the pumpkin is fork-tender.
3. Drain pumpkin. Cool slightly and scoop flesh from peel into same saucepan. With potato masher or slotted spoon, mash pumpkin; drain well.
4. Over low heat, heat pumpkin about 3 minutes, shaking pan occasionally to evaporate excess liquid. Stir in butter, honey and allspice; mix well.

Radishes

Season: All year.
Look for: Uniformly shaped radishes that are free of blemishes, firm and bright, red or white, depending upon variety.
To store: Refrigerate in crisper or in plastic bag. Use radishes within a week.
To prepare: See below.
To serve: Eat radishes fresh as a snack or relish, sliced or cut up in salads.

Preparing radishes: Rinse in cold water. With small sharp knife, cut off stems and tails. Slice for salads. If using as garnish or relish, see below or Salad Garnishes (page 327). (If radishes have leafy tops, leave some tops on for garnish.)

Radish Spread

Color index page 18

Begin 15 mins ahead

2 cups

1 cup mayonnaise
1 cup minced radishes
¼ cup sour cream
½ teaspoon salt
thin radish slices for garnish

1. In medium bowl with spoon, mix well mayonnaise, minced radishes, sour cream and salt.
2. Use mixture to spread on rye bread for appetizers. Garnish with radish slices.

MAKING RADISH GARNISHES

Carved radish: Cut off root and stem end of large radish. Insert tip of knife slightly beyond center point of one end. Carve out small petal-shaped wedges, ⅛ inch deep, around radish. Carve other end, cutting first wedge between tips of two petals already made. Chill in iced water.

Radish rose: *Early in day:* Leave tops on radishes, if you like. Make 5 thin cuts almost to stem end of radish, all equidistant. Cut another 5 slices just above first slices. Place radish in iced water in bowl; cover and refrigerate until "petals" open.

Spinach

Season: All year.
Look for: Bright green, fresh tender leaves. Avoid spinach that is yellowish and wilted or gritty.
To store: Refrigerate spinach in crisper or wrapped. Use within 1 or 2 days.
To prepare: See below.
To cook: In saucepan over medium heat, in ¼ inch boiling, salted water, heat spinach to boiling. Reduce heat to low; cover and simmer 1 to 3 minutes until wilted, stirring occasionally. Or use in recipes.
Seasonings: Cook spinach with allspice, bacon drippings, lemon, onion or nutmeg.
To serve: Eat raw in salads. Or use leaves to garnish other salads. Serve hot, with or without a sauce.

Preparing spinach: Wash leaves well under running cold water.

Trim any tough ribs or stems; drain; pat dry on paper towels.

Baked Creamed Spinach

Color index page 67

Begin 1 hr ahead

8 servings

2 tablespoons butter or margarine
1 small onion, finely chopped
2 tablespoons all-purpose flour
1 teaspoon salt
⅛ teaspoon pepper
1 cup milk
2 eggs, separated
2 10-ounce bags spinach, finely chopped, cooked as above and well drained

1. Grease 8″ by 8″ baking dish. In 2-quart saucepan over medium heat, in hot butter, cook onion until tender, about 5 minutes. Stir in flour, salt and pepper until blended. Gradually stir in milk; cook, stirring, until sauce boils and is slightly thickened.
2. Preheat oven to 350°F. In small bowl with fork, beat egg yolks slightly. Into yolks, stir small amount of hot sauce; slowly pour yolk mixture into sauce, stirring rapidly to prevent lumping. Cook, stirring constantly, until thickened (do not boil). Remove from heat; stir in spinach.
3. In small bowl with mixer at high speed, beat egg whites until stiff peaks form. With wire whisk, gently fold egg whites into spinach mixture. Pour into baking dish; bake 20 to 25 minutes until a knife inserted in center comes out clean.

Squash, hard-skinned

Squash, soft-skinned

BUTTERNUT SQUASH

HUBBARD SQUASH

ZUCCHINI

YELLOW STRAIGHTNECK SQUASH

Acorn, banana, butternut, Des Moines, green and golden delicious, green and blue Hubbard.

Season: All year. Best supplies are in fall.

Look for: Squash heavy for its size, with a hard skin. Tender skin indicates immaturity or poor quality.

To store: Refrigerate or store at cool room temperature. Use within a few weeks.

To prepare: See below.

To cook: *Boiled squash:* In saucepan over medium heat, in 1 inch boiling, salted water, heat squash, cut side down, to boiling. Reduce heat to low; cover and simmer about 15 minutes or until pulp is tender. Drain; cool slightly and eat from shell, or scoop out pulp and use in recipes for vegetables, pies or desserts. *Baked squash:* Bake squash in jelly-roll pan in 325° to 375°F. oven 45 minutes to 1½ hours till fork-tender. Or use in recipes.

Seasonings: Basil, cloves, ginger, mustard seed, nutmeg.

To serve: Eat as cooked vegetable.

Varieties include Italian marrow, yellow straightneck, pattypan, zucchini.

Season: All year.

Look for: Small young squash, heavy for their size, with skin tender enough to yield easily to thumb pressure.

To store: Refrigerate. Use within a few days.

To prepare: See below

To cook: In saucepan over medium heat, in 1 inch boiling, salted water, heat squash to boiling. Reduce heat to low; cover and simmer halved squash about 5 minutes and sliced squash, 3 minutes.

Seasonings: Garlic, onion, sesame seed, salt and pepper.

To serve: Serve hot; eat fresh as a snack, in salads.

Preparing squash: Rinse the squash in cold water. Cut in half lengthwise; remove the seeds. If large squash, cut in wedges or medium-sized chunks.

Preparing squash: Scrub gently with vegetable brush in cold water. Cut slice off stem and blossom ends.

Without removing the skin or seeds, cut into slices or chunks. Cut pattypan in wedges.

Mashed Butternut Squash

2 small butternut squash
water
salt

¼ cup packed brown sugar
2 tablespoons butter

Color index page 72

Begin 45 mins ahead

6 servings

1. Halve squash lengthwise; remove seeds.
2. In 10-inch skillet over medium heat, in 1 inch boiling water, heat squash, cut side down, and ½ teaspoon salt to boiling. Reduce heat to low; cover; simmer 15 minutes or until fork-tender.
3. Drain; cool slightly. Scoop out pulp into large bowl; with mixer at low speed, beat squash, ½ teaspoon salt and remaining ingredients till smooth.

Baked Acorn Squash

1 medium acorn squash
4 tablespoons butter

2 tablespoons brown sugar or maple syrup

Color index page 72

Begin 1 hr ahead

2 servings

1. Preheat oven to 350°F. Halve squash lengthwise; remove seeds; place, cut side up, in roasting pan.
2. Spoon butter and brown sugar equally into halves. Bake 45 minutes or until fork-tender.

Stir-fried Zucchini

3 medium zucchini
1 tablespoon salad oil
¼ cup water

1½ teaspoons salt
½ teaspoon sugar

Color index page 67

Begin 15 mins ahead

4 servings

1. Cut zucchini into ¼-inch pieces.
2. In 5-quart Dutch oven over high heat, in very hot salad oil, cook zucchini, stirring quickly and frequently (stir-frying) until well coated.
3. Add water, salt and sugar. Reduce heat to medium-high; continue stir-frying 7 to 8 minutes until tender-crisp.

Summer Squash Medley

1 pound small zucchini
1 pound small yellow straightneck squash
water
salt

½ cup chopped parsley
¼ cup butter
2 tablespoons lemon juice
¼ teaspoon pepper

Color index page 67

Begin 15 mins ahead

6 servings

1. Cut zucchini and straightneck squash into strips about 2 inches long.
2. In 3-quart saucepan over medium heat, in 1 inch boiling water, heat zucchini, squash and 2 teaspoons salt to boiling. Reduce heat to low; cover and simmer 3 minutes or until vegetables are tender-crisp; drain.
3. Return vegetables to saucepan; over low heat, stir in 1 teaspoon salt, chopped parsley, butter, lemon juice and pepper until butter is melted.

Sweet potatoes

Season: All year. Best supplies are in November.

Look for: Firm, uniformly shaped sweet potatoes, free of blemishes. Yams are not botanically related to sweet potatoes, but in the United States, canned sweet potatoes are often labeled yams; use in recipes in the same way as sweet potatoes.

To store: Store sweet potatoes in a cool, dry place. Use within a week or so.

To prepare: Scrub. When possible, do not peel before cooking (to save nutrients).

To cook: *Boiled sweet potatoes:* In saucepan over high heat, heat unpeeled sweet potatoes and enough salted water to cover to boiling. Reduce heat to low; cover and simmer 30 to 40 minutes or until fork-tender. Drain and peel. *Baked sweet potatoes:* Bake unpeeled medium sweet potatoes in 450°F. oven about 1 hour until fork-tender. Or use in recipes.

Seasonings: Cinnamon, cloves, nutmeg, allspice.

To serve: Eat as cooked vegetable.

Sherried Sweet Potatoes

Color index page 67

Begin 50 mins ahead

6 servings

3 pounds sweet potatoes (about 6 medium)
salt
water
¼ cup butter or margarine

¼ cup packed brown sugar
2 tablespoons cream sherry
⅛ teaspoon pepper

1. In 4-quart saucepan over high heat, heat sweet potatoes, 1 teaspoon salt and water to cover potatoes to boiling. Reduce heat to low; cover; simmer 30 to 40 minutes until fork-tender; drain. Peel.
2. In large bowl with mixer at low speed, beat sweet potatoes and butter until smooth, scraping bowl constantly with rubber spatula. Add remaining ingredients and ¾ teaspoon salt. At medium speed, beat 2 minutes longer or until sweet potato mixture is light and fluffy.

Candied Sweet Potatoes

Color index page 67

Begin 30 mins ahead

6 servings

6 medium sweet potatoes, cooked and halved lengthwise or 2 16-ounce cans whole sweet potatoes, drained

½ cup packed brown sugar
½ cup dark corn syrup
¼ cup butter or margarine

1. Preheat oven to 350°F. Arrange sweet potatoes in cook-and-serve baking dish.
2. In 1-quart saucepan over medium heat, combine brown sugar, corn syrup and butter; heat to boiling. Reduce heat to low; simmer, stirring occasionally, 5 minutes. Pour syrup over sweet potatoes.
3. Bake 20 minutes or until potatoes are well glazed, basting often with syrup.
4. To serve: Spoon syrup over potatoes.

Tomatoes

CHERRY TOMATOES

Season: All year.

Look for: Firm, unblemished tomatoes with good red color. Size does not indicate quality.

To store: If not fully ripe, leave them, stem end up, at room temperature out of sunlight until they turn red. Then refrigerate and use within 1 or 2 days.

To prepare: It is not necessary to peel tomatoes before using them. Simply rinse in cold water. If you wish to peel them, see below.

To cook: Use tomatoes in recipes for vegetables, or in soups and main dishes.

Seasonings: Basil, celery seed, chives, parsley, oregano, tarragon, thyme, coarsely ground black pepper.

To serve: Eat fresh in salads, as sandwich filling or as a cooked vegetable.

Peeling tomatoes: Dip tomato in boiling water for a minute, then into cold water. Or, with long-handled fork, rotate tomato over flame until skin pops.

With sharp knife, pull away loosened skin. Cut out stem end.

Fried Green Tomatoes

Color index page 72

Begin 30 mins ahead

8 to 10 servings

⅔ cup all-purpose flour
2 teaspoons salt
⅛ teaspoon pepper

3 pounds green tomatoes, cut in ½-inch slices
salad oil

1. In pie plate, combine flour, salt and pepper. Dip in tomato slices to coat both sides.
2. In 12-inch skillet over medium heat, in ¼ cup hot salad oil, fry slices, a few at a time, until golden on both sides and heated through. Drain on paper towels. Repeat, adding more oil as needed.

Stewed Fresh Tomatoes

Color index page 72

Begin 30 mins ahead

6 servings

2 pounds tomatoes, peeled
2 tablespoons butter or margarine
4 green onions, chopped

1½ teaspoons sugar
1½ teaspoons garlic salt
¼ teaspoon seasoned pepper

1. Cut tomatoes into wedges.
2. In 10-inch skillet over medium heat, in hot butter or margarine, cook green onions 1 minute. Add tomatoes and remaining ingredients; cook about 10 minutes, stirring occasionally.

Turnips

Baked Herbed Tomatoes

Color index
page 72

Begin 25 mins
ahead

4 servings

2 medium tomatoes
¼ teaspoon salt
¼ teaspoon rosemary

¼ teaspoon basil
2 teaspoons butter or
margarine

1. Preheat oven to 350°F. Cut tomatoes horizontally in half into sawtooth pattern.
2. In cup, mix salt, rosemary and basil. Sprinkle each tomato half with some herb mixture and dot with butter or margarine.
3. Place tomato halves in 9-inch round cake pan. Bake 15 minutes or until heated through.

Scalloped Tomatoes

Color index
page 72

Begin 45 mins
ahead

6 servings

¼ cup butter or
margarine
1 small onion, chopped
2 cups fresh bread
crumbs
1 teaspoon salt
½ teaspoon basil
¼ teaspoon pepper
5 medium tomatoes,
sliced
4 teaspoons sugar

1 Preheat oven to 375°F. In 2-quart saucepan over medium heat, in hot butter, cook onion until tender, then stir in crumbs, salt, basil and pepper.

2 Into 1½-quart shallow casserole, place ¼ of tomato slices; sprinkle with 1 teaspoon sugar and ¼ of bread-crumb mixture. Repeat, ending with bread-crumb mixture.

3 Cover casserole and bake 30 minutes or until hot and bubbly. Uncover casserole and bake 5 minutes longer or until crumbs are golden.

Season: All year.
Look for: Firm, unblemished turnips, heavy for their size, with fresh tops.
To store: Remove tops, if any. Refrigerate tops and turnips in crisper or wrapped. Use turnips within a week or so. Use tops as soon as possible (see Lettuce and other greens, page 288).
To prepare: Rinse in cold water. Peel thinly. Leave whole or cut into slices or pieces.
To cook: In saucepan over medium heat, in 1 inch boiling, salted water, heat turnips to boiling. Reduce heat to low; cover and simmer whole turnips 20 to 30 minutes, cut-up turnips, 10 to 20 minutes. Or, use in recipes for soups, stews, main dishes.
Seasonings: Cook with bay leaf, cloves.
To serve: Eat as cooked vegetable.

Mashed Turnips

Color index
page 68

Begin 40 mins
ahead

6 to 8 servings

water
2½ pounds turnips,
peeled and diced
¼ cup butter or
margarine

2½ teaspoons salt
1 teaspoon sugar
¼ teaspoon pepper
parsley for garnish

1. In 4-quart saucepan over high heat, in 1 inch boiling water, heat turnips to boiling. Reduce heat to low; cover and simmer 15 minutes or until tender. Remove from heat; drain.
2. Mash. Add butter, salt, sugar and pepper; stir until well mixed. Serve garnished with parsley.

RUTABAGA

The rutabaga, a yellow-fleshed relative of the turnip, is also in season the year round, but is most plentiful from September to May. Look for rutabagas free of decay and heavy for their size. Store them at cool room temperature and keep dry for use within a week or so. Prepare and cook as for turnips and serve as a cooked vegetable with White Sauce (page 461) or Cheese Sauce (page 461) or in recipes for soups, stews and casseroles.

CHERRY TOMATOES

Cherry tomatoes are small, red tomatoes sold by the box in many markets. Although too small to peel they can be used like other tomatoes in recipes.

Sautéed Cherry Tomatoes

Color index
page 72

Begin 10 mins
ahead

4 servings

1 tablespoon salad
oil
1 pint cherry tomatoes

salt
pepper

In 3-quart saucepan over medium heat, in hot oil, cook cherry tomatoes 5 minutes or until heated through, shaking saucepan occasionally. To serve, sprinkle with salt and pepper to taste.

Combination dishes

Ratatouille

Color index
page 67

Begin 45 mins
ahead or
early in day

8 servings

½ cup olive or salad oil
1 large onion, diced
1 large garlic clove, cut in
    half
1 medium eggplant, cut in
    1-inch chunks
1 large green pepper, cut
    in 1-inch pieces
3 medium zucchini, cut in
    1-inch-thick slices
½ cup water
1 tablespoon salt
2 teaspoons oregano
    leaves
1 teaspoon sugar
2 large tomatoes, cut in
    wedges

1 In 6-quart Dutch oven
or saucepot over med-
ium heat, in hot olive oil,
cook onion and garlic until
tender, about 10 minutes,
stirring occasionally;
discard garlic.

2 Add eggplant and the
green pepper; cook for
5 minutes, stirring the
mixture frequently.

3 Stir in zucchini, water,
salt, oregano and
sugar; heat to boiling.
Reduce heat to medium-
low; cook 30 minutes or
until vegetables are tender,
stirring occasionally.

4 Stir in tomato wedges;
heat through; serve hot
or follow step 5.

5 Cover vegetable
mixture and refrigerate
to serve cold later.

Confetti Vegetables

Color index
page 71

Begin 30 mins
ahead

12 servings

¾ cup water
⅓ cup butter or
    margarine
1 tablespoon sugar
2 teaspoons salt
4½ cups shredded
    zucchini (about 1½
    pounds)

3 cups coarsely shredded
    carrots (about 1½
    pounds)
3 cups shredded parsnips
    or turnips (about 1½
    pounds)

In 5-quart Dutch oven or large saucepot, in boiling
water, heat all ingredients to boiling. Cover and
simmer about 5 minutes until vegetables are tender-
crisp, stirring occasionally.

Summer Vegetable Bowl

Color index
page 69

Begin 1 hr
ahead

8 servings

4 bacon slices
12 small white onions
1 small green pepper,
    diced
2 cups hot water
1 pound green beans
6 ears corn, broken in
    thirds
1 tablespoon salt

2 teaspoons sugar
¼ teaspoon white pepper
6 small zucchini, cut in
    1-inch chunks
2 large celery stalks, cut
    in 1-inch slices
1 large tomato, cut in
    wedges

1. In 6-quart Dutch oven over medium heat, fry
bacon until crisp; drain on paper towels.
2. To drippings in Dutch oven, add onions and green
pepper; cook until golden; add hot water and next 5
ingredients. Heat to boiling; reduce heat to low;
cover; simmer 10 minutes.
3. Add zucchini and celery; cover and cook 8 to 10
minutes until all vegetables are tender.
4. With slotted spoon, arrange vegetables on large
platter or in large, shallow bowl; crumble bacon and
sprinkle over top. Arrange tomato wedges on top.

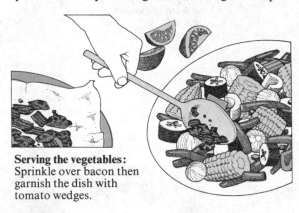

Serving the vegetables:
Sprinkle over bacon then
garnish the dish with
tomato wedges.

Carrots and Celery

Color index
page 70

Begin 30 mins
ahead

8 servings

2 tablespoons salad
    oil
1 16-ounce bag carrots,
    diagonally sliced
1¼ teaspoons salt

¼ teaspoon sugar
¼ cup water
1 small bunch celery,
    diagonally sliced

1. In 5-quart Dutch oven or 12-inch skillet over high
heat, in hot salad oil, heat carrots, salt, sugar and
water to boiling. Reduce heat to medium; cover and
cook 7 minutes.
2. Uncover; add celery; cook 5 to 7 minutes until
vegetables are tender-crisp, stirring frequently.

Vegetable Trio

Color index
page 69

Begin 25 mins
ahead

5 servings

½ pound carrots (about
    4 large carrots), cut in
    matchstick-thin strips
½ pound green beans, cut
    in 1-inch pieces
¼ pound mushrooms,
    sliced

1 teaspoon salt
½ teaspoon thyme
    leaves
3 tablespoons butter or
    margarine

In 2-quart saucepan over medium heat, place all
ingredients. Cover and cook 15 minutes or until
vegetables are tender-crisp, stirring occasionally.

Stir-fried Cabbage and Zucchini

Color index
page 69

Begin 15 mins
ahead

8 servings

1/4 cup salad oil
1 large garlic clove, sliced
6 cups packed sliced
    cabbage
2 medium zucchini
    (about 1 pound),
    thinly sliced
2 1/4 teaspoons salt
1 teaspoon sugar

1 In 5-quart Dutch oven over high heat, in hot oil, cook garlic until browned; discard garlic.

2 Add cabbage and zucchini, stir-frying (stirring quickly and frequently) until they are well coated with oil.

3 Add salt and sugar; reduce heat to medium-high; continue stir-frying 7 to 8 minutes until vegetables are tender-crisp.

Green Beans with Zucchini

Color index
page 67

Begin 30 mins
ahead

6 servings

1 9-ounce package frozen
    cut green beans
4 bacon slices
1/4 cup butter or
    margarine

1 small onion, minced
2 medium zucchini, sliced
    1/4 inch thick
3/4 teaspoon salt
1/8 teaspoon pepper

1. Prepare beans as label directs, but halve cooking time; drain. In 12-inch skillet over medium heat, fry bacon until crisp; drain; crumble. Pour off fat.
2. Wipe skillet clean. In skillet, in butter, cook onion until tender, about 3 minutes. Increase heat to medium-high; cook zucchini, stirring quickly and frequently, until tender-crisp, about 4 minutes.
3. Stir in bacon, green beans, salt and pepper and cook just until beans are hot.

Stir-fried Vegetable Mix

Color index
page 70

Begin 25 mins
ahead

6 servings

3 tablespoons salad
    oil
2 medium carrots,
    cut in matchstick-
    thin strips
1 medium onion, thinly
    sliced

1 small bunch broccoli,
    cut in 2" by 1/2" pieces
3/4 teaspoon salt
1/2 teaspoon sugar
1 4-ounce can whole
    mushrooms

1. In 12-inch skillet over high heat, in hot oil, cook carrots, onion and broccoli, stirring quickly and frequently, about 3 to 4 minutes.
2. Add salt, sugar and mushrooms with their liquid; cover and cook 5 to 6 minutes until vegetables are tender-crisp, stirring occasionally.

Pepper-and-Tomato Sauté

Color index
page 70

Begin 30 mins
ahead

10 servings

1/4 cup salad oil
6 large green peppers, cut
    into large chunks
2 medium onions,
    chopped

5 large tomatoes, peeled
    and cut into large
    chunks
2 1/2 teaspoons salt
1 1/4 teaspoons basil

1. In 12-inch skillet over medium heat, in hot salad oil, cook green pepper chunks and chopped onions 10 minutes.
2. Add the peeled tomato chunks together with the salt and basil; cover and simmer until the vegetables are fork-tender, stirring the mixture occasionally, about 15 minutes.

Eggplant Parmigiana

Color index
page 33

Begin 1 1/2 hrs
ahead

6 main-dish
servings

olive oil
1 garlic clove, minced
1 large onion,
    chopped
2 16-ounce cans
    tomatoes
2 teaspoons sugar
1/2 teaspoon oregano
    leaves
1/2 teaspoon basil
1/2 teaspoon salt
1 cup dried bread
    crumbs

2 eggs
2 tablespoons water
1 large eggplant,
    cut into
    1/2-inch slices
1/2 cup grated Parmesan
    cheese
1 8-ounce package
    mozzarella cheese,
    cut into 1/4-inch
    slices

1 In 9-inch skillet over medium heat, in 2 tablespoons hot oil, cook garlic and onion until tender, then add next 5 ingredients. Reduce heat; cook, covered, 30 minutes.

2 On waxed paper, place bread crumbs; in small dish with fork, beat eggs and water. Dip eggplant slices in egg then in bread crumbs. Repeat to coat slices twice.

3 Grease 13" by 9" baking dish. In 12-inch skillet over medium heat, in 2 tablespoons hot oil, cook a few eggplant slices at a time till golden brown. Add more oil as needed.

4 Preheat oven to 350°F. Arrange 1/2 eggplant slices in baking dish; cover with 1/2 tomato mixture; sprinkle with 1/2 Parmesan; top with 1/2 mozzarella; repeat. Bake 25 minutes.

Combination dishes

Caponata

Color index
page 20

Begin 4 hrs
or up to
1 wk ahead

12 first-course
or accompani-
ment servings

³/₄ cup olive or salad oil
1 large eggplant, cut into
bite-size pieces
(2 pounds)
6 medium zucchini, cut
into bite-size pieces
(2 pounds)
¹/₂ pound mushrooms,
thickly sliced
1¹/₂ cups chopped
onions
1 cup sliced celery
1 garlic clove,
crushed
¹/₂ cup red wine
vinegar

¹/₄ cup capers,
drained
2 tablespoons sugar
2 teaspoons salt
¹/₄ teaspoon pepper
3 large tomatoes,
cut into bite-size
chunks
1 4¹/₂-ounce jar pimento-
stuffed olives,
drained and halved
crosswise

1. In 8-quart Dutch oven or large saucepot over high heat, in hot olive oil, cook eggplant, zucchini, mushrooms, onions, celery and garlic 10 minutes, stirring occasionally.
2. Stir red wine vinegar, capers, sugar, salt and pepper into mixture in Dutch oven. Reduce heat to low; cover and simmer 5 to 10 minutes until vegetables are fork-tender.
3. Stir in tomato chunks and halved olives; over high heat, heat to boiling.
4. Spoon vegetable mixture into large bowl; cover and refrigerate at least 3 hours or until mixture is well chilled.
5. Serve cold as a first-course or as an accompaniment for cold, sliced meats.

Vegetable-stuffed Green Peppers

Color index
page 70

Begin 15 mins
ahead

4 servings

2 large green peppers
salt
water

2 cups seasoned hot
cooked corn or mixed
vegetables

1. Cut peppers in half lengthwise; remove stem, seeds and membrane.
2. In 3-quart saucepan over medium heat, in 1 inch boiling, salted water, heat green peppers to boiling; cover and simmer for 5 minutes or until peppers are tender-crisp. Drain.
3. Spoon seasoned hot cooked corn or a selection of cooked and chopped mixed vegetables into the pepper halves. Serve hot.

Preparing the peppers:
With sharp knife, cut
peppers in half lengthwise;
remove stem, seeds and
white membrane.

Stuffing the peppers: Fill
pepper halves with
seasoned hot cooked corn
or with chopped and diced
mixed vegetables.

Sauces and toppings

Butter Sauce

Begin 5 mins
ahead

¹/₂ cup

liquid from cooked
vegetables
water
1 tablespoon butter or
margarine, softened

1 tablespoon all-purpose
flour
salt
pepper

1. Into measuring cup, pour liquid from cooked vegetables; add water to make ¹/₂ cup liquid, if necessary. Return liquid to vegetables in pan. In cup, stir butter or margarine and flour to make smooth paste.
2. Stir mixture into vegetables and liquid; over medium heat, cook, stirring gently, until sauce is thickened and smooth. Add salt and pepper to taste.

Vinaigrette Sauce

Begin 10 mins
ahead

1¹/₄ cups

³/₄ cup salad oil
¹/₃ cup cider or red wine
vinegar
3 tablespoons sweet
pickle relish

2 tablespoons chopped
parsley
1 teaspoon salt
³/₄ teaspoon sugar

1. In covered blender container at low speed, blend all ingredients 1 minute. (Or, in medium bowl, combine vinegar with next 4 ingredients; slowly pour in oil, beating with fork until well mixed.) Just before serving beat with fork.
2. Serve on chilled fresh or cooked vegetables. Any leftover sauce may be refrigerated, covered.

Sour Cream-Mustard Sauce

Begin 10 mins
ahead

1 cup

1 cup sour cream
1 tablespoon minced
onion
1 tablespoon prepared
mustard

¹/₄ teaspoon salt
¹/₈ teaspoon pepper
1 tablespoon chopped
parsley

1. In 1-quart saucepan over very low heat, heat sour cream, onion, prepared mustard, salt and pepper just until hot.
2. Sprinkle sauce with chopped parsley.

Buttered Crumbs

Begin 10 mins
ahead

Topping for
4 servings

2 tablespoons butter or
margarine
¹/₂ cup fresh bread crumbs
¹/₈ teaspoon thyme or
basil

1 tablespoon lemon juice
or ¹/₂ cup shredded
Cheddar or grated
Parmesan cheese
(optional)

1. In 1-quart saucepan over medium heat, melt butter or margarine.
2. Add fresh bread crumbs; cook, tossing lightly, until crumbs are golden. Stir in thyme or basil until well mixed.
3. If you like, add lemon juice or Cheddar cheese.
4. Sprinkle Buttered Crumbs over drained, hot cooked vegetables.

POLONAISE SAUCE: Prepare Buttered Crumbs with lemon juice as above. Stir in *1 hard-cooked egg,* chopped, *1 tablespoon chopped parsley* and *¹/₄ teaspoon salt* until thoroughly mixed together.

FRUIT

Fruit makes the perfect finale to the most sophisticated dinner, but it can also be included in every course of any meal, from soup to dessert. Or fruit can be eaten as a satisfying, healthy snack, at any time.

All unripe fresh fruit should be stored in a cool, dark place (avoid direct sunlight) and allowed to ripen at room temperature. Citrus fruit never needs further ripening but other fruits do, so buy them ahead of time. But remember that, in general, fresh fruit is highly perishable and requires refrigeration once it is ripe.

Specific directions for buying and using fruit are given in the following pages.

Apples

Season: All year. Best supplies are in October, lowest in June, July and August.

Look for: Firm, crisp, well-colored fruit, the color depending on variety. Avoid any apples which have brown spots or any fruit which is shriveled or soft. Select apples according to their use (see below).

To store: Refrigerate. Use within 2 weeks.

To prepare: Wash, peel and core, depending on use. To prevent browning, if apples are sliced and are to stand, sprinkle with lemon juice or ascorbic-acid mixture.

To serve: Eat out of hand, peeled or unpeeled; use in pies, salads, sauces, desserts and coffeecakes.

BEST WAYS OF USING APPLES

	York Imperial	Winesap	Stayman	Rome Beauty	Red Delicious	Northern Spy	Newtown Pippin	McIntosh	Jonathan	Gravenstein	Golden Delicious	Cortland
Eating		●	●		●	●		●	●	●	●	●
Baking	●	●	●	●		●	●			●		●
Cooking	●	●				●	●	●	●	●	●	●
Sauces	●	●				●	●	●	●	●	●	●
Salads		●	●		●		●	●	●		●	●
Pies	●	●	●	●		●	●	●	●	●	●	●

Color index page 101

Begin 30 mins ahead

4 cups

Applesauce

½ cup boiling water
2 pounds cooking apples, peeled, cored and sliced
⅛ teaspoon ground cinnamon
⅛ teaspoon ground cloves
½ cup sugar

1. In 2-quart saucepan over medium heat, heat first 4 ingredients to boiling.
2. Reduce heat to low; cover and simmer 8 to 10 minutes until the apples are tender for chunky applesauce, 12 to 15 minutes for smoother applesauce. During last minutes of cooking time, stir sugar into applesauce mixture.

Color index page 101

Begin 1 hr ahead or early in day

6 servings

Baked Apples

6 medium cooking apples
1 cup light corn syrup
cream or ice cream

1. Preheat oven to 350°F. Core apples and starting from stem end, peel them ⅓ of the way down. Arrange in a shallow baking dish, peeled end up, and pour corn syrup over them.
2. Bake apples 45 minutes or until fork-tender, spooning syrup from pan over them occasionally. Serve hot or cold with cream or ice cream.

Color index page 72

Begin 15 mins ahead

4 servings

Pan-fried Apple Wedges

2 red cooking apples, cored
2 tablespoons butter or margarine
½ cup apple jelly

1. Cut apples into ½-inch-thick wedges.
2. In 12-inch skillet over medium heat, in hot butter or margarine, cook apple wedges about 5 to 7 minutes until apples are tender-crisp; with pancake turner, turn wedges once during cooking.
3. Stir in apple jelly; heat through. Serve with baked ham or with breakfast pancakes.

Apples

Candy Apples

**8 wooden ice-cream-bar
sticks
8 small Red Delicious
apples, washed and
dried
1 cup water
3 cups sugar
½ cup light corn syrup
¼ cup red-hot candies
½ teaspoon red food
color**

Color index
page 106

Begin 2 hrs
ahead or
early in day

8 candy
apples

1 Insert a wooden stick part way through stem end of apples. Grease large cookie sheet; set aside.

2 In 2-quart saucepan, combine remaining ingredients. Over medium heat, heat mixture to boiling, without stirring.

3 Boil, without stirring, until candy thermometer reads 290°F., or when a little of mixture dropped into cold water separates into thin hard threads, about 20 minutes.

4 With brush dipped in hot water, occasionally brush sugar from side of pan as mixture cooks.

5 When cooked, remove syrup from heat. Tip saucepan; swirl each apple in mixture to coat.

6 Lift apple out of syrup mixture and swirl it over the saucepan a few more seconds to allow any drips to fall back into saucepan.

7 Place apples on cookie sheet to cool. Work quickly before syrup hardens. To soften, place over very low heat. Cool at least 1 hour before serving.

Apricots

Season: June and July.
Look for: Plump, juicy, orange-yellow apricots. Ripe fruit yield to gentle pressure on the skin. Avoid dull-looking, shriveled or soft fruit.
To store: Refrigerate. Use within 2 to 3 days.
To prepare: Wash, cut in half and remove seed; peel if desired. To prevent browning, if cut apricots are not eaten immediately, sprinkle with lemon juice or ascorbic-acid mixture for fruit.
To serve: Eat out of hand, peeled or unpeeled. Use in recipes for salads, desserts.

Cinnamon Apricots in Cream

Color index
page 100

Begin 35 mins
ahead

4 servings

**1 pound apricots,
unpeeled
⅓ cup sugar
⅓ cup water**

**½ teaspoon ground
cinnamon
¼ cup heavy or whipping
cream**

1. Preheat oven to 375°F. Halve and remove seeds from apricots. Place in 1-quart casserole.
2. In small bowl, combine sugar, water and cinnamon; pour over fruit. Bake 20 minutes or until apricots are tender.
3. Pour on cream and bake 5 minutes longer.

DRIED FRUITS

Packaged dried fruits come in 8-, 11-, 12- or 16-ounce packages depending on variety. Store tightly wrapped, at room temperature, for up to 6 months. After opening, transfer to tightly closed container.

Eat out of hand or use in recipes for sauces, coffeecakes, breads and desserts or stews, according to label directions. Or, cook following the chart below, adding sugar during last minutes of cooking.

STEWING DRIED FRUITS*

Fruit	Package size (in ounces)	Water (in cups)	Sugar (in cups)	Cooking time (in minutes)
Apples	8	3½ + ⅛ teaspoon salt	¼	25
Apricots	8 11 or 12	2½ 3	¼ ½	15 15
Figs	12	3 + 1 tablespoon lemon juice		35
Mixed fruit	11 or 12	4	½	25
Peaches	11 or 12	4	¼	25
Pears	11	3	¼	25
Prunes	16	4	0	20

Makes 4 to 6 servings

Avocados

Season: All year.

Look for: Pear-shaped, round or egg-shaped fruit, green or purplish-black, depending on variety. Avoid any with dark spots or broken skin. Avocados yield to gentle pressure when ripe.

To store: Refrigerate avocados after ripening and use within 3 to 5 days.

To prepare: See below. To prevent browning, if sliced avocados are not to be served immediately, sprinkle with lemon juice or ascorbic-acid mixture for fruit.

To serve: Use in dips, appetizers (below). Serve slices with French dressing, or toss with green or fruit salads.

Preparing avocados: Cut avocado lengthwise around the seed; twist gently to separate halves.

To remove seed, strike it with blade of sharp knife so blade lodges in seed; twist knife gently to lift out seed.

Peel and slice or cut up, depending on use. Or use unpeeled as shell for salads or filling.

Appetizer Avocados

Color index page 21

Begin 35 mins ahead

6 first-course servings

2 tablespoons water
2 tablespoons sugar
2 tablespoons white vinegar
2 tablespoons Worcestershire
¼ cup chili sauce

2 tablespoons butter or margarine
3 medium avocados, peeled and sliced
4 bacon slices, cooked and crumbled

1. In 1-quart saucepan over medium heat, heat first 6 ingredients to boiling. Reduce heat to low; simmer 15 minutes, stirring occasionally.

2. Arrange avocado slices on 6 appetizer or salad plates; spoon hot sauce over avocados and sprinkle with the crumbled bacon slices.

Bananas

Season: All year.

Look for: For immediate use, solid yellow bananas lightly flecked with brown. Fruit with some green will ripen in a few days at room temperature. Brown skins usually indicate overripened fruit.

To store: Refrigerate ripe fruit; use within 3 days.

To prepare: Peel skin from top. Slice or cut up fruit as required. To prevent browning, if cut bananas are not eaten immediately, sprinkle with a little lemon juice or ascorbic-acid mixture.

To serve: Eat out of hand or use in recipes.

Baked Bananas

Color index page 72

Begin 25 mins ahead

4 servings

3 tablespoons butter
4 slightly unripe medium bananas, peeled
salt

1. Preheat oven to 450°F. In oven, in pie plate or baking dish, melt butter.

2. Remove plate from oven and roll bananas in melted butter; sprinkle lightly with salt.

3. Bake 10 to 12 minutes or until bananas are fork-tender. Serve hot as a vegetable.

Banana Pops

Color index page 101

Begin 2 hrs ahead or early in day

12 banana pops

3 tablespoons water
2 teaspoons ascorbic-acid mixture for fruit
4 large bananas, peeled and sliced crosswise into thirds
1 package wooden ice-cream-bar sticks

½ cup shredded coconut
½ cup toasted shredded coconut
1 6-ounce package semisweet-chocolate pieces
2 tablespoons salad oil

1. In large bowl, in water, stir ascorbic-acid mixture until dissolved; gently toss bananas in mixture until coated. Insert a stick about 1 inch deep into end of each banana piece. Place on cookie sheet; freeze until firm, about 45 minutes.

2. Meanwhile, place each kind of coconut on a small plate. In double boiler, over hot, not boiling, water, melt chocolate pieces with salad oil, stirring occasionally. Pour into pie plate.

3. Remove bananas from freezer and quickly roll each in chocolate; roll some bananas in shredded coconut and some in toasted shredded coconut.

4. Return banana pops to cookie sheet and freeze for at least 30 minutes before serving.

FRUIT
Berries

GOOSEBERRIES

BLUEBERRIES

RASPBERRIES   BLACKBERRIES   STRAWBERRIES

Blackberries, Blueberries, Boysenberries, Dewberries, Gooseberries, Loganberries, Raspberries, Strawberries, Youngberries. (See also Cranberries, page 306.)
Season: Summer months, mostly June and July. Strawberries are available all year round, best supplies from April to July.
Look for: Plump, fresh, uniformly colored fruit, free of stems or leaves. Avoid fruit that is moldy, crushed or bruised, or that has leaked moisture through carton.
To store: Refrigerate. Use within 1 or 2 days.
To prepare: See below.
To serve: Serve with sugar and milk or over cereal. Eat out of hand. Use in recipes for salads, pies, muffins, coffeecakes, desserts, jams and sauces.

Preparing berries: Wash berries under running cold water, discarding any crushed or bruised ones. Drain well in a colander or strainer.

Remove stems (hulls) from berries such as strawberries.

Using kitchen scissors, cut top and tail from gooseberries.

Sugaring perfect berries for garnish: Wash and drain; roll in sugar while still wet.

Very-Berry Compote

Color index page 100

Begin 2½ hrs ahead

8 to 10 servings

3 pints strawberries, halved
½ cup sugar
1 cup raspberries
1 cup blueberries

1½ pints vanilla ice cream, softened
2 tablespoons grated orange peel

1. In large bowl, gently toss strawberries with sugar; cover and refrigerate about 2 hours, tossing occasionally.
2. *Just before serving:* Alternately spoon strawberries, raspberries and blueberries into large glass serving bowl.
3. In medium bowl, combine ice cream with orange peel; spoon some on top of berries to garnish. Pass remainder in small bowl. Serve immediately.

Blueberry Sauce

Color index page 100

Begin 20 mins ahead

2¾ cups

1 cup water
1 pint blueberries
¾ cup sugar

1 tablespoon cornstarch
⅛ teaspoon salt
1 teaspoon lemon juice

1. In 2-quart saucepan over medium heat, heat water to boiling; add blueberries; return to boiling.
2. Meanwhile, in a small bowl, combine sugar, cornstarch and salt; stir into blueberries and cook, stirring constantly, until thick. Add lemon juice.

Blackberry Sauce

Begin early in day

2⅔ cups

1 20-ounce bag frozen unsweetened blackberries
½ cup packed light brown sugar

2 tablespoons lemon juice
½ teaspoon ground cinnamon

In 2-quart saucepan over medium heat, heat berries, sugar, lemon juice and cinnamon, stirring occasionally, until hot and bubbly. Cover; chill. Serve over ice cream, cake and other fruits.

Freezer Strawberry Topping

Color index page 100

Begin 2 days or up to 1 year ahead

Six 8-ounce jars

1 quart fully ripened strawberries
4 cups sugar (about 1¾ pounds)
2 tablespoons orange juice

1 1¾-ounce package powdered fruit pectin
¾ cup water
about 6 8-ounce freezer-proof containers

1. In large bowl with potato masher or slotted spoon, thoroughly crush berries, one layer at a time. Stir in sugar and orange juice until thoroughly mixed; let stand 10 minutes.
2. In 1-quart saucepan over medium heat, heat fruit pectin with water until boiling; boil 1 minute, stirring constantly. Stir pectin mixture into fruit; continue stirring 3 minutes to blend well (a few sugar crystals will remain).
3. Ladle mixture into containers to ½ inch from top; cover with lids. Let stand at room temperature for 24 hours or until set. Freeze to use within 1 year. For use within 3 weeks, store in refrigerator. Use to top plain or toasted slices of poundcake, angel cake; serve on rice pudding or ice cream; spoon over cheesecake; stir into plain yogurt.

Strawberries Romanoff

Color index page 100

Begin 1½ hrs ahead

4 servings

¼ cup orange-flavored liqueur
¼ cup orange juice
2 tablespoons brandy
1 pint strawberries

½ cup heavy or whipping cream
1½ tablespoons confectioners' sugar

1. In small bowl, combine liqueur, juice and brandy. Cut strawberries in halves; add to mixture and chill at least 1 hour, spooning liquid over berries occasionally.
2. In another small bowl with mixer at high speed, whip cream until frothy; add sugar and beat until soft peaks form. Spoon strawberries into sherbet dishes and top with whipped cream.

See descriptions, page 16

Cherries

Season: May to August.

Look for: Plump, bright-looking cherries ranging in color from light to bright red to purplish-black, depending on variety. Tart or sour cherries are best for cooking. Sweet cherries may be eaten fresh or used in cooking. Avoid fruit which is too soft or shriveled in appearance.

To store: Refrigerate; use within 2 or 3 days.

To prepare: Remove any stems; wash and drain well. Remove pits as shown below.

To serve: Eat out of hand. Use in recipes for salads, pies, desserts, jams and sauces.

Pitting cherries: Cut into the center of the cherry with a sharp knife and remove the pit.

Or, you can remove the pit using a cherry or olive pitter.

Brandied Cherry Sauce

Color index page 100

Begin 30 mins or up to 3 days ahead

2 cups

1 pound sweet cherries, pitted
½ cup brandy
½ cup sugar

2 teaspoons cornstarch
¼ teaspoon almond extract

1. In 2-quart saucepan combine first 4 ingredients. Over medium heat, cook, stirring constantly, until mixture is thickened and boils; remove from heat. Stir in almond extract.

2. Serve warm or cover and refrigerate. Serve over vanilla ice cream, crêpes, bread pudding, or pound or sponge cake.

MAKING A MARASCHINO CHERRY BLOSSOM

Cut canned red maraschino cherries into 6 or 8 sections, cutting about ¾ of the way through; with hand, spread open petals.

Add leaves, cut from candied green cherries or angelica, around sides of cherry "blossom"

Coconuts

Season: All year. Best supplies are from October to December.

Look for: Coconuts that are heavy for their size, filled with juice that sloshes around when coconut is shaken. Avoid fruit with moldy or wet eyes.

To store: Refrigerate and use within a week. (Fresh shredded coconut will keep in refrigerator 1 to 2 days.)

To prepare: See below.

To serve: Use coconut juice in beverages, salad dressings. Eat the coconut meat out of hand or shred it (see below) for use in recipes for salads, pies, pastries and cakes, and in desserts.

Preparing coconuts: With a skewer and hammer, puncture eyes of the coconut.

Drain the coconut juice into measuring cup (it may take some time for all the juice to drain through); reserve the juice and drink as is; or use in recipes for salads.

Open the shell by cracking very hard with a hammer at the widest part. Hit firmly all around middle.

Pry out coconut meat in pieces from the shell with a small sharp knife.

Shredding coconut: Use a small sharp knife to peel the brown skin from coconut meat (left); shred meat with a coarse grater. For *toasted shredded coconut*, preheat oven to 350°F. and spread coconut in shallow pan. Bake 20 to 30 minutes, stirring occasionally.

See descriptions, page 16

Cranberries

Season: September to January.

Look for: Plump, firm berries with a high luster. Some varieties are rather large, bright red in color and quite tart; others are smaller, darker and sweeter. Avoid cranberries which are shriveled, discolored or moist. Cranberries are sold prepackaged by brands.

To store: Refrigerate. Use within 1 to 2 weeks.

To prepare: Wash and drain well.

To serve: Use in recipes below, and for sauces, salads, pies, sherbets and quick breads.

Cranberry Sauce

Color index page 72

Begin 10 mins or day ahead

5 cups

2 cups sugar
1½ cups water

1 16-ounce package cranberries

1. In 2-quart saucepan over medium heat, heat sugar and water to boiling.

2. Add cranberries and return to boiling. Reduce heat to low; cover and simmer 7 minutes or until cranberries pop. Serve hot, or chill to serve cold.

Cranberry Relish

Color index page 72

Begin 3 hrs or day ahead

14 relish servings

3 15- or 16-ounce packages fresh or frozen cranberries

4½ cups packed brown sugar
¾ cup orange juice

1. In 5-quart saucepan over high heat, heat all ingredients to boiling, stirring occasionally. Reduce heat to low; cover and simmer 30 minutes or until berries pop.

2. Spoon mixture into medium bowl, cover and refrigerate until well chilled.

CRANBERRY RELISH IN ORANGE CUPS: *About 1 hour before serving:* With sharp knife, cut each of *7 large oranges* in half. Scoop out pulp to use in salad another day. With kitchen shears, trim rim of each orange shell into sawtooth pattern. Fill orange shells with cranberry mixture.

Cranberry Chutney

Color index page 72

Begin 2 hrs or up to 1 wk ahead

7 cups

1 16-ounce package cranberries
2 cups sugar
1 cup water
1 tablespoon grated orange peel
1 cup orange juice
1 cup golden or dark seedless raisins

1 cup California walnuts, chopped
1 cup chopped celery
1 medium apple, chopped
1 teaspoon ground ginger

1. In 3-quart saucepan over medium heat, heat cranberries, sugar and water to boiling, stirring the mixture frequently. Reduce heat to low and simmer 15 minutes.

2. Remove from heat; stir in remaining ingredients. Cover and refrigerate chutney.

Grapes

Season: All year. Best grape supplies are available from July to November.

Look for: Plump, fresh-looking grapes with individual berries firmly attached to stems. A high color for the variety usually means good flavor. Avoid grapes with dry, brittle stems or any that are shriveled or leaking moisture and staining the carton.

To store: Refrigerate. Use within 1 to 2 weeks.

To prepare: Wash and seed fruit.

To serve: Eat out of hand. Use in recipes for salads, fish and poultry dishes, desserts, sauces, jellies and jams. Or sugar and use as a garnish (below).

Seeding grapes: With a small sharp knife, carefully cut each grape lengthwise in half.

Scoop out the seeds, either with the point of the knife or using the point of a small teaspoon.

Sugaring grapes: Dip a small bunch of grapes into egg white taking care to coat evenly. Then, dip the grapes in sugar.

Place grapes on rack until sugar coating is dry.

Minted Grapes

Color index page 101

Begin early in day

4 servings

1 bunch seedless green grapes
½ cup honey
2 tablespoons lime juice

2 tablespoons finely chopped mint

1. Stem grapes and arrange them in 4 sherbet or dessert dishes.

2. In small bowl, combine remaining ingredients; pour over grapes and refrigerate to marinate.

Grapefruit

Season: All year. Best supplies October to May.
Look for: Well-shaped, firm fruit that is springy-to-touch and heavy for its size. Discolored spots on the skin rarely affect eating quality. Varieties include seedless, with seeds, pink- or white-fleshed. Avoid fruit which is soft or discolored at stem end.
To store: Refrigerate. Use within 1 to 2 weeks.
To prepare: See below.
To serve: Eat fresh, with sugar or salt, or bake with cinnamon or ginger. Use in recipes below, and for main dishes. For segments, peel like an orange.

Preparing grapefruit: Cut fruit in half between blossom and stem ends. With sharp pointed knife, cut sections from membrane, leaving them in place if serving in the shell.

Cut out the core; remove any seeds.

Broiled Grapefruit

1 grapefruit   *butter or margarine,*
brown sugar   *softened*

Color index
page 23

Begin 15 mins
ahead

2 servings

1. Preheat broiler if manufacturer directs. Cut grapefruit in half, section and remove seeds.
2. Sprinkle each half with a little brown sugar; dot with softened butter or margarine. Broil 10 minutes or until golden and heated through.

BAKED GRAPEFRUIT: Prepare as above but bake in 450°F. oven for 20 minutes.

VARIATIONS: Instead of sugar, use honey, maple-flavored syrup or dark corn syrup.

Grapefruit Ambrosia

1 16-ounce can   *¼ cup honey*
grapefruit   *½ cup flaked coconut*
sections

Color index
page 100

Begin 5 mins
ahead

4 servings

1. Thoroughly drain liquid from grapefruit sections; set aside for use another day.
2. In bowl, toss well grapefruit sections, honey and coconut. Serve immediately.

Kiwi Fruit

Also known as Chinese Gooseberries.
Season: June to December.
Look for: Small, slightly firm fruit with fairly fuzzy skin. When fully ripened, kiwi fruit should yield to gentle pressure on the skin.
To store: Refrigerate after the fruit has ripened and use within 1 or 2 days.
To prepare and serve: See below.

Preparing kiwi fruit: With a small sharp knife, carefully peel off the skin.

Using the same knife, carefully cut the flesh of the fruit into small wedges.

Or cut the fruit crosswise into thin slices.

Serving suggestion: Arrange slices from 1 or 2 kiwi fruit on a plate; garnish with fresh mint leaves and serve at once as a first course.

Gingered Kiwi Fruit

3 tablespoons sugar   *¼ teaspoon vanilla*
3 tablespoons water   *extract*
2 tablespoons minced   *4 large kiwi fruit*
crystallized ginger   *2 medium oranges*

Color index
page 101

Begin 2½ hrs
ahead

4 servings

1. In 1-quart saucepan over medium-high heat, heat sugar, water and ginger to boiling, stirring constantly. Boil until mixture reaches light syrup consistency, about 3 minutes. Remove from heat; stir in vanilla. Cool slightly.
2. Meanwhile, peel and slice kiwi fruit. With knife, peel and section oranges. In dessert dish, gently fold sliced kiwi fruit, orange sections and ginger syrup until well mixed. Cover the dish with plastic wrap; refrigerate until well chilled, about 2 hours.

307

Kumquats

Season: November to February.
Look for: Small, firm bright orange kumquats, with smooth, shiny skins. Avoid blemished or shriveled fruit.
To store: Keep a few days at room temperature or refrigerate and use within a week.
To prepare: See below.
To serve: Eat out of hand, peel and all. Add cut-up kumquats to fruit salads; use as a garnish or in recipes for jams and marmalades. Use canned, preserved kumquats, drained, as garnish for main dishes, especially those made with poultry or ham.

Preparing kumquats: Wash the kumquats under running cold water and remove any stems.

Serve whole, or, with a small sharp knife, cut the kumquats in half lengthwise and with the tip of the knife, remove the seeds.

Lemons and limes

Season: All year.
Look for: Bright, firm fruits that are heavy for their size. Pale or greenish-yellow lemons usually indicate fruit of higher acidity. Limes should be glossy skinned; irregular purplish-brown marks on skins do not affect quality. Avoid soft, shriveled or hard-skinned fruits.
To store: Keep a few days at room temperature. Or refrigerate and use within 2 weeks.
To prepare: See below.
To serve: Use lemon or lime juice in recipes for sauces for seafood, poultry, vegetables or fruits, and in beverages, salad dressings and desserts. Use slices or peel to garnish soups, main dishes, desserts, beverages.

Preparing lemons and limes: For squeezing, cut in half between blossom and stem ends. Squeeze on a juice reamer. Discard seeds. Fruit at room temperature gives more juice. For garnishes, slice into rings or cut into chunky wedges. See left and below.

PREPARING CITRUS FRUIT PEEL

Lemon, lime and orange peel can all be grated, slivered or minced as illustrated here.

Grated peel: Wash fruit; dry. With grater over waxed paper, using quick downward strokes, remove outer colored layer of peel only. Measure lightly in spoon. Do not pack.

Slivered peel: Score peel of fruit into quarters; remove with fingers. With tip of spoon, scrape most of white membrane from peel. Stack 2 or 3 pieces at a time on cutting board. Cut into thinnest possible strips.

Minced peel: Prepare slivered peel, then finely chop with a sharp knife to mince.

MAKING LEMON AND LIME GARNISHES

Twists: Cut fruit crosswise in thin slices. Cut each slice once from center to edge, then twist the cut edges in opposite directions.

Cartwheels: Cut thin crosswise slices. Cut small V-shaped notches in peel around each slice.

Roses: Cut a thin crosswise slice from both ends of fruit. With a vegetable peeler, peel a continuous ½-inch-wide strip of peel.

Roll peel tightly, skin side out. Hold end in place with toothpick.

Lemon boats: Cut lemon in half lengthwise. Ream out juice; scrape clean. Edges may be notched with kitchen shears. To prevent tipping, cut small slice from bottom.

Mangoes

Season: April to September.

Look for: Oval or round, yellowish or orange fruit, sometimes with speckled skin. Ripe mangoes should yield slightly to gentle thumb pressure on the skin. (Unripe fruit are hard and have very poor flavor.) Avoid any bruised, soft or shriveled fruit.

To store: Allow to ripen at room temperature. Then refrigerate and use within 2 or 3 days.

To prepare: See below.

To serve: Eat out of hand; use sliced pieces for adding to fruit salads.

Preparing mangoes: With a sharp knife, cut a single lengthwise slice from each side of the long flat seed as close to the seed as possible; set aside the middle section of the mango containing the seed.

With a spoon, carefully scoop out the mango flesh in long curved slices for serving.

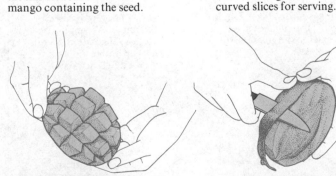

Or, for eating out of hand, score crosswise and then lengthwise the flesh of the slices without cutting through the skin. Gently push it out to eat the cubes.

Peel the skin from the inner section of the mango and either eat out of hand or carefully slice the flesh from the seed lengthwise and serve in recipes for fruit salad.

Melons

Season: April to November, depending on variety.

Look for: Fully ripened fruit for best sweetness and flavor. Avoid bruised or cracked melons. Follow these guidelines when selecting varieties:

Cantaloupe: Should be smooth at stem end, without a sign of any stem remaining. Rind around the blossom end should yield slightly to gentle thumb pressure. Cantaloupes should have a pleasant odor. The coarse, corky netting (veining) should stand out over the rind, which should not be green. Cantaloupes may be firm at store but ripen well at home.

Casaba: Gold yellow color indicates ripeness. Rind at blossom end should yield slightly to gentle thumb pressure. Casabas have no aroma.

Crenshaw: Rind should be deep golden yellow, sometimes with small areas of lighter yellow. The rind, especially around the blossom end, should yield slightly to gentle thumb pressure. Crenshaws should have a pleasant aroma.

Honey Ball: Follow tips for *honeydew,* except that honey ball is smaller and has slight, irregular netting over surface of rind.

Honeydew: Yellowish to creamy-white in color, with a soft, velvety feel. Ripeness is difficult to judge, but a honeydew should be slightly soft around the blossom end and have a faint, agreeable aroma.

Persian: Follow tips for *cantaloupe.* Persian melon is rounder and has fine netting.

Watermelon: Should be firm and symmetrically shaped (round or oblong, depending on variety). Ripeness is not always easy to judge so look for melons sold in halves or quarters. Flesh should be firm, of good red color, with dark brown or black seeds. Avoid melons with hard white streak running through flesh.

To store: Ripen at room temperature, then refrigerate and use within 2 to 3 days. Melons with strong aroma should be stored well wrapped to prevent aroma transferring to other foods in refrigerator. After cutting melons, tightly cover cut surfaces.

To prepare: See following page.

To serve: Serve melon with lemon or lime wedges as appetizer or dessert. Use in fruit and poultry salads.

Melons

Preparing melons: To serve cantaloupe or honeydew halves, cut melon in half between blossom and stem ends. Remove seeds with spoon. For decorative effect, with a knife, mark sawtooth design around melon shell (see Making a Watermelon Bowl, right).

For rings, with a sharp knife, cut crosswise into thick slices. Discard seeds.

For wedges, with a sharp knife, cut melon in half from stem to blossom end; discard seeds. Slice thickly lengthwise.

Scoop out balls of melon flesh either with a measuring half teaspoon or melon baller.

Gingered Melon Wedges

Color index page 23

Begin 2 hrs ahead

8 servings

1 large honeydew melon	*½ teaspoon ground*
2 tablespoons	*ginger*
confectioners' sugar	

1. Cut melon in half lengthwise and remove seeds; slice each half into 4 wedges. Slash the pulp of wedges criss-cross into bite-size pieces, then cut pulp loose from rind, leaving pulp in place.
2. In cup, combine sugar and ginger; sprinkle over melon. Cover melon and refrigerate.

Cantaloupe Ice

Color index page 101

Begin day or several days ahead

5 cups

2 medium cantaloupes	*2 tablespoons lemon juice*
½ cup sugar	*½ teaspoon salt*

1. Cut cantaloupes in half and remove seeds. With sharp knife, cut halves into thick slices and remove rind. Cut slices into chunks to make 6 cups.
2. In covered blender container at low speed, blend sugar, lemon juice, salt and about 1 cup of melon chunks until smooth; add remaining melon and blend a few seconds until smooth.
3. Pour into jelly-roll pan or large, shallow baking pan and place in freezer until partially frozen or mushy, about 2 hours.
4. Spoon mixture into chilled bowl; with mixer at high speed, beat until fluffy. Return to pan; freeze until firm. For easier serving, let stand at room temperature until soft enough to scoop.

Marinated Watermelon

Color index page 101

Begin 4 hrs ahead or early in day

16 servings

3 cups cranberry-juice cocktail	*1 small honeydew melon*
1 cup light corn syrup	*1 10-pound oval-shaped watermelon*
2 tablespoons lime juice	

1. In large bowl, mix well first 3 ingredients. Cut honeydew in half; discard seeds; scoop pulp into balls; add to cranberry mixture.
2. Prepare watermelon bowl (see below): Cut lengthwise slice, 3 inches from top of melon; scoop out and cut pulp from both sections into 1-inch pieces; discard seeds and top rind. Add melon to cranberry mixture. Cut sawtooth edge around shell; cut thin slice off bottom.
3. Spoon melon mixture into watermelon bowl; cover. Refrigerate at least 3 hours. Serve the mixture in individual bowls.

Filling watermelon bowl: Spoon melon mixture into bowl; cover and chill thoroughly.

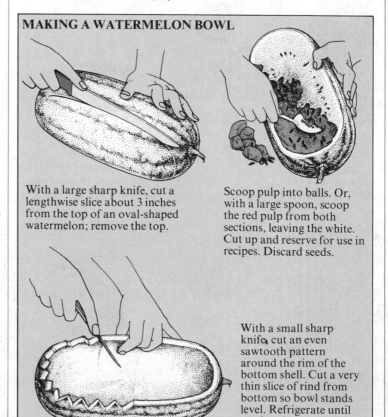

MAKING A WATERMELON BOWL

With a large sharp knife, cut a lengthwise slice about 3 inches from the top of an oval-shaped watermelon; remove the top.

Scoop pulp into balls. Or, with a large spoon, scoop the red pulp from both sections, leaving the white. Cut up and reserve for use in recipes. Discard seeds.

With a small sharp knife, cut an even sawtooth pattern around the rim of the bottom shell. Cut a very thin slice of rind from bottom so bowl stands level. Refrigerate until serving time.

Nectarines

Season: June to September.

Look for: Plump, rich-colored fruit with slight softening along the seam side. Color can be reddish to yellowish, depending on variety. Slightly firm fruit ripens well at room temperature. Avoid hard, soft or shriveled fruit, or any with a large proportion of green skin.

To store: Ripen at room temperature. Refrigerate and use within 3 to 5 days.

To prepare: See below. To prevent browning, if cut nectarines are not to be eaten immediately, sprinkle with a little lemon juice or ascorbic-acid mixture for fruit.

To serve: Eat out of hand. Use in salads, desserts, relishes, pies; or use in recipes below.

Preparing nectarines: Wash the nectarine under running cold water; peel if you like. Cut nectarine in half; remove the seed.

Fresh Nectarine Relish

Color index page 72

Begin 4 hrs or up to 3 days ahead

4 cups

2 pounds nectarines, seeded and diced
1 cup California walnuts, chopped
½ cup dark seedless raisins
½ cup packed dark brown sugar
¼ cup diced crystallized ginger
2 tablespoons lemon juice
½ teaspoon salt

In large bowl combine all ingredients. Cover with plastic wrap; refrigerate at least 3½ hours to blend flavors. Serve relish as accompaniment to chicken, pork, duck or ham.

Spiced Nectarine Slices

Color index page 72

Begin early in day

16 relish servings

1½ cups water
¾ teaspoon whole cloves
¼ teaspoon ground cinnamon
¼ teaspoon ground ginger
¼ teaspoon salt
4 large nectarines, peeled and thinly sliced
½ cup sugar
3 tablespoons lemon juice

1. In 10-inch skillet over medium heat, heat water with cloves, cinnamon, ginger and salt to boiling; boil 2 minutes.
2. Add nectarine slices and cook until fork-tender, about 10 minutes, stirring occasionally. During last minutes of cooking time, stir in sugar and lemon juice. Refrigerate until well chilled. Serve as accompaniment to meat or poultry.

Oranges

Season: All year. Best in winter and early spring.

Look for: Firm oranges, heavy for their size. Strict state regulations help assure tree-ripened fruits. Slight greenish color or russeting of skin of some varieties does not affect quality. Navel and Temple oranges peel and section easily; Valencia, Parson Brown, Pineapple and Hamlin are juicy. Avoid dry, soft or spongy fruit.

To store: Keep at room temperature a few days or refrigerate and use within 2 weeks.

To prepare: Peel; slice, cut up or section (see below). See also Preparing Citrus Fruit Peel, page 308.

To serve: Eat out of hand. Use in recipes for salads, desserts, beverages, sauces, cakes.

Peeling and sectioning oranges: With a sharp knife, cut off peel and white portion, being sure to remove thin membrane that covers pulp.

Cut along both sides of each dividing membrane and lift out sections from center of orange.

Candied Orange Peel

Color index page 102

Begin day or up to 2 wks ahead

2 pounds

4 cups long thin orange peel strips, lightly packed (about 3 large oranges)
water
½ cup light corn syrup
sugar
1 3-ounce package orange-flavor gelatin

1. In 5-quart saucepot over high heat, heat peel and 8 cups hot water to boiling; boil 15 minutes. Drain peel in colander and rinse. With 8 more cups of hot water, boil peel 15 minutes again; drain.
2. In same saucepot over high heat, heat corn syrup, 1¾ cups sugar and 1½ cups water until boiling and sugar is dissolved, stirring frequently. Stir in peel. Reduce heat to medium-low; cook until most of syrup has been absorbed, about 40 minutes, stirring.
3. Remove from heat; gently stir in gelatin until gelatin is dissolved; cool 10 minutes. (Mixture will be thick and sticky.)
4. Onto waxed paper, place 1 cup sugar. Lightly roll pieces of peel, a few at a time, in sugar, adding more sugar if necessary.
5. Place sugar-coated peel in single layer on wire racks; let dry overnight or about 12 hours. Store in tightly covered container.

Papayas

Season: All year.
Look for: Greenish-yellow to almost-yellow fruit that yields to gentle thumb pressure. Avoid shriveled or bruised fruit.
To store: Refrigerate. Use within 3 to 4 days.
To prepare: Cut in half lengthwise and scoop out seeds. Peel and slice or cut up.
To serve: Serve unpeeled halves with lemon or lime wedges for appetizer or dessert. Or fill with ice cream or sherbet, or flavored cream (see recipe below); use cut up in salads or desserts.

Papayas with Lemon Cream

Color index
page 100

Begin 1 hr
ahead

6 servings

3 medium papayas
1 cup heavy or whipping
* cream*
2 egg yolks
⅓ cup sugar

3 tablespoons lemon
* juice*
⅛ teaspoon salt
lemon slices for garnish

1 Cut each papaya in half lengthwise and scoop out seeds. In small bowl with mixer at medium speed, beat the heavy or whipping cream until stiff peaks form.

2 In another small bowl with mixer at high speed, beat egg yolks, sugar, lemon juice and salt until sugar dissolves. Gently fold mixture into whipped cream.

3 Spoon mixture into center of each papaya. Refrigerate until cream is slightly set, about 30 minutes.

4 *To serve:* Garnish papaya halves with lemon slices made into twists. (To make lemon twists, see page 308.)

Peaches

Season: May to October.
Look for: Fairly firm to slightly soft, yellow or cream-colored fruit with, depending on variety, a red blush. Avoid green, shriveled or bruised fruit. Pulp of free-stone varieties is easily removed from the seed.
To store: Refrigerate. Use within 3 to 5 days.
To prepare: Peel (see below) and halve to remove seed. To prevent browning, if cut peaches are not eaten immediately, sprinkle with lemon juice or a little ascorbic-acid mixture for fruit.
To serve: Eat out of hand. Use in recipes below and for salads, desserts, pies, preserves.

Peeling peaches: To peel a peach, dip it into rapidly boiling water for about 15 seconds; dip immediately in pan of cold water.

With a small sharp knife, peel off the skin.

Stewed Peaches

Color index
page 100

Begin 20 mins
ahead

6 servings

¼ cup sugar
¾ cup water
4 whole cloves

1½ pounds peaches,
* peeled and halved*

1. In 2-quart saucepan over medium heat, heat sugar, water and cloves to boiling.
2. Add peaches; return to boiling. Reduce heat to low; cover and simmer 10 minutes or until tender.

Buttery Baked Peaches

Color index
page 100

Begin 1 hr
ahead

6 servings or
12 garnishes

6 peaches
½ cup sugar
2 tablespoons lemon juice
2 tablespoons butter or
* margarine*

1 cup water
mint jelly (optional)

1. Preheat oven to 350°F. Peel, halve and seed peaches. In 1-quart saucepan over medium-high heat, heat sugar, lemon juice, butter or margarine and water to boiling; simmer 5 minutes.
2. Place peaches in 3-quart casserole; add syrup. Cover and bake 30 minutes or until peaches are tender. Place a little mint jelly in center of each half, if you like. Serve, drained, as a garnish for meat dishes or warm as a dessert.

Pears

Season: All year, but best from August to December.
Look for: Well-shaped fruit which yields to soft pressure. Color depends upon variety. Avoid shriveled, discolored or bruised fruit. Bartlett, Anjou and Bosc pears can be used both for eating fresh and cooking; Comice, Seckel, Nelis and Kieffer are for eating fresh.
To store: Ripen firm pears at room temperature a few days, then refrigerate and use within 3 to 5 days.
To prepare: Wash; peel; halve and remove core and stem. For even slices, use a pear slicer (see below).
To serve: Eat out of hand; or with Roquefort, Cheddar or other cheese. Use in salads, pies, desserts.

Using a pear slicer: Press the cutter firmly down on top of the pear; slices fall away from the core, which remains intact.

Poached Pears in Sauterne

Color index
page 101

Begin 4 hrs
or day ahead

6 servings

3 large pears	*½ cup sauterne*
water	*¼ cup sugar*

1. Peel, halve and core each pear. In 10-inch skillet over medium-high heat, heat ½ inch water to boiling; add pears; heat to boiling. Reduce heat to low; cover and simmer 20 minutes or until tender.
2. With slotted spoon, remove pears from skillet and place in 9" by 9" baking dish.
3. To liquid in skillet, add sauterne and sugar; heat to boiling. Reduce heat to low; simmer 8 minutes; pour over pears; cover and refrigerate. Serve chilled.

Pears in Chocolate Sauce

Color index
page 101

Begin 30 mins
ahead or
early in day

2 servings

2 ripe medium pears, chilled	*1 square unsweetened chocolate*
¼ cup sugar	*2 tablespoons milk*
2 tablespoons brandy	*½ cup thawed frozen whipped topping*
1 egg yolk	
⅛ teaspoon salt	

1. Remove cores from bottom of pears (do not remove stems). Stand pears on plate. In small bowl, mix well sugar, brandy, egg yolk and salt.
2. In 1-cup liquid measuring cup, place chocolate and milk. In 1-quart saucepan over low heat, in 1 inch hot, not boiling, water, place cup; heat until chocolate is melted, stirring constantly.
3. Stir in sugar mixture until slightly thickened; pour over pears. If prepared ahead, refrigerate.
4. Spoon topping on 2 dessert plates; stand pears in topping. Serve pears with knives and forks.

Pineapples

Season: All year.
Look for: Firm fruit, heavy for its size, with distinct aroma and plump, glossy eyes. Color depends on variety but green usually indicates that pineapple is unripe.
To store: Ripen pineapple at room temperature a few days; then refrigerate. Use within 1 to 2 days.
To prepare: See below.
To serve: Use as appetizer or dessert. Use in recipes for salads and pies (do not use fresh pineapple in gelatin because it prevents jelling).

Cutting rings: With a sharp knife, cut off crown and stem end; cut fruit into crosswise slices ½ to 1 inch thick, depending on recipe.

Carefully cut off the peel from the fruit.

Remove the eyes with the tip of a sharp knife.

Core with a biscuit cutter or sharp knife; serve as is or cut up in chunks.

Cutting wedges: With a sharp knife, slice pineapple in half lengthwise from bottom through crown; cut in quarters, leaving on leafy crown for decoration. Cut off core. With small sharp knife, loosen fruit by cutting close to peel. To serve in shell, cut fruit crosswise into slices and stagger slices.

Plums

Season: June to October.
Look for: Plump, well-colored fruit that yields to gentle pressure on the skin. Depending on variety, color varies from bright yellow-green to reddish-purple to purplish-black. Avoid hard, shriveled, soft or cracked fruit.
To store: Refrigerate. Use within 3 to 5 days.
To prepare: See below.
To serve: Eat out of hand. Serve sliced or cut up, with or without skins, with milk and sugar. Use in salads, desserts, sauces, jams, coffeecakes.

Preparing plums: Wash plums; with a small sharp knife, cut in half then remove seed.

Stewed Plums

Color index page 100

Begin 20 mins ahead

2½ cups

½ cup water
1 pound plums, halved and seeded
⅓ cup sugar

1. In 2-quart saucepan over medium heat, heat water and plums to boiling. Reduce heat to low; cover and simmer 5 minutes.
2. During last minutes of cooking time, stir in sugar.

Creamy Plum Dressing

Color index page 100

Begin 1¼ hrs ahead

1¾ cups

4 plums, seeded
½ cup confectioners' sugar
1 8-ounce package cream cheese, softened

1. In covered blender container at low speed, blend the plums and sugar until the mixture is of sauce consistency, about 1 minute.
2. Add cream cheese; blend for 30 seconds or just until smooth.
3. Refrigerate at least 1 hour. Serve well chilled over fresh fruit salad.

Plums in Port Sauce

Color index page 100

Begin day or up to 4 days ahead

6 servings

2 pounds small plums, halved and seeded
2 cups ruby port
6 whole cloves
1 cinnamon stick
1½ teaspoons grated orange peel
1 cup sugar

1. In 4-quart saucepan over high heat, heat plums, port, cloves, cinnamon and orange peel to boiling. Reduce heat to low; cover and simmer 3 to 5 minutes until plums are tender.
2. Gently stir in sugar until sugar is dissolved. Spoon plum mixture into large bowl; cover and refrigerate mixture overnight.
3. Serve the plums well chilled with their syrup or with vanilla ice cream spooned over.

Pomegranates

Season: September to December.
Look for: Fresh-looking fruit, heavy for its size. Avoid shriveled fruit or fruit with broken peel.
To store: Refrigerate. Use within 1 week.
To prepare: See below.
To serve: Use juice in beverages. Eat kernels out of hand, add them to fruit salads or use them as a garnish.

Preparing pomegranates: With sharp knife, 1 inch from and parallel to blossom end, make shallow cut all around.

With fingers, pull off top. Kernels are juicy.

Score fruit, through peel only, in about 6 wedges.

Break the pomegranate into separate sections.

Gently remove pomegranate kernels.

To extract the juice, with spoon, press kernels through sieve; discard seeds.

Rhubarb

Season: January to July, but some areas may have rhubarb all year.

Look for: Firm, crisp, fairly thick stalks, either red or pink, depending on variety. Avoid limp stalks.

To store: Refrigerate. Use within 3 to 5 days.

To prepare: Cut off and discard any leaves. Trim discolored ends. With vegetable brush, scrub rhubarb under running cold water. Cut stalks into pieces for use in cooking.

To serve: Use in recipes below, and for pies, desserts, or sauces to accompany meat or poultry.

Rhubarb Sauce

Color index page 101

Begin 20 mins ahead or early in day

2²/₃ cups

1¹/₂ pounds rhubarb, cut up
³/₄ cup water
²/₃ cup sugar

1. In 2-quart saucepan over medium heat, heat rhubarb and water to boiling. Reduce heat to low; cover and simmer 5 minutes or until rhubarb is tender, but not broken up.
2. During last minutes of cooking time, stir sugar into sauce. Serve hot or refrigerate to serve cold.

Rhubarb Crumble

Color index page 101

Begin 50 mins ahead

6 servings

1¹/₂ pounds rhubarb, cut into 1-inch pieces (about 4 cups)
¹/₄ cup water
1 teaspoon lemon juice sugar
1¹/₄ cups all-purpose flour
¹/₂ cup butter or margarine
half-and-half or vanilla ice cream

1. In 4-quart saucepan over medium heat, heat rhubarb, water, lemon juice and ¹/₂ cup sugar to boiling. Reduce heat to low; cover and simmer 10 minutes or until rhubarb is tender. Pour mixture into 8″ by 8″ baking dish. Preheat oven to 425°F.
2. In medium bowl with fork, stir flour and ¹/₄ cup sugar. With pastry blender or 2 knives used scissor-fashion, cut butter or margarine into flour mixture until mixture resembles coarse crumbs.
3. Sprinkle flour mixture over rhubarb. Bake in oven 25 minutes or until crumbs are golden. Serve warm with half-and-half or ice cream.

Tangerines and tangelos

TANGERINE

TANGELO

Season: Tangelos are in season from November to February, tangerines from October to April.

Look for: Firm tangelos, heavy for their size, with good orange color. They peel and section easily (see below), are juicy and have few seeds. Tangerines are deep yellow to deep orange in color, heavy for their size, and often have loose skins which can easily be pulled away.

To store: Keep tangelos at room temperature a few days or refrigerate and use within 1 week. Refrigerate tangerines and use within 1 or 2 days.

To prepare: See below.

To serve: Eat out of hand. Use in salads.

Peeling and sectioning: Starting from the stem end, with fingers, pull off the skin.

Break the fruit into its natural sections; cut center of each section to remove seeds.

Zesty Tangelo Salad

Color index page 77

Begin 40 mins ahead

6 servings

4 large tangelos or 6 large tangerines
1 cup thinly sliced celery
¹/₄ cup bottled Italian salad dressing
2 tablespoons sliced pimento
³/₄ teaspoon salt romaine leaves

1. Peel tangelos; separate into sections; remove seeds, if any.
2. In large bowl combine celery, salad dressing, pimento and salt; add tangelos and gently toss to coat with dressing.
3. To serve: Line salad bowl with romaine leaves. Spoon tangelo mixture onto romaine.

315

SALADS

Salads are for serving the year round, as appetizers, accompaniment dishes, substantial main dishes and desserts. Most are quick and easy to make and take little or no cooking. They can be tossed in anything from a regular salad bowl to an earthenware casserole and served from the kitchen or at the table. For variety with few calories, there's a wide range of low-calorie greens to use in salads and as garnishes.

Appetizer salads are light and tangy, to stimulate the palate for heartier foods to follow. The favorite is a simply dressed mixture of tossed greens, sometimes with vegetables or fruit added for color and flavor contrast.

Accompaniment salads may be a mixture of greens, or a heartier combination of greens and vegetables or fruit. Recipes in this chapter are for accompaniment servings, unless otherwise specified.

Main-dish salads provide the same quantity of high-quality protein to be found in hot main dishes based on meat, poultry, seafood, cheese or eggs.

Dessert salads are made of fruit, often with nuts or cheese, and a sweet dressing.

CHOOSING SALAD GREENS

Always use fresh, crisp-looking greens, free from wilted or discolored leaves, for salads. (For details of choosing and storing lettuce and other greens, see page 288.) Select firm, heavy heads of iceberg lettuce and cabbage. Besides the familiar lettuces there are many other greens from which to choose: romaine, escarole, chicory (curly endive), Belgian endive, green and red cabbage, Chinese cabbage, kale, spinach, watercress, sorrel. Young beet greens, celery and turnip tops add special flavor interest to the salad bowl, too. For tempting variety of color, texture and flavor, plan to combine tangy greens with mild-flavored ones, crisp leaves with tender ones, dark leaves with pale ones. Experiment until you find the combination of greens you like.

Greens also add good nutrition to your menus – vitamins, minerals and few calories. Don't discard outer, darker green leaves of romaine or lettuce that are not wilted or bruised. Although often less tender than the inner leaves, they are especially nutritious. Wash, dry and shred the outer leaves and add to the salad bowl, or use in sandwiches or as a garnish for cold dishes or hot clear soups or consommé.

CLEANING AND STORING SALAD GREENS

Store prepared greens in the refrigerator, in plastic bags, in covered containers, in the crisper drawer, or wrapped in plastic wrap. Use them within a day or two.

Preparing firm heads (such as iceberg lettuce, red or green cabbage): Holding lettuce firmly, insert a sharp knife alongside core and cut all the way around the core in cone shape.

Or place lettuce, core up, on counter and with heel of hand, strike core firmly to loosen.

Then, holding lettuce firmly with one hand, twist out the loosened core with the other hand; discard core.

Washing a firm lettuce: Hold head, cut side up, under running cold water to clean and help separate the leaves.

Place, cored end down, on rack or in colander; allow to drain thoroughly.

Preparing loose heads (Boston lettuce, romaine): Break off individual leaves.

Place in a colander or French lettuce basket. Hold colander under running cold water; shake, then drain well.

PREPARING OTHER GREENS

Wash greens such as chicory, Swiss chard, kale, spinach or leafy broccoli in cold water. Drain them thoroughly, pat dry, trim tough ribs or stems.

With a small sharp knife, trim any tough ribs or stems from the washed greens.

CRISPING SALAD GREENS

Gently pat leaves dry with paper towels, taking care not to damage the leaves.

Place in plastic bags and refrigerate. Place washed and dried fresh parsley, watercress and mint, stems down, in a little water in covered jars; refrigerate.

DRESSING THE SALAD

As a general rule, light oil-and-vinegar dressings go best with tender greens such as Boston lettuce, and creamy or mayonnaise dressings with very crisp greens such as romaine or iceberg lettuce. For the weight-conscious, cut down on the quantity of salad oil used and toss the greens with freshly squeezed lemon juice, or use instead a low-calorie ingredient such as cottage cheese, sour cream or yogurt.

It's a good idea to mix the dressing ingredients well in advance to allow flavors to develop. While cooked vegetable salads absorb more flavor if part of the dressing is mixed in while they are still warm, don't dress green salads until just before serving, or the leaves will become limp and garnishes such as croutons will become soggy.

When dressing a salad, unless the recipe directs otherwise, start by adding about ⅔ of the dressing to the mixture and mix or toss gently until the dressing is well incorporated. Then, if necessary, add the rest of the dressing until the ingredients are just coated. Avoid overdressing salads – it makes them soggy.

Leftover dressings keep well in the refrigerator, and often small amounts can be combined with mayonnaise or sour cream to make enough new dressing for another meal's salad.

MOLDED SALADS

Shimmering gelatin salads, which can be shaped either individually or in a large, attractive mold, add a decorative touch to any table.

They should be prepared at least 4 hours ahead of serving, to give the gelatin time to set fully. To keep large molded mixtures from breaking, unmold them directly onto the serving platter and then surround with greens. Wet the platter first with a little cold water so the salad can be moved easily to the platter's center if needed; individual salads can simply be unmolded right onto the salad greens. Once unmolded, a gelatin salad should be taken straight to the table and served immediately.

UNMOLDING GELATIN SALADS

Carefully loosen edges of gelatin from mold with a small metal spatula or knife.

Fill the sink or a large bowl with *warm* water; dip mold into water just to rim for about 10 seconds. Be careful not to melt gelatin.

Lift mold from water and shake gently to loosen gelatin. Invert platter on top of mold and quickly invert mold and platter; gently lift off mold.

Tossed salads

Caesar Salad

Color index
page 75

Begin 30 mins
ahead

6 servings

Garlic Croutons (below)
2 medium heads romaine
  lettuce or the
  equivalent in iceberg or
  leaf lettuce
1/3 cup olive or salad oil
1/3 cup grated Parmesan
  cheese

2 tablespoons lemon juice
1/4 teaspoon salt
1/8 teaspoon cracked
  pepper
1 2-ounce can anchovy
  fillets, drained
1 egg

1 Prepare the Garlic
Croutons; set aside.
Wash romaine under
running cold water; drain
thoroughly in colander
or French lettuce basket;
pat dry with paper towels.

2 Into chilled large salad
bowl, tear the romaine
into bite-size pieces.

3 Add olive oil and toss
together gently until
the romaine leaves are
thoroughly coated

4 Add Parmesan cheese,
lemon juice, salt, crack-
ed pepper, anchovies and
uncooked egg; toss again
gently to mix well.

5 Garnish salad with
Garlic Croutons. Serve
salad immediately.

GARLIC CROUTONS: Trim crusts from *3 white
bread slices;* cut slices into 1/2-inch cubes. In 10-inch
skillet over medium heat, heat *1/4 cup salad oil;* add *1
small garlic clove* and cook until golden, about 2
minutes; discard garlic. Add bread cubes; cook,
stirring frequently, until the cubes are crisp and
golden. Drain well on paper towels.

Tossed Salad
with Lemony-Mustard Dressing

Color index
page 75

Begin 45 mins
ahead

10 servings

2 10-ounce bags spinach
1 medium head Boston
  lettuce
2 small Belgian endives
1/2 pound medium
  mushrooms

Dressing:
1 large lemon

2/3 cup olive or salad oil
2 teaspoons sugar
1 1/2 teaspoons salt
1 teaspoon dry mustard
1 teaspoon fresh or
  frozen chopped chives
1/4 teaspoon cracked
  pepper

1. Into chilled large salad bowl, tear spinach and
Boston lettuce into bite-size pieces. Cut endives in
half crosswise; separate top leaves; cut bottom into
wedges. Thinly slice mushrooms. Add endives and
mushrooms to spinach mixture.
2. Prepare the dressing: Grate 2 teaspoons peel from
lemon; squeeze juice from lemon to make 1/4 cup. In
small bowl with wire whisk or fork, mix lemon peel,
lemon juice, olive oil and remaining ingredients.
3. Pour dressing over salad; gently toss to mix well
and thoroughly coat vegetables.

Colonel's Lady's Salad Bowl

Color index
page 75

Begin 20 mins
ahead

12 servings

1/2 10-ounce package
  frozen peas
boiling water
1 small head romaine
  lettuce
1 small head iceberg
  lettuce
1 small cucumber,
  thinly sliced
3 green onions,
  chopped
1 stalk celery,
  sliced

Dressing:
1/4 cup salad oil
3 tablespoons white wine
  vinegar
1 tablespoon sugar
1 tablespoon chopped
  parsley
1/2 teaspoon garlic salt
1/2 teaspoon salt
1/4 teaspoon oregano
  leaves
1/8 teaspoon seasoned
  pepper

1. In medium bowl, place frozen peas; cover with
boiling water and let stand 5 minutes.
2. Meanwhile, in large bowl, tear lettuce into bite-
size pieces; drain peas and add to bowl with remaining salad ingredients.
3. Prepare the dressing: In cup, combine dressing
ingredients; stir with fork to mix well.
4. Toss salad gently with dressing to coat lettuce.

California Salad

Color index
page 75

Begin 30 mins
ahead

8 servings

1/4 cup salad oil
1 tablespoon sugar
2 tablespoons white wine
  vinegar
2 teaspoons minced
  parsley
1/2 teaspoon garlic salt
1/2 teaspoon seasoned salt
1/4 teaspoon oregano
  leaves

1/8 teaspoon seasoned
  pepper
1/2 large head iceberg
  lettuce
1/2 large head Boston
  lettuce
2 large avocados, peeled
  and sliced
1/2 cup California walnuts

1. To make the dressing, in large salad bowl, mix
thoroughly first 8 ingredients.
2. Into dressing, tear iceberg and Boston lettuce into
bite-size pieces. Add avocados; gently toss to coat
avocados and lettuce. Garnish with walnuts.

Vegetable salads

Deluxe Coleslaw

Color index
page 76

Begin 1½ hrs
ahead or
early in day

8 servings

Dressing:
½ cup mayonnaise or
   cooked salad dressing
1 tablespoon milk
1 tablespoon vinegar or
   lemon juice
½ teaspoon sugar
¼ teaspoon salt
⅛ teaspoon paprika
⅛ teaspoon pepper

1 medium head
   cabbage
1 small green pepper
1 large celery stalk
1 large carrot
2 tablespoons minced
   onion

1 Prepare dressing: Into cup, measure all dressing ingredients; with fork or wire whisk, stir until well blended. Set aside.

2 With sharp knife, shred cabbage and thinly slice green pepper.

3 With a sharp knife, first cut the celery stalk into ¼-inch-wide pieces. Then, using a grater, finely shred the carrot.

4 In large bowl, gently toss prepared cabbage, green pepper, celery, carrot, onion and dressing. Cover and refrigerate.

COLESLAW BOWL

Spread apart several outer leaves of cabbage. With sharp knife, carefully cut out center of cabbage and set aside, leaving center "bowl" about ¾ inch thick.

Use cut-out cabbage to make coleslaw as above. Spoon salad into cabbage "bowl" to serve.

Cucumbers in Sour Cream

Color index
page 75

Begin 20 mins
ahead or
early in day

6 servings

1 cup sour cream
3 tablespoons minced
   chives or onion
2 tablespoons lemon
   juice

1½ teaspoons salt
⅛ teaspoon pepper
3 large cucumbers

1. In large bowl, combine sour cream, minced chives, lemon juice, salt and pepper.
2. Peel and thinly slice cucumbers; add and mix well. Cover and refrigerate.

Danish Cucumber Salad

Color index
page 75

Begin 5 hrs
ahead or
early in day

8 servings

4 medium cucumbers
salt
½ cup white vinegar
¼ cup sugar

2 tablespoons chopped
   fresh dill
¼ teaspoon white
   pepper

1. With sharp knife, cut cucumbers into paper-thin slices. In large bowl, mix slices with 2 teaspoons salt. Let stand at room temperature 1 hour.
2. Drain liquid from cucumbers. Stir in vinegar, sugar, chopped dill, pepper and 1 teaspoon salt until thoroughly mixed.
3. Cover with plastic wrap and refrigerate salad at least 3 hours before serving.

Tomatoes Vinaigrette

Color index
page 75

Begin 2 hrs
ahead

6 servings

6 medium tomatoes
2 tablespoons salad oil
1 teaspoon wine vinegar
½ teaspoon sugar
½ teaspoon oregano
   leaves

½ teaspoon salt
½ teaspoon pepper
chopped parsley for
   garnish (optional)

1. Slice tomatoes and arrange in serving dish in overlapping slices.
2. In small bowl, combine salad oil, wine vinegar, sugar, oregano leaves, salt and pepper. Stir thoroughly to blend and sprinkle over tomatoes. Cover and refrigerate until serving time.
3. *To serve:* Garnish Tomatoes Vinaigrette with parsley, if you like.

Marinated Artichoke Hearts and Mushrooms

Color index
page 20

Begin early
in day or
day ahead

8 first-course
servings

2 9-ounce packages
   frozen artichoke
   hearts
¾ cup salad oil
½ cup lemon juice
1 tablespoon sugar
2 teaspoons salt
1 teaspoon dry
   mustard

½ teaspoon pepper
½ teaspoon basil
1 small garlic clove,
   crushed
1 pound mushrooms,
   sliced
1 tablespoon diced
   pimento

1. Prepare artichoke hearts as the labels direct; drain them thoroughly.
2. In large bowl, mix salad oil with lemon juice, sugar, salt, mustard, pepper, basil and garlic until well blended.
3. Stir in artichoke hearts, sliced mushrooms and diced pimento. Cover with plastic wrap and refrigerate, tossing mixture occasionally.

Vegetable salads

Greek Salad

Color index
page 77

Begin 30 mins
ahead

10 servings

1 medium head chicory
1 medium head iceberg
  lettuce
2 medium cucumbers
2 large tomatoes
1 5½-ounce jar Greek
  olives or 1 6-ounce can
  pitted ripe olives,
  drained
1 2-ounce can anchovy
  fillets, drained
  (optional)

2 green onions, chopped
2 tablespoons capers
½ pound feta cheese,
  crumbled
½ cup olive or salad oil
3 tablespoons red wine
  vinegar
1 teaspoon oregano
  leaves
½ teaspoon salt
⅛ teaspoon pepper

1. Into chilled large salad bowl, tear chicory and iceberg lettuce into bite-size pieces.
2. Peel lengthwise strips of skin from cucumbers, to give striped effect; slice the cucumbers thinly; cut tomatoes into wedges.
3. Add cucumbers and tomatoes to lettuce mixture with olives, anchovy fillets; if you are using them, green onions, capers and feta cheese.
4. In cup, combine olive oil with the remaining ingredients; pour over salad; toss to mix well.

Preparing cucumber: Peel strips of skin from cucumbers, then slice cucumbers thinly.

Adding feta cheese: Add coarsely crumbled cheese to salad ingredients then add dressing and mix well.

Potato-Vegetable Salad

Color index
page 75

Begin 1 hr
ahead

8 servings

8 medium potatoes,
  unpeeled
water
2 10-ounce packages
  frozen peas and carrots
2 small cucumbers

salt
1 cup mayonnaise
⅓ cup milk
¼ teaspoon pepper
leaf lettuce

1. In 4-quart saucepan over high heat, heat potatoes and enough water to cover to boiling. Reduce heat to medium-low; cover; cook 20 to 30 minutes until tender; drain.
2. Cool potatoes slightly; with a sharp knife, peel and cut into ½-inch cubes.
3. Meanwhile, prepare peas and carrots as labels direct. Cut cucumbers into paper-thin slices. In medium bowl, gently toss cucumbers with ¼ teaspoon salt; set aside.
4. In large bowl with rubber spatula, gently toss potatoes, peas and carrots, mayonnaise, milk, pepper and 1½ teaspoons salt until well mixed.
5. To serve: Line large platter with lettuce leaves; spoon salad onto center of platter. Arrange cucumbers, overlapping, on top of salad.

German Hot-Potato Salad

Color index
page 75

Begin 45 mins
ahead

6 servings

6 medium potatoes,
  unpeeled (2 pounds)
water
6 slices bacon, cut into
  ½-inch pieces
½ cup chopped onion
2 teaspoons sugar
2 teaspoons salt
1 teaspoon all-purpose
  flour
⅛ teaspoon pepper
3 tablespoons red wine
  vinegar
minced parsley for
  garnish

1 In 4-quart saucepan over high heat, heat potatoes and water to cover to boiling. Reduce heat to low; cover; simmer 20 to 30 minutes until fork-tender.

2 Drain potatoes and allow to cool slightly. With sharp knife, peel and dice potatoes.

3 Meanwhile, in 10-inch skillet over medium heat, cook bacon until crisp; remove bacon to paper towels to drain.

4 Spoon off all but 2 tablespoons bacon fat from skillet. Add onion; cook until tender, about 5 minutes, stirring often.

5 Stir in sugar, salt, flour and pepper until mixture is well blended.

6 Gradually stir in red wine vinegar and ½ cup water. Cook, stirring the mixture constantly, until it is slightly thickened and boiling.

7 Gently stir in potatoes and bacon; heat through then transfer salad to warm bowl or platter. Garnish with minced parsley.

Celery Hearts Vinaigrette

Color index page 20

Begin 6 hrs or day ahead

8 first-course servings

4 medium bunches celery
water
1 chicken-flavor bouillon cube or envelope
1 4-ounce jar pimentos, drained and minced
²/₃ cup white vinegar
¹/₃ cup salad oil

3 tablespoons minced green pepper
1 teaspoon sugar
1 teaspoon salt
1 teaspoon dry mustard
³/₄ teaspoon seasoned pepper
romaine lettuce leaves

1 Remove outer rows of celery ribs; trim root ends. Cut tops and leaves from celery 6 to 8 inches from root ends; discard. Halve bunches lengthwise.

2 In 5-quart Dutch oven over medium heat, in 1 inch boiling water, heat celery and bouillon to boiling. Cover and cook 15 minutes until tender.

3 Meanwhile, in 13″ by 9″ baking dish, combine pimentos with the remaining ingredients except lettuce.

4 Drain celery; arrange in baking dish, turning to coat with marinade. Cover and refrigerate at least 4 hours or overnight, turning occasionally.

5 To serve: Line 8 salad plates with romaine leaves and arrange celery on top. Spoon some marinade over salad.

VARIATION: Prepare and cook *celery* as in steps 1 and 2 above. In 13″ by 9″ baking dish, combine *pimentos* with *Classic French Dressing* or *Mixed Herb Dressing* (page 326); omit remaining ingredients except romaine lettuce leaves. Drain and marinate celery; serve on lettuce leaves as above.

BRAISED LEEKS VINAIGRETTE: Cut off roots and trim leaf end of *8 medium leeks* (about 3 pounds). Cut each leek crosswise in half; then cut root end of each leek lengthwise in half. Rinse leeks well under running cold water to remove all sand. Divide leeks into 4 portions; tie loosely with string into 4 bundles. Cook leeks in *chicken broth* about 30 minutes until tender. Untie bundles; marinate and serve as for Celery Hearts Vinaigrette.

Color index page 76

Begin 6 hrs ahead

8 servings

Three-Bean Salad

Color index page 76

Begin early in day or several days ahead

8 servings

¹/₂ cup sugar
¹/₂ cup salad oil
¹/₂ cup cider vinegar
1 teaspoon salt
1 16-ounce can cut green beans, drained

1 16-ounce can cut wax beans, drained
1 16-ounce can red kidney beans, drained
¹/₂ cup chopped onion

1. In large bowl, stir sugar with salad oil, vinegar and salt until blended. Add beans and onion; toss to coat beans and onion thoroughly.
2. Cover and refrigerate at least 6 hours before serving to blend flavors.

Turkish Bean Salad

Color index page 76

Begin 5 hrs or day ahead

10 servings

1 16-ounce package dry Great Northern, navy or pea beans
6 cups water
3 chicken-flavor bouillon cubes or envelopes
1 bay leaf
1 6-ounce can pitted ripe olives, drained and halved
2 large tomatoes, chopped

¹/₂ cup olive or salad oil
¹/₂ cup lemon juice
2 tablespoons crumbled dried mint or ¹/₃ cup chopped fresh mint
1 tablespoon salt
1 tablespoon sugar
¹/₄ teaspoon white pepper
mint leaves for garnish

1. Rinse beans under running cold water and discard any stones or shriveled beans.
2. In 7-quart Dutch oven over high heat, heat beans, water, bouillon and bay leaf to boiling; boil 2 minutes. Remove from heat; cover and allow to stand 1 hour.
3. Over high heat, return beans to boiling. Reduce heat to low; cover and simmer beans 1 hour or until tender but firm, stirring occasionally. Drain beans; discard bay leaf.
4. In large bowl with rubber spatula, gently combine beans, olives and remaining ingredients except mint leaves. Cover; refrigerate until well chilled.
5. *To serve:* Spoon into salad dish and garnish.

German Sauerkraut Salad

Color index page 76

Begin 1¹/₂ hrs or up to 3 days ahead

8 servings

1 27-ounce can sauerkraut (4 cups)
2 red eating apples
¹/₃ cup olive oil

2 teaspoons sugar
¹/₂ teaspoon cracked pepper

1. Drain sauerkraut; set aside. With grater, grate eating apples, including the peel.
2. In large bowl, combine sauerkraut, grated apples, olive oil, sugar and pepper.
3. Cover and refrigerate salad at least 1 hour.

Fruit salads

Waldorf Salad

Color index page 77

Begin 20 mins ahead

8 servings

1 cup mayonnaise
¼ cup lemon juice
1 pound red eating apples
2 cups thinly sliced celery
1 cup California walnuts, chopped
1 cup dark seedless raisins
lettuce leaves

1 In medium bowl with fork, mix mayonnaise with lemon juice.

2 With small sharp knife, dice eating apples (do not peel them); discard cores and stems.

3 Add diced apples to mayonnaise and lemon juice mixture and with spoon, stir to coat well.

4 Add sliced celery, walnuts and raisins; toss gently to mix well.

5 Arrange lettuce leaves on serving platter and spoon salad into center.

Hawaiian Fruit Salad

Color index page 21

Begin 20 mins ahead

8 first-course servings

preserved ginger in syrup
¼ cup lime juice
¼ cup light corn syrup
¼ teaspoon salt

4 medium papayas
4 medium bananas
¼ cup shredded coconut

1. Mince enough drained, preserved ginger to make ¼ cup; set aside.
2. In small bowl, combine lime juice, corn syrup, salt and ¼ cup syrup from preserved ginger; set aside.
3. With sharp knife, cut papayas lengthwise in half and scoop out seeds. Slice off thin piece from rounded side of each papaya half, so that each will stand evenly. With paring knife, score flesh.
4. With small sharp knife, slice bananas crosswise; arrange on papaya halves.
5. Spoon syrup mixture over bananas and papayas, then sprinkle with shredded coconut; top mixture with the drained minced preserved ginger.

Sacramento Fruit Bowl

Color index page 101

Begin early in day

10 to 12 first-course or dessert servings

2 cups water
1½ cups sugar
3 tablespoons lemon juice
2 tablespoons anise seed
½ teaspoon salt
1 small pineapple
1 small honeydew melon
1 small cantaloupe
2 oranges
2 nectarines or 4 apricots
2 purple plums
1 cup seedless green grapes
1 lime, sliced

1 In 2-quart saucepan over medium heat, cook water with sugar, lemon juice, anise seed and salt 15 minutes or until mixture becomes a light syrup. Chill syrup well.

2 Meanwhile, cut peel from pineapple, melon, cantaloupe and oranges and cut pulp from all into bite-size chunks.

3 Cut nectarines or apricots and purple plums into halves and remove seeds; slice.

4 In large bowl or large container, combine cut-up fruits with grapes and lime slices.

5 Pour chilled syrup through strainer over fruits. Cover and refrigerate, stirring the salad frequently.

Fresh Fruit Bowl with Cardamom Dressing

Color index page 101

Begin 30 mins ahead

12 first-course or dessert servings

Cardamom Dressing (page 326)
1 small honeydew melon
1 medium cantaloupe

6 medium plums
2 medium pears
3 medium peaches

1. Prepare Cardamom Dressing; set aside.
2. With a sharp knife, peel melon and cantaloupe; cut into bite-size pieces. Slice plums and pears; peel and slice peaches.
3. In large bowl, gently toss melon, plums, pears and peaches. Serve fruit with Cardamom Dressing.

Molded salads

Tomato Aspic

7 medium tomatoes
2 medium celery stalks
1 medium onion
2½ teaspoons salt
1 bay leaf
2 envelopes unflavored
  gelatin
½ cup water
3 tablespoons sugar
2 tablespoons lemon juice
½ teaspoon Worcestershire
⅛ teaspoon hot pepper
  sauce

vegetable cooking spray
1 8-ounce container plain
  yogurt (1 cup)
2 tablespoons chopped
  fresh dill
1 teaspoon grated lemon
  peel
lettuce leaves for garnish

Color index page 76
Begin 4 hrs or day ahead
8 servings

1 With sharp knife, cut tomatoes into bite-size chunks. Slice celery, onion.

2 In 3-quart saucepan over medium heat, cook tomatoes, celery, onion, salt and bay leaf about 20 minutes until vegetables are very tender, stirring frequently.

3 In 1-cup measuring cup, mix gelatin with water; let gelatin stand 5 minutes to soften.

4 Into blender container, spoon tomato mixture; cover container; blend at high speed until pureed.

5 Into same saucepan, press tomato mixture through coarse sieve or food mill; discard seeds and skin. Stir in sugar, lemon juice, Worcestershire and pepper sauce.

6 Add gelatin mixture to tomato mixture. Over medium heat, cook, stirring frequently, until the gelatin is completely dissolved.

7 Lightly spray 6-cup mold or Bundt pan with vegetable cooking spray and pour in gelatin mixture. Cover and refrigerate until set, 3 hours.

8 Meanwhile, prepare dressing: In small bowl, mix yogurt, dill and lemon peel. Cover bowl with plastic wrap; chill.

9 Unmold gelatin mixture onto salad platter; tuck lettuce leaves under for garnish. Serve aspic with yogurt dressing.

Color index page 76
Begin 4 hrs or day ahead
8 servings

Perfection Salad

water
4 envelopes unflavored
  gelatin
1 cup sugar
2 teaspoons salt
1 cup cider vinegar
¼ cup lemon juice

3 cups finely shredded
  cabbage
1⅓ cups diced celery
1 4-ounce jar diced
  pimentos
lettuce leaves for garnish

1. In 1-quart saucepan, heat 2 cups water to boiling. In medium bowl, mix gelatin with sugar and salt. Stir in boiling water until gelatin is dissolved. Stir in vinegar, lemon juice and 3 cups cold water. Refrigerate until mixture mounds slightly when dropped from a spoon.
2. Fold in cabbage, celery and pimentos with their liquid; pour into 2-quart bowl; cover and chill until set, about 3½ hours.
3. *To serve:* Unmold salad onto plate. Garnish with lettuce leaves.

Color index page 76
Begin 6 hrs or day ahead
10 servings

Cranberry Nut Mold

1 15- or 16-ounce
  package fresh or
  frozen cranberries
1½ cups sugar
1½ cups dry red wine
water
1 envelope unflavored
  gelatin
1 6-ounce package
  lemon-flavor
  gelatin

1½ cups diced celery
¾ cup California
  walnuts, chopped

Dressing:
1 8-ounce container sour
  cream (1 cup)
¾ cup mayonnaise

orange peel for garnish

1. In 3-quart saucepan combine cranberries, sugar, wine and ½ cup water; lightly sprinkle unflavored gelatin over cranberry mixture.
2. Over medium heat, heat mixture to boiling, stirring constantly. Reduce heat to low; simmer 3 minutes, stirring constantly.
3. Stir in lemon-flavor gelatin until gelatin is completely dissolved. Remove saucepan from heat; stir in 1 cup *cold* water.
4. Refrigerate until mixture mounds slightly when dropped from a spoon, about 2 hours.
5. Gently fold celery and walnuts into gelatin mixture; pour into 8-cup mold. Cover and refrigerate until set, about 3½ hours.
6. Meanwhile, prepare dressing: In small bowl, stir sour cream and mayonnaise until blended; cover and refrigerate.
7. *To serve:* Unmold gelatin onto chilled platter. With kitchen shears, cut orange peel into flower petals to garnish top of gelatin. Serve Cranberry Nut Mold with sour-cream dressing.

Main dish salads

Color index page 66

Begin 30 mins ahead

6 servings

Chef's Salad

1 garlic clove, halved
1 large head romaine or iceberg lettuce
¼ pound cooked chicken or turkey meat
1 8-ounce package sliced Swiss cheese
1 6-ounce package sliced cooked ham

2 medium tomatoes
2 hard-cooked eggs
Classic French Dressing (page 326), Russian Dressing (page 326) or Thousand Island Dressing (page 326)

1 Rub large, shallow salad bowl well with the halved garlic clove; discard both pieces.

2 Into salad bowl, tear romaine lettuce into bite-size pieces.

3 With knife, cut chicken or turkey, cheese and ham into thin strips. Cut tomatoes into wedges. Peel and then quarter the hard-cooked eggs.

4 On lettuce, arrange chicken, cheese, ham, tomato and egg. Just before serving, toss together with dressing.

Herring Salad

Color index page 66

Begin early in day

6 servings

1 cup heavy or whipping cream
1½ cups diced cooked potatoes
1 16-ounce can sliced pickled beets, drained
1 medium apple, diced
½ cup pickled herring in wine sauce, drained and chopped

¼ cup diced dill pickle
¼ cup minced onion
1½ teaspoons salt
¼ teaspoon pepper
2 hard-cooked eggs, cut in wedges for garnish
parsley for garnish

1. In medium bowl with mixer at medium speed, beat cream until soft peaks form.
2. Gently fold in potatoes, pickled beets, apple, pickled herring, diced dill pickle, minced onion, salt and pepper.
3. Cover the bowl with plastic wrap and refrigerate at least 6 hours before serving.
4. To serve: Arrange salad on platter; garnish with wedges of hard-cooked eggs and parsley.

Salade Niçoise

Color index page 66

Begin early in day

4 servings

3 medium potatoes, unpeeled
3 eggs
2 medium tomatoes
1 12½- to 13-ounce can tuna
1 2-ounce can anchovy fillets
2 small heads Boston lettuce
1 16-ounce can French-style green beans, drained

1 5½-ounce jar Greek olives or 1 6-ounce can pitted ripe olives
Classic French Dressing (page 326) or Sauce Vinaigrette (page 326)

1 Cook potatoes until fork-tender. Hard-cook eggs. Refrigerate cooked potatoes and hard-cooked eggs until they are thoroughly chilled.

2 About 45 minutes before serving: Peel cooked potatoes and cut them into bite-size pieces; set aside.

3 Peel hard-cooked eggs under running cold water (take care not to peel white away with shell); cut each egg into 4 wedges. Cut medium tomatoes into wedges.

4 Drain can of tuna; separate into bite-size pieces. Drain anchovies and carefully separate the fillets; set aside.

5 Into large salad bowl, tear lettuce into bite-size pieces. On lettuce, arrange in separate piles potatoes, tuna, eggs, tomatoes, beans, anchovies.

6 With spoon, sprinkle olives over top of salad for garnish. Let each person help himself to a portion of salad. Pass dressing separately.

Pineapple-Cheese Salad

Color index
page 66

Begin 30 mins
ahead

4 servings

1 large pineapple
*8 ounces sharp Cheddar
cheese*
³/₄ cup mayonnaise
2 tablespoons milk
½ teaspoon salt

½ cup sliced celery
*½ medium green pepper,
diced*
*8 ounces Swiss cheese,
cut into bite-size pieces*

1. With sharp knife, slice pineapple into 4 wedges from bottom through crown, leaving on leafy crown for decoration. Cut off hard core from each wedge; then with paring knife, loosen fruit by cutting close to rind, leaving ½-inch-thick shell; cover with plastic wrap and refrigerate shells. Cut fruit into bite-size pieces.
2. Shred ½ cup Cheddar cheese for garnish; set aside. Cut remaining cheese into bite-size pieces.
3. In medium bowl with fork, blend mayonnaise, milk and salt. Stir in celery, green pepper, pineapple and the Cheddar and Swiss cheese pieces. Mound mixture in the chilled pineapple shells; sprinkle shredded cheese over the top.

Crab Louis

Color index
page 66

Begin 1 hr
ahead

4 servings

1 cup mayonnaise
3 tablespoons catchup
*2 tablespoons chopped
green onion*
*1 tablespoon
Worcestershire*
*1 tablespoon red wine
vinegar*
2 teaspoons lemon juice
½ teaspoon salt
*⅛ teaspoon white
pepper*

*1 pound cooked fresh
crab or 3 6-ounce
packages frozen
Alaska King crab,
thawed and drained
lettuce leaves*
*3 hard-cooked eggs,
sliced*
1 cucumber, sliced
1 tomato, sliced

1. In medium bowl, combine mayonnaise, catchup, onion, Worcestershire, wine vinegar, lemon juice, salt and pepper; refrigerate 30 minutes.
2. In center of salad platter, heap crab; encircle it with lettuce, egg, cucumber and tomato slices; pass the dressing separately.

Shrimp Salad

Color index
page 66

Begin 1 hr
ahead

4 servings

*2 cups cooked, shelled
and deveined shrimp,
chilled*
1½ cups sliced celery
*½ cup California
walnuts, chopped
(optional)*

*¼ cup sliced stuffed
olives*
¼ cup French dressing
¼ cup mayonnaise
*1 teaspoon minced onion
lettuce leaves*

1. Into large bowl, cut shrimp in half lengthwise.
2. Add all ingredients except lettuce leaves; toss to mix well; cover with plastic wrap and refrigerate. Serve on lettuce leaves.

TUNA SALAD: Prepare as above but substitute *two 6½- or 7-ounce cans tuna,* flaked, for shrimp.

SALMON SALAD: Prepare as for Shrimp Salad but substitute *one 16-ounce can salmon,* drained and coarsely flaked, for shrimp; omit walnuts; add *2 cut-up hard-cooked eggs.*

Ham with Rice Salad

Color index
page 66

Begin 3 hrs
ahead

6 servings

⅓ cup salad oil
1 medium onion, diced
*1 cup regular long-grain
rice*
1 ⅔ cups water
¼ cup catchup
*2 chicken-flavor bouillon
cubes or envelopes*

1 teaspoon thyme leaves
*1 pound cooked ham, cut
into ½-inch cubes*
*1 large green pepper,
diced*
*¼ cup red wine vinegar
lettuce leaves*

1. In 10-inch skillet over medium heat, in hot oil, cook onion until tender, stirring frequently. Stir in the rice, water, catchup, bouillon cubes and thyme leaves; heat to boiling. Reduce heat to low; cover; simmer 25 minutes or until rice is tender.
2. With fork, stir in ham, green pepper and vinegar. Cover; refrigerate 2 hours or until chilled.
3. *To serve:* Spoon ham mixture over lettuce.

Chunky Egg Salad

Color index
page 66

Begin 1 hr
ahead or
early in day

4 servings

¼ cup mayonnaise
*1 tablespoon cider
vinegar*
1¼ teaspoons salt
1 teaspoon minced onion
*½ teaspoon
Worcestershire*

⅛ teaspoon pepper
6 hard-cooked eggs
1 cup thinly sliced celery
*2 tablespoons minced
green pepper*
lettuce leaves
parsley for garnish

1. In medium bowl, stir mayonnaise and next 5 ingredients until well mixed.
2. Cut eggs into big pieces; add eggs, celery and green pepper to mayonnaise mixture; mix well. Cover and refrigerate.
3. *To serve:* Spoon mixture onto lettuce leaves and garnish with parsley.

Buffet Salad

Color index
page 66

Begin 2½ hrs
or day ahead

6 servings

*6 ounces Swiss cheese,
shredded*
*6 ounces sharp Cheddar
cheese, shredded*
*3 4-ounce or 2 6-ounce
packages sliced cooked
ham*
*1 large head Boston
lettuce*

*4 medium tomatoes
parsley sprigs for garnish*

Mustard Sauce:
1 cup mayonnaise
½ cup prepared mustard
½ teaspoon sugar
½ teaspoon garlic salt
¼ teaspoon paprika

1. Line 2½-quart mixing bowl with plastic wrap. In same bowl combine Swiss cheese and Cheddar cheese. With hand, firmly pat cheese mixture on bottom and up side of bowl.
2. Slice ham into 1-inch strips. Remove 4 to 6 large leaves from Boston lettuce; set aside for garnish later. Tear remaining lettuce into bite-size pieces. Thinly slice tomatoes.
3. Arrange ⅓ of ham over cheese mixture; top with ⅓ of bite-size lettuce pieces and ⅓ of tomatoes, patting firmly after each layer. Repeat layering two more times. Cover and refrigerate 2 hours.
4. Meanwhile prepare Mustard Sauce: In small bowl, mix well all ingredients. Cover; refrigerate.
5. *To serve:* Unmold salad onto chilled plate. Tuck reserved lettuce leaves under salad; garnish with parsley. Cut salad into wedges. Serve with sauce.

Dressings and sauces

Classic French Dressing

Begin 10 mins
or day ahead

1 cup

*¾ cup olive or
salad oil*
*¼ cup cider or
wine vinegar*

¾ teaspoon salt
⅛ teaspoon pepper

Into a small bowl or a covered jar, measure all ingredients; stir with fork or cover and shake until thoroughly mixed. Cover and chill. Stir or shake the dressing just before serving.

FLAVORED FRENCH DRESSINGS

GARLIC: Prepare as for Classic French Dressing but add *1 garlic clove,* crushed. (Makes 1 cup.)

ROQUEFORT OR BLUE CHEESE: Prepare as for Classic French Dressing but add *½ cup crumbled Roquefort or blue cheese.* (Makes 1⅓ cups.)

MIXED HERB: Prepare as for Classic French Dressing but add *2 teaspoons chopped parsley* and *½ teaspoon tarragon* or basil. (Makes 1 cup.)

ANCHOVY: Prepare as above but stir in *1 tablespoon anchovy paste.* (Makes 1 cup.)

Thousand Island Dressing

Begin 10 mins
ahead

1⅓ cups

1 cup mayonnaise
*2 tablespoons chili
sauce*
*2 tablespoons minced
green pepper*

*1 tablespoon chopped
parsley*
*1 teaspoon grated
onion*

In small bowl, stir all ingredients until·well mixed. Serve on tossed greens or Chef's Salad (page 324).

Poppy-Seed Dressing

Begin early
in day
or up to
1 wk ahead

1½ cups

1 cup salad oil
½ cup sugar
⅓ cup cider vinegar
*1 tablespoon poppy
seed*

*1 tablespoon grated
onion*
1 teaspoon salt
*1 teaspoon dry
mustard*

1. In covered blender container at medium speed, blend the salad oil, sugar, vinegar, poppy seed, grated onion, salt and mustard until thoroughly mixed. Dressing will be thick.
2. Store in tightly covered jar in refrigerator. Stir well before using. Serve dressing on tossed greens or fruit salad, or cottage cheese.

Green Goddess Dressing

Begin 10 mins
or day ahead

1 cup

¾ cup mayonnaise
*2 anchovy fillets,
minced*
*1 tablespoon chopped
parsley*
*1 tablespoon chopped
chives*

*1 tablespoon chopped
green onion*
*1 tablespoon tarragon
vinegar*
¾ teaspoon tarragon

1. In small bowl, stir together mayonnaise, anchovies, parsley, chives, green onion, vinegar and tarragon until well mixed.
2. Cover and refrigerate. Serve on tossed greens, chilled vegetables or cold seafood or poultry.

Deluxe Garlic French Dressing

Begin 15 mins
or up to
1 wk ahead

1¾ cups

1¼ cups olive or salad oil
*½ cup cider vinegar or
lemon juice*
3 tablespoons chili sauce
2¼ teaspoons salt
1 teaspoon sugar
1 teaspoon horseradish

*1 teaspoon prepared
mustard*
½ teaspoon paprika
¼ teaspoon pepper
*2 garlic cloves,
crushed*

Into small bowl or covered jar, measure all ingredients; stir with fork or cover and shake until well blended. Cover and refrigerate. Stir before serving.

Blender Mayonnaise

Begin 10 mins
ahead

1¼ cups

olive or salad oil
1 egg
*2 tablespoons cider
vinegar*

1 teaspoon sugar
1 teaspoon dry mustard
¾ teaspoon salt
⅛ teaspoon white pepper

1. In covered blender container at low speed, blend ¼ cup oil and remaining ingredients for 1 or 2 seconds until thoroughly mixed.
2. Remove center of cover (or cover) and, at low speed, very slowly pour ¾ cup oil in steady stream into mixture; continue blending until well mixed.

Russian Dressing

Begin 10 mins
ahead

1 cup

1 cup mayonnaise
*3 tablespoons chili
sauce*

*1 teaspoon minced onion
or chopped chives*

In small bowl, stir mayonnaise, chili sauce and minced onion until well mixed.

Cardamom Dressing

Begin 15 mins
ahead

1½ cups

*1 8-ounce package cream
cheese, softened*
¼ cup milk
3 tablespoons sugar

3 tablespoons lemon juice
*¾ teaspoon ground
cardamom*

In small bowl with mixer at low speed, beat all ingredients just until mixed. Increase speed to medium; beat until smooth.

Creamy Anise Sauce

Begin 15 mins
ahead or
early in day

1 cup

*1 8-ounce package cream
cheese*
4 to 5 tablespoons milk

1 teaspoon sugar
*½ teaspoon anise
seed*

In covered blender container with blender at high speed, blend all ingredients until smooth and of thick pouring consistency. If prepared early in day, sauce will thicken when refrigerated; stir in additional milk until of pouring consistency. Spoon over cut-up fruit as first course or dessert.

Sauce Vinaigrette

Begin 10 mins
ahead

1 cup

⅔ cup olive or salad oil
¼ cup red wine vinegar
2 teaspoons salt

½ teaspoon chervil
½ teaspoon tarragon
⅛ teaspoon pepper

In small bowl, mix thoroughly oil, vinegar, salt, chervil, tarragon and pepper.

Decorative ideas

GARNISHES

Cucumber slices: With sharp-tined fork, completely score peeled or unpeeled cucumber. Cut crosswise into thin slices.

Radish accordions: Cut radish crosswise into thin slices, almost all the way through. In bowl, on ice, refrigerate; drain.

Ruffled green onions: Cut off all but 3 inches green tops; shred tops down to white. Chill in ice water to curl; drain.

Melon clusters: Peel honeydew. Halve crosswise; slice into thin rings. Cut one edge of each ring.

Roll each ring into cone shape; secure with toothpick.

Place parsley in center of each cone. Make cluster with 3 cones; secure with toothpicks.

Pepper chains: Cut crosswise slices of red or green pepper. Cut one edge of each ring. Slip together to make chain.

Celery fans: Cut celery stalks into 3-inch pieces; slit each piece, almost to end, into narrow strips. Place on ice in bowl until ends curl; drain.

Cheese balls: With hands, shape softened cream cheese into balls. Roll in chopped nuts.

Vegetable cutouts: Cut peeled turnip, kohlrabi or rutabaga into thin crosswise slices. Cut shapes with canapé cutters. To make flower shapes, cut V-shaped notches around circle; cut off corners to form rounded petals. Cut thinly sliced carrots with smaller canapé cutters or knife.

CARROT FLOWER

With vegetable peeler, cut around thick end of carrot three times to make spiral strip. Cut cucumber slice; make decoration from edge to center.

Lap one cut edge over the other to make cone; secure with half-toothpick. Twist to ruffle carrot strip; place in cucumber to make "flower"

SHELLS FOR SALADS

These fruit and vegetable shells make attractive serving dishes for salads.

Apple cup: Cut top off apple. Scoop out inside, leaving 1/4-inch-thick shell. With pointed small knife, mark petal shapes; cut along marking. Brush cut surface with lemon juice.

Avocado half: Slice avocado lengthwise in half. Remove seed. Cut thin slice from underside so avocado stays even. Brush cut surface with lemon juice.

Grapefruit or orange zig-zag: Remove flesh from grapefruit or orange half. Cut zig-zag edge for special effect.

Tomato shells: Cut top off tomato and scoop out flesh. Or cut tomato into 8 wedges, being careful not to cut all the way through; spoon filling into center. Or, cut 3 slices from top almost to bottom; fill between slices.

Pepper flower: Cut top off small pepper. Remove seeds and white membrane. Cut petal shapes as for the apple cup (above).

Pineapple half: Cut pineapple lengthwise in half. Cut out core and flesh. Cut thin slice from underside so pineapple stays upright.

PASTA

The term pasta covers a rich variety of Italian-style noodles and dough shapes, of which macaroni and spaghetti are the best known. Spaghetti is available in various thicknesses and macaroni can be short or long, curved or straight. Noodles are usually flat. Apart from these familiar shapes, there are corkscrews, ribbons, stars, fans, rings and bow ties and shapes that are filled such as ravioli, cannelloni, shells, tortellini and mani-cotti. Pasta products provide hearty, delicious eating at relatively low cost. They combine readily with other foods ranging in flavor from sweet and mild to savory and highly seasoned.

All types are made from what is essentially the same flour and water dough, except noodles which also contain eggs. Although dried pasta is widely available in packaged form, many people are discovering how easy it is to make fresh pasta at home. With homemade pasta, the same dough can be rolled out into wide, flat sheets to make lasagna, or cut into pieces for cannelloni or ravioli. Our Homemade Pasta Dough (opposite), is made with eggs for a rich flavor and tender texture.

Pasta can be served plain or with a sauce. Different types of pasta are interchangeable in most recipes, but if the size or thickness is different, so will be the proportion of pasta to sauce or other ingredients. Dry pasta should be substituted by weight. Do not use a cup measure, as a cupful of one uncooked product may weigh more or less than a cupful of another kind. Different kinds of cooked pasta may be substituted cup for cup.

How much pasta you plan to serve per portion is very much a matter of personal preference. Eight ounces of spaghetti is usually sufficient for 4 to 6 servings, especially if the dish is to be served as a first course or accompaniment, but for a main dish you may well find that you need up to a pound of pasta for the same number of servings.

CHOOSING PASTA

The best pasta is made from durum (hard) wheat which has a high gluten content and makes an elastic dough which shapes easily. Look for the term "enriched" on the labels of pasta products. This tells you that they are

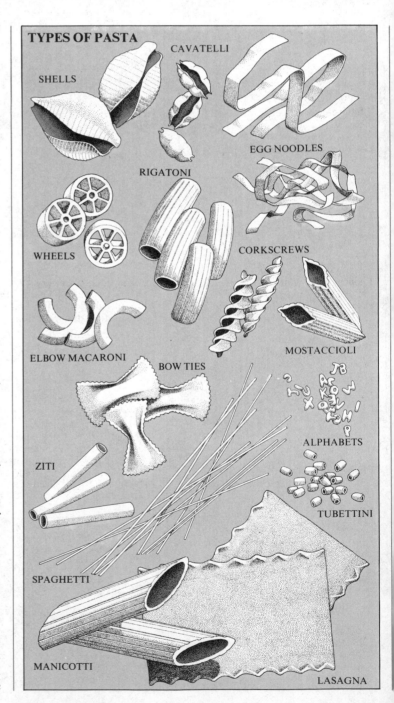

TYPES OF PASTA

SHELLS

CAVATELLI

EGG NOODLES

RIGATONI

WHEELS

CORKSCREWS

ELBOW MACARONI

BOW TIES

MOSTACCIOLI

ZITI

ALPHABETS

TUBETTINI

SPAGHETTI

MANICOTTI

LASAGNA

rich in B vitamins and iron. Other ingredients are sometimes added to change the color of the pasta: eggs will turn it golden, spinach puree makes it green.

COOKING PASTA

Use a large, deep saucepot containing at least 8 cups water and about 1 teaspoon salt for every 8 ounces pasta. Let the water come to a rolling boil, then add pasta gradually so that water does not stop boiling. Hold spaghetti vertically in the boiling water until you feel the ends begin to soften. Then press them down, coiling the strands around until they are totally submerged in the water. You can also break the spaghetti into pieces into the boiling water.

Cook pasta uncovered, stirring occasionally to separate, until tender but still firm (al dente). Be guided by the cooking times suggested on the package; small pasta may take only 2 minutes while large pasta may take 15 minutes. The average cooking time is 8 to 10 minutes. Cook for a shorter time if the pasta is to be used in a casserole and cooked further.

As soon as the pasta is done to your taste, drain it thoroughly in a colander or strainer. Do not rinse. Add a tablespoon of salad oil, softened butter or margarine to prevent pasta sticking.

Adding spaghetti to water: Gradually add spaghetti to boiling water, pushing it down as the ends soften. Be sure water keeps boiling.

SERVING PASTA

A dish of pasta dressed with sauce is at its best served as soon as it is cooked. Heap drained pasta on a warm serving plate and pour the sauce over the top. For individual servings you can use a large fork and spoon to divide the pasta between the plates, then spoon a portion of sauce over each one. Another way of serving pasta with sauce is to toss the two together thoroughly. As an alternative to a topping of sauce, toss cooked pasta with one of the following: tomato chunks or halved cherry tomatoes; drained canned or cooked mushrooms; shredded raw carrot; drained canned or cooked peas and diced canned pimento; whole or diced stuffed or ripe olives.

If you are planning to serve grated cheese with the dish, sprinkle a little over the top and pass around more in a separate bowl or let each person grate some himself.

STORING PASTA

Cover and store uncooked pasta and noodles at room temperature in a cool, dry place. Spaghetti and macaroni will keep up to a year, noodles should be used within about 6 months.

Toss leftover cooked pasta with a small amount of salad oil and refrigerate in a covered container. It can be reheated in a pot of boiling water, just long enough to heat through, and then drained.

PASTA MACHINES

Although all pasta is available in packaged form, many people make their own by hand or with the help of a pasta machine.

Noodle machines knead the dough, then roll it into sheets between two smooth steel rollers. Cutters at the other end of the machine then cut the dough into strips. Most machines have two sizes of cutter for broad or fine noodles. Other shapes such as ravioli or lasagna have to be handcut out of the rolled sheet of dough.

To make ravioli, you can either use an attachment to a noodle machine or use a specially built ravioli machine. Place a rolled sheet of dough, cut to width, in the hopper. The two edges of the dough are opened and the filling added. When the handle is turned, the sealed ravioli emerges.

Pasta makers work like meat grinders with different dies for shaping the various pastas. They can make spaghetti and macaroni as well as noodles; just press the dough into the hopper and crank.

Homemade Pasta Dough

1 pound dough for recipes, pages 330 to 335

2¼ to 2½ cups all-purpose flour	2 eggs
⅓ cup water (if using pasta machine, follow manufacturer's directions)	1 egg yolk
	1 tablespoon olive or salad oil
	1 teaspoon salt

1. In large bowl, combine 1 cup flour and remaining ingredients. With mixer at low speed, beat 2 minutes, occasionally scraping bowl.
2. With wooden spoon, stir in enough additional flour to make a soft dough.
3. Turn dough onto lightly floured surface, knead until smooth and elastic, about 10 minutes. Cover dough and let rest 30 minutes.

Kneading the dough: On a lightly floured board with floured hands, fold furthest edge of dough toward you; then push the dough away in a rolling motion with heels of hands. Give dough a quarter turn and repeat.

Noodles

Homemade Egg Noodles

Color index page 74

Begin 3½ hrs ahead

6 accompaniment servings

Homemade Pasta Dough (page 329)
3 quarts water
9 chicken- or beef-flavor bouillon cubes or envelopes, or 3 tablespoons beef-flavor stock base, or 1 tablespoon salt
1 tablespoon butter or margarine

1 Prepare Homemade Pasta Dough and knead until smooth and elastic, about 10 minutes. Wrap in waxed paper and let stand 30 minutes as directed; cut dough in half.

2 On floured surface with floured rolling pin, roll half of dough into 20″ by 14″ rectangle, then fold in half crosswise and in half again crosswise to form 5″ by 14″ rectangle.

3 Cut into ⅛-inch strips for narrow noodles, ¼-inch strips for medium noodles or ½-inch strips for wide noodles.

4 Open dough strips and place them in a single layer on clean cloth towels. Repeat with remaining dough. Let the strips dry at least 2 hours before cooking them.

5 *About 20 minutes before serving:* In 8-quart saucepot over high heat, heat to boiling water, bouillon and butter or margarine. Break noodles in smaller lengths, if desired, and add to saucepot; heat to boiling and cook 12 to 15 minutes until tender, then drain in colander. Serve the noodles with more butter or margarine, if you like.

Color index page 74

Begin 45 mins ahead

6 accompaniment servings

NOODLE RING: Preheat oven to 375°F. In 3-quart saucepan, cook *one 8-ounce package egg noodles* as label directs; drain well in colander or strainer. Return noodles to saucepan and toss with *¼ cup butter* or margarine and *¼ teaspoon salt;* pack into 5½-cup ring mold. Set mold in shallow roasting pan on oven rack; pour boiling water in pan to come halfway up side of mold. Bake in oven 20 minutes. To unmold ring, place warm platter over ring mold; invert both platter and mold and lift off mold. Serve noodle ring immediately.

Homemade Spinach Noodles

Color index page 74

Begin 3 hrs ahead

8 accompaniment servings

1 10-ounce bag fresh spinach
water
salt
2 eggs
2½ to 3 cups all-purpose flour
1 tablespoon salad oil
½ cup butter or margarine

1. Wash spinach; trim off tough ribs and stems. In 3-quart saucepan over medium heat, heat to boiling ¼ inch water and ½ teaspoon salt. Add spinach and return to boiling; cover; cook 3 minutes. Drain well; blot excess moisture with paper towels. Puree spinach with blender or food mill and place in large bowl. Or, into large bowl press through a coarse strainer with back of spoon or rubber spatula.

2. With fork, stir in eggs, 2½ cups flour and 1 teaspoon salt until mixture resembles coarse crumbs. Shape dough into ball. On well-floured surface, knead until smooth and not sticky, about 10 minutes, kneading in more flour if needed. Wrap in waxed paper; let stand 30 minutes; cut dough in 2 equal pieces.

3. On floured surface with rolling pin, roll half of dough into 20″ by 14″ rectangle. With knife, cut into 20″ by ½″ strips. Place in single layer on clean cloth towels. Repeat with remaining dough. Let noodles dry at least 2 hours.

4. *About 20 minutes before serving:* In 8-quart saucepot over high heat, heat to boiling 4 quarts water, 2 tablespoons salt and oil. Add noodles and return to boiling; cook 8 minutes or until tender but firm. In colander, drain noodles; return to pot. Add butter; toss until melted. Serve on heated platter.

Drying spinach: Drain cooked spinach; with paper towels, blot excess moisture from leaves.

Making spinach puree: Puree the spinach in a blender or a food mill.

Fettucini Alfredo

Color index page 74

Begin 30mins ahead

8 accompaniment servings

1 8-ounce package fettucini or medium egg noodles
¼ cup butter, melted
¼ cup grated Parmesan cheese
2 tablespoons half-and-half
¼ teaspoon salt
⅛ teaspoon pepper

1. Prepare noodles as label directs; drain noodles in colander and keep hot.

2. Meanwhile, in warm serving dish, combine butter, cheese, half-and-half, salt and pepper.

3. Toss hot noodles with cheese mixture to coat well. Serve immediately. Pass more grated cheese, if you like, to sprinkle over servings.

Spaghetti

Spaghetti and Meatballs

Color index page 32

Begin 2¼ hrs ahead

6 main-dish servings

Spaghetti Sauce (page 337)
1½ pounds lean ground beef
1 cup fresh bread crumbs
1 egg
½ teaspoon oregano leaves
⅛ teaspoon pepper
salt
salad oil
4 quarts water
1 16-ounce package spaghetti
grated Parmesan cheese

1 Prepare Spaghetti Sauce. Prepare meatballs: In large bowl, combine ground beef, crumbs, egg, oregano, pepper and 2 teaspoons salt.

2 With hands, shape ground-beef mixture into 1-inch balls.

3 In 12-inch skillet over medium-high heat, in 2 tablespoons oil, cook meatballs until browned. Spoon off drippings from the skillet.

4 Add Spaghetti Sauce; heat to boiling. Reduce heat to low; cover skillet and simmer sauce and meatballs for 10 minutes.

5 Meanwhile, in 8-quart saucepot, heat to boiling water and 2 teaspoons salt. Add spaghetti; cook until spaghetti is tender but firm (al dente).

6 Drain spaghetti in colander. Toss with 1 tablespoon oil to prevent spaghetti sticking.

7 Arrange on warm plate. Serve meatballs and sauce over spaghetti. Pass grated cheese.

Bacon and Eggs Spaghetti

Color index page 32

Begin 30 mins ahead

4 main-dish servings

1 16-ounce package spaghetti
8 bacon slices, cut up
2 medium onions, coarsely chopped
4 eggs, slightly beaten
½ 8-ounce package pasteurized process cheese spread, cubed

1. Prepare spaghetti as label directs; drain well in colander and keep warm.
2. Meanwhile, in 12-inch skillet over medium heat, cook bacon until crisp; with slotted spoon, remove to paper towels; set aside.
3. In drippings in skillet, cook onions until tender, about 5 minutes. Add spaghetti and bacon to onions; toss until well mixed; stir in eggs and cheese; heat until cheese is melted.

Spaghetti with Four Cheeses

Color index page 32

Begin 45 mins ahead

4 main-dish servings

1 8-ounce package spaghetti
¼ cup butter or margarine
1 tablespoon all-purpose flour
1½ cups half-and-half or light cream
1 cup shredded mozzarella or scamorze cheese
1 cup shredded fontina cheese
½ cup grated provolone cheese
¼ cup grated Parmesan or Romano cheese
¼ teaspoon salt
¼ teaspoon cracked pepper
2 tablespoons chopped parsley

1. Prepare spaghetti as label directs; drain well in colander and keep hot.
2. Meanwhile, in 3-quart saucepan over medium heat, in hot butter, stir in flour until blended; cook 30 seconds. Gradually stir in half-and-half; cook, stirring, until mixture boils and slightly thickens. Stir in mozzarella, fontina, provolone and Parmesan cheeses, salt and pepper until smooth and cheeses are melted.
3. Pour hot spaghetti into warm, large bowl. Pour cheese sauce over spaghetti; sprinkle with parsley. Toss until spaghetti is well coated.

Spaghetti with Ham and Peas

Color index page 32

Begin 45 mins ahead

4 main-dish servings

1 8-ounce package spaghetti
¼ cup butter or margarine
1 tablespoon all-purpose flour
¼ teaspoon salt
¼ teaspoon cracked pepper
1½ cups half-and-half
1 10-ounce package frozen peas, thawed
1 cup shredded fontina cheese
1 cup shredded mozzarella cheese
1 4-ounce package sliced cooked ham, cut into ⅛-inch strips

1. Prepare spaghetti as label directs. Drain spaghetti in colander and keep warm.
2. Meanwhile, in 3-quart saucepan over low heat, melt butter; stir in flour, salt and pepper; gradually stir in half-and-half; cook, stirring, until thickened. Add peas and cheeses, stirring until cheeses are melted; stir in ham; heat.
3. In large bowl, toss spaghetti and cheese mixture until spaghetti is well coated and serve immediately.

Macaroni and cavatelli

The short curved elbow macaroni is the most popular. Other types of macaroni or its special shapes such as bow ties, corkscrews and rigatoni can be substituted for elbow macaroni in recipes. All are delicious with a sauce or piping hot with a homemade cheese topping.

Baked Macaroni and Cheese

Color index page 32

Begin 45 mins ahead

6 accompaniment or 4 main-dish servings

2 quarts water
salt
1 8-ounce package elbow macaroni
4 tablespoons butter or margarine
3/4 cup fresh bread crumbs

1 small onion, minced
1 tablespoon all-purpose flour
1/4 teaspoon dry mustard
1/8 teaspoon pepper
1 1/2 cups milk
2 cups shredded Cheddar cheese

1 In 3-quart saucepan, heat to boiling water and 1 teaspoon salt. Add macaroni; cook until tender but firm; drain. Grease 2-quart baking dish. Preheat oven to 350°F.

2 In 1-quart saucepan over medium heat, melt 2 tablespoons butter or margarine; add bread crumbs and toss to coat; set aside.

3 Meanwhile, in 2-quart saucepan over medium heat, melt remaining butter; add onion and cook until tender, about 5 minutes.

4 Blend in flour, mustard, pepper and 1 teaspoon salt. Stir in milk; cook, stirring, until thickened. Remove from heat; stir in cheese.

5 Place macaroni in baking dish. Pour cheese mixture over macaroni.

6 Sprinkle crumb mixture over top. Bake in oven 20 minutes.

Skillet Macaroni and Cheese

Color index page 32

Begin 45 mins ahead

4 main-dish servings

1/2 cup butter or margarine
2 cups elbow macaroni
1/4 cup minced onion
2 tablespoons minced green pepper
1 teaspoon salt

1/4 teaspoon dry mustard
2 cups water
2 cups shredded Cheddar cheese
10 medium pimento-stuffed olives, sliced

1. In 10-inch skillet over medium heat, in hot butter, cook uncooked macaroni and next 4 ingredients for 5 minutes, stirring frequently.
2. Stir in water; heat to boiling. Reduce heat to low; cover; simmer 10 to 15 minutes until macaroni is tender, stirring occasionally.
3. Remove from heat; stir in cheese and olives until cheese is melted.

Cavatelli with Meat Sauce

Color index page 32

Begin 4 hrs ahead

4 main-dish servings

Meat Sauce (page 337)
Homemade Pasta Dough (page 329)
4 quarts water
2 tablespoons salt
1 tablespoon salad oil
grated Parmesan or Romano cheese for topping

1 Prepare Meat Sauce and dough; cut dough into 8 pieces. Roll each piece into 15-inch rope.

2 Cut ropes into 1/2-inch pieces. Press each piece in center; draw finger toward you to flatten slightly and curl ends.

3 Place cavatelli in single layer on floured, clean cloth towels. Let dry 2 hours before cooking.

4 In 8-quart saucepot, heat to boiling water, salt and oil; add cavatelli; cook until tender but firm, about 10 minutes.

5 Drain well and arrange on heated platter. Spoon heated sauce over cavatelli; sprinkle with grated Parmesan cheese.

Stuffed pasta

Ravioli, tortellini, manicotti, shells and cannelloni are popular shapes that are stuffed with fillings. They can all be stuffed with meat, cheese or vegetable fillings. Ravioli and tortellini are usually boiled, while cannelloni, shells and manicotti are baked.

Ravioli

Color index page 32

Begin 3 hrs ahead

4 main-dish servings

Cheese, Meat or Spinach Filling (below right)
Homemade Pasta Dough (page 329)
Marinara Sauce (page 337)

6 quarts water
2 tablespoons salt
1 tablespoon salad oil
¼ cup grated Parmesan cheese

1 Prepare filling and dough; cut dough into 6 pieces. On floured surface with floured rolling pin, roll 1 piece into 18″ by 4″ rectangle; cut nine 4″ by 2″ pieces.

2 Drop scant teaspoonful of filling on 2-inch side of each piece of dough to within ½ inch of edges. Brush dough edges lightly with water.

3 Fold dough over filling, bringing edges together. With 4-tined fork dipped in flour, press edges together.

4 Place ravioli in one layer on floured, clean cloth or paper towels. Repeat, making 54 ravioli in all. Let dry 30 minutes. Make Marinara Sauce.

5 In 8-quart saucepot, heat water, salt and oil to boiling. Add ravioli; stirring occasionally, heat to boiling. Reduce heat; cook about 5 minutes till tender.

6 Drain well in colander. Arrange on warm platter. Reheat Marinara Sauce and spoon evenly over ravioli; sprinkle with grated cheese.

Jumbo Ravioli

Color index page 32

Begin 2½ hrs ahead

4 main-dish servings

Cheese, Meat or Spinach Filling (below)
Homemade Pasta Dough (page 329)
Marinara Sauce (page 337)

4 quarts water
2 tablespoons salt
1 tablespoon salad oil
¼ cup grated Parmesan cheese

1. Prepare Cheese, Meat or Spinach Filling
2. Prepare dough; cut into 4 pieces. On well-floured surface with floured rolling pin, roll 1 piece into 15″ by 6″ rectangle; with sharp knife, cut rectangle crosswise into five 6″ by 3″ pieces.
3. Spread rounded tablespoonfuls of filling on 3-inch side of each piece of pasta to within ¼ inch of edges. Fold dough over filling, bringing ends together; with fork dipped in flour, firmly press edges together. Place ravioli in single layer on floured, clean cloth towels. Repeat with remaining pasta and filling making 20 ravioli in all. Let dry 30 minutes. Meanwhile, make Marinara Sauce.
4. In 8-quart saucepot over high heat, heat to boiling water, salt and oil. Cook ravioli a few at a time, 10 minutes or until tender but firm; drain. Arrange on heated platter.
5. Reheat Marinara Sauce and spoon evenly over ravioli; sprinkle with Parmesan Cheese.

Forming the shape: Fold dough over filling, bringing ends together.

Sealing edges: With fork dipped in flour, press edges together to seal.

FILLINGS FOR RAVIOLI

CHEESE FILLING: In small bowl, combine *8 ounces ricotta cheese* (1 cup), *3 tablespoons minced parsley, 2 tablespoons grated Parmesan cheese, 1 egg white* and *¼ teaspoon salt.* Stir ingredients until they are well mixed.

MEAT FILLING: In 10-inch skillet over medium-high heat, cook *½ pound ground beef, ⅓ cup minced onion, 1 garlic clove,* minced, until meat is browned; remove from heat; spoon off juices. Stir in *1 egg, ¼ cup minced parsley, 2 tablespoons grated Parmesan cheese* and *½ teaspoon salt.* Stir ingredients until well mixed.

SPINACH FILLING: In small bowl, combine *one 10-ounce package frozen chopped spinach,* thawed and well drained, *⅓ cup grated Parmesan cheese, 2 egg yolks, 1 tablespoon butter,* softened, *¼ teaspoon salt, ⅛ teaspoon pepper, ⅛ teaspoon ground nutmeg.* Stir ingredients until well mixed.

Stuffed pasta

Manicotti

Spaghetti Sauce
(page 337)

Pancakes:
*1 cup all-purpose
   flour
4 eggs
1 tablespoon salad oil
1 teaspoon salt
1 cup water*

Manicotti Sauce:
*2 tablespoons butter
1 pound ground veal or
   ground uncooked
   turkey*

Filling:
*2 cups ricotta or creamed
   cottage cheese
2 tablespoons grated
   Parmesan cheese
¾ teaspoon salt
¼ teaspoon pepper
2 eggs
1 8-ounce package
   mozzarella cheese,
   coarsely shredded*

Color index page 33

Begin 3 hrs ahead

8 main-dish servings

1 Prepare Spaghetti Sauce. For pancakes: In small bowl with mixer at low speed, blend pancake ingredients; at medium speed, beat 1 minute.

2 Lightly brush 7-inch skillet with salad oil. Over medium-high heat, heat skillet.

3 Pour in about 2 tablespoons pancake batter; tip pan to coat bottom evenly with batter.

4 Cook until top is set and dry and underside lightly browned, about 30 seconds. Lift pancake onto waxed paper. Repeat.

5 Prepare sauce: In 10-inch skillet over medium-high heat, in hot butter, cook ground veal until well browned then add Spaghetti Sauce.

6 Heat sauce through then spoon ⅓ of hot sauce evenly into a 15½" by 10½" roasting pan.

7 Prepare filling: In medium bowl, mix ricotta cheese, Parmesan cheese, salt, pepper and eggs until well blended. Preheat oven to 375°F.

8 Spoon heaping tablespoon of cheese mixture down center of each pancake; top with some shredded mozzarella.

9 Fold pancake edges over cheese. Arrange filled pancakes, seam side down, in roasting pan.

10 Spoon remaining sauce over pancakes. Bake 30 minutes or until sauce is hot and bubbly.

Color index page 33

Begin 2½ hrs ahead

10 main-dish servings

Stuffed Shells

Spaghetti Sauce
(page 337)
*1 16-ounce package
   jumbo shell macaroni
   (about 40)
4 cups ricotta or cottage
   cheese
1 8-ounce package
   mozzarella cheese,
   shredded*

*2 eggs
⅓ cup dried bread
   crumbs
¼ cup chopped
   parsley
1 teaspoon salt
¼ teaspoon pepper
½ cup grated Parmesan
   cheese*

1. Prepare Spaghetti Sauce.

2. Prepare shells as label directs; drain well in colander. Preheat oven to 350°F. In large bowl, combine ricotta and next 6 ingredients. Stuff rounded tablespoonful of cheese mixture into each shell.

3. Spoon ¾ cup sauce into each of two 13" by 9" baking dishes. Place shells, seam side down, over sauce in one layer. Spoon over remaining sauce; sprinkle with Parmesan. Bake 30 minutes.

Color index page 33

Begin 2½ hrs ahead

8 main-dish servings

Hearty Manicotti

*water
1 pound Italian sweet
   sausage links
1 pound ground beef
1 medium onion, chopped
2 16-ounce cans tomato
   puree
1 6-ounce can tomato
   paste
1 teaspoon sugar
½ teaspoon pepper*

*basil
salt
1 8-ounce package
   manicotti shells (16)
4 cups ricotta cheese
1 8-ounce package
   mozzarella cheese,
   diced
2 tablespoons chopped
   parsley
grated Parmesan cheese*

1. In covered 5-quart Dutch oven over medium heat, in ¼ cup water, cook sausage links 5 minutes. Uncover; brown well; drain on paper towels.

2. Spoon fat from Dutch oven; over medium heat, brown ground beef and onion well; stir in tomato puree, tomato paste, sugar, pepper, 1 teaspoon basil, 1 teaspoon salt and 1 cup water; simmer, covered, 45 minutes.

3. Cut sausage into bite-size pieces; add to mixture; cook 15 minutes, stirring occasionally. Meanwhile, cook manicotti as label directs; drain in colander. Preheat oven to 375°F.

4. In large bowl, combine ricotta and mozzarella cheeses, parsley, ¾ teaspoon basil and ½ teaspoon salt; stuff into shells.

5. Spoon half of meat sauce into one 13" by 9" baking dish. Place half of shells over sauce in one layer. Spoon remaining sauce except ¾ cup over shells; top with remaining shells in one layer. Spoon reserved meat sauce over top. Sprinkle with Parmesan. Bake 30 minutes.

FILLING PASTA SHELLS

A pastry bag without a tip is a convenient tool for filling pasta shapes. Use it to stuff manicotti and jumbo shells if you are cooking in large quantities.

Color index page 23
Begin 3 hrs ahead
10 first-course or 5 main-dish servings

Tortellini in Cream Sauce

salad oil	1/8 teaspoon pepper
2 small whole chicken	1/8 teaspoon ground
breasts, boned, skinned	nutmeg
and diced	Homemade Pasta Dough
1/4 pound sliced	(page 329)
prosciutto, mortadella	5 quarts water
or cooked ham, cut up	1/2 cup butter
(about 1 1/2 cups)	1 cup heavy cream
salt	1 cup grated Parmesan
1 egg	cheese

1. In 10-inch skillet over medium-high heat, in 1 tablespoon hot oil, cook chicken until tender, stirring, about 5 minutes. Remove from heat.

2. In covered blender container at medium speed, blend chicken and prosciutto until finely ground. Add salt to taste. Add egg, pepper and nutmeg; blend until paste forms; set aside.

3. Prepare dough; cut into 3 pieces. On floured surface with rolling pin, roll 1 piece (keep others covered) into 26″ by 9″ rectangle. With 2-inch round cookie cutter, cut out as many circles as you can. Remove trimmings; reserve.

4. Place scant 1/2 teaspoon chicken filling in center of each circle. Brush edges with water; fold in half with edges not quite meeting; press to seal. Place straight edge of half-circle at right angle to a finger; bend around finger until two ends meet to form fan shape; press to seal ends.

5. Place in single layer on floured cloth or paper towels. Repeat with remaining pasta and filling; reroll all trimmings and cut as above, making about 125 tortellini. Let dry 30 minutes.

6. In 8-quart saucepot over high heat, heat water, 2 tablespoons salt and 1 tablespoon oil to boiling. Add tortellini. Stir to prevent sticking; heat to boiling. Reduce heat to medium-low; cook 5 minutes until tender but firm. Drain.

7. In same saucepot over low heat, melt butter. Add tortellini and cream; heat to boiling, stirring gently until cream thickens slightly. Sprinkle with cheese. Stir to mix well; spoon onto heated platter.

Cannelloni

Homemade Pasta Dough	1 egg, beaten
(page 329)	1 tablespoon dry sherry
2 tablespoons butter or	1/4 teaspoon ground
margarine	ginger
1 tablespoon chopped	salt
green onion	salad oil
1 10-ounce package	5 quarts water
frozen chopped	Parmesan-Cheese Sauce
spinach, cooked and	(page 463)
drained	chopped parsley for
1 cup finely chopped	garnish
cooked chicken	
1/2 cup finely chopped	
cooked ham	
1/2 cup grated Parmesan	
cheese	

Color index page 33
Begin 2 hrs ahead
8 main-dish servings

1 Prepare dough; cut into 3 pieces. On well-floured surface with floured rolling pin, roll 1 piece into 16″ by 8″ rectangle.

2 With knife, cut the dough rectangle into eight 4-inch squares.

3 Place squares on floured, clean cloth towel. Repeat with remaining dough, making 24 squares in all. Cover; let stand 30 minutes.

4 In 2-quart saucepan over medium heat, in butter, cook onion until tender. Stir in next 7 ingredients and 1/4 teaspoon salt; heat; set aside.

5 Preheat oven to 350°F. Grease 13″ by 9″ metal pan or broiler-safe baking dish.

6 In 8-quart saucepot, heat to boiling water, 2 tablespoons salt and 1 tablespoon oil. Cook squares a few at a time, 5 minutes.

7 Remove pasta with slotted spoon; drain in colander and assemble while warm.

8 To assemble cannelloni: With spoon, spread rounded tablespoon of meat mixture across center of warm pasta square.

9 Roll jelly-roll fashion. Place, seam side down, in pan. Repeat with remaining pasta squares and meat mixture.

10 Prepare cheese sauce; pour over cannelloni; sprinkle with parsley. Bake in oven 20 minutes then broil 5 minutes.

Lasagna

Lasagna

Color index
page 33

Begin 2½ hrs
ahead

8 main-dish
servings

1 pound ground beef
1 small onion, diced
1 28-ounce can tomatoes
1 12-ounce can tomato
   paste
1 tablespoon sugar
1½ teaspoons salt
½ teaspoon oregano
   leaves
½ teaspoon thyme
   leaves
½ teaspoon crushed red
   pepper

¼ teaspoon garlic
   salt
1 bay leaf
⅔ 16-ounce package
   lasagna noodles (about
   14 noodles)
2 eggs
1 15-ounce container
   ricotta cheese
1 16-ounce package
   mozzarella cheese,
   diced

1 In 5-quart Dutch oven over high heat, cook ground beef and onion until pan juices evaporate and beef is browned. Add tomatoes, their liquid, and next 8 ingredients.

2 Heat mixture to boiling, stirring to break up tomatoes. Reduce heat to low; cover and simmer 30 minutes, stirring mixture occasionally.

3 Discard bay leaf. Tilt pan and spoon off any fat which accumulates on top of sauce. Cook lasagna noodles as label directs; drain well in colander.

4 In 13″ by 9″ baking dish, arrange half of drained lasagna noodles, overlapping to fit. Preheat oven to 375°F.

5 In a small bowl with spoon, combine eggs and ricotta cheese and spoon one-half of this mixture over lasagna noodles in baking dish.

6 Sprinkle with one-half mozzarella; top with one-half sauce. Repeat layers. Bake in oven 45 minutes. Remove from oven and let stand 10 minutes before serving.

Veal Lasagna

Color index
page 33

Begin 2½ hrs
ahead

10 main-dish
servings

1 3-pound rolled veal
   shoulder roast
   boneless
salad oil
½ 16-ounce package
   lasagna noodles
   (12 noodles)
⅓ cup butter or
   margarine
2 large onions, minced
⅓ cup all-purpose flour
4 cups milk

⅓ cup medium sherry
1 tablespoon salt
¼ teaspoon white
   pepper
¼ teaspoon ground
   nutmeg
1 3-ounce can grated
   Parmesan and
   Romano cheese
chopped parsley for
   garnish

1. Cut veal into ½-inch cubes, discarding fat. In 12-inch skillet over medium-high heat, in 2 tablespoons hot oil, cook veal until lightly browned, stirring occasionally. Reduce heat to low; cover; simmer 30 minutes or until tender, stirring occasionally.

2. Meanwhile, cook lasagna noodles as label directs, adding 1 tablespoon salad oil to cooking water; drain well in colander.

3. In heavy 3-quart saucepan over medium heat, in hot butter, cook onions until tender, about 5 minutes, stirring occasionally. Stir in flour until blended. Stir in milk; cook, stirring, until thickened. Drain meat; add to mixture; stir in sherry, salt, pepper and nutmeg.

4. Arrange 4 noodles lengthwise in baking dish; spoon ½ of meat mixture evenly over noodles. Repeat layers, ending with noodles Cover dish tightly with foil.

5. Preheat oven to 350°F. Bake lasagna, covered, 30 minutes. Remove cover; sprinkle with grated cheese. Continue baking 15 minutes or until lasagna mixture is lightly browned. Sprinkle with chopped parsley. Let stand 10 minutes before serving.

Eggplant Lasagna

Color index
page 33

Begin 2¼ hrs
ahead

8 main-dish
servings

Spaghetti Sauce
   (page 337)
½ 16-ounce package
   lasagna noodles
   (12 noodles)
1 cup dried bread
   crumbs
⅛ teaspoon pepper
salt
2 eggs

2 tablespoons water
1 medium eggplant, cut in
   ½-inch slices
salad oil
1 16-ounce package
   mozzarella cheese,
   thinly sliced
¼ cup grated Parmesan
   cheese

1. Prepare Spaghetti Sauce. Cook lasagna noodles as label directs; drain.

2. On waxed paper, combine crumbs, pepper and ½ teaspoon salt. In small dish with fork, beat eggs with water. Dip eggplant into egg mixture, then crumb mixture.

3. In 12-inch skillet over medium heat, in 2 tablespoons hot salad oil, cook eggplant slices, a few at a time, until tender, adding more oil when necessary. Drain on paper towels. Preheat oven to 350°F.

4. In 13″ by 9″ baking pan layer half of noodles, eggplant slices, mozzarella and Spaghetti Sauce; repeat. Sprinkle with Parmesan cheese. Bake 30 minutes or until hot.

Sauces for pasta

Spaghetti Sauce

Begin 1 hr ahead
4 cups

2 tablespoons salad oil
1 medium onion, diced
1 medium garlic clove, minced
2 15-ounce cans tomato sauce
1 12-ounce can tomato paste
2 teaspoons brown sugar
2 tablespoons chopped parsley
1 teaspoon oregano leaves
1 teaspoon salt
⅛ teaspoon cracked pepper
1 bay leaf

1. In 3-quart saucepan over medium heat, in hot salad oil, cook onion and garlic until tender, stirring frequently, about 10 minutes.
2. Add tomato sauce and remaining ingredients; over high heat, heat to boiling.
3. Reduce heat to medium-low; partially cover and cook 30 minutes. Discard bay leaf.

Meat Sauce

Begin 1¼ hrs ahead
4 cups

2 tablespoons olive or salad oil
1 pound ground beef
1 medium onion, chopped
1 garlic clove, minced
1 16-ounce can tomatoes
1 12-ounce can tomato paste
4 teaspoons sugar
2 teaspoons oregano leaves
1¾ teaspoons salt
⅛ teaspoon cayenne pepper
1 bay leaf, crumbled

1. In 5-quart Dutch oven over medium heat, in hot olive oil, cook ground beef, onion and garlic until meat is well browned; spoon off excess fat.
2. Stir in tomatoes, their liquid, and remaining ingredients. Reduce heat to low; partially cover and simmer tomato meat mixture 35 minutes or until very thick, stirring occasionally.

White Clam Sauce

Begin 20 mins ahead
3 cups

3 8-ounce cans minced clams
¼ cup olive or salad oil
1 garlic clove, minced
¾ cup chopped parsley
2 tablespoons white wine (optional)
1 teaspoon basil
½ teaspoon salt

1. Drain juice from clams, reserving juice.
2. In 2-quart saucepan over medium heat, in hot oil, cook garlic until tender. Stir in reserved clam juice and remaining ingredients except clams; cook 10 minutes, stirring occasionally.
3. Stir in drained clams; cook sauce just until clams are heated through.

Anchovy Sauce

Begin about 20 mins ahead
½ cup

¼ cup olive or salad oil
1 small garlic clove, halved
1 2-ounce can anchovy fillets, drained and chopped
2 tablespoons minced parsley
2 tablespoons grated Parmesan cheese
1 teaspoon lemon juice

1. In 1-quart saucepan over medium-high heat, in hot olive oil, brown garlic. Remove from heat; discard garlic.
2. Stir in remaining ingredients until well mixed.

Marinara Sauce

Begin 30 mins ahead
3 cups

2 tablespoons olive or salad oil
2 garlic cloves, minced
1 small onion, chopped
1 16-ounce can tomatoes
1 6-ounce can tomato paste
1 tablespoon sugar
2 teaspoons basil
1½ teaspoons salt

1. In 2-quart saucepan over medium heat, in oil, cook garlic and onion until tender, 5 minutes.
2. Stir in tomatoes, their liquid, and remaining ingredients. Reduce heat to low; cover; cook 20 minutes or until thickened, stirring occasionally.

Shrimp Marinara Sauce

Begin 30 mins ahead
4 cups

1 tablespoon olive oil
1 garlic clove, minced
1 15-ounce can tomato sauce
1 6-ounce can tomato paste
2 tablespoons chopped parsley
1 tablespoon sugar
¾ teaspoon salt
½ teaspoon oregano leaves
¼ teaspoon pepper
1 pound frozen shelled and deveined shrimp

1. In 10-inch skillet over medium-high heat, in hot olive oil, lightly brown garlic.
2. Add tomato sauce and next 6 ingredients; heat to boiling. Reduce heat to low; cover and simmer sauce mixture over low heat 10 minutes.
3. Add frozen shrimp and cook until shrimp are tender, about 8 minutes, stirring occasionally.

Spinach Sauce

Begin 15 mins ahead
2½ cups

¼ cup butter or margarine
1 10-ounce package frozen chopped spinach
1 teaspoon salt
1 cup ricotta cheese
¼ cup grated Parmesan cheese
¼ cup milk
⅛ teaspoon ground nutmeg

1. In 2-quart saucepan over medium heat, in hot butter, cook spinach and salt 10 minutes.
2. Reduce heat to low; add remaining ingredients; mix sauce well; cook sauce until just heated through (do not boil).

Walnut Sauce

Begin 15 mins ahead
1⅓ cups

¼ cup butter or margarine
1 cup California walnuts, coarsely chopped
½ cup milk
2 tablespoons minced parsley
1 teaspoon salt

In 9-inch skillet over medium heat, in hot butter, lightly brown walnuts, about 5 minutes, stirring occasionally. Stir in remaining ingredients; heat.

Pesto

Begin 5 mins ahead
½ cup

⅓ cup olive or salad oil
¼ cup grated Parmesan cheese
¼ cup chopped parsley
1 small garlic clove, quartered
2 tablespoons basil or ½ cup fresh basil
1 teaspoon salt
¼ teaspoon ground nutmeg

In blender container, place all ingredients; cover and blend at medium speed until well mixed.

RICE

The delicate flavor of rice combines readily with foods ranging in taste from sweet and mild to highly seasoned. Cook rice, tightly covered, in a measured amount of liquid, so all liquid is absorbed. Check for doneness by tasting a grain: it should be tender throughout.

For different flavors, prepare your favorite kind of rice, but vary the liquid. Substitute chicken or beef broth for all of the water; or use half water and half tomato juice or cocktail vegetable juice; or substitute ½ cup orange or apple juice for ½ cup water.

Hot Fluffy Rice

Color index page 73

Begin 20 mins ahead

3 cups or 4 servings

2 cups water
1 cup regular long- or medium-grain rice
1 teaspoon salt

1 tablespoon butter or margarine (optional)

1 In 3-quart saucepan with tight-fitting lid, over high heat, heat water, rice, salt and butter or margarine, if you wish, to boiling.

2 Reduce heat until mixture just simmers; with fork, stir once or twice.

3 Cover pan and simmer without stirring or lifting lid, about 14 minutes or until rice is tender and all liquid is absorbed. Check tenderness by tasting a grain.

4 For drier rice, remove pan from heat; fluff with fork; cover and let stand 5 to 10 minutes. Or, spoon cooked rice into warm serving dish and fluff with fork before serving.

BROWN RICE: *About 50 minutes ahead:* Prepare as above but use *2½ cups water, 1 cup brown rice* and *1 teaspoon salt* and simmer mixture about 45 minutes. Or, prepare brown rice as the label directs. (Makes 4 cups or 5 or 6 servings.)

Oven Dinner Rice

Color index page 73

Begin 35 mins ahead

3 cups or 4 servings

2 cups boiling water
1 cup regular long-grain rice or ³/₄ cup parboiled rice

2 tablespoons butter or margarine
1 teaspoon salt

1. Preheat oven to 350°F. Grease a 1½-quart casserole. In casserole, combine boiling water, rice, butter or margarine and salt.
2. Cover and bake mixture 30 minutes or until rice is tender and all liquid is absorbed. Fluff rice with fork just before serving.

Red-and-Green Rice

Color index page 73

Begin 30 mins ahead

6 servings

4 cups hot cooked rice
¼ cup chopped green pepper
¼ cup sliced green onions
1 canned pimento, chopped

2 tablespoons butter or margarine
½ teaspoon seasoned salt

In warm serving bowl, toss hot cooked rice with all ingredients until butter or margarine is melted. Serve rice immediately.

Herbed Orange Rice

Color index page 74

Begin 45 mins ahead

6 servings

¼ cup butter or margarine
²/₃ cup chopped celery (with leaves)
2 tablespoons minced onion
1½ cups water
1 tablespoon grated orange peel

1 cup orange juice
1 teaspoon salt
⅛ teaspoon thyme leaves
1 cup regular long-grain rice or ³/₄ cup parboiled rice

1. In 2-quart saucepan over medium heat, in hot butter or margarine, cook celery and onion until tender, about 5 minutes.
2. Add water, grated orange peel, orange juice, salt and thyme leaves. Heat to boiling; stir in rice. Reduce heat to low; cover and simmer mixture 15 to 20 minutes until rice is tender and all liquid is absorbed. Fluff lightly with fork before serving.

Accompaniment dishes

Rice Pilaf with Peas

Color index
page 73

Begin 40 mins
ahead

12 servings

8 bacon slices, diced
1 medium onion, finely
*   chopped*
2 cups regular long-grain
*   rice*
2 10-ounce packages
*   frozen green peas*
2 cups water
1 13 ³/₄-ounce can
*   chicken broth*
2 teaspoons salt
¹/₄ teaspoon pepper

1 In 12-inch skillet over medium heat, cook bacon until crisp. With slotted spoon, remove bacon to paper towels; set aside.

2 Pour off all but ¹/₄ cup bacon drippings from the skillet.

3 Add chopped onion to skillet and cook until tender, about 5 minutes, stirring occasionally.

4 Stir rice, frozen peas, water, chicken broth, salt and pepper into mixture; heat to boiling. Reduce heat to low; cover and simmer about 20 minutes until rice is tender.

5 To serve, toss rice mixture together with the reserved bacon until well mixed. Transfer mixture to warm serving dish and serve immediately.

Curried Rice and Onions

Color index
page 74

Begin 35 mins
ahead

4 servings

2 tablespoons butter or
*   margarine*
2 small onions, sliced
*   ¹/₄ inch thick*
¹/₂ teaspoon curry
*   powder*

¹/₂ teaspoon salt
¹/₈ teaspoon ground
*   nutmeg*
2 cups hot cooked rice
¹/₂ cup half-and-half

1. In 2-quart saucepan over low heat, in hot butter or margarine, cook onions, curry, salt and nutmeg, stirring mixture often, until onions are tender, about 7 minutes.
2. Stir in cooked rice and half-and-half; then heat the curried mixture through to serve.

Risotto alla Milanese

Color index
page 74

Begin 45 mins
ahead

6 servings

¹/₄ cup butter
¹/₃ cup minced onion
1 ¹/₂ cups regular long-
*   grain rice*
2 13 ³/₄-ounce cans
*   chicken broth, heated*

³/₄ teaspoon salt
¹/₈ teaspoon saffron
¹/₈ teaspoon pepper
¹/₃ cup grated Parmesan
*   cheese*

1 In 3-quart ovensafe saucepan over medium heat, in hot butter, cook onion until golden.

2 Add rice, stirring until butter is absorbed. Preheat oven to 350°F.

3 Stir in broth, salt, saffron and pepper and heat, stirring, to boiling. Bake 30 minutes or until liquid is absorbed and rice is tender.

4 Stir in Parmesan cheese until well blended. Serve in heated dish as first course or as an accompaniment to veal.

TYPES OF RICE

REGULAR WHITE RICE: Milled to remove outer coating of bran and sometimes polished; available as long-, medium- or short-grain. Long-grain rice is best in curries, stews, salads and main dishes. Medium- and short-grain rice is preferred for puddings and rice rings. May be nutrient-enriched; check label. One cup uncooked regular rice yields about 3 cups cooked.

PRECOOKED RICE: Fully cooked and dehydrated, milled, long-grain rice with short preparation time. Follow label directions for preparation and yield.

PARBOILED RICE: A long-grain rice subjected to a special process before milling so it retains vitamins and minerals. It requires slightly longer cooking than regular rice. One cup uncooked parboiled rice yields about 4 cups cooked.

BROWN RICE: Unmilled so grains retain most of their food value. Brown absorbs more liquid and takes longer to cook than white rice. Nutty in flavor. One cup uncooked brown rice yields about 4 cups cooked.

WILD RICE: Not a true rice but served as an accompaniment like rice. Cook as label directs. One cup uncooked wild rice yields about 3 cups cooked.

Accompaniment dishes

Rice-and-Mushroom Casserole

Color index
page 73

Begin 1 hr
ahead

4 servings

*½ cup regular long-grain
   rice*
*4 tablespoons butter or
   margarine*
*¼ pound mushrooms,
   sliced*
½ cup chopped onion
½ cup chopped celery
1¼ cups water
*1 beef-flavor bouillon
   cube or envelope*
½ teaspoon salt
⅛ teaspoon thyme leaves

1 Preheat oven to 350°F. In 10-inch skillet over medium heat, cook rice, stirring constantly, until rice is golden, about 5 minutes. Pour into 1-quart casserole.

2 In same skillet, in 2 tablespoons hot butter, cook mushrooms, onion and celery until tender, about 5 minutes. Add remaining ingredients; heat to boiling.

3 Over rice in casserole, pour mixture from skillet. Cover and bake 35 minutes or until all liquid is absorbed.

4 With fork, lightly toss 2 tablespoons butter into rice mixture until butter is melted and mixture is fluffy.

Party Rice and Noodles

Color index
page 73

Begin 1¼ hrs
ahead

12 servings

butter or margarine
*2 medium onions,
   chopped*
*2 cups regular
   long-grain
   or 1½ cups
   parboiled rice*
*½ pound mushrooms,
   sliced*
½ teaspoon curry powder
⅛ teaspoon pepper
4 cups chicken broth
1½ teaspoons salt
*½ 8-ounce package
   medium noodles
   (2 heaping cups)*

1. In 5-quart Dutch oven over medium heat, in ¼ cup butter, cook onions until tender, about 5 minutes. Preheat oven to 350°F.
2. Add rice, mushrooms, curry and pepper and cook 5 minutes, stirring frequently. Stir in broth, ¼ cup butter and salt and heat to boiling. Gently stir in uncooked noodles.
3. Pour mixture into 3-quart casserole; cover and bake 35 to 40 minutes until rice and noodles are tender and all liquid is absorbed. Just before serving, fluff rice and noodle mixture with fork.

Baked Spanish Rice

Color index
page 73

Begin 1 hr
ahead

6 servings

4 bacon slices
1 cup chopped onions
½ cup diced green pepper
1 16-ounce can tomatoes
water
*1 8-ounce can tomato
   sauce*
2 teaspoons sugar
1 teaspoon salt
*1⅓ cups regular long-
   grain rice*
*½ cup shredded Cheddar
   cheese*

1 Preheat oven to 350°F. In 12-inch skillet over medium heat, fry bacon crisp; drain on paper towels; crumble and set aside. Pour off all but 2 tablespoons drippings.

2 In hot drippings, cook onions and green pepper until tender, stirring often, about 5 minutes.

3 Into measuring cup, drain tomatoes; add enough water to tomato liquid to make 1¾ cups. Cut up tomatoes.

4 To onion mixture, add liquid, tomatoes, tomato sauce, sugar and salt; heat to boiling. Grease 1½-quart casserole.

5 Remove from heat and stir in rice; pour into casserole. Cover; bake 35 minutes or until rice is tender and liquid absorbed.

6 Fluff rice with fork; sprinkle with cheese and bake 5 minutes. Garnish with bacon.

Boiled Wild Rice

*1¹⁄₃ cups wild rice
(8 ounces)*
2²⁄₃ cups water

1¹⁄₂ teaspoons salt
*2 tablespoons butter or
margarine*

1. Wash wild rice well; drain thoroughly.
2. In 2-quart saucepan over high heat, heat water to boiling. Stir in wild rice and salt. Reduce heat; cover and simmer 45 to 50 minutes until rice is tender and all liquid is absorbed.
3. With fork, lightly toss butter or margarine into rice until butter is melted.

Rice Ring

*6 cups hot cooked
rice*
¹⁄₄ cup chopped parsley

*3 tablespoons butter or
margarine*

1. Thoroughly grease a 5¹⁄₂-cup ring mold.
2. In large bowl, toss hot cooked rice, chopped parsley and butter or margarine; lightly pack in ring mold; let stand 1 minute.
3. Loosen edges; invert plate on top of mold; holding mold and plate, quickly invert rice ring onto plate. Lift off mold.

Packing in rice: Lightly pack hot cooked rice into greased ring mold.

Turning out rice ring: Invert rice ring onto warm serving plate.

Chinese Fried Rice

*1 cup regular long-grain
rice (or 3 cups cold,
cooked rice)*
6 eggs
¹⁄₄ teaspoon salt
salad oil

*1 8-ounce package sliced
bacon, cooked and
crumbled*
1 tablespoon soy sauce
*2 tablespoons chopped
green onions*

1. Prepare rice as label directs. Refrigerate cooked rice until well chilled.
2. In medium bowl with fork, beat eggs and salt lightly. In 12-inch skillet over high heat, heat 3 tablespoons salad oil until very hot. Pour in egg mixture; cook, stirring quickly and constantly with spoon, until eggs are the size of peas and leave side of pan. Reduce heat to low.
3. Push eggs to one side of skillet. In same skillet, gently stir rice and 2 tablespoons salad oil until rice is well coated with oil. Add bacon and soy sauce; gently stir to mix all ingredients in skillet; heat mixture through.
4. To serve, spoon fried rice into warm bowl and sprinkle with chopped green onions.

Rice pudding

Rice Pudding

6 cups milk
*1 cup regular medium-
grain rice*
¹⁄₂ cup sugar
*2 tablespoons butter or
margarine*

¹⁄₄ teaspoon salt
*2 teaspoons vanilla
extract*
*¹⁄₄ teaspoon ground
nutmeg*

1 Add milk, rice, sugar, butter or margarine and salt to 3-quart saucepan.

2 Over medium heat, heat milk mixture until tiny bubbles form around the edge, stirring mixture frequently.

3 Reduce heat to low; cover; simmer 1 hour or until rice is very tender, stirring occasionally.

4 Stir in vanilla. Cover and refrigerate until well chilled, about 3 hours.

5 *To serve:* Spoon rice pudding into dessert dishes; sprinkle each serving with nutmeg.

CREAMY RICE PUDDING: Prepare as above but omit butter. Refrigerate. In small bowl with mixer at medium speed, beat *1 cup heavy or whipping cream* into soft peaks. With rubber spatula, fold cream into pudding; spoon into dessert dish; sprinkle with nutmeg. (Makes 10 servings.)

FRUIT RICE PUDDING: Prepare Rice Pudding as above but omit nutmeg. On top of each serving, place *canned peach half*, cut side down, then over each peach half pour some *Melba Sauce* (page 465). (Makes 8 servings.)

PIES

Pies lend themselves to infinite variation. You can make baked or unbaked pastry or crumb crusts filled with fruit, custard or cream, chiffon, even ice cream.

The best pie plates to use are those made of anodized aluminum, tin-coated or enamel-coated steel, porcelain-coated aluminum with a non-stick finish or glass; these materials all absorb heat and help the piecrusts to brown. Crusts baked in shiny, heat-reflecting metal pans tend to be pale; place these on cookie sheets to help the crust to brown. For a golden glaze, brush the top crust (not the edge) with milk, half-and-half, undiluted evaporated milk or slightly beaten egg white and sprinkle the crust with sugar, if you like. If the top crust seems to be browning too much cover the pie loosely with foil for the last 15 minutes of baking time.

Make sure your pie plates are the diameter specified in the recipe. Pie plates which are of the same diameter may be of different capacity. Our recipes fill those which are of a larger capacity. Any leftover filling can be baked in a custard cup, covered with foil if the pie has a top crust, for about a third of the pie baking time.

Don't grease the pie plate unless specifically directed to do so, for the crust will not stick to the plate. To loosen an unbaked crumb crust, wrap a cloth wrung out in hot water around the plate for a minute or two before cutting the pie. A pie with an ice cream or frozen filling will not only be easier to cut, but also have more flavor, if allowed to stand at room temperature for 15 minutes after removal from the freezer.

MAKING PASTRY

For best results, use cold water; if the water from the cold tap feels rather lukewarm, first chill it with an ice cube. If using lard instead of shortening, use it from the refrigerator also.

Handle pastry as little as possible. Cut in shortening with a pastry blender or two knives used scissor-fashion. Stir in water with a fork, stopping as soon as the ingredients hold together. Then, with hands, gently press the pastry into a ball. If, on a hot day, the pastry becomes too soft to handle, wrap it in waxed paper and refrigerate for 30 minutes, or until firm again.

If making a 1-crust pie, prepare enough pastry for 2 crusts (or more). Refrigerate or freeze unused pastry.

ROLLING PASTRY

Pastry should be rolled with a stockinette-covered rolling pin on a lightly floured surface. First roll the pin over the floured surface so that the stockinette cover absorbs some of the flour. Then slightly flatten the ball of pastry and roll it out as shown below.

Rolling the pastry: Roll it out from the center to the edges, keeping it circular. Push the sides in occasionally by hand, if necessary, and lift the rolling pin slightly as you near the edges to avoid making them too thin.

Lift the pastry from time to time to make sure that it is not sticking. If it does stick, loosen it with a spatula and sprinkle a little more flour on the surface underneath. Mend any cracks or breaks as they appear, patching tears with a strip of pastry cut from the edge. Moisten the torn edges, lay the patch over the tear and press it carefully into position.

LINING THE PIE PLATE

If you are making a 2-crust pie, divide your pastry into 2 pieces, one slightly larger than the other. Use the larger piece for the bottom crust. For 2 bottom crusts, divide the dough evenly in half.

Roll the pastry into a circle about 1/8 inch thick and 2 inches larger all around than the pie plate. Roll half of the circle loosely around the rolling pin and lift the pastry on to the pie plate, centering it over the plate. Unroll the pastry and ease it into the pie plate, pressing it lightly onto the bottom and side with your fingertips. Do not stretch the pastry at any point; it will just shrink back while baking. Make a decorative edge (opposite) and fill the pie, or make a top crust.

MAKING A TOP CRUST

Use a smaller ball of pastry to make the top crust. Roll it out into a circle like the bottom crust. Then, with a sharp knife, cut a few short slashes or a design in the center. Roll the pastry around a rolling pin as above and transfer it to the pie, centering it over the filling. Make one of the decorative edges shown opposite.

DECORATIVE PIE EDGES

Old-fashioned fork edge: Trim pastry even with plate rim. With floured 4-tined fork, press pastry to rim all around pie edge.

Fluted edge: Trim pastry, leaving a 1-inch overhang. Fold overhang under to make a stand-up edge. Place one index finger on inside edge and with index finger and thumb of other hand, pinch pastry to make a curved flute. Repeat, leaving ¼ inch between flutes.

Rope edge: Make a stand-up edge as for fluted edge then press thumb into pastry at an angle and pinch pastry between this thumb and knuckle of index finger. Place thumb in groove left by index finger and repeat all around edge.

Modified fluted edge: Make as fluted edge but leave ½ inch between flutes; flatten each flute with a floured 4-tined fork.

Turret edge: Make a stand-up edge as for fluted edge. With knife, cut through pastry to pie plate rim at ½-inch intervals. Press alternate strips of pastry flat around edge.

Scalloped edge: Make a stand-up edge as for fluted edge. Put thumb and index finger of one hand about 1¼ inches apart on outside of pie edge; with a floured round-bowl measuring tablespoon, press pastry outward to make scallops. Pinch points in between.

DECORATIVE TOPS FOR 2-CRUST PIES

Lattice top: Fill bottom crust and trim edge, leaving a 1-inch overhang. Roll pastry for top crust into a circle and cut it into ½-inch strips. Moisten edge of bottom crust with water. Place strips about 1¼ inches apart across filling. Trim strips even with overhang. Press ends of each strip to overhang to seal them. Lay an equal number of pastry strips at right angles to first layer. Turn overhang up over strips. Pinch edges to seal and make a high, stand-up edge. Make a fluted edge.

Twisted lattice top: Make as above but twist strips.

Diamond lattice top: Make a lattice top but attach cross-strips diagonally to make a diamond pattern.

WOVEN LATTICE TOP

Cut pastry strips as for lattice top. Place layer of strips on filling; fold every other strip back. Place center cross-strip on pie and replace folded strips. Fold back alternate strips; position second cross-strip. Repeat to weave lattice. Seal ends. Make a fluted edge.

STORING PIES AND PASTRY

Keep pies with cream, custard, whipped cream or chiffon fillings in the refrigerator; use within a day or so. Store fruit pies at room temperature and use within 2 or 3 days. Balls of unbaked pastry, wrapped in plastic wrap or foil, may be stored in the refrigerator for a day or two.

FREEZING PIES AND PASTRY

Pastry: Freeze balls of uncooked pastry, freezer-wrapped, up to 2 months. Thaw, wrapped, at room temperature 2 to 4 hours. Or roll pastry into circles 3 inches larger all around than pie plates, stack with 2 sheets of waxed paper between each, wrap and freeze. To use, place circle on pie plate; thaw 10 to 15 minutes before shaping.

Piecrusts: Freeze baked or unbaked piecrusts in their pie plates. Wrap, then stack with crumpled waxed paper between each. Store baked piecrusts 4 to 6 months; thaw, unwrapped, at room temperature 15 minutes. Store unbaked crusts 2 to 3 months; bake without thawing either unfilled, for about 20 minutes in a 425°F. oven, or filled and baked as directed in the recipe.

Fruit pies: Freeze baked or unbaked fruit pies 3 to 4 months. To freeze unbaked fruit pies, if fruit is very juicy, add 1 to 2 tablespoons extra thickening per pie. Do not cut slits in top crust. Freezer-wrap and freeze. Or, if pie is fragile, first freeze until firm, then cover top with a paper plate for protection, freezer-wrap and store. To use an unbaked fruit pie, unwrap, cut slits in top crust and bake still frozen, allowing 15 to 20 minutes additional baking time or until fruit is bubbling. Thaw baked pies at room temperature 30 minutes, then bake in a 350°F. oven 30 minutes or until warm.

Pumpkin pies: Bake pumpkin pies before freezing, or the crust may become soggy. Use within 4 to 6 months. Thaw as for fruit pies. Or freeze filling and unbaked crust separately; thaw and complete pie as recipe directs.

Chiffon pies: Freeze until firm, wrap and store. Use within 1 month. To thaw, unwrap and let stand at room temperature 2 to 4 hours, or in refrigerator overnight.

Don't freeze cream and custard pies, fillings may separate; or meringue topping, it may shrink.

Pie crusts

Pastry for 2-Crust Pie

2 cups all-purpose flour
1 teaspoon salt
¾ cup shortening
5 to 6 tablespoons cold
water

Pastry for one 2-crust pie
or two 8- or 9-inch piecrusts

1 In medium bowl with fork, lightly stir together flour and salt.

2 With pastry blender or 2 knives used scissor-fashion, cut in shortening until mixture resembles coarse crumbs.

3 Sprinkle in cold water, a tablespoon at a time, mixing lightly with a fork after each addition until pastry just holds together.

4 With hands, shape pastry into a ball. (If it is a hot day, wrap in waxed paper and refrigerate 30 minutes.)

5 For a 2-crust pie, divide pastry into 2 pieces, one slightly larger, and then gently shape each piece into a ball.

6 On lightly floured surface with lightly floured stockinette-covered rolling pin, roll larger ball into a ⅛-inch-thick circle, 2 inches larger all around than pie plate.

7 Roll half of circle onto rolling pin; transfer pastry to pie plate and unroll, easing into bottom and side of plate. Fill as recipe directs.

8 For top crust, roll smaller ball as for bottom crust; with sharp knife, cut a few slashes or a design in center of circle; center over filling in the bottom crust.

9 With scissors or a sharp knife, trim the pastry edges, leaving 1-inch overhang all around the pie plate rim.

10 Fold overhang under; pinch a high edge; make a decorative edge (page 343). Bake pie as recipe directs.

Making 2 piecrusts:
Prepare pastry as directed in steps 1 to 4 then divide pastry evenly in half, shaping each half into a ball. On a lightly floured surface with a lightly floured stockinette-covered rolling pin, roll out each ball and line 2 pie plates as directed in steps 6 and 7. Trim pastry edge and make a decorative edge as in steps 9 and 10. Fill and bake or bake and fill as recipe directs.

UNBAKED PIECRUST: Prepare as steps 1 to 3 of Pastry (left) but use only *1 cup all-purpose flour, ½ teaspoon salt, ¼ cup plus 2 tablespoons shortening* and *2 to 3 tablespoons water.* Shape all of pastry into one ball. On lightly floured surface with lightly floured stockinette-covered rolling pin, roll pastry into circle ⅛ inch thick and about 2 inches larger all around than pie plate. Roll pastry circle gently onto rolling pin; transfer to pie plate and unroll, easing into bottom and side of plate. With kitchen scissors or sharp knife, trim pastry edges, leaving a 1-inch overhang. Fold overhang under; pinch to form a high edge, then make a decorative edge. Fill and bake as directed in recipe. (Makes one 8- or 9-inch piecrust.)

BAKED PIECRUST: Preheat oven to 425°F. Prepare as above for Unbaked Piecrust. With 4-tined fork, prick bottom and side of crust in many places to prevent puffing during baking. Bake for 15 minutes or until golden. Cool. (Makes one 8- or 9-inch piecrust.)

Pricking the crust: To prevent puffing during baking, prick the bottom and side with a fork.

COBBLER OR TOP CRUST: Prepare pastry for one Unbaked Piecrust (above). Roll 2 inches larger all around than 9½" by 1½" deep pie plate; place over filling; trim edges leaving a 1-inch overhang; pinch to form a high edge and make a decorative edge. Cut a 4-inch "X" in center of crust; fold back points from center of "X" to make a square opening. Bake as directed in recipe.

Making a cobbler crust: First cut a 4-inch "X" in center of top crust.

Fold back the 4 points to make a square opening and reveal the filling.

Begin 1½ hrs ahead

One 9-inch piecrust

Baked Graham-Cracker Crumb Crust

about 18 graham crackers (1½ cups graham-cracker crumbs)
¼ cup sugar
⅓ cup melted butter or margarine

1 In covered blender container, blend crackers, ¼ at a time, until finely crumbed; or place crackers in strong bag and roll fine with rolling pin.

2 Preheat oven to 375°F. In medium bowl, mix well crumbs, sugar and melted butter. If you like, set aside 3 tablespoons mixture for garnish.

3 With back of spoon, press rest of mixture to bottom and side of 9-inch pie plate, making a small rim.

4 Bake 8 minutes then remove crumb crust to wire rack to cool.

5 Fill as recipe directs; garnish with reserved crumb mixture or as recipe directs.

8-INCH GRAHAM-CRACKER: Prepare as above but use *14 graham crackers* (1¼ cups crumbs), *3 tablespoons sugar* and *¼ cup melted butter.*

VANILLA- OR CHOCOLATE-WAFER: Prepare as above but for 8-inch crust use about *24 vanilla or 14 chocolate wafers* (1¼ cups crumbs) and *¼ cup melted butter;* for 9-inch crust use about *35 vanilla or 18 chocolate wafers* (1½ cups crumbs) and *⅓ cup melted butter.*

GINGERSNAP: Prepare as above but for 8-inch crust use about *18 gingersnaps* (1¼ cups crumbs) and *¼ cup melted butter;* for 9-inch crumb crust use about *24 gingersnaps* (1½ cups crumbs) and *⅓ cup melted butter.*

Begin 1½ hrs ahead

One 9-inch piecrust

Unbaked Crumb Crust

1½ cups graham-cracker crumbs
⅓ cup packed brown sugar
½ teaspoon ground cinnamon
⅓ cup melted butter or margarine

Prepare as Baked Graham-Cracker Crumb Crust (left) but do not make rim and do not bake. Chill well; fill as recipe directs or with chilled filling; top with reserved crumb mixture. Refrigerate.

8-INCH CRUST: Prepare as above but decrease quantities. Use *1⅛ cups graham-cracker crumbs, ¼ cup packed brown sugar, ¼ teaspoon ground cinnamon* and *¼ cup melted butter.*

Begin 1¾ hrs ahead

12 tart shells

Baked Tart Shells

1½ cups all-purpose flour
1 tablespoon sugar
¼ teaspoon salt
⅓ cup shortening
3 to 4 tablespoons cold water

1. In medium bowl with fork, mix flour, sugar and salt. With pastry blender or 2 knives used scissor-fashion, cut in shortening.
2. Sprinkle in cold water, a tablespoon at a time, mixing lightly with fork after each addition, until pastry just holds together.
3. Shape dough into a ball; divide into 12 equal pieces; carefully shape each into a ball. Preheat the oven to 425°F.

4 Roll each ball into circle, ⅛ inch thick and 5 inches in diameter.

5 Press pastry circles into 3¼″ by 1¼″ deep fluted tart pans.

6 With knife, trim each pastry shell even with top of tart pan.

7 With 4-tined fork, prick the bottom of each tart shell.

8. Bake 10 to 12 minutes until light golden. Turn shells out of pans onto wire rack; cool completely. Fill with chilled filling.

UNBAKED: Prepare dough and line pans as above; do not prick. Fill and bake as recipe directs.

Fruit pies

Fruit pie is always in season and if fresh fruit is unavailable, canned and frozen products can be substituted. Follow the guidelines below.

The best apples for pies are York Imperial, Winesap, Stayman, Rome Beauty, Northern Spy, Newtown Pippin, McIntosh, Jonathan, Gravenstein, Golden Delicious and Cortland. One pound of apples is equal to 3 medium apples or 3 cups sliced.

Tart or sour cherries are used most for pies. Two cups pitted cherries equal one 16-ounce can or 20 ounces frozen cherries. One pint blackberries, blueberries or cranberries is equal to 1¾ cups.

Use Bartlett, Anjou or Bosc pears for cooking. One 29-ounce can of pears equals 3 fresh ones or about 2 cups peeled and sliced. Two 29-ounce cans of sliced cling peaches equals 5 cups sliced fresh peaches or about 2½ pounds whole.

Apple Pie

Pastry for 2-Crust Pie
  (page 344)
⅔ to ¾ cup sugar
2 tablespoons all-purpose flour
½ teaspoon ground cinnamon
¼ teaspoon ground nutmeg
½ teaspoon grated lemon peel
1 to 2 teaspoons lemon juice

6 to 7 cups thinly sliced, peeled and cored cooking apples (2 pounds)
1 tablespoon butter or margarine
milk

Color index page 86

Begin 2 hrs ahead or early in day

6 servings

1 Prepare pastry. Roll out half of pastry and line 9-inch pie plate.

2 In small bowl, combine sugar (amount depends on tartness of apples) and next 5 ingredients.

3 Place half of thinly sliced apples in piecrust; sprinkle with half of sugar mixture. Top with rest of apples, then rest of sugar mixture.

4 Dot the filling with butter or margarine. Preheat oven to 425°F.

5 Roll out remaining pastry for top crust and using a floured leaf-shaped cookie cutter, cut out design. Place crust over pie; trim edges.

6 Fold pastry overhang under then bring up over pie-plate rim. Pinch to form a high edge then make your choice of decorative edge.

7 For a golden glaze, brush the top crust (not the edge) lightly with some milk. Bake pie for 40 to 50 minutes or until crust is golden.

Color index page 86
Begin 2 hrs ahead
6 servings

Cherry Pie

Pastry for 2-Crust Pie (page 344)
1 cup sugar
¼ cup cornstarch
½ teaspoon salt

5 cups pitted fresh tart cherries
1 tablespoon butter or margarine

1. Prepare pastry. Roll out half of pastry and line 9-inch pie plate. Preheat oven to 425°F.
2. For filling, combine sugar, cornstarch, salt and pitted cherries. Place filling in piecrust; dot with butter or margarine.
3. Roll out remaining pastry for top crust and cut a few slashes; cover with slashed top crust; flute edge. Bake 50 to 60 minutes until golden.

Color index page 87
Begin 2 hrs ahead
6 to 8 servings

Blueberry Cobbler

Cobbler or Top Crust (page 344)
⅔ cup sugar
¼ cup all-purpose flour
½ teaspoon ground cinnamon
¼ teaspoon ground nutmeg

½ teaspoon grated lemon peel
2 teaspoons lemon juice
⅛ teaspoon salt
6 cups blueberries
1 tablespoon butter or margarine

1. Prepare Cobbler or Top Crust as directed. Preheat oven to 425°F.
2. For filling, toss together sugar, flour, cinnamon, nutmeg, lemon peel, lemon juice, salt and blueberries. Place filling in 9½" by 1½" deep pie plate; dot with butter or margarine. Top with crust. Bake 50 minutes or until golden brown.

Color index page 86
Begin 2 hrs ahead
6 servings

Blackberry Pie

Pastry for 2-Crust Pie (page 344)
⅔ to ¾ cup sugar
¼ cup all-purpose flour
½ teaspoon ground cinnamon
¼ teaspoon ground nutmeg

½ teaspoon grated lemon peel
⅛ teaspoon salt
5 cups blackberries
1 tablespoon butter

1. Prepare pastry. Roll out half of pastry and line 9-inch pie plate. Preheat oven to 425°F.
2. For filling, toss together sugar, flour, cinnamon, nutmeg, lemon peel and salt with blackberries. Place filling in piecrust; dot with butter.
3. Roll out remaining pastry for top crust; cut a few slashes and cover filling with slashed top crust; make a decorative edge. Bake 50 minutes or until the piecrust is golden brown.

Color index
page 88

Begin 2 hrs
ahead or
early in day

6 servings

Peach Pie

Pastry for 2-Crust Pie
(page 344)
6 cups peeled, sliced
peaches
¾ to 1 cup sugar
⅓ cup all-purpose
flour
1 tablespoon lemon juice

½ teaspoon grated lemon
peel
½ teaspoon ground
cinnamon
milk

1 Prepare pastry. Roll out
half of pastry and line
9-inch pie plate.

2 Toss sliced peaches in
large bowl with remain-
ing ingredients except milk
then spoon peach mixture
into piecrust.

3 Roll remaining pastry
into 11-inch-diameter
circle and cut into 6 strips
of equal width. Preheat
oven to 425°F

4 Place pastry strips
parallel across pie;
twist, then fasten ends to
the piecrust.

5 Trim the pastry edges.
Fold overhang over
strip ends; pinch to form a
high edge, then make a
decorative edge.

6 Brush strips with milk.
Bake 45 to 50 minutes
or until crust is golden.
Serve pie warm or cold.

Begin 2 hrs
ahead or
early in day

6 servings

PEAR PIE: Prepare as Peach Pie (above) but for
filling combine *6 pears*, peeled, cored and sliced,
*¾ cup sugar, 3 tablespoons quick-cooking tapioca,
2 tablespoons lemon juice, 2 tablespoons butter* or
margarine, *1 teaspoon grated lemon peel, ½ teaspoon
ground nutmeg, ½ teaspoon ground cinnamon* and *¼
teaspoon salt.* Bake in preheated 425°F. oven 50 to
60 minutes until pears are tender.

Color index
page 88

Begin 2 hrs
ahead or
early in day

8 servings

Streusel-topped Pear Pie

2¼ cups all-purpose flour
salt
1 cup butter or margarine
2½ to 3 tablespoons
cold water
5 medium pears
½ cup sugar
2 tablespoons lemon
juice
½ cup packed light
brown sugar

1 teaspoon ground
cinnamon
¼ teaspoon ground
nutmeg
¼ teaspoon ground
cloves
½ cup shredded Cheddar
cheese

1. In medium bowl with fork, stir 2 cups flour and
1 teaspoon salt. With pastry blender or 2 knives
used scissor-fashion, cut in ¾ cup butter until
mixture resembles coarse crumbs. Measure 1 cup
mixture into medium bowl; reserve.
2. To remaining flour mixture, add cold water, 1
tablespoon at a time, mixing lightly with a fork
after each addition until moist enough to hold
together. With hands, shape pastry into a ball.
3. On lightly floured surface with lightly floured
rolling pin, roll pastry into an 11-inch circle; use to
line 9-inch pie plate. Trim pastry edges, leaving 1-
inch overhang. Fold overhang under; bring up
over pie-plate rim; pinch to form a high edge;
make a fluted edge.
4. Peel, core and cut pears into thick slices to
measure about 4½ cups. In large bowl, toss pears
with sugar, lemon juice, ¼ cup flour and ¼ teaspoon salt; put in crust. Preheat oven to 425°F.
5. In medium bowl, combine reserved flour mixture, brown sugar and next 3 ingredients. With
pastry blender or 2 knives used scissor-fashion, cut
in cheese and ¼ cup butter until mixture resembles
coarse crumbs and ingredients are well blended.
Sprinkle over pears. Bake 40 minutes; cover with
foil and bake 20 minutes more. Serve warm or
refrigerate to serve cold.

Prune and Apricot Pie

Color index
page 86

Begin early
in day or
day ahead

8 servings

1 9-inch Baked Piecrust
(page 344)
water
1 12-ounce package
pitted prunes (about
2 cups)
1 cup dried apricots
¼ cup chopped
California walnuts

3 tablespoons cornstarch
¼ cup sugar
1 tablespoon finely
grated lemon
peel
1 teaspoon ground
cinnamon
⅛ teaspoon salt

1. Prepare piecrust; cool. Preheat oven to 375°F.
2. In 2-quart saucepan over medium-high heat,
heat 3 cups water, prunes and apricots to boiling;
reduce heat to low and simmer 15 minutes or until
fruits are tender.
3. Meanwhile, spread walnuts on cookie sheet; toast
in oven 8 to 10 minutes until lightly browned.
4. In cup, blend cornstarch and ½ cup water;
gradually stir into simmering fruit and cook, stirring
constantly, until thickened. Stir in sugar, lemon
peel, cinnamon and salt. Pour mixture into piecrust.
Sprinkle with walnuts. Cool.

Fruit pies

Color index page 86

Begin early in day or day ahead

10 servings

Deep-Dish Peach Pie

1 cup sugar	*Pastry for 2-Crust Pie*
¼ cup cornstarch	*(page 344)*
½ teaspoon ground	*10 cups sliced peaches*
cinnamon	*(about 5 pounds)*
⅛ teaspoon salt	*3 tablespoons butter*

1. In medium bowl, combine sugar, cornstarch, cinnamon and salt; set aside. Prepare pastry; cut off one-fourth; set aside.
2. Roll three-fourths of pastry into 17″ by 13″ rectangle. Use to line 12″ by 8″ baking dish. Add peaches to dish; dot with butter; sprinkle with sugar mixture. Preheat oven to 425°F.
3. Roll remaining pastry into 10″ by 6″ rectangle; cut into six 1-inch-wide strips; place the strips crosswise over the peach filling, twisting them. Make a high, fluted edge.
4. Bake 50 minutes or until filling is bubbly and crust is golden brown.
5. Let stand 15 minutes, then serve warm. Or cool to serve cold.

Color index page 87

Begin 2 hrs ahead or early in day

10 servings

Deep-Dish Plum Pie

Pastry for 2-Crust Pie	*4 tablespoons butter or*
(page 344)	*margarine*
4 pounds plums, halved	*1½ cups sugar*
and pitted	*6 tablespoons all-purpose*
½ teaspoon almond	*flour*
extract	*1 egg white or milk*

1. Prepare pastry. Roll three-fourths of pastry into 18″ by 14″ rectangle; use to line 13″ by 9″ baking dish. Arrange the plums in pastry lining; sprinkle with almond extract and dot with butter.
2. In small bowl, combine sugar and flour; sprinkle over plums. Preheat oven to 425°F.
3. Roll remaining pastry into 15″ by 5″ rectangle; cut into ten ½-inch-wide strips; use to make a lattice top (page 343); make a rope edge. Brush pastry with egg white or milk. Bake 45 to 50 minutes until filling is bubbly and crust is golden brown. Serve the pie warm or cool to serve cold later.

PREVENTING OVERBROWNING

If the piecrust edges begin to brown too much during baking, cover them with strips of foil to prevent burning.

Deluxe Apple Tart

1 cup all-purpose flour
5 tablespoons butter,
softened
⅛ teaspoon salt
sugar
water
9 medium Golden
Delicious apples
(3 pounds)
1 teaspoon lemon juice
1 10- or 12-ounce jar
apricot preserves

Color index page 88

Begin early in day or day ahead

8 servings

1 In medium bowl, knead flour, butter, salt, 2 tablespoons sugar and 2 tablespoons water until dough forms a ball, adding a little more water if it is needed.

2 Pat pastry into bottom and up side of 9-inch tart pan with removable bottom, or in 9″ by 3″ springform pan to within 2 inches from top of pan; refrigerate piecrust.

3 Quarter 3 apples; with sharp knife, peel, core and cut in ⅛-inch-thick slices to make 3 cups.

4 In medium bowl with spoon, toss apples with lemon juice and 2 tablespoons sugar.

5 Make applesauce: Peel and core remaining apples; cut into chunks. In blender, puree ¼ cup water and ⅓ of apple chunks. Add remaining chunks, ⅓ at a time; blend until smooth. In 3-quart pan, heat puree, ⅓ cup apricot preserves and ¼ cup sugar to boiling. Reduce heat; cook, uncovered, 20 minutes or until very thick, stirring frequently.

6 Spread applesauce (about 1½ cups) evenly over piecrust. Preheat oven to 400°F.

7 Place apple slices, closely overlapping, in concentric circles on pie. Bake 45 minutes or until apple is tender and lightly browned. Remove to rack.

8 Strain remaining apricot preserves through sieve into 1-quart saucepan and stir in 1 tablespoon sugar.

9 Over medium-high heat, heat to boiling; cook 2 minutes more or until mixture coats spoon.

10 Brush the apricot mixture evenly over pie. Cool pie on wire rack. Remove pan side to serve.

Custard pies

Unbaked custard pie fillings are very thin mixtures and it is advisable to rub the crust of our Custard Pie with butter or margarine before adding the filling to prevent the unbaked piecrust from becoming soggy. Avoid spilling any mixture by placing the pie on the oven rack before pouring in the filling, then carefully push the rack back in place. Bake a custard pie until the filling has set and a knife inserted into filling comes out clean. Garnish with chocolate curls, chopped nuts, whipped cream or shredded or flaked coconut.

Custard Pie

Color index page 88

Begin early in day

6 servings

1 9-inch Unbaked Piecrust (page 344)
1 tablespoon butter or margarine, softened
2½ cups milk
½ cup sugar
3 eggs
1 teaspoon vanilla extract
½ teaspoon salt
¼ teaspoon ground nutmeg
chopped nuts, ground nutmeg or whipped cream for garnish

1 Prepare piecrust. Rub unbaked piecrust with softened butter or margarine; refrigerate. Preheat oven to 425°F.

2 In medium bowl with wire whisk or hand beater, beat remaining ingredients except garnish.

3 Place pie plate on oven rack and pour milk mixture into piecrust.

4 Bake 20 to 25 minutes until knife inserted about 1 inch from edge comes out clean. Cool.

5 Garnish cooled pie with chopped nuts, ground nutmeg or whipped cream to serve.

COCONUT-CUSTARD PIE: Prepare pie as above but sprinkle *½ cup shredded or flaked coconut* over the bottom of the prepared piecrust before pouring in the milk mixture.

Pumpkin Pie

Color index page 86

Begin early in day or day ahead

6 servings

1 9-inch Unbaked Piecrust (page 344)
3 eggs, separated
1 16-ounce can pumpkin (2 cups)
1 cup evaporated milk
1 cup sugar
1 teaspoon ground cinnamon
½ teaspoon ground ginger
¼ teaspoon ground nutmeg
¼ teaspoon ground cloves
¼ teaspoon salt
Brandy Hard Sauce (below)

1 Prepare unbaked piecrust with your choice of decorative edge. Preheat oven to 375°F.

2 In small bowl with mixer at high speed, beat egg whites just until soft peaks form.

3 In large bowl with same beaters and with mixer at low speed, beat together egg yolks, pumpkin and next 7 ingredients until well blended.

4 With wire whisk or rubber spatula, gently fold beaten egg whites into pumpkin mixture.

5 To avoid spilling pumpkin mixture, place pie plate on oven rack and pour filling into crust; carefully push rack back.

6 Bake 45 minutes until filling is set and knife inserted 1 inch from edge comes out clean; refrigerate. Serve with sauce.

BRANDY HARD SAUCE: In small bowl with mixer at medium speed, beat *¼ cup butter* or margarine, softened, until light and fluffy. Gradually beat in *¾ cup confectioners' sugar, 1 tablespoon brandy* and *¼ teaspoon vanilla extract* until creamy. Refrigerate. (Makes ½ cup.)

Cream pies

Cream pie fillings are usually cooked separately and then added to a baked pastry or crumb crust. If the recipe calls for the filling to be chilled, press plastic wrap or waxed paper to the surface of the cream filling to prevent a skin forming; be sure to remove the covering before adding a topping.

Whipped cream and meringue are the most popular toppings for cream pies. Remember that meringue toppings require special care to keep them from shrinking. Spread the meringue over the pie, making sure it touches the crust at all points and after baking, be sure to allow the pie to cool away from any drafts.

Chocolate Cream Pie

*1 9-inch Baked Piecrust
(page 344) or 9-inch
Baked Vanilla or
Chocolate-Wafer
Crumb Crust
(page 345)
1/2 cup sugar
1/3 cup all-purpose
flour
1/4 teaspoon salt
2 cups milk
2 squares unsweetened
chocolate, coarsely
chopped
3 egg yolks*

*3 tablespoons butter or
margarine
1 teaspoon vanilla
extract
1 cup heavy or whipping
cream*

Color index page 86

Begin 5½ hrs ahead or early in day

8 servings

1 Prepare piecrust; cool. In 2-quart saucepan with spoon, mix together sugar, flour and salt; stir in milk.

2 Stir in chocolate and over low heat, cook mixture, stirring constantly, until chocolate is completely melted.

3 With wire whisk, beat until chocolate is blended; increase heat to medium: cook, stirring till mixture is thickened and boils (about 10 minutes); remove at once from heat.

4 In cup with wire whisk, beat egg yolks with small amount of hot chocolate mixture.

5 Slowly pour egg mixture into saucepan, stirring rapidly. Over low heat, cook, stirring, until *very* thick (do not boil) and mixture mounds when dropped from spoon.

6 Remove from heat; stir in butter and vanilla then pour into piecrust. Cover surface with plastic wrap to prevent skin forming. Refrigerate until set, about 4 hours.

7 *Just before serving:* In small bowl with mixer at medium speed, beat cream until stiff peaks form. Discard plastic wrap on filling. Spread whipped cream on top of pie.

350

MERINGUE-TOPPED CHOCOLATE CREAM PIE: Prepare as Chocolate Cream Pie (left) but omit whipped cream. Do not cool pie. Top with *3-Egg-White Meringue Topping* (opposite); bake as directed. Cool; refrigerate. (Makes 8 servings.)

Color index page 89

Begin 5½ hrs ahead or early in day

8 servings

Vanilla Cream Pie

*1 9-inch Baked Piecrust
(page 344) or 9-inch
Baked Graham-
Cracker Crumb
Crust (page 345)
1/2 cup sugar
1/3 cup all-purpose flour*

*1/4 teaspoon salt
2¼ cups milk
4 egg yolks
1 tablespoon butter
2 teaspoons vanilla
extract
1 cup heavy cream*

1. Prepare piecrust or crumb crust; cool.
2. In 2-quart saucepan with spoon, mix sugar, flour and salt. Stir in milk until smooth. Over medium heat, cook mixture, stirring constantly, until mixture is thickened and begins to boil (about 10 minutes). Boil 1 minute. Remove immediately from heat and set aside.
3. In cup with wire whisk, beat egg yolks with small amount of hot milk mixture. Slowly pour egg mixture into saucepan, stirring rapidly to prevent lumping. Over low heat, cook, stirring constantly, until *very* thick (do not boil) and mixture mounds when dropped from spoon.
4. Remove from heat; stir in butter and vanilla; pour into piecrust. Cover surface of mixture with plastic wrap to prevent skin forming. Refrigerate until set, about 4 hours.
5. *Just before serving:* In small bowl with mixer at medium speed, beat cream until stiff peaks form. Discard plastic wrap. Spread cream on pie.

BANANA CREAM PIE: Prepare piecrust and filling as above but do not pour filling into crust. Cover surface of filling with plastic wrap; refrigerate until cool, about 2 hours. Peel and slice *3 medium bananas* over bottom of piecrust; top with filling; chill until set, about 2 hours. Spread whipped cream evenly on top. To garnish, grate peel of *1 lemon*; sprinkle around top edge of pie. Cut lemon in half and squeeze juice into bowl. Into juice, peel and slice *1 large banana*; toss to coat; drain on paper towels. Arrange banana slices in center of top of pie. In 1-quart saucepan over low heat, heat *1/3 cup apple jelly* until just melted; brush over banana slices. Chill.

LEMON CREAM PIE: Prepare piecrust and filling as above but increase sugar to 2/3 cup and reduce milk to 1¾ cups. Omit vanilla but stir in *1/4 cup lemon juice* and *1 teaspoon grated lemon peel.* Fill and top pie with whipped cream as above.

BUTTERSCOTCH CREAM PIE: Prepare crust and filling as above but substitute *3/4 cup packed light brown sugar* for sugar; reduce milk to 2 cups and increase butter to 3 tablespoons. Fill and top pie with whipped cream as above.

Lemon Meringue Pie

Color index
page 89

Begin 6 hrs
ahead or
early in day

6 servings

1 9-inch Baked Piecrust
   (page 344)
⅓ cup cornstarch
sugar
salt
1½ cups warm water
grated peel of 1 lemon
½ cup lemon juice
4 eggs, separated
1 tablespoon butter
or margarine
4-Egg-White
   Meringue Topping
   (right)

1 Prepare piecrust. Into 2-quart saucepan, measure cornstarch, 1 cup sugar and ⅛ teaspoon salt; stir together.

2 Stir in water, lemon peel and juice; cook over medium heat, stirring, until mixture boils; remove from heat.

3 In small bowl with wire whisk or spoon, beat egg yolks; then stir in small amount of hot sauce.

4 Slowly pour egg mixture into sauce, stirring rapidly to prevent lumping. Return to heat; cook, stirring, until mixture is thick (do not boil).

5 Add butter or margarine to thickened mixture and stir until melted and thoroughly blended.

6 Pour mixture into piecrust. Preheat oven to 400°F. Make 4-Egg-White Meringue Topping (right) with egg whites.

7 Spread meringue over filling, touching piecrust all around. Bake as directed; cool and refrigerate pie.

MAKING A MERINGUE TOPPING

3-EGG-WHITE MERINGUE TOPPING: Prepare topping as below, using *3 egg whites, ¼ teaspoon salt* and *6 tablespoons sugar.*

4-EGG-WHITE MERINGUE TOPPING: Prepare topping as below, using *4 egg whites, ¼ teaspoon salt* and *½ cup sugar.*

Preheat oven to 400°F. Have egg whites at room temperature. Be sure bowl and beaters are completely free of fat. In small bowl with mixer at high speed, beat egg whites and salt until soft peaks form.

At high speed, sprinkle in sugar, 2 tablespoons at a time, beating after each addition until sugar is dissolved. Rub a bit of meringue between fingers; if it doesn't feel grainy, sugar is dissolved. Whites should stand in stiff, glossy peaks.

With back of spoon, spread meringue over filling; seal to piecrust all around edge. Swirl up points to make attractive top. Bake 10 minutes or until golden. Cool away from drafts.

8-INCH LEMON MERINGUE PIE: Prepare as Lemon Meringue Pie but use ¾ cup sugar, ¼ cup cornstarch, ⅛ teaspoon salt, 1¼ cups water, grated peel of 1 lemon, ⅓ cup lemon juice, 3 eggs, separated, and 1 tablespoon butter or margarine for filling; turn into 8-inch Baked Piecrust. Make 3-Egg-White Meringue Topping.

LEMON SNOW PIE: Prepare as Lemon Meringue Pie but fold meringue into hot filling; pour into piecrust; don't bake. Refrigerate until set.

ORANGE MERINGUE PIE: Prepare as Lemon Meringue Pie but reduce sugar to ⅓ cup, water to ½ cup, lemon juice to 2 tablespoons; substitute *grated peel of 1 orange* for lemon peel; add *1 cup orange juice* with water.

PINEAPPLE MERINGUE PIE: Drain *one 8-ounce can crushed pineapple,* reserving liquid. To liquid, add water to make 1½ cups; use as liquid in filling. Prepare as Lemon Meringue Pie but reduce sugar to ½ cup, lemon juice to 1 tablespoon; add drained pineapple to the hot filling.

Chiffon pies

Chiffon pies depend upon both gelatin and beaten egg whites for their lightness and height. Some also have whipped cream folded into their fillings. They are always served cold and are made in baked pastry or crumb crusts or unbaked crumb crusts. Store them in the refrigerator. Because they can be made a day ahead they are an ideal choice for a party dessert.

In most of our recipes, sugar is mixed with the gelatin or cornstarch before the liquid is added. This helps to separate the granules and prevent clumps forming. Remember to cook egg mixtures over medium-low heat, stirring constantly to prevent curdling. The whites should be beaten until soft peaks form and then gently folded into the gelatin mixture. If stirred too much the egg whites will lose volume and may even become runny again. For further tips on using egg whites, see page 139.

Garnish chiffon pies with shredded lemon, lime or orange peel, whipped cream, small amounts of fresh berries or orange sections, angelica, chocolate curls or shaped chocolate and candied fruits.

For easy serving of pies with unbaked crumb crusts, dip a dish cloth in warm water, wring it out and wrap it around the pie plate for a minute or two. Then cut the pie and serve straight away. The heat will loosen the crust so that the pieces come out easily.

Lemon Chiffon Pie

1 9-inch Baked Piecrust (page 344) or 9-inch Baked Vanilla-Wafer or Graham-Cracker Crumb Crust (page 345)
1 envelope unflavored gelatin
¼ teaspoon salt
sugar
4 eggs, separated
⅓ cup water
1 tablespoon grated lemon peel
¼ cup lemon juice

½ cup heavy or whipping cream, whipped
shredded lemon peel for garnish

Color index page 87

Begin early in day or day ahead

8 servings

1 Prepare piecrust. In 1-quart saucepan, mix well gelatin, salt and ⅓ cup sugar.

2 In small bowl with wire whisk, beat egg yolks with water, lemon peel and lemon juice, then stir this mixture into the gelatin mixture.

3 Cook over medium-low heat, stirring, until mixture is thickened and coats spoon; remove saucepan from heat.

4 In large bowl with mixer at high speed, beat whites until soft peaks form; gradually sprinkle in ½ cup sugar, beating until sugar is completely dissolved.

5 With rubber spatula, gently fold lemon mixture into egg whites just until blended.

6 Spoon mixture into piecrust; refrigerate pie until lemon chiffon filling is set.

7 *To serve:* Spoon whipped cream in mounds around pie edge. Sprinkle with shredded lemon peel.

LIME-SWIRL PIE: Prepare as Lemon Chiffon Pie (left) but omit the ⅓ cup sugar; substitute **1 teaspoon grated lime peel** for lemon peel, and **lime juice** for lemon juice. Swirl whipped cream through filling in shell; top pie with **shredded lime peel**. (Makes 8 servings.)

Color index page 88

Begin early in day or day ahead

8 servings

Orange Chiffon Pie

1 9-inch Baked Piecrust (page 344) or Unbaked Crumb Crust (page 345)
1 envelope unflavored gelatin
¼ teaspoon salt
sugar
3 eggs, separated

1 teaspoon grated orange peel
1 cup orange juice
2 tablespoons lemon juice
few drops yellow food color
1½ cups heavy cream
orange sections, drained, for garnish

1. Prepare piecrust; cool crust if baked.
2. In 1-quart saucepan, stir gelatin with salt and ½ cup sugar until well mixed. In small bowl with wire whisk or hand beater, beat egg yolks with orange peel, orange juice and lemon juice until mixed; stir into gelatin mixture.
3. Cook over medium-low heat, stirring constantly, until mixture is thickened and coats spoon; remove from heat. Stir in food color; refrigerate, stirring occasionally, until mixture mounds when dropped from spoon, about 45 minutes.
4. In large bowl with mixer at high speed, beat egg whites until soft peaks form; beating at high speed, gradually sprinkle in ¼ cup sugar; beat until sugar is completely dissolved. With wire whisk or rubber spatula, gently fold gelatin mixture into whites.
5. In small bowl with same beaters and with mixer at medium speed, beat ½ cup heavy cream until soft peaks form; fold into gelatin mixture. Spoon mixture into crust; refrigerate pie until set, about 30 minutes.
6. *To serve:* In small bowl with mixer at medium speed, beat remaining heavy cream with 2 tablespoons sugar until stiff peaks form. Spoon on pie; garnish with orange sections.

Color index
page 87

Begin early
in day or
day ahead

8 servings

Rich Bavarian Pie

*1 9-inch Baked Piecrust
(page 344)*
*1 envelope unflavored
gelatin*
⅛ teaspoon salt
sugar
3 eggs, separated
1¼ cups milk
*1 teaspoon vanilla
extract*
*¾ to 1 cup heavy cream,
whipped*
*¼ teaspoon ground
nutmeg*
*shaved unsweetened
chocolate for garnish*

1 Prepare piecrust; cool. Into 1-quart saucepan, measure gelatin, salt and ¼ cup sugar and stir thoroughly until they are well mixed.

2 In small bowl with wire whisk, beat egg yolks with milk until mixed, then with spoon, stir into gelatin mixture.

3 Cook over medium-low heat, stirring, until mixture is thickened and coats spoon. Remove from heat and stir in vanilla.

4 Refrigerate until mixture mounds when dropped from spoon, about 40 minutes. With hand beater, beat the mixture smooth.

5 In large bowl with mixer at high speed, beat egg whites into soft peaks; gradually sprinkle in ¼ cup sugar; beat until sugar is dissolved.

6 With rubber spatula, fold whipped cream and gelatin mixture into beaten egg whites.

7 Spoon into crust; sprinkle with nutmeg. Chill. To serve, garnish with chocolate shavings.

RICH BAVARIAN PIE VARIATIONS

COFFEE: Prepare Rich Bavarian Pie as left but add *2 tablespoons instant coffee powder* to egg whites before beating. Omit whipped cream and shaved chocolate. For topping melt *¾ cup semisweet-chocolate pieces* over hot, *not boiling,* water; stir in *¼ cup water* until smooth; drizzle over top of pie.

STRAWBERRY: Prepare pie as left but fold *1 cup sliced strawberries* into filling. Omit chocolate; garnish top of pie with *whole strawberries.*

EGGNOG: Prepare pie as left but omit vanilla extract; add *½ teaspoon rum extract* and increase ground nutmeg to 1 teaspoon.

COCONUT: Prepare pie as left but omit nutmeg; add *½ cup flaked or grated fresh coconut* with gelatin mixture. If fresh coconut, add *¼ teaspoon almond extract* with vanilla.

CRANBERRY-TOPPED: Prepare the pie as left but substitute *almond extract* for vanilla; use only ½ cup heavy cream; omit nutmeg and chocolate. For topping, in 2-quart saucepan over medium heat, cook *one 16-ounce can whole-cranberry sauce* with *1 tablespoon cornstarch* until clear and thickened; cool; spread on pie when filling is set.

Chocolate Chiffon Pie

Color index
page 87

Begin 4 hrs
ahead

8 servings

*1 9-inch Baked
Chocolate-Wafer
Crumb Crust
(page 345)*
3 eggs, separated
½ teaspoon salt
1 cup water
sugar
*2 squares unsweetened
chocolate*

*1 envelope unflavored
gelatin*
*½ teaspoon vanilla
extract*
*¼ teaspoon cream of
tartar*
*whipped cream for
garnish*

1. Prepare crust; set aside. In heavy 2-quart saucepan with fork, mix well egg yolks, salt, water and ¾ cup sugar; add chocolate and sprinkle gelatin over mixture. Cook over medium heat, stirring, until gelatin is dissolved and chocolate melts. Remove from heat; stir in vanilla.

2. Pour mixture into large bowl. With mixer at high speed, beat 1 minute (the mixture may look slightly speckled). Refrigerate until mixture is cold and mounds when dropped from a spoon, stirring occasionally, about 45 minutes.

3. In small bowl with mixer at high speed, beat egg whites and cream of tartar into soft peaks; beating at high speed, gradually sprinkle in ¼ cup sugar. Whites should stand in stiff peaks. Do not scrape side of bowl during beating.

4. Using same beaters, beat chocolate mixture until fluffy, about 2 minutes. With wire whisk, fold in beaten egg whites until well blended.

5. Carefully pour mixture into piecrust so mixture does not run over edge of piecrust; refrigerate at least 2 hours or until set. Garnish the edge of the pie with dollops of whipped cream.

Chiffon pies

Raspberry Ribbon Pie

Color index
page 89

Begin early
in day or
day ahead

8 servings

*1 9-inch Baked
Piecrust
(page 344)*
*1 3-ounce package
raspberry-flavor
gelatin*
¼ cup sugar
*1¼ cups boiling
water*
*1 10-ounce package
frozen raspberries*
*1 tablespoon lemon
juice*

*1 3-ounce package cream
cheese or Neufchâtel
cheese, softened*
*⅓ cup confectioners'
sugar*
*1 teaspoon vanilla
extract*
⅛ teaspoon salt
1 cup heavy cream
*fresh raspberries or
whipped cream for
garnish*

1 Prepare piecrust. In medium bowl, stir gelatin and sugar with boiling water until gelatin and sugar are dissolved; then add frozen raspberries and lemon juice.

2 Stir mixture until berries thaw. Cover and refrigerate, stirring frequently, until mixture mounds when dropped from a spoon.

3 In small bowl with wire whisk, mix cream cheese with confectioners' sugar, vanilla extract and salt until smooth.

4 In second small bowl with mixer at medium speed, beat heavy cream into soft peaks; then with wire whisk or rubber spatula, gradually fold cream-cheese mixture into cream.

5 Spread half of the whipped-cream mixture in the prepared piecrust then spoon half of raspberry mixture over it.

6 Repeat with rest of cream mixture and berries. Refrigerate until set then garnish with raspberries or whipped cream.

Coffee Cordial Pie

Color index
page 89

Begin 4½ hrs
or day ahead

8 servings

*1 9-inch Baked
Chocolate-Wafer
Crumb Crust
(page 345)*
*1 envelope unflavored
gelatin*
⅛ teaspoon salt
sugar
3 eggs, separated

½ cup water
*½ cup coffee-flavor
liqueur*
*1 tablespoon instant
coffee*
*2 teaspoons vanilla
extract*
1 cup heavy cream

1. Prepare crust; cool. In 2-quart saucepan, mix gelatin, salt and ¼ cup sugar. With wire whisk, beat in egg yolks and water until well mixed. Cook over low heat, stirring, until gelatin is dissolved and mixture is slightly thickened, about 10 minutes (do not boil). Remove from heat; stir in liqueur, coffee and vanilla extract.
2. Refrigerate, stirring often, until mixture is consistency of unbeaten egg white, about 20 minutes.
3. In large bowl with mixer at high speed, beat egg whites into soft peaks; gradually sprinkle in ¼ cup sugar, beating until sugar is dissolved and whites stand in stiff peaks. With wire whisk, gently fold in gelatin mixture.
4. In small bowl at medium-high speed, beat cream into stiff peaks; fold into gelatin mixture. Spoon into crust. Chill until set, about 3 hours.

Pumpkin Chiffon Pie

Color index
page 88

Begin early
in day or
day ahead

10 servings

*1 3½-ounce can flaked
coconut*
*¼ cup finely crushed
graham-cracker
crumbs*
*⅓ cup melted butter or
margarine*
sugar
*1 envelope unflavored
gelatin*
*¾ teaspoon ground
cinnamon*

*½ teaspoon ground
ginger*
*½ teaspoon ground
nutmeg*
½ teaspoon salt
3 eggs, separated
½ cup milk
1¼ cups canned pumpkin
*whipped heavy or
whipping cream, for
garnish*

1. Preheat oven to 375°F. Spread coconut on cookie sheet; bake 8 to 10 minutes until lightly browned; reserve 2 tablespoons for garnish. In 9-inch pie plate, mix remaining coconut, crumbs, butter and 2 tablespoons sugar; press firmly to bottom and side of pie plate. Bake crust for 6 to 8 minutes until golden; cool.
2. In double-boiler top, mix well gelatin, cinnamon, ginger, nutmeg, salt and ½ cup sugar. In small bowl with wire whisk, beat egg yolks with milk until well mixed; stir into gelatin mixture; stir in pumpkin. Cook over boiling water 20 minutes or until thickened, stirring frequently. Refrigerate the mixture until cool but not set.
3. In large bowl with mixer at high speed, beat egg whites into soft peaks; gradually sprinkle in ¼ cup sugar beating at high speed. With wire whisk, gently fold pumpkin mixture into whites. Pour into crust; refrigerate until set.
4. *To serve:* Top with whipped cream; sprinkle cream with reserved coconut.

Nesselrode Pie

Color index
page 89

Begin early
in day or
day ahead

8 servings

1 9-inch Baked Graham-
 Cracker Crumb Crust
 (page 345)
1 envelope unflavored
 gelatin
1/4 teaspoon salt
sugar
4 eggs, separated
1 1/4 cups milk
1 tablespoon rum

1 teaspoon grated lemon
 peel
1 4-ounce jar diced mixed
 candied fruit (about
 1/2 cup)
1 cup heavy or whipping
 cream, whipped
red and green candied
 pineapple, cut in
 slivers, for garnish

1. Prepare crust. In 2-quart saucepan, mix well gelatin, salt and 3 tablespoons sugar. In small bowl with wire whisk, beat egg yolks with milk until mixed; stir into gelatin mixture.
2. Cook mixture over medium-low heat, stirring, until thickened and it coats spoon. Remove from heat; stir in rum and lemon peel. Refrigerate until cold but not firm, about 40 minutes.
3. In large bowl with mixer at high speed, beat egg whites into soft peaks; gradually sprinkle in 1/4 cup sugar, beating until sugar is dissolved and whites stand in stiff peaks. Gently fold gelatin mixture into whites with mixed candied fruit. Spoon into piecrust; refrigerate about 1 hour or until set.
4. *To serve:* Top with whipped cream. Garnish with candied pineapple.

Black Bottom Pie

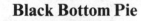

Color index
page 89

Begin early
in day or
day ahead

8 servings

1 9-inch Baked
 Gingersnap Crumb
 Crust (page 345)
2 squares unsweetened
 chocolate
1 envelope unflavored
 gelatin
2 1/4 teaspoons cornstarch

sugar
3 eggs, separated
1 1/4 cups milk
1 teaspoon vanilla
 extract
1 tablespoon light rum
1/2 cup heavy or whipping
 cream, whipped

1. Prepare crust; cool. In 1-quart saucepan over very low heat, melt 1 1/2 squares of the unsweetened chocolate; set aside.
2. In second 1-quart saucepan, mix gelatin, cornstarch and 1/4 cup sugar. In small bowl with fork, beat egg yolks with milk; stir into gelatin mixture. Cook over medium-low heat, stirring, until mixture is thickened and coats the back of a spoon. Remove from heat.
3. Divide custard in half. Into one half, stir melted chocolate and vanilla; with spoon, beat smooth; refrigerate until it mounds when dropped from spoon. Pour into crust; refrigerate. Chill remaining custard until it mounds when dropped from spoon.
4. In small bowl with mixer at high speed, beat egg whites into soft peaks; gradually sprinkle in 1/4 cup sugar, beating until sugar is dissolved. Gently fold whites and rum into chilled custard.
5. Pour as much custard mixture as crust will hold into crust. Refrigerate pie a few minutes, then pour rest of mixture on top. Refrigerate until set.
6. *To serve:* Garnish pie with whipped cream. Shave the remaining half square of chocolate and sprinkle over the top of the pie.

Cherry Cream Tart

Color index
page 88

Begin early
in day

8 servings

1 1/4 cups all-purpose flour
3/4 cup butter, softened
3/4 cup sugar
4 egg yolks
1 envelope unflavored
 gelatin
2 cups half-and-half
1/4 cup cherry-flavor
 liqueur
1/2 cup heavy or whipping
 cream, whipped
1 pound sweet cherries,
 pitted

1 In small bowl with mixer at low speed, beat flour, butter, 1/4 cup sugar and 1 egg yolk until well mixed; cover and refrigerate 1 hour. Preheat oven to 400°F. Press dough onto bottom and 1 inch up side of 10-inch round quiche pan with removable bottom or 10-inch springform pan. Bake 10 minutes or until lightly browned. Cool completely on wire rack.

2 In 2-quart saucepan, combine gelatin and 1/2 cup sugar; stir in half-and-half. Over medium heat, cook, stirring constantly, until the gelatin is completely dissolved.

3 In small bowl with wire whisk or fork, beat remaining 3 egg yolks, then stir in a small amount of hot gelatin mixture.

4 Slowly pour egg mixture into sauce, stirring rapidly to prevent lumping; cook, stirring constantly, until thickened (do not boil).

5 Remove from heat and stir in liqueur, then refrigerate until custard mounds slightly when dropped from a spoon, about 1 hour, stirring frequently.

6 Gently fold whipped cream into custard then pour filling into the cooled piecrust.

7 Arrange cherries on top. Refrigerate until set, about 1 hour. Remove side of pan to serve.

Nut pies

Pecans, peanuts and California walnuts are the most popular nuts for fillings. The nut crusts below are good with the filling from any of the following: Rich Bavarian Pie or Chocolate Chiffon Pie (page 353); Vanilla or Chocolate Cream Pie (page 350).

Allow nut pies to cool on a wire rack before serving them garnished with your choice of either ice cream or whipped cream.

For further information about the preparation of nuts and cooking with nuts, see the Index.

Pecan Pie

Color index
page 86

Begin early
in day

10 servings

*1 9-inch Unbaked
  Piecrust (page 344)*
3 eggs
*1 cup dark corn
  syrup*
1/2 cup sugar

*1/4 cup butter or
  margarine, melted*
*1 teaspoon vanilla
  extract*
1 cup pecan halves

1 Prepare piecrust with your choice of decorative edge, then preheat oven to 350°F.

2 In medium bowl with wire whisk or hand beater, beat eggs well.

3 Beat in corn syrup, sugar, butter or margarine and vanilla extract until well blended.

4 Arrange pecan halves in single layer in bottom of piecrust.

5 Pour egg mixture over the pecans in piecrust being careful not to disturb the nuts.

6 Bake pie 1 hour or until knife inserted about 1 inch from edge comes out clean. Cool.

Double Peanut Pie

Color index
page 88

Begin early
in day

12 servings

*1 9-inch Unbaked
  Piecrust (page 344)*
3 eggs
1 cup dark corn syrup
1/2 cup sugar
*1/2 cup creamy peanut
  butter*

*1/2 teaspoon vanilla
  extract*
*1 cup salted peanuts
whipped cream for
  garnish*

1. Prepare piecrust. Preheat oven to 350°F.
2. In large bowl with mixer at medium speed, beat eggs with corn syrup, sugar, peanut butter and vanilla until smooth. Stir in peanuts.
3. Place pie plate on oven rack; pour mixture into crust. Bake 55 to 60 minutes or until knife inserted about 1 inch from edge comes out clean. Cool. Garnish servings with whipped cream.

Fudge-Nut Pie

Color index
page 88

Begin early
in day

8 servings

*1 9-inch Unbaked Piecrust
  (page 344)*
*2 squares unsweetened
  chocolate*
1/4 cup butter or margarine
3/4 cup sugar
*1/2 cup packed light
  brown sugar*
1/2 cup milk
*1/4 cup corn syrup or
  maple-flavor syrup*

*1 teaspoon vanilla
  extract*
1/4 teaspoon salt
3 eggs
*1 cup finely chopped
  California walnuts
coffee, vanilla or
  chocolate ice cream
  for garnish*

1. Prepare piecrust. Preheat oven to 350°F.
2. In 2-quart saucepan over low heat, heat chocolate with butter or margarine just until melted; remove saucepan from heat.
3. Add sugar and brown sugar, milk, corn syrup, vanilla, salt and eggs; with hand beater or wire whisk, beat until well mixed. Stir in the chopped California walnuts.
4. Pour mixture into piecrust. Bake 45 to 55 minutes until filling is puffed. Cool. To serve, top each serving with a small scoop of ice cream.

NO-ROLL NUT CRUSTS

WALNUT PASTRY CRUST: Preheat oven to 400°F. In 9-inch pie plate with hands, mix *1 cup all-purpose flour, 1/2 cup butter* or margarine, softened, *1/4 cup confectioners' sugar* and *1/4 cup finely chopped California walnuts* until soft and pliable. Press against bottom and side of pie plate. With fork, prick bottom of crust well. Bake 12 minutes or until golden; then cool crust on wire rack. (Makes one 9-inch piecrust.)

GROUND NUT CRUST: Preheat oven to 400°F. In small bowl with spoon, mix *1 1/2 cups finely ground Brazil nuts,* pecans, California walnuts, blanched almonds or peanuts with *3 tablespoons sugar* and *2 tablespoons butter* or margarine, softened. With back of spoon, press to bottom and side of pie plate; do not spread on rim. Bake about 8 minutes, just until golden. Cool on wire rack. (Makes one 9-inch piecrust.)

Tarts

Fruit Cream Tarts

Color index page 87

Begin early in day or day ahead

12 tarts

Baked Tart Shells (page 345)
¼ cup sugar
2 tablespoons cornstarch
¼ teaspoon salt
1 cup milk
1 egg
1 teaspoon vanilla extract
½ cup heavy or whipping cream, whipped

Garnish: *whole or sliced strawberries, blueberries, raspberries, peach slices, apricot halves or mandarin-orange sections, drained*

1 cup currant jelly (optional)
1 tablespoon water (optional)

1 Prepare tart shells. In 2-quart saucepan, mix sugar, cornstarch and salt; stir in milk until smooth. Over medium heat, cook, stirring, until mixture boils; boil 1 minute.

2 In 1-cup measure with fork, beat egg slightly, then slowly stir in small amount of the hot sauce.

3 Slowly pour egg mixture into sauce, stirring rapidly to prevent lumping. Cook, stirring, until thickened (do not boil).

4 Cover with waxed paper and refrigerate. When the custard is cold (after about 40 minutes), stir in vanilla extract; then, with wire whisk, fold in whipped cream.

5 Spoon custard into shells. Top with fruit. If you like, in 1-quart saucepan, melt jelly and water; cool slightly; spoon over fruit. Refrigerate until jelly sets.

Walnut Tarts

Color index page 87

Begin early in day

12 tarts

Unbaked Tart Shells (page 345)
3 eggs
1 cup dark corn syrup
½ cup sugar
¼ cup butter or margarine, melted

1 teaspoon vanilla extract
1 cup coarsely chopped California walnuts
whipped cream for garnish

1. Prepare tart shells. Preheat oven to 350°F. In medium bowl with wire whisk, beat eggs well. Beat in next 4 ingredients until well blended.
2. Distribute chopped walnuts evenly among tart shells; carefully pour filling over walnuts.
3. Bake 25 to 30 minutes. Cool 10 minutes; remove from pans and cool on wire rack. Serve topped with whipped cream.

Mince Tarts

Color index page 89

Begin day ahead

12 tarts

1 18-ounce jar prepared mincemeat (2 cups)
1½ cups coarsely broken California walnuts
2 large apples, cored and diced
½ cup packed brown sugar

¼ cup brandy or rum (optional)
1 tablespoon lemon juice
Unbaked Tart Shells (page 345)
Brandy Hard Sauce (page 349)

1. In medium bowl, stir first 6 ingredients until well mixed; cover and refrigerate overnight to allow flavors to blend.
2. *About 3 hours before serving:* Prepare tart shells. Preheat oven to 425°F. Fill shells with undrained mincemeat mixture. Bake 20 to 25 minutes until golden. Serve warm, each topped with some sauce.

Begin day ahead

8 servings

MINCE PIE: Prepare as above but use Pastry for 2-Crust Pie (page 344). Roll out half of pastry to line 9-inch pie plate. Fill crust and use remaining pastry to make a lattice top (page 343). Bake in preheated 425°F. oven 30 to 40 minutes until crust is golden. Serve warm with Brandy Hard Sauce.

Peach Meringue Tarts

Color index page 89

Begin 3 hrs ahead

12 tarts

4 cups sliced ripe peaches (about 2 pounds)
3 tablespoons quick-cooking tapioca
2 tablespoons lemon juice
¼ teaspoon almond extract

sugar
Unbaked Tart Shells (page 345)
2 egg whites

1. In medium bowl with rubber spatula, gently stir peaches, tapioca, lemon juice, almond extract and ½ cup sugar; let stand 20 minutes. Meanwhile, prepare tart shells. Preheat oven to 425°F.
2. Gently stir peach mixture again; spoon into tart shells; place on cookie sheet. Bake 30 to 35 minutes until juices are bubbly.
3. Beat egg whites until foamy; gradually beat in 2 tablespoons sugar, until stiff peaks form. Remove tarts from oven; spoon dollop of meringue on top of each; bake about 4 minutes longer, just until tarts are lightly browned.

DESSERTS

Our recipes for desserts fall into the following categories: Custards, Bavarian Cream, Cold Soufflés, Mousse, Hot Soufflés, Meringues, Crêpes and Blintzes, Cream Puffs and Eclairs and Other Desserts. The recipes range from simple everyday desserts to internationally popular ones calling for special techniques.

THICKENING WITH EGGS

Many desserts and sauces call for using eggs as a thickening agent. The key to successful custard preparation is low heat; high heat causes the eggs to curdle, resulting in lumpy, thin mixtures. Either cook custard in a double boiler or if cooking over direct heat, always use a heavy saucepan. Stir the mixture constantly with a whisk until it thickens and coats a metal spoon (do not boil). Check thickness by lifting the spoon from custard and holding it up for 15 to 20 seconds; if the spoon does not show through mixture the custard has thickened to the correct consistency.

Testing consistency: Hold up spoon for 15 to 20 seconds; spoon should not show through mixture.

USING GELATIN

Many desserts – fruit molds, Bavarian creams, cold soufflés – call for gelatin, both flavored and unflavored.
Dissolving gelatin: For properly set jelled mixtures, the gelatin must be dissolved completely; no granules of gelatin should remain in the mixture. Stirring is essential to dissolve gelatin. To prevent granules from splashing up the side of the bowl or saucepan, always be sure to stir steadily but not too vigorously.

Checking dissolving: Run a rubber spatula through the mixture, next to the side of the pan, to see if the granules are all dissolved.

Flavored gelatins are stirred with hot or boiling water, depending on the package directions. Recipes using unflavored gelatin vary slightly in the dissolving technique, depending on the other ingredients used. The rule of thumb is this: never add unflavored gelatin directly to hot liquid because the gelatin will become lumpy and will not dissolve completely. Usually, unflavored gelatin is sprinkled over a small amount of cold liquid, left to stand a minute to soften, then stirred with hot liquid or cooked over low heat to dissolve. In recipes with more than a cup of liquid, as for many sauces, unflavored gelatin is sprinkled over cold liquid; cook it without standing, stirring until the gelatin is completely dissolved. In recipes which call for sugar, the sugar is sometimes mixed with the gelatin and then at least a cup of boiling liquid is stirred in.

Gelatin consistency: Allow gelatin to partially set before adding fruits, whipped cream or other solids. A partially set mixture holds them in suspension, keeps them uniformly distributed throughout. Some recipes, especially ones with cut-up fruit added, call for mixtures jelled to the consistency of "an unbeaten egg white." Other recipes, especially ones with whipped cream or whipped egg whites added, call for mixtures jelled until "mixture mounds when dropped from a spoon." Then the whipped cream or whipped egg whites are folded in.

Hastening setting: Put the saucepan or bowl of gelatin mixture into a bowl of ice and stir to hasten setting.

Testing consistency: Take up a spoonful of mixture and drop it back on top. It should "mound," not disappear.

As an alternative to the method explained and illustrated above, if you want to hasten the setting of a gelatin mixture, you can put the bowl of gelatin mixture in the freezer, and stir occasionally until partially set. Do not try to freeze the mixture until it has set, as ice crystals may form, making the gelatin watery.

Custards

Egg custards are really quite simple to prepare, provided you follow recipe directions. Avoid using excessive heat which will ruin the texture of the dish. If cooking over direct heat, stir the custard constantly and watch the mixture carefully as it thickens.

Crème Brûlée

Color index page 97

Begin early in day or day ahead

10 servings

3 cups heavy or whipping cream
6 egg yolks
⅓ cup sugar
1 teaspoon vanilla extract
⅓ cup packed brown sugar

sliced strawberries, bananas, fresh or canned pineapple chunks and canned mandarin-orange sections

1 In 1-quart saucepan over medium heat, heat cream until tiny bubbles form around edge of pan.

2 Meanwhile, in 2-quart saucepan with wire whisk, blend yolks with sugar. Slowly stir in cream.

3 Over medium-low heat, cook the mixture, stirring constantly, until it just coats back of metal spoon, about 15 minutes (do not boil). Stir in vanilla.

4 Pour mixture into 1½-quart broilersafe casserole; refrigerate until well chilled, about 6 hours.

5 Preheat broiler if manufacturer directs. Sift brown sugar over chilled cream mixture; broil 3 to 4 minutes until sugar melts. Refrigerate.

6 *To serve:* Place casserole in center of large tray; surround with fruit. Serve portions of mixed fruit with Crème Brûlée spooned over.

Crème Caramel

Color index page 96

Begin early in day or day ahead

8 servings

sugar
5 eggs
¼ teaspoon salt
3 cups milk
1½ teaspoons vanilla extract

1 Butter eight 6-ounce custard cups. In small skillet over medium heat, melt ½ cup sugar, stirring, till it is a light brown syrup.

2 Pour syrup into buttered cups. Place cups in shallow baking pan for easy handling. Preheat oven to 300°F.

3 In large bowl with mixer at low speed, beat eggs, salt and ½ cup sugar until lemon-colored. Gradually beat in milk and vanilla extract.

4 Pour mixture in cups; put hot water in pan to within 1 inch of top of cups; bake 1 hour until knife inserted in center comes out clean.

5 Cool on wire racks; refrigerate; with knife, loosen custard from cups and invert onto dessert dishes, letting syrup run down sides onto dish.

BAKED CUSTARD: Prepare as for Crème Caramel (above) but omit making syrup in steps 1 and 2. Before baking, sprinkle with *ground nutmeg*.

Custard Sauce

Begin early in day

1½ cups

3 tablespoons sugar
1¾ cups half-and-half
1 egg yolk
1 tablespoon cornstarch

⅛ teaspoon salt
½ teaspoon vanilla extract

In heavy, 2-quart saucepan, combine all ingredients except vanilla. Cook over medium heat, stirring, until mixture coats back of spoon, about 15 minutes. Remove from heat; stir in vanilla. Chill.

Custards

Apricot-Cream Flan

Color index
page 95

Begin 5 hrs
ahead or
early in day

8 servings

1 cup all-purpose flour
*¾ cup California
walnuts, finely ground*
*6 tablespoons butter or
margarine, softened*
*¼ teaspoon ground
cinnamon*
sugar
salt
8 egg yolks

2 cups milk
¼ cup cornstarch
*¾ teaspoon almond
extract*
*1 17-ounce can apricot
halves, drained or
7 large apricots,
halved and pitted*
¼ cup apple jelly

1. In large bowl with mixer at low speed, beat flour, walnuts, butter or margarine, cinnamon, 3 tablespoons sugar, ¼ teaspoon salt and 2 egg yolks until well mixed.
2. Preheat oven to 400°F. Pat mixture evenly onto bottom and side of fluted 10-inch tart pan with removable bottom or into 10-inch springform pan (pat mixture only 1 inch up side of pan). With fork, prick bottom of crust well. Bake 20 minutes or till golden brown. Cool on wire rack.
3. Meanwhile, in 2-quart saucepan, stir milk, cornstarch, ⅓ cup sugar and ¼ teaspoon salt until smooth. Cook over medium heat, stirring constantly, until mixture is thickened and boils, about 5 minutes; remove pan from heat. In small bowl with wire whisk, beat remaining 6 egg yolks; stir in small amount of hot milk mixture. Slowly pour yolk mixture into milk mixture, stirring rapidly to prevent lumping.
4. Return the saucepan to the heat; cook, stirring constantly with whisk, until mixture thickens and coats a spoon (do not boil). (To check thickness, lift metal spoon from custard and hold up 15 to 20 seconds; spoon should not show through mixture when it is the correct consistency.)
5. Stir in almond extract; cover the custard surface with waxed paper; refrigerate 30 minutes until mixture is cool but not set. Pour cooled custard mixture into cooled crust; refrigerate until custard is completely set, about 4 hours.
6. *To serve:* Remove side from pan; transfer flan to large flat serving dish. Arrange apricot halves on custard. In 1-quart saucepan, melt apple jelly; brush melted jelly over apricots.

Zabaglione

Color index
page 97

Begin 20 mins
ahead

6 servings

6 egg yolks
¼ cup sugar

*½ cup dry or sweet
Marsala*

1. In double-boiler top, not over water, with portable mixer at high speed, beat egg yolks and sugar until of a thick consistency and light colored, about 5 minutes. Reduce the speed to medium and beat in the Marsala.
2. Place mixture over simmering water in double-boiler bottom; cook, beating constantly at medium speed, until mixture is fluffy, warm and mounds slightly on the surface when the beater is lifted, about 10 minutes.
3. Serve at once as dessert or spoon over fresh berries or sliced fruit as a sauce.

Bavarian cream

A light mixture of gelatin, custard, egg whites and cream, classic Bavarian Cream is an elegant molded dessert, often served with sliced fruit such as peaches, strawberries or canned pineapple. Sometimes the fruit is folded into the flavored cream mixture before jelling.

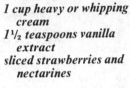

Bavarian Cream

Color index
page 95

Begin early
in day or
day ahead

8 servings

*1 envelope unflavored
gelatin*
½ teaspoon salt
sugar
2 eggs, separated
1¼ cups milk

*1 cup heavy or whipping
cream*
*1½ teaspoons vanilla
extract*
*sliced strawberries and
nectarines*

1 In 3-quart saucepan, stir gelatin, salt and 2 tablespoons sugar until well mixed. In small bowl with wire whisk, mix together egg yolks and milk.

2 Stir milk mixture into gelatin mixture; over low heat, cook, stirring constantly, until mixture coats spoon. Refrigerate until mixture mounds when dropped from spoon.

3 In small bowl at high speed, beat egg whites until soft peaks form; at high speed, gradually beat in ¼ cup sugar until dissolved.

4 Spoon whites over gelatin mixture. In same bowl, beat cream with vanilla until soft peaks form; add to gelatin mixture in pan.

5 With wire whisk, gently fold whites and cream into gelatin; pour into 6-cup mold; refrigerate till set, about 3 hours.

6 *To serve:* Carefully unmold Bavarian Cream onto chilled serving plate. Serve with sliced strawberries and nectarines.

Cold soufflés

Raised high with beaten egg whites and whipped cream, light, fluffy dessert soufflés can be made in almost any deep serving dish. To make a cold soufflé look like a hot soufflé which rises above the top of its dish, add a collar of foil which extends beyond the top of the dish to support the soufflé mixture during the setting process; remove the collar just before the soufflé is served.

Unlike hot soufflés, cold soufflés can be made well ahead of time and kept in the refrigerator ready to be brought to the table; add the decorative garnish, such as slivered citrus peel, whipped cream or chocolate curls, just before serving.

Strawberry Soufflé

2 pints strawberries
2 envelopes unflavored
* gelatin*
sugar
4 teaspoons lemon juice
6 egg whites
¼ teaspoon salt
2 cups heavy or whipping
* cream*

Color index page 94
Begin 6 hrs or day ahead
12 servings

1 Reserve 6 strawberries for garnish. Wash and hull remainder. Place in covered blender container; puree them at medium speed.

2 In 2-quart saucepan, stir gelatin with 3 tablespoons sugar; gradually stir in one third of pureed strawberries. Cook over low heat, stirring, till gelatin dissolves.

3 Remove from heat; stir in remaining puree and lemon juice; pour into bowl. Chill in freezer, about 20 minutes, until mixture mounds when dropped from spoon.

4 Prepare foil collar for 2-quart soufflé dish or casserole (right). In large bowl with mixer at high speed, beat egg whites and salt until soft peaks form; beating at high speed, gradually sprinkle in ⅓ cup sugar, 2 tablespoons at a time, until the whites form stiff glossy peaks. (Do not scrape side of bowl during beating.)

5 Beat chilled strawberry mixture until fluffy, about 2 minutes. In another small bowl at medium speed, using same beaters, beat cream until stiff peaks form.

6 With rubber spatula, gently fold the strawberry mixture and whipped cream into the beaten egg whites.

7 Spoon folded mixture into prepared soufflé dish. Refrigerate the mixture until it has set, about 2 hours.

8 Remove foil collar from dish. Wash and hull 6 reserved strawberries and use whole or halved to garnish top of soufflé.

Color index page 96
Begin early in day
12 servings

Chocolate-Cherry Soufflé

2 16½- to 17-ounce cans *sugar*
* pitted dark sweet*   *4 squares semisweet*
* cherries, drained*   * chocolate*
6 tablespoons Kirsch   *2 envelopes unflavored*
* (cherry-flavor brandy)* * gelatin*
3 eggs, separated   *2 cups heavy or whipping*
2 cups milk   * cream*

1. Prepare foil collar for 1½-quart soufflé dish (see instructions below).

2. Reserve 3 cherries; cut remaining cherries in half. In medium bowl, mix cherry halves and 3 tablespoons Kirsch; set aside.

3. In 2-quart saucepan with wire whisk, beat egg yolks, milk and ½ cup sugar until well mixed. Add chocolate; sprinkle gelatin evenly over mixture. Over low heat, cook, stirring constantly, until gelatin is completely dissolved, chocolate is melted and mixture coats a spoon, about 15 minutes. Stir in remaining 3 tablespoons Kirsch; cover and refrigerate until mixture mounds when dropped from a spoon, about 1 hour.

4. In small bowl with mixer at high speed, beat egg whites until stiff peaks form. Beating at high speed, gradually sprinkle in ¼ cup sugar, beating mixture until sugar is completely dissolved.

5. In large bowl, using same beaters, beat 1¾ cups heavy cream until soft peaks form. With rubber spatula, fold chocolate mixture, egg whites and cherry halves into whipped cream until blended. Pour the mixture into the prepared soufflé dish. Cover with plastic wrap and refrigerate until it has set, about 4 hours.

6. *To serve:* Remove collar from soufflé dish. In small bowl with mixer at medium speed, beat remaining ¼ cup heavy cream until stiff peaks form. Garnish top of soufflé with whipped cream and reserved cherries.

MAKING A FOIL COLLAR

Cut piece of 12-inch-wide foil to fit around soufflé dish and overlap by about 2 inches (about 24 inches long for 2-quart dish). Then fold the foil in half lengthwise.

Carefully wrap foil strip around outside of dish so that collar stands about 3 inches above rim. Fasten the foil collar securely with a short piece of cellophane tape.

Cold soufflés

Color index page 97

Begin early in day

8 servings

Frosty Lime Soufflé

1 envelope unflavored gelatin
sugar
½ teaspoon salt
4 eggs, separated
½ cup cold water

⅓ cup lime juice
grated peel of 1 lime
⅛ teaspoon green food color
1 cup heavy or whipping cream

1. In double boiler, stir gelatin with ¼ cup sugar and salt until well mixed.

2. In small bowl with wire whisk, beat egg yolks with cold water and lime juice until mixed; stir into gelatin mixture. Cook over hot, *not boiling,* water, stirring constantly, until mixture thickens and coats a spoon. Remove from heat; stir in 1 teaspoon of grated peel and food color; pour into large bowl and cool to room temperature, stirring occasionally. Meanwhile, prepare collar for a 1-quart soufflé dish (page 361).

3. In small bowl with mixer at high speed, beat egg whites until soft peaks form; beating at high speed, gradually sprinkle in ½ cup sugar; beat until sugar is completely dissolved. Whites should stand in stiff peaks. Spoon into bowl with lime mixture.

4. In small bowl with mixer at medium speed, whip cream; gently fold with beaten egg whites into lime mixture. Pour into prepared soufflé dish; chill until firm, at least 3 hours. Carefully remove foil collar and garnish with remaining peel.

Color index page 98

Begin early in day

8 to 10 servings

Cranberry Soufflé

2 cups cranberries
1½ cups cranberry juice
sugar
3 envelopes unflavored gelatin
Sugared Cranberries (below)

4 egg whites, at room temperature
¼ teaspoon salt
1 cup heavy or whipping cream

1. Into 2-quart saucepan, measure cranberries, cranberry juice and 1 cup sugar; evenly sprinkle with gelatin. Cook over medium-high heat, stirring constantly, until gelatin is completely dissolved and cranberries pop, about 7 minutes. Refrigerate until mixture mounds slightly when dropped from a spoon, about 45 minutes.

2. Meanwhile, make collar for a 1-quart soufflé dish (page 361). Prepare Sugared Cranberries.

3. In large bowl with mixer at high speed, beat egg whites and salt until soft peaks form. Beating at high speed, gradually sprinkle in ½ cup sugar, 2 tablespoons at a time, beating until each addition is dissolved. Whites should stand in stiff peaks.

4. In small bowl with same beaters and with mixer at medium speed, beat cream until soft peaks form. With rubber spatula, gently fold cranberry mixture and whipped cream into beaten whites until well blended. Pour into soufflé dish; cover and refrigerate until set, about 4 hours. Carefully remove the foil collar; top with Sugared Cranberries.

SUGARED CRANBERRIES: In cup, beat *1 egg white* till frothy. Dip *18 whole cranberries* into egg white; roll in *sugar* to coat; dry on rack.

Mousse

Many people judge restaurants or cooks by the quality of their chocolate mousse, that rich, light, whipped cream dessert. This all-time favorite, served in little cups, is called, literally, "pots of cream."

Color index page 94

Begin 5 hrs or day ahead

6 servings

Pots de Crème au Chocolat

2 cups half-and-half (1 pint)
4 squares semisweet chocolate
6 egg yolks
¼ cup sugar

½ teaspoon salt
vanilla extract
¼ cup heavy or whipping cream
2 tablespoons confectioners' sugar

1 In 1-quart saucepan over medium heat, heat half-and-half until tiny bubbles form around edge of saucepan (do not allow half-and-half to boil). Set saucepan aside. In double boiler over hot, *not boiling,* water, melt semisweet chocolate squares, stirring occasionally with rubber spatula.

2 Remove double-boiler top to work surface and, with rubber spatula, beat egg yolks into the melted chocolate until smooth; then stir in sugar and salt.

3 Gradually stir half-and-half into the chocolate mixture until thoroughly blended. Replace double-boiler top over simmering (not boiling) water.

4 Cook, stirring constantly, until mixture coats back of a spoon, about 15 minutes. Stir in 2 teaspoons vanilla extract.

5 Pour mixture into six 6-ounce *pots de crème* cups or stemmed glasses. Refrigerate for about 4 hours or just until the mixture is set.

6 In small bowl with mixer at low speed, beat cream, confectioners' sugar and ¼ teaspoon vanilla until stiff; use to top *pots de crème.*

Hot soufflés

Timing is the key to success when making hot soufflés and since they tend to collapse if left to stand for more than a few minutes, they should always be served as soon as they come from the oven. It helps to avoid a lot of last-minute work when preparing the meal and this is easy to arrange with hot soufflés because both the basic sauce and the soufflé dish itself can be prepared well in advance; let the egg whites stand in the mixer bowl, at room temperature, ready to be beaten and folded with the sauce just before baking. Do not open the oven door before the end of baking time; cold air could cause the soufflé to fall.

Chocolate Soufflé

⅓ cup all-purpose flour
sugar
1½ cups milk
3 squares unsweetened
  chocolate, coarsely
  chopped or grated
6 eggs, separated
¼ teaspoon salt
2 teaspoons vanilla
  extract

Color index page 95
Begin 2 hrs ahead
8 servings

1 In 2-quart saucepan, into flour and ¼ cup sugar, slowly stir milk. Cook over medium heat, stirring constantly, until the mixture thickens and starts to boil.

2 Cook mixture 1 minute more. Remove pan from heat and stir in chocolate until melted.

3 With wooden spoon, rapidly beat in egg yolks, all at once, beating until thoroughly blended; refrigerate to cool the mixture to lukewarm, stirring occasionally.

4 Grease 2-quart soufflé dish or round casserole with butter or margarine and lightly sprinkle dish with sugar. Preheat the oven to 375°F.

5 In large bowl with mixer at high speed, beat egg whites and salt until soft peaks form.

6 With the mixer at high speed, gradually sprinkle in ¼ cup sugar; beat well until the sugar is completely dissolved. The whites should stand in stiff glossy peaks.

7 With wire whisk or rubber spatula, gently fold chocolate mixture, one third at a time, and vanilla into egg whites, until blended. Pour mixture into soufflé dish.

8 With back of spoon, 1 inch from edge of dish, make 1-inch indentation all around soufflé. Bake 35 to 40 minutes until knife inserted under "top hat" comes out clean.

Color index page 95
Begin 1 hr ahead
6 servings

Individual Chocolate Soufflés

sugar
¼ cup all-purpose
  flour
1¼ cups milk
3 squares unsweetened
  chocolate
5 eggs, separated

¼ teaspoon salt
2 teaspoons vanilla
  extract
½ cup heavy or whipping
  cream, whipped
½ cup chocolate syrup

1. Grease six 10-ounce soufflé dishes or custard cups with butter or margarine and then lightly sprinkle them with sugar.
2. In 2-quart saucepan, combine flour and ¼ cup sugar; gradually add milk, stirring constantly until mixture is smooth. Cook mixture over medium heat, stirring constantly, until mixture is thickened; remove from heat.
3. Stir chocolate into mixture until melted. Rapidly beat in egg yolks all at once, until well mixed; set aside and allow to cool to lukewarm.
4. Preheat oven to 375°F. In large bowl with mixer at high speed, beat egg whites, salt and vanilla until soft peaks form; beating at high speed, gradually add ½ cup sugar, 2 tablespoons at a time. Whites should stand in stiff peaks. With rubber spatula, gently fold chocolate mixture into beaten egg whites until blended; spoon into the prepared soufflé dishes or custard cups.
5. Place filled cups in 15½" by 10½" jelly-roll pan for easier handling. Bake soufflés 30 to 35 minutes until puffy and brown.
6. Serve soufflés immediately. Pass whipped cream and chocolate syrup to spoon over top.

CHOCOLATE TIPS

Melting chocolate: Use any of these ways: Place in top of double boiler and melt over hot, *not boiling*, water. Or place in custard cup and set in pan of hot water. Or place in heavy, 1-quart saucepan; melt over low heat – if the pan is too thin, it will transfer heat too fast and burn the chocolate.

To speed melting: Break up chocolate into smaller pieces; stir frequently. If you are melting the chocolate in a double boiler or in a custard cup set in a pan of water, do not boil the water to speed melting as this will only thicken or curdle the chocolate.

If chocolate thickens or curdles, add vegetable shortening (not butter or margarine) a little at a time and stir until of the desired consistency.

In an emergency you can substitute cocoa for unsweetened chocolate in recipes. The proportions to use are 3 tablespoons cocoa plus 1 tablespoon shortening or salad oil (not butter or margarine) for each square of chocolate called for in the recipe.

Do not substitute semisweet or milk chocolate in recipes calling for unsweetened.

Hot soufflés

Color index
page 97

Begin 1¼ hrs
ahead

6 servings

Orange Liqueur Soufflé

¼ cup butter or margarine	1 tablespoon grated orange peel
⅓ cup all-purpose flour	6 egg whites, at room temperature
⅛ teaspoon salt	¼ teaspoon cream of tartar
1½ cups milk sugar	1 cup heavy or whipping cream, whipped
4 egg yolks	
⅓ cup orange-flavor liqueur	

1. In 3-quart saucepan over low heat, melt butter. Stir in flour and salt until well blended; gradually stir in milk; cook, stirring, until mixture is thickened. Remove pan from heat.

2. With wire whisk, beat 3 tablespoons sugar into milk mixture. Rapidly beat in egg yolks, all at once. Stir in liqueur and orange peel; set aside.

3. Preheat oven to 375°F. Grease 2-quart soufflé dish or round casserole with butter or margarine and sprinkle lightly with sugar.

4. In large bowl with mixer at high speed, beat egg whites and cream of tartar until stiff peaks form. With rubber spatula or wire whisk, gently fold egg-yolk mixture, one third at a time, into egg whites until blended.

5. Pour the mixture into the prepared soufflé dish; with back of spoon, about 1 inch from edge of dish, make 1-inch indentation all around. Bake 30 to 35 minutes until knife inserted under "top hat" comes out clean.

6. Serve soufflé immediately and pass bowl of whipped cream separately to spoon over top.

Color index
page 95

Begin 1 hr
ahead

8 servings

Banana Soufflé

3 large bananas	¾ cup milk
1 tablespoon lemon juice	3 large eggs, separated
⅓ cup sugar	2 tablespoons melted butter or margarine
1 tablespoon cornstarch	1½ teaspoons vanilla extract
½ teaspoon ground nutmeg	1 cup heavy or whipping cream, whipped
¼ teaspoon grated lemon peel	
⅛ teaspoon salt	

1. Grease bottom of 1½-quart soufflé dish. Peel and slice bananas. In covered blender container at medium speed, blend bananas and lemon juice until well mixed and creamy.

2. In 3-quart saucepan, mix sugar, cornstarch, nutmeg, lemon peel and salt. Stir in milk until blended. Over medium heat, cook milk mixture until thickened, stirring constantly. Remove from heat.

3. Preheat oven to 375°F. In small bowl with fork, beat egg yolks well. Add a little of hot-milk mixture; mix together well. Mix egg-yolk mixture well with remaining hot-milk mixture. Stir in butter or margarine, vanilla extract and banana mixture.

4. In small bowl with mixer at high speed, beat egg whites until stiff peaks form. Carefully fold into banana mixture; pour into soufflé dish. Bake 35 minutes or until golden brown. Serve immediately with whipped cream to spoon over the top.

Meringues

Meringue, a mixture of stiffly beaten egg whites and sugar, is baked into small or large shells to be served with either ice cream or another filling. Soft meringue, which is beaten with less sugar, is baked on top of pies or can be poached for Floating Island.

Meringue Shells

Begin early
in day or
up to 5 days
ahead

6 shells

3 egg whites, at room temperature	¾ cup sugar
⅛ teaspoon cream of tartar	½ teaspoon vanilla extract

1. Preheat oven to 275°F. In small bowl with mixer at high speed, beat egg whites and cream of tartar until soft peaks form.

2. Gradually sprinkle in sugar, 2 tablespoons at a time, beating after each addition for about 2 minutes or until sugar is completely dissolved, about 15 minutes. To test, rub meringue between fingers; if grainy, continue beating. Add vanilla, beating at high speed until mixture stands in stiff, glossy peaks.

3. Onto large greased cookie sheet, spoon mixture into 6 mounds. Spread each mound into a 4-inch circle, heaping mixture to form a nest shape.

4. Bake 45 minutes until meringues are crisp and very lightly browned. Turn off oven; let meringues stand in oven 45 minutes longer to dry. Cool completely on cookie sheet. Store loosely wrapped in waxed paper; keep at room temperature.

Shaping meringue: Spoon on cookie sheet; spread into 4-inch circles.

Forming nests: Heap mixture at edge of each circle to form nest shape.

MAKING A MERINGUE PIE SHELL

Preheat oven to 275°F. Prepare steps 1 and 2 of Meringue Shells (above) then shape as shown below. Bake 1 hour. Turn off oven; let stand in oven 1 hour.

Into greased 9-inch pie plate, spoon mixture, smoothing it at center.

Pile meringue high on the sides to form a pie "shell."

Surprise Angel Pecan Pie

Color index
page 95

Begin 4 hrs or
day ahead

8 servings

*3 egg whites, at room
temperature*
*⅛ teaspoon salt
sugar
vanilla extract*
¾ cup chopped pecans

*¾ cup crushed soda
crackers*
*1 teaspoon double-acting
baking powder*
*1 cup heavy or whipping
cream*

1. Preheat oven to 350°F. Grease 9-inch pie plate; line with foil; grease foil.
2. In small bowl with mixer at high speed, beat egg whites and salt until soft peaks form. Gradually sprinkle in 1 cup sugar, 2 tablespoons at a time, beating well after each addition. Whites should stand in stiff glossy peaks. Lightly beat in 1 teaspoon vanilla extract.
3. Into egg-white mixture, fold pecans, crackers and baking powder. Spread evenly in pie plate. Bake 35 minutes or until light golden but not brown. Cool on wire rack 2 hours. Using foil, lift pie from plate; refrigerate until pie is thoroughly chilled, at least 1 hour or overnight.
4. *To serve:* Remove foil; place pie on plate. In small bowl with hand beater or mixer at medium speed, beat cream with 2 tablespoons sugar and 1 teaspoon vanilla extract until stiff peaks form. Spread whipped cream mixture over pie.

Strawberry Meringues

Color index
page 97

Begin early
in day

6 servings

*Meringue Shells
(opposite)*
*1½ pints vanilla ice
cream*

1½ pints strawberries
⅓ cup sugar

1. Prepare Meringue Shells.
2. Using ice-cream scoop or large spoon, scoop ice cream into 6 balls onto cookie sheet; freeze.
3. Thinly slice strawberries; place in medium bowl. Stir sugar into berries; refrigerate.
4. *To serve:* Top each meringue shell with ice-cream ball and spoon on strawberries and juice.

Chocolate Angel Pie

Color index
page 97

Begin early
in day

10 servings

*1 Meringue Pie Shell
(opposite)*
*2 squares unsweetened
chocolate*
3 tablespoons water
3 egg yolks

¼ cup sugar
⅛ teaspoon salt
*1½ cups heavy or
whipping cream*
*1 teaspoon vanilla
extract*

1. Prepare Meringue Pie Shell.
2. Meanwhile, in double boiler over hot, *not boiling*, water, combine chocolate, water, egg yolks, sugar and salt. Cook until chocolate melts and mixture is very thick and mounds when dropped from a spoon, about 5 minutes, stirring constantly. Remove from heat and set aside.
3. In large bowl with mixer at medium speed, beat heavy cream and vanilla extract until soft peaks form. With wire whisk, gently fold chocolate mixture into whipped-cream mixture.
4. Spoon mixture into meringue shell. Refrigerate until filling is set, about 4 hours.

Floating Island

Color index
page 94

Begin 1½ hrs
ahead

4 servings

5 egg yolks
2 cups milk
*¼ teaspoon salt
sugar*
*½ teaspoon vanilla
extract*
*1 egg white, at room
temperature*
water

1 In double boiler over hot, *not boiling*, water, combine egg yolks, milk, salt and ¾ cup sugar. Cook, stirring constantly, until mixture thickens and coats spoon, about 15 minutes. (To test consistency, lift metal spoon; hold up 15 to 20 seconds; spoon should not show through mixture.) Stir in vanilla extract.

2 Pour custard into 4 wine goblets or into dessert dishes. Cover; refrigerate until well chilled, about 1 hour.

3 Meanwhile, in small bowl with mixer at high speed, beat egg white until soft peaks form. Gradually sprinkle in 2 tablespoons sugar, beating till completely dissolved.

4 Preheat oven to 350°F. Onto ½ inch cold water in 8″ by 8″ baking dish, drop beaten egg white in 4 mounds. Bake 7 to 10 minutes until lightly browned.

5 With slotted spoon, remove each light brown meringue from water; drain on spoon over paper towels. Slip onto custard in wine goblet.

6 In heavy, 1-quart saucepan over high heat, heat 3 tablespoons sugar, stirring constantly, until smooth and amber, about 3 minutes.

7 Remove saucepan from heat; let stand 2 minutes then, with spoon, quickly drizzle the sugar syrup over each dessert in thin strands.

365

Cream puffs and éclairs

Based on *choux* paste, a butter, egg and flour mixture, cream puffs and éclairs have a lightly browned, crisp and tender shell with a slightly moist hollow interior.

Cream Puffs

Color index page 95

Begin early in day or day ahead

12 servings

Choux paste:
1/2 cup butter or margarine
1 cup water
1/4 teaspoon salt
1 cup all-purpose flour
4 eggs

Vanilla or Almond Pastry Cream (right)
confectioners' sugar

1 Grease 2 large cookie sheets. Prepare *choux* paste: In 2-quart saucepan over medium heat, heat butter, water and salt until butter mixture boils. Remove from heat.

2 Add flour all at once. With wooden spoon, vigorously stir until mixture forms a ball and leaves side of pan. Preheat oven to 375°F.

3 Add eggs to flour mixture, one at a time, beating well after each addition, until smooth. Cool mixture slightly.

4 Using large spoon and rubber spatula, drop batter onto cookie sheets in 12 large mounds, 3 inches apart, swirling top of each. Bake 50 minutes.

5 Remove from oven; cut slit in side of each puff. Return to oven; bake 10 minutes. Turn off oven; dry puffs in oven 10 minutes. Cool. Prepare filling; cover and chill.

6 When puffs are cool, slice top off each. Fill each shell with the chilled Vanilla Pastry Cream; replace top. Sprinkle tops of cream puffs with some confectioners' sugar.

FILLINGS AND GLAZE

VANILLA PASTRY CREAM: In 2-quart saucepan, combine *3/4 cup sugar, 1/4 cup all-purpose flour* and *1/4 teaspoon salt;* stir in *1 1/2 cups milk.* Over medium heat, cook, stirring, until mixture thickens and boils, about 10 minutes; boil 1 minute. In small bowl with fork, beat *6 egg yolks* slightly; beat small amount of milk mixture into yolks; slowly pour egg mixture back into milk mixture, stirring. Cook over medium-low heat, stirring until mixture thickens and coats spoon well, about 8 minutes (do not boil). (To check thickness, lift metal spoon from mixture and hold up 15 seconds; spoon should not show through mixture.) Remove from heat; stir in *1 1/2 teaspoons vanilla extract.* Cover surface with plastic wrap; chill well, about 2 hours. In small bowl with mixer at medium speed, beat *1 1/2 cups heavy or whipping cream* until stiff peaks form. With rubber spatula, gently fold cream into custard. (Makes 4 2/3 cups.)

ALMOND PASTRY CREAM: Prepare as above but substitute *1 teaspoon almond extract* for vanilla.

SEMISWEET CHOCOLATE GLAZE: In 1-quart saucepan over low heat, melt *2 squares semisweet chocolate* and *2 tablespoons butter,* stirring constantly. Stir in *1 cup confectioners' sugar* and *3 tablespoons milk* until smooth. (Makes 1 cup.)

Eclairs

Color index page 97

Begin early in day or day ahead

10 éclairs

choux paste from Cream Puffs (left)
Vanilla Pastry Cream (above)

Semisweet Chocolate Glaze (above)

1. Preheat oven to 375°F. Make *choux* paste as for Cream Puffs in steps 1 to 3; drop by 1/4 cupfuls onto cookie sheet 2 inches apart, and in rows 6 inches apart, to make 10. Spread each mound into rectangle, rounding edges. (Or use pastry bag as below.) Bake 40 minutes or until lightly browned. Cut slit in side of each shell and bake 10 minutes longer. Turn off oven; dry shells in oven 10 minutes. Cool on rack.
2. Meanwhile, prepare Vanilla Pastry Cream and Semisweet Chocolate Glaze.
3. Slice about 1/3 from top of each shell and fill bottom of shells with cream filling; replace tops and spread with glaze. Refrigerate until serving time.

Shaping *choux* paste: With a small spatula, spread paste in 5" by 3/4" rectangles.

Piping *choux* paste: Or, use a pastry bag with plain round tube to form éclairs.

Cream Puff Ring

Color index
page 94

Begin early
in day or
day ahead

10 servings

*choux paste from Cream
Puffs (opposite)*
*Almond Pastry Cream
(opposite)*
*Semisweet Chocolate
Glaze (opposite)*
*1 pint strawberries,
hulled and washed*

1 On greased, lightly
floured cookie sheet,
using a 7-inch plate as a
guide, trace a circle.
Preheat oven to 400°F.
Prepare *choux* paste as in
Cream Puffs, steps 1 to 3.

2 Drop heaping table-
spoonfuls of *choux*
paste just inside circle to
form ring. Bake 40 minutes
or until golden and firm.
Turn off heat; leave in
oven 15 minutes; cool.

3 With sharp knife, carefully cut puff ring in
half horizontally.

4 With spoon, remove
soft interior; discard,
leaving hollow ring shell.

5 Prepare Almond Pastry
Cream; fill bottom shell
with cream; replace top
shell; refrigerate.

6 Prepare Semisweet
Chocolate Glaze;
spread on top of ring.
Refrigerate ring.

7 *To serve:* Fill center of
Cream Puff Ring with
fresh strawberries.
Serve immediately.

Swans

Color index
page 95

Begin early
in day

36 pastries

*choux paste from Cream
Puffs (opposite)*   *Vanilla Filling (below)*

1. Grease large cookie sheet. Preheat oven to 375°F.
Make *choux* paste as for Cream Puffs in steps 1 to 3.
Spoon scant ¾ cupful mixture into pastry bag with
⅛″ round tube. Onto sheet, pipe thirty-six 2-inch
long "question marks" for swans' necks, making a
small dollop at end of each for head.
2. Spoon remaining mixture into large pastry bag
with ½″ round tube. Pipe thirty-six 1½″ by 1″
teardrops for swans' bodies, about 1 inch apart.
Bake 10 minutes until swans' necks are golden;
remove to rack; cool. Continue baking bodies 20 to
25 minutes longer until golden. Remove to wire
racks to cool. Prepare Vanilla Filling.
3. Cut off top third of swans' bodies; set aside.
Spoon filling into pastry bag with large fluted tube.
Pipe some filling mixture into bottom pieces. Cut
top pieces of swans' bodies lengthwise in half; set
into filling for wings. Place necks into filling. Chill.

VANILLA FILLING: In 3-quart saucepan, mix
well *1 envelope unflavored gelatin* with ½ *cup sugar*
and *2 tablespoons all-purpose flour.* In small bowl
with wire whisk, beat *4 egg yolks* with *1 cup milk*
until well mixed; stir into gelatin mixture. Cook over
medium-low heat, stirring constantly, until mixture
is very thick and coats a spoon well, about 10
minutes (do not boil). Remove pan from heat; stir in
1 teaspoon vanilla extract. Cover and refrigerate
until mixture is cold but not set, about 45 minutes.
In small bowl with mixer at medium speed, beat *1
cup heavy cream* into soft peaks; fold into custard.

Piping *choux* paste: Pipe
necks then teardrop
shapes for bodies.

Adding filling: Cut off
top third of bodies then
pipe in filling. Cut top
pieces lengthwise in half.

Forming swans: Set top
half-pieces into filling
for wings, then add necks

Crêpes and blintzes

Crêpes Suzette

Color index
page 94

Begin early
in day

12 crêpes or
6 servings

Crêpes:
butter or margarine,
melted
1½ cups milk
⅔ cup all-purpose flour
½ teaspoon salt
3 eggs

Suzette Sauce (below)
¼ cup orange-flavor
liqueur

1. In medium bowl with wire whisk, beat 2 tablespoons butter and remaining crêpe ingredients until smooth. Cover; chill 2 hours.
2. Brush bottom of 7-inch crêpe pan and 10-inch skillet with melted butter. Over medium heat, heat pans; pour scant ¼ cup batter into crêpe pan, tip pan to coat bottom; cook 2 minutes till top is set, underside slightly browned.
3. Loosen crêpe; invert into hot 10-inch skillet; cook other side 30 seconds. Slip crêpe onto waxed paper. Meanwhile, start cooking another crêpe. Stack crêpes between waxed paper. Use immediately or wrap in foil and refrigerate.
4. *About 30 minutes before serving:* Prepare Suzette Sauce. Fold crêpes in quarters; arrange in Suzette Sauce. Simmer over medium-low heat 10 minutes; pour liqueur in center (do not stir). Heat liqueur a minute or two; light with a long match and flame. Or, in 1-quart saucepan over low heat, heat liqueur just until warm. Carefully light the warm liqueur with a long match and pour over crêpes in chafing dish. Serve the crêpes immediately.

SUZETTE SAUCE: In chafing dish or 10-inch skillet over low heat, heat *⅓ cup orange juice, ¼ cup butter* or margarine, *2 tablespoons sugar* and *¼ teaspoon grated orange peel* until butter melts.

SERVING CREPES SUZETTE

Fold crêpes in quarters; arrange in sauce in chafing dish. Simmer 10 minutes.

Pour the liqueur in center of chafing dish over the crêpes (do not stir).

Heat liqueur a minute or two, then light with a long match. Let liqueur flame. Or, heat liqueur in 1-quart saucepan; ignite; pour over crêpes. Serve crêpes and sauce immediately.

Dessert Crêpes with Orange Sauce

Color index
page 94

Begin 1 hr
ahead

6 servings

Orange Sauce (below)
1½ cups milk
¾ cup all-purpose flour
½ teaspoon double-
acting baking powder
½ teaspoon salt
6 eggs, separated

salad oil
1 8-ounce container sour
cream (1 cup)
2 medium oranges,
peeled, seeded and
diced

1. Prepare Orange Sauce; keep warm.
2. In large bowl with wire whisk or fork, mix milk, flour, baking powder, salt and egg yolks until smoothly blended.
3. In small bowl with mixer at high speed, beat egg whites until stiff peaks form. With wire whisk or rubber spatula, gently fold the beaten egg whites into the flour mixture.
4. Heat 12-inch skillet over medium heat; lightly brush with salad oil. Making 3 crêpes at a time, pour batter by ½ cupfuls into hot skillet; spread batter into 4-inch circles. Cook crêpes until golden on both sides, about 3 minutes, turning once. With pancake turner, remove crêpes to cookie sheet; keep warm. Repeat, making 12 crêpes in all, brushing skillet with more salad oil if it becomes too dry.
5. To serve, spread some sour cream over each crêpe. Roll each crêpe, jelly-roll fashion; arrange on warm large platter. Spoon Orange Sauce over crêpes; top with diced oranges.

ORANGE SAUCE: In 1-quart saucepan over low heat, melt *¼ cup butter* or margarine. Stir in *1½ cups confectioners' sugar, ⅓ cup orange juice* and *2 tablespoons grated orange peel.* Cook over low heat, stirring frequently, until heated through.

Cheese Blintzes

Color index
page 98

Begin early
in day

6 servings

12 crêpes from
Crêpes Suzette (left)
1 8-ounce container
creamed cottage
cheese (1 cup)
1 3-ounce package cream
cheese, softened
¼ cup sugar

½ teaspoon vanilla
extract
2 tablespoons butter or
margarine
1 10-ounce package
frozen strawberries,
thawed

1. Prepare crêpes as in steps 1 to 3 of Crêpes Suzette.
2. *About 30 minutes before serving:* In a small bowl with mixer at medium speed, beat cottage cheese, cream cheese, sugar and vanilla extract until smooth. Spread about a tablespoon of mixture on each crêpe to within ½ inch of edge; fold two sides of each crêpe slightly toward the center then roll in opposite direction, jelly-roll fashion.
3. Preheat oven to 350°F. In 15½″ by 10½″ jelly-roll pan in the oven, melt butter or margarine. Remove from oven. Arrange blintzes in one layer in pan. Bake 10 minutes until heated through. Serve topped with strawberries.

CHERRY BLINTZES: Prepare Cheese Blintzes but omit strawberries. Prepare Cherry Sauce (page 464) in cook-and-serve skillet; add filled crêpes. Over low heat, simmer 10 minutes to heat through.

See descriptions, page 16

Other desserts

Strawberry Shortcake

Color index
page 97

Begin 45 mins
ahead

8 servings

sugar
1³/₄ cups all-purpose
    flour
½ cup shortening
⅓ cup milk
1 egg
1 tablespoon double-
    acting baking
    powder

1 teaspoon grated lemon
    peel
¾ teaspoon salt
2 pints strawberries
butter or margarine,
    softened
1 cup heavy or whipping
    cream, whipped

1. Preheat oven to 450°F. Prepare shortcake: Grease 9-inch round cake pan. Into medium bowl, measure ¼ cup sugar and next 7 ingredients. With mixer at medium speed, beat mixture until well combined and a soft dough forms. Pat the dough evenly into the prepared cake pan. Bake 15 minutes or until golden on top.
2. Wash and hull strawberries, reserving a few for garnish. Sprinkle the remainder with ⅓ cup sugar; mash slightly.
3. Invert the shortcake onto platter; with long, sharp knife, carefully split hot shortcake horizontally. Spread both cut surfaces evenly with softened butter or margarine.
4. Onto bottom half, spoon half of strawberries; top with other cake half; spoon remaining strawberries over top.
5. Spread the whipped cream over the mashed strawberries and then garnish with the reserved whole strawberries.

Splitting the cake: Using a long, sharp knife, halve the cake horizontally; spread both cut surfaces with softened butter or margarine.

Layering the cake: Spoon half of the mashed strawberries on cake half; top with the second layer and spoon over the rest of the strawberries.

INDIVIDUAL SHORTCAKES: Prepare as above but onto greased cookie sheet, drop dough in 8 equal mounds about 2 inches apart. Bake 10 minutes or until golden. Split and serve as above.

Syllabub

Color index
page 94

Begin 10 mins
ahead

8 cups or
16 servings

5 cups half-and-half
2 cups Chablis
1 cup sugar
½ cup brandy

⅓ cup lemon juice
shredded peel of 1 lemon
    for garnish

In large bowl with mixer at low speed, beat half-and-half until frothy; gradually beat in remaining ingredients except lemon peel until well mixed; pour into chilled stemmed glasses. Lightly sprinkle the shredded lemon peel over the top.

Deluxe Strawberry Shortcake

Color index
page 94

Begin 4 hrs
ahead or early
in day

12 servings

4 eggs, separated, at
    room temperature
¼ teaspoon cream of
    tartar
sugar
1 cup all-purpose flour
⅓ cup water
¼ cup salad oil
1½ teaspoons double-
    acting baking powder

½ teaspoon vanilla
    extract
2 pints strawberries,
    hulled
1½ cups heavy or
    whipping cream,
    whipped

1. In large bowl with mixer at high speed, beat egg whites and cream of tartar until soft peaks form. Beating at high speed, sprinkle in ¼ cup sugar, 2 tablespoons at a time, beating well after each addition until sugar is completely dissolved. Whites should stand in stiff peaks.
2. Preheat oven to 325°F. In small bowl with mixer at medium speed, beat yolks, flour, water, oil, baking powder, vanilla and ½ cup sugar until well mixed. With wire whisk, fold flour mixture into beaten egg whites, just until blended. Pour mixture into ungreased 9-inch tube pan.
3. Bake 1 hour or until top of cake springs back when lightly touched with finger. Invert cake in pan on bottle; cool completely.
4. Cut strawberries lengthwise in half. Remove cake from pan; with serrated knife, slice in two horizontally. Place bottom layer on platter; spread with half whipped cream; top with one third berries; top with second layer. Spread remaining cream on top of cake; garnish with remaining berries.

YOGURT DESSERTS

Yogurt is a versatile ingredient for all kinds of cooking, especially for desserts. Try some of these ideas for serving light, refreshing desserts.

Combine plain yogurt with honey (below left) or fresh berries or other fruit (below right).

Coffee flavored yogurt is delicious with chocolate syrup on top, and layered with chopped nuts, cake or cookie crumbs (above).

Use sherbet dishes, parfaits or tall glasses and alternate layers of sweetened fresh or canned fruits with plain, vanilla or fruit flavored yogurt (left).

See descriptions, page 16

Other desserts

Color index page 95

Begin 2 hrs ahead or early in day

8 servings

Chocolate Cups with Strawberry Cream

1 6-ounce package semi-sweet-chocolate pieces	*1 cup heavy or whipping cream*
1 tablespoon shortening	*⅓ cup confectioners' sugar*
1 pint strawberries	

1. Place a fluted paper baking cup in each of eight 3-inch cups of muffin pan; set aside.

2. In double boiler over hot, *not boiling*, water (or in heavy, 1-quart saucepan over low heat), heat the chocolate pieces together with shortening until melted and smooth, about 5 minutes, stirring chocolate mixture occasionally.

3. Lift one paper cup and tilt slightly; drizzle chocolate, 1 heaping teaspoonful at a time, down side of cup to cover sides evenly. About 3 of these teaspoonfuls will cover the entire inside of each cup. Repeat with remaining paper cups. Refrigerate the chocolate-coated cups until chocolate is firm, about 30 minutes.

4. *About 30 minutes before serving:* With cool hands, remove 1 cup at a time from refrigerator; gently but quickly peel paper from each, leaving a chocolate cup. Set the chocolate cups on chilled dessert platter and refrigerate.

5. Wash and hull strawberries; pat dry with paper towels. Cut berries into ⅛-inch-thick slices. Reserve ½ cup sliced strawberries for garnish.

6. In small bowl with mixer at medium speed, beat heavy or whipping cream and confectioners' sugar until stiff peaks form. With rubber spatula, gently fold strawberries into whipped-cream mixture; spoon into chocolate cups. Arrange a few reserved strawberry slices on each.

Making cups: Lift cup, tilting slightly, and drizzle chocolate over cup to cover inside.

Filling cups: Spoon strawberry and cream mixture into cups; top with strawberry slices.

Begin 2 hrs ahead or early in day

8 servings

CHOCOLATE CUPS WITH COCOA CREAM: Prepare Chocolate Cups as above. For filling, omit strawberries; instead, beat **¼ cup cocoa** and **¼ teaspoon vanilla extract** with the heavy or whipping cream and confectioners' sugar.

Apple Strudel

2 pounds tart cooking apples, thinly sliced (about 6 cups)	*about 1 cup dry bread crumbs*
½ cup dark seedless raisins or currants	*½ pound phyllo (strudel leaves)*
½ cup chopped California walnuts or pecans	*½ cup butter or margarine, melted*
⅓ cup sugar	
½ teaspoon ground cinnamon	
¼ teaspoon ground nutmeg	
¼ teaspoon salt	

Color index page 94

Begin 3 hrs ahead or early in day

10 servings

1 Grease 15½" by 10½" jelly-roll pan. In large bowl, mix first 7 ingredients and ½ cup bread crumbs; set apple mixture aside.

2 Cut two 25-inch lengths of waxed paper; overlap two long sides about ½ inch; fasten with cellophane tape.

3 On waxed paper, place one sheet of phyllo; brush with some butter then sprinkle with scant tablespoon of remaining bread crumbs.

4 Preheat oven to 375°F. Layer remaining sheets of phyllo to make an 18-inch square, brushing each sheet with butter and sprinkling with crumbs.

5 About 3 inches from one edge of phyllo, evenly spoon apple mixture in a 12" by 4" row, leaving 3 inches of phyllo at each end.

6 Fold ends over apples. Starting with edge by apples, roll phyllo jelly-roll fashion, lifting waxed paper as you roll.

7 Place roll in jelly-roll pan seam side down. Brush with melted butter. Bake 40 minutes or just until golden brown.

8 Remove cooked strudel from oven and allow to cool in jelly-roll pan on wire rack about 30 minutes.

9 With sharp knife, cut strudel crosswise into individual serving pieces; serve warm or cold.

Baklava

Color index
page 96

Begin 3 hrs
or up to
1 wk ahead

24 servings

4½ cups California
  walnuts (1 16-ounce
  package), finely
  chopped
½ cup sugar
1 teaspoon ground
  cinnamon

1 pound phyllo (strudel
  leaves)
1 cup butter or
  margarine, melted
1 cup honey

1. Grease 13" by 9" baking pan. In large bowl, mix walnuts, sugar and cinnamon; set aside.
2. In baking pan, place 1 sheet of phyllo, allowing it to extend up sides of pan; brush with butter or margarine. Repeat to make 5 more layers; sprinkle with 1 cup walnut mixture. Cut remaining phyllo into approximately 13" by 9" rectangles. Preheat oven to 300°F.
3. Place one phyllo rectangle in pan; brush with butter or margarine. Repeat to make at least 6 layers, overlapping small strips of phyllo to make rectangles, if necessary. Sprinkle with 1 cup of the walnut mixture.
4. Repeat step 3 three more times. Place remaining phyllo on top of last walnut layer. Trim any phyllo that extends over top of pan. With sharp knife, cut just halfway through all layers in a diamond pattern to make 24 servings. Bake 1¼ hours or until top is golden brown.
5. Meanwhile, in 1-quart saucepan over medium-low heat, heat honey until hot, not boiling. Spoon hot honey evenly over baklava. Cool in pan on wire rack at least 1 hour, then cover and leave at room temperature until serving time.
6. *To serve:* Finish cutting through layers.

LAYERING THE BAKLAVA

Place 1 sheet phyllo in pan letting sheet extend up pan sides; brush with butter. Repeat to make 5 more layers.

Sprinkle phyllo with 1 cup of the chopped walnut mixture. Cut the remaining phyllo sheets into 13" by 9" rectangles.

Place phyllo rectangle in pan; brush with butter; repeat to make at least 6 layers. Top with 1 cup of the walnut mixture. Repeat this step three more times.

Place remaining phyllo on top of last walnut layer, then trim any phyllo that extends above sides of pan. Before baking, cut just halfway through all layers in diamond pattern.

Galatoboureko

Color index
page 96

Begin 2½ hrs
or up to
2 days ahead

24 servings

4 cups milk
2 cups heavy or whipping
  cream
½ cup plus 1 tablespoon
  quick enriched
  farina
½ cup sugar
6 egg yolks

1 tablespoon vanilla
  extract
½ pound phyllo
  (strudel leaves)
¾ cup butter or
  margarine, melted
Syrup (below)

1. Grease a 13" by 9" baking pan. In 3-quart saucepan over medium-high heat, heat milk and heavy cream just until boiling. In small bowl, mix together the farina and sugar; gradually sprinkle into milk and cream, stirring with wire whisk or spoon; heat to boiling. Reduce heat to medium-low; continue cooking, stirring constantly, until mixture is slightly thickened, 5 to 10 minutes; remove the saucepan from the heat.
2. In large bowl with mixer at high speed, beat the egg yolks with the vanilla extract until thoroughly blended. Reduce speed to medium and gradually beat in the farina mixture to blend well. Preheat oven to 375°F.
3. In baking pan, place 1 sheet of phyllo, allowing it to extend up the sides of the pan; brush with butter or margarine. Repeat to make about 5 more layers; pour the farina and egg-yolk mixture into phyllo-lined baking pan.
4. Cut remaining phyllo into approximately 13" by 9" rectangles. Place one sheet of phyllo on farina mixture; brush with butter or margarine. Repeat with remaining phyllo and butter. (If necessary, overlap small strips of phyllo to make rectangles.) With sharp knife, cut the top phyllo layer into 2¼-inch squares.
5. Bake 35 minutes or until top is golden brown and puffy. Pour the hot, lemon-flavored Syrup over the top. Let Galatoboureko cool on wire rack at least 1 hour before serving.
6. *To serve:* Finish cutting through the layers. Galatoboureko may be served either warm or cold. Refrigerate to serve cold.

SYRUP: In 1-quart saucepan over medium heat, heat ¾ *cup sugar* and ⅓ *cup water* to boiling, stirring occasionally. Reduce heat to low; simmer for about 8 minutes or until the syrup is thickened then stir in *1 tablespoon lemon juice.*

Making phyllo rectangles: Using a sharp knife, carefully cut 13" by 9" sheets of phyllo.

Cutting dessert: Before baking, cut the top phyllo layer into 2¼-inch squares.

Other desserts

Sherry Trifle

6 tablespoons all-purpose flour
½ teaspoon double-acting baking powder
¼ teaspoon salt
2 egg whites
sugar
6 egg yolks
vanilla extract
½ cup raspberry jam
¼ cup cream sherry
½ cup crushed macaroons (about 6)
2 cups milk

1 cup heavy or whipping cream, whipped
candied red cherries (optional)
toasted slivered almonds (optional)

Color index page 97

Begin early in day or day ahead

8 servings

1 Grease bottom of 9-inch round cake pan; line with waxed paper. In cup with fork, mix flour, baking powder and salt. In small bowl with mixer at high speed, beat egg whites until soft peaks form; gradually sprinkle in 3 tablespoons sugar, beating until sugar is dissolved and whites stand in stiff glossy peaks. In medium bowl at high speed, beat 2 egg yolks, ¼ cup sugar and ¼ teaspoon vanilla extract just until thick.

2 Preheat oven to 375°F. Sprinkle flour mixture over beaten yolk mixture in medium bowl.

3 Add beaten egg whites to mixtures in medium bowl, then with rubber spatula, gently fold until blended. Spread batter evenly in pan.

4 Bake 15 minutes until top springs back when touched with finger. Cool in pan on wire rack 10 minutes; remove from pan and cool on wire rack.

5 With knife, cut cake horizontally in half; spread lower half with jam. Replace top.

6 Cut layers into bite-size pieces and place randomly in bottom of deep, 1½-quart glass bowl.

7 Sprinkle with sherry. Reserve 2 tablespoons macaroons; sprinkle remainder over cake; set aside.

8 In 2-quart saucepan over low heat, cook milk, 4 egg yolks and 3 tablespoons sugar, stirring, until thickened. Remove from heat; add ½ teaspoon vanilla extract.

9 Pour custard over cake pieces in bowl. Cover surface with plastic wrap; refrigerate about 2 hours. Sprinkle the reserved crushed macaroons over custard surface.

10 Spoon whipped cream into pastry bag with large rosette tube; use to decorate custard. Garnish with candied red cherries and the toasted slivered almonds.

Color index page 98

Begin 5 hrs ahead or early in day

8 turnovers

Apple Turnovers

2 cups all-purpose flour
1 teaspoon salt
1 cup butter or margarine
½ cup iced water
2 apples, peeled, cored and sliced
½ cup sugar
1 tablespoon cornstarch

1 teaspoon lemon juice
¼ teaspoon ground cinnamon
1 egg
water
½ cup confectioners' sugar

1. In medium bowl with pastry blender, combine flour and salt. Cut in ½ cup butter until mixture resembles coarse crumbs. Sprinkle with iced water. With fork, mix well. Shape dough into a ball; with lightly floured rolling pin on lightly floured surface, roll into an 18″ by 8″ rectangle. Cut ¼ cup butter into thin slices. Starting at one of the 8-inch sides, place butter slices over ⅔ of rectangle to within ½ inch of edges.

2. Fold unbuttered ⅓ of pastry over middle ⅓; fold opposite end over to make an 8″ by 6″ rectangle. Roll dough into an 18″ by 8″ rectangle.

3. Slice remaining ¼ cup butter; place slices on dough and fold as in steps 1 and 2; wrap in plastic wrap. Chill 15 minutes. Roll folded dough into an 18″ by 8″ rectangle. Fold lengthwise then crosswise; wrap and chill 1 hour.

4. Prepare filling: In saucepan with spoon, mix apples, sugar, cornstarch, lemon juice and cinnamon. Cook over low heat, stirring frequently, until apples are tender. Chill.

5. Preheat oven to 450°F. Cut dough crosswise in half; roll one half into a 12-inch square (keep rest chilled); cut into four 6-inch squares. In cup, beat egg with 1 tablespoon water. Brush mixture over squares. Spoon ⅛ of apple mixture in center of each and fold in half; press edges to seal. Place on ungreased cookie sheet. Chill while preparing other half of pastry.

6. Brush turnovers with egg mixture. Cut a few slashes on each. Bake 20 minutes or until golden. Cool on wire rack.

7. In bowl, combine confectioners' sugar and 1 tablespoon water; drizzle over turnovers.

Adding butter to dough: Dot slices of butter over ⅔ of the dough rectangle to within no more than ½ inch of the edges.

Folding dough: Fold unbuttered ⅓ of pastry over middle ⅓; fold opposite end over top making a rectangle.

Chocolate-Cinnamon Torte

Color index
page 96

Begin up to
3 days ahead

16 servings

2 cups sugar
1½ cups butter, softened
2 eggs
2 tablespoons ground
  cinnamon
2⅔ cups all-purpose
  flour

3 squares semisweet
  chocolate
4 cups heavy or whipping
  cream
¾ cup cocoa

1. Tear 14 sheets of waxed paper, each about 9½ inches long. On one sheet, trace bottom of 9-inch round cake pan. Evenly stack all sheets with pattern on top. With kitchen shears, cut out circles.

2. Into large bowl, measure sugar, butter, eggs, cinnamon and 2 cups flour. With mixer at low speed, beat ingredients until well mixed, constantly scraping bowl with rubber spatula. Increase speed to medium; beat mixture 3 minutes or until very light and fluffy, occasionally scraping bowl. With spoon, stir in remaining flour to make a soft dough.

3. Preheat oven to 375°F. With damp cloth, moisten 1 large or 2 small cookie sheets. Place 2 waxed-paper circles onto large cookie sheet or 1 on each small cookie sheet. With metal spatula, spread a scant ⅓ cup dough in a very thin layer onto each circle. Bake layers 8 to 12 minutes or until lightly browned around the edges.

4. Remove cookie sheet to wire rack; cool 5 minutes. With pancake turner, carefully remove cookie still on waxed paper to wire rack to cool completely. (Allow cookie sheet to cool before spreading waxed-paper circles with more dough. The more sheets you have the faster you can bake the cookies.) Repeat until all dough is baked. Carefully stack cooled cookies on a flat plate; cover with plastic wrap and store in a cool, dry place.

5. Early in day or day ahead: Coarsely grate chocolate squares; set aside. In large bowl with mixer at medium speed, beat cream and cocoa until soft peaks form.

6. Carefully peel off paper from one cookie; place on flat cake plate; spread with about ½ cup whipped mixture. Repeat layering until all cookies are used, ending with whipped mixture on top.

7. Pile grated chocolate on top of cake; refrigerate until serving time or at least 3 hours before serving so cookies soften for easier cutting.

Shaping cookies: With metal spatula, spread dough in very thin layer on each of the waxed-paper circles.

Assembling torte: Peel off paper and layer cookies spread with whipped mixture, ending with mixture on top.

GARNISHES FOR DESSERTS

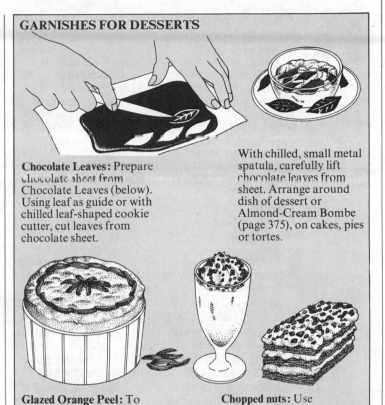

Chocolate Leaves: Prepare chocolate sheet from Chocolate Leaves (below). Using leaf as guide or with chilled leaf-shaped cookie cutter, cut leaves from chocolate sheet.

With chilled, small metal spatula, carefully lift chocolate leaves from sheet. Arrange around dish of dessert or Almond-Cream Bombe (page 375), on cakes, pies or tortes.

Glazed Orange Peel: To prepare, see below. Use to top cold soufflés, cheesecake or ice cream.

Chopped nuts: Use favorite kind to top creamy and frozen desserts, cakes and tortes.

GLAZED ORANGE PEEL: With vegetable peeler, cut peel from **2 medium oranges** in 1-inch-wide strips. With knife, cut peel crosswise in ⅛-inch-wide strips. In 1-quart saucepan over high heat, heat peel and **½ cup water** to boiling; reduce heat to low; simmer 5 minutes, stirring often. Drain. To peel, add **½ cup light corn syrup;** over medium heat, heat to boiling; reduce heat to low and simmer 5 minutes, stirring often. With fork, lift peel onto waxed paper; cool 10 minutes. (Use syrup on pancakes.)

WHIPPED CREAM: With hand beater or mixer at medium speed, beat well-chilled **heavy or whipping cream** just until soft or stiff peaks form, depending on use. (Overbeating causes cream to turn to butter.) On hot days, chill bowl and beaters. Cream doubles in volume when beaten.

SWEETENED WHIPPED CREAM: For **each cup heavy or whipping cream,** add **1 to 2 tablespoons sugar** and **1 teaspoon vanilla extract** or ¼ teaspoon almond extract or dry sherry to taste. Beat as above.

CHOCOLATE WHIPPED CREAM: Place **2 tablespoons instant-cocoa mix** (or 2 tablespoons sugar and 2 tablespoons cocoa) in small bowl; add **1 cup heavy or whipping cream.** With hand beater or mixer at low speed, beat just until soft peaks form.

CHOCOLATE LEAVES: In double boiler over hot, not boiling, water, heat **one 6-ounce package semisweet-chocolate pieces** (1 cup) and **1 tablespoon shortening** until smooth, stirring occasionally. With small metal spatula, spread a thin layer of chocolate mixture on sheet of waxed paper. Place chocolate-coated sheet on cookie sheet; refrigerate 20 minutes or until firm. Cut into leaf shapes as directed above.

Other desserts

Chocolate Fancy

Color index page 96

Begin early in day or day ahead

16 servings

Strawberry-Almond Cream:
2 pints strawberries, hulled
4 envelopes unflavored gelatin
¾ teaspoon salt
sugar
6 eggs, separated
3½ cups milk
2 teaspoons almond extract
1 cup heavy or whipping cream

Chocolate Cake:
1 cup cake flour
¾ cup sugar

1½ teaspoons double-acting baking powder
½ teaspoon salt
¼ cup salad oil
3 eggs, separated
1 square unsweetened chocolate, melted
¼ cup water
¼ teaspoon cream of tartar

Chocolate Coating (right)

1. Prepare Strawberry-Almond Cream: In covered blender container, blend 1 pint strawberries until pureed. Dice remaining strawberries.
2. In heavy, 3-quart saucepan, combine gelatin, salt and ½ cup sugar. In small bowl with wire whisk, beat egg yolks and milk; gradually stir into gelatin mixture until blended. Cook over medium-low heat, stirring, until mixture thickens and coats a spoon, about 20 minutes. Stir in almond extract, strawberry puree and diced strawberries. Remove pan from heat; cool slightly; place in large bowl; fill bowl with ice cubes and cold water to come halfway up side. (Add more ice if needed to keep water *very* cold.) Stir mixture often until mixture mounds from spoon, about 30 minutes.
3. Meanwhile, line 2½-quart bowl (about 9 inches in diameter) with plastic wrap, leaving overhang.
4. In large bowl with mixer at high speed, beat egg whites until soft peaks form. Beating at high speed, sprinkle in ¾ cup sugar, beating until sugar is dissolved. Using same beaters, in small bowl with mixer at medium speed, beat half the heavy cream until soft peaks form. With wire whisk, gently fold whipped cream and strawberry mixture into egg-white mixture. Spoon into prepared bowl; cover and refrigerate until firm, about 2 hours.
5. Prepare Chocolate Cake: Preheat oven to 350°F. In large bowl with spoon, stir flour, sugar, baking powder and salt until blended. Stir in salad oil, egg yolks, chocolate and water until smooth.
6. In large bowl with mixer at high speed, beat egg whites and cream of tartar until stiff peaks form; fold in chocolate mixture. Pour batter into an ungreased 9-inch round cake pan. Bake 30 minutes or until cake springs back when lightly touched. Invert cake *with pan* on rack; cool 1 hour. Meanwhile, prepare Chocolate Coating (right).
7. Remove cake from pan; place on cake plate. In small bowl with mixer at medium speed, beat remaining cream until soft peaks form; spread over top of cake. Assemble dessert (right) and chill.
8. *To serve:* Remove dessert from refrigerator; let stand about 20 minutes to soften chocolate slightly for easier slicing. Dip sharp knife in hot water then carefully cut cake into even-sized wedges.

CHOCOLATE COATING: Cut waxed paper into five 8″ by 7″ sheets and one 17″ by 5″ sheet. Place sheets on 3 large cookie sheets; set aside. In double boiler over hot, *not boiling*, water (or in heavy, 1-quart saucepan over low heat), heat *one 12-ounce package semisweet-chocolate pieces, ¼ cup butter* or margarine, *¼ cup light corn syrup* until chocolate is melted and mixture is smooth, about 5 minutes. Remove double boiler from heat. On each 8″ by 7″ waxed paper sheet, with metal spatula, spread about ¼ cup chocolate mixture. Spread remaining chocolate mixture on 17″ by 5″ sheet. Chill 2 hours.

ASSEMBLING CHOCOLATE FANCY

Invert strawberry cream onto whipped-cream-topped cake. Peel off plastic wrap; discard.

Gently press chocolate onto cream and cake. Repeat with remaining sheets, overlapping them to cover side of dessert.

Remove 8″ by 7″ chocolate sheets from refrigerator; let stand 3 to 5 minutes to soften slightly. Carefully place chocolate side of one sheet, vertically, against side of strawberry cream and cake. Peel off paper.

Remove 17″ by 5″ chocolate sheet from refrigerator; let soften slightly. Fold chocolate sheet lengthwise in half to make 2½-inch-wide strip, with waxed paper outside; peel off paper.

Loosely roll up chocolate from narrow end, jelly-roll fashion, to about 4 inches in diameter; place on top of dessert. Refrigerate until serving time.

Steamed Pudding

2¼ cups all-purpose
flour
1 cup sugar
1 cup fresh bread crumbs
1 teaspoon double-acting
baking powder
1 teaspoon salt
½ teaspoon ground
cinnamon
½ teaspoon ground
cloves
butter or margarine
1 cup chopped pitted
dates
1 cup peeled chopped
apple

½ cup chopped
California walnuts
1 cup buttermilk
½ cup dark molasses
2 eggs
1 cup confectioners'
sugar
½ teaspoon vanilla
extract
½ cup brandy or liqueur
holly leaves for garnish

Color index page 96
Begin 4 hrs ahead
12 servings

1 Heavily grease a 2½-quart bowl; cut foil with 1-inch overhang to cover bowl. Grease well one side of foil circle. Set aside.

2 In large bowl, combine flour, sugar, bread crumbs, baking powder, salt, cinnamon and cloves.

3 With pastry blender, cut in 1 cup butter until mixture resembles coarse crumbs; add dates.

4 Add apple and nuts, then stir in buttermilk, molasses and eggs. Pour into prepared bowl.

5 With foil, greased side down, cover mixture in bowl. Tie foil to bowl tightly with string.

6 Place metal trivet in 12-quart saucepot. Set bowl on trivet. Pour water into pot to about 1 inch below rim of foil. Cover pot. (If needed, add more water during cooking.)

7 Over high heat, heat water to boiling. Reduce heat to low; simmer 3½ hours or until toothpick inserted through foil comes out clean.

8 For sauce, in small bowl with mixer at medium speed, beat ⅓ cup butter, confectioners' sugar and vanilla until creamy.

9 Cool pudding in bowl on rack 5 minutes. In 1-quart pan, heat brandy to lukewarm. Invert pudding onto warm platter.

10 Top with holly; pour brandy over and ignite; when alcohol burns off, serve Steamed Pudding with sauce.

Color index page 96
Begin day ahead
8 servings

Almond-Cream Bombe

1 4-ounce can blanched
whole almonds
(about ¾ cup)
1 10¾- or 12-ounce
ready-to-serve frozen
pound cake,
thawed
¼ cup almond-flavor
liqueur

½ 6-ounce package
semisweet-chocolate
pieces (½ cup)
2 cups heavy or whipping
cream
⅔ cup confectioners'
sugar
⅛ teaspoon salt

1. In 9″ by 9″ baking pan, toast the blanched whole almonds in 375°F. oven until golden, about 10 minutes, stirring occasionally; cool thoroughly; with a sharp knife, chop almonds coarsely.

2. Meanwhile, line 1½-quart round-bottom bowl with plastic wrap; set aside. Cut pound cake into ¼-inch-thick slices; cut each slice diagonally in half to make 2 triangles. Sprinkle with almond-flavor liqueur. Use triangles with top brown cake crust first to line bowl, with narrow points at bottom of bowl, so that brown crusts form a pinwheel design. Complete lining bowl by placing more cake triangles around inside of bowl, making sure there are no spaces between triangles. Reserve any remaining cake triangles.

3. In heavy, 1-quart saucepan over low heat, place chocolate pieces; stir occasionally until chocolate is melted; cool slightly.

4. In large bowl with mixer at medium speed, beat heavy or whipping cream, confectioners' sugar and salt until the mixture stands in soft peaks. Fold in the toasted chopped almonds.

5. Spread ⅔ whipped cream evenly over cake in bowl. Fold melted chocolate into remaining whipped-cream mixture; use to fill center of dessert. Top the dessert with the remaining cake triangles. Cover the dish with plastic wrap and leave in the refrigerator overnight.

6. *To serve:* Remove top sheet of plastic wrap. Invert bowl onto chilled serving plate; remove and discard plastic wrap. With a sharp knife, carefully cut dessert into wedges.

Lining the bowl: Arrange cake triangles in pinwheel design then completely line bowl with triangles making sure that there are no spaces.

Covering the filling: Top dessert with remaining cake triangles. Cover the bowl with plastic wrap and leave to chill overnight.

ICE CREAM AND SHERBET

Ice cream, ice milk and sherbet are all favorite frozen desserts. Commercial *ice cream* and *ice milk* are basically mixtures of milk fat, non-fat milk solids, sweeteners and flavorings. Ice cream has the highest butterfat content of all frozen desserts. Ice milk has about half the butterfat of ice cream but contains more sweetener. *Sherbet* is virtually fat-free while *fruit ices* are a fat-free mixture of water, sugar and fruit. *Frozen, low-fat yogurts* are made with skim milk, non-fat milk solids, yogurt cultures, fruit, fruit flavorings and jelling agents or emulsifiers and stabilizers.

Frozen desserts are easy to make at home. When using a churn-type ice-cream freezer, fill the freezer can only as full as the manufacturer directs, to allow for expansion—any excess mixture may be frozen in an ice-cube tray. After freezing, transfer the mixture from the ice-cream freezer to a chilled container and place in home freezer a few hours to harden or pack in ice-cream freezer as directed in recipe. If using an ice-cube tray, about 1 hour before serving, remove mixture to a bowl and beat at medium speed until smooth; return to tray; keep frozen until serving time. To serve, stand at room temperature 10 minutes for easier scooping.

Keep some trays specially for desserts since ice cubes tend to stick in trays previously used for freezing desserts. You can tell when a mixture is partially frozen because it will be frozen firm to 1 inch in from the edge, with a soft, mushy center.

Ice cream

Homemade Vanilla Ice Cream

2 cups sugar
6 tablespoons all-purpose
* flour*
1 teaspoon salt
5 cups milk
6 eggs
4 cups half-and-half
3 tablespoons vanilla
* extract*
20 pounds cracked ice
2 to 3 pounds rock salt

Color index page 102

Begin early in day or
up to 1 month ahead

3 quarts or 12 servings

1 In heavy, 3-quart saucepan with spoon, combine sugar, flour and salt. In medium bowl with hand beater or wire whisk, beat milk and eggs together until well blended; stir into sugar mixture until smooth. Cook over low heat, stirring constantly, until the mixture thickens and coats a spoon, about 30 to 45 minutes, being sure custard does not boil or it will curdle. Remove saucepan from the heat.

2 Cover the surface of the thickened mixture with waxed paper and refrigerate until thoroughly cooled, approximately 2 hours.

3 Pour the half-and-half, vanilla extract and cooled custard mixture into 4-quart ice-cream freezer can.

4 Place dasher in the ice-cream freezer can; put lid on can and place can in bucket; attach motor or hand crank to the freezer can.

5 Fill bucket half full with ice; sprinkle with ¼ cup rock salt. Add 1 inch ice and ¼ cup salt; repeat to 1 inch below can lid.

6 Freeze according to manufacturer's directions, adding more ice and salt as needed. Freezing will take 35 to 45 minutes.

7 Remove motor or hand crank; wipe can lid and remove; remove dasher. With spoon, pack down the soft ice cream.

8 Cover opening of the freezer can with waxed paper and then replace the can lid; put cork in the hole in center.

9 Add more ice and salt to cover can lid. Let stand to harden ice cream, 2 to 3 hours, adding more ice and salt as needed.

Ice cream

ICE CREAM VARIATIONS

HOME-FREEZER METHOD: Prepare egg mixture as in step 1 of Homemade Vanilla Ice Cream, but use *1 cup sugar, 3 tablespoons all-purpose flour, ½ teaspoon salt, 2½ cups milk* and *3 eggs;* cook about 15 minutes; cool. Stir in *2 cups heavy or whipping cream* and *5 teaspoons vanilla extract*. Pour into 9″ by 9″ pan; cover; freeze until frozen but still soft, 3 to 4 hours; spoon into large bowl. Beat at medium speed until smooth but still frozen; return to pan; cover; freeze until firm. (Makes 6 cups or 6 servings.)

Color index
page 102

CHOCOLATE: Prepare egg mixture as in step 1 of Homemade Vanilla Ice Cream, but omit 1 cup milk. While mixture is cooling, in 1-quart saucepan over low heat, melt *8 squares unsweetened chocolate;* stir in *¾ cup sugar* and *1 cup hot water* until blended; chill. In 4-quart freezer can, combine egg mixture, chocolate mixture, half-and-half and vanilla; freeze. (Makes 3 quarts or 12 servings.)

Color index
page 102

PEACH: Prepare egg mixture as in step 1 of Homemade Vanilla Ice Cream; while mixture is cooling, in covered blender container at low speed, blend *10 to 12 ripe peaches,* peeled and cut up, and *½ cup sugar* until smooth. In 4-quart freezer can, stir peaches, egg mixture, only *2 cups half-and-half* and *¾ teaspoon almond extract* instead of vanilla; freeze. (Makes 7 pints or 14 servings.)

Color index
page 102

STRAWBERRY: Prepare as for Homemade Vanilla Ice Cream but, while egg mixture is cooling, in medium bowl with potato masher, crush *1½ pints strawberries,* hulled, *1 cup sugar* and *2 tablespoons lemon juice;* let stand about 1 hour. In 4-quart freezer can, stir well egg mixture, half-and-half, strawberries and *¼ teaspoon red food color;* freeze. (Makes 4 quarts or 16 servings.)

Color index
page 102

PISTACHIO: Prepare egg mixture as in step 1 of Homemade Vanilla Ice Cream, but use *1 cup sugar, 3 tablespoons all-purpose flour, ½ teaspoon salt, 2½ cups milk* and *3 eggs* and cook about 15 minutes. In step 3, use only *2 cups half-and-half* and, for vanilla, substitute *⅛ teaspoon green food color* and *¼ teaspoon almond extract;* freeze about 20 minutes. While mixture is freezing, coarsely chop *1½ cups salted pistachio nuts*. Remove dasher. With long-handled spoon, stir in nuts. Cover can and harden. (Makes 3 pints or 6 servings.)

Color index
page 102

SPICED BANANA: Prepare egg mixture as in step 1 of Homemade Vanilla Ice Cream, but use *1 cup sugar, 3 tablespoons all-purpose flour, ½ teaspoon salt, 2½ cups milk* and *3 eggs;* cook about 15 minutes. While mixture is cooling, in blender container, dissolve *1 tablespoon ascorbic-acid mixture for fruit* in *¼ cup water;* add *6 ripe, firm, medium bananas,* cut up, to mixture. (Too-ripe bananas will over-flavor and color ice cream.) Add *⅓ cup sugar* and *1½ teaspoons ground cinnamon;* cover and blend until smooth. In 4- to 6-quart freezer can, stir egg and banana mixtures, only *2 cups half-and-half;* omit vanilla. Freeze 20 minutes. (Makes 5 pints or 10 servings.)

Peppermint-Candy Ice Cream

Color index
page 102

Begin 6 hrs
or up to
1 month ahead

6 quarts or
24 servings

6 cups half-and-half	*3 tablespoons vanilla*
3 14-ounce cans	*extract*
sweetened condensed	*1 cup water*
milk	*2 cups coarsely crushed*
2 cups milk	*peppermint candies*

1. In 6-quart ice-cream freezer can, stir first 5 ingredients with 1 cup peppermint candies; refrigerate 1 hour or until thoroughly chilled.
2. Remove can from refrigerator and prepare as in steps 4 to 9 of Homemade Vanilla Ice Cream but in step 7, with spoon, stir in remaining candies.

HOME-FREEZER METHOD: In large bowl, stir *one 14-ounce can sweetened condensed milk, 1 cup water, 1 tablespoon vanilla extract* and half of *⅔ cup coarsely crushed peppermint candies;* fold in *2 cups heavy or whipping cream*, whipped. Pour into 12″ by 8″ pan; cover; freeze 1 hour. Spoon into large bowl. With mixer at medium speed, beat until smooth; fold in remaining candies. Refreeze until firm. (Makes 6 cups or 6 servings.)

PARFAIT IDEAS

Parfaits are layers of ice cream and dessert sauce, fruit, jelly or candy; serve them in parfait, sherbet or small iced-tea glasses.

For chocolate parfaits, alternate layers of vanilla ice cream with Chocolate Sauce (page 464). Garnish with whipped cream and shaved chocolate.

For fruit-cocktail parfaits, alternate layers of vanilla ice cream with chilled canned fruit cocktail mixed with seedless grapes and grated orange peel.

For raspberry-macaroon parfaits, layer vanilla ice cream and thawed frozen raspberries. Top each individual serving with crumbled macaroons.

Ice milk

Ice-cream desserts

Strawberry Ice Milk

1 quart milk
1 envelope unflavored
  gelatin
¾ cup sugar
2 teaspoons vanilla
  extract

¼ teaspoon salt
1 pint strawberries,
  hulled
6 drops red food color
  (optional)

1 In 3-quart saucepan, over 1 cup milk, evenly sprinkle gelatin. Cook over medium-low heat, stirring, until gelatin is dissolved.

2 Remove saucepan from heat; stir in remaining milk, sugar, vanilla extract and salt.

3 Pour into 13" by 9" baking pan; cover with foil and freeze about 3 hours until partially frozen. Crush strawberries; set aside.

4 In covered blender container at medium speed, blend half of milk mixture until smooth but still frozen. Pour into chilled bowl; repeat.

5 Fold crushed strawberries and red food color into milk mixture just until mixed.

6 Return mixture to baking pan; cover; freeze 2 hours until firm, stirring occasionally. *To serve:* Let stand 10 minutes before scooping.

PEACH ICE MILK: Prepare milk mixture as above but use ½ *teaspoon almond extract* for vanilla; omit berries and food color. In blender, blend **4 cups peeled, diced peaches** and **¼ cup lemon juice**. Stir into milk mixture; pour into pan; freeze 3 hours. Spoon into large bowl; with mixer at medium speed, beat until smooth. Freeze 2 hours. Beat again and freeze. Serve as above.

Baked Alaska Pie

18 ladyfingers, split
⅓ cup orange-flavor
  liqueur
1 10-ounce package
  frozen raspberries,
  slightly thawed
3 pints vanilla ice cream,
  slightly softened
4 egg whites, at room
  temperature
¼ teaspoon salt
⅛ teaspoon cream of
  tartar
⅔ cup sugar

1 Line 9-inch pie plate with about ⅔ of ladyfingers, allowing ends to extend over rim; sprinkle with half of liqueur.

2 In medium bowl with potato masher, crush raspberries to make a paste consistency.

3 In large bowl, stir ice cream slightly. Spoon on berries; cut through mixture to create "ripple"

4 Keeping ripples, spoon ½ mixture into plate. Layer remaining fingers on top; sprinkle with remaining liqueur. Spoon on remaining ice cream. Freeze until firm, 4 hours.

5 *About 20 minutes before serving:* Preheat oven to 500°F. In large bowl with mixer at high speed, beat egg whites, salt and cream of tartar until soft peaks form.

6 Beat in sugar, 2 tablespoons at a time, beating at high speed till sugar is dissolved and whites stand in stiff peaks.

7 Quickly spread meringue over top of pie, sealing to edge; swirl up points. Bake 3 to 4 minutes till light brown. Serve at once.

Ice-Cream Bombe Les Dames d'Escoffier

*3 pints vanilla or coffee
 ice cream
2 pints strawberry ice
 cream or raspberry
 sherbet
½ 7.8-ounce bag almond
 brickle chips for
 baking
1 cup heavy or whipping
 cream
¼ teaspoon vanilla
 extract
2 tablespoons
 confectioners' sugar
 strawberries for
 garnish*

Chocolate Sauce:
*¾ cup sugar
½ cup cocoa
½ cup heavy or whipping
 cream
¼ cup butter or
 margarine
1¼ teaspoons vanilla
 extract*

Color index page 103

Begin early in day or up to
2 wks ahead

12 servings

1 Remove vanilla ice cream from freezer; let stand in refrigerator until softened; then, spread the ice cream evenly to line deep, 2½-quart mold or bowl.

2 Cover and freeze about 30 minutes or until ice cream is firm. Meanwhile, soften strawberry ice cream in same way.

3 Spread strawberry ice cream evenly over vanilla ice cream, leaving a well in center of mold; freeze until firm.

4 Spoon almond brickle chips into the well in center of mold.

5 In sink of warm water, quickly dip mold to loosen ice-cream bombe.

6 Invert large, chilled platter on top of mold; invert mold and platter; gently lift off mold; freeze.

7 In small bowl with mixer at medium speed, beat cream, vanilla and sugar till stiff peaks form.

8 Spoon whipped-cream mixture into pastry bag fitted with large rosette tube; use to decorate bombe; freeze.

9 *About 10 minutes before serving:* Remove bombe from freezer; garnish top of bombe with strawberries; let stand 10 minutes for easier slicing. Prepare Chocolate Sauce: In heavy, 2-quart saucepan over medium heat, cook sugar, cocoa, cream and butter or margarine until the mixture is smooth and boils. Remove from heat; stir in vanilla extract. Keep the Chocolate Sauce warm until ready to serve bombe.

10 *To serve:* Cut a wedge; place on a dessert plate. Spoon over some candy from center of bombe. Serve with sauce.

Color index page 102

Begin day or up to 2 wks ahead

10 servings

Nesselrode Ice Cream Mold

*⅓ cup diced candied
 orange peel
⅓ cup candied cherries,
 chopped
⅓ cup golden raisins,
 chopped
⅓ cup black walnuts,
 chopped*

*3 pints French vanilla ice
 cream, slightly
 softened
1 3-ounce package
 ladyfingers
6 tablespoons brandy or
 orange-flavor
 liqueur*

1. In large bowl, stir first 5 ingredients until just mixed. Spoon ⅓ of ice-cream mixture into 7-cup mold. Split ⅓ of ladyfingers and press lightly into ice-cream mixture, overlapping slightly if necessary; drizzle with 2 tablespoons brandy. Repeat layering twice. Cover and freeze.
2. *About 1 hour before serving:* With metal spatula, loosen edges of frozen mixture from mold. In large bowl of hot water, quickly dip mold almost to top to loosen; dry mold with towel. Unmold onto freezer-safe platter. Return to freezer.

OTHER COMBINATIONS: Instead of candied orange peel, cherries and golden raisins, use *two 4-ounce jars mixed candied fruit.* Substitute *California walnuts,* almonds or pecans for black walnuts; use *rum* instead of brandy.

Color index page 103

Begin early in day or up to 1 month ahead

12 servings

Rainbow Ice-Cream Torte

*2 pints chocolate ice
 cream
2 pints chocolate-chip-
 mint ice cream
2 pints strawberry ice
 cream
2 pints vanilla ice cream
2½ cups gingersnap
 crumbs*

*½ cup butter or
 margarine, melted
2 17-ounce cans pitted
 dark sweet cherries,
 drained
½ cup chopped
 California walnuts*

1. Soften ice cream in refrigerator about 30 minutes. Meanwhile, in 10-inch springform pan, combine gingersnap crumbs and butter or margarine. With hands, firmly press crumb mixture into bottom of springform pan; chill in freezer 10 minutes or until mixture is firm.
2. On top of crumb mixture, evenly spread the chocolate ice cream, then the chocolate-chip-mint ice cream, drained sweet cherries, strawberry ice cream and end with the vanilla ice cream. Sprinkle the top evenly with chopped California walnuts. Cover the torte and freeze until firm.
3. *To serve:* Run knife or metal spatula, dipped in hot water, around edge of pan to loosen ice cream. Remove side of springform pan. Allow the ice cream torte to stand at room temperature 10 minutes for easier slicing.

Sherbet

Pineapple Sherbet

³/₄ cup sugar
¹/₂ cup water
1 large pineapple
3 tablespoons lemon juice
2 egg whites, at room temperature

Color index
page 102

Begin early
in day or
day ahead

5 cups or
8 servings

1 In 1-quart saucepan over medium heat, heat sugar and water to boiling, stirring the mixture constantly. Remove saucepan from heat.

2 With sharp knife, cut crown and stem end off pineapple; cut off rind; remove eyes. Cut pineapple in half; remove core. Cut pineapple into small chunks.

3 In covered blender container at medium speed, blend pineapple until smooth. Strain into large bowl; with spoon, press out all juice and discard fibers.

4 Stir sugar mixture and lemon juice into pineapple. In small bowl with mixer at high speed, beat egg whites into stiff peaks.

5 Fold beaten egg whites into pineapple mixture. Pour into 13″ by 9″ baking pan. Cover with foil and freeze until firm, 3 hours.

6 Spoon pineapple mixture into chilled large bowl; with mixer at low speed, beat until softened. Increase speed to medium and beat until fluffy but still frozen; return to baking pan. Cover with foil. Freeze 2 hours until partially frozen. Spoon into chilled large bowl and beat again as above. Return mixture to baking pan; cover again with foil and freeze until firm.

7 *To serve:* Let sherbet stand at room temperature 10 minutes. Scoop into serving dishes.

Cantaloupe Sherbet

1 small very ripe cantaloupe
1 quart milk
2 envelopes unflavored gelatin
³/₄ cup light corn syrup

¹/₂ cup sugar
³/₄ teaspoon salt
3 drops yellow food color
1 drop red food color

Color index
page 102

Begin early
in day or
up to 1 month
ahead

2 quarts or
12 servings

1. Cut cantaloupe in half; discard seeds and peel. Cut cantaloupe into bite-size chunks. In covered blender container at medium speed, blend cantaloupe and 1 cup milk until smooth; set aside.

2. In 3-quart saucepan over 1 cup milk, evenly sprinkle gelatin. Cook over medium-low heat, stirring, until gelatin is dissolved. Remove from heat; stir in cantaloupe mixture, remaining milk and remaining ingredients (mixture may look curdled). Pour mixture into 13″ by 9″ baking pan. Cover and freeze until partially frozen, about 3 hours, stirring mixture occasionally.

3. Spoon cantaloupe mixture into chilled large bowl; with mixer at medium speed, beat until smooth but still frozen; return to pan. Cover; freeze until firm, about 3 hours.

4. *To serve:* Let sherbet stand at room temperature 10 minutes for easier scooping.

Minted Sherbet Ring with Berries

3 pints lemon sherbet, slightly softened
¹/₃ cup green crème de menthe

2 pints strawberries, hulled
shredded coconut for garnish

Color index
page 103

Begin early
in day or
day ahead

8 to 10
servings

1. In large bowl with mixer at medium speed, beat sherbet with crème de menthe until smooth; spoon into a 5½-cup ring mold; freezer-wrap; freeze.

2. *To serve:* With metal spatula, loosen edges of frozen mixture from mold. In sink of hot water, quickly dip frozen mixture almost to top to loosen; dry mold with towel. Invert mold onto platter; remove mold. Fill center of ring with strawberries; sprinkle with coconut.

Orange Milk Sherbet

5 cups milk
1 envelope unflavored gelatin
1¹/₂ cups sugar
1 cup orange juice
¹/₄ cup grated orange peel

¹/₄ cup lemon juice
³/₄ teaspoon salt
¹/₄ teaspoon yellow food color
¹/₈ teaspoon red food color

Color index
page 102

Begin early
in day or
up to 1 month
ahead

2 quarts or
12 servings

1. In 3-quart saucepan over 1 cup milk, evenly sprinkle gelatin. Cook over medium-low heat, stirring, until gelatin is dissolved. Remove pan from heat; stir in remaining ingredients and milk (mixture may look curdled). Pour mixture into 13″ by 9″ baking pan. Cover; freeze until partially frozen, about 3 hours, stirring occasionally.

2. Spoon mixture into chilled large bowl; with mixer at medium speed, beat until smooth but still frozen; return to pan. Cover; freeze until firm.

3. *To serve:* Let sherbet stand at room temperature 10 minutes for easier scooping.

Fruit ices

Lemon Ice in Lemon Cups

6 large lemons
1 envelope unflavored
**   gelatin**
1 cup sugar
2¼ cups water
mint sprigs
**   for garnish**

Color index page 103

Begin early in day or
day ahead

1 quart or 6 servings

1 With sharp knife, cut off
⅓ of each lemon from
one end. Grate peel from
top ⅓ pieces.

2 Squeeze juice from all
pieces of lemon to
make approximately ¾
cup. Discard tops.

3 Remove all crushed
pulp and membrane
from lemon cups; cut a
thin slice off bottom of
each so they can stand.
Place in plastic bag;
refrigerate cups.

4 In 1-quart saucepan
over low heat, cook
gelatin, sugar and water,
stirring constantly, until
gelatin is dissolved.

5 Remove saucepan from
heat; stir in lemon juice
and grated lemon peel.

6 Pour mixture into 9" by
9" baking pan; cover
with foil or plastic wrap;
freeze about 3 hours until
partially frozen.

7 Spoon lemon mixture
into chilled large bowl;
with mixer at medium
speed, beat until smooth
but still frozen.

8 Return lemon mixture
to baking pan; cover;
freeze about 2 hours until
partially frozen.

9 Spoon mixture into
chilled large bowl and
with mixer at medium
speed, beat again as in step
7. Freeze until firm.

10 *To serve:* Let ice
stand at room tem-
perature 10 minutes.
Scoop into lemon cups;
garnish with mint sprigs.

Begin early in day or day ahead

1 quart or 6 servings

ORANGE ICE: In 1-quart saucepan, combine *1
envelope unflavored gelatin* and *½ cup sugar*; stir in *1
cup water*. Over medium heat, heat until gelatin is
completely dissolved, stirring constantly. Remove
saucepan from heat; stir in *2 cups orange juice, 1
teaspoon grated lemon peel* and *1 tablespoon lemon
juice*. Pour into 9" by 9" baking pan and freeze.
Spoon orange and lemon mixture into chilled large
bowl; beat and serve as Lemon Ice, left, but omit
lemon cups and mint sprigs.

Color index page 103

Begin early in day or up to 1 month ahead

10 cups or 20 servings

Strawberry-Orange Ice

1½ cups orange juice   **3 pints strawberries,**
½ cup lemon juice   **   hulled**
¼ cup orange-flavor   **2 cups sugar**
**   liqueur**

1. In covered blender container at high speed, blend
all ingredients until smooth, blending about half at a
time; pour mixture into a 9" by 9" baking pan and
mix well. Cover with foil or plastic wrap and freeze
until partially frozen, about 4 hours.
2. Spoon strawberry-orange mixture into chilled
large bowl and, with mixer at medium speed, beat
until smooth but still frozen; return mixture to
baking pan. Cover with foil or plastic wrap and
freeze mixture until firm.
3. *To serve:* Remove mixture from freezer and allow
it to stand at room temperature about 10 minutes for
easier scooping.

Color index page 103

Begin early in day or up to 1 month ahead

5 cups or 10 servings

Watermelon Ice

½ small watermelon,   **3 tablespoons**
**   peeled, seeded and**   **   confectioners' sugar**
**   cut into 1-inch**   **1 tablespoon lemon juice**
**   chunks (about 6 cups)**   **¼ teaspoon salt**

1. In covered blender container at low speed, blend 1
cup watermelon chunks with confectioners' sugar,
lemon juice and salt until the mixture is smooth; add
remaining watermelon chunks and blend a few
seconds longer until smooth. Pour into 9" by 9"
baking pan; cover with foil or plastic wrap and
freeze until partially frozen, about 2 hours.
2. Into chilled large bowl, spoon watermelon mixture. With mixer at high speed, beat until fluffy.
Return mixture to baking pan and freeze until firm,
about 1½ hours.
3. *To serve:* Remove Watermelon Ice from freezer
and let it stand at room temperature 10 minutes for
easier scooping.

CAKES

The cakes in this chapter all follow one of two basic methods. Most of our layer cakes, loaves and cupcakes contain solid shortening, butter or margarine and are mixed and beaten in one bowl. Others, such as angelfood, chiffon and sponge cakes, depend on beaten egg whites or eggs to make them high, light and fluffy. Whichever type you bake, if you follow directions carefully you can be assured of success.

BEFORE MAKING CAKES
Before you start, read the recipe carefully and assemble all ingredients and equipment. Prepare pans, set oven racks in position and preheat the oven. Have all ingredients at room temperature.
Ingredients: Don't substitute; different ingredients give different results. We use Large eggs and double-acting baking powder in our recipes in this book.
Measuring: Measure dry and liquid ingredients in the same way as for Quick Breads (page 421).
Pans: Use shiny metal pans or pans with a non-stick finish. Avoid dull, dark or enamel pans which can cause uneven and excessive browning. If using glass or porcelain-coated aluminum pans with non-stick finish, reduce the oven temperature 25°F. Be sure your pans are the size called for and prepare them as directed. If to be greased and floured, grease bottom and sides generously with solid shortening, using crumpled waxed paper or with melted shortening, using a pastry brush. Then sprinkle the pan with a little flour, shake it until coated, invert it and tap it to remove excess flour. Don't grease pans for angel, chiffon and sponge cakes.
Oven space: Set your oven rack so the center of cake or layers is close to the center of the oven. If using two racks, arrange them so they divide the oven into thirds. Make sure the pans do not touch each other or the sides of the oven and if using more than one rack, stagger the pans so that one is not directly underneath another.

MIXING CAKES
Shortening cakes: Beat ingredients with a mixer for the time and at the speed specified, scraping the bowl often so ingredients are mixed well. If you beat with a wooden spoon, use *150 vigorous strokes for every minute of beating time.* Before baking, cut through batter in pan with knife to remove air bubbles.

Angel, chiffon and sponge cakes: Be sure the bowl for egg whites is free from grease and no traces of yolk are present in the whites. With a rubber spatula, fold ingredients into the beaten egg whites by cutting down through the whites, across the bottom and up the side of the bowl. Give the bowl a quarter turn and repeat just until dry ingredients are no longer visible. Don't overfold or egg whites will break down. Before baking, cut through the batter in the pan with a rubber spatula several times to remove any large air bubbles.
Fruitcake: Toss about ½ cup of the flour with fruits and nuts to coat them so they won't sink in the batter.

TESTING FOR DONENESS
Do not open the oven door to test a cake until the minimum baking time has passed, or the cake might fall.

Test shortening cakes and fruitcakes by inserting a toothpick into the center. It should come out clean and dry. Test angel, chiffon and sponge cakes by pressing the top lightly with a finger. Top should spring back and any cracks on surface should look dry.

COOLING CAKES
Shortening cakes: Leave in the pan on a wire rack for 10 minutes, then run a spatula around the edges to loosen them from the pan and turn the cake out as below.

Invert a second rack over top of cake in pan on rack.

Turn two racks upside down. Remove upper rack; lift off pan.

Replace rack; turn two racks over again so cake rests top up.

Remove top rack; let cake cool before frosting or storing.

Angel, chiffon and sponge cakes: If baked in tube pan, invert pan on a bottle or funnel, so top of cake does not touch counter. Cool completely in pan, then gently cut around pan side and tube with a knife. Invert and shake the cake onto a plate.

Fruitcakes: Cool completely in the pan on a wire rack.

FROSTING CAKES

Allow your cake to cool completely. Before frosting, trim off any crisp edges with kitchen scissors and brush away all loose crumbs. Keep the cake plate clean by covering the edges with strips of waxed paper arranged in a square. Lay the cake on the paper strips, centering it on the plate. After frosting the cake, carefully slide out the paper strips.

Keeping plate clean: Lay cake on waxed paper strips arranged in square, and frost.

After frosting, carefully slide out strips. If needed, touch up base with a little more frosting.

It's easier to frost a cake evenly if you can turn it as you work. Place cake on a plate on a turntable, lazy Susan or top of a large bowl. Spread frosting with a broad-bladed knife or spatula.

Cutting a cake in layers: With a ruler and toothpicks, mark the cutting line(s) all around a layer or tube cake. With a long, sharp knife, using toothpicks as a guide, cut the layers. Remove toothpicks. If you make a shallow vertical cut in one side of the cake before splitting it, it will be easier to reassemble the layers in their original position; just align the marks when putting the cake together again.

Frosting a layer cake: Place one layer, top side down, on the plate. Spread the layer with filling or frosting almost to edge. If the filling is soft, spread it only to within an inch of the edge – the weight of the top layer will push it to the edge. Place the second layer, top side up, on the filling, so that the flat bottoms of the two layers face each other, keeping the top layer from cracking or sliding off. Frost sides of cake thinly to set any loose crumbs, then apply a second, generous layer of frosting, swirling it up to make a ½-inch ridge above rim of cake. Finally, frost the top of the cake, swirling the frosting or leaving it smooth, as you like. Decorate if desired.

Frosting an oblong cake: Frost top and sides as layer cake; or, leave in pan and frost top only.

Frosting a tube or ring cake: Frost sides then top and inside center of cake as layer cake.

Glazing a cake: Brush crumbs from top only, then drizzle glaze over top with spoon, so it runs down sides.

Frosting cupcakes: Dip the top of each cupcake in frosting, turning it slightly to coat it evenly.

CUTTING CAKES

Use a long, thin, sharp knife with a sawing motion to cut layer cakes and loaves. Fruitcakes are easier to slice thinly if first chilled. For angel, chiffon and sponge cakes, use a serrated knife or cake breaker.

STORING CAKES

Cakes left in the pan, frosted or unfrosted, should be covered tightly with a lid, plastic wrap or foil.

Layer cakes and frosted tube cakes are best stored in a cake keeper or under a large, inverted bowl. However, a cake with fluffy frosting should be frosted and served on the same day, as the frosting gradually disintegrates during storage. Leftovers may be put in a cake keeper or under an inverted bowl with a spoon or knife handle inserted under the top to hold it open, so that air will be able to circulate freely and help keep the frosting fluffy. Store cakes with whipped-cream frosting or cream filling in the refrigerator. Most cakes are best eaten within 1 or 2 days.

Wrap fruitcakes closely in plastic wrap or foil; if you like, sprinkle them first with brandy or wine, or wrap them in a wine- or brandy-dampened cloth, then overwrap with foil and store for up to 2 months. Redampen the cloth weekly. Glaze or decorate just before serving.

FREEZING CAKES

Unfrosted cakes should be wrapped in freezer wrap, plastic wrap or foil, and sealed with tape. They will keep from 4 to 6 months, fruitcake up to 12 months.

Freeze frosted cakes, unwrapped, on a sheet of cardboard covered with foil until frosting hardens. Then wrap and seal as above, and return to freezer. Frosted cakes can be kept frozen for 2 to 3 months.

Don't freeze cakes which have a custard or fruit filling; they may become soggy when thawed. Never freeze uncooked batter.

THAWING CAKES

Thaw unfrosted cakes and cakes with butter-cream or with fudge frosting, wrapped, at room temperature. Unfrosted cakes will take about 1 hour; frosted tube cakes and layer cakes, 2 to 3 hours; cupcakes will thaw in about 30 minutes.

Cakes with a whipped-cream topping or filling, or a fluffy frosting, should be unwrapped before they are thawed. Thaw cakes with whipped-cream topping or filling in the refrigerator for 3 to 4 hours. Thaw cakes with fluffy frosting at room temperature.

Shortening cakes

Yellow Cake

2¼ cups cake flour
1½ cups sugar
¾ cup shortening
¾ cup milk
3 eggs
2½ teaspoons double-acting baking powder
1 teaspoon salt
1 teaspoon vanilla extract
½ teaspoon almond extract
Butter-Cream Frosting (page 400)

Color index page 92

Begin early in day

8 to 10 servings

1 Preheat oven to 375°F. Prepare pans: First grease and then flour two 9-inch round cake pans.

2 Into large bowl, measure all ingredients except frosting.

3 With mixer at low speed, beat until well mixed, constantly scraping bowl with rubber spatula. Increase speed to medium; beat 5 minutes, occasionally scraping bowl.

4 Pour batter into prepared cake pans, smoothing top with rubber spatula. Cut through batter with knife to remove any air bubbles.

5 Bake layers 25 minutes or until toothpick inserted deep into center comes out clean.

6 Cool in pans on wire racks 10 minutes then remove from pans and cool completely on racks.

7 Meanwhile, prepare frosting. When layers are completely cooled, fill and frost cake.

Pineapple-Upside-Down Cake

Color index page 92

Begin early in day

12 servings

½ cup butter or margarine
2 cups packed brown sugar
1 15½-ounce can pineapple chunks
maraschino cherries, drained
Yellow Cake batter (left)
cream, whipped cream or vanilla ice cream

1. Preheat oven to 375°F. Before making cake batter, prepare topping: In 13″ by 9″ baking pan, place butter or margarine; place pan in oven until butter melts. Sprinkle brown sugar over butter. Meanwhile, drain pineapple chunks; use pineapple to form "flowers" in sugar mixture. Use a cherry for center of each flower.
2. Prepare cake batter as recipe directs but carefully spoon over design in baking pan.
3. Bake 35 to 40 minutes until toothpick inserted in center comes out clean. Cool in pan on wire rack 10 minutes. Then loosen cake from sides of pan; place platter on top of pan and invert both; lift off pan. (If fruit sticks to pan, lift off with spatula and replace in design on cake.) Serve topped with cream, whipped cream or vanilla ice cream.

Making sugar mixture: Sprinkle the brown sugar over melted butter in the baking pan.

Arranging pineapple: Form flowers with pineapple chunks. Place cherry in center of each.

Devil's Food Cake

Color index page 90

Begin early in day

8 to 10 servings

2 cups cake flour
1½ cups sugar
1¼ cups buttermilk
½ cup shortening
3 eggs
3 squares unsweetened chocolate, melted
1½ teaspoons baking soda
1 teaspoon salt
1 teaspoon vanilla extract
½ teaspoon double-acting baking powder
Quick Fudge Frosting (page 400), Snow Peak Frosting (page 401) or Mocha Butter-Cream Frosting (page 400)

1. Preheat oven to 350°F. Grease and flour two 9-inch round cake pans.
2. Into large bowl, measure all ingredients except frosting. With mixer at low speed, beat until well mixed, constantly scraping bowl with rubber spatula. Increase speed to high; beat 5 minutes, occasionally scraping bowl.
3. Pour batter into pans. Bake 25 to 30 minutes until toothpick inserted in center comes out clean. Cool on wire racks 10 minutes then remove from pans; cool completely on racks.
4. Prepare chosen frosting. Fill and frost cake.

Silver-White Cake

Color index
page 90

Begin early
in day

8 servings

4 egg whites
1½ cups sugar
2¼ cups cake flour
1 cup milk
½ cup shortening
1 tablespoon
double-acting
baking powder
1 teaspoon salt
1 teaspoon vanilla
extract

¼ teaspoon almond
extract
Mocha Butter-Cream
Frosting (page 400),
or Fresh Lemon Filling
(page 401) and Snow
Peak Frosting
(page 401)

1. Preheat oven to 375°F. Grease and flour two 8-inch round cake pans; line pans with waxed paper.

2 In small bowl with mixer at high speed, beat egg whites until soft peaks form.

3 Beating at high speed, sprinkle in ½ cup sugar, 2 tablespoons at a time; beat until sugar is dissolved and whites stand in stiff peaks (do not scrape bowl). Set aside.

4 In large bowl at low speed, beat 1 cup sugar and remaining ingredients except frosting, constantly scraping bowl. At medium speed, beat 3 minutes longer.

5 At low speed, beat in whites. Pour into pans; bake 25 minutes. Cool in pans on wire racks 10 minutes; remove from pans and cool completely on wire racks.

6. Meanwhile, prepare chosen frosting and filling. Fill and frost with Mocha Butter-Cream Frosting or alternatively, fill with Fresh Lemon Filling and frost with Snow Peak Frosting.

Begin early
in day

10 servings

LADY BALTIMORE CAKE: Prepare and cool *Silver-White Cake* as above. With sharp knife, cut each cake layer horizontally in half. In small bowl, combine *½ cup candied cherries,* chopped, *⅓ cup dried figs,* chopped, *⅓ cup raisins,* chopped, and *¼ cup chopped pecans;* set fruit mixture aside. Prepare *2 packages fluffy white-frosting mix* as label directs; stir fruit mixture into 3 cups of frosting; use this mixture to fill cake layers. Spread remaining frosting on top and sides of cake.

Chocolate Cupcakes

Color index
page 93

Begin early
in day

24 cupcakes

2 cups cake flour
1 ¾ cups sugar
¾ cup cocoa
1¼ cups milk
¾ cup shortening
3 eggs
1¼ teaspoons baking
soda
1 teaspoon salt

1 teaspoon vanilla
extract
½ teaspoon double-acting baking
powder
Coffee Cream-
Cheese Frosting
(page 400)

1 Preheat oven to 350°F. Place liners in 2 dozen 3-inch muffin-pan cups or grease and flour cups.

2 Into large bowl, measure all cupcake ingredients except frosting.

3 With mixer at low speed, beat until well mixed, constantly scraping bowl; at high speed, beat 5 minutes, scraping the bowl occasionally.

4 Spoon into muffin-pan cups, filling each half full. Bake 20 minutes or until toothpick inserted in center of one comes out clean and dry.

5 Cool in pans on wire racks 10 minutes, then remove from pans and cool completely on racks.

6 Prepare frosting then dip tops of cupcakes into frosting and turn slightly to coat.

Color index
page 93

Begin early
in day

8 to 10 servings

CHOCOLATE CAKE: Preheat oven to 350°F. Grease and flour two 9-inch round cake pans. Prepare batter as above but pour into pans; bake 30 to 35 minutes. Cool layers in pans on wire racks 10 minutes; remove from pans and cool completely on racks. Fill and frost the chocolate cake layers with your choice of either *Coffee Cream-Cheese Frosting (page 400)* or *Fluffy Boiled Frosting (page 400).*

Shortening cakes

Deluxe Marble Cake

Color index
page 90

Begin early
in day

10 to 12
servings

*2 squares unsweetened
  chocolate*
1¼ cups sugar
¼ cup water
1 teaspoon vanilla extract
½ cup butter, softened
2 cups all-purpose flour
¾ cup evaporated milk
3 eggs
*2 teaspoons double-acting
  baking powder*
1 teaspoon orange extract
½ teaspoon salt
½ teaspoon baking soda
confectioners' sugar

1 Preheat oven to 350°F.
Grease well a 9-inch
springform pan. In 1-quart
saucepan over very low
heat, melt chocolate and ¼
cup sugar with water, stirring. Stir in vanilla; cool.

2 Into large bowl,
measure 1 cup sugar
and all ingredients except
chocolate mixture and confectioners' sugar.

3 With mixer at low
speed, beat until well
mixed, constantly scraping
bowl; at high speed, beat 5
minutes, scraping the bowl
occasionally. Remove 2½
cups batter.

4 Beat chocolate mixture
into remaining batter;
alternately spoon plain and
chocolate batters into pan.

5 With knife, cut through
batter a few times, then
bake 55 to 60 minutes (top
will be cracked).

6 Cool in pan on rack 10
minutes; remove sides of
pan and cool cake on rack.

7 Sprinkle top of cooled
cake lightly with some
confectioners' sugar.

Fresh Coconut Cake

Color index
page 92

Begin 3 hrs
or day ahead

16 servings

2¼ cups cake flour
1½ cups sugar
¾ cup shortening
¾ cup milk
3 eggs
*2½ teaspoons double-
  acting baking powder*
1 teaspoon salt
*1 teaspoon vanilla
  extract*

Custard Filling (below)
*meat from 1 medium
  coconut, shredded
  (3 to 4 cups; to extract
  meat, see page 305)*
*Snow Peak Frosting
  (page 401)*
*candied orange slices for
  garnish*

1. Preheat oven to 375°F. Grease and flour two 9-
inch round cake pans.
2. In large bowl with mixer at low speed, beat first 8
ingredients until well mixed, constantly scraping
bowl. Beat at medium speed 5 minutes, occasionally
scraping bowl.
3. Pour into pans; bake 25 to 30 minutes until
toothpick inserted in center of cakes comes out
clean. Cool in pans on wire racks 10 minutes;
remove from pans and cool completely on racks.
4. Meanwhile, prepare Custard Filling. Stir 1 cup
shredded coconut into chilled Custard Filling.
Prepare Snow Peak Frosting.
5. With sharp knife, cut each cake horizontally in
half. Place first layer on cake plate, cut side up;
spread cake with ⅓ of filling. Repeat layering,
ending with a cake layer, top side up.
6. Frost side and top of cake with frosting. Sprinkle
side and top of cake with about 2 cups shredded
coconut. Garnish top with candied orange slices.
Refrigerate until serving time.

CUSTARD FILLING: In heavy, 2-quart saucepan
with wire whisk, mix well *4 egg yolks, 2 cups milk, ½
cup sugar, ⅓ cup cornstarch* and *3 tablespoons
orange-flavor liqueur* until well blended; then, over
medium heat, cook, stirring constantly, until mixture thickens, about 10 minutes. Cover custard
surface with waxed paper; refrigerate until well
chilled, about 1½ hours.

German Gold Poundcake

Color index
page 90

Begin early
in day

16 servings

2 cups sugar
*1 cup butter,
  softened*
3½ cups cake flour
1 cup milk
6 egg yolks

*1½ teaspoons double-
  acting baking powder*
*2 teaspoons vanilla
  extract*
⅛ teaspoon salt

1. Preheat oven to 350°F. Grease and flour 10-inch
Bundt pan or two 9″ by 5″ loaf pans.
2. In large bowl with mixer at high speed, beat sugar
and butter until light and fluffy.
3. Add flour and rest of ingredients; at low speed,
beat until well mixed, constantly scraping bowl with
rubber spatula. Beat at high speed 4 minutes, occasionally scraping bowl.
4. Pour batter into Bundt pan and bake 1 hour or, if
using loaf pans, 45 to 50 minutes until toothpick
inserted in center comes out clean. Cool cake in pan
on wire rack 10 minutes; remove from pan; cool
completely on rack.

Spicy Gingerbread

Color index
page 90

Begin early
in day

9 servings

2½ cups all-purpose flour
1 cup molasses
½ cup sugar
½ cup shortening
1 egg
1½ teaspoons baking soda
1 teaspoon ground
cinnamon
1 teaspoon ground ginger
¾ teaspoon salt
½ teaspoon ground
cloves
1 cup boiling water
whipped cream for
topping

1 Preheat oven to 350°F. Grease one 9-inch square cake pan then sprinkle with flour.

2 In large bowl with mixer at low speed, mix well all ingredients except cream; then beat at medium speed 3 minutes.

3 Pour gingerbread batter into greased and floured cake pan.

4 Bake 55 to 60 minutes until toothpick inserted in cake comes out clean.

5 Cool cake in pan on wire rack then top cake with whipped cream.

Merryfield Apple Cake

Color index
page 91

Begin early
in day

18 servings

3 cups all-purpose flour
2 cups sugar
1 cup salad oil
1 teaspoon baking soda
1 teaspoon salt
2 teaspoons vanilla
extract

3 eggs
3 cups diced, peeled
cooking apples
1 cup chopped California
walnuts
½ cup chopped raisins
confectioners' sugar

1. Preheat oven to 325°F. Grease well and flour two 8-inch square cake pans.
2. In large bowl with mixer at low speed, mix well first 7 ingredients, constantly scraping bowl. Beat 3 minutes more, occasionally scraping bowl. Stir in apples, nuts and raisins.
3. Spread in pans. Bake 1 hour. Cool on wire racks. Place paper doily on each cake; sprinkle with confectioners' sugar; remove doilies.

Spice Cake

Color index
page 91

Begin early
in day

8 servings

2 cups cake flour
¾ cup sugar
¾ cup milk
½ cup packed brown
sugar
½ cup shortening
2 eggs
2½ teaspoons double-
acting baking powder
1 teaspoon salt
1 teaspoon ground
cinnamon

1 teaspoon ground
allspice
½ teaspoon ground
cloves
½ teaspoon ground
nutmeg
1 teaspoon vanilla
extract
Whipped-Cream
Frosting (page 400) or
Buttermilk Icing
(page 401)

1. Preheat oven to 350°F. Grease and flour two 8-inch round cake pans.
2. In large bowl with mixer at low speed, beat all ingredients except frosting just until blended. Beat 3 minutes at high speed.
3. Pour batter into pans. Bake 25 to 30 minutes. Cool on racks. Prepare frosting; fill and frost cake.

Lane Cake

Color index
page 90

Begin early
in day

16 servings

8 eggs, at room
temperature
2 cups sugar
2¾ cups cake flour
1 cup milk
1 cup butter or
margarine

3 teaspoons double-
acting baking powder
1 teaspoon salt
1 teaspoon vanilla
extract
Filling (below)
Frosting (below)

1. Preheat oven to 375°F. Separate eggs, placing 6 whites in large bowl, 2 whites in small bowl and all the yolks in 2-quart saucepan. Grease two 9-inch round cake pans; line bottoms of cake pans with waxed paper; grease.
2. In large bowl with mixer at high speed, beat egg whites until soft peaks form. Beating at high speed, sprinkle in 1 cup sugar, 2 tablespoons at a time. Beat until stiff peaks form.
3. In another large bowl at low speed, mix flour, next 5 ingredients and 1 cup sugar. At medium speed, beat 4 minutes; fold in whites.
4. Pour into pans; bake 35 minutes. Cool in pans on wire racks 10 minutes; remove from pans; discard paper; cool. Prepare Filling. Cut each layer in half horizontally; assemble 4-layer cake with filling. Prepare Frosting; frost cake.

FILLING: Into 8 yolks, stir *1¼ cups sugar* and *½ cup butter.* Over medium heat, cook, stirring until slightly thickened, about 5 minutes. Stir in *one 4-ounce can shredded coconut, 1 cup pecan halves,* chopped, *1 cup candied red cherries,* chopped, *1 cup dark seedless raisins,* chopped and *⅓ cup bourbon.*

FROSTING: In 1-quart saucepan over medium heat, heat *1½ cups sugar, 1 tablespoon dark corn syrup, ⅓ cup water* and *½ teaspoon salt* to boiling. Boil, without stirring, to 240°F. on candy thermometer. Remove from heat. With mixer at high speed, beat reserved 2 egg whites until soft peaks form. Pour syrup in thin stream into whites, beating constantly. Add *1 teaspoon vanilla extract;* continue beating until very thick.

Shortening cakes

Banana Cake

Color index page 92

Begin early in day

8 to 10 servings

2¼ cups cake flour
1¼ cups sugar
1½ cups well-mashed ripe bananas (3 to 4)
½ cup shortening
2 eggs
2½ teaspoons double-acting baking powder
1 teaspoon vanilla extract
½ teaspoon baking soda
½ teaspoon salt
Whipped-Cream Frosting (page 400)
banana slices for garnish
lemon juice

1 Preheat oven to 375°F. Prepare two 8-inch round cake pans: First grease and then flour the bottom and sides of the cake pans.

2 Into large bowl, measure all ingredients except frosting, banana slices and lemon juice.

3 With mixer at low speed, beat until well mixed, constantly scraping bowl, then beat at high speed 5 minutes, occasionally scraping bowl.

4 Pour batter into pans and bake 25 minutes or until toothpick inserted deep into center of cake comes out clean.

5 Cool layers in pans on wire racks 10 minutes, then remove from pans and cool completely on racks before filling and frosting cake.

6 Prepare Whipped-Cream Frosting then, with metal spatula, fill and frost cake layers.

7 Just before serving, dip banana slices in lemon juice; use to garnish top of Banana Cake.

Walnut-Fudge Cake

Color index page 92

Begin early in day or day ahead

16 servings

8 eggs, separated
1½ cups confectioners' sugar
1 cup unsalted butter, softened
2 cups California walnuts, finely chopped
6 squares semisweet chocolate, melted

3 tablespoons all-purpose flour
1½ teaspoons vanilla extract
Chocolate-Walnut Filling (below)
Thin Chocolate Glaze (below)
California walnut halves for garnish

1. Preheat oven to 325°F. Grease and flour three 9-inch round cake pans.

2. In large bowl with mixer at high speed, beat egg whites until soft peaks form; beating at high speed, sprinkle in ½ cup sugar, 2 tablespoons at a time; beat until sugar is completely dissolved and whites stand in stiff, glossy peaks.

3. In another large bowl at low speed, mix well yolks, remaining sugar, butter, chopped walnuts, chocolate, flour and vanilla, constantly scraping bowl. Beat 4 minutes at medium speed, occasionally scraping bowl. With rubber spatula, gently fold in egg whites until just blended.

4. Pour batter into pans; bake 35 minutes or until toothpick inserted in center comes out clean. Cool in pans on wire racks 10 minutes; remove from pans and cool completely on racks.

5. Prepare Chocolate-Walnut Filling and fill between layers; place cake on cake plate. Prepare glaze; spread over top and sides of cake. Garnish with walnut halves; refrigerate. Cut cake into wedges to serve

CHOCOLATE-WALNUT FILLING: In double boiler, over hot, *not boiling*, water, melt **2 squares semisweet chocolate.** Stir in **⅓ cup sugar, 2 cups California walnuts,** chopped, and **½ cup milk.** Cook over boiling water 5 minutes until sugar is completely dissolved. Remove from heat; with spoon, beat in **¼ cup butter** or margarine, softened, and **1 teaspoon vanilla extract** just until blended. Refrigerate just until cool.

THIN CHOCOLATE GLAZE: In double boiler over hot, *not boiling*, water, melt **one 6-ounce package semisweet-chocolate pieces** with **2 tablespoons shortening**; remove from heat. Beat in **2 tablespoons light corn syrup** and **3 tablespoons milk** until smooth; spread while still warm.

Adding glaze: Spread glaze over top and down sides of filled cake.

Chiffon cakes

Orange Chiffon Cake

Color index page 90

Begin early in day

16 servings

1 cup egg whites, at room temperature
½ teaspoon cream of tartar
sugar
2¼ cups cake flour
¾ cup orange juice
½ cup salad oil

5 egg yolks
1 tablespoon double-acting baking powder
3 tablespoons grated orange peel
1 teaspoon salt
Fluffy Orange Frosting (below)

1 Preheat oven to 325°F. In large bowl with mixer at high speed, beat egg whites and cream of tartar into soft peaks.

2 At high speed, beat in ½ cup sugar, 2 tablespoons at a time, until dissolved and whites stand in stiff, glossy peaks. Do not scrape the bowl.

3 In another large bowl at low speed, beat 1 cup sugar and remaining ingredients except frosting.

4 With rubber spatula, gently fold mixture into beaten whites. Pour batter into ungreased 10-inch tube pan.

5 Bake 1¼ hours or until top springs back when lightly touched. Invert in pan on funnel; cool.

6 Meanwhile, prepare frosting. Remove cake from pan; frost top and sides. Keep refrigerated.

FLUFFY ORANGE FROSTING: In 1-quart saucepan over medium heat, heat *one 12-ounce jar sweet orange marmalade* to boiling. In large bowl with mixer at high speed, beat *2 egg whites, ½ teaspoon vanilla extract, 10 drops yellow food color* and *⅛ teaspoon salt* until soft peaks form. Slowly pour in hot marmalade, beating 6 to 8 minutes until peaks form.

Sugar Bush Walnut Cake

Color index page 90

Begin early in day

12 servings

1 cup egg whites, at room temperature (7 or 8 egg whites)
½ teaspoon cream of tartar
1½ cups sugar
2¼ cups all-purpose flour
¾ cup water

7 egg yolks
⅔ cup California walnuts, finely chopped
½ cup salad oil
1 tablespoon double-acting baking powder
1 teaspoon vanilla extract
1 teaspoon maple extract

1. Preheat oven to 325°F. In large bowl with mixer at high speed, beat egg whites and cream of tartar until soft peaks form; beating at high speed, sprinkle in ½ cup sugar, 2 tablespoons at a time; beat until sugar is dissolved and whites stand in stiff peaks. Do not scrape bowl during beating.
2. In another large bowl with mixer at medium speed, beat flour with water, 1 cup sugar, egg yolks, finely chopped California walnuts, salad oil, baking powder, vanilla extract and maple extract until thoroughly blended.
3. Pour flour mixture over whites and, with rubber spatula, gently fold until just blended.
4. Pour batter into ungreased 10-inch tube pan and bake 1¼ hours or until top springs back when lightly touched with finger.
5. Invert cake in pan on funnel or bottle; cool completely in the pan.
6. With metal spatula, carefully loosen cake from tube pan; place on cake plate.

Chocolate Chiffon Cake

Color index page 92

Begin early in day or day ahead

12 servings

2 cups cake flour
½ cup cocoa
1 tablespoon double-acting baking powder
1 teaspoon salt
sugar
¾ cup water
½ cup salad oil

1 teaspoon vanilla extract
6 eggs, separated, at room temperature
½ teaspoon cream of tartar
confectioners' sugar

1. In medium bowl with wire whisk or spoon, stir flour, cocoa, baking powder, salt and 1¼ cups sugar until thoroughly blended. With same wire whisk or spoon stir in water, salad oil, vanilla and egg yolks until smooth.
2. Preheat oven to 350°F. In large bowl with mixer at high speed, beat egg whites and cream of tartar until soft peaks form; beating at high speed, gradually sprinkle in ½ cup sugar, 2 tablespoons at a time; beat until sugar is completely dissolved and whites stand in stiff peaks. Do not scrape side of bowl during beating.
3. With rubber spatula, gently fold flour mixture into beaten egg whites until just blended.
4. Pour batter into ungreased 10-inch tube pan. Bake 60 to 65 minutes until top springs back when lightly touched with finger.
5. Invert cake in pan on funnel or bottle; cool completely in the pan.
6. With spatula, loosen cake from pan; place on cake plate. Sprinkle cake with confectioners' sugar.

Angel-food cake

Sponge cakes

Angel-Food Cake

Color index page 91

Begin early in day

12 servings

1¼ cups confectioners' sugar
1 cup cake flour
1½ cups egg whites, at room temperature (12 to 14 egg whites)
1½ teaspoons cream of tartar
1½ teaspoons vanilla extract
¼ teaspoon salt
¼ teaspoon almond extract
1 cup sugar

1 Preheat oven to 375°F. In small bowl, stir confectioners' sugar and cake flour; set aside.

2 Add egg whites, cream of tartar, vanilla extract, salt and almond extract to large bowl and, with mixer at high speed, beat until well mixed.

3 Beating at high speed, sprinkle in sugar, 2 tablespoons at a time; beat just until sugar dissolves and whites form stiff peaks. Do not scrape bowl during beating.

4 With rubber spatula, fold in flour mixture, about ¼ at a time, just until flour disappears.

5 Pour mixture into ungreased 10-inch tube pan and with spatula, cut through batter to break any large air bubbles.

6 Bake 35 minutes or until top of cake springs back when lightly touched with finger. Any cracks on surface should look dry.

7 Invert cake in pan on funnel; cool completely. With spatula, loosen cake from pan and remove to plate.

Daffodil Cake

Color index page 93

Begin early in day or day ahead

12 servings

1¼ cups egg whites
1½ teaspoons cream of tartar
1 teaspoon vanilla extract
¼ teaspoon salt
1½ cups sugar
1 cup cake flour

4 egg yolks
1 tablespoon grated orange peel
2 teaspoons grated lemon peel
Orange-Lemon Icing (below)
orange sections

1 Preheat oven to 375°F. Into large bowl, measure egg whites, cream of tartar, vanilla and salt. With mixer at high speed, beat until soft peaks form.

2 Sprinkle in sugar, 2 tablespoons at a time, beating at high speed until sugar dissolves and whites stand in stiff glossy peaks. Do not scrape bowl.

3 Reduce mixer speed to low; gradually beat in flour until just blended.

4 In another large bowl at high speed, beat yolks until thick and lemon-colored; fold in half of egg-white mixture and orange and lemon peel.

5 In 10-inch tube pan, drop heaping tablespoons of white and yellow batters to form a checkerboard pattern; bake 35 to 40 minutes.

6 Invert cake and cool in pan for 1 hour. Meanwhile, prepare icing. Remove cake from pan and frost; garnish with orange sections; refrigerate.

ORANGE-LEMON ICING: In small bowl with mixer at medium speed, beat *1½ cups confectioners' sugar* with *¾ cup butter*, softened, *3 egg yolks* and *⅛ teaspoon salt* until fluffy; stir in *2 tablespoons grated orange peel* and *4 teaspoons grated lemon peel*.

Jelly Roll

Color index
page 91

Begin early
in day

10 servings

¾ cup all-purpose flour
1 teaspoon double-acting
  baking powder
½ teaspoon salt
4 eggs, separated, at
  room temperature
sugar

½ teaspoon vanilla
  extract
confectioners' sugar
1 10-ounce jar favorite
  jam or jelly

1 Preheat oven to 375°F. Grease 15½" by 10½" jelly-roll pan; line with waxed paper. In small bowl, combine flour, baking powder and salt. In another small bowl with mixer at high speed, beat whites into soft peaks; gradually sprinkle in ⅓ cup sugar, beating until sugar is completely dissolved and stiff peaks form.

2 In large bowl at high speed, beat egg yolks until thick and lemon-colored; at same speed, gradually sprinkle in ½ cup sugar then vanilla extract. Sprinkle flour mixture over yolks; add beaten whites; with rubber spatula, gently fold mixture to blend thoroughly.

3 Spread batter in pan; bake 15 minutes or until top springs back when lightly touched with finger.

4 Meanwhile, sprinkle cloth towel with ⅓ cup confectioners' sugar.

5 Immediately invert hot cake onto towel; gently remove waxed paper and cut off crisp edges of cake, if you like.

6 While still warm, carefully roll up cake and towel from narrow end.

7 Cool cake completely on rack, then unroll and spread with jam.

8 Reroll without towel and sprinkle roll with confectioners' sugar.

Mocha-Cream Roll

Color index
page 91

Begin 2 hrs
or day ahead

10 servings

5 eggs, separated,
  at room
  temperature
1 cup confectioners'
  sugar
⅛ teaspoon salt

cocoa
Mocha-Cream Filling
  (below)
Chocolate Icing (below)
Confectioners'
  ·Sugar Glaze (below)

1. Preheat oven to 400°F. Grease 15½" by 10½" jelly-roll pan; line bottom of pan with waxed paper; grease and flour paper.

2. In large bowl with mixer at high speed, beat egg whites until soft peaks form. Beating at high speed, gradually sprinkle in ½ cup confectioners' sugar, beating thoroughly after each addition. Continue beating until the egg whites stand in stiff, glossy peaks. Set aside.

3. In small bowl with same beaters and with mixer at high speed, beat egg yolks until thick and lemon-colored. Reduce speed to low; beat in salt, ½ cup confectioners' sugar and 3 tablespoons cocoa, occasionally scraping bowl with rubber spatula. With wire whisk or rubber spatula, gently fold yolk mixture into beaten whites just until the mixture is blended.

4. Spread batter evenly in pan and bake 15 minutes or until top springs back when lightly touched with finger. Prepare a clean cloth towel by sprinkling it with cocoa.

5. When cake is done, with small spatula, immediately loosen edges from side of pan; invert cake onto prepared towel. Gently peel waxed paper from bottom of cake. Roll towel with cake from narrow end, jelly-roll fashion. Cool completely, placing it seam side down, on wire rack. Meanwhile, prepare Mocha-Cream Filling.

6. When cake is cool, unroll from towel. Evenly spread Mocha-Cream Filling on cake almost to edges. Starting at same narrow end, roll up cake without the towel this time. Place the cake, seam side down, on platter.

7. Prepare Chocolate Icing. Spread icing over top and down sides of roll.

8. Prepare Confectioners' Sugar Glaze; use to drizzle over top of the roll to make a decorative design. Keep the roll in the refrigerator until you are ready to serve it.

MOCHA-CREAM FILLING: In medium bowl with mixer at medium speed, beat *1½ cups heavy or whipping cream, ½ cup cocoa, ¼ cup confectioners' sugar* and *2 tablespoons coffee-flavor liqueur* until stiff peaks form.

CHOCOLATE ICING: In double boiler, over hot, *not boiling*, water, melt *one-half 6-ounce package semisweet-chocolate pieces* with *1 tablespoon butter* or margarine; remove from heat; then beat in *1 tablespoon light corn syrup* and *3 tablespoons milk* until smooth.

CONFECTIONERS' SUGAR GLAZE: In small bowl, stir ½ *cup confectioners' sugar* and *2 to teaspoons water* until smooth.

Sponge cakes

Holiday Petits Fours

Cake:
4 eggs
¾ cup sugar
¾ cup all-purpose flour
1 teaspoon double-acting baking powder
½ teaspoon salt
½ teaspoon almond extract
1 10-ounce jar apple jelly (1 cup)
Almond Paste (right)

Sugar Icing:
1 16-ounce package confectioners' sugar

5 tablespoons water
1 teaspoon almond extract
2 drops red food color

Decorations: *red candied cherries, dragées, candied flowers, nonpareils*

Color index page 91

Begin early in day

30 petits fours

1 Grease 15½" by 10½" jelly-roll pan; line with waxed paper and grease paper. Preheat oven to 350°F. Prepare cake: In large bowl with mixer at high speed, beat eggs until foamy. Gradually sprinkle in sugar, beating until mixture is fluffy and very pale yellow, about 7 minutes. At low speed, beat in flour, baking powder, salt and almond extract. Spread evenly in pan.

2 Bake 20 minutes or until cake springs back when lightly touched. Cool on rack 10 minutes; invert from pan onto rack; peel off paper; cool completely.

3 In 1-quart saucepan over low heat, melt jelly, then with pastry brush, glaze cake with some jelly. Cut cake crosswise in half into two 10½" by 7¾" rectangles.

4 Between 2 sheets of waxed paper, roll Almond Paste to about 10½" by 7¾" rectangle. Peel off top sheet.

5 Invert bottom sheet with Almond Paste onto one cake rectangle and peel off paper.

6 Top with second cake rectangle, glazed side down, pressing layers together firmly.

7 Cut lengthwise into six 1¼-inch-wide strips. Then cut each strip crosswise into five pieces.

8 Brush cut surfaces of pieces with remaining jelly; place 1 inch apart on racks over waxed paper. Combine icing ingredients.

9 Drizzle icing over pieces. Return dripped icing to bowl; beat smooth to re-use, adding ½ teaspoon water if needed.

10 When icing is dry, decorate petits fours with your choice of candied cherries, candied flowers, dragées and nonpareils.

Begin 20 mins ahead
1 cup

Almond Paste

1 cup ground almonds
1 cup confectioners' sugar
1 egg yolk

2 teaspoons lemon juice
½ teaspoon almond extract

1. In small bowl, mix well the ground almonds, confectioners' sugar, egg yolk, lemon juice and almond extract.
2. Sprinkle work surface generously with confectioners' sugar; with sugared hands, knead mixture until smooth and not sticky.

Color index page 92

Begin early in day

12 servings

Coffee Cloud Cake

¾ cup egg whites, at room temperature
½ teaspoon cream of tartar
2 cups sugar
6 egg yolks
2 cups all-purpose flour
1 cup cold coffee

1 tablespoon double-acting baking powder
1 teaspoon vanilla extract
½ teaspoon salt
1 cup California walnuts, finely chopped

1. Preheat oven to 350°F. In large bowl with mixer at high speed, beat egg whites and cream of tartar until soft peaks form; beating at high speed, gradually sprinkle in ½ cup sugar, 2 tablespoons at a time; beat until sugar is completely dissolved and whites stand in stiff peaks. Do not scrape side of bowl during beating. Set aside.
2. In another large bowl with mixer at medium speed, beat 1½ cups sugar, egg yolks, flour, coffee, baking powder, vanilla and salt until light and fluffy.
3. Sprinkle egg whites with nuts; with rubber spatula, gently fold flour mixture into whites, just until blended.
4. Pour batter into ungreased 10-inch tube pan and bake 60 to 70 minutes until top springs back when lightly touched with finger. Invert cake in pan on bottle; cool completely. Loosen cake in pan and turn out as shown below.

Loosening cake in pan: Gently cut around pan side and tube with knife.

Turning out cake: Invert pan and shake cake out onto a plate.

Fruitcakes

Golden Fruitcake

2 cups golden raisins
1½ cups chopped dried figs
1 cup diced candied citron
1 cup diced candied lemon peel
1 cup diced candied orange peel
1 cup chopped pitted dates
1 cup slivered blanched almonds or pecans
½ cup diced candied pineapple

½ cup candied cherries, halved
½ cup dried currants
all-purpose flour
1 cup butter, softened
2 cups sugar
2 teaspoons double-acting baking powder
½ teaspoon salt
6 eggs
1 teaspoon lemon or orange extract
1 cup dry sherry or orange juice

¼ cup apple jelly
candied cherries
and blanched
whole almonds
for garnish

Color index page 93

Begin day or several wks ahead

One 7-pound fruitcake

1 Preheat oven to 300°F. Line 10-inch tube pan with aluminum foil.

2 In large bowl, combine first 10 ingredients; toss lightly with ¾ cup flour until fruits and nuts are well coated to prevent them sinking in batter.

3 In another large bowl with mixer at medium speed, beat butter with sugar until light and fluffy.

4 Add 3 cups flour, baking powder, salt, eggs, extract and sherry or orange juice and beat at low speed until well mixed, constantly scraping bowl.

5 Increase speed to medium and beat 4 minutes longer, occasionally scraping bowl.

6 With spoon, stir fruit mixture into batter until well mixed.

7 Spoon batter evenly into foil-lined tube pan then bake fruitcake 3 hours or until toothpick inserted in center of cake comes out clean.

8 Cool completely in pan on rack; remove from pan; peel off foil. Flavor improves on storing. To wrap and store fruitcake, see page 383.

9 Before serving: In small saucepan over low heat, melt jelly; brush on cake. Press in cherries and almonds in flower design. Let glaze set.

Color index page 91

Begin several wks ahead

One 5-pound fruitcake

Dark Christmas Fruitcake

3 cups dark seedless raisins
1½ cups diced candied citron
1 cup candied cherries, halved
1 cup diced candied pineapple
1 cup pecan halves
1 cup slivered blanched almonds
1 cup dried currants
½ cup diced candied orange peel
½ cup diced candied lemon peel

all-purpose flour
6 eggs, separated, at room temperature
sugar
1½ teaspoons ground cinnamon
1½ teaspoons ground cloves
1 teaspoon ground nutmeg
½ teaspoon baking soda
1 cup shortening
½ square unsweetened chocolate, melted
¼ cup lemon juice
¼ cup orange juice
¼ cup apple jelly

1. Preheat oven to 300°F. Line 10-inch tube pan with foil. In large bowl, combine first 9 ingredients; toss fruit and nuts with 1 cup flour to coat well.
2. In another large bowl with mixer at high speed, beat egg whites until soft peaks form; at high speed, beat in ½ cup sugar, 1 tablespoon at a time, until sugar is dissolved and whites stand in stiff peaks.
3. In medium bowl at low speed, mix well 1 cup flour, ½ cup sugar, yolks and rest of ingredients except apple jelly, constantly scraping bowl. Beat at high speed 5 minutes, occasionally scraping bowl.
4. Stir batter into fruit mixture. Fold in whites.
5. Pour batter into pan; bake 2 hours 10 minutes or until toothpick inserted in center comes out clean. Cool cake completely in pan on wire rack; remove from pan; peel off foil. Wrap and store.
6. Before serving: Melt jelly; brush on cake; let set.

Color index page 92

Begin several wks ahead

One 3-pound fruitcake

Brazil-Nut Sensation Fruitcake

3 cups Brazil nuts
2 cups whole pitted dates
1 cup maraschino cherries, well drained
¾ cup all-purpose flour
¾ cup sugar

½ teaspoon double-acting baking powder
½ teaspoon salt
3 eggs
1 teaspoon vanilla extract

1. Preheat oven to 300°F. Grease 9" by 5" loaf pan; line with foil. In large bowl, stir nuts, dates and cherries. Add flour, sugar, baking powder and salt; mix to coat nuts and fruits.
2. In small bowl with mixer at medium speed, beat eggs and vanilla until foamy; stir into nut mixture; mix well. Pour into pan; level top.
3. Bake 2½ hours or until toothpick inserted in center comes out clean. Cool in pan on wire rack 15 minutes. Turn out cake; peel off foil; allow to cool completely on wire rack. Wrap well; refrigerate.

Very special cakes

Sachertorte

Color index
page 90

Begin 6 hrs
ahead

12 servings

**5 squares semisweet
chocolate**
½ cup butter, softened
**1 teaspoon vanilla
extract**
¼ teaspoon salt
**6 eggs, separated, at
room temperature**

¾ cup sugar
1 cup cake flour
**1 10- or 12-ounce jar
apricot preserves**
Chocolate Glaze (below)
**1 cup heavy cream,
whipped**

1. In double boiler over hot, *not boiling*, water, melt
chocolate; remove from heat. Stir in butter, vanilla
and salt until mixture is smooth and cool. Add egg
yolks; stir until blended.
2. Lightly grease and flour 9″ by 3″ springform pan.
Preheat oven to 350°F. In large bowl with mixer at
high speed, beat egg whites until soft peaks form.
Beating at high speed, sprinkle in sugar, 2 tablespoons at a time, beating until sugar is dissolved and
whites stand in stiff, glossy peaks.
3. Gently fold chocolate mixture into beaten whites.
While folding, sprinkle in flour, about ⅓ at a time;
fold gently until blended. Pour batter into pan; with
spatula, cut through batter a few times to break any
air bubbles. Bake 45 minutes or until cake springs
back when lightly touched with finger. Cool cake in
pan on wire rack 10 minutes; remove side of pan;
cool completely.
4. Assemble torte as shown below, then refrigerate
torte until chocolate is firm.
5. *To serve:* With 2 pancake turners, transfer torte
to cake plate; let stand about 30 minutes. Serve torte
with whipped cream.

CHOCOLATE GLAZE: In double boiler over hot,
not boiling, water, melt *1 cup semisweet chocolate
pieces* and *2 tablespoons butter;* stir in *1 tablespoon
milk* and *1 tablespoon light corn syrup* until smooth.

ASSEMBLING THE SACHERTORTE

Cut cake in half horizon-
tally. Place top layer, cut
side up, on wire rack over
waxed paper.

Spread cut side of top layer with
apricot preserves, then add
bottom layer, cut side down.
Remove bottom of springform
pan from cake.

Prepare Chocolate Glaze. With
metal spatula, frost cake, letting
excess glaze drip onto paper.

MAKING CHOCOLATE CURLS

Make chocolate curls as shown below and use them to garnish
frosted cakes, pies or whipped-cream desserts.

Soften square or bar of unsweetened or semisweet chocolate
with heat of your hands or in
just-warm oven. Slowly and
firmly pull vegetable peeler across
wide side of chocolate for wide
curls, thin side for thin curls.

Or you can use the shred-
der side of a grater to
make curly shreds.

Six-Layer Eggnog Cake

Color index
page 93

Begin 4 hrs
or day ahead

12 servings

2 cups all-purpose flour
**2 teaspoons double-
acting baking powder**
**½ teaspoon ground
nutmeg**
½ teaspoon salt
**1½ cups heavy or
whipping cream**
**½ teaspoon rum
extract**

4 eggs
1¼ cups sugar
**Buttery Chocolate
Frosting (page 401)**
**4 squares semisweet
chocolate made into
chocolate curls
(above)**

1. Preheat oven to 350°F. Grease and flour three 9-
inch round cake pans.
2. In small bowl with fork, combine first 4 ingredients; set aside. In another small bowl with
mixer at medium speed, beat heavy or whipping
cream and rum extract until stiff peaks form.
3. In large bowl using same beaters, with mixer at
high speed, beat eggs and sugar until thick and
lemon-colored, about 5 minutes. With wire whisk or
rubber spatula, gently fold flour mixture and whipped heavy cream into egg mixture until blended;
pour batter into cake pans.
4. Stagger pans on 2 oven racks so no pan is
directly above another. Bake 20 to 25 minutes until
toothpick inserted in center of cakes comes out
clean. Cool cake layers on wire racks 10 minutes;
carefully remove cakes from pans and cool completely, about 1 hour.
5. Prepare Buttery Chocolate Frosting. With sharp
knife, cut each cake layer horizontally in half. Place
first layer on cake plate, cut side up; spread with a
scant ½ cup frosting. Repeat until 4 more frosted
layers are stacked on top. Top with last layer, top
side up. Frost side and top of cake with remaining
chocolate frosting.
6. Garnish top of cake with chocolate curls, transferring them to cake with toothpick to avoid breaking
them. Refrigerate until serving time.

Black Forest Cherry Torte

*2 15- or 16-ounce cans
  pitted tart cherries,
  drained
about ½ cup kirsch
  (cherry-flavor
  brandy)
Chocolate Cake layers
  (page 385)
2 cups heavy or whipping
  cream
½ cup confectioners'
  sugar
1 square semisweet
  chocolate, grated*

*12 maraschino cherries,
  well drained
2 squares semisweet
  chocolate made into
  chocolate curls
  (opposite)*

Color index page 92

Begin 4 hrs ahead

12 servings

1 In medium bowl, place cherries and ⅓ cup kirsch; leave at room temperature for 2½ hours, stirring occasionally.

2 Meanwhile, preheat oven to 350°F. Prepare cake layers as recipe directs but pour batter into 3 greased and floured 9-inch round cake pans. Stagger pans on 2 oven racks so no pan is directly above another. Bake cake layers 20 to 25 minutes until toothpick inserted in center comes out clean. Cool on wire racks 10 minutes; remove layers from pans and cool them completely on wire racks, about 2 hours.

3 With fork, prick well top of each cake, then drain cherries well and sprinkle cherry liquid over cake layers.

4 In small bowl with mixer at medium speed, beat heavy or whipping cream, confectioners' sugar and 2 tablespoons kirsch until the cream stands in stiff peaks.

5 Place one cake layer on cake platter. Spread with one-fourth whipped-cream mixture; top with half of cherries.

6 Repeat with the second layer and then top with the third one.

7 Frost side of cake with half of remaining whipped-cream mixture.

8 With spoon, gently press grated semisweet chocolate onto whipped-cream mixture all around the side of the cake.

9 Garnish with dollops of remaining whipped-cream mixture; top each dollop with a drained maraschino cherry.

10 Pile chocolate curls in center; keep refrigerated. (Chocolate curls may turn slightly gray in color.)

Color index page 91

Begin 3 hrs ahead

12 servings

Filbert Torte

*6 eggs, separated
sugar
⅓ cup dried bread
  crumbs
¼ cup all-purpose flour*

*1 cup ground filberts
2 cups heavy or whipping
  cream
1 teaspoon vanilla
  extract*

1. Preheat oven to 325°F. In large bowl with mixer at high speed, beat egg whites until soft peaks form. Beating at high speed, gradually sprinkle in ¼ cup sugar, beating well after each addition. Whites should stand in stiff peaks.

2. In small bowl with mixer at medium speed, beat egg yolks until thick and lemon-colored. Gradually beat in ½ cup sugar until blended. Stir in bread crumbs, flour and ⅔ cup ground nuts; with wire whisk or rubber spatula, fold into beaten egg whites. Pour batter into 10″ by 3″ springform pan and spread evenly.

3. Bake 40 minutes or until cake springs back when lightly touched with finger. Invert cake in pan on wire rack; cool completely.

4. In small bowl with mixer at medium speed, beat heavy or whipping cream, vanilla extract and 2 tablespoons sugar until stiff peaks form.

5. Remove cake from pan; with a long sharp knife, slice cake horizontally into 2 layers. Place bottom layer on cake platter; spread with one-fourth whipped-cream mixture; top with second layer. Frost side of cake with half of remaining whipped-cream mixture. With hand, gently press remaining ⅓ cup ground nuts onto cream.

6. Spoon remaining cream mixture into a pastry bag with a large star tube; use to decorate top of cake.

DECORATING THE FILBERT TORTE

Spread bottom layer of cake with whipped-cream mixture. Top with second layer and frost sides of cake. With hand, gently press ground nuts into cream on side.

Using pastry bag with large star tube, decorate top of cake with the remaining whipped-cream mixture.

Very special cakes

Party Cake

Color index page 93

Begin day or up to 1 wk ahead

62 servings

12 eggs, at room temperature
5 cups sugar
6 cups cake flour
2½ cups milk
1½ cups butter or margarine, softened
2 tablespoons double-acting baking powder

1 tablespoon vanilla extract
2 teaspoons salt
Lemon Butter-Cream Filling (below)
Pink Butter-Cream Frosting (below right)
Vanilla Butter-Cream Frosting (below right)
Decorations (opposite)

1. Generously grease and flour 14-inch, 10-inch and 6-inch round cake pans. Separate eggs, placing whites in a large bowl and yolks in another large bowl. Be sure to have wire racks large enough to cool cake layers. If necessary, use a refrigerator wire rack or several racks taped together for the 14-inch layer. Also have large cookie sheets on hand for handling the layers.
2. In large bowl with mixer at high speed, beat egg whites until soft peaks form. Beating at high speed, sprinkle in 1 cup sugar, 2 tablespoons at a time. Beat until stiff peaks form; set aside.
3. Into second large bowl with yolks, measure cake flour, milk, butter, baking powder, vanilla, salt and remaining 4 cups sugar. With mixer at low speed, beat until well mixed, constantly scraping bowl. Beat at medium speed 10 to 15 minutes or until mixture is fluffy.
4. Place upper oven rack one-third from top and lower rack two-thirds down from top, then preheat oven to 375°F.
5. Pour yolk mixture into 8-quart bowl or saucepot; fold in beaten egg whites. Pour batter evenly into the three pans. Place 14-inch layer on lower oven rack and the other two on the upper rack with the 6-inch layer in front. Bake 6-inch layer 40 minutes or until toothpick inserted in center comes out clean. Quickly remove from oven to wire rack; cool 10 minutes; remove from pan; cool completely. Bake 10-inch layer 15 minutes longer than small layer or 55 minutes in all. Quickly remove from oven; cool on wire rack 10 minutes; remove from pan; cool completely. Bake 14-inch layer 20 minutes longer than the second layer or 1¼ hours in all. Cool in pan on wire rack 10 minutes; remove from pan; cool completely. If cakes are made 1 week ahead, freeze layers on cookie sheets; wrap with plastic wrap. To thaw cake layers, unwrap and leave them to stand 2 hours at room temperature.
6. *Early in day:* Prepare filling and assemble layers in three tiers (right). Prepare Pink Butter-Cream Frosting and Vanilla Butter-Cream Frosting and frost cake (opposite). Make decorations and decorate cake (opposite).

LEMON BUTTER-CREAM FILLING: In large bowl with mixer at medium-low speed, beat *two 16-ounce packages confectioners' sugar,* ¾ *cup butter* or margarine, softened, and *6 to 8 tablespoons lemon juice* until the filling is smooth and of a good spreading consistency.

ASSEMBLING THE LAYERS

With long serrated knife, cut each cooled cake layer in half. Place top half of 14-inch layer upside down on large platter or foil-covered heavy cardboard.

Spread layer on platter with about 2 cups filling to edge. Place second half of layer, cut side down, over filled layer.

Spread filling thinly in center of 14-inch tier to about 2 inches from edge; then, for easier cutting, place 10½-inch foil-covered round cardboard in center.

Place half of 10-inch layer in center of 14-inch tier, on foil-covered cardboard. Fill and top with other half.

Spread filling thinly in center of 10-inch layer; place 6½-inch foil-covered cardboard on top.

Place half of 6-inch layer on 10-inch tier, on cardboard. Fill and top with other half.

FROSTINGS

PINK BUTTER-CREAM FROSTING: In large bowl with mixer at medium-low speed, beat *two 16-ounce packages confectioners' sugar,* ¾ *cup butter* or margarine, softened, *6 to 8 tablespoons milk, 1 tablespoon vanilla extract,* ¼ *teaspoon salt* and enough *red food color* until the frosting is tinted a pretty pale pink color.

VANILLA BUTTER-CREAM FROSTING: In medium bowl with mixer at medium-low speed, beat *one 16-ounce package confectioners' sugar, 6 tablespoons butter* or margarine, softened, *3 to 4 tablespoons milk, 1½ teaspoons vanilla extract* and ⅛ *teaspoon salt* until the frosting is smooth and of easy spreading consistency.

FROSTING THE CAKE

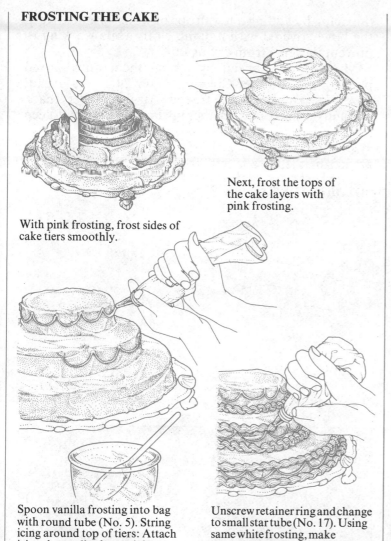

With pink frosting, frost sides of cake tiers smoothly.

Next, frost the tops of the cake layers with pink frosting.

Spoon vanilla frosting into bag with round tube (No. 5). String icing around top of tiers: Attach icing then pull tube straight away letting string drop; move along; reattach icing; repeat.

Unscrew retainer ring and change to small star tube (No. 17). Using same white frosting, make borders around both top and bottom edges of cake tiers. Allow frosting to harden.

ADDING DECORATIONS

With small round tube and green frosting, pipe stems onto cake then press on roses. Change to leaf tube and make leaves on stems.

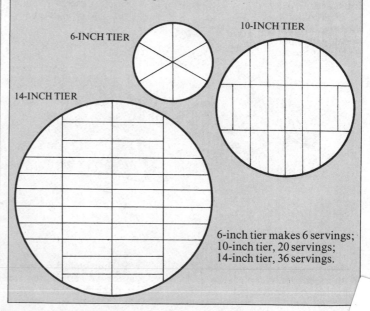

MAKING DECORATIONS: In small bowl with mixer at low speed, beat *one 16-ounce package confectioners' sugar, ¹/₂ teaspoon cream of tartar* and *3 egg whites,* at room temperature, until just mixed. Increase speed to high and beat until mixture is very stiff and knife drawn through mixture leaves a clean-cut path. Remove about one-fourth to small bowl; with *green food color,* tint green; cover with plastic wrap. Into remaining three-fourths of mixture, beat enough *red food color* to tint a rose-pink color. With rose-pink frosting in decorating bag fitted with small petal tube (No. 103), make a small rose (page 399); let dry at least 30 minutes. Repeat to make more. Spoon green frosting in to decorating bag fitted with small round tube (No. 5); pipe stems onto cake. Arrange roses on stems. Change round tube to leaf tube (No. 70); make leaves on stems.

CUTTING THE CAKE

Using a long, thin knife with a sawing motion, cut the cake into 62 servings following the guide below.

6-INCH TIER

10-INCH TIER

14-INCH TIER

6-inch tier makes 6 servings; 10-inch tier, 20 servings; 14-inch tier, 36 servings.

Cake decorating

With a decorating bag fitted with a coupler, and a selection of tubes and flower nails, you can make a wide range of shapes and designs. Each tube is numbered to indicate the design it makes. Except for shapes which require flower nails, practice on an inverted jelly-roll pan, scraping up the icing to re-use. Butter-Cream, Fluffy Boiled and Ornamental Frostings are the best to use.

The consistency of the icing is very important. Use a stiff icing for flowers, a medium-stiff icing for borders, and a thinner icing for leaves and writing; if necessary, thin icing by adding a few drops of water or milk. Keep the bowl covered with a damp cloth while working to prevent the icing from drying out.

Make flowers ahead by piping them onto waxed paper. Freeze Butter-Cream flowers 24 hours ahead; they'll keep a week in the freezer. Air-dry flowers made of Fluffy Boiled or Ornamental Frosting; they'll keep for months in a tightly covered container.

Our instructions are for right-handed cooks. If you are left-handed, read "left" for "right" and vice versa.

BASIC EQUIPMENT

DECORATING BAG

COUPLER

COUPLER RING

FLAT-HEAD FLOWER NAIL

TIPS OR TUBES

HOLDING THE BAG

90° ANGLE

45° ANGLE

For a perfect shape, hold icing bag at 90° or 45° to the surface being decorated, as directed. Use the fingertips of your other hand to steady the bag.

FITTING AND FILLING THE BAG

1 Unscrew coupler ring; drop coupler, narrow end first, into bag and position so that two threads show through bag opening, trimming opening if needed.

2 Fit chosen decorating tube over coupler and screw retainer ring in place. To change tube, simply unscrew retainer ring and replace tube.

3 Fold down open end of bag to make deep cuff. With rubber spatula, push icing deep into the bag, filling it half full.

4 Keep the bag twisted shut while decorating and as you apply pressure to it the icing will flow down the tube.

TYPES OF TUBE

Star: This decorating tube is used for making stars, rosettes or shells.

Round: The circular opening of this tube makes dots, beads and flower stems and is also used for stringwork.

Petal: Petal tubes are used for flower petals as well as ribbons and bows.

Drop flower: This tube forms a complete flower with one simple action. The number of openings determines the number of flower petals.

Leaf: The open "V" of this tube gives flat and stand-up leaves their veins and pointed tips.

MAKING STARS, ROSETTES AND SHELLS

Stars: With star tube at 90° and almost touching surface, squeeze to form star, then lift slightly keeping tip in icing. Stop pressure and lift tube.

Rosettes: Position star tube as for stars, but as you squeeze move tube up and to left in a circular motion. Stop pressure and lift tube away from icing.

Shells: With star tube at 45° and touching surface, squeeze, lifting slightly as icing fans out. Then relax pressure, bringing tube down and toward you.

MAKING DOTS AND BEADS

Dots: With round tube at 90° and almost touching surface, squeeze to form dot, then lift tube slightly keeping tip in icing. Stop pressure and lift tube.

Beads: With round tube, follow the technique for making shells. Slightly overlap beads, starting each bead on the point of the preceding one.

WRITING MESSAGES

Use a round tube and thinned icing which will flow smoothly. With tube at 45°, touch surface to secure icing then slightly lift tube as it moves to form letters. Use even pressure and guide tube with your entire arm. To finish a letter or word, just stop pressure and lift tube.

MAKING RIBBONS, SWAGS AND BOWS

Ribbon: With petal tube at 45°, place wide end of opening at surface of cake, narrow end slightly up. Squeeze, while making a series of curves.

Ribbon swag: Follow the ribbon technique, as shown above, but as you complete each curve, move the tube up and down in 3 short strokes.

Bow: Work with bag pointing toward you. Hold petal tube at 45° with wide end of opening on surface and narrow end straight up. Squeezing evenly, make loop to left. Stop pressure as you cross starting point. Squeeze again to make loop to right, stopping at starting point. From center, make 2 streamers.

MAKING A ROSE

Attach 2-inch square of waxed paper to flat-head flower nail with dab of frosting; hold nail between thumb and forefinger of left hand. With round tube at 90°, pipe mound of icing. Now use nail as turntable, always turning nail to left (counterclockwise) as you form petals to right.

With petal tube at 45°, touch wide end to just below top of mound with narrow end straight up; turn nail to left as you pipe band of icing up, around and back down to starting point to make bud.

Touch wide end to base, narrow end up; move tube up and down in arc. Make two more petals.

With narrow end pointing out a little, pipe row of 4 petals under the first row.

With narrow end of tube pointing out, pipe final row of 5 to 7 petals under previous row. Slip finished rose off nail to dry.

MAKING LEAVES

Plain leaf: Hold leaf tube at 45°. Squeeze until icing fans out, then relax pressure and draw leaf to a point. Stop pressure and pull tube away.

Stand-up leaf: Hold leaf tube at 90°. Squeeze until icing fans out, then relax pressure as you raise tube, drawing leaf up to a point. Stop pressure and lift tube.

Frostings and fillings

Fluffy frostings should be made just before use but most uncooked creamy frostings can be made in advance and stored until needed in a tightly covered container to prevent a crust forming on top. If creamy frostings are refrigerated and as a result become too firm to spread easily, let them stand at room temperature or stir well to soften to spreading consistency. Each of the frosting recipes that follows makes enough frosting to frost a 13″ by 9″ cake, tube cake or 24 cupcakes, or to fill and frost a 2-layer cake. Each of the filling recipes makes enough filling for a 2-layer cake.

Butter-Cream Frosting

Begin 15 mins ahead

1 16-ounce package confectioners' sugar
6 tablespoons butter or margarine, softened
3 to 4 tablespoons milk or half-and-half

1½ teaspoons vanilla extract
⅛ teaspoon salt

In large bowl with spoon or with mixer at medium speed, beat all ingredients until very smooth, adding more milk if necessary to make the icing of good spreading consistency.

LEMON: Prepare as above but substitute *lemon juice* for milk and omit vanilla.

MOCHA: Prepare as above but add *½ cup cocoa;* substitute *⅓ cup hot coffee* for milk and reduce vanilla to ½ teaspoon.

ORANGE: Prepare as above but add *2 egg yolks* and *1 teaspoon grated orange peel* and use only about 2 tablespoons milk.

CHOCOLATE: Increase butter to ½ cup. Melt, then cool, *3 squares unsweetened chocolate*; add with *2 egg yolks* to rest of above ingredients.

Whipped-Cream Frosting

Begin 15 mins ahead

2 cups heavy or whipping cream
¼ cup confectioners' sugar

⅛ teaspoon salt
1 teaspoon vanilla extract

In small bowl with mixer at medium speed, beat cream with sugar and salt until stiff peaks form; fold in vanilla extract. Keep frosted cake refrigerated until serving time.

CHOCOLATE: Over hot, *not boiling*, water, melt *one 6-ounce package semisweet-chocolate pieces* (1 cup); cool completely. Prepare frosting as above but fold in cooled chocolate.

COFFEE: Prepare as above but add *1 teaspoon instant coffee* with sugar.

ORANGE: Prepare as above but add *1 teaspoon shredded orange peel* with vanilla.

PEPPERMINT: Beat cream and salt together (no sugar) as above and fold in *¼ cup crushed peppermint candy*; omit vanilla extract.

Quick Fudge Frosting

Begin 30 mins ahead

1 12-ounce package semisweet-chocolate pieces (2 cups)
¼ cup shortening

3 cups confectioners' sugar
½ cup milk

1. In double boiler, over hot, *not boiling*, water, melt chocolate pieces with shortening.
2. Stir in sugar and milk; remove from heat. With spoon, beat until smooth.

Cream-Cheese Frosting

Begin 15 mins ahead

2 3-ounce packages cream cheese, softened
2 tablespoons evaporated milk
1 teaspoon vanilla extract

⅛ teaspoon salt
1 16-ounce package confectioners' sugar

1. In small bowl with mixer at medium speed, beat together the softened cream cheese and evaporated milk just until smooth.
2. Beat in vanilla, salt and sugar until blended.

COFFEE: Prepare as above but, with sugar, add *4 teaspoons instant coffee*.

Ornamental Frosting

Begin 30 mins ahead

1 16-ounce package confectioners' sugar
½ teaspoon cream of tartar

3 egg whites, at room temperature
½ teaspoon vanilla or almond extract

1. Into large bowl, sift sugar and cream of tartar.
2. With mixer at low speed, beat in egg whites and vanilla; at high speed, beat until knife drawn through mixture leaves clean-cut path. On humid days it may be necessary to beat in more confectioners' sugar.
3. Cover bowl with damp cloth. Use to make cake and cookie decorations with decorating bag fitted with tubes. To tint, in small bowl, place some of frosting; stir in food color a drop at a time.

Fluffy Boiled Frosting

Begin 45 mins ahead

1¼ cups sugar
⅛ teaspoon cream of tartar
⅛ teaspoon salt
6 tablespoons water

3 egg whites, at room temperature
1 teaspoon vanilla extract

1. In 1-quart saucepan over medium heat, heat sugar, cream of tartar, salt and water to boiling; set candy thermometer in place and boil, without stirring, until temperature reaches 260°F. or until a little mixture dropped in cold water forms hard ball. Remove from heat.
2. In small bowl with mixer at high speed, beat egg whites until soft peaks form.
3. Pour syrup in thin stream into whites, beating constantly; add vanilla and continue beating until mixture forms stiff peaks.

EASY DECORATIVE TOUCHES
With back of spoon, swirl circles, S-shapes or wavy lines in frosting, or pull frosting up in peaks. Or make patterns below.

For spiral, place cake on turntable or lazy Susan. Press tip of spatula into center of frosting and, turning cake in one direction, slowly move spatula outward.

On creamy frosted cake, draw tines of fork across top in parallel rows; repeat rows at right angles.

Buttery Chocolate Frosting

Begin 20 mins ahead

1 cup egg whites (7 or 8 egg whites)
1 cup sugar
½ teaspoon rum extract
1¾ cups butter
¾ cup cocoa

1. In heavy, 1-quart saucepan over medium heat, heat whites, sugar and rum extract until sugar is dissolved, about 2 minutes, stirring constantly (over-heating will cause egg whites to coagulate).
2. In large bowl with mixer at medium speed, beat butter until light and fluffy, about 4 minutes (if butter becomes too warm, frosting will separate).
3. *Gradually* beat egg-white mixture into butter; beat in cocoa. At high speed, beat until the mixture is light and fluffy, about 2 minutes.

"Seven-Minute" Frosting

Begin 20 mins ahead

1½ cups sugar
½ cup water (for crusty surface, use only ⅓ cup water)
2 egg whites
1 tablespoon light corn syrup
1 teaspoon vanilla extract
½ teaspoon salt

1. In top of double boiler with mixer at high speed, beat all ingredients about 1 minute.
2. Place over rapidly boiling water; beat at high speed until the mixture forms soft peaks (this may take longer than 7 minutes).
3. Pour into large bowl; beat until the mixture is thick enough to spread.

Snow Peak Frosting

Begin 20 mins ahead

1¼ cups light corn syrup
2 egg whites, at room temperature
⅛ teaspoon salt
1 teaspoon vanilla extract

1. In 1-quart saucepan over medium heat, heat corn syrup to boiling; remove from heat.
2. In large bowl with mixer at high speed, beat egg whites until foamy; add salt and continue beating just until soft peaks form.
3. Slowly pour in hot syrup, beating 6 to 8 minutes until the mixture is fluffy and peaks form when beater is raised. Beat in vanilla extract.

Buttermilk Icing

Begin 30 mins ahead

3 cups sugar
1 cup butter
1 cup buttermilk
2 tablespoons light corn syrup
1 teaspoon baking soda
1 cup finely chopped pecans

1. In 4- quart saucepan over medium heat, heat first 5 ingredients to boiling, stirring constantly. Set candy thermometer in place; cook, stirring occasionally, until temperature reaches 238°F. or until a little of the mixture dropped in a cup of cold water forms a soft ball.
2. Pour mixture into large bowl; with mixer at high speed, beat to spreading consistency, about 7 minutes, occasionally scraping bowl with a rubber spatula. Fold in chopped pecans.

Fresh Lemon Filling

Begin 1½ hrs ahead

½ cup water
¼ cup sugar
1 tablespoon grated lemon peel
¼ cup lemon juice
4 teaspoons cornstarch
¼ teaspoon salt
1 tablespoon butter

1. In 1-quart saucepan, stir first 6 ingredients until blended. Over medium heat, cook until very thick and boiling briskly, stirring constantly. Reduce heat; simmer 1 minute, stirring occasionally.
2. Remove from heat; stir in butter. Cool mixture at room temperature.

Creamy Mocha Filling

Begin 20 mins ahead

2 eggs, separated, at room temperature
confectioners' sugar
⅓ cup water
1 cup butter or margarine, softened
2 squares unsweetened chocolate, melted
2 teaspoons instant coffee
1 teaspoon vanilla extract

1. In small bowl with mixer at high speed, beat egg whites until soft peaks form; gradually sprinkle in ¼ cup confectioners' sugar, beating until sugar is dissolved and whites stand in stiff peaks. Do not scrape bowl during beating.
2. In large bowl with same beaters and at medium speed, mix well 1¼ cups confectioners' sugar with yolks, water and remaining ingredients.
3. With rubber spatula, fold in egg whites.

Pineapple Filling

Begin 1½ hrs ahead

¼ cup sugar
3 tablespoons cornstarch
⅛ teaspoon salt
¾ cup canned pineapple juice
2 tablespoons butter or margarine
1 tablespoon lemon juice
1 teaspoon grated lemon peel

In 1-quart saucepan, mix sugar, cornstarch and salt; stir in juice; add remaining ingredients. Over low heat, heat to boiling, stirring constantly; boil 1 minute until smooth and thickened; cool.

COOKIES

Cookies are quick and easy to make, and are an excellent introduction to the more complicated techniques of cake and bread making. All cookies are made from basically the same ingredients – flour, sugar, shortening, possibly eggs and leavening, plus liquid and flavoring – they vary in texture and taste according to the proportions and flavorings used.

Measure ingredients carefully so dough is the right consistency. Most cookie doughs can be whipped up in the mixer in minutes with our one-bowl method. Use low or medium speed as directed and beat only as long as the recipe indicates. For mixing by hand, use a long-handled wooden spoon so you can mix, stir and beat the ingredients easily. Don't overmix; this could make cookies tough or hard. When rolling dough, use as little extra flour as possible so cookies won't look floury and rerolled trimmings won't be tough. Be sure that the cookies you place on a cookie sheet are of the same size and thickness so they will be uniformly cooked and browned and ready at the same time.

BAKING COOKIES

For best results, use clean, shiny aluminum cookie sheets 2 inches smaller all around than the oven so that the heat will be able to circulate evenly. If baking one sheet of cookies at a time, place it in the center of the oven; when baking 2 sheets, stagger the oven racks so that they divide the oven into thirds, switching the sheets once, about half-way through baking time, to make certain that cookies brown evenly. Don't grease cookie sheets unless indicated in the recipe, or cookies will tend to spread too much.

When baking several batches in succession, plan ahead so that while the first sheet is in the oven, you are preparing the second one. Let sheets cool before placing more dough on them, or the dough will soften and spread, and finished cookies will be misshapen If you don't have enough spare cookie sheets, use inverted baking pans. Or, place unbaked cookies on a sheet of heavy-duty foil and, as soon as baked cookies have been transferred to wire racks, place the foil on the cookie sheet and return it to the oven.

Cookies bake quickly, so test them for doneness at the end of the minimum baking time given; correctly baked, the cookies will feel set and dry to the touch.

TYPES OF COOKIE

There are six types of cookie, made from doughs of varying degrees of stiffness. Bar and drop cookies are made from soft unchilled dough. For pressed cookies, dough should be moderately stiff; for refrigerator, molded and rolled cookies, dough must be stiff, chilled if necessary to make it easy to handle.

 Bar cookies are simplest of all to make. Just spread the dough evenly in a well-greased shallow pan, bake, then cut the slab into bars or squares with a sharp, thin-bladed knife once it has cooled slightly.

 Drop cookies are formed by scooping up teaspoonfuls of soft dough and dropping them about 2 inches apart onto a cookie sheet; use a small spatula to shape them.

 Refrigerator cookie dough can be made a week or more ahead, shaped into a smooth roll, wrapped in waxed paper and refrigerated until needed. To bake, slice the roll thinly and evenly with a sharp knife, and arrange slices slightly apart on cookie sheet.

 Molded cookie dough should always be firm enough for shaping in a mold or by hand into balls, crescents and wreaths. Chill dough just until easy to handle.

 Pressed cookies are forced through a cookie press or decorating bag. Dough should be soft enough to go through the press but firm enough to hold its shape. Chill only if directed.

 Rolled cookie dough should be stiff, chilled if necessary, then rolled out and cut into shapes with lightly floured cookie cutters, a pastry wheel, or knife and a pattern. Or, dough can be rolled out directly onto a cookie sheet, and the cookies cut and trimmings removed. Cut cookies as close together as possible, so that you reduce the amount of rerolling that is necessary.

COOLING COOKIES

Unless the recipe directs otherwise, empty cookie sheets as soon as they come out of the oven, or the cookies will continue to bake on the hot sheet. Loosen cookies carefully with a pancake turner, transfer them to wire racks, and let cool in a single layer; don't overlap them or they will soften. Wait until they are quite cold before decorating or storing them. Cool bar cookies in the pan.

STORING AND FREEZING COOKIES

Crisp cookies and soft cookies must be stored separately in containers with tight-fitting lids. To keep soft cookies moist, add a piece of apple to the storage jar and replace it often. Crisp cookies which have turned soft can be re-crisped by heating them for 3 to 5 minutes in a 300°F. oven. Bar cookies can be stored in the pan. Allow the slab to cool slightly before cutting it into bars (otherwise the edges tend to crumble), and leave until quite cold. Then cover the whole pan tightly with foil or plastic wrap and store at room temperature.

Cookies can be stored in the freezer for up to 6 months, either baked, or as unbaked dough. Pack unbaked dough in freezer containers or, for refrigerator cookies, shape it into rolls or bars and wrap tightly in foil or plastic wrap.

Baked cookies should be quite cold before they are packed for the freezer. Use sturdy containers, and cushion fragile cookies with crumpled foil or waxed paper. If the cookies have been decorated or have a soft frosting, lay them out on cookie sheets and freeze them hard, then pack them. Thaw baked cookies, unwrapped, at room temperature for about 10 minutes. When you are ready to bake frozen cookie dough, thaw it until it is soft enough to handle, then shape the cookies and bake as usual. Frozen refrigerator cookie dough should be left in the refrigerator to soften until it slices easily.

DECORATING COOKIES

To decorate cookies you can use homemade ornamental or butter cream frosting; canned, ready-to-spread frostings; and decorating icings sold in tubes to which different tips are attached. Colored decorating gels in tubes are also attractive. To use homemade frosting in a decorating bag, see Cake Decorating, pages 398 to 399

Assemble all frostings and tools before starting to decorate cookies. Useful items include a soft pastry brush to brush crumbs from cookies; a decorating bag and tubes; a small cutting board for chopping nuts or candied fruit; small, sharp knives and metal spatulas; custard cups to keep decorations separate, and wire racks on which to decorate cookies.

DECORATIVE IDEAS

It is easy to transform the plainest cookies into something special. Everything you need can be found in the supermarket – frostings, icings, nuts, candies, multicolored sugar decorations, chocolate for melting, chocolate sprinkles or chips, candied fruit and decorative cereals. Here are some basic decorated cookies you can adapt as required.

Double star: Frost 2 star-shaped cookies with white icing; press together so all points show. Decorate top with multicolored sprinkles.

Chessboard: Frost oblong cookie with white icing. With round tube attached to decorating bag, crosshatch with dark frosting; fill in alternate squares with dark frosting.

Love kiss: Frost heart-shaped cookie with white icing. Decorate the 2 halves of the heart with contrasting colored sugar flowerets, sprinkles or dragées.

Pine cone: Frost oval cookie and press unblanched sliced nuts into the frosting to resemble a pine cone.

Letter cookie: Using a decorating bag with star tube cover letter with rippled lines of frosting; fill in with contrasting gel.

Doughnut sprinkle: Frost top of doughnut-shaped cookie; toss in multicolored sprinkles; press well to coat cookie completely in sprinkles.

Bar cookies

Fudgy Brownies

1 cup butter or margarine
4 squares unsweetened chocolate
2 cups sugar
4 eggs
1 cup all-purpose flour
1 teaspoon vanilla extract
½ teaspoon salt
2 cups coarsely chopped nuts

Color index page 104

Begin early in day

24 brownies

1 Preheat oven to 350°F. Grease 13″ by 9″ baking pan. In 3-quart saucepan over very low heat, melt butter or margarine and chocolate, stirring the mixture constantly.

2 Remove pan from heat and with a spoon, stir the sugar into the chocolate. Allow the mixture to cool slightly.

3 Add eggs, one at a time, beating until well blended after the addition of each egg.

4 Add the flour, vanilla and salt to the mixture and stir in well.

5 Add the chopped nuts to the mixture and stir to blend well.

6 Pour chocolate-nut mixture into greased baking pan, scraping the side of saucepan with a rubber spatula; bake in oven 30 to 35 minutes.

7 Brownies are done when toothpick inserted in center comes out clean. Cool in pan on wire rack; with a sharp knife, cut brownies into pieces.

Backpacking Bars

¾ cup all-purpose flour
½ cup uncooked quick-cooking oats
½ cup butter, softened
¼ cup toasted wheat germ
1 tablespoon grated orange peel
brown sugar
2 eggs
1 4¼-ounce can blanched whole almonds
½ cup shredded coconut

Color index page 104

Begin 3 hrs or up to 1 wk ahead

12 cookies

1. Preheat oven to 350°F. In large bowl with mixer at low speed, beat first 5 ingredients and ½ cup packed brown sugar until just mixed; at medium speed, beat 2 minutes (mixture will look dry).
2. With lightly floured hands, shape mixture into a ball, then pat into 8″ by 8″ baking pan.
3. In small bowl with hand beater, beat eggs with ¼ cup packed brown sugar; stir in almonds and coconut. Pour evenly over mixture in pan.
4. Bake 35 minutes or until toothpick comes out clean. Cool in pan on rack. Cut into 12 pieces.

Luscious Apricot Squares

Color index page 105

Begin 3 hrs ahead

16 cookies

water
⅔ cup dried apricots
½ cup butter, softened
¼ cup sugar
all-purpose flour
1 cup packed light brown sugar
2 eggs
½ cup chopped California walnuts
½ teaspoon double-acting baking powder
½ teaspoon vanilla extract
¼ teaspoon salt
confectioners' sugar

1. In covered 1-quart saucepan over low heat, in enough water to cover apricots, cook apricots 15 minutes; drain and finely chop.
2. Preheat oven to 350°F. Grease 8″ by 8″ baking pan. In large bowl with mixer at medium speed, beat butter, sugar and 1 cup flour until well mixed and crumbly; pat into pan. Bake 25 minutes or just until layer is golden.
3. Meanwhile, in same bowl at medium speed, mix well apricots, brown sugar, ⅓ cup flour and remaining ingredients except confectioners' sugar.
4. Pour over baked layer; bake 25 minutes longer.
5. Cool in pan; cut into squares. Sprinkle with confectioners' sugar.

Toffee Bars

Color index page 105

Begin 3 to 5 days ahead

50 cookies

1¾ cups all-purpose flour
1 cup sugar
1 cup butter or margarine, softened
1 teaspoon vanilla extract
1 egg, separated
½ cup finely chopped California walnuts

1. Preheat oven to 275°F. Grease 15½″ by 10½″ jelly-roll pan. In large bowl with mixer at medium speed, beat all ingredients except egg white and walnuts until well mixed; pat evenly into pan.
2. In cup with fork, beat egg white slightly; brush over top of dough and sprinkle with nuts.
3. Bake 1 hour and 10 minutes or until golden. Immediately cut into 50 bars and remove from pan to cool on wire racks. Store in tightly covered container for at least 3 days before serving.

Shortbread

Color index
page 104

Begin early
in day

14 cookies

**2 cups all-purpose flour
1 cup butter or
margarine, softened
½ cup confectioners'
sugar
¼ teaspoon salt**

**¼ teaspoon double-
acting baking powder
1 teaspoon vanilla
extract
2 tablespoons sugar**

1 Preheat oven to 350°F.
In large bowl with
mixer at medium speed,
beat first 6 ingredients until
well mixed, occasionally
scraping the bowl.

2 Pat dough into 9-inch
round cake pan and
with fork, prick well.

3 With spoon, sprinkle
sugar over dough.
Bake 30 to 35 minutes.

4 Cut into wedges while
warm. Cool on wire
rack; separate cookies.

Marbled Fudge Bars

Color index
page 104

Begin 2 hrs
or up to
1 wk ahead

36 cookies

**1 cup butter or margarine
4 squares unsweetened
chocolate
sugar
4 eggs
1 cup all-purpose flour**

**½ teaspoon salt
1 cup chopped California
walnuts
vanilla extract
1 8-ounce package cream
cheese, softened**

1. Grease a 13″ by 9″ baking pan. In 2-quart heavy
saucepan over low heat, melt butter and chocolate.
With wire whisk or spoon, beat in 2 cups sugar and 3
eggs until well blended. With wooden spoon, stir in
flour, salt, nuts and 1 teaspoon vanilla extract.
Spread evenly in pan.
2. Preheat oven to 350°F. In small bowl with mixer
at low speed, beat cream cheese, ½ cup sugar, 1 egg
and 1 teaspoon vanilla extract until just mixed; at
medium speed, beat 2 minutes, occasionally scraping bowl with rubber spatula.
3. With large spoon, drop mixture in dollops on top
of batter. Using tip of knife, lightly score top surface
in a crisscross pattern.
4. Bake 40 to 45 minutes until toothpick comes out
clean. Cool on rack. Cut into bars. Refrigerate.

Prune-Ribbon Cookies

Color index
page 105

Begin 3 hrs
or up to
2 wks ahead

27 cookies

**1 12-ounce package
pitted prunes (2 cups)
1 cup water
¼ cup honey
¼ large lemon, unpeeled
2 cups all-purpose flour
1¼ cups packed light
brown sugar**

**¾ cup butter or
margarine, softened
1 teaspoon double-acting
baking powder
1 teaspoon vanilla
extract
½ teaspoon salt
1 egg**

1. In 2-quart saucepan over medium-high heat, heat
prunes and water to boiling. Reduce heat to low;
cover saucepan and simmer 3 minutes; drain prunes
well. In covered blender container at high speed,
blend prunes, honey and lemon until smooth.
2. Meanwhile, preheat oven to 350°F. Grease 9″ by
9″ baking pan. Into large bowl, measure remaining
ingredients; with mixer at low speed, beat until just
mixed. At medium speed, beat until smooth.
3. Divide dough into thirds. With greased fingers,
pat one piece into bottom of baking pan. With
spoon, spread half of prune mixture on dough;
repeat layering, ending with dough.
4. Bake 1 hour or until browned and cookie pulls
away from side of pan. Cool in pan on wire rack.
With sharp knife, cut into 3″ by 1″ bars.

Linzer Cookies

Color index
page 105

Begin 4 hrs
or up to
3 days ahead

30 cookies

**1 3½- to 4-ounce can
blanched slivered
almonds, ground
1 egg
2 cups all-purpose flour
1 cup sugar
¾ cup butter, softened**

**1 teaspoon cinnamon
1 teaspoon grated lemon
peel
⅛ teaspoon ground
cloves
½ 12-ounce jar raspberry
preserves**

1. In large bowl with mixer at low speed, beat all
ingredients except preserves until well mixed, occasionally scraping bowl. (Mixture will be crumbly.)
Shape dough into ball; wrap; chill until easy to
handle, about 2 hours.
2. Preheat oven to 350°F. Grease 11″ by 7″ baking
pan. Press half of dough into pan (keep remainder
chilled). Spread preserves over dough in pan.
3. Roll half of remaining dough into six 11-inch-long
ropes; arrange lengthwise, one inch apart on preserves. Roll remaining dough into eight 7-inch-long
ropes; arrange crosswise over preserves.
4. Bake 40 minutes or until top is golden. Cool in
pan on wire rack. Cut into 2″ by 1″ bars.

Making ropes: With hands,
roll chilled dough into
ropes on countertop.

Arranging ropes: Position
11-inch ropes lengthwise,
then 7-inch ropes crosswi

Drop cookies

Chocolate Chip Cookies

Begin 2¼ hrs ahead

48 cookies

1¼ cups all-purpose flour
½ cup packed light brown sugar
½ cup butter, softened
¼ cup sugar
1 egg
1 teaspoon vanilla extract
½ teaspoon baking soda
½ teaspoon salt
1 6-ounce package semisweet-chocolate pieces
½ cup chopped California walnuts

1 Preheat oven to 375°F. Grease cookie sheets. Into large bowl, measure all ingredients except chocolate pieces and nuts.

2 With mixer at medium speed, beat until well mixed, scraping bowl.

3 Add the chocolate pieces and chopped nuts. Stir in well.

4 Drop by rounded teaspoonfuls, 2 inches apart, on sheets. Bake 10 to 12 minutes until cookies are lightly browned.

5 With pancake turner or spatula, remove cookies to wire racks; cool.

Soft Molasses Cookies

Begin 2 hrs ahead

30 cookies

2 cups all-purpose flour
½ cup sugar
½ cup shortening
½ cup light molasses
1 egg
2 teaspoons baking soda
1 teaspoon ground ginger
1 teaspoon ground cinnamon
¼ teaspoon salt
⅓ cup cold water
raisins for garnish

1. Preheat oven to 400°F. Grease cookie sheets. In large bowl with mixer at medium speed, beat all ingredients except raisins until well mixed.
2. Drop mixture by rounded tablespoonfuls, at least 2 inches apart, onto cookie sheets; place 4 or 5 raisins on top of each cookie.
3. Bake 8 minutes or until top springs back when lightly pressed with finger. With pancake turner, remove cookies to wire racks; cool.

Double Chocolate Drops

Begin 2½ hrs or up to 1 wk ahead

48 cookies

1¾ cups all-purpose flour
¾ cup sugar
½ cup milk
½ cup butter or margarine, softened
1 teaspoon vanilla extract
½ teaspoon salt
½ teaspoon baking soda
1 egg
2 squares unsweetened chocolate, melted
Chocolate Butter-Cream Frosting (below)
1 cup pecan halves

1. Preheat oven to 400°F. Into large bowl, measure all ingredients except Frosting and pecans; with mixer at low speed, beat just until blended, scraping bowl constantly with rubber spatula. Increase mixer speed to medium; beat 3 minutes, scraping bowl occasionally, until well blended.
2. Drop batter by heaping teaspoonfuls onto cookie sheets, about 1 inch apart. Bake 8 to 10 minutes until cookies are puffy and slightly cracked on top. Cool.
3. Top cookies with frosting; garnish with pecans.

CHOCOLATE BUTTER-CREAM FROSTING: In small bowl with mixer at medium speed, beat together *1½ cups sifted confectioners' sugar, ¼ cup butter* or margarine, softened, and *⅛ teaspoon salt* until light and fluffy. Add *1½ squares unsweetened chocolate,* melted, *1 to 2 tablespoons milk* and *1 teaspoon vanilla extract,* beating until well blended. (Makes 1¼ cups.)

Raisin-Granola Cookies

Begin 1¾ hrs or up to 1 wk ahead

48 cookies

1¾ cups regular granola
1½ cups all-purpose flour
1 cup butter or margarine, softened
¾ cup sugar
¾ cup packed dark brown sugar
1 teaspoon baking soda
1 teaspoon salt
1 teaspoon vanilla extract
1 egg
1 cup dark seedless raisins
½ cup unsalted peanuts, coarsely chopped

1. Preheat oven to 375°F. Grease cookie sheets. Into large bowl, measure all ingredients except raisins and peanuts. With mixer at low speed, beat ingredients just until mixed; increase speed to medium and beat 2 minutes, occasionally scraping bowl with rubber spatula. Stir in raisins and peanuts until mixture is well blended.
2. Drop dough by heaping teaspoonfuls, about 2 inches apart, on cookie sheets.
3. Bake 12 to 15 minutes until cookies are lightly browned around edges.
4. With pancake turner, remove cookies to wire racks and allow to cool completely. Store cookies in a tightly covered container up to 1 week.

CHOCOLATE-GRANOLA COOKIES: Prepare dough as for Raisin-Granola Cookies, above, but substitute *one 6-ounce package semisweet-chocolate pieces* for seedless raisins.

DATE-GRANOLA COOKIES: Prepare dough as for Raisin-Granola Cookies, above, but substitute *1 cup chopped, pitted dates* for seedless raisins.

Almond Lace Rolls

Begin 1³/₄ hrs ahead

30 cookies

²/₃ cup blanched almonds, ground
¹/₂ cup sugar
¹/₂ cup butter or margarine
1 tablespoon all-purpose flour
2 tablespoons milk

1 Preheat oven to 350°F. Grease and flour cookie sheet. In 10-inch skillet over low heat, cook all ingredients, stirring just until mixture is blended.

2 Keeping mixture warm over very low heat, drop 4 heaping teaspoonfuls, 2 inches apart, on sheet. Bake 5 minutes.

3 When cookies are golden, remove cookie sheet from oven and, with pancake turner, loosen and lift cookies one by one.

4 Roll each cookie around handle of wooden spoon and cool. If cookies get too hard quickly reheat in oven.

5 Finish cooling on rack. Repeat steps 2–5, greasing and flouring cookie sheet each time.

Oatmeal Cookies

Begin 1³/₄ hrs ahead

48 cookies

1 cup uncooked quick-cooking oats
³/₄ cup all-purpose flour
¹/₂ cup packed brown sugar
¹/₂ cup chopped California walnuts
¹/₂ cup shortening
¹/₄ cup sugar
1 egg
¹/₂ teaspoon salt
¹/₂ teaspoon baking soda
¹/₂ teaspoon vanilla extract

1. Preheat oven to 375°F. In large bowl with mixer at medium speed, beat all ingredients until well mixed, occasionally scraping bowl.
2. Drop by teaspoonfuls, 1 inch apart, on sheet.
3. Bake for 12 minutes or until lightly browned. Immediately remove cookies to wire racks; cool.

Walnut Clusters

Begin 2 hrs ahead

36 cookies

1¹/₂ squares unsweetened chocolate, melted
¹/₂ cup all-purpose flour
¹/₂ cup sugar
¹/₄ cup butter or margarine, softened
1 egg
¹/₂ teaspoon salt
1¹/₂ teaspoons vanilla extract
¹/₄ teaspoon double-acting baking powder
2 cups chopped California walnuts
confectioners' sugar

1. Preheat oven to 350°F. Grease cookie sheets. In large bowl with mixer at medium speed, beat all ingredients except walnuts and confectioners' sugar until well mixed, occasionally scraping bowl with rubber spatula. Stir in walnuts.
2. Drop mixture by rounded teaspoonfuls, ¹/₂ inch apart, onto cookie sheets.
3. Bake 10 minutes. Remove cookies to wire racks; cool. Sprinkle with confectioners' sugar.

Choco-Peanut Drops

Begin 2 hrs ahead

48 cookies

all-purpose flour
2 squares unsweetened chocolate, melted
¹/₂ cup sugar
¹/₂ cup shortening
1 egg
1 teaspoon salt
1 teaspoon vanilla extract
¹/₂ cup packed light brown sugar
¹/₄ cup peanut butter
2 tablespoons butter or margarine, softened

1. Preheat oven to 325°F. In large bowl with mixer at medium speed, beat 1 cup flour and next 6 ingredients until well mixed, occasionally scraping bowl with rubber spatula. Wash beaters.
2. In small bowl with mixer at medium speed, beat 3 tablespoons flour and remaining ingredients until well mixed (mixture will be crumbly).
3. Drop chocolate dough by teaspoonfuls, 1 inch apart, onto cookie sheet; top each with ¹/₂ teaspoon peanut-butter dough. Dip a fork into flour and press gently across top of each cookie.
4. Bake 12 minutes or until firm. With pancake turner, remove cookies to racks; cool.

Raisin-Orange Cookies

Begin 1¹/₂ hrs or up to 2 wks ahead

30 cookies

2¹/₄ cups all-purpose flour
1¹/₂ cups sugar
1 cup butter or margarine, softened
3 eggs
1 teaspoon double-acting baking powder
1 teaspoon salt
1 teaspoon vanilla extract
1¹/₂ cups dark seedless raisins
2 tablespoons grated orange peel

1. Preheat oven to 375°F. Grease 2 large cookie sheets. Into large bowl, measure all ingredients except raisins and orange peel. With mixer at low speed, beat ingredients until just mixed. Increase speed to medium and beat 2 minutes, occasionally scraping bowl with rubber spatula. Stir in raisins and orange peel.
2. Drop batter by heaping tablespoonfuls, about 2 inches apart, on cookie sheets.
3. Bake 15 minutes or until cookies are golden brown. Remove cookies to wire racks to cool.

Drop cookies

Almond Macaroons

Color index
page 105

Begin 1 hr
or up to
2 wks ahead

36 cookies

**2 cups sliced blanched
almonds (about
9 ounces)**
³/₄ cup sugar
**2 teaspoons almond
extract**
**2 egg whites, at
room temperature**

1 In covered blender
container, blend
almonds half at a time
until finely ground.

2 Line cookie sheet with
heavy-duty foil.
Preheat oven to 350°F.

3 In medium bowl,
combine all ingredients
until well mixed and stiff.

4 Drop in 1-inch
mounds, 1 inch apart,
on sheet. Bake 20 minutes
or until firm at edges but
soft in center and golden.

5 Remove from oven and
lift foil with macaroons
to wire rack to cool. When
cool, peel off foil. Store in
tightly covered container.

Coconut Meringues

Color index
page 104

Begin 1½ hrs
or up to
3 wks ahead

24 cookies

**2 egg whites, at room
temperature**
**¹/₈ teaspoon cream of
tartar**
**³/₄ cup confectioners'
sugar**

**¹/₄ cup shredded
coconut**
**¹/₄ teaspoon almond
extract**

1. Preheat oven to 250°F. In small bowl with mixer
at high speed, beat egg whites and cream of tartar
until soft peaks form. Beating at high speed,
gradually sprinkle in sugar, 2 tablespoons at a time,
beating until sugar is completely dissolved. (Whites
should stand in stiff glossy peaks.) With rubber
spatula, fold in coconut and extract until mixed.
2. Drop mixture by rounded teaspoonfuls onto large
cookie sheet, about 1 inch apart.
3. Bake 1 hour or until dry. Remove to rack to cool.

Molded cookies

Peanut-Butter Cookies

Color index
page 105

Begin 2¼ hrs
or up to
2 wks ahead

36 cookies

**2¹/₄ cups all-purpose
flour**
**1 cup creamy peanut
butter**
²/₃ cup honey
¹/₂ cup sugar

**¹/₂ cup butter or
margarine, softened**
2 eggs
**¹/₂ teaspoon double-
acting baking powder**

1 Preheat oven to 350°F.
Into large bowl,
measure all ingredients.
With mixer at medium
speed, beat until well
mixed, occasionally
scraping bowl.

2 With hands, shape
dough into 1½-inch
balls; place 3 inches apart
on cookie sheets.

3 Dip a fork into flour
and press deeply across
top of each cookie; repeat
in opposite direction.
Bake in oven 15 minutes
or just until cookies
are lightly browned.

4 With pancake turner,
immediately remove
cookies to wire racks;
allow to cool. Store in
tightly covered container.

Filbert Drops

Color index
page 105

Begin 3 hrs
ahead or
early in day

24 cookies

**1 cup all-purpose
flour**
¹/₂ cup shortening
¹/₄ cup sugar
1 tablespoon water
**1 teaspoon grated orange
peel**

**¹/₂ teaspoon grated lemon
or lime peel**
¹/₄ teaspoon salt
1 egg, separated
**²/₃ cup finely ground
filberts**

1. Into large bowl, measure all ingredients except
egg white and filberts. With mixer at medium speed,
beat ingredients until well mixed, occasionally
scraping bowl with rubber spatula. Refrigerate
dough until easy to handle.
2. Preheat oven to 350°F. Put egg white in saucer;
put nuts on waxed paper. With hands, shape dough
into 1-inch balls; roll in egg white, then in ground
nuts. Place 1 inch apart on cookie sheets.
3. Bake 18 to 20 minutes until cookies are firm.
Immediately remove to wire racks; cool completely.
Store cookies in tightly covered container.

Danish Almond Cakes

Color index
page 104

Begin 4 hrs
ahead

42 cookies

1²/₃ cups all-purpose flour
½ cup sugar
½ cup diced toasted
  almonds
½ cup butter or
  margarine, softened
½ cup shortening
1 egg
1 tablespoon ground
  cinnamon

½ teaspoon double-
  acting baking
  powder
½ teaspoon ground
  cardamom
1 egg yolk, beaten
1 tablespoon water
blanched almonds,
  halved

1. Into large bowl, measure all ingredients except 1 egg yolk, water and almonds. With mixer at medium speed, beat ingredients until well mixed, occasionally scraping bowl with rubber spatula. Cover; refrigerate 2 hours.
2. Preheat oven to 375°F. With hands, shape dough into 1-inch balls; place 2 inches apart on cookie sheets. Cover the bottom of a flat-bottomed glass with a damp cloth and use to flatten slightly each ball of dough.
3. In cup, blend remaining egg yolk with water; brush egg yolk glaze on tops of cookies and top with an almond half.
4. Bake 10 minutes or until golden. With pancake turner, immediately remove cookies to wire racks and allow to cool. Store in tightly covered container.

Shaping the dough: Use a flat-bottomed glass covered with a damp cloth to flatten slightly each ball.

Decorating the cakes: Brush on egg yolk glaze and top each cookie with half a blanched almond.

Cardamom Cookies

Color index
page 105

Begin 3 hrs
or up to
2 wks ahead

72 cookies

3³/₄ cups all-purpose
  flour
2 cups butter or
  margarine, softened
1 cup chopped
  California walnuts

1½ teaspoons almond
  extract
1 teaspoon ground
  cardamom
⅛ teaspoon salt
confectioners' sugar

1. Preheat oven to 350°F. Into large bowl, measure flour, butter, walnuts, almond extract, cardamom, salt and 1½ cups confectioners' sugar.
2. With hand, knead until well blended; shape dough into 1-inch balls. Place balls of dough, 2 inches apart, on cookie sheets.
3. Bake cookies 20 minutes or until lightly browned. With pancake turner, immediately remove cookies to wire racks; cool.
4. If you like, just before serving, roll cookies in confectioners' sugar. Store tightly covered.

Madeleines

Color index
page 105

Begin 1 hr
or up to
3 days ahead

30 cookies

2 eggs
⅓ cup sugar
½ teaspoon vanilla
  extract
1 teaspoon grated lemon
  peel

1 cup all-purpose flour
¾ cup butter or
  margarine, melted and
  cooled
3 tablespoons salad oil

1. Grease and flour well each 3³/₈″ by 2″ shell of one 12-shell Madeleine pan to prevent dough sticking. Preheat oven to 425°F.
2. In small bowl with mixer at high speed, beat eggs, sugar and vanilla; beating at high speed, beat until mixture becomes thick and lemon-colored, about 5 minutes, occasionally scraping the bowl with a rubber spatula.
3. With rubber spatula, fold in lemon peel. Sprinkle flour, about 2 tablespoons at a time, over egg mixture and gently fold into mixture. Fold in butter and salad oil, about 1 tablespoon at a time.
4. Fill shells about three-fourths full. Bake 8 minutes or until golden. Immediately remove from shells to wire rack; allow cookies to cool completely. Repeat until all the Madeleine batter is used.

Christmas Wreaths

Color index
page 104

Begin 2½ hrs
or up to
2 wks ahead

54 cookies

sugar
2½ cups all-purpose
  flour
1 cup butter or
  margarine, softened
2 teaspoons grated
  orange peel

2 egg yolks
¼ teaspoon salt
1 egg white,
  beaten
red and green candied
  cherries, chopped

1. In large bowl, measure ½ cup sugar and next 5 ingredients. With mixer at low speed, beat ingredients until just mixed; increase speed to medium and beat 4 minutes, occasionally scraping bowl with rubber spatula. (Mixture may look dry.)
2. Preheat oven to 400°F. Take a heaping teaspoonful of dough at a time and roll it into a 6-inch rope. Place each dough rope on cookie sheet in a circle, crossing ends over.
3. Brush cookies with egg white and sprinkle on some sugar. Decorate with red and green cherries.
4. Bake 10 to 12 minutes until light golden. Allow wreaths to cool on cookie sheet. Store cookies in a tightly covered container.

Shaping the wreaths: Arrange dough rope in a circle but cross one end over the other with ½ inch extending at each end.

Decorating the cookies: Press pieces of red and green candied cherries into cookies before baking to make a pretty decoration.

Molded and Pressed cookies

Spritz

3³⁄₄ cups all-purpose flour
1¹⁄₃ cups butter or margarine, softened
³⁄₄ cup sugar
¹⁄₄ cup orange juice
1 egg yolk

Color index page 106

Begin 3¹⁄₂ hrs ahead or early in day

108 cookies

1 Into large bowl, measure flour, butter, sugar, orange juice and egg yolk. With mixer at medium speed, beat ingredients until well mixed, occasionally scraping bowl with rubber spatula. Cover; refrigerate about 1 hour. Preheat oven to 375°F. Use part of dough at a time; keep rest of dough refrigerated.

2 Using cookie press fitted with bar-plate tip, press dough in long strips, about 1 inch apart, down length of cookie sheets.

3 With sharp knife, cut each strip into 2¹⁄₂-inch pieces. Leave pieces in place. Bake 8 minutes or until light golden, being careful not to overbake.

4 Remove from oven and immediately cut again between cookies to separate any cookies which are still joined together.

5 With pancake turner, immediately remove cookies to wire racks. Allow cookies to cool completely. Store tightly covered.

RASPBERRY THUMBPRINTS

Use ¹⁄₂ *of chilled Spritz dough* (above). Shape rounded tea-spoonfuls of dough into balls. Place 1 inch apart on cookie sheets.

Press thumb into centers of cookies, making deep indentations. Bake 10 minutes.

Remove from oven and with ¹⁄₃ *cup red raspberry preserves* fill indentations. Bake 5 minutes more; immediately remove and cool cookies on racks. (72 cookies.)

RINGLETS

With sharp knife, divide chilled *Spritz dough* (above) into quarters; refrigerate ³⁄₄ of dough. Divide remainder into 16 pieces.

On lightly floured surface, with hands, roll each piece into thin rope about 7 inches long.

Twist 2 ropes together tightly; shape into ring. Place 1 inch apart on sheet; brush with *1 egg,* slightly beaten. Bake 12 minutes or until golden; remove to racks to cool. Repeat with remaining dough. (32 cookies.)

Color index page 106
Begin 4 hrs or up to 2 wks ahead
120 cookies

Chocolate-dipped Butter Cookies

4¹⁄₃ cups all-purpose flour
1¹⁄₂ cups butter or margarine, softened
1 cup sugar
¹⁄₂ cup sour cream
2 egg yolks
¹⁄₂ teaspoon almond extract
¹⁄₄ teaspoon salt

Chocolate Glaze:
1¹⁄₂ cups sugar
¹⁄₄ cup light corn syrup
2 tablespoons butter or margarine
¹⁄₂ cup water
1 6-ounce package semisweet-chocolate pieces

1. Preheat oven to 375°F. Into large bowl, measure all ingredients except glaze; with mixer at low speed, beat until just mixed. Increase speed to medium; beat 2 minutes, occasionally scraping bowl with rubber spatula.

2. With cookie press fitted with 1¹⁄₂-inch Christmas tree plate, fill cookie press cylinder with dough. Refrigerate remaining dough. Press dough shapes onto cookie sheets, about ¹⁄₂ inch apart.

3. Bake 12 to 15 minutes until lightly browned around edges.

4. With pancake turner, immediately remove to wire racks and allow to cool completely. (Wash and cool cookie sheets completely before reusing, or cookies will not have a nice shape.)

5. Prepare Chocolate Glaze: In a 2-quart heavy saucepan over high heat, heat sugar, light corn syrup, butter or margarine and water to a full rolling boil; boil mixture for 2 minutes then remove saucepan from heat. Into mixture in saucepan stir semisweet-chocolate pieces until pieces are melted and glaze is smooth. Keep glaze warm over low heat while dipping cooled cookies.

6. With fork, gently lower one cookie at a time, flat side down, into Chocolate Glaze, to allow mixture to coat back and approximately ¹⁄₈ inch up sides of each of the cookies.

7. Carefully lift cookie out and allow excess glaze to drain off. Place cookies chocolate side up on wire racks to allow glaze to cool and harden. Store in a tightly covered container.

Dipping in chocolate: With fork, lower cookie flat side down into glaze to coat one side; lift out; allow excess to drain off.

Hardening the glaze: Carefully place each cookie, chocolate side up, on a wire rack. Leave until glaze is completely hard.

Refrigerator cookies

Color index
page 103

Begin 6 hrs
or up to
1 wk ahead

96 cookies

Refrigerator Cookies

2½ cups all-purpose flour
1½ cups sugar
1 cup butter or
margarine, softened
1 egg
1½ teaspoons double-
acting baking powder
1 teaspoon vanilla
extract
½ teaspoon salt

1. With mixer at low speed, beat all ingredients until just mixed. At medium speed, beat 3 minutes.
2. Shape dough into rolls about 1½ inches in diameter. Wrap in waxed paper; refrigerate until firm, at least 4 hours or up to 1 week.
3. Preheat oven to 375°F. Cut rolls into ¼-inch-thick slices; rewrap and refrigerate rest of roll.
4. Place slices 1 inch apart on cookie sheet. Bake 8 minutes or until lightly browned. Immediately remove cookies to wire racks; cool.

Color index
page 105

Begin 6 hrs
ahead

96 cookies

Citrus Pinwheels

Refrigerator Cookies
dough (above)
1 teaspoon milk
(optional)
confectioners' sugar
¼ teaspoon lemon
extract
½ teaspoon yellow food
color
½ teaspoon orange
extract
10 drops red food
color

1. Prepare Refrigerator Cookies dough as directed in step 1. If dough is too dry, add milk. Divide dough into 4 equal portions. On waxed paper covered with confectioners' sugar, with lightly sugared rolling pin, roll one dough portion into 12″ by 6″ rectangle.
2. Into small bowl, spoon another dough portion; stir in lemon extract and ¼ teaspoon yellow food color; mix well. On another sheet of sugared paper, roll lemon dough to 12″ by 6″ rectangle.
3. Invert lemon dough on to basic dough; peel off top paper. Trim doughs to same size.
4. Starting with a long end, roll doughs jelly-roll fashion, peeling back waxed paper while rolling. Wrap and refrigerate until firm, about 4 hours.
5. Repeat steps 1–4 using remaining 2 portions of dough. For step 2, flavor and color portion of dough with orange extract, remaining yellow food color and red food color.
6. Preheat oven to 350°F. Unwrap rolls and cut each roll crosswise into ¼-inch-thick slices.
7. Place slices, cut side up, on cookie sheets, 1 inch apart. Bake 12 to 15 minutes until light brown. Remove cookies to wire racks to cool.

Inverting the dough: Invert lemon-flavored dough on top of basic dough.

Rolling the dough: Peel back waxed paper while rolling jelly-roll fashion.

Neapolitan Cookies

Color index
page 105

Begin 6 hrs
ahead

72 cookies

Refrigerator Cookies
dough (left)
½ teaspoon almond
extract
5 drops red food
color
1 square unsweetened
chocolate
¼ cup chopped
California
walnuts

1 Prepare dough and divide among 3 small bowls. Add almond extract and red food color to one portion; stir until thoroughly mixed.

2 In 1-quart saucepan over low heat, melt chocolate. Mix chocolate into second portion; mix California walnuts with remainder.

3 Line 9″ by 5″ loaf pan with waxed paper and spread almond dough evenly in pan. Then spread walnut dough and finally, chocolate dough.

4 Cover layered dough in pan with waxed paper and place it in the refrigerator until firm, about 4 hours.

5 Preheat oven to 350°F. Invert pan over board to turn out chilled dough and peel off waxed paper.

6 With sharp knife, cut dough lengthwise in half. Slice each half of dough crosswise into ¼-inch slices.

7 Place slices on cookie sheet, 1 inch apart. Bake 10 to 12 minutes until light brown. Remove to wire racks to cool.

Rolled cookies

Sugar Cookies

*3¹/₄ cups all-purpose
flour
1¹/₂ cups sugar
²/₃ cup shortening
2 eggs
2¹/₂ teaspoons double-
acting baking powder
2 tablespoons milk
1 teaspoon vanilla
extract
¹/₂ teaspoon salt*

*heavy or whipping cream
or 1 egg white slightly
beaten with
1 tablespoon water*

Decorative toppings:
*nonpareils, sugar,
chopped nuts, shredded
coconut, cut-up
gumdrops or butterscotch
pieces*

Color index
page 105

Begin 6 hrs
ahead

72 cookies

1 Into large bowl,
measure first 8 in-
gredients. With mixer at
medium speed, beat until
well mixed, occasionally
scraping bowl.

2 Shape dough into ball;
wrap with waxed
paper; refrigerate 2 to 3
hours until easy to
handle. Preheat oven to
400°F. Lightly grease
cookie sheets.

3 On lightly floured
surface, roll half of
dough at a time, keeping
rest refrigerated. For crisp
cookies, roll paper thin.
For softer cookies, roll
¹/₈ inch to ¹/₄ inch thick.

4 With floured cookie
cutters, cut dough into
various shapes. Reroll
dough trimmings and
continue to cut shapes.

5 Place cookies ¹/₂ inch
apart on greased
cookie sheets. To glaze:
Brush tops of cookies with
heavy or whipping cream or
with the beaten egg white
and water mixture.

6 Sprinkle cookies with
your choice of
toppings; bake 8 minutes
or until very light brown.
With pancake turner
remove cookies to racks;
cool completely.

Sandwich Cookies

*2 egg yolks
2 tablespoons milk
2¹/₄ cups all-purpose flour
³/₄ cup sugar
³/₄ cup butter or
margarine, softened
1 teaspoon vanilla
extract
¹/₄ teaspoon salt*

*Butter-Cream Frosting
(page 400)
4 drops green food
color
3 drops red food
color
3 drops yellow food
color*

Color index
page 106

Begin 3 hrs
or up to
2 wks ahead

42 cookies

1. Preheat oven to 375°F. In large bowl with mixer
at low speed, beat egg yolks and milk until well
blended. Add flour, sugar, butter or margarine,
vanilla and salt; beat ingredients until just mixed;
increase speed to medium and beat 2 minutes,
occasionally scraping bowl. Divide dough in half.
2. On floured pastry cloth, with lightly floured,
stockinette-covered rolling pin, roll one dough half
¹/₈ inch thick. With 2¹/₄-inch fluted-edged cookie
cutter, cut dough into rounds; with ¹/₂-inch round
cutter, cut out centers from half of rounds. Reserve
the dough scraps.
3. Place rounds about ¹/₂ inch apart on cookie
sheets; bake 8 to 10 minutes until lightly browned.
With pancake turner, remove cookies to wire racks
to cool completely. Repeat steps 2 and 3 with
remaining dough, rerolling scraps.
4. Prepare frosting as recipe directs; divide mixture
into thirds; place portions in separate bowls. Tint
portions with food color.
5. On bottom side of a cookie without a hole, spread
teaspoonful of either green, pink or yellow frosting;
top with a cookie with a hole in it, top side up, to
make a "sandwich". Repeat with remaining cookies
and frosting. (Use any leftover frosting for graham
crackers or cupcakes.)

Almond Butter Cookies

*1³/₄ cups all-purpose flour
³/₄ cup butter or
margarine, softened
1 teaspoon almond
extract
¹/₈ teaspoon salt
sugar*

*1 egg white, slightly
beaten
¹/₈ teaspoon ground
cinnamon
¹/₃ cup toasted diced and
buttered almonds*

Color index
page 105

Begin 1³/₄ hrs
or day ahead

36 cookies

1. Into large bowl, measure flour, butter or margarine, almond extract, salt and ¹/₄ cup sugar. With
mixer at medium speed, beat ingredients until well
mixed, occasionally scraping bowl with rubber
spatula. (Mixture will be crumbly.)
2. With hands, shape into ball. (If dough is too soft
to roll, cover and refrigerate until firm.)
3. Preheat oven to 325°F. On lightly floured surface,
with floured rolling pin, roll dough into 12″ by 8″
rectangle. With pastry wheel or knife, cut into 3″ by
1″ strips; place on cookie sheets; brush with slightly
beaten egg white.
4. In small bowl, mix a scant ¹/₄ cup sugar with
cinnamon and almonds; sprinkle on cookies. Bake
15 minutes or until golden. With pancake turner,
remove cookies to wire racks; allow to cool.

Gingerbread-Men Cookies

2¼ cups all-purpose
   flour
½ cup sugar
½ cup shortening
½ cup light molasses
1 egg
1½ teaspoons ground
   cinnamon
1 teaspoon double-acting
   baking powder
1 teaspoon ground
   ginger
1 teaspoon ground
   cloves

½ teaspoon ground
   nutmeg
½ teaspoon baking
   soda
½ teaspoon salt
dried currants
Ornamental Cookie
   Frosting (right)

Color index page 104
Begin 6 hrs ahead
24 cookies

1 Into large bowl measure all ingredients except currants and frosting. With mixer at medium speed, beat ingredients until well mixed. Cover and refrigerate 1 hour.

2 On lightly floured surface, with floured rolling pin, roll chilled dough ⅛ inch thick. Preheat oven to 350°F.

3 With 5-inch long cutter, cut out men. Reroll trimmings and cut more cookies. With pancake turner, place ½ inch apart on cookie sheets.

4 On each cut out, place currants to represent buttons, eyes and mouth. (Or, omit currants and mark with frosting after cookies have been baked.)

5 Bake 8 minutes or until browned, then, with pancake turner, remove cookies to racks. Cool before decorating.

6 With paper cone or cake decorator and frosting, outline feet, sleeves and other features as you wish.

MAKING A PATTERN

To make Gingerbread Men if you have no special cutter, draw a man about 5 inches long and 4 inches wide on cardboard. Cut out the shape.

Put it on the rolled dough and carefully cut around it with a sharp pointed knife.

ORNAMENTAL COOKIE FROSTING: Into small bowl, sift *1¼ cups confectioners' sugar* and *⅛ teaspoon cream of tartar* through very fine sieve; add *1 egg white.* With mixer at high speed, beat mixture so stiff that knife drawn through leaves clean path. (On humid days you may need to beat in more confectioners' sugar.)

Color index page 105
Begin day ahead
108 cookies

Spice Cookies

sugar
3⅔ cups all-purpose flour
1 cup butter or
   margarine, softened
2 eggs
1 tablespoon milk
1½ teaspoons baking
   soda

1½ teaspoons ground
   cinnamon
½ teaspoon ground
   nutmeg
¼ teaspoon ground
   cloves
1 cup dried currants

1. Into large bowl, measure 1½ cups sugar and remaining ingredients except currants. With mixer at medium speed, beat ingredients until well mixed, occasionally scraping bowl with rubber spatula. Stir in currants. Cover; refrigerate overnight.
2. Preheat oven to 375°F. On lightly floured board, with floured rolling pin, roll dough as thin as possible; lightly sprinkle with sugar.
3. With pastry wheel or knife, cut dough into 2-inch diamond; place on cookie sheets.
4. Bake 8 minutes or until very lightly browned.
5. With pancake turner, remove cookies to wire racks and allow to cool completely.

Color index page 104
Begin 4 hrs or up to 2 wks ahead
72 cookies

Cinnamon Cookies

2 cups all-purpose flour
1 cup sugar
½ cup butter or
   margarine, softened
3 egg yolks
2 tablespoons milk

2 teaspoons ground
   cinnamon
½ teaspoon double-
   acting baking powder
½ teaspoon salt

1. Into large bowl, measure all ingredients. With mixer at medium speed, beat ingredients until well mixed, about 3 minutes, occasionally scraping bowl.
2. Wrap the dough in plastic wrap then put it in the refrigerator for 2½ hours or until easy to handle.
3. With lightly floured rolling pin, directly onto *cold* cookie sheet, roll half of dough to ⅛-inch thickness. Keep remaining dough refrigerated.
4. With floured 2¼-inch cookie cutters, cut cookies, spacing 1 inch apart. Chill about 1 hour; remove dough from between cookies. Meanwhile, preheat oven to 350°F.
5. Bake 15 minutes or until lightly browned. Immediately remove cookies to wire racks; cool. Repeat with remaining dough and trimmings.

413

CANDY

Homemade candies are family favorites at any time; if you are afraid that they will dull the appetite for meals, you can always serve them as an alternative to dessert.

COOKING CANDY

Use a heavy saucepan for candies, one large enough to allow the mixture to boil freely without running over; stir with a long wooden spoon – a metal one would become too hot to handle.

Undissolved sugar crystals will make a candy grainy. You can either grease the sides of the saucepan first to prevent crystals clinging to them, or keep brushing down any crystals with a pastry brush dipped in hot water and shaken dry. Once the sugar has dissolved, stop stirring the mixture immediately, unless the recipe specifically directs otherwise.

USING A CANDY THERMOMETER

The most reliable way of testing a candy mixture is to check the temperature with a candy thermometer. Always cook the mixture to the exact temperatures specified. If you suspect that your thermometer is not quite accurate, stand it in boiling water for a few minutes. It should register 212°F. If it rises above (or does not reach) this temperature, add the difference to (or subtract it from) that specified in the recipe. Hold the thermometer upright, keeping the bulb totally immersed in the boiling (not foaming) mixture, yet *well clear of the bottom of the pan*. When you have finished with the thermometer, always be sure that you allow it to cool before washing it, otherwise it might break.

Reading a candy thermometer: Always read the temperature of candy mixture at eye level. Watch carefully once it reaches 220°F. as it rises rapidly from this point.

COLD-WATER TEST

If you do not own a candy thermometer, with practice you can soon learn how to recognize the different consistencies of candy by using the cold-water test. Have ready a measuring cup of very cold, not iced, water. Remove the candy from the heat and, with a clean spoon, drop about ½ teaspoon of the hot mixture into the water. Let it stand a minute then test the firmness of the mixture with your fingers. Use this chart as your guide when you make candy.

CANDY COOKING TEMPERATURES		
Stage	**Temperature**	**Consistency**
Thread	230° to 234°F.	Syrup spins 2-inch thread in the air as it falls from spoon
Soft ball	234° to 240°F.	Syrup (in cold water) forms soft ball which flattens on removal from water
Firm ball	244° to 248°F.	Syrup (in cold water) forms firm ball which does not flatten on removal from water
Hard ball	250° to 266°F.	Syrup (in cold water) forms hard, yet pliable ball
Soft crack	270° to 290°F.	Syrup (in cold water) separates into threads which are hard but not brittle
Hard crack	300° to 310°F.	Syrup (in cold water) separates into hard, brittle threads

COOLING CANDY

For recipes that call for a mixture to be cooled to lukewarm, let it stand undisturbed, off the heat, until the temperature falls to 110°F., or until the bottom of the saucepan feels lukewarm to the touch. Never move the pan or beat the mixture while it is hot or large sugar crystals will form, giving the candy a grainy texture.

When the mixture is ready for pouring out, do it quickly, holding the saucepan close to the pan. Use a rubber spatula for pushing out the mixture; always avoid scraping the saucepan since the mixture on the sides may be sugary.

Allow the candy to cool before cutting or breaking it up and do not store it until it is completely cold.

STORING CANDY

Sugar readily absorbs moisture so most candies are best stored in a cool place in tightly covered containers. Creamy candies such as fudge and penuche, chewy caramels and taffy should be individually wrapped in plastic wrap, waxed paper or foil. Refrigerated candies should always be wrapped or covered and kept well chilled until you are ready to serve them.

Fudges

Chocolate Fudge

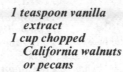

Color index
page 106

Begin 2½ hrs
ahead

36 pieces or
1¼ pounds

3 cups sugar
1 cup milk
2 tablespoons light corn
syrup
2 squares unsweetened
chocolate
3 tablespoons butter or
margarine

1 teaspoon vanilla
extract
1 cup chopped
California walnuts
or pecans

1 In 3-quart saucepan over medium heat, heat sugar, milk, corn syrup and chocolate to boiling, stirring constantly. Wash crystals from pan side with damp pastry brush.

2 Set candy thermometer in place and continue cooking mixture, stirring occasionally, until temperature reaches 238°F. (soft-ball stage).

3 Remove pan from heat; add butter and vanilla. Cool, without stirring, to 110°F., or until outside of saucepan feels lukewarm.

4 Meanwhile, butter 8″ by 8″ pan. With spoon, beat until the mixture becomes thick and begins to lose its gloss.

5 Quickly stir in chopped walnuts or pecans until evenly mixed. Pour into pan. (Don't scrape saucepan; mixture on side may be sugary.)

6 Cool chocolate fudge in pan; when the fudge has cooled completely, cut it into small even-sized squares with a sharp knife.

PEANUT BUTTER FUDGE: Prepare as above but use *¼ cup creamy peanut butter* instead of butter or margarine and substitute *1 cup chopped salted peanuts* for the California walnuts or pecans.

Nutty Butterscotch Fudge

Color index
page 106

Begin 1½ hrs
ahead

49 pieces or
1¼ pounds

1 cup sugar
¼ cup butter or
margarine
¾ teaspoon salt
1 7½-ounce jar
marshmallow cream
1 5.33-ounce can
evaporated milk,
undiluted

1 12-ounce package
butterscotch-flavored
pieces
½ teaspoon vanilla
extract
½ cup salted peanuts,
pecans or cashews,
chopped

1. Grease 9″ by 9″ baking pan; set aside.
2. In heavy, 3-quart saucepan, combine sugar, butter or margarine, salt, marshmallow cream and undiluted milk. Over medium-high heat, heat to a rolling boil; cook 5 minutes, stirring.
3. Remove saucepan from heat. Quickly stir in butterscotch-flavored pieces and vanilla extract until butterscotch pieces are melted and well blended; stir in peanuts. Pour mixture into pan. Cool. Cut into small squares with a sharp knife.

Pecan Penuche

Color index
page 107

Begin 2½ hrs
ahead

36 pieces or
2 pounds

2 cups packed light
brown sugar
2 cups sugar
1 cup milk
3 tablespoons butter

1½ teaspoons vanilla
extract
1 cup coarsely chopped
pecans

1. In 3-quart saucepan over medium heat, heat sugars and milk to boiling, stirring constantly. Set candy thermometer in place and continue cooking, without stirring, until temperature reaches 238°F. or until a small amount of mixture dropped into very cold water forms a soft ball. Remove from heat; add butter and vanilla.
2. Cool mixture, without stirring, to 110°F. or until outside of saucepan feels lukewarm to hand. Meanwhile, butter 8″ by 8″ pan.
3. With spoon, beat until mixture becomes thick and begins to lose its gloss; quickly stir in pecans. Pour into pan. (Don't scrape saucepan; mixture on side may be sugary.) Cool in pan on wire rack; when cold, cut into squares with a sharp knife.

Maple Kisses

Color index
page 106

Begin 1½ hrs
or up to
1 wk ahead

24 pieces or
¾ pound

1 cup packed light brown
sugar
½ cup sugar
½ cup evaporated milk
¼ cup light corn syrup

1 tablespoon butter or
margarine
1 teaspoon maple flavor
1½ cups chopped
California walnuts

1. In 2-quart saucepan over very low heat, heat sugars, undiluted milk and corn syrup to boiling, stirring constantly. Set candy thermometer in place and continue cooking, stirring constantly, until temperature reaches 235°F. or until a small amount of mixture dropped into very cold water forms a soft ball. (This takes about 30 minutes.) Remove candy mixture from heat.
2. With spoon, beat butter, maple flavor and nuts into mixture. Quickly drop mixture by teaspoonfuls onto waxed paper; cool on wire racks.

Other candies

Molasses Taffy

1 14-ounce can sweetened
condensed milk
(1⅓ cups)
½ cup light molasses
⅛ teaspoon salt

Color index
page 107

Begin 2 hrs
or day ahead

50 pieces or
¾ pound

1 Butter an 8″ by 8″ pan or large platter. In 2-quart saucepan over medium heat, heat all ingredients to boiling, stirring occasionally.

2 Set candy thermometer in place and continue cooking the mixture, stirring constantly, until the temperature reaches 244°F. (firm-ball stage), about 20 minutes.

3 Remove saucepan from heat; pour mixture into pan. Let stand until cool enough to handle.

4 With buttered fingers, pull the candy mixture until it becomes shiny and light colored.

5 With fingers, twist taffy into continuous rope about ¾ inch thick.

6 With kitchen shears, cut rope into 1-inch pieces. Wrap each piece in plastic wrap.

Orange-Almond Caramels

Color index
page 107

Begin 1½ hrs
or up to
1 wk ahead

50 pieces or
1½ pounds

3 cups sugar
¼ cup boiling water
1 cup evaporated
milk
⅛ teaspoon salt

2 teaspoons grated
orange peel
1⅓ cups toasted slivered
almonds

1. In heavy, 2-quart saucepan over medium heat, heat 1 cup sugar, stirring constantly, until entirely melted and a deep golden color. Stirring constantly, slowly add boiling water; cook until mixture is a smooth syrup. Stir in remaining 2 cups sugar, undiluted evaporated milk and salt.
2. Set candy thermometer in place and continue cooking over medium heat, stirring constantly, until temperature reaches 238°F. or soft-ball stage. Remove from heat; add orange peel and stir until mixture cools slightly; add 1 cup slivered almonds and continue stirring until a little of the mixture retains its shape and looks slightly dull when dropped on waxed paper.
3. Drop by heaping teaspoonfuls onto waxed paper; press a few more nuts on top of each piece; wrap individually in plastic wrap, waxed paper or foil.

Nougats

Color index
page 107

Begin day
or up to
2 wks ahead

2¼ pounds

½ pound hard gum candy
(not sugar coated)
cornstarch
2 cups sugar
1½ cups light corn
syrup
¼ teaspoon salt
¼ cup water

2 egg whites
1 teaspoon vanilla
extract
¼ cup butter or
margarine, softened
1 cup coarsely chopped
California walnuts

1. With kitchen shears, cut gum candy into small pieces; set aside. Grease well 9″ by 9″ baking pan; sprinkle lightly with cornstarch. In 2-quart saucepan with candy thermometer in place, over medium-high heat, heat sugar, corn syrup, salt and water to boiling, stirring constantly. Continue cooking, stirring occasionally, until temperature reaches 250°F. or hard-ball stage.
2. Meanwhile, in large bowl with mixer at high speed, beat egg whites until stiff peaks form. Beating at high speed, gradually pour about one-fourth of hot syrup into egg whites. Continue beating while heating remaining syrup to 300°F. or hard-crack stage. Egg-white mixture should stand in stiff, glossy peaks; beat in vanilla extract.
3. With mixer at high speed, gradually beat remaining syrup into egg-white mixture, then beat in butter or margarine until well blended. If mixture becomes too thick for the mixer to beat, continue beating with a wooden spoon.
4. With wooden spoon, stir in walnuts and gum candy; spoon evenly into baking pan. With pastry brush, lightly brush mixture with some cornstarch.
5. Let nougat cool in pan on wire rack for about 12 hours or overnight. Remove nougat from pan; with kitchen shears or knife, cut into 1-inch squares, wiping shears as needed with damp cloth. To store, wrap each piece in plastic wrap.

Lollipops

12 8-ounce paper hot-drink cups
36 ³/₄-inch-long oval hard candies in assorted colors
about 2 ounces cinnamon red-hot or other small red candies
2 cups sugar
1 cup water
³/₄ cup light corn syrup
¹/₂ teaspoon oil of lemon
10 drops yellow food color
12 lollipop sticks

Color index
page 106

Begin 3 hrs
or up to
1 wk ahead

Twelve 3-inch
lollipops

1 Cut off top of each cup to make 1¹/₂-inch-deep ring mold; cut ¹/₈-inch-wide slit from cut edge to, but *not* through, rim.

2 Grease well molds and 2 cookie sheets; put molds, rim side down, in rows on sheets, leaving space for sticks.

3 Arrange a flower pattern of 3 hard candies and two clusters of 3 cinnamon red-hot candies in each mold; set aside.

4 In heavy, 2-quart pan, stir sugar, water and syrup until sugar dissolves. With damp pastry brush, wipe side of pan to remove sugar crystals.

5 With candy thermometer in place, over high heat, without stirring, heat mixture to 300°F. or hard-crack stage.

6 Remove from heat and stir in oil of lemon and food color then, working quickly, pour about ¹/₄ cup mixture into each mold.

7 Press sticks through slits into candy; cool completely. With spatula, loosen lollipops from sheets; discard molds.

Divinity

3 cups sugar
¹/₂ cup light corn syrup
¹/₂ cup water
2 egg whites, at room temperature
1 teaspoon vanilla extract

Color index
page 107

Begin 1¹/₂ hrs
or up to
1 wk ahead

60 candies or
1¹/₂ pounds

1. Avoid making Divinity on a humid day; candy will not harden. In 2-quart saucepan over medium-high heat, heat sugar, syrup and water to boiling, stirring until sugar is dissolved. Set candy thermometer in place and continue cooking, without stirring, until temperature reaches 248°F.

2. Meanwhile, in medium bowl with mixer at high speed, beat egg whites until stiff peaks form. Beating at medium speed, slowly pour half of syrup into whites. Continue beating while heating other half of syrup to 272°F.

3. While turning bowl and continuing beating, slowly pour remaining hot syrup into mixture (mixture will be stiff). (Don't scrape saucepan; mixture on side may be sugary.) Add vanilla; beat until mixture holds stiff, glossy peaks. Working quickly, drop by heaping teaspoonfuls onto waxed paper. Cool completely before storing.

Fondant

4 cups sugar
¹/₄ cup light corn syrup
¹/₄ teaspoon cream of tartar
¹/₈ teaspoon salt
1 cup water
peppermint or favorite extract
green, red or yellow food color

Color index
page 107

Begin 5 hrs
or up to
1 wk ahead

60 pieces or
1 pound

1. In heavy, 2-quart saucepan with candy thermometer in place, over high heat, heat first 5 ingredients until boiling and sugar is dissolved, stirring occasionally. Reduce heat to medium; continue cooking, without stirring, until temperature reaches 238° to 240°F. or soft-ball stage, about 10 to 15 minutes. (If mixture takes too long to reach desired temperature, it will not become stiff after beating in step 3.) During cooking, wipe down sides of pan with damp pastry brush to remove sugar crystals. Remove pan from heat.

2. Set thermometer in large bowl; add mixture. (Don't scrape mixture from side of pan; it may be sugary.) Cool the mixture, *without stirring*, until temperature reaches about 125°F., about 1 hour.

3. With wooden spoon, beat mixture till white and stiff, about 10 minutes. If it does not stiffen after beating 10 minutes, it has cooled too much. Reheat in pan just to boiling; beat again.

4. Divide fondant into several portions; keep covered tightly with plastic wrap as you work with each portion in turn. Flatten one portion; add flavoring extract to taste and a drop or two of food color; knead to blend well. Repeat with remaining fondant. Shape fondant into balls and other shapes.

5. Place shapes on waxed paper and let stand 1¹/₂ hours or until a light crust has formed, then place on wire rack so light crust will form on bottom also. Cover and store or you can use the fondant for dipping into melted chocolate or for Bonbons (page 418).

Other candies

Bonbons

Color index
page 107

Begin 7 hrs
or up to
1 wk ahead

30 bonbons and
6 or 8 patties or
1 pound

Fondant (page 417)
¼ teaspoon peppermint,
almond extract or
other flavoring

red, yellow or green food
color
½ to 1 teaspoon hot
water

1. Prepare Fondant as in steps 1 through 3; divide in two; tightly wrap one portion in plastic wrap. Flatten other and add peppermint extract to taste; knead until well blended. Shape into ¾-inch balls. Place on waxed paper and let stand 1½ hours or until a light crust has formed; place on wire rack about 1½ hours so crust forms on bottom also. (Crust helps prevent distortion of coating and centers when dipping.)

2. In double-boiler top over simmering water, melt reserved fondant portion with one or two drops food color to make a delicate pastel color, stirring constantly until mixture is hot and thin. A crust will begin to appear as soon as stirring stops, so work steadily to dip fondant pieces.

3. Dip one fondant piece at a time: Drop, flat side down, into melted fondant. With long-handled, 2-tined fork, quickly turn to coat rounded side; immediately lift piece, rounded side down and rap fork on rim of pan two or three times; scrape fork across rim to remove excess fondant, but do not scrape fondant from bonbon.

4. Onto waxed paper, invert fork to place bonbon rounded side up. Hold fork in contact with bonbon for a few seconds, then lift off, pulling fondant up to make a "curl." During dipping, keep stirring fondant to remove crust. Let dipped bonbons stand at least 1 hour before removing from paper.

5. To any melted fondant left in pan, add hot water, and heat over simmering water, stirring until mixture is thin and well melted. Pour mixture onto waxed paper in little patties; let dry as above.

Popcorn Balls

Color index
page 106

Begin 2 hrs or
day ahead

12 balls

12 cups popped corn
(about ¾ cup
popcorn)
½ pound candied
cherries, halved
1 16-ounce bottle light
corn syrup (2 cups)

1 tablespoon white
vinegar
1 teaspoon salt
2 teaspoons vanilla
extract

1. In greased 8-quart saucepot toss popped corn with cherries until well mixed. In 2-quart saucepan over medium-high heat, heat to boiling corn syrup, vinegar and salt, stirring occasionally. Set candy thermometer in place; continue cooking, without stirring, until temperature reaches 250°F. or until a small amount dropped in very cold water forms a hard but pliable ball. Remove syrup mixture from heat and stir in vanilla extract.

2. Slowly pour syrup over popped-corn mixture, tossing until kernels are coated. With greased hands, shape mixture into 3-inch balls, using as little pressure as possible, so balls will not be too compact. (If mixture hardens, place saucepot over very low heat until mixture is pliable.)

Peanut Brittle

Color index
page 106

Begin 2 hrs or
up to 2 wks
ahead

1 pound

1 cup sugar
½ cup light corn syrup
¼ teaspoon salt
¼ cup water
1 cup shelled raw
peanuts

2 tablespoons butter or
margarine,
softened
1 teaspoon baking
soda

1. Grease large cookie sheet. In heavy, 2-quart saucepan over medium heat, heat to boiling sugar, corn syrup, salt and water, stirring until sugar is dissolved. Stir in peanuts. Set candy thermometer in place and continue cooking, stirring frequently, until temperature reaches 300°F. or until a small amount of mixture dropped into very cold water separates into hard and brittle threads.

2. Remove from heat; immediately stir in butter or margarine and baking soda; pour at once onto cookie sheet.

3. With 2 forks, lift and pull peanut mixture into rectangle about 14″ by 12″; cool. With hands, snap candy into small pieces.

Walnut Crunch

Color index
page 107

Begin 3½ hrs
ahead

1½ pounds

1¼ cups sugar
¾ cup butter or
margarine
1½ teaspoons salt
¼ cup water
1½ cups coarsely
chopped California
walnuts

½ teaspoon baking soda
⅓ cup semisweet-
chocolate pieces,
melted
½ cup finely chopped
California walnuts

1. Butter 15″ by 10″ jelly-roll pan. In 2-quart saucepan over medium heat, heat sugar, butter or margarine, salt and water to boiling, stirring often. Set candy thermometer in place and continue cooking, stirring often, until temperature reaches 290°F. or until a small amount of mixture dropped into very cold water separates into threads which are hard but not brittle.

2. Remove mixture from heat; stir in coarsely chopped walnuts and soda; pour at once into pan. (Don't scrape saucepan; side may be sugary.)

3. Spread mixture with chocolate and sprinkle with finely chopped walnuts; cool. With hands, snap candy into small pieces.

Testing sugar mixture: Cook to 290°F. or until small amount dropped into very cold water separates into hard but not brittle threads.

Adding chocolate: Use a spatula to spread melted chocolate over the walnut layer, then sprinkle the top with finely chopped walnuts.

Color index
page 107

Begin 3 hrs
or up to
2 wks ahead

64 patties or
2½ pounds

Peppermint Patties

1 14-ounce can sweetened condensed milk
2 teaspoons peppermint extract
12 drops red food color

1½ to 2 16-ounce packages confectioners' sugar
1½ cups pecan halves

1. In large bowl, mix sweetened condensed milk, peppermint extract and food color. With spoon, stir in 1½ packages confectioners' sugar.
2. On cutting board generously sprinkled with confectioners' sugar, gradually knead in enough additional sugar so that mixture forms a smooth, firm ball that doesn't stick to hands or board.
3. Pat mixture into 8″ by 8″ square. With knife, cut into 1-inch squares. Shape each piece into a ball and, with fingers, flatten into 2-inch patty; top with pecan half. Repeat with remaining pieces. (Keep pieces covered with plastic wrap while preparing patties.) Let patties dry at least 1 hour.

Color index
page 107

Begin day
or up to
2 wks ahead

4¼ pounds

Marzipan Fruits

Marzipan Dough:
2 cups canned almond paste
4 egg whites
about 12 cups confectioners' sugar

Glossy Sugar Glaze (below)

1. Prepare Marzipan Dough: In large bowl, knead almond paste with egg whites; slowly knead in confectioners' sugar or enough to make a stiff dough; cover to keep moist for easy handling.
2. Shape the Marzipan Dough into apples, bananas, pears, oranges or strawberries (right); make only one shape or a selection, if you wish. Allow the fruits to dry on a tray. Meanwhile, prepare glaze.
3. Place Marzipan Fruits (do not let them touch) on a rack in shallow, open pan. With spoon, carefully remove any crystallized sugar on top of glaze. To coat fruits, evenly pour on glaze with as little agitation as possible to prevent glaze crystallizing. Dry overnight.

GLOSSY SUGAR GLAZE: In 2-quart saucepan over medium heat, cook **4½ cups sugar** with **1 cup water** just until sugar dissolves and candy thermometer reads 223°F. Remove from heat very gently; do not stir. Let stand undisturbed until cool.

Preparing Marzipan Dough: Knead almond paste with egg whites, then with confectioners' sugar.

Coating Marzipan Fruits: Pour glaze over fruits on rack; be sure to avoid agitating the syrup.

SHAPING THE FRUITS

14 apples

APPLES: On waxed paper, knead about **2 drops green food color** into **1½ cups Marzipan Dough**. Divide dough into 14 pieces and shape into apples; insert knobs of **whole cloves** part way into tops of apples. Using fine brush, tint apples with **red food color** diluted with **water**. Dry on tray.

Adding stems: Insert knobs of whole cloves part way into tops of apples.

Tinting apples: Use a fine brush to apply diluted red food color.

7 bananas

BANANAS: On waxed paper, knead about **6 drops yellow food color** into **½ cup Marzipan Dough**. Divide dough into 7 pieces and shape into bananas. Prepare brown color as label of food color directs; using brush, paint lines. Dry on tray.

12 pears

PEARS: On waxed paper, knead about **4 drops green and 4 drops yellow food color** into **1 cup Marzipan Dough**. Divide dough into 12 pieces and shape into pears. In top of each pear, insert a leaf of **dried rosemary** part way. Dry on tray.

9 oranges

ORANGES: On waxed paper, knead about **6 drops yellow and 4 drops red food color** into **1 cup Marzipan Dough.** Divide dough into 9 pieces and shape into oranges. Roll oranges over grater to make surface texture. Insert **stems from whole cloves** into tops of oranges. Dry on tray.

20 berries

STRAWBERRIES: Divide ¾ **cup Marzipan Dough** into 20 pieces and shape into strawberries. Roll strawberries over grater to make surface texture. Using fine brush, tint berries with **red food color** diluted with **water**. On waxed paper, knead about **5 drops green food color** into ¼ **cup Marzipan Dough**. Using lightly cornstarch-dusted cutting board and rolling pin, roll dough ⅛ inch thick. With 1¼-inch star-shaped canapé cutter, cut 20 stars; press a star on large end of each berry. Dry on tray.

Making surface texture: Roll berry over grater to mark strawberry seeds.

Adding stars: Press star on large end of each berry to complete the fruit.

Chocolates

Melt-Away Chocolate Mints

Color index
page 107

Begin 2½ hrs
or up to
2 wks ahead

1 pound

**2 8-ounce packages
    semisweet chocolate
    squares
2 tablespoons shortening**

**½ cup heavy cream
1 tablespoon peppermint
    extract
cocoa**

1. Line bottom of 8" by 8" baking pan with waxed paper; set aside. Chop chocolate into small pieces. Place chocolate and shortening in double-boiler top (not over water). Set candy thermometer in place; set aside. Heat water to boiling in double-boiler bottom; remove from heat. Place double-boiler top over hot water; melt chocolate, stirring with rubber spatula, until temperature reaches 130°F.
2. Immediately discard water from double-boiler bottom and refill with cold water. Set top in place and cool chocolate, stirring constantly but gently, until chocolate reaches 83°F. on special 40° to 120°F. thermometer.
3. Meanwhile, in 1-quart saucepan over medium heat, heat heavy cream just to boiling; remove saucepan from heat.
4. In small bowl with mixer at low speed, beat chocolate, cream and peppermint until blended. Increase speed to medium; beat 2 minutes, occasionally scraping bowl with rubber spatula.
5. Pour mixture into prepared pan; set aside until firm, about 2 hours.
6. *To serve:* With metal spatula, loosen chocolate mixture from sides of pan. Invert pan onto cutting board; discard waxed paper. Lightly dust sharp knife with cocoa; cut chocolate mixture into diamonds or 1-inch squares.

Truffles

Color index
page 107

Begin 2 hrs or
up to 1 wk
ahead

36 truffles or
1½ pounds

**1 12-ounce package
    semisweet-chocolate
    pieces
¾ cup sweetened
    condensed milk
1 teaspoon vanilla
    extract**

**⅛ teaspoon salt
½ cup cocoa or 1 cup
    chopped, flaked
    coconut for
    garnish**

1. In double boiler over hot, *not boiling*, water (or in heavy, 2-quart saucepan over low heat), melt chocolate pieces. Stir in condensed milk, vanilla and salt until well mixed. Refrigerate mixture about 45 minutes or until easy to shape.
2. With buttered hands, shape mixture into 1-inch balls. Roll balls in cocoa or coconut.

Shaping balls: With buttered hands, shape mixture into balls.

Coating balls: Roll the balls in cocoa or chopped, flaked coconut.

Chocolate-dipped Fruit

Color index
page 107

Begin 1½ hrs
ahead or early
in day

60 fruit and
12 clusters

**2 large oranges
2 pints large strawberries
1 cup salted peanuts**

**2 8-ounce packages
    semisweet-chocolate
    squares**

1. Peel oranges and separate them into their sections; wrap sections with plastic wrap so fruits will not dry out. Rinse strawberries under running cold water but do not remove stems, being sure to pat berries completely dry with paper towels. Set fruit aside. (For dipping, fruit should be at room temperature.) In small bowl, place peanuts.
2. Into double-boiler top (not over water) grate semisweet-chocolate squares. Set candy thermometer in place; set aside. Heat water to boiling in double-boiler bottom; remove from heat. Place double-boiler top over hot water; melt chocolate, stirring chocolate constantly with rubber spatula, until temperature reaches 130°F.
3. Immediately discard hot water from double-boiler bottom and refill with cold water to come one-third way up side of double boiler. Set top in place and cool chocolate, stirring constantly, until chocolate temperature reaches 83°F. on special 40° to 120°F. thermometer.
4. Remove double-boiler top and replace cold water in bottom with warm water (about 85°F.). This will keep chocolate at dipping consistency longer.
5. With fingers, hold 1 piece of fruit at a time and dip it into chocolate, leaving part of fruit uncovered. Shake off excess chocolate or gently scrape one side of fruit across rim of double boiler being careful not to scrape too much chocolate from fruit; place on waxed paper.
6. Working quickly, stir peanuts into leftover chocolate in pan. Drop mixture by tablespoonfuls onto waxed paper. Let chocolate-covered fruit and peanut clusters stand until chocolate is set (about 10 minutes) before removing from waxed paper. Serve dipped fresh fruit same day. Store peanut clusters in tightly covered container; use within 1 week.

DIPPING THE FRUIT

Dip fruit into chocolate, leaving part uncovered. Gently scrape off excess chocolate across rim of double boiler; place fruit on waxed paper. Stir peanuts into remaining chocolate; drop by tablespoonfuls onto paper.

QUICK BREADS

Unlike yeast breads, quick breads are made with quick-acting leavening and are mixed, shaped and baked in one uninterrupted process. Some, such as muffins, loaves and soda bread, can accompany a meal like ordinary bread, while waffles and pancakes make a delicious meal in themselves. Doughnuts are a tasty snack at any time of the day.

Most quick breads are raised with baking powder, baking soda, or both. The double-acting baking powder used in all our recipes produces gas bubbles twice, first when it comes in contact with liquid and again when subjected to heat; the mixture can, therefore, be left to stand for a little while after mixing, if necessary. Baking soda is usually used in mixtures containing an acid ingredient such as buttermilk, sour cream, fruit juice, molasses or even chocolate. Baking soda starts reacting as soon as it comes in contact with liquid, so mixtures containing it should be baked immediately.

MAKING QUICK BREADS

By following our recipe directions to the letter – measuring carefully, mixing and handling doughs and batters as lightly and quickly as possible, and by baking at the temperature given – you will turn out a perfect quick bread every time.

Measuring: Ingredients should be measured accurately. For dry ingredients, use a graduated measuring cup set; for liquids, use glass or plastic measuring cups with a pouring lip. The same measuring spoons are used for both. Spoon unsifted flour into the measuring cup and level off lightly with the straight edge of a knife or metal spatula. Measure granulated white or brown sugar in the same way, but press regular brown sugar lightly into the cup so that it holds its shape when turned out.

Mixing: The secret of a perfect quick bread lies in the lightness and speed with which the ingredients are handled. To make a dough, first mix the dry ingredients well. Then cut in the shortening with a pastry blender or two knives used scissor-fashion until the mixture resembles coarse crumbs. Next, add the liquid and stir just enough to moisten dry ingredients and hold them together. When making batters, unless otherwise directed, stir in the liquid only until dry ingredients are moistened. Muffin and pancake batters will be lumpy but, if overmixed, the breads will be tough and won't

rise to full volume and muffins will have unattractive "tunnels." For some breads, however, ingredients should be well mixed. In each case, always be sure to follow the directions carefully.

Cutting in shortening: With a pastry blender or two knives used scissor-fashion, cut in shortening.

Kneading and rolling: A dough which is to be kneaded should be mixed just long enough to come away from the side of the bowl (it will still be sticky). Turn it out onto a lightly floured surface and knead it lightly – 6 to 8 strokes will be enough to make it manageable and knead ingredients. Roll it gently with a floured rolling pin. Biscuit dough doubles in height when baked; so for high biscuits, roll dough out ½ inch thick. For thin, crusty biscuits, roll it ¼ inch thick. After cutting out the first batch, press the trimmings together gently; reroll lightly. Don't knead again or the biscuits will be tough.

Testing for doneness: Biscuits are done when they are well risen and golden; muffins, when they are golden. To test loaves for doneness, pierce them deeply with a toothpick; it should come out clean and dry. For some very moist loaves, however, the recipe may describe the toothpick as "almost clean," meaning that there will be a few crumbs sticking to it when the bread is done. Turn pancakes when the little bubbles on top start to burst and the edges look dry; cook until underside is golden. If your waffle baker doesn't have a signal light, wait until it stops steaming, then lift the cover and wait a few seconds so waffles will be crisp. Using a slotted spoon, tongs or a two-tined fork, turn doughnuts as soon as they rise to the surface of the fat; don't pierce them or they will soak up fat. Fry until golden on both sides.

BAKING EQUIPMENT

Shiny metal cookie sheets and baking pans are best for browning biscuits and muffins. For loaves, use dull metal, anodized aluminum or glass loaf pans.

Always check pan sizes and if the dimensions are different from those called for, directions will have to be adapted – the muffin cups we use are generally 2½ inches in diameter, for example. If yours are different, fill them no more than two-thirds full (only half full for popovers). Wipe muffin pans clean of any spills and if any greased cups remain empty, half-fill them with water to protect them from burning. Loaf pans that are larger than specified will result in thin loaves. If they are smaller than required, fill them no more than two-thirds full and bake remaining batter in custard cups, filling them two-thirds full; bake 20 minutes or until done.

SERVING QUICK BREADS

Most quick breads are at their best fresh from the oven. Bring them to the table in an attractive baking dish, or serve in a basket or on a napkin-lined plate. Turn muffins out of their cups as soon as they are ready, or they will steam and become soggy. If they are not to be served at once, keep them warm by leaving them in their cups, slightly tipped to allow the steam to escape. Fruit and nut loaves, on the other hand, may be hard to slice soon after they come from the oven. Allowed to cool, then wrapped and left overnight, they often develop a mellower flavor and are easier to slice.

STORING AND REHEATING LEFTOVERS

Quick breads quickly turn stale. To retain moisture, store, tightly wrapped, at room temperature. Reheat them in one of the following ways to restore their fresh-baked flavor.

Wrap biscuits in foil and reheat in a 375°F. oven about 20 minutes. Or pour 2 tablespoons water into a large skillet and arrange biscuits on a rack in skillet. Cover and heat over low heat 8 to 10 minutes until hot. Biscuits can also be toasted. Split them, spread with butter or margarine and top with any of the following: shredded cheese, celery seed, poppy seed or caraway seed, cinnamon sugar, cheese spread, garlic spread, softened plain or flavored cream cheese or jelly. Then toast the biscuits in the broiler, split sides up, until they are hot and golden.

Wrap muffins in foil and reheat in a 400°F. oven about 15 minutes. Both muffins and corn bread can be toasted in the broiler like biscuits.

Place Boston Brown Bread, out of its can, in a double boiler or a colander set over a pan of water; cover and heat. Or, slice the bread, spread with butter or margarine and toast in broiler.

Reheat coffeecake either wrapped in foil, in a 400°F. oven for 20 to 30 minutes, or in a covered skillet as directed for biscuits (above).

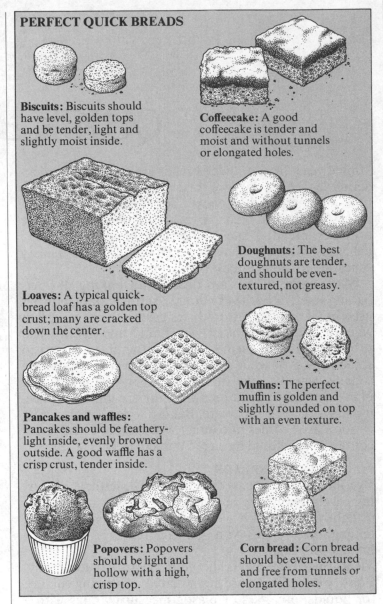

PERFECT QUICK BREADS

Biscuits: Biscuits should have level, golden tops and be tender, light and slightly moist inside.

Coffeecake: A good coffeecake is tender and moist and without tunnels or elongated holes.

Loaves: A typical quick-bread loaf has a golden top crust; many are cracked down the center.

Doughnuts: The best doughnuts are tender, and should be even-textured, not greasy.

Muffins: The perfect muffin is golden and slightly rounded on top with an even texture.

Pancakes and waffles: Pancakes should be feathery-light inside, evenly browned outside. A good waffle has a crisp crust, tender inside.

Popovers: Popovers should be light and hollow with a high, crisp top.

Corn bread: Corn bread should be even-textured and free from tunnels or elongated holes.

FREEZING QUICK BREADS

Biscuits and muffins are so quick to make that there is nothing to be gained by making them ahead for the freezer. Fruit loaves, nut loaves and coffeecakes are a different matter. To freeze them, cool completely, then wrap in foil, heavy-duty plastic wrap or freezerwrap. Freeze for up to 3 months; thaw wrapped at room temperature, about 1½ hours. If they are to be frosted, frost them after they are thawed.

If you plan to freeze waffles, bake them until only lightly browned. Cool, wrap and freeze as above; or freeze, unwrapped, on cookie sheets, then pack in heavy-duty plastic bags. Store in the freezer for 1 or 2 months. Thaw in a toaster at medium setting.

Doughnuts, packed in freezer cartons or in heavy-duty plastic bags, can be stored in the freezer for 4 to 6 months. Thaw, wrapped in foil, in a 400°F. oven.

Biscuits

Biscuits

**2 cups all-purpose
 flour
1 tablespoon double-
 acting baking
 powder
1 teaspoon salt
¼ cup shortening
¾ cup milk**

Color index
page 85

Begin 35 mins
ahead

18 biscuits

1 Preheat oven to 450°F. In large bowl with fork, mix flour, baking powder and salt. With pastry blender, cut in shortening until mixture resembles coarse crumbs.

2 Add milk and with fork, mix just until mixture forms soft dough that leaves side of bowl.

3 Turn onto lightly floured surface; knead 6 to 8 strokes to mix dough thoroughly.

4 Roll out the dough, ½ inch thick for high, fluffy biscuits, ¼ inch thick if you are making thin, crusty ones.

5 With floured 2-inch biscuit cutter, cut biscuits, using straight downward motion. Do not twist the cutter.

6 Place biscuits on ungreased cookie sheet, 1 inch apart for crusty biscuits, nearly touching for soft-sided ones.

7 Press dough trimmings together (don't knead); reroll and cut until all dough is used. Bake 12 to 15 minutes until golden.

BUTTERMILK BISCUITS: Prepare Biscuits (left) but use *buttermilk* in place of milk and use only *2 teaspoons baking powder*; add *¼ teaspoon baking soda* to flour mixture. (Makes 18 biscuits.)

SPEEDY BISCUITS: Prepare Biscuits (left) but after rolling dough, cut with knife into different shapes including squares, triangles or diamonds; bake biscuits as directed.

DROP BISCUITS: Prepare Biscuits (left) but increase milk to 1 cup. With fork, stir the dough until thoroughly mixed but do not knead it. Onto ungreased cookie sheet, drop heaping tablespoonfuls of the mixture 1 inch apart. Bake biscuits as directed. (Makes 20 biscuits.)

Mixing dough: With fork, stir the dough until it is thoroughly mixed; don't knead.

Shaping drop biscuits: Drop heaping table-spoonfuls of the mixture onto cookie sheet.

BLUEBERRY DROP BISCUITS: Grease cookie sheet. Make Drop Biscuits (above) but stir *1 cup fresh or frozen unsweetened blueberries* into flour mixture. Sprinkle tops of biscuits with *sugar* before placing in the oven. (Makes 20 biscuits.)

FRUITED DROP BISCUITS: Grease cookie sheet. Make Drop Biscuits (above) but add *¼ cup sugar* and *½ teaspoon ground cinnamon* to flour mixture. Add *one 8¾-ounce can fruit cocktail*, well drained, with milk or water. (Makes 20 biscuits.)

CUTTING OUT BISCUITS

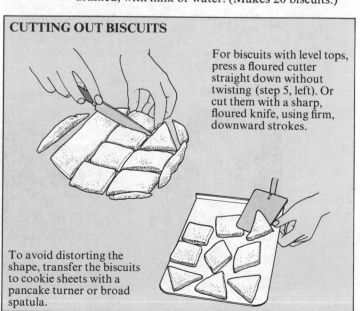

For biscuits with level tops, press a floured cutter straight down without twisting (step 5, left). Or cut them with a sharp, floured knife, using firm, downward strokes.

To avoid distorting the shape, transfer the biscuits to cookie sheets with a pancake turner or broad spatula.

Muffins

Muffins

*2 cups all-purpose
  flour
2 tablespoons sugar
1 tablespoon double-
  acting baking
  powder
1/2 teaspoon salt
1 egg
1 cup milk
1/4 cup salad oil*

Color index
page 85

Begin 35 mins
ahead

12 muffins

1 Preheat oven to 400°F. With pastry brush, grease well twelve 2½-inch muffin-pan cups.

2 In large bowl with fork, mix flour, sugar, baking powder and salt.

3 In small bowl with fork, beat egg slightly, then stir milk and salad oil into beaten egg.

4 Add egg mixture all at once to flour mixture and with spoon, stir just until flour is moistened. (Avoid overmixing which causes toughness; batter should be lumpy.)

5 Spoon batter into greased muffin-pan cups. Be sure to wipe pan clean of any spills.

6 Bake muffins 20 to 25 minutes until they are well risen and golden and toothpick inserted in center of one comes out clean and dry.

7 Immediately remove muffins from pan onto wire rack; serve at once, or keep warm by leaving in cups, slightly tipped to allow steam to escape.

ORANGE MUFFINS: Prepare Muffins (left) but use ¼ cup sugar; use only ¾ cup milk. Add *¼ cup orange juice* and *1 tablespoon finely shredded orange peel* to the egg mixture.

BLUEBERRY MUFFINS: Prepare Muffins (left) but use ½ cup sugar and add *¾ cup fresh or frozen unsweetened blueberries* with egg mixture.

WHOLE-WHEAT MUFFINS: Prepare Muffins (left) but use only ¾ cup flour; add *1 cup whole-wheat flour*. Increase sugar to ¼ cup and baking powder to 4 teaspoons.

Bran Muffins

*3 cups bran flakes
1¼ cups all-purpose flour
½ cup sugar
1¼ teaspoons baking
  soda
¼ teaspoon salt
1 egg
1 cup buttermilk
¼ cup salad oil*

Color index
page 85

Begin 45 mins
ahead

Eight 3-inch
muffins or
sixteen
2½-inch
muffins

1. Preheat oven to 400°F. Grease eight 3-inch muffin-pan cups or sixteen 2½-inch muffin-pan cups and set them aside.
2. In bowl, mix first 5 ingredients. In small bowl with fork, beat egg, buttermilk and salad oil until they are thoroughly blended.
3. Stir egg mixture into flour mixture just until flour is moistened. Spoon batter into muffin-pan cups. Bake 25 minutes for 3-inch cups, 15 minutes for 2½-inch cups, or until lightly browned. Immediately remove muffins from pan.

MAKING BUTTER SHAPES

Early in day or several days ahead, make the butter or margarine shapes below. Keep refrigerated in covered bowl of iced water until time to use; drain shapes thoroughly and arrange in a chilled serving dish.

Butter balls: In iced water, chill wooden butter paddles well. Cut firm ¼-pound bar of butter into ½-inch-thick pats. Place a pat between paddles; holding the bottom paddle steady, rotate top paddle to form ball. For cylinders, flatten balls and roll between paddles.

Butter curls: Let butter curler stand in hot water 10 minutes to heat. Pulling lightly, scrape curler over top of a ¼-pound bar of firm butter (if the bar is too cold, the curls will break). Reheat the curler briefly in hot water each time.

Doughnuts

Doughnut dough should be soft and shaped lightly and quickly or doughnuts will be tough. After mixing, refrigerate the dough at least 1 hour to make it easier to handle and remember to cut doughnuts close together to reduce the amount of rerolling.

Doughnuts can be plain or varied by adding such ingredients as chocolate, nuts or whole-wheat flour. Try them sprinkled with sugar or coated with a glaze.

You can fry doughnuts in either an electric skillet or deep-fat fryer, or in a large saucepan or Dutch oven using a deep-fry thermometer to check the temperature.

Doughnuts are best eaten the day they are made.

Old-fashioned Doughnuts

Color index
page 85

Begin 2½ hrs
ahead

24 doughnuts

**3 cups all-purpose
    flour
1 cup sugar
¾ cup buttermilk
2 eggs
2 tablespoons shortening
2 teaspoons double-acting
    baking powder
1 teaspoon baking soda
1 teaspoon salt
½ teaspoon ground
    nutmeg
salad oil
confectioners' sugar or
    Nutmeg Sugar (right)**

1 Into large bowl, measure 1½ cups flour and remaining ingredients except salad oil and confectioners' sugar; with mixer at low speed, beat just until smooth, constantly scraping bowl. At medium speed, beat 1 minute, constantly scraping bowl. Stir in remaining flour to make soft dough. Refrigerate at least 1 hour to make it easier to handle.

2 On well-floured surface with floured rolling pin, roll dough ½ inch thick.

3 With floured doughnut cutter, cut out doughnuts. Reroll and cut trimmings until all the dough is used.

4 In deep-fat fryer, heat 3 or 4 inches salad oil to 370°F. Fry 4 or 5 rings at a time. Turn with a pancake turner as they rise to surface then turn often until golden brown.

5 Lift them from fat with slotted spoon and drain on paper towels. Serve as is or sprinkle with confectioners' sugar or shake in Nutmeg Sugar while still warm.

NUTMEG SUGAR: In paper bag, combine *1 cup sugar* and *¾ teaspoon ground nutmeg;* shake warm doughnuts in mixture, a few at a time, to coat well.

DOUGHNUT "HOLES": Use centers cut from doughnuts; or, using small biscuit cutter, cut all dough into small circles. Fry as directed (left). Toss in *sugar* or shake in Nutmeg Sugar (above).

CHOCOLATE DOUGHNUTS: In double boiler over hot, not boiling, water, melt *1½ squares unsweetened chocolate*. Prepare dough (left) but use 1¼ cups sugar and omit nutmeg; add melted chocolate and *1 teaspoon vanilla extract* with milk. Roll, cut and fry; cool. Serve doughnuts as is or, if you like, sprinkle doughnuts with confectioners' sugar.

NUTTED DOUGHNUTS: Prepare dough (left) but add *½ cup chopped California walnuts* with remaining flour.

WHOLE-WHEAT DOUGHNUTS: Prepare as left but substitute *1½ cups whole-wheat flour* for 1½ cups of the all-purpose flour, stirring it in after beating dough 1 minute. Roll dough about ⅜ inch thick. Fry. Make glaze: In small bowl with fork, stir *½ cup honey* with *⅔ cup confectioners' sugar* thoroughly until glaze is smoothly blended. Spread over warm Whole-Wheat Doughnuts.

Beignets

Color index
page 85

Begin 45 mins
ahead

8 servings

**1 cup water
½ cup butter or
    margarine
1 teaspoon sugar
¼ teaspoon salt
1 cup all-purpose flour
4 eggs**

**1 teaspoon vanilla
    extract
salad oil
confectioners' sugar
Cinnamon-Maple Syrup
    (below)**

1. In 2-quart saucepan over medium heat, heat water, butter or margarine, sugar and salt until butter melts and mixture boils.

2. Remove pan from heat and add flour all at once. With wooden spoon, vigorously stir until the ingredients are thoroughly combined and mixture leaves side of pan and forms a ball.

3. Add eggs, one at a time, beating thoroughly after each addition until the mixture is smooth and glossy. Add vanilla.

4. Meanwhile, in another 2-quart saucepan over medium heat, heat about 1½ inches salad oil to 375°F. on deep-fat thermometer, or heat oil in deep-fat fryer set at 375°F. Drop heaping teaspoonfuls of dough into hot oil and fry beignets, a few at a time, until golden. Drain on paper towels; keep warm.

5. To serve: Sprinkle warm beignets lightly with some confectioners' sugar. Serve with Cinnamon-Maple Syrup poured over them or pass syrup separately in a sauce boat.

CINNAMON-MAPLE SYRUP: In 1-quart saucepan over low heat, heat *one 12-ounce bottle maple-flavored syrup* and *2 tablespoons cinnamon red hot candies* until the candies are completely melted, stirring the mixture occasionally.

Pancakes and waffles

Basic pancake and waffle recipes can be varied by adding whole-wheat flour, nuts, fruit or other ingredients. Serve with butter or margarine and your choice of syrup, honey, preserves or confectioners' sugar.

Remember that you can thin a batter which has become too thick while standing with extra milk. Refrigerate any leftover batter to use the next day.

If you are using an electric griddle, skillet or waffle baker, preheat it following manufacturer's directions. Test a non-automatic model by sprinkling with a few drops of water; drops should sizzle.

Pancakes

1¼ cups all-purpose flour
2 tablespoons sugar
2 teaspoons double-
*   acting baking powder*
¾ teaspoon salt
1 egg
1⅓ cups milk (for
*   thicker pancakes, use*
*   only 1 cup milk)*
salad oil
butter or margarine
maple or maple-flavor
*   syrup, honey,*
*   preserves, marmalade,*
*   apple butter as desired*

Color index
page 84

Begin 30 mins
ahead

Twelve 4-inch
pancakes
or 8 thick
pancakes

1 In large bowl, mix first 4 ingredients. In small bowl, beat egg slightly; stir in milk and 3 tablespoons oil; add to flour mixture and stir just until flour is moistened.

2 Heat skillet or griddle over medium-high heat until drop of water sizzles. Brush lightly with oil.

3 Pour batter by scant ¼ cupfuls onto hot skillet or griddle, making a few pancakes at a time.

4 Cook until bubbly and bubbles burst; edges will look dry. With pancake turner, turn and cook until underside is golden.

5 Place on heated platter; keep warm. Repeat, brushing skillet with more oil, if needed. Serve with butter and syrup.

Potato Pancakes

cold water
4 large potatoes
*   (3 pounds), peeled*
*   and rinsed*
1 small onion, peeled
2 eggs
⅓ cup all-purpose flour
2 teaspoons salt
⅛ teaspoon pepper
⅓ cup salad oil
parsley sprigs for
*   garnish*

Color index
page 84

Begin 1¼ hrs
ahead

16 pancakes

1 Into large bowl half filled with cold water, coarsely shred potatoes and small onion.

2 In colander lined with clean towel or cheese-cloth, drain shredded potatoes and onion.

3 Wrap potatoes and onion in towel; squeeze towel to remove as much water as possible.

4 In same large bowl, beat eggs; add the shredded potatoes and onion, flour, salt and pepper and toss together until well mixed.

5 In 12-inch skillet over medium heat, in hot salad oil, drop mixture by scant ¼ cupfuls into 4 mounds.

6 With pancake turner, flatten each mound to make a 4-inch pancake. Cook until golden brown on one side, about 4 minutes; turn pancake and brown other side.

7 Remove to paper-towel-lined cookie sheet to drain; keep warm. Repeat to make about 12 more pancakes, stirring mixture occasionally; garnish with parsley sprigs.

Popovers

Buttermilk Waffles

1³/₄ cups all-purpose flour
1 teaspoon double-acting
 baking powder
1 teaspoon baking soda
¹/₂ teaspoon salt
2 cups buttermilk
¹/₃ cup salad oil
3 eggs

Color index
page 84

Begin 30 mins
ahead

4 cups batter
or 5 waffles

1 Preheat waffle baker as manufacturer directs. In large bowl with whisk, mix flour, baking powder, baking soda and salt.

2 Add buttermilk, salad oil and eggs to flour mixture and beat until thoroughly blended.

3 Pour batter into center of lower half of baker until it spreads to about 1 inch from edges.

4 Cover and bake as manufacturer directs; do not lift the cover during baking time.

5 Loosen baked waffle carefully with fork. Reheat baker before pouring next waffle.

PANCAKE AND WAFFLE VARIATIONS

BUCKWHEAT PANCAKES: Prepare Pancakes (opposite) but substitute *¹/₂ cup buckwheat flour* for ¹/₂ cup all-purpose flour.

SILVER DOLLAR PANCAKES: Prepare Pancakes (opposite) but pour batter by measuring tablespoonfuls onto hot griddle. (Color index, page 84; makes twenty-four 2-inch pancakes.)

SWEET-MILK WAFFLES: Prepare Buttermilk Waffles (above) but substitute *regular milk* for buttermilk; use 1 tablespoon baking powder and omit the baking soda.

OTHERS: To pancake or waffle batter, add drained canned whole-kernel corn, drained canned crushed pineapple, chopped nuts, flaked coconut, raisins or currants, or fresh fruit, as desired.

Giant Popovers

6 eggs
2 cups milk
6 tablespoons butter or
 margarine,
 melted
2 cups all-purpose
 flour
1 teaspoon salt
Butter Curls or Balls
 (page 424)

Color index
page 85

Begin 1¹/₂ hrs
ahead

8 popovers

1 Preheat oven to 375°F. Grease 8 deep 7-ounce pottery custard cups.

2 Set greased custard cups in jelly-roll pan for easier handling.

3 In large bowl with mixer at low speed, beat eggs until frothy; beat in milk and butter.

4 At low speed, beat flour and salt into egg, milk and butter mixture.

5 Pour about ³/₄ cup batter into each of 8 greased custard cups.

6 Bake 1 hour; make slit in each to let out steam; bake 10 minutes more.

7 Immediately remove from cups. Serve hot with Butter Curls or Balls.

REGULAR POPOVERS: Prepare as above but grease eight 6-ounce custard cups and use *3 eggs, 1 cup milk, 3 tablespoons melted butter, 1 cup all-purpose flour* and *¹/₂ teaspoon salt;* bake 50 minutes before cutting slit in each popover to allow steam to escape. (Makes 8 popovers.)

Loaves

Nut Bread

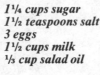

3 cups all-purpose flour
1½ cups coarsely chopped California walnuts
5 teaspoons double-acting baking powder

1¼ cups sugar
1½ teaspoons salt
3 eggs
1½ cups milk
⅓ cup salad oil

Color index page 84

Begin day ahead

1 loaf

1 Preheat oven to 350°F. Grease 9″ by 5″ loaf pan. In large bowl with fork, mix the flour and next 4 ingredients.

2 In small bowl, beat eggs slightly; stir in milk and salad oil; stir this mixture into flour mixture just until flour is moistened.

3 Pour batter into pan; bake 1 hour and 20 minutes or until bread pulls away from sides of pan.

4 Cool in pan on wire rack 10 minutes then remove from pan and cool completely on rack.

Lemon Loaf

1 medium lemon
2¼ cups all-purpose flour
1½ teaspoons double-acting baking powder
¾ teaspoon salt

sugar
¾ cup butter or margarine
3 eggs
¾ cup milk

Color index page 84

Begin 2 hrs or up to 3 days ahead

1 loaf

1. Preheat oven to 350°F. From lemon, grate 1 tablespoon peel and squeeze 4½ teaspoons lemon juice; set aside. Grease 9″ by 5″ loaf pan.
2. In large bowl with fork, mix flour, baking powder, salt and 1½ cups sugar. With pastry blender or 2 knives used scissor-fashion, cut in butter until mixture resembles coarse crumbs. Stir in peel.
3. In small bowl with fork, beat eggs slightly and stir in milk; then stir this mixture into flour mixture just until flour is moistened.
4. Spoon into pan. Bake 1¼ hours. Cool in pan on wire rack 10 minutes; remove from pan.
5. In 1-quart saucepan over medium-high heat, heat lemon juice and 2 tablespoons sugar to boiling. Cook, stirring, until slightly thickened, about 5 minutes. With pastry brush, brush sugar mixture evenly over top of bread. Serve warm; or cool loaf completely to serve later.

Corn Bread

1 cup all-purpose flour
¾ cup cornmeal
2 to 4 tablespoons sugar
1 tablespoon double-acting baking powder
1 teaspoon salt

1 egg
⅔ cup milk
⅓ cup butter or margarine, melted, or salad oil

Color index page 84

Begin 35 mins ahead

9 servings

1 Preheat oven to 425°F. Grease 8″ by 8″ baking pan. In medium bowl with fork, mix together flour, cornmeal, sugar, baking powder and salt.

2 In small bowl with fork, beat together egg, milk and butter or margarine and pour egg mixture all at once into flour mixture.

3 Stir just until flour is moistened and quickly pour batter into the prepared baking pan.

4 Spread batter evenly and bake 25 minutes or until golden. Cut into squares to serve.

 CORN-BREAD RING: Grease a 5½-cup ring mold. Prepare as above but spoon batter into ring mold. Bake about 25 minutes; invert from mold onto serving platter. Slice and serve as bread or fill center with creamed ham, chicken, shrimp or favorite curry mixture and serve as main dish for 8. (Makes 1 corn-bread ring.)

 CORN MUFFINS: Grease twelve 2½-inch muffin-pan cups. Prepare batter as above, then spoon into greased cups, filling each cup two-thirds full. Bake muffins about 20 minutes. (Color index, page 85; makes 12 muffins.)

 BLUEBERRY CORN MUFFINS: Grease sixteen 2½-inch muffin-pan cups. Prepare as above but, to flour mixture, add *1 cup fresh or frozen unsweetened blueberries*. Spoon batter into greased muffin-pan cups, filling each two-thirds full. Bake 20 minutes. (Makes 16 muffins.)

 CORN STICKS: Grease 14 corn-stick molds very well with *salad oil*. Prepare batter as above; spoon batter into molds, filling each mold three-fourths full. Bake corn stick for 15 to 20 minutes. (Color index, page 84; makes 14 corn sticks.)

Chocolate Date-Nut Loaf

Color index
page 84

Begin day
ahead

1 loaf

¾ cup boiling water
1 cup sliced pitted dates
1 6-ounce package semi-
  sweet-chocolate
  pieces
¼ cup butter
1 egg
¾ cup milk
1 teaspoon vanilla
  extract

2½ cups all-purpose flour
1 cup coarsely chopped
  California walnuts or
  pecans
⅓ cup sugar
1½ teaspoons salt
1 teaspoon double-acting
  baking powder
1 teaspoon baking soda

1. Preheat oven to 350°F. Grease 9" by 5" loaf pan. In small bowl, pour boiling water over dates. In double boiler, over hot, not boiling, water, melt chocolate with butter. In small bowl with fork, beat egg, milk and vanilla just until mixed.
2. In large bowl with spoon, mix flour and next 5 ingredients; add dates and liquid, chocolate and milk mixtures; mix just until blended.
3. Pour mixture into loaf pan. Bake 1 hour and 10 minutes. Cool in pan on wire rack 10 minutes; remove from pan; cool on rack.

Irish Soda Bread

Color index
page 83

Begin 5 hrs
ahead

1 loaf

4 cups all-purpose flour
3 tablespoons sugar
1 tablespoon double-
  acting baking powder
1 teaspoon salt
¾ teaspoon baking soda
6 tablespoons butter or
  margarine

1½ cups dark seedless
  raisins
1 tablespoon caraway
  seed
2 eggs
1½ cups buttermilk

1. Preheat oven to 350°F. Grease 2-quart round casserole. In large bowl with fork, mix flour and next 4 ingredients. With pastry blender, cut in butter until mixture resembles coarse crumbs; stir in raisins and caraway seed.
2. In small bowl with fork, beat eggs slightly; remove 1 tablespoon and reserve. Stir buttermilk into remaining egg; stir into flour mixture just until flour is moistened (dough will be sticky).
3. Turn dough onto well-floured surface; knead about 10 strokes to mix thoroughly. Shape into a ball; place in casserole. In center of ball, cut 4-inch cross ¼ inch deep. Brush dough with reserved egg.
4. Bake about 1 hour and 20 minutes. Cool in casserole on wire rack 10 minutes; remove from casserole and cool completely on rack.

Shaping the bread: Shape dough into a ball; place in greased casserole.

Making the cross: With sharp knife, carefully cut 4-inch cross ¼ inch deep.

Boston Brown Bread

Color index
page 85

Begin 2¼ hrs
ahead

2 small loaves

1 cup whole-wheat flour
1 cup rye flour
1 cup cornmeal
1½ teaspoons baking
  soda
1½ teaspoons salt
2 cups buttermilk
¾ cup dark molasses
1 cup dark seedless
  raisins (optional)

1 Line 2 tall 1-pound coffee cans with foil (it should stand 1 inch above top); cut foil for lids; grease.

2 Into large bowl, measure all ingredients; with spoon, mix well.

3 Pour batter into cans; cover with foil and tie foil to can with string.

4 Place cans on rack in deep saucepot; add boiling water to come halfway up sides of cans. Cover saucepot.

5 Over low heat, simmer 2 hours. When tooth-pick inserted in center comes out almost clean, invert onto wire rack to cool.

Zucchini Bread

Color index
page 83

Begin 2 hrs
or up to
3 days ahead

2 loaves

3 cups all-purpose flour
1½ cups sugar
1 cup California walnuts,
  chopped
4½ teaspoons double-
  acting baking powder

1 teaspoon salt
4 eggs
⅔ cup salad oil
2 cups grated zucchini
2 teaspoons grated lemon
  peel

1. Preheat oven to 350°F. Grease two 8½" by 4½" loaf pans. In large bowl with fork, mix flour, sugar, walnuts, baking powder and salt.
2. In medium bowl with fork, beat eggs slightly; stir in salad oil, zucchini and lemon peel.
3. Stir liquid mixture into flour mixture just until flour is moistened; spread evenly in pans.
4. Bake bread 1 hour. Cool in pans on wire racks 10 minutes; remove from pans. Serve warm or cold.

Coffeecakes

Cherry Coffeecake

all-purpose flour
sugar
1 teaspoon double-acting baking powder
¼ teaspoon baking soda
¼ teaspoon salt
10 tablespoons butter, melted
½ cup milk
1 egg
1 teaspoon vanilla extract
¼ teaspoon lemon extract
1 21- or 22-ounce can cherry-pie filling

Color index page 85

Begin 2 hrs ahead

9 servings

1 Preheat oven to 350°F. Grease and flour 9″ by 9″ baking pan. In large bowl with fork, mix 1¼ cups flour, ½ cup sugar, baking powder, baking soda and salt.

2 To flour mixture, add ½ cup melted butter, milk, egg and vanilla.

3 With spoon, beat until well mixed then pour batter evenly into greased and floured baking pan.

4 In small bowl with fork, combine ½ cup flour, ¼ cup sugar and remaining 2 tablespoons butter until mixture resembles coarse crumbs.

5 Sprinkle half of crumb mixture evenly over top of batter in pan.

6 Stir lemon extract into cherry-pie filling; then spread pie-filling mixture on crumb mixture in pan.

7 Sprinkle with rest of crumb mixture. Bake 1 hour or until top is golden. Cut into squares.

Peach-filled Coffeecake

1½ cups all-purpose flour
1 cup sugar
2 teaspoons double-acting baking powder
2 teaspoons grated lemon peel
⅛ teaspoon salt
1 cup butter or margarine, softened
4 eggs
1 29-ounce can sliced cling peaches, well drained
Topping (below)

Color index page 85

Begin 1½ hrs ahead

12 servings

1. Preheat oven to 350°F. Grease 13″ by 9″ baking pan. In large bowl with mixer at low speed, beat first 7 ingredients until well mixed, constantly scraping bowl. Increase speed to high; beat 4 minutes, occasionally scraping bowl.
2. Spread batter evenly in baking pan. Arrange peaches on top of batter. Sprinkle with Topping. Bake 45 to 50 minutes until light golden and toothpick inserted in center comes out clean.

TOPPING: In 1-quart saucepan over medium heat, melt ½ cup butter or margarine; remove from heat. Stir in **1 cup all-purpose flour, ¼ cup sugar** and **1 tablespoon grated lemon peel** to form a soft dough.

Sour-Cream Coffeecake

½ cup finely chopped California walnuts
1 teaspoon ground cinnamon
sugar
½ cup butter or margarine
2 cups all-purpose flour
1 cup sour cream
2 eggs
1 teaspoon double-acting baking powder
1 teaspoon baking soda
1 teaspoon vanilla extract

Color index page 85

Begin 2 hrs or day ahead

8 to 10 servings

1. In small bowl, combine nuts, cinnamon and ½ cup sugar; set aside. Preheat oven to 350°F. Grease 9-inch tube pan.
2. In large bowl with mixer at medium speed, beat 1 cup sugar with butter until light and fluffy. Add remaining ingredients; beat at low speed until blended, constantly scraping bowl. At medium speed, beat 3 minutes, occasionally scraping bowl.
3. Spread half of batter in pan; sprinkle with half of nut mixture; repeat layers. Bake 60 to 65 minutes until cake pulls away from side of pan. Cool in pan on wire rack 10 minutes; loosen inside edge; invert from pan onto rack to cool; serve warm or cold.

Assembling batter and nut mixtures: Spread half of batter in pan; sprinkle with half of nut mixture. Repeat.

Cooling the cake: Cool in pan on rack 10 minutes then loosen inside edge and invert onto rack.

Flat breads

Corn Tortillas

Color index page 109

Begin 45 mins ahead

12 tortillas

2 cups instant corn masa (specially treated, finely ground corn sold in Mexican and gourmet foodstores)
½ teaspoon salt
about 1 cup warm water

1 In medium bowl with fork, stir together instant corn masa and salt. Gradually add water to corn masa mixture, mixing lightly with fork until dough is just moist enough to hold together. If necessary, add a little more water, a tablespoon at a time.

2 With hands, gather dough into a ball; knead a few times in bowl until smooth.

3 Divide the dough into 12 pieces then, with hands, shape each piece into a small ball. Keep dough covered with plastic wrap while you are shaping into tortillas.

4 To shape: Flatten one ball to about ¼-inch thickness; place between sheets of waxed paper. With rolling pin, roll into 6-inch circle. Leave in paper until all are rolled.

5 Remove top sheet of paper and invert the tortilla onto hot, ungreased 8-inch skillet over medium heat. Peel off bottom sheet. Cook about 30 seconds.

6 Turn; press gently with pancake turner until bubbles form in tortilla (this will make a lighter tortilla). Turn again; cook 1 minute longer or until bottom of tortilla has small brown specks.

7 Remove to foil and wrap to keep warm, stacking tortillas as each is made. Serve warm with Chili con Carne (page 209); or use in recipes for Tacos (page 456) or Tostada Appetizers (page 118).

Poori

Color index page 85

Begin 1¾ hrs ahead

20 poori

(fried Indian bread)

1 cup all-purpose flour
1 cup whole-wheat flour
1 teaspoon salt
½ cup water
salad oil

1. In medium bowl, stir flours, salt, water and 1½ teaspoons salad oil until thoroughly blended (the mixture will be very dry).

2. In bowl, knead dough until it holds together and is smooth, about 10 minutes. Shape into ball; place in greased bowl, turning to grease top. Cover with plastic wrap; let rest 10 minutes.

3. Meanwhile, in electric skillet, heat 1 inch salad oil to 400°F. With hands, shape dough into 20 balls. On lightly floured surface with lightly floured rolling pin, roll each ball into paper-thin circle, 4 inches in diameter (edges will be ragged). Keep remaining dough and finished circles covered with plastic wrap to keep them from drying out.

4. Drop circles, one at a time, into hot oil. With back of slotted spoon, gently hold circle under surface of oil until it puffs up, about 10 seconds. Fry about 20 seconds more, turning once. With slotted spoon, remove poori to paper towels; drain. Serve warm or store and reheat to serve later.

5. *To reheat:* Preheat oven to 325°F. Wrap poori in foil in one layer; heat 5 minutes (they will be flat).

Onion Thins

Color index page 85

Begin 1½ hrs or up to 3 days ahead

32 crackers or 16 servings

2 cups all-purpose flour
½ cup cornmeal
2 tablespoons sugar
½ teaspoon baking soda
½ teaspoon salt
¼ cup butter or margarine
about ½ cup cold water
2 tablespoons cider vinegar
⅓ cup instant minced onion

1. In large bowl with fork, stir flour, cornmeal, sugar, baking soda and salt. With pastry blender or 2 knives used scissor-fashion, cut in butter or margarine until mixture resembles coarse crumbs. Stir water and vinegar into mixture, mixing lightly with fork until pastry is just moist enough to hold together. If necessary, gradually add more water, a tablespoon at a time.

2. Shape dough into a ball; knead a few times in bowl until well mixed; divide into 32 pieces; shape each into a ball. Keep dough covered with plastic wrap while rolling each piece.

3. Preheat oven to 375°F. On floured board with floured rolling pin, roll one piece of dough into paper-thin 4½-inch circle (edges may be ragged). Sprinkle circle with ½ teaspoon instant minced onion. With rolling pin, roll again to press onion into dough. With pancake turner, remove circle to ungreased cookie sheet. Repeat until enough dough pieces are rolled to fill sheet.

4. Bake circles 8 to 10 minutes until golden brown. Cool on wire rack. Repeat with remaining dough pieces. Store in tightly covered container or wrapped in plastic wrap. Serve Onion Thins as an accompaniment to salads or entrees.

YEAST BREADS

The delicious aroma of fresh bread is a pleasure many families are rediscovering. It is not difficult to make a perfect loaf, if you keep the following points in mind.

Do not add ingredients to speed up the yeast, or increase the amount of flour, sweetener or salt. These additions will make the bread heavier. All ingredients should be at room temperature.

Use baking pans of the proper size. If they are too small, the dough will spill over the sides; if they are too large, the bread will not rise sufficiently above the sides.

INGREDIENTS
Yeast: Yeast, which makes dough rise, is available in active dry granule form or as fresh (compressed) cakes. One package of active dry yeast equals one 0.6-ounce cake of fresh yeast. In our recipes only dry yeast is used. Store it in a cool, dry place and it will stay fresh and retain its leavening power until the expiration date stamped on the package. In all our recipes the yeast should be mixed with some of the dry ingredients and dissolved later when the liquid is added.

Flour: The texture of a yeast bread largely depends on the gluten in the flour. The gluten content varies from flour to flour: "hard" wheat flour is richer in gluten than "soft" flour, and will give a better rise and more open, even-textured loaf; whole-wheat flour has less gluten than white flour, and unless a proportion of white is added, the loaf will be heavy and close-textured. Some flours, such as soy, rice and corn, contain no gluten and can only be used in combination with white flour. Good Housekeeping yeast breads are made with all-purpose flour which is a blend of hard and soft wheats.

Liquid: Water or milk (whole, skimmed, evaporated or reconstituted nonfat dry), or a combination of the two are most often used for breads. Water makes the crust crisp, while milk produces a soft crust and a creamy-white crumb. The liquid must be at the correct temperature: if it is too hot, it will kill the yeast; if it is too cold, the dough will take longer to rise.

Sugar: A little sugar helps the yeast to grow and produce gas to leaven the dough but extra sugar retards the action of the yeast, so sweet doughs take longer to rise than plain ones. Sugar also adds flavor and makes the crust brown. Brown sugar, molasses and honey will give good results when used as the recipe directs.

Salt: Salt adds and enhances flavor. It also controls the growth of the yeast, making the dough or batter rise more slowly, so it is important not to add too much.

Fat: Many different kinds of fat – butter, margarine, shortening, salad oil or lard – can be added to improve flavor and make the dough stretch more easily. The resulting bread has a tender crumb and stays soft longer.

Egg: Eggs are added to a yeast dough for their flavor and color. They make it richer and more nutritious, soften the crust and give the interior a fine crumb.

Other ingredients: Small quantities of herbs, seeds, fruit and nuts may be added to a dough for their flavor and texture, and to increase its food value; however, they may slow the rising time.

MAKING A YEAST DOUGH
Dissolving dry yeast: Mix active dry yeast with some of the dry ingredients, then gradually add liquid heated to 120° to 130°F. (the temperature of very hot tap water). Beat the batter for about 2 minutes, either in an electric mixer at medium speed or with a wooden spoon.

Adding flour to make a dough: Add only enough flour to make a dough that can be handled. Additional flour will be worked in during kneading. On very humid days, the dough may need more flour than the recipe indicates.

KNEADING
Lightly sprinkle a board or countertop with flour and rub some onto your hands. If the dough remains sticky, a little more flour may be added while kneading. Follow the folding, rolling and turning instructions set out below. The duration of kneading will depend on the development of gluten during beating, the stickiness of the dough and the strength with which you knead.

Kneading the dough: Shape the dough into a ball and, on a lightly floured surface, fold it toward you.

Using the heels of your hands, push it away with a rolling motion and give the dough a quarter turn.

Continue kneading 8 to 10 minutes until dough is smooth and elastic and doesn't stick, with little blisters under surface.

YEAST BREADS
Everyday breads

In this section, we give recipes for conventional breads shaped as loaves, rounds or rolls which can be served with meals every day. Today's breadmaking techniques are easily acquired, yet thanks to modern ingredients and equipment, give the same good flavor, texture and appearance as older, more complicated methods.

All bread tastes best fresh from the oven. However, if it has gone slightly stale, you can "refresh" it by wrapping it in foil and putting it in a 375°F. oven for 15 minutes. For a crisp crust, unwrap it and put it back in the oven for 5 minutes more.

Here are ways to glaze bread before baking. For a dark, shiny glaze, brush on 1 beaten egg yolk. For a light shiny glaze, beat the whole egg or brush on melted butter or margarine. For shine with no color, brush on 1 egg white beaten with 1 tablespoon water.

To slice fresh bread, use a sharp knife or serrated knife and slice with a sawing motion.

White Bread

3 tablespoons sugar
2 teaspoons salt
1 package active dry yeast
5½ to 6½ cups all-purpose flour
2 cups milk
butter or margarine

Color index page 78

Begin 4 hrs ahead

2 loaves

1 In large bowl, combine sugar, salt, yeast and 2 cups flour. In 2-quart saucepan over low heat, heat milk and 3 tablespoons butter until very warm (120° to 130°F.).

2 With mixer at low speed, gradually beat liquid into dry ingredients, until just blended. Increase speed to medium; beat 2 minutes, occasionally scraping bowl.

3 Beat in ¾ cup flour or enough to make a thick batter; continue beating 2 minutes, scraping bowl often. With spoon, stir in enough flour (about 3 cups) to make soft dough.

4 On floured surface, knead dough until elastic, about 10 minutes. Shape into ball; turn over in greased bowl to grease top. Cover; let rise until doubled, about 1 hour.

5 Punch down dough by pushing fist into center and pulling in edges. Transfer to a lightly floured surface; cut in half; cover with bowl; let dough rest 15 minutes.

6 Grease two 9" by 5" loaf pans. Roll each dough half into 12" by 8" rectangle. Shape into loaf (page 433); place, seam side down, in loaf pan.

7 Cover with a towel; let dough rise in a warm place (80° to 85°F.), away from draft, until doubled (dough will double in about 1 hour).

8 Preheat oven to 400°F. If liked, brush loaves with 2 tablespoons melted butter. Bake 25 to 30 minutes until loaves test done Remove from pans; cool.

Color index page 78

Begin 4½ hrs ahead

2 loaves

Whole-Wheat Bread

3 tablespoons sugar
4 teaspoons salt
2 packages active dry yeast
4 cups whole-wheat flour

3 to 3½ cups all-purpose flour
2¼ cups milk
⅓ cup butter or margarine
⅓ cup molasses

1. In large bowl, combine sugar, salt, yeast, 2 cups whole-wheat flour and 1 cup all-purpose flour. In 2-quart saucepan over low heat, heat milk, butter or margarine and molasses until very warm (120° to 130°F.). (Butter does not need to melt completely.)
2. With mixer at low speed, gradually beat liquid into dry ingredients. Increase speed to medium; beat 2 minutes, occasionally scraping bowl with rubber spatula. Beat in ½ cup whole-wheat flour and ½ cup all-purpose flour or enough to make a thick batter; continue beating 2 minutes, occasionally scraping bowl with rubber spatula.
3. With spoon, stir in 1½ cups whole-wheat and additional all-purpose flour (about 1½ cups) to make a soft dough.
4. Turn dough onto lightly floured surface and knead until smooth and elastic, about 10 minutes. Shape dough into ball and place in greased large bowl, turning dough to grease top. Cover with towel; let rise in warm, draft-free place (80° to 85°F.), until doubled, about 1 hour.
5. Punch down dough; turn onto lightly floured surface; cut in half; cover with bowl; let dough halves rest 15 minutes for easier shaping. Grease 2 9" by 5" loaf pans.
6. With lightly floured rolling pin, roll one dough half into a 12" by 8" rectangle. Starting at a narrow end, roll dough up tightly and pinch the edge with your fingers. Seal ends by pressing them with the sides of your hands and fold them under. Place the roll, seam side down, in loaf pan.
7. Repeat step 6 with remaining dough. Cover loaves with towel; let rise in warm place, away from draft, until loaves are doubled, about 1 hour.
8. Preheat oven to 400°F. Bake loaves 30 to 35 minutes or until golden and loaves sound hollow when top is tapped lightly with fingers. Remove from pans immediately so bottoms don't become soggy, and cool on wire racks.

RISING

Cover the dough with a clean cloth, while you wash, dry and lightly grease the mixing bowl. Replace dough in mixing bowl, smooth side (top) down, and turn to lightly grease the top and prevent it drying out. Cover the bowl with a towel and put in a draft-free place at a temperature of 80° to 85°F. In a cool kitchen, place bowl (1) in an unheated oven with a large pan of hot water on the shelf below, replenishing water as it cools; or (2) on a wire rack set over a large pan filled two-thirds full with hot water; or (3) in a deep pan of warm, not hot, water; or (4) near, but not on, a warm range or radiator. Let the dough rise until doubled in bulk and test as below.

Testing the rising: The dough is doubled when two fingertips pressed ½ inch into it leave dents that remain. If dents fill in quickly, let rise 15 minutes longer and test again. A batter should look light and bubbly, with an uneven, slightly rounded top.

PUNCHING OR STIRRING DOWN

When a dough has doubled in bulk it is punched down by hand; batters are stirred down. To punch down dough, push your fist deep into the center of the dough, pull edges to the center and turn the dough over.

Stir batter with a wooden spoon until it has fallen to about its original size.

RESTING

Dough is easier to handle if it is allowed to rest before shaping. Turn it out on a lightly floured surface, divide pieces as required and put it aside for 10 to 15 minutes, covered with the bowl or a towel.

SHAPING BREAD

For a round loaf, hold ball of dough and pull sides under until ball is evenly rounded and smooth on top. Place on a cookie sheet; flatten slightly. For a loaf shape, follow the directions set out below.

Shaping a loaf: With a lightly floured rolling pin, roll dough into a rectangle.

Starting at narrow end, roll dough up tightly and pinch the edge with your fingers to seal.

Seal ends by pressing with the sides of your hands; fold under. Place roll, seam side down, in loaf pan.

After shaping, cover the loaf with a towel and leave in a warm, draft-free place until it has redoubled and a finger pressed into it lightly leaves a dent.

BAKING

Place loaf pans on the middle shelf of a preheated oven, 2 inches apart so heat circulates. If baking on 2 shelves, stagger pans. If tops brown too quickly, cover loosely with foil. Test bread after the minimum specified baking time. If it is not ready, return it to the oven; retest the bread a few minutes later.

Testing for doneness: Tap top of loaf lightly with your fingertips. If it sounds hollow and is well browned on top, the bread is ready.

Cooling: Remove loaves from pans (or cookie sheet) immediately so bottoms don't become soggy; cool on wire racks away from drafts.

HIGH ALTITUDE BAKING

Yeast doughs rise faster and higher at high altitudes. At 5,000 feet use only half the yeast specified. Punch down the dough as soon as it tests doubled, even if it does not look as if it has doubled in size.

THE PERFECT LOAF

Top is evenly rounded and well browned.

Nuts, raisins and similar ingredients are evenly dispersed throughout the loaf.

Interior is soft and moist, and easily pulled apart.

Bread has an even texture; holes are small and uniform in size from top to bottom.

Color of bread is uniform.

STORING BREAD

To keep bread fresh, wrap each cooled loaf in foil or plastic wrap, or seal in a plastic bag; store in a cool, dry cupboard or bread box. Bread may be stored in the refrigerator but it goes stale more quickly.

Bread keeps in the freezer for up to 3 months if tightly wrapped in foil, heavy-duty plastic wrap or freezer wrap, or if sealed in plastic bags. Always make sure to press out as much air as possible.

Slices of frozen bread can be toasted without thawing. To thaw a loaf, leave it at room temperature for 2 to 3 hours, unwrapped for a crisp crust. Or, wrap in foil and thaw in a preheated 375°F. oven for 20 minutes. For a crisp crust, remove wrapping for last 5 minutes.

Round Rye Bread

Color index page 78

Begin 4½ hrs ahead

2 loaves

4 cups all-purpose flour
2 cups rye flour
2 packages active dry yeast
1½ teaspoons salt

2 tablespoons caraway seed
2 cups buttermilk
⅓ cup light molasses
butter or margarine

1. In medium bowl, combine all-purpose flour and rye flour. In large bowl, combine 2 cups flour mixture, yeast, salt and caraway seed. In 2-quart saucepan over low heat, heat buttermilk, molasses and ⅓ cup butter or margarine until very warm (120° to 130°F.). (Butter or margarine does not need to melt, and mixture will appear curdled.)

2. With mixer at low speed, gradually beat liquid into dry ingredients. Increase speed to medium; beat mixture 2 minutes, occasionally scraping bowl with rubber spatula.

3. Gradually beat in ½ cup flour mixture or enough to make a thick batter; continue beating 2 minutes, occasionally scraping bowl with rubber spatula. With spoon, stir in enough additional flour mixture (about 2½ cups) to make a soft dough.

4. Turn dough onto well-floured surface and knead until smooth and elastic, about 10 minutes. Shape the dough into a ball and place it in a greased large bowl, turning dough over to grease top. Cover with towel; let rise in warm place (80° to 85°F.), away from draft, until doubled, about 1 hour. (Dough is doubled when two fingers pressed lightly into dough leave a dent.)

5. Punch down dough by pushing down the center with fist, then pushing edges of dough into center. Turn dough onto lightly floured surface; cut dough in half; cover with bowl and let rest for 15 minutes.

6. Grease large cookie sheet. Shape each dough half into a smooth round ball by pulling the sides of the dough underneath; place balls of dough on cookie sheet and flatten slightly. Cover with towel; let rise in warm place, away from draft, until the dough has doubled, about 1 hour.

7. Preheat oven to 350°F. Brush loaves with 2 tablespoons melted butter or margarine. Bake loaves 35 minutes or until loaves sound hollow when lightly tapped with fingers. Remove loaves from cookie sheet immediately so the bottoms don't become soggy and leave them to cool completely on wire racks away from draft.

Shaping the dough: Pull sides of each dough half under to form a smooth, round ball.

Flattening the balls: Place balls on cookie sheet and with hand, flatten each one slightly.

Marbled Loaf

Color index page 78

Begin 4½ hrs ahead

2 loaves

Dark Dough:
2 cups whole-wheat flour
2 cups rye flour
about 3 cups all-purpose flour
1 tablespoon sugar
1 tablespoon salt
2 packages active dry yeast
2¼ cups water
¾ cup yellow cornmeal
⅓ cup dark molasses
3 tablespoons butter
1 tablespoon caraway seed

Light Dough:
3 tablespoons sugar
2½ teaspoons salt
1 package active dry yeast
about 6 cups all-purpose flour
1½ cups water
½ cup milk
5 tablespoons butter
1 egg white, beaten

1. Prepare Dark Dough: In medium bowl, combine whole-wheat flour, rye flour and 2½ cups all-purpose flour. In large bowl, combine sugar, salt, yeast and 1½ cups flour mixture. In 2-quart saucepan, combine water, cornmeal and molasses; add butter and caraway seed; over low heat, heat until very warm (120° to 130°F.).

2. With mixer at low speed, gradually beat liquid mixture into dry ingredients until just blended. Increase speed to medium; beat 2 minutes, occasionally scraping bowl. Gradually beat in 1 cup flour mixture or enough to make a thick batter. Continue beating 2 minutes, occasionally scraping bowl. Stir in enough additional flour mixture (about 3 cups) to make a soft dough.

3. On lightly floured surface, knead dough about 10 minutes, until smooth and elastic, working in remaining flour mixture while kneading. Shape into ball; place in greased large bowl, turning dough over to grease top. Cover; let rise in warm place until doubled, about 1½ hours.

4. Meanwhile, prepare Light Dough as for Dark Dough in steps 1–3, but for dry mixture combine sugar, salt, yeast and 2 cups flour and for liquid mixture, in 1-quart saucepan, combine water, milk and butter. After first 2 minutes' beating, beat in ¾ cup flour and after second 2 minutes' beating, stir in about 3 cups flour. Let dough rise in warm place until doubled, about 1 hour.

5. Punch down Dark Dough and turn onto lightly floured surface; cut into 2 equal pieces; cover with bowl and let rest 15 minutes for easier shaping. Meanwhile, repeat with Light Dough.

6. Grease 2 large cookie sheets. Carefully knead together 1 piece Dark Dough with 1 piece Light Dough about 15 times. With lightly floured rolling pin, roll into 16″ by 9″ rectangle. Starting at 16-inch end, tightly roll dough jelly-roll fashion; pinch seam to seal and tuck ends under; place, seam down, diagonally across cookie sheet. Repeat with remaining dough; place on second cookie sheet. Cover; let rise until doubled, about 1 hour.

7. Preheat oven to 400°F. Brush loaves with egg white. Bake on 2 oven racks 20 minutes; switch sheets between oven racks so loaves brown evenly; bake 20 minutes more, or until loaves sound hollow when tapped. Remove to wire racks to cool.

Everyday breads

Italian Bread

Color index page 79

Begin 4 hrs or day ahead

2 loaves

1 tablespoon sugar
2 teaspoons salt
2 packages active dry yeast
about 5 cups all-purpose flour
1 tablespoon butter or margarine
water
cornmeal
salad oil
1 egg white

1. In large bowl, combine sugar, salt, yeast and 2 cups flour. In 1-quart saucepan over low heat, heat butter or margarine and 1¾ cups water until very warm (120° to 130°F.). (Butter or margarine does not need to melt.)

2. With mixer at low speed, gradually beat liquid into dry ingredients until just blended. Increase speed to medium; beat 2 minutes, occasionally scraping bowl with rubber spatula.

3. Beat in ½ cup flour to make thick batter; continue beating mixture at medium speed 2 minutes, scraping bowl often with rubber spatula. With wooden spoon, stir in enough additional flour (about 1¾ cups) to make a soft dough.

4. Turn dough onto floured surface; knead until smooth and elastic, about 10 minutes, adding flour while kneading.

5. Cut dough in half; cover pieces with bowl; let dough rest 20 minutes for easier shaping.

6. Grease large cookie sheet; sprinkle cookie sheet with cornmeal.

7 On floured surface with floured rolling pin, roll each half into 15″ by 10″ rectangle. From 15-inch side, tightly roll dough, jelly-roll fashion; pinch seam to seal.

8 Place loaves, seam side down, on cookie sheet and taper ends. Brush loaves with oil; cover loosely with plastic wrap. Refrigerate 2 to 24 hours.

9 Preheat oven to 425°F. Meanwhile, remove loaves from refrigerator; uncover; let stand 10 minutes. Cut 3 or 4 diagonal slashes on top of each loaf. Bake 20 minutes.

10 In small bowl with fork, beat egg white with 1 tablespoon water. Remove loaves from oven; brush with egg-white mixture; return to oven and bake 5 minutes.

Whole-Grain Bread

Color index page 78

Begin 5 hrs ahead

1 loaf

2 cups rye flour
1 cup unprocessed bran
½ cup wheat germ
about 4¼ cups whole-wheat flour
3 tablespoons sugar
4 teaspoons salt
2 packages active dry yeast
¾ cup milk
½ cup butter or margarine
⅓ cup dark molasses
water
2 eggs
2 tablespoons yellow cornmeal
1 teaspoon caraway seed

1. In large bowl, combine rye flour, bran, wheat germ and 3 cups whole-wheat flour. In another large bowl, combine sugar, salt, yeast and 3 cups flour mixture. In 2-quart saucepan over low heat, heat milk, butter or margarine, molasses and 1 cup water until very warm (120° to 130°F.).

2. With mixer at low speed, gradually beat liquid into dry ingredients until just blended. Increase speed to medium; beat 2 minutes, occasionally scraping bowl. Reserve 1 egg white; beat in remaining eggs and 2 cups flour mixture; continue beating 2 minutes, occasionally scraping bowl. With spoon, stir in remaining flour mixture and enough additional whole-wheat flour (about ¾ cup) to make the mixture a soft dough.

3. Lightly flour surface with whole-wheat flour; turn dough onto surface; knead until smooth and elastic, about 10 minutes, adding more whole-wheat flour while kneading. Shape dough into ball; place in greased large bowl, turning dough to grease top. Cover; let rise in warm place, away from draft, until doubled, about 1 hour. (Dough is doubled when two fingers pressed lightly into dough leave a dent.)

4. Punch down dough; turn onto surface lightly floured with whole-wheat flour; cover with bowl; let dough rest for 15 minutes.

5. Sprinkle cookie sheet with cornmeal. Shape dough into oval, tapering ends; place on cookie sheet. Cover with towel; let rise in warm place until doubled, about 1 hour. (Dough is doubled when one finger very lightly pressed against it leaves a dent.)

6. Preheat oven to 350°F. Cut 3 diagonal slashes on top of loaf. In cup, mix reserved egg white with 1 tablespoon water. With pastry brush, brush bread with egg-white mixture. Sprinkle bread with caraway seed. Bake 50 to 60 minutes until loaf sounds hollow when lightly tapped with fingers. Immediately remove loaf from cookie sheet; cool.

Shaping the dough: Form dough into an oval with tapering ends.

Adding caraway seed: Sprinkle seed over loaf brushed with mixture of egg white and water.

Pumpernickel and Whole-Wheat Braid

Color index
page 78

Begin 4½ hrs
ahead

1 loaf

Pumpernickel Dough:
4½ teaspoons sugar
1½ teaspoons salt
1 package active dry
  yeast
about 1¼ cups
  all-purpose flour
1 square unsweetened
  chocolate
⅓ cup molasses
2 tablespoons butter or
  margarine
¾ cup water
1½ cups rye flour or
  pumpernickel rye
  flour

Whole-Wheat Dough:
2¼ teaspoons sugar
2 teaspoons salt
1 package active dry
  yeast
about 1¾ cups whole-
  wheat flour
about 1½ cups all-
  purpose flour
⅓ cup milk
2 tablespoons honey
2 tablespoons butter
¾ cup water

Egg Glaze:
1 egg yolk
2 teaspoons water

1. Prepare Pumpernickel Dough: In large bowl, combine sugar, salt, yeast and 1 cup all-purpose flour. In heavy 1-quart saucepan over low heat, melt chocolate; stir in molasses, butter and water and heat until very warm (120° to 130°F.). (Butter does not need to melt completely.)
2. With mixer at low speed, gradually beat liquid into dry ingredients until just mixed. Increase speed to medium; beat 2 minutes, occasionally scraping bowl with rubber spatula.
3. Gradually beat in ¾ cup rye flour or enough to make a thick batter; continue beating 2 minutes occasionally scraping bowl with rubber spatula. With wooden spoon, stir in remaining rye flour and enough additional all-purpose flour (about ¼ cup) to make a soft dough.
4. Turn dough onto lightly floured surface and knead until elastic, about 7 minutes, adding as little flour as possible while kneading. (Dough will be slightly sticky.) Shape into ball; place in greased large bowl, turning to grease top. Cover bowl loosely with towel; let rise in warm place (80° to 85°F.), away from draft, until doubled, 2 hours.
5. Meanwhile, prepare Whole-Wheat Dough as for Pumpernickel Dough in steps 1–4, but for dry ingredients combine sugar, salt, yeast, ¾ cup whole-wheat flour and ½ cup all-purpose flour, and for liquid ingredients combine milk, honey, butter and water. After first 2 minutes' beating, beat in ¼ cup whole-wheat flour and ¼ cup all-purpose flour and after second 2 minutes' beating, stir in ¾ cup whole-wheat and about ½ cup all-purpose flour. Knead dough about 10 minutes. Dough will double in about 1 hour.
6. Punch down Pumpernickel Dough. Turn onto lightly floured surface; cover with towel; let rest 15 minutes. Repeat with Whole-Wheat Dough.
7. Grease a large cookie sheet. Divide Whole-Wheat Dough in half. On lightly floured surface, roll Whole-Wheat pieces and Pumpernickel Dough into 20-inch ropes and braid (right); let rise 1 hour.
8. Preheat oven to 350°F. Prepare Egg Glaze: In cup, beat egg yolk with water. Brush braid with mixture. Bake 45 minutes or until loaf sounds hollow when tapped. Let loaf cool on wire rack.

Braided Herb Bread

Color index
page 78

Begin 4 hrs
ahead

2 loaves

1 tablespoon salt
1 tablespoon rosemary
  leaves
2 packages active dry
  yeast
about 7 cups all-purpose
  flour

2½ cups water
1 tablespoon butter or
  margarine, softened
1 egg, slightly beaten

1. In large bowl, combine salt, rosemary leaves, yeast and 2½ cups flour. In 2-quart saucepan over low heat, heat water and butter until very warm (120° to 130°F.). (Butter does not need to melt.)
2. With mixer at medium speed, gradually beat liquid into dry ingredients. Beat 2 minutes, scraping bowl occasionally. Add 1 cup flour or enough to make a thick batter; beat 2 minutes at high speed, scraping bowl occasionally. With spoon, stir in 3½ cups flour to make a soft, sticky dough.
3. Place in greased bowl; cover with towel. Let dough rise in warm place, away from draft, until doubled, about 1½ hours.
4. Punch down dough and turn out onto well-floured surface. Knead until smooth and elastic, about 10 minutes. Divide dough into 6 equal pieces; roll each piece into an 18-inch rope. On one side of a large cookie sheet, braid 3 ropes (below). Repeat with remaining ropes. Cover with towel; let rise in warm place until doubled, about 30 minutes.
5. Preheat oven to 450°F. Brush tops of loaves with egg. Bake 30 minutes or until loaves sound hollow when tapped with fingers. Remove to racks to cool.

BRAIDING

Shape dough pieces into ropes of equal length.

On cookie sheet, lay ropes of dough side by side. Braid ropes, starting at center and working to ends.

Press each end firmly and tuck under. Cover braid with plastic wrap; let rise in warm place until dough is doubled.

Everyday breads and rolls

Sesame Pan Bread

Color index
page 79

Begin 3 hrs
ahead

2 loaves

3 tablespoons sugar
1 tablespoon salt
2 packages active dry
yeast
about 6 cups all-purpose
flour

2 cups water
¼ cup butter or
margarine
milk
1 egg, slightly beaten
¼ cup sesame seed

1. In large bowl, combine sugar, salt, yeast and 2 cups flour. In 2-quart saucepan over low heat, heat water, butter and 1 cup milk until very warm (120° to 130°F.). (Butter does not need to melt.)
2. With mixer at low speed, gradually beat liquid into dry ingredients until just mixed. Increase speed to medium; beat 2 minutes, occasionally scraping bowl. Beat in egg and ½ cup flour or enough to make a thick batter; continue beating 2 minutes at medium speed, occasionally scraping bowl. With wooden spoon, stir in enough additional flour (about 3 cups) to make a soft dough.
3. Turn dough onto lightly floured surface; knead until smooth and elastic, about 10 minutes, adding more flour while kneading, if needed. Shape into ball; cover with bowl; let rest 15 minutes. Grease two 9-inch round cake pans.
4. Cut dough in half; with fingers, press into pans evenly. Cover with towel; let rise in warm place until doubled, about 40 minutes.
5. Preheat oven to 350°F. Brush loaves with milk; sprinkle with sesame seed. Bake 40 minutes or until golden and loaves sound hollow when tapped with fingers. Remove from pans; cool.

Oatmeal Batter Bread

Color index
page 79

Begin 4½ hrs
ahead

2 loaves

2 teaspoons salt
2 packages active dry
yeast
about 5 cups all-purpose
flour

2¼ cups water
1 cup quick-cooking oats,
uncooked
½ cup light molasses
butter or margarine

1. In large bowl, combine salt, yeast and 2 cups flour. In 2-quart saucepan with spoon, mix water, oats and molasses; add 1 tablespoon butter; over low heat, heat until very warm (120° to 130°F.).
2. With mixer at low speed, gradually beat liquid mixture into dry ingredients until just blended. Increase speed to medium; beat 2 minutes, occasionally scraping bowl. Beat in ½ cup flour to make a thick batter; continue beating 2 minutes, scraping bowl often. Stir in enough additional flour (about 2½ cups) to make a stiff dough that leaves side of bowl.
3. Cover bowl with towel; let rise in warm place until doubled, about 1 hour.
4. Stir down dough; divide in two and turn into 2 greased 2-quart round, straight-sided, shallow casseroles. With greased fingers, turn dough over to grease top; shape into ball. Cover; let rise in warm place until doubled, about 45 minutes.
5. Preheat oven to 350°F. Bake 40 minutes or until loaves sound hollow when tapped. Remove from casseroles immediately. If you like, rub tops with softened butter; cool on racks.

Cheese Casserole Bread

Color index
page 79

Begin 4½ hrs
ahead

1 loaf

2 tablespoons sugar
2 teaspoons salt
2 packages active dry
yeast
about 5 cups all-purpose
flour

2¼ cups milk
¼ pound sharp
Cheddar cheese,
shredded (1 cup)
1 tablespoon butter or
margarine, melted

1. In large bowl, combine sugar, salt, yeast and 2 cups flour. In 2-quart saucepan over low heat, heat milk and cheese until very warm (120° to 130°F.). (Cheese does not need to melt.)
2. With mixer at low speed, beat liquid mixture into dry ingredients until just blended. At medium speed, beat 2 minutes, occasionally scraping bowl with rubber spatula. Beat in 1 cup flour to make a thick batter; beat 2 minutes more, scraping bowl often. Stir in enough additional flour (about 2 cups) to make a stiff dough that leaves side of bowl.
3. Cover bowl with towel; let rise in warm place until doubled, about 45 minutes.
4. Stir down dough; turn into greased 2-quart round, straight-sided, shallow casserole. Cover; let rise in warm place until doubled, about 45 minutes.
5. Preheat oven to 375°F. Brush loaf with melted butter. Bake 30 to 35 minutes until golden and loaf sounds hollow when tapped. Cool on wire rack.

Potato Bread

Color index
page 79

Begin 4½ hrs
ahead

2 loaves

2 tablespoons sugar
4 teaspoons salt
2 packages active dry
yeast
about 8 cups all-purpose
flour

½ cup water
1½ cups mashed potatoes
milk
¼ cup butter or
margarine
2 eggs

1. In large bowl, combine sugar, salt, yeast and 1½ cups flour. In 2-quart saucepan, mix water, mashed potatoes and 1½ cups milk; add butter; over low heat, heat until very warm (120° to 130°F.), stirring often. (Butter does not need to melt.)
2. With mixer at low speed, gradually beat liquid into dry ingredients just until blended; beat in eggs. At medium speed, beat 2 minutes, occasionally scraping bowl. Beat in 1 cup flour to make a thick batter; continue beating 2 minutes, scraping bowl often. Stir in enough additional flour (about 3¼ cups) to make a soft dough.
3. On well-floured surface, knead dough about 10 minutes, until smooth and elastic, kneading in about 1½ cups flour. Shape into ball; place in greased large bowl, turning to grease top. Cover; let rise until doubled, about 1 hour.
4. Punch down dough; turn onto lightly floured surface; cut in half; cover; let rest 15 minutes.
5. Grease two 2-quart round, straight-sided, shallow casseroles. Shape 1 piece of dough into ball; place in casserole. Cut 2 parallel slashes on top. Repeat. Cover; let rise until doubled, about 1 hour.
6. Preheat oven to 400°F. Brush each loaf with milk. Bake 40 minutes or until well browned and loaves sound hollow when tapped with fingers. Remove loaves to cool on wire racks.

Old-fashioned Rolls

Color index
page 83

Begin 3½ hrs
ahead

24 rolls

⅓ *cup sugar*
1½ *teaspoons salt*
2 *packages active dry
yeast*
4½ *to 5½ cups all-
purpose flour*
1 *cup milk*
¼ *cup butter*
2 *eggs*
*melted butter or Egg
Glaze (below)*

1 In large bowl, combine sugar, salt, yeast and 1½ cups flour. In 1-quart saucepan, heat milk and butter until very warm (120° to 130°F.). With mixer at low speed, gradually beat liquid into dry ingredients. At medium speed, beat 2 minutes, occasionally scraping bowl, with a rubber spatula.

2 Beat in eggs and about ½ cup flour to make a thick batter; continue beating 2 minutes. Stir in flour (2 to 2½ cups) to make a soft dough.

3 On lightly floured surface, knead dough until smooth and elastic, about 10 minutes. Shape dough into ball.

4 Turn in greased large bowl to grease top. Cover; let rise in warm place until doubled, 1 hour.

5 Punch down dough. Transfer to lightly floured surface; cut in half; cover; let rest 15 minutes.

6 Cut each half into 12 pieces; shape into balls. Place 2 inches apart on greased cookie sheets. Cover; let rise until doubled, about 30 minutes.

7 Preheat oven to 400°F. Brush with melted butter or Egg Glaze. Bake 10 minutes or until golden. Cool slightly on wire racks. Serve warm.

EGG GLAZE: In small bowl with fork, beat *1 egg* with *1 tablespoon milk.*

Dinner Rolls

Color index
page 80

Begin 3½ hrs
ahead

12 to 24 rolls

*Old-fashioned Rolls
dough (left)*

*melted butter or Egg
Glaze (below left)*

1. Prepare dough as in steps 1-5 but in step 6, cut and shape dough as directed and shown below or on the next page. Brush with melted butter or glaze.
2. Preheat oven to 400°F. Bake 12 to 18 minutes or until golden, depending on the shape selected.

DINNER BUNS

Shape one half of dough into 12 oval balls, tapering ends slightly. Place 2 inches apart on greased cookie sheet. Cover; let rise until doubled.

With sharp, floured knife, slash lengthwise halfway through center of each roll.

VIENNA ROLLS

Prepare as for Dinner Buns (above). Beat *1 egg white* with *1 tablespoon water* until frothy; brush egg-white mixture over rolls.

Sprinkle with *caraway seed.*

DOUBLE TWISTS

Divide one half of dough into 12 equal pieces. Roll each piece into 6-inch-long rope. Pinch 2 ropes together at one end.

Then, carefully twist together, pinching bottom ends to seal. Overlap ends; tuck under center of twist. Place on greased cookie sheet.

Brush with Egg Glaze; sprinkle with *sesame seed.* Cover; let rise until dough is doubled.

439

Everyday breads and rolls

KNOTS

Divide one half of dough into 6 equal pieces. Roll each piece into 6-inch-long rope shape.

Carefully tie each rope into a knot. Arrange on greased cookie sheet. Brush with *melted butter.* Cover; let rise until doubled.

CRESCENTS

Roll one half of dough into 9-inch circle. Cut circle into 12 wedges; brush with *melted butter.*

Roll up each wedge toward point; place wedges on lightly greased cookie sheet.

Curve ends. Cover with towel; let crescents rise until doubled.

PAN ROLLS

Shape one half of dough into 2-inch balls by tucking ends under.

Dip balls into melted butter. In greased 8" by 8" baking pan, place balls letting them just touch each other. Let rise until doubled.

PINWHEELS

Roll one half of dough into 12½" by 10" rectangle. Cut into 2½-inch squares. Place 2 inches apart on greased cookie sheets. Cut 1½ inches deep from corners to center of each square, making 8 points (right).

Fold every other point into center of square.

Gently press points to center to secure them in position. Brush with melted butter or Egg Glaze; let rise until doubled.

FAN-TANS

Roll one half of dough into ⅛-inch-thick rectangle. Brush with melted butter. Cut dough into 1½-inch-wide strips (right).

Stack 6 or 7 strips together (left); cut stacks into 1½-inch pieces.

Place, cut side up, in greased 2½- or 3-inch muffin-pan cups (left). Let rise until doubled.

POSIES

Shape one half of dough into 6 balls. Place on greased cookie sheet. Flatten slightly.

With scissors, make six ¼-inch-deep cuts in edge of each ball.

Brush lightly with Egg Glaze ; sprinkle with *poppy seed.* Let rise until dough is doubled.

Sourdough bread

Color index page 80

Begin 6 hrs or up to 1 wk ahead

30 rolls

Refrigerator Pan Rolls

½ cup sugar	*2 cups water*
2 teaspoons salt	*butter or margarine,*
2 packages active dry	*softened*
yeast	*1 egg*
6 to 6½ cups all-purpose	*salad oil*
flour	

1. In large bowl, combine sugar, salt, yeast and 2¼ cups flour. In 2-quart saucepan over low heat, heat water and ½ cup butter until very warm (120° to 130°F.). (Butter does not need to melt.)

2. With mixer at low speed, gradually beat liquid into dry ingredients. Add egg; increase speed to medium; beat 2 minutes, occasionally scraping bowl with rubber spatula. Beat in ¾ cup flour or enough to make a thick batter; continue beating 2 minutes, occasionally scraping bowl with rubber spatula. Stir in about 2½ cups flour to make a soft dough.

3. Turn dough onto lightly floured surface and knead until smooth and elastic, about 10 minutes. Shape into ball; place in greased large bowl, turning over to grease top. Cover with towel; let rise in warm place, until doubled, about 1½ hours.

4. Punch down dough. Turn dough over; brush with oil. Cover bowl tightly with plastic wrap and refrigerate at least 2 hours or until ready to use, punching down dough occasionally.

5. *About 2½ hours before serving:* Grease 15½" by 10½" open roasting pan. Cut dough into 30 equal pieces; shape into balls and place in pan. Cover with towel; let rise in warm place, away from draft, until doubled, about 1½ hours.

6. Preheat oven to 400°F. Bake 15 to 20 minutes until golden brown. Brush rolls with softened butter. Remove from pan and serve hot.

PARKER HOUSE ROLLS

Prepare *dough for Refrigerator Pan Rolls* (above) in steps 1–4. Roll dough ½ inch thick. With floured 2¾-inch round cutter, cut circles. Knead trimmings; reroll; cut more.

Melt *½ cup butter* in 17¼" by 11½" pan; dip both sides of each circle in fat and fold in half.

Arrange closely in rows in pan. Cover; let rolls rise until doubled. Preheat oven to 400°F. Bake 18 to 20 minutes until browned. (Makes 40 rolls.)

Sourdough Bread

Sourdough Starter:
2 cups all-purpose flour
1 package active dry yeast
2 cups warm water

Dough:
2 tablespoons sugar
1 tablespoon salt
1 teaspoon baking soda
water

6 to 8 cups all-purpose flour
3 tablespoons butter or margarine, melted

Color index page 79

Begin 4 days ahead

2 loaves

1 Make Starter: In large bowl, combine flour and yeast; stir in water; beat until smooth. Cover bowl with waxed paper.

2 Let stand 48 hours in warm place, stirring occasionally. If it does not rise, form bubbles and separate, start again. Stir well before using Starter.

3 *Day before serving, make dough:* In large bowl with mixer at medium speed, beat well sugar, salt, soda, 2 cups warm water, 1 cup Starter and 3 cups flour.

4 Cover bowl with towel; let batter rise at room temperature, away from draft, at least 18 hours.

5 *About 4½ hours before serving:* Stir in 3½ to 4 cups flour to make a soft dough. On floured surface, knead until smooth and elastic, 8 to 10 minutes.

6 Cut dough in half; shape into 2 flat, round loaves, measuring about 7 inches in diameter.

7 Place loaves on well-greased cookie sheets; cover with towels and let rise in warm place until doubled, about 2 hours.

8 Preheat oven to 400°F. Brush loaves with water; with a sharp knife, cut 3 to 5 crisscross slashes across top of each loaf.

9 Bake 45 to 50 minutes until golden and loaves sound hollow when tapped. Remove to racks; brush with melted butter.

To replenish Starter:
If you plan to make Sourdough Bread regularly (at least once a week), remaining Starter may be replenished, if there is at least 1 cup of it left. Combine *1 cup all-purpose flour* with *1 cup warm water* and beat until smoothly blended. Stir into remaining Starter. Leave at room temperature a few hours until mixture begins to bubble. Cover bowl loosely; refrigerate replenished Starter until needed.

Sweet breads and rolls

A sweet dough is no more difficult to make than any plain bread. With one recipe, Sweet Dough (below), many different breads and buns can be made by adding in a few other ingredients – fruit, nuts and spices – and varying the shapes. Also included are other interesting breads, some with icing. Wait until sweet breads have cooled at least slightly before adding icing or the icing will melt and flow off. Store them as ordinary bread.

Dough for breads, pages 442 to 444

Sweet Dough

1 cup sugar
1 teaspoon salt
3 packages active dry yeast
8 to 9 cups all-purpose flour

2 cups milk
1 cup butter or margarine
2 eggs

1 In large bowl, combine sugar, salt, yeast and 2 cups flour. In 2-quart saucepan over low heat, slowly heat milk and butter until very warm (120° to 130°F.) (Butter does not need to melt.) With mixer at low speed, gradually beat liquid into dry ingredients. Increase speed to medium; beat 2 minutes more, occasionally scraping bowl with rubber spatula.

2 Beat in eggs and 2 cups flour; continue beating 2 minutes, occasionally scraping bowl.

3 With spoon, stir in enough additional flour (about 4¼ cups) to make a soft dough.

4 Turn dough onto lightly floured surface; knead until smooth and elastic, about 10 minutes. Shape into a ball.

5 Turn over in greased large bowl to grease top. Cover; let rise in warm place until dough is doubled, about 1 hour.

6 Punch down dough. On lightly floured surface, divide into pieces as recipes (pages 442 to 444) direct. Cover; let rest 15 minutes.

Raisin Bread

Color index page 81
Begin 4½ hrs ahead
1 loaf

⅓ Sweet Dough (left)   *¾ cup raisins*

1. Prepare Sweet Dough. Grease 9" by 5" loaf pan. Roll dough piece into 12" by 9" rectangle. Sprinkle raisins on dough.
2. From 9-inch end, roll dough jelly-roll fashion; pinch seam to seal. Press ends to seal and tuck under; place, seam side down, in pan.
3. Cover; let rise until doubled, about 1½ hours. Preheat oven to 350°F. Bake 35 minutes or until loaf sounds hollow when tapped. Let cool on rack.

Turtle Bread

Color index page 81
Begin 4½ hrs ahead
1 loaf

¼ Sweet Dough (left)   *1 egg water*

1. Prepare Sweet Dough. Cut off ½-cup piece from dough; set aside. Shape remaining piece into 5-inch oval ball. Place on greased cookie sheet.
2. Roll reserved piece into 7-inch rope. From rope cut 2-inch piece for head; with scissors, snip eyes and mouth. Cut four 1-inch legs from rope; snip toes. Make pointed tail with remainder. Assemble body and shape shell as shown below.
3. Beat egg with a little water; brush turtle; let rise until doubled. Preheat oven to 375°F. Bake 20 to 25 minutes until browned.

Assembling the body: Tuck head, legs and tail under oval ball and pinch to seal.

Shaping the shell: With scissors, snip design in top of body. Pinch edge to resemble shell.

Hot Cross Buns

Color index page 81
Begin 4½ hrs ahead
12 buns

½ Sweet Dough (left)
½ cup dark seedless raisins
⅓ cup chopped candied orange peel
1 egg yolk
1 teaspoon water

Sugar Icing:
¾ cup confectioners' sugar
1 tablespoon milk
1 tablespoon butter, softened
⅓ teaspoon lemon juice

1. Grease a 13" by 9" baking pan. Into dough knead raisins and peel. Divide dough into 12 pieces; shape into balls; place evenly in pan. Cover with towel; let rise in warm place, away from draft, until doubled, about 1 hour. Preheat oven to 350°F.
2. In small bowl, combine egg yolk with water. Brush buns with egg-yolk mixture. Bake buns 30 minutes or until brown and glazed.
3. Meanwhile, prepare icing: In small bowl with mixer at low speed, beat all ingredients until smooth. Make icing cross on buns. Serve warm.

Kolacky

Color index page 81

Begin 4½ hrs ahead

12 coffeecake servings

| ¼ Sweet Dough (opposite) | Kolacky Toppings (below) |

1. Prepare Sweet Dough. On lightly floured board with lightly floured rolling pin, roll Sweet Dough into a 12-inch circle; place the circle on a greased cookie sheet and let it rise until it has nearly *tripled* in volume, about 1½ hours.

2. Meanwhile, prepare Kolacky Toppings.

3. Preheat oven to 375°F. With hands, firmly press raised dough to within ½ inch of edges, being sure that you have pressed out all large bubbles. With back of knife, lightly mark pressed dough into 6 wedge-shaped sections.

4. Into each section, spoon one of toppings; spread evenly to fill section. Bake 20 to 25 minutes.

Shaping the dough: Press dough to within ½ inch of edges. With back of knife, mark 6 wedge shapes.

Adding the toppings: Evenly spoon a different topping into each of the marked sections.

KOLACKY TOPPINGS

BLUEBERRY: In small bowl, stir *⅓ cup canned blueberry-pie filling* and *¼ teaspoon grated lemon peel* until mixed. (Use leftover filling on ice cream.)

CHERRY: In small bowl, stir *½ cup canned cherry-pie filling* and *1 tablespoon shredded coconut* until mixed. (Use leftover filling on ice cream.)

CREAM CHEESE: In small bowl, stir *one 3-ounce package cream cheese,* softened, *1 tablespoon sugar, 1 tablespoon milk* and *⅛ teaspoon ground cinnamon* until mixture is smooth.

LEMON: Prepare one *3¼- to 3⅝-ounce package lemon pudding mix* as label directs. Set aside ⅓ cup lemon-pudding mixture for Kolacky. Pour remaining mixture into 3 dessert dishes and refrigerate to serve another day.

ORANGE: Use *¼ cup orange marmalade.*

PINEAPPLE: In small bowl, stir *¼ cup pineapple preserves, 1 tablespoon chopped California walnuts* and *⅛ teaspoon salt* until mixed.

Begin 4½ hrs ahead

8 servings

INDIVIDUAL KOLACKY: Cut Sweet Dough into 8 pieces; shape into balls. Place balls on 2 greased cookie sheets, 3 inches apart. Cover; let rise about 1½ hours. Meanwhile, prepare only *2 Kolacky Toppings* (above). Pat balls to make 4-inch circles with ¼-inch rim around edges; fill each with 1 tablespoon topping. Bake as above 15 minutes.

Apricot Coffeecake

Color index page 81

Begin 4½ hrs ahead

8 coffeecake servings

¼ *Sweet Dough (opposite)*
1 8-ounce package dried apricots
¾ cup water
¼ cup sugar
¼ teaspoon ground cinnamon

Glaze:
½ cup confectioners' sugar
¼ teaspoon vanilla extract
2 teaspoons water

1 Prepare Sweet Dough. In 2 quart saucepan over medium heat, heat apricots and water to boiling. Reduce heat to low; cover; simmer 30 minutes.

2 In covered blender container at high speed, blend apricots, sugar and cinnamon until smooth (if mixture is too tart, add more sugar to taste).

3 Grease large cookie sheet. On lightly floured surface with floured rolling pin, roll dough into 15″ by 12″ rectangle. Place on sheet.

4 Spread apricot mixture in 4-inch-wide strip lengthwise down center of dough rectangle.

5 With knife, cut dough on sides of mixture crosswise into 1-inch-wide strips; fold strips alternately across mixture.

6 Cover; let rise in warm place, away from draft, until doubled, about 1 hour. Preheat oven to 375°F. Bake cake 20 minutes or until golden.

7 Cool on sheet on wire rack 15 minutes. Meanwhile, in small bowl, combine glaze ingredients and stir until smooth. Drizzle over cake.

Sweet breads and rolls

Fruited Braid

Color index
page 81

Begin 4½ hrs
ahead

1 loaf

½ Sweet Dough
  (page 442)
1 cup golden raisins
¾ cup finely chopped
  candied orange peel
¼ cup finely chopped
  candied citron

1 tablespoon all-purpose
  flour
1 egg yolk, slightly
  beaten
½ cup confectioners'
  sugar
1 tablespoon water

1. Prepare Sweet Dough. Grease large cookie sheet.
Cut dough into 3 pieces. Roll each dough piece into
a 12″ by 4″ strip.
2. In medium bowl, toss raisins, orange peel and
citron with flour. Spread ⅓ of mixture lengthwise on
center of each strip; brush edges with egg yolk. Fold
edges of each strip over fruit and each other,
forming a roll; pinch seams to seal. On greased
cookie sheet, braid the 3 rolls, tucking ends under.
Cover; let rise until doubled, about 1 hour. Brush
braid with beaten egg yolk.
3. Preheat oven to 350°F. Bake 35 minutes or until
golden and loaf sounds hollow when tapped.
Remove to cool on wire rack. In small bowl, mix
sugar and water; brush over braid.

Cinnamon Rolls

Color index
page 81

Begin 4½ hrs
ahead

15 rolls

½ Sweet Dough
  (page 442)
½ cup packed light
  brown sugar
½ cup pecans, chopped
½ cup dark seedless
  raisins

1 teaspoon ground
  cinnamon
¼ cup butter or
  margarine, melted
Sugar Glaze (below)
  (optional)

1. Prepare Sweet Dough. Grease well 13″ by 9″
baking pan. In small bowl, combine brown sugar,
pecans, raisins and cinnamon; set aside. Roll dough
into 18″ by 12″ rectangle. Brush with melted butter;
sprinkle with sugar mixture.
2. Starting at an 18-inch side, roll dough jelly-roll
fashion. Pinch seam to seal. With roll seam side
down, cut dough crosswise into 15 slices; place in
pan, cut side down. Cover; let rise in warm place
until doubled, about 40 minutes.
3. Preheat oven to 400°F. Bake 25 minutes or until
lightly browned. Cool slightly in pan on wire rack.
Spread with glaze. To serve: Pull apart with forks.
SUGAR GLAZE: In small bowl, stir **2 cups confectioners' sugar, ½ teaspoon vanilla extract** and
about **3 tablespoons water** until smooth.

Placing rolls in pan:
Arrange slices in baking
pan, cut side down.

Serving rolls: Glaze rolls if
you wish, then use forks to
pull rolls apart.

Lemon Bubble Ring

Color index
page 81

Begin 4 hrs
ahead

1 loaf

2 packages active dry
  yeast
1 teaspoon salt
5 to 6 cups all-purpose
  flour
sugar

1½ cups milk
butter or margarine
2 eggs
grated peel from
  2 lemons
¼ teaspoon ground mace

1. In large bowl, combine yeast, salt, 2 cups flour and
½ cup sugar. In 1-quart saucepan over low heat,
heat milk and ¼ cup butter until very warm (120° to
130°F.). (Butter does not need to melt.)
2. With mixer at low speed, beat liquid into dry
ingredients. Add eggs; at medium speed, beat 2
minutes, occasionally scraping bowl with rubber
spatula. Beat in ½ cup flour or enough to make a
thick batter; continue beating 2 minutes. Stir in
about 2 cups flour to make a soft dough.
3. On floured surface, knead dough until smooth
and elastic, about 10 minutes. Shape into ball; place
in greased large bowl, turning to grease top. Cover;
let rise until doubled, about 1 hour.
4. In small bowl, combine lemon peel, mace and ½
cup sugar; set aside. In 1-quart saucepan, melt 2
tablespoons butter.
5. Punch down dough. Turn dough onto lightly
floured surface; cover with bowl; let rest 15 minutes.

6 Cut dough in half; cut
each half into 16 pieces.
Shape each piece into a
ball by tucking ends under.

7 In greased 10-inch tube
pan, place half of balls.
Brush with half of melted
butter or margarine.

8 Sprinkle balls in tube
pan with half of lemon-
peel mixture.

9 Put remaining balls in
ring, brush with melted
butter and sprinkle with
lemon mixture.

10. Cover with towel; let rise in warm place until
doubled, about 45 minutes. (Dough is doubled when
one finger pressed lightly into dough leaves a dent.)
11. Preheat oven to 350°F. Bake 35 minutes or until
golden and bread sounds hollow when tapped with
fingers. Cool in pan 5 minutes; remove bread from
pan to wire rack to cool.

Whole-Wheat "Sugar" Bears

Color index
page 82

Begin 4 hrs
ahead

3 bears

1¼ cups sugar	4 cups whole-wheat flour
1½ teaspoons salt	2 cups milk
2 packages active dry yeast	1 cup butter or margarine
about 4 cups all-purpose flour	2 eggs
	1 tablespoon water

1. In large bowl, combine sugar, salt, yeast, 1 cup all-purpose flour and 2 cups whole-wheat flour. In 2-quart saucepan over low heat, heat milk and butter until very warm (120° to 130°F.).

2. With mixer at low speed, beat liquid into dry ingredients until blended. At medium speed, beat 2 minutes. Reserve 1 egg white; beat in remaining eggs and 1 cup of each of flours; beat 2 minutes more. Stir in remaining whole-wheat flour and enough additional all-purpose flour (about 1½ cups) to make a soft dough.

3. On floured surface, knead dough about 10 minutes, adding all-purpose flour while kneading. Shape into ball; turn in greased large bowl to grease top. Cover; let rise until doubled, about 1 hour.

4. Punch down dough; turn onto floured surface; cover; let rest 15 minutes. Grease 2 large cookie sheets. In cup, combine egg white with water.

5. Divide dough into thirds. Cut one dough piece into one half and two quarters. Shape half-piece and one quarter-piece into balls for body and head.

6 Slightly flatten body on cookie sheet. Brush side of head with egg white; tuck it slightly under body.

7 Roll remaining ¼-piece into 7-inch rope. Cut 2-inch snout and piece for nose. Brush with egg white. Place on head.

8 Cut two ½-inch pieces for ears and four 1-inch pieces for legs. Tuck under bear; pinch to seal.

9 With scissors, snip fingers, toes, eyes, mouth and belly button. Repeat for other 2 bears.

10. Cover; let rise in warm place away from draft until doubled, about 1 hour.

11. Preheat oven to 375°F. Brush bears with egg white. Bake 25 minutes until brown.

Apricot Butterfly Rolls

Color index
page 82

Begin 4½ hrs
ahead

20 rolls

½ cup sugar	1 cup milk
1 teaspoon salt	butter or margarine
1 package active dry yeast	2 eggs
4 to 4½ cups all-purpose flour	2 teaspoons almond extract
	Apricot Filling (below)

1. In large bowl, combine sugar, salt, yeast and 1 cup flour. In 1-quart saucepan over low heat, heat milk and ½ cup butter until very warm (120° to 130°F.).

2. With mixer at low speed, beat liquid mixture into dry ingredients; beat until just mixed. At medium speed, beat 2 minutes. Beat in 1 egg, almond extract and 1 cup flour or enough to make thick batter; continue beating 2 minutes. Stir in enough flour (about 2 cups) to make a soft dough.

3. On floured surface, knead dough 10 minutes until smooth and elastic, adding more flour while kneading. Shape dough into ball; place in greased large bowl, turning to grease top. Cover; let rise until doubled, about 2 hours. Prepare Apricot Filling.

4. Punch down dough; turn onto lightly floured surface; cut in half; cover for 15 minutes. With lightly floured rolling pin, roll one piece into 20″ by 14″ rectangle. Brush generously with melted butter; spread half of filling to within ½ inch of edges. From 20-inch edge, tightly roll dough, jelly-roll fashion; pinch edges to seal. With roll seam side down, cut into 10 wedges, each about 2½ inches at wide side, about 1 inch at short side.

5. Grease 2 large cookie sheets. Place wedges, short side up, on sheet; with finger, across top of each wedge, press to form butterfly-like wings. Repeat with remaining dough and filling. Let rise until doubled, about 30 minutes. In cup, beat remaining egg slightly; use to brush tops of rolls.

6. Preheat oven to 350°F. Bake 20 minutes or until golden. Immediately remove butterfly rolls to cool on wire racks.

APRICOT FILLING: In 2-quart saucepan over high heat, heat *one 8-ounce package dried apricots* and *2½ cups water* to boiling. Reduce heat to low; cover and simmer 15 minutes or until apricots are tender; drain. With fork or wire whisk, beat in *¾ cup sugar* until apricots are mashed; allow Apricot Filling to cool before using.

Cutting the wedges: Cut roll into 10 wedges, each 2½ inches at wide side, 1 inch at short side.

Making butterfly shape: Place wedges, short side up, on cookie sheet; press top with finger to form butterfly-like wings.

Special breads

In addition to everyday breads and rolls, there are many more fine yeast doughs to try. Some of them are served as breads for breakfast, brunch or luncheon and between meal snacking. Some special breads, like Fondue Bread, are main dishes; some, like Babas au Rhum, are served as dessert. And some, such as croissants, doughnuts and brioches, call for special techniques.

Color index page 31

Begin 2 hrs ahead

1 loaf or 8 main-dish servings

Fondue Bread

3½ teaspoons sugar
2 teaspoons salt
2 packages active dry yeast
about 4 cups all-purpose flour
½ cup butter or margarine

1 cup milk
2 eggs
2 pounds Muenster cheese, shredded
about 2 teaspoons sliced blanched almonds for garnish

1. In large bowl, combine sugar, salt, yeast and 1 cup flour. In 1-quart saucepan over low heat, heat butter and milk until very warm (120° to 130°F.).
2. With mixer at low speed, gradually beat liquid into dry ingredients until just mixed. Increase speed to medium; beat 2 minutes, occasionally scraping bowl. Beat in 1 cup flour or enough to make a thick batter; continue beating 2 minutes, occasionally scraping bowl. With spoon, stir in enough additional flour (about 2 cups) to make a soft dough.
3. Turn dough onto lightly floured surface and knead until smooth and elastic, about 10 minutes, adding more flour while kneading, if necessary. Shape dough into ball; cover with bowl and let dough rest 15 minutes for easier shaping.
4. Meanwhile, reserve 1 egg white. In large bowl, thoroughly combine remaining eggs with cheese; set aside. Grease 9-inch round cake pan.
5. On lightly floured surface, with lightly floured rolling pin, roll dough into a 24″ by 6″ rectangle.

6 Lengthwise along center of dough, shape cheese mixture into cylinder. Fold dough over filling, making about 1- to 1½-inch overlap; pinch seam to seal.

7 Place roll, seam side down, in pan to make a ring, overlapping ends slightly; pinch ends together to seal. Cover with towel; let rest in warm place 10 minutes.

8. Preheat oven to 375°F. Brush loaf with reserved egg white. Garnish top with almonds. Bake 1 hour or until golden and bread sounds hollow when lightly tapped. Remove bread from pan immediately; let stand 15 minutes for easier cutting. Cut bread into wedges.

English Muffins

Color index page 83

Begin 3½ hrs ahead

18 muffins

2 tablespoons sugar
1 teaspoon salt
1 package active dry yeast
about 5 cups all-purpose flour
1½ cups milk

butter or margarine
1 egg
2 tablespoons yellow cornmeal
salad oil

1. In large bowl, combine sugar, salt, yeast and 1½ cups flour. In 1-quart saucepan over medium heat, heat milk and ¼ cup butter or margarine until very warm (120° to 130°F.).
2. With mixer at low speed, gradually beat liquid into dry ingredients until just blended. Increase speed to medium; beat 2 minutes, occasionally scraping bowl with rubber spatula.
3. Gradually beat in egg and 1 cup flour or enough to make a thick batter; continue beating 2 minutes, occasionally scraping bowl with rubber spatula. With spoon, stir in enough additional flour (about 2 cups) to make a stiff dough.
4. Turn dough onto lightly floured surface and knead just until well mixed, about 2 minutes. Shape dough into a ball and place in greased large bowl, turning dough over to grease top. Cover with towel; let rise in warm place, away from draft, until dough is doubled, about 1½ hours.
5. Punch down dough. Turn dough onto lightly floured surface; cover with bowl for 15 minutes and let dough rest for easier shaping. Meanwhile, place cornmeal in a pie plate.
6. With lightly floured rolling pin, roll dough about ⅜ inch thick. With 3-inch round cookie cutter, cut dough into circles; reroll scraps to make 18 circles in all.
7. Dip both sides of each circle in cornmeal; place cornmeal-coated circles about 1 inch apart on 2 small cookie sheets. Cover cookie sheets with towel; let circles rise in warm place, away from draft, until doubled, about 45 minutes.
8. Lightly brush 12-inch skillet with salad oil. Over medium heat, heat skillet until hot. Place 6 circles in skillet; cook 8 minutes on each side or until browned. Repeat with remaining circles. Cool muffins on wire rack. To store muffins for later use, wrap cooled muffins with plastic wrap or foil.
9. *Just before serving*: With tines of fork, split each muffin horizontally in half; toast the muffin halves in toaster until golden and piping hot; serve them spread with butter or margarine.

Coating circles: Dip dough circles in cornmeal in pie plate to coat well.

Splitting muffins: Use tines of fork to split each muffin in half.

Brioches

¼ cup sugar
1 teaspoon salt
2 packages active dry
  yeast
about 4½ cups all-
  purpose flour
1 cup milk
1 cup butter or margarine
5 eggs
1 teaspoon lemon extract
2 egg yolks
2 teaspoons water

Color index page 82

Begin day ahead

36 brioches

1 In large bowl, combine sugar, salt, yeast and 1½ cups flour. In 1-quart saucepan over medium heat, heat milk and butter or margarine until very warm (120° to 130°F.).

2 With mixer at low speed, gradually beat liquid into dry ingredients until just blended. At medium speed, beat 2 minutes, occasionally scraping bowl.

3 Beat in eggs, lemon extract and 1½ cups flour to make thick batter; beat 2 minutes more. Stir in 1½ cups flour to make soft dough. Beat dough 5 minutes more.

4 Place dough in greased large bowl. Cover; let rise until doubled, about 1 hour. Stir down dough; cover tightly with foil or plastic wrap. Refrigerate overnight.

5 About 2 hours before serving: Punch down dough. Turn onto floured surface; cover with bowl; let rest 15 minutes. Grease 36 brioche pans.

6 Cut off ⅙ of dough; set aside. Cut rest of dough into 36 pieces. Shape each piece into a ball and place in a brioche pan.

7 Cut reserved dough into 36 pieces; shape into small balls. With finger, make depression in center of each large ball.

8 Place small ball in depression. Cover; let rise in warm place until doubled, about 1 hour.

9 Preheat oven to 375°F. In small bowl, combine egg yolks with water. Brush brioches with egg mixture.

10 Bake 20 minutes until golden brown and brioches sound hollow when tapped. Remove from pans; serve hot.

Color index page 82

Begin 3 hrs ahead

6 pocket breads

Pita (Pocket Bread)

3½ to 3¾ cups all-
  purpose flour
1 teaspoon salt
1 package active dry
  yeast

¼ teaspoon sugar
1⅓ cups water
1 tablespoon salad oil
cornmeal
favorite filling

1. In large bowl, combine 1½ cups flour, salt, yeast and sugar. In 1-quart saucepan over medium heat, heat water and salad oil until very warm (about 120° to 130°F.).

2. With mixer at low speed, beat liquid into dry ingredients; beat until just mixed. Increase speed to medium; beat 2 minutes, occasionally scraping bowl. Stir in enough additional flour (about 2 cups) to make a soft dough.

3. On floured surface, knead dough until smooth and elastic, about 5 minutes, adding more flour as needed. Shape into ball; place in greased medium bowl, turning over to grease top. Cover; let dough rise in warm place, away from draft, until doubled, about 1 hour.

4. Punch down dough; turn onto floured surface.

5 Cut dough into 6 pieces; cover; let rise 30 minutes. Meanwhile, lightly sprinkle 3 ungreased cookie sheets with cornmeal.

6 On lightly floured surface with lightly floured rolling pin, roll each piece of dough into a 7-inch circle.

7 Place 2 circles on each cookie sheet. Cover with towel; let rise in warm place 45 minutes or until doubled in height.

8 Preheat oven to 475°F. Bake 8 to 10 minutes until pitas are puffed and golden brown. Serve pitas immediately with favorite filling.

9. To serve later: Cool 5 minutes then place warm bread in plastic bags to keep moist and pliable. To reheat: Preheat oven to 375°F. Wrap pocket breads in foil and heat 10 minutes or until hot.

Special breads

Croissants

2 tablespoons sugar
1½ teaspoons salt
2 packages active dry
*   yeast*
about 3 cups all-purpose
*   flour*
1¼ cups milk
1 cup butter
1 egg
1 tablespoon water

Color index page 82

Begin 8 hrs or day ahead

12 croissants

1 In large bowl, combine sugar, salt, yeast and 1 cup flour. In 1-quart saucepan over low heat, heat milk until very warm (120° to 130°F.). With mixer at low speed, beat liquid into dry ingredients until just blended. At medium speed, beat 2 minutes, occasionally scraping bowl. Beat in ½ cup flour to make thick batter; beat 2 minutes more. Stir in about 1 cup flour to make soft dough.

2 On floured surface, knead dough until smooth and elastic, about 10 minutes, adding more flour while kneading. Shape into ball; place in greased large bowl, turning over to grease top. Cover; let rise in warm place (80° to 85°F.), away from draft, until doubled, about 1½ hours. Punch down dough; turn onto lightly floured surface; cover with a bowl; let rest 30 minutes.

3 Roll butter between 2 sheets of waxed paper to 10″ by 7″ rectangle. Turn over for even rolling; lift top sheet frequently to remove wrinkles. Chill butter with waxed paper.

4 On floured surface, roll dough to 18″ by 9″ rectangle. Remove 1 sheet of paper from butter; invert butter on ⅔ of dough, leaving 1-inch margin on 3 sides.

5 Remove other sheet from butter. Fold unbuttered dough over butter. Fold buttered dough over center to make 9″ by 6″ rectangle.

6 Press edges to seal. Carefully roll layered dough to 18″ by 9″ rectangle ; do not press edges too hard or butter may ooze out.

7 Fold in thirds to make a 9″ by 6″ rectangle; sprinkle with flour; wrap; chill 1 to 2 hours. Roll, fold and chill twice more (dough may be left overnight after final fold).

8 Cut dough in half. Roll one piece to 21″ by 10″ rectangle. (Chill other piece.) Cut triangles 7 inches wide at base; join ends for sixth triangle.

9 From 7-inch base, roll up triangles. Place, pointed tip down, on ungreased cookie sheet, 2 inches apart.

10 Bend ends around toward pointed tip to form crescent shape. Repeat with the remaining dough.

11 Cover croissants loosely with plastic wrap; let rise in warm place until doubled, about 1 hour. In hot weather, set dough in refrigerator from time to time to prevent butter oozing out. Preheat oven to 425°F. In cup with pastry brush, beat egg and water; brush over croissants. Bake 15 minutes or until puffed and browned. Immediately remove croissants to cool on wire rack 10 minutes.

Color index page 83

Begin 6 hrs ahead

2 loaves

Poppy-Seed Poticas

½ cup sugar
2 teaspoons grated lemon
*   peel*
½ teaspoon salt
1 package active dry
*   yeast*
3½ to 4 cups all-purpose
*   flour*

1 cup milk
½ cup butter or
*   margarine*
1 egg
Poppy-Seed Filling
*   (below)*
1 egg yolk, beaten

1. In large bowl, combine sugar, lemon peel, salt, yeast and 1 cup flour. In 1-quart saucepan over low heat, heat milk and butter until very warm (120° to 130°F.). (Butter does not need to melt.)
2. With mixer at low speed, beat liquid into dry ingredients; beat until just mixed. Increase speed to medium: beat 2 minutes, occasionally scraping bowl with rubber spatula. Beat in egg and 1 cup flour or enough to make thick batter; beat 2 minutes more, occasionally scraping bowl. With spoon, stir in enough additional flour (about 1½ cups) to make soft dough.
3. On lightly floured surface, knead dough until smooth and elastic, about 5 minutes. Shape into ball; place in greased large bowl, turning to grease top. Cover; let rise until doubled, about 1 hour.
4. Punch down dough. Turn onto lightly floured surface; cut in half; cover; let rest 15 minutes.
5. Grease 2 cookie sheets. With lightly floured rolling pin, roll one dough half into 18″ by 12″ rectangle. Spread half filling on dough, to within ½ inch of sides. From 18-inch edge, tightly roll dough, jelly-roll fashion; pinch ends to seal. Arrange dough in flat coil, seam side down, on a cookie sheet. Repeat with remaining dough. Cover with towel; let rise until doubled, about 1½ hours.
6. Preheat oven to 350°F. Brush loaves with beaten yolk. Bake 25 to 30 minutes until loaves sound hollow when tapped. Remove to wire racks to cool.

POPPY-SEED FILLING: In medium bowl, combine *one 12-ounce can poppy-seed cake-and-pastry filling, ½ cup finely chopped California walnuts, 1 tablespoon grated lemon peel* and *1 teaspoon ground cinnamon;* set aside. In small bowl with mixer at high speed, beat *1 egg white* until soft peaks form; fold into poppy-seed mixture.

Making dough roll: From 18-inch edge, tightly roll dough. Pinch ends to seal.

Forming the shape: Place roll in a flat coil, seam side down, on cookie sheet.

Color index
page 82

Begin 4 hrs
ahead

36 doughnuts

Jelly Doughnuts

5 to 6 cups all-purpose
  flour
1/3 cup sugar
2 teaspoons ground
  nutmeg
1 teaspoon salt
1/2 teaspoon ground
  cinnamon
2 packages active dry
  yeast

1 1/4 cups milk
1/3 cup butter or
  margarine
2 eggs
about 4 cups salad oil
2 cups apple, blackberry,
  grape or other jelly (2
  10-ounce jars)
confectioners' sugar

1. In large bowl, combine 1 1/2 cups flour and next 5 ingredients. In 1-quart saucepan over low heat, heat milk and butter until very warm (120° to 130°F.). (Butter does not need to melt completely.)
2. With mixer at low speed, beat liquid into dry ingredients. At medium speed, beat in eggs; beat 2 minutes more. Beat in 3/4 cup flour or enough to make thick batter; beat 2 minutes more. Stir in about 1 3/4 cups flour to make soft dough.
3. On floured surface, knead dough until smooth and elastic, about 10 minutes. Shape into ball; place in greased large bowl; turn to grease top. Cover with towel; let rise in warm place, away from draft, until doubled, about 1 hour.
4. Punch down dough; turn onto lightly floured surface. Cut dough in half; cover with bowl; let rest 15 minutes. Grease 2 cookie sheets.
5. Roll one half of dough 1/4 inch thick. Using 2 3/4-inch round biscuit cutter, cut circles. Repeat with remaining dough and trimmings.

6 Place circles on cookie sheets; cover with towels and let rise in warm place (80° to 85°F.), until doubled, about 1 hour.

7 In deep-fat fryer, heat 1 inch oil to 370°F. Fry 4 or 5 doughnuts at a time until golden brown, 45 seconds to 1 minute on each side, turning once with slotted spoon.

8 Drain on paper towels. With sharp, thin knife, pierce doughnuts from one side almost to other side.

9 With pastry bag with 1/4-inch hole in end, press a little jelly into doughnuts through slit. Sprinkle with confectioners' sugar.

SUGARED DOUGHNUTS: Prepare *dough for Jelly Doughnuts* (left) as in steps 1–5 but, with lightly floured doughnut cutter, cut out doughnuts. Reroll trimmings and "holes" (or fry "holes" separately). Let rise, then fry as in steps 6 and 7. Drain. Sprinkle warm doughnuts with *sugar* or shake with sugar in a plastic bag and omit jelly. Or, spread a glaze of *1/2 cup honey* and *2/3 cup confectioners' sugar* on top.

Shaping the doughnuts: Cut out the doughnuts as close together as possible.

Sugaring: Sprinkle warm doughnuts with sugar or shake with sugar in a bag.

CREAM DOUGHNUTS: Prepare as for Jelly Doughnuts but omit jelly. For filling, use *canned vanilla or chocolate pudding* or pudding prepared with regular vanilla, chocolate, butterscotch or lemon pudding mix as label directs. Store doughnuts in refrigerator.

Color index
page 82

PARTY DOUGHNUTS: Prepare *Cream Doughnuts* (above). Make glaze: In small bowl, beat *2 cups confectioners' sugar*, *1/2 teaspoon vanilla extract* and *3 tablespoons water* until smooth. Spread glaze over doughnuts; top with *chopped nuts,* flaked or shredded coconut, or chocolate shot or nonpareils.

Coating with glaze: With spoon, spread glaze over tops of doughnuts.

Adding a topping: Sprinkle glazed doughnuts with toppings of your choice.

DOUGHNUT TIPS

Doughnuts can also be fried in a Dutch oven. Use medium heat and heat oil to 370°F.

Do not roll doughnut dough too many times or the last doughnuts will be tough.

Lift raised, ready-to-fry dough circles with a pancake turner so they keep their shape and do not stretch.

Use a slotted spoon to remove doughnuts from fat.

A cookie press or cake decorator can be used instead of a pastry bag to add a filling.

Special breads

Color index page 82
Begin 4 hrs or day ahead
24 babas

Babas au Rhum

¼ cup sugar	*6 eggs*
¼ teaspoon salt	*1 4-ounce jar candied*
2 packages active dry	*citron or 1 cup dried*
yeast	*currants*
about 3½ cups all-	*Rum Sauce (below)*
purpose flour	*⅓ cup apricot jam*
½ cup water	*1 tablespoon lemon*
½ cup butter or	*juice*
margarine	

1. Grease twenty-four 2-inch-deep, 2-inch-diameter baba molds or 3-inch muffin-pan cups; set aside. In large bowl, combine sugar, salt, yeast and ¾ cup flour. In 1-quart saucepan over low heat, heat water and butter until very warm (120° to 130°F.). (Butter does not need to melt completely.)
2. With mixer at low speed, gradually beat liquid into dry ingredients; beat just until mixed. At medium speed, beat 2 minutes, occasionally scraping bowl with rubber spatula. Beat in eggs and 1 cup flour or enough to make a thick batter; continue beating 2 minutes, occasionally scraping bowl. Stir in citron or currants and enough additional flour (about 1¾ cups) to make a soft dough.
3. Place a heaping tablespoonful of dough in each mold. Cover with towel; let rise in warm place (80° to 85°F.), until center of dough is slightly above tops of molds, about 1 hour.
4. Preheat oven to 375°F. Bake babas 15 to 20 minutes until golden brown. Meanwhile, prepare Rum Sauce. Slightly cool babas in molds on wire racks; remove from molds; place, top side up, in large, shallow roasting pan; spoon on sauce. Cover; let babas stand at least 2 hours, turning several times to absorb sauce evenly.
5. To serve: Into small bowl, press apricot jam through a sieve and stir in lemon juice until smooth. Spread over top of each baba.

RUM SAUCE: In 2-quart saucepan over medium heat, heat *3 cups water, 2¼ cups sugar, 6 thin orange slices* and *6 thin lemon slices* to boiling. Reduce heat to low; cover; simmer 5 minutes. Cool sauce to lukewarm; discard orange and lemon slices. Stir *1¼ cups light rum* into sauce.

Turning babas: During a 2-hour period, turn babas several times to absorb sauce evenly.

Making topping: With spoon, press jam through a sieve before stirring in lemon juice.

Danish Pastry Dough

¼ cup sugar
1 teaspoon salt
1 teaspoon ground
cardamom
2 packages active dry
yeast
about 4 cups all-purpose
flour
1¼ cups milk
1 egg
1½ cups butter

Begin 5 hrs or up to 1 wk ahead

Dough for Danish Pastry (opposite)

1 In large bowl, combine sugar, salt, cardamom, yeast and 1½ cups flour. In 1-quart saucepan over low heat, heat milk until very warm (120° to 130°F.).

2 With mixer at low speed, beat liquid into dry ingredients until just blended; beat in egg. Increase speed to medium; beat 2 minutes.

3 Beat in ½ cup flour to make thick batter; continue beating 2 minutes. Stir in enough additional flour (about 1½ cups) to make soft dough.

4 On well-floured surface, knead dough until smooth and elastic, about 10 minutes, adding more flour if needed. Shape into ball; cover 30 minutes.

5 Roll butter between 2 sheets of waxed paper to 12″ by 8″ rectangle; turn over for even rolling and lift top sheet frequently to remove wrinkles. Chill.

6 On floured surface with floured rolling pin, roll dough into 18″ by 9″ rectangle.

7 Remove top sheet of paper from butter; invert over ⅔ of dough, leaving ½-inch margin on 3 sides. Remove other sheet.

8 Fold unbuttered ⅓ of dough over middle ⅓; fold opposite end over middle to make 9″ by 6″ rectangle.

9 With rolling pin, press dough together around edges to seal in butter.

10 Roll dough to 18″ by 9″ rectangle. Fold rectangle crosswise into thirds to make 9″ by 6″ rectangle.

11 Wrap; chill 30 minutes. Roll, fold, wrap and chill twice more. Dough will keep 1 week. Use in recipe opposite.

Danish Pastry

Danish Pastry Dough (left) **1 egg**
Fillings (right) **1 tablespoon water**

Color index page 82
Begin 5 hrs ahead
24 pastries

1. Prepare Danish Pastry Dough. Prepare one of fillings. Cut dough into quarters; roll one piece to 12″ by 8″ rectangle (keep other pieces chilled). Cut rectangle into six 4-inch squares. In cup, beat egg with water; brush over squares. Place on ungreased cookie sheet about 2 inches apart; shape and fill as shown below. Repeat with remaining dough.
2. Cover loosely; let rise in refrigerator 1 hour.
3. Preheat oven to 400°F. Brush egg mixture over pastries. Bake 15 to 18 minutes or until puffed and golden brown. Remove to wire rack to cool. If folded portions on pastries open slightly during baking, while pastries are still hot, reshape them.

FILLINGS

JAM FILLING: *One 10- to 12-ounce jar raspberry or apricot jam* (about 1½ cups jam) will fill 24 Danish Pastries.

ALMOND FILLING: In small bowl with spoon, blend well *one 8-ounce can almond paste* and *1 egg yolk.* (Makes 1¼ cups or enough for 24 pastries.)

CREAM CHEESE FILLING: In small bowl with mixer at low speed, beat *one 8-ounce package cream cheese,* softened, *½ cup confectioners' sugar, 1 egg yolk* and *1 teaspoon grated lemon peel* until blended. Stir *¼ cup dried currants* into cream-cheese mixture. (Makes 1⅓ cups or enough filling for 24 pastries.)

PINWHEELS

With sharp knife, cut 1½ to 2 inches from each corner toward center, making 8 points.

Fold alternate points to center; press dough firmly in center to seal.

If using jam, fill center with 1 tablespoon jam after baking for better appearance. With other fillings, spoon about 1 tablespoon in center just before baking.

FOLDOVERS

Place 1 tablespoon jam or Almond Filling in center; bring one corner over filling; bring opposite corner to center of fold; press gently to seal.

ENVELOPES

Place 1 tablespoon jam or other filling in center of square. Bring corners to center to enclose filling.

COCKSCOMB

Use only Almond Filling: Spread 1 tablespoon filling on half of square to within ½ inch of edges.

Fold square in half; across folded edge make 4 slashes ¾ way through.

Open slashes to form cockscomb.

Holiday breads

These breads are usually baked at a special time of year: Kulich is traditionally eaten at Easter time (see also Hot Cross Buns, page 442), and Stollen, heavy with fruit and nuts, is traditionally baked for Christmas. However, they can be enjoyed all year round, whether there is a holiday or not, so try them whenever you like.

Stollen

Color index
page 83

Begin 5 hrs
ahead

3 stollens

½ cup sugar	3 eggs
1½ teaspoons salt	1 cup toasted slivered
2 packages active dry	almonds
yeast	1 cup cut-up candied
5½ to 6½ cups all-	cherries
purpose flour	⅓ cup golden raisins
1¼ cups milk	confectioners' sugar
⅔ cup butter or	
margarine	

1. In large bowl, combine sugar, salt, yeast and 2 cups flour. In 1-quart saucepan over low heat, heat milk and butter until very warm (120° to 130°F.). (Butter does not need to melt.)
2. With mixer at low speed, gradually beat liquid into dry ingredients. Increase speed to medium; beat 2 minutes, occasionally scraping bowl with rubber spatula. Beat in eggs and ½ cup flour or enough to make a thick batter; continue beating 2 minutes, occasionally scraping bowl. With spoon, stir in enough flour (about 2¾ cups) to make a soft dough.
3. On lightly floured surface, knead dough until smooth and elastic, about 10 minutes. Shape dough into ball; place in greased large bowl, turning to grease top. Cover with towel; let rise in warm place until doubled, about 1 hour. In small bowl, mix almonds, cherries and raisins.
4. Punch down dough. Turn onto lightly floured surface; knead nut mixture into dough. Cut dough into 3 pieces. Cover 2 pieces; refrigerate.
5. With lightly floured rolling pin, roll 1 piece into 12″ by 7″ oval; fold in half lengthwise. Place on large cookie sheet. Cover. Repeat with second piece of dough. Let both rise in warm place until doubled, about 1 hour. After 30 minutes of rising time, repeat with third piece of dough.
6. Preheat oven to 350°F. Bake first 2 stollens 25 to 30 minutes until they sound hollow when tapped with fingers. Remove to cool on wire racks. Bake third stollen; cool on wire rack. Sprinkle 3 stollens with confectioners' sugar.

Adding nut mixture: Knead almond, cherry and raisin mixture into dough.

Shaping bread: Roll dough into 12″ by 7″ oval; fold in half lengthwise.

Kulich

Color index
page 83

Begin 5 hrs
ahead

3 loaves

½ cup sugar	milk
½ teaspoon salt	3 eggs
¼ teaspoon ground	½ cup dark seedless or
cardamom	golden raisins
2 packages active dry	½ cup mixed candied
yeast	fruit
about 6½ cups all-	¼ cup diced roasted
purpose flour	almonds
½ cup butter or	1½ cups confectioners'
margarine	sugar
1 teaspoon vanilla	½ teaspoon lemon juice
extract	

1. In large bowl, combine sugar, salt, cardamom, yeast and 1 cup flour. In 1-quart saucepan over low heat, heat butter, vanilla and 1 cup milk until very warm (120° to 130°F.).
2. With mixer at low speed, beat liquid into dry ingredients until just blended. At medium speed, beat 2 minutes, scraping bowl often with rubber spatula. Beat in eggs and 2 cups flour to make a thick batter; beat 2 minutes longer. Stir in about 3 cups flour to make a soft dough.
3. On floured surface, knead dough 5 minutes, adding more flour while kneading. Add raisins, candied fruit and almonds; knead until smooth and elastic, about 5 minutes. Shape into ball; place in greased large bowl, turning to grease top. Cover with towel; let rise until doubled, about 1½ hours.
4. Prepare and fill three 1-pound (5½-inch high) coffee cans, as shown below. Then cover; let rise until doubled, about 1 hour.
5. Preheat oven to 350°F. Brush each loaf with milk. Bake 50 minutes or until loaves sound hollow when tapped. (If tops brown too quickly, cover loosely with foil.) Remove loaves from cans immediately; cool them on wire racks.
6. Meanwhile prepare icing: In small bowl, with spoon, beat confectioners' sugar, 2 tablespoons milk and lemon juice until smooth.
7. Frost tops of loaves with icing, letting some drip down side of loaves.

PREPARING THE CANS

Line inside of each can with foil; grease foil. Punch down dough; divide into 3 pieces and shape to fit cans; place in cans, smooth side up.

Cut one 14-inch piece of 12-inch foil for each can; fold in fourths lengthwise; grease one side and with this side inward, wrap around outside of can leaving 2 inches extending above rim.

Challah

Color index
page 82

Begin 5½ hrs
ahead

2 loaves

2 tablespoons sugar
1½ teaspoons salt
2 packages active dry
   yeast
6½ to 7 cups all-purpose
   flour

1½ cups water
6 tablespoons salad
   oil
6 eggs

1. In large bowl, combine sugar, salt, yeast and 2 cups flour. In 1 quart saucepan over low heat, heat water and oil until very warm (120° to 130°F.).
2. With mixer at low speed, gradually beat liquid into dry ingredients; beat until just mixed. Increase speed to medium; beat 2 minutes, occasionally scraping bowl with rubber spatula.
3. Reserve 2 egg yolks; add egg whites, remaining eggs and 1½ cups flour or enough to make a thick batter; continue beating 2 minutes, occasionally scraping bowl with rubber spatula. Stir in about 2½ cups flour to make a soft dough.
4. On lightly floured surface, knead dough until smooth and elastic, about 5 minutes, adding more flour while kneading. Shape dough into ball; place in greased large bowl, turning to grease top. Cover with towel; let rise in warm place (80° to 85°F.), until doubled, about 1 hour.
5. Punch down dough. Turn dough onto lightly floured surface; cover; let rest 15 minutes. Meanwhile, grease 1 large cookie sheet.
6. Prepare braided loaves.

Pinch ends of braid to seal. Place on cookie sheet for bottom part of loaf. Repeat with another piece for another loaf. Cut remaining dough into 6 pieces; roll each piece into 17-inch-long rope. Braid each set of 3 ropes as above; pinch ends to seal.

Braiding loaves: Divide the dough into 3 pieces. Cut 1 piece into thirds; with hands, roll each third into a 16-inch-long rope. Place ropes side by side and braid.

Place each smaller braid on top of a large braid; tuck ends of top braid under bottom braid, stretching top braid if it is necessary.

7. Arrange loaves at least 5 inches apart on cookie sheet; cover; let rise in warm place, away from draft, until doubled, about 1 hour.
8. Preheat oven to 375°F. Brush top and sides of loaf with reserved egg yolks. Bake 35 minutes or until loaves sound hollow when lightly tapped. Remove from cookie sheet and cool on wire racks.

Cardamom Christmas Wreath

Color index
page 83

Begin 4½ hrs
ahead

1 wreath

1 cup sugar
1 teaspoon salt
1 teaspoon ground
   cardamom
2 packages active dry
   yeast
about 7 cups all-purpose
   flour
1 cup butter or margarine

milk
3 eggs
1 tablespoon grated
   lemon peel
½ teaspoon almond
   extract
about 1 yard decorative
   ribbon

1. In large bowl, combine sugar, salt, cardamom, yeast and 2 cups flour. In 1-quart saucepan over low heat, heat butter or margarine and 1½ cups milk until very warm (120° to 130°F.). (Butter does not need to melt completely.)
2. With mixer at low speed, beat liquid into dry ingredients until just blended. At medium speed, beat 2 minutes. Reserve 1 egg white. Beat in remaining eggs, lemon peel, almond extract and 2 cups flour; beat 2 minutes longer. Stir in about 2½ cups flour to make a soft dough.
3. On floured surface, knead dough until smooth and elastic, about 10 minutes, adding more flour while kneading, if needed. Shape dough into ball; place in greased large bowl, turning to grease top. Cover dough with towel; let rise in warm place (80° to 85°F.), until doubled, about 1 hour.
4. Punch down dough. Turn onto lightly floured surface; cover with towel and let dough rest for 15 minutes for easier shaping.
5. Grease large cookie sheet and outside of 2-quart, straight-sided, ovensafe bowl. Invert bowl; place in center of sheet. In small bowl, combine reserved egg white and 1 tablespoon milk; set aside. Cut off about ½ cup of dough; set aside.
6. With rolling pin, roll dough into 30″ by 10″ rectangle. From 30-inch side, with hands, roll jelly-roll fashion into rope; twist slightly. Wrap rope around bowl on sheet; press ends of rope together to seal and tuck them under.
7. Roll reserved dough ⅛ inch thick. Decorate loaf:

Cutting decorations:
With floured 2½-inch leaf-shaped cookie cutter, cut about 15 leaves. Shape scraps into about fifteen ¼-inch balls.

Applying decorations:
Brush some egg-white mixture on back of leaves and balls. Place 3 leaves together and top with 3 balls as shown.

8. Cover wreath; let rise in warm place, away from draft, until doubled, about 45 minutes. Preheat oven to 350°F. Brush wreath with remaining egg-white mixture. Bake 1 hour or until golden. Remove bowl; cool wreath on wire rack. Tie ribbon around it.

Pizza

Pizza dough is as easy to make as the simplest yeast dough. Just follow the same basic techniques. By using water as the liquid ingredient, not milk as in most yeast doughs, you make the crust crisp. When the dough has risen, been punched down and allowed to rest for 15 minutes, you are ready to roll it into thin circles.

To transfer dough circles easily to pizza pans, fold them into quarters, transfer, then unfold in pans. If you don't have special pizza pans use large cookie sheets. As soon as the topping has been arranged on the dough, bake the pizza. Unlike most yeast breads, pizza does not have to rise again before being baked.

Pizza can be served as a main dish, for between-meal snacks and as party fare.

Cutting baked pizza: Use scissors to cut pizza easily into wedge-shaped slices if you don't have a straight-edge pastry wheel.

PIZZA TOPPINGS

Prepare the Cheese Pizza (right) but use only *½ pound mozzarella cheese.* Add one or more of the following to the pizzas before baking:

MUSHROOM: *½ pound mushrooms,* sliced.

PEPPERONI: *1 pound pepperoni,* thinly sliced.

ANCHOVY: *Two 2-ounce cans anchovy fillets,* well-drained.

SAUSAGE: *Two 8-ounce packages brown-and-serve sausages,* cut into ½-inch chunks; or *1 pound pork sausage,* cooked in skillet until browned, then drained well.

ITALIAN SAUSAGE: *1 pound sweet or hot Italian sausages,* cooked and cut into thin slices.

BEEF: *1 pound lean ground beef,* cooked in skillet until browned, then drained.

OLIVE: *1 cup sliced pitted ripe or pimento-stuffed green olives.*

GREEN PEPPER: *2 small green peppers,* sliced in thin strips.

ONION: *2 small onions,* minced.

PIMENTO: *½ cup chopped canned pimentos.*

Cheese Pizza

1 package active dry yeast
about 4½ cups all-purpose flour
salt
1½ cups water
olive or salad oil
1 medium onion, diced
1 garlic clove, minced
1 16-ounce can tomatoes
1 6-ounce can tomato paste
1½ teaspoons sugar

1 teaspoon Italian herb seasoning mix
¼ teaspoon crushed red pepper
1 16-ounce package mozzarella cheese, shredded

Color index page 31
Begin 2½ hrs ahead
8 main-dish servings

1 In large bowl, combine yeast, 2 cups flour and 1 teaspoon salt. In 1-quart saucepan over low heat, heat water until very warm (120° to 130°F.). With mixer at low speed, just blend water into dry ingredients. At medium speed, beat 2 minutes, occasionally scraping bowl with rubber spatula. Beat in ½ cup flour to make a thick batter; beat 2 minutes more. Stir in about 1½ cups flour to make a soft dough.

2 On floured surface, knead dough about 8 minutes, adding more flour if needed. Shape into ball; place in greased large bowl; cover; let rise until doubled, about 1 hour.

3 In 2-quart saucepan over medium heat, in 1 tablespoon hot oil, cook onion and garlic until tender. Add tomatoes and tomato paste. Stir to break up tomatoes.

4 Add sugar, herb seasoning mix, red pepper and 1 teaspoon salt; heat to boiling, stirring. Reduce heat to low; cover partially; simmer sauce 20 minutes.

5 Punch down dough; cut in half; turn onto lightly floured surface. Cover 15 minutes. Preheat oven to 450°F. Grease 2 large cookie sheets or 12-inch pizza pans.

6 With floured rolling pin, roll each dough half into 13-inch circle.

7 Fold circles of dough into quarters; lift onto cookie sheets and unfold.

8 Pinch up edges of dough circle to form rim; brush circle with olive or salad oil.

9 Sprinkle dough circles with half of shredded mozzarella cheese. Top with tomato sauce.

10 Sprinkle with rest of cheese. Bake 20 minutes or until crust is golden. Cut into wedges.

SANDWICHES

Sandwiches can be anything from a light snack to a meal in themselves. For large quantities, use production-line techniques. Line up the bread slices in rows, two by two, and spread them with softened butter. Spread the filling on one row; top with remaining slices; cut and wrap sandwiches. When making more than one variety, cut and wrap one type before proceeding to another. Always add lettuce, tomato and similar ingredients just before serving. If added ahead, these can make the bread soggy and may moisten the filling. Many sandwiches can be prepared and frozen up to 2 weeks before serving. Always use fresh bread and the freshest filling ingredients.

Hot sandwiches

Croque Monsieur

Color index page 108

Begin 45 mins ahead or early in day

16 sandwiches or 8 servings

**16 thin white-bread slices, crusts removed
prepared mustard
1 8-ounce package sliced
Swiss cheese**

**½ pound thinly sliced
cooked ham
⅓ cup melted butter or
margarine**

1 Spread half of bread slices with mustard; trim cheese slices to fit and place on top.

2 Trim ham slices to fit bread; place on cheese. Top with remaining bread slices. Arrange sandwiches on cookie sheet. Wrap; refrigerate, if made ahead.

3 *About 20 minutes before serving:* Preheat oven to 450°F. Brush sandwiches with some of melted butter; toast in oven about 5 minutes until lightly browned.

4 Turn; brush other side with butter; toast 3 minutes more. Cut sandwiches into halves and serve warm wrapped individually in small paper napkins.

Mozzarella Loaf

Color index page 108

Begin 40 mins ahead

6 servings

**1 long loaf Italian bread
with sesame seed
1 16-ounce package
mozzarella cheese**

**½ cup olives for salad
1½ teaspoons
oregano**

1. Preheat oven to 400°F. Cut Italian bread crosswise into 1-inch slices, being careful not to cut through bottom crust. Cut mozzarella cheese into ¼-inch slices. Place cheese slices and olives between bread slices.
2. Place bread on cookie sheet and bake about 15 minutes or until cheese is melted and bread is heated through. Sprinkle loaf with oregano. With a sharp knife, divide loaf into slices by cutting through bottom crust. Serve Mozzarella Loaf immediately.

Barbecued Pork Sandwiches

Color index page 108

Begin 3½ hrs ahead

10 sandwiches

**2½ pounds pork shoulder
blade roast boneless,
cut into 1½-inch
chunks
2 medium onions,
chopped
2 medium green peppers,
chopped
1 6-ounce can tomato
paste
½ cup packed brown
sugar**

**½ cup water
¼ cup cider vinegar
3 tablespoons chili
powder
2 teaspoons salt
2 teaspoons
Worcestershire
1 teaspoon dry mustard
10 6-inch-long hard rolls
lettuce leaves
1 large tomato, diced**

1. In 5-quart Dutch oven, combine first 11 ingredients. Over high heat, heat to boiling. Reduce heat to low; cover and simmer about 3 hours or until pork is *very* tender, stirring occasionally.
2. When pork is done, skim off any fat. With wire whisk, stir mixture until meat is shredded.
3. To serve, cut each roll horizontally in half but not all the way through. Line rolls with lettuce leaves; fill with pork mixture. Sprinkle with tomato.

Hot sandwiches

Reuben

Color index
page 108

Begin 45 mins
ahead

4 sandwiches

½ cup mayonnaise
1 tablespoon minced
　green pepper
1 tablespoon chili
　sauce
8 rye-bread slices
4 Swiss-cheese slices

½ pound sliced corned
　beef
½ 16-ounce package
　sauerkraut, drained
　(1 cup)
butter or margarine

1. In small bowl, combine first 3 ingredients. Spread about 1 tablespoon mayonnaise mixture on each bread slice. Halve cheese slices crosswise. On each of 4 bread slices, place a cheese slice, ¼ of corned beef, ¼ of sauerkraut, another cheese slice and another bread slice, mayonnaise side down.

2. In 12-inch skillet over medium heat, in 2 tablespoons hot butter, brown sandwiches on one side. Turn and cook until bread is browned and cheese is melted, adding more butter if needed. Cut each sandwich crosswise in half.

Layering the filling: On 4 bread slices, place cheese, corned beef, sauerkraut and more cheese.

Cooking the sandwiches: Fry sandwiches in butter until bread is brown and cheese melted.

Canadian-Bacon Buns

Color index
page 108

Begin 15 mins
ahead

6 sandwiches

1 16-ounce package
　Canadian-bacon slices
6 hamburger buns

butter or margarine,
　softened

Preheat broiler if manufacturer directs. In 10-inch skillet over medium-high heat, fry bacon just until heated. Meanwhile, split buns and spread with butter or margarine; broil until golden brown. To serve: Place 2 or 3 slices bacon in each bun; cut in half. Serve hot.

Western Sandwiches

Color index
page 108

Begin 35 mins
ahead

4 sandwiches

3 tablespoons butter
1 6-ounce package sliced
　cooked ham, diced
　(about 1 cup)
½ medium green pepper,
　diced

½ medium onion, diced
6 eggs
2 tablespoons milk
¾ teaspoon salt
8 white-bread slices,
　toasted

1. In 10-inch skillet over medium heat, in butter, cook ham, green pepper and onion until the vegetables are tender, about 5 minutes.

2. Meanwhile, in large bowl, beat eggs, milk and salt until well mixed; stir into ham mixture. Reduce heat to low; cover and cook 12 to 15 minutes, until top is set and underside is lightly browned. Serve between the toasted white-bread slices.

Sloppy Joes

Color index
page 108

Begin 30 mins
ahead

6 sandwiches

1 pound lean ground beef
1 medium green pepper,
　diced
1 medium onion, diced
1 16-ounce can pork and
　beans
½ cup catchup
½ teaspoon salt
½ teaspoon chili
　powder
6 8-inch-long rolls
lettuce leaves

1 In 10-inch skillet over medium-high heat, cook first 3 ingredients 10 minutes till ground beef is well browned.

2 Stir in next 4 ingredients; heat to boiling. Reduce heat to low; simmer, uncovered, 10 minutes, stirring occasionally.

3 Halve rolls horizontally. On bottom halves arrange lettuce leaves; add ⅔ cup ground beef and pork and beans mixture; replace top halves.

Tacos

Color index
page 109

Begin 1 hr
ahead

12 sandwiches

Chicken or Beef Filling
　(below)
12 taco shells or
　Homemade Taco
　Shells (below)
shredded lettuce

2 cups shredded
　Cheddar cheese
4 medium tomatoes,
　chopped
hot red pepper sauce

Prepare filling. Stuff each shell with 2 or 3 tablespoons filling; add remaining ingredients.

CHICKEN FILLING: In 10-inch skillet over medium-high heat, cook 2 medium onions, chopped, in ¼ cup butter until limp; add 4 cups cooked diced chicken, 4 medium tomatoes, chopped, 2 teaspoons salt and 1 teaspoon pepper; heat until piping hot.

BEEF FILLING: In 10-inch skillet over medium-high heat, brown 2 pounds ground beef and 2 medium onions, chopped; spoon off any excess fat. Add 4 medium tomatoes, chopped, 2 teaspoons oregano, 2 teaspoons salt, 1 teaspoon pepper and 2 garlic cloves, crushed; heat until piping hot.

HOMEMADE TACO SHELLS: About 1¾ hours ahead: Prepare Corn Tortillas (page 431). In 10-inch skillet over medium heat, in about ½ inch hot salad oil, fry a tortilla just until it softens. With tongs, fold in half, holding it open about an inch. Fry one side crisp; turn and fry other side. Drain on paper towels. Repeat with rest of tortillas.

Cold sandwiches

Curried Beef in Pita

Color index page 108

Begin 3 hrs ahead

12 sandwiches or 6 servings

Pita (page 447)
1 pound lean ground beef
½ cup chopped onion
1 medium Delicious apple, chopped
¼ cup dark seedless raisins

1¼ teaspoons salt
1 teaspoon curry powder
1 8-ounce container plain yogurt

1. Prepare Pita. Prepare Curried Beef: In 10-inch skillet over medium-high heat, cook ground beef and onion until meat is browned and onion is tender; spoon off any excess fat. Add apple, raisins, salt and curry. Reduce heat to low; cover and simmer 5 minutes or until apple is tender-crisp.
2. Cut each piece of pita bread in half to make 2 "pockets." Fill each half with about ⅓ cup beef mixture. Pass the plain yogurt separately to spoon into each sandwich.

Italian Hero Sandwiches

Color index page 109

Begin 45 mins ahead

4 sandwiches

12 sweet Italian sausages
¼ cup water
2 medium onions
5 green or red peppers

2 tablespoons olive or salad oil
4 5-inch-long hard rolls

1. In 12-inch skillet, place sausages; add water. Cover; simmer 5 minutes. Remove cover and continue cooking about 15 minutes longer or until sausages are browned, turning occasionally.
2. Meanwhile, cut onions into thin slices; cut peppers into ½-inch strips. In hot oil, in another 12-inch skillet, sauté onions until just limp. Add peppers and continue cooking over medium heat, stirring occasionally, until peppers are tender, about 10 minutes. Add cooked sausages.
3. Split hard rolls in half lengthwise. Layer bottom of each roll with some of pepper and onion mixture and 3 of the sausages, then add top part of roll.
4. To serve: Cut each roll crosswise into halves for easier eating.

Open-face Steak Sandwiches

Color index page 108

Begin 20 mins ahead

4 servings

4 white-bread slices
butter or margarine
4 beef cubed steaks
unseasoned meat tenderizer
1 envelope beef-flavor bouillon

¾ cup water
2 teaspoons all-purpose flour
watercress sprigs for garnish

1. Toast bread slices; spread one side of each with butter or margarine; arrange each on a warm dinner plate; keep warm.
2. Sprinkle steaks with tenderizer as label directs. In 12-inch skillet over high heat, in 3 tablespoons hot butter or margarine, cook steaks 1 minute on each side or until of desired doneness. Place a steak on each toast slice.
3. Reduce heat to medium. In cup, blend bouillon, water and flour. Stir into drippings in skillet; cook, stirring, until thickened. Pour gravy over sandwiches. Garnish plates with watercress.

Club Sandwiches

Color index page 109

Begin 20 mins ahead

2 servings

6 bacon slices
6 white-bread slices, toasted
mayonnaise
lettuce leaves

2 large cooked turkey slices
salt
pepper
1 large tomato, sliced

1 In 10-inch skillet over medium heat, cook bacon slices until crisp; drain on paper towels. Spread one side of each bread slice with mayonnaise.

2 Arrange lettuce leaves on 2 slices; top with turkey; sprinkle with salt and pepper then cover each with another bread slice, mayonnaise side up.

3 Top each sandwich with more lettuce, half of tomato slices, 3 cooked bacon slices and remaining white-bread slice, mayonnaise side down.

4 Cut sandwiches diagonally into fourths; secure each quarter with decorated toothpicks. Arrange, cut sides up, on individual plates.

VARIATIONS: Prepare as above but instead of turkey, use *2 large slices cooked ham*, corned beef, pastrami or roast beef. Instead of bacon, use *2 slices Swiss cheese* or 4 slices cooked Canadian bacon.

Poor Boy

Color index page 109

Begin 20 mins ahead

6 servings

1 1-pound long loaf unsliced French bread
¼ cup Russian dressing (page 326)
2 hard-cooked eggs, finely chopped
2 tablespoons chopped green onions
2 tablespoons mayonnaise

½ teaspoon seasoned salt
1 small cucumber, sliced
2 6-ounce packages sliced cooked ham
1 8-ounce package natural Swiss-cheese slices
1 large tomato, sliced

1. With sharp knife, cut bread horizontally in half. In small bowl, mix Russian dressing with chopped eggs, green onions, mayonnaise and seasoned salt.
2. On bottom bread half, arrange cucumber slices and remaining ingredients in layers; evenly spread Russian-dressing mixture on top. Replace top bread half. Slice in equal pieces to serve.

Cold sandwiches

OPEN SANDWICHES

The open sandwich, originally a Scandinavian idea, is now internationally enjoyed. The most popular bread to use is pumpernickel or rye. Butter it and choose fillings and garnishes with eye appeal. Here are a few suggestions.

Top rye bread with marinated herring on lettuce; garnish with onion rings and a tomato wedge.

Rare roast beef slices on rye bread, topped with cucumber twist, tomato wedge and crumbled fried onions.

Slices of salami and cucumber twists arranged on rye bread.

Shrimp with mayonnaise on white bread, garnished with cucumber twist and lemon twist.

On white bread, slices of smoked salmon on lettuce decorated with lemon twists.

Sliced cold roast pork on white bread, decorated with orange twist and crumbled cooked bacon.

Slices of hard-cooked egg topped with black caviar and red pepper rings, served on pumpernickel.

On pumpernickel bread, slices of Danish Blue cheese topped with halved black grapes and a walnut half.

Watercress-Walnut Sandwiches

Color index page 109

Begin 30 mins ahead

4 sandwiches

½ bunch watercress
¼ cup California walnuts, chopped
¼ teaspoon seasoned salt

1 8-ounce package Neufchâtel cheese, softened
4 thin pumpernickel-bread slices

1. Chop enough watercress to make ⅓ cup; reserve remaining watercress for garnish.
2. In medium bowl with fork, mix well walnuts, salt, cheese and chopped watercress. Spread cheese mixture on bread slices.
3. To serve: Cut each slice diagonally in half; garnish each half with 2 or 3 sprigs watercress.

Color index page 109

KEEP TRIM SANDWICHES

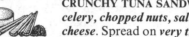

CRUNCHY TUNA SANDWICH: To *tuna*, add *minced celery, chopped nuts, salt* and *a bit of blended cottage cheese*. Spread on *very thin slices of date-nut bread*.

CURRIED SHRIMP SANDWICH: Mix *canned shrimp* and *chopped apple* with *low-calorie mayonnaise* and *curry powder*. Spread on *dark bread*.

CHICKEN LIVER SPECIAL SANDWICH: Chop *cooked chicken livers* with *stuffed olives*. Spread on *pumpernickel bread*.

PEPPERY SANDWICH: Make a sandwich of *thinly sliced green pepper* and *ham slices* on *dark bread*.

PEANUT-BUTTER-PLUS SANDWICHES

Make peanut-butter sandwiches varied and interesting by adding other ingredients. Use creamy or chunky-style peanut butter and spread it on pumpernickel or white bread, or try whole wheat, raisin or rye.

PEANUT-BUTTER AND BANANA SANDWICH: Spread *peanut butter* on both *bread slices*. Use *thinly sliced ripe bananas* as filling.

PEANUT-BUTTER AND CANADIAN-BACON SANDWICH: Cook *2 slices Canadian bacon* for each sandwich. Arrange bacon on a *bread slice* spread with *peanut butter*; sprinkle with *finely chopped parsley*; top with *bread slice*.

PEANUT-BUTTER AND CRANBERRY-SAUCE SANDWICH: Spread a *bread slice* with *2 tablespoons crushed jellied cranberry sauce*. Top with a tender *lettuce leaf*, then add *another bread slice* spread with *peanut butter*, butter side down.

PEANUT-BUTTER AND COLESLAW SANDWICH: In small bowl, combine *2 cups finely shredded cabbage, 2 tablespoons diced pimentos, 2 tablespoons mayonnaise, 1 teaspoon wine vinegar, ½ teaspoon salt* and *¼ teaspoon sugar*. Toss together well. Use as filling with *peanut butter*.

PEANUT-BUTTER AND DATE-NUT SANDWICH: Combine *½ cup diced pitted dates* and *¼ cup chopped pecans*. Use as filling with *peanut butter*.

Tea sandwiches

Color index
page 109

Begin 30 mins
ahead or
early in day

30 tea
sandwiches

Deviled Ham Pinwheels

*1 4½-ounce can deviled
ham*
*1 tablespoon grated
orange peel*
*1 tablespoon prepared
mustard*

2 teaspoons horseradish
*1 1-pound loaf unsliced
white bread (8 inches
long), crust removed*

1. In bowl, combine first 4 ingredients.
2. Cut bread lengthwise into five ¼-inch-thick slices. With rolling pin, lightly flatten each slice. Spread about 2 tablespoons ham mixture over surface of each slice. From short side, roll each slice jelly-roll fashion; cut each slice evenly crosswise to make 6 pinwheel sandwiches.

Spreading the mixture:
Cover each bread slice
with about 2 tablespoons
of ham mixture.

Making the pinwheels: Roll
each bread slice jelly-roll
fashion; cut crosswise to
make pinwheels.

Color index
page 109

Begin 3½ hrs
ahead or
early in day

50 tea
sandwiches

Ribbon Sandwiches

½ cup butter, softened
*3 tablespoons minced
parsley*
*2 5-ounce cans chunk
white chicken*
⅓ cup mayonnaise

1 tablespoon lemon juice
¼ teaspoon salt
¼ teaspoon pepper
*1 1-pound loaf unsliced
white bread (8 inches
long)*

1. In small bowl, mix butter and parsley. In another bowl, mix chicken and next 4 ingredients.
2. Trim crusts from bread. Cut bread horizontally into six ½-inch slices. On first slice, spread ¼ of parsley butter. Place second slice on first; spread with ½ of chicken mixture. Spread third slice with ¼ of parsley butter; place, butter side down, on second slice. Wrap. Repeat. Refrigerate both loaves until well chilled.
3. Cut each loaf into ½-inch-thick slices; cut each slice crosswise in half.

Completing the layers: Add
third bread slice to others,
butter side down.

Cutting the loaves: Cut
loaves into ½-inch-thick
slices; halve slices.

Fillings

CHEESE-AND-RAISIN: Combine *1½ 4-ounce packages shredded Cheddar cheese* (1½ cups) with *3 tablespoons raisins*. (Makes 2 cups.)

DEVILED-HAM-AND-RELISH: Combine *three 4½-ounce cans deviled ham* with *⅓ cup sweet relish*. (Makes 2 cups.)

SALMON-AND-PARSLEY: Combine *one 15-ounce can salmon*, drained, with *3 tablespoons chopped parsley, 2 tablespoons pineapple juice* and *¼ teaspoon salt*. (Makes 2 cups.)

TUNA SALAD: Combine *one 6½- or 7-ounce can tuna*, drained, *½ cup diced celery, ⅓ cup mayonnaise, 2 tablespoons minced onion, 2 tablespoons pickle relish, ¼ teaspoon salt* and *⅛ teaspoon pepper*. (Makes 2 cups.)

SHRIMP SALAD: Mix *1½ cups chopped, cooked shrimp, 2 chopped hard-cooked eggs, ½ cup bottled relish sandwich spread, ¼ cup diced celery, 2 tablespoons milk* and *¼ teaspoon salt*. (Makes 2 cups.)

EGG SALAD: Mix *6 chopped hard-cooked eggs, ¼ cup minced onion, ½ cup mayonnaise, 3 tablespoons prepared mustard* and *1 teaspoon salt* until thoroughly combined. (Makes 2 cups.)

TANGY PINEAPPLE: Combine *one 3-ounce package cream cheese*, softened, with *¼ cup drained canned crushed pineapple* and *1 teaspoon horseradish*. (Makes ⅔ cup.)

CHEESE-AND-ANCHOVY: Combine *one 8-ounce package cream cheese*, softened, *6 tablespoons half-and-half, 1 teaspoon Worcestershire, 1 tablespoon anchovy paste* and *½ cup chopped stuffed olives*. (Makes 1½ cups.)

TURKEY-CHUTNEY: Mix together well *1¼ cups diced cooked turkey, 1 cup thinly sliced celery, ⅓ cup mayonnaise, 2 tablespoons minced chutney, 1 teaspoon finely grated onion* and *¾ teaspoon salt*. (Makes 2⅓ cups.)

TONGUE SALAD: Mix well *2 cups ground cooked beef tongue, 1 cup mayonnaise, 2½ teaspoons bottled horseradish, ½ teaspoon salt* and *⅛ teaspoon pepper*. (Makes 2 cups.)

NIPPY SALMON: Mix *1 cup flaked canned salmon, 3 tablespoons mayonnaise, 1 tablespoon horseradish, 2 teaspoons bottled capers* and *2 teaspoons lemon juice*. (Makes 1 cup.)

CHICKEN-CRANBERRY: Combine *2 cups diced cooked or canned chicken* with *3 tablespoons cranberry-orange relish, 1 tablespoon orange juice* and *¼ teaspoon salt*. (Makes 2 cups.)

CHEESE SALAD: Combine *2 cups diced natural or pasteurized process Swiss cheese, ¾ cup mayonnaise, ½ cup diced green pepper, 1 tablespoon chili sauce* and *⅛ teaspoon pepper*. (Makes 2½ cups.)

DEVILED-HAM-CHEESE: Mix *one 2¼-ounce can deviled ham* with *one 3-ounce package cream cheese*, softened, *½ teaspoon each lemon juice* and *horseradish*. (Makes ½ cup.)

SAUCES

A repertoire of sauces is invaluable, enabling a cook to add the finishing touch to a wide variety of both sweet and savory dishes. Serve sauces with eggs, seafood, vegetables, meat, poultry and desserts.

Sauces that are especially appropriate for certain dishes, and which are traditionally associated with them, such as gravy for roast beef or meat sauce for spaghetti, are to be found in the chapters dealing with those particular foods; check the Index. More versatile sauces that can be served with a variety of dishes are given in the following pages.

INGREDIENTS
White and brown sauces usually consist of a mixture of butter or margarine, flour and liquid – either milk, half-and-half, cream, meat, fish or vegetable broth – plus seasoning. With some classic sauces, such as béarnaise or hollandaise, egg yolks act as the thickening agent.

In many recipes for sweet dessert sauces, cornstarch is used as a thickening agent because it makes a clearer sauce than flour. Sweet dessert sauces can also be thickened with beaten egg yolks.

COOKING SAUCES
When preparing sauces, always use a heavy saucepan and stir the mixture constantly. There are two ways of adding flour to the other ingredients to thicken white or brown sauces. In some recipes, the flour and butter or margarine are cooked together (this is known as the *roux* method), just until smooth for white sauces or, for brown sauces, until the mixture is evenly browned; the liquid is then added gradually while the mixture is stirred vigorously to prevent it from lumping. In other recipes, flour is combined with a small amount of liquid to make a smooth, pourable mixture; this mixture is then slowly poured into the rest of the liquid in the saucepan. The sauce must be stirred constantly to prevent lumping, then heated to boiling and cooked over medium heat until thick and smooth.

MAKING SAUCES SMOOTH
Curdled mayonnaise or lumpy white sauce are problems which beset even the most experienced cooks. By vigorous beating or stirring, lumpy sauces are quickly made smooth again, or if the lumps persist, the mixture can be blended smooth in the blender.

Mayonnaise or any other cold egg-based sauce may curdle if the oil is added too quickly, particularly in the early stages. You can save the sauce by adding the curdled mixture, just a teaspoon at a time, to a freshly beaten egg yolk; as you add the mixture, the sauce will return to a smooth consistency.

Overheating can curdle a hollandaise sauce. To rescue it, if this does happen, place a teaspoon of lemon juice and a tablespoon of curdled sauce in a bowl. With a wire whisk, beat vigorously until the mixture is creamy and thickened, then gradually beat in the remaining sauce, a tablespoon at a time, making sure that each addition has thickened before adding the next.

KEEPING SAUCES HOT
It is sometimes necessary to prepare a sauce ahead and keep it warm for serving. Sauces to be served hot can be kept in a double boiler over hot water; hollandaise and other egg-based sauces should be kept over *warm* water, otherwise they will become thin or curdled.

Preventing a skin forming : If sauce is made ahead, cover surface with waxed paper, pressing paper to surface.

Or dot surface with tiny pieces of butter. Just before serving, beat in the butter until the sauce is smooth and creamy.

FREEZING SAUCES
Many sauces freeze well, among them tomato, barbecue, mushroom, hollandaise, mornay and béarnaise. Those made with flour may separate on thawing; however, if they are thoroughly stirred during reheating they should return to the correct consistency.

To prepare sauces for the freezer, package them in meal-size amounts, in freezer containers, leaving head space for expansion. Reheat frozen sauces either in a heavy saucepan over very low heat, stirring often, or in a double boiler. Use sauces within 1 to 3 months.

460

Accompaniment sauces

White or Cream Sauce

Begin 15 mins ahead

1 cup

2 tablespoons butter or margarine
2 tablespoons all-purpose flour
½ teaspoon salt
⅛ teaspoon pepper
⅛ teaspoon paprika
1 cup milk or half-and-half

1 In heavy, 1-quart sauce-pan over low heat, melt butter or margarine.

2 Add flour, salt, pepper and paprika to melted butter or margarine. Over low heat, stir together until smooth.

3 Gradually stir in milk; cook, stirring constantly, until thickened and smooth. Serve hot on cooked vegetables, fish, poultry, seafood or hard-cooked eggs.

THIN WHITE SAUCE: Prepare as above but use 1 tablespoon butter or margarine and 1 tablespoon flour. (Makes 1 cup.)

THICK WHITE SAUCE: Prepare as above but use ¼ cup butter and ¼ cup flour. (Makes 1 cup.)

BECHAMEL SAUCE: Prepare as above but substitute ½ *cup chicken broth* for ½ cup of the milk. (Makes 1 cup.)

CHEESE SAUCE: Prepare White Sauce as above but halve ingredients and, into hot sauce, stir ½ *cup shredded American or Cheddar cheese* and ⅛ *teaspoon dry mustard;* or half of a 5-ounce jar sharp pasteurized process cheese spread. Cook over very low heat, stirring constantly, just until the cheese is melted. (Makes 1¼ cups.)

CURRY SAUCE: When preparing White Sauce, to butter or margarine, add ¼ *cup minced onion, 2 teaspoons curry powder, ¾ teaspoon sugar* and ⅛ *teaspoon ground ginger.* Just before you are ready to serve the sauce, stir in *1 teaspoon lemon juice.* (Makes 1¼ cups.)

EGG SAUCE: When preparing White Sauce, use ¼ cup butter and 2 teaspoons flour; stir in *2 sliced hard-cooked eggs* and *2 teaspoons prepared mustard* or ½ teaspoon dry mustard. (Makes 1¼ cups.)

HOT THOUSAND ISLAND SAUCE: In cup, stir ¼ *cup mayonnaise* with ¼ *cup chili sauce;* stir into hot White Sauce. (Makes 1½ cups.)

Mornay Sauce

Begin 20 mins ahead

2⅓ cups

3 tablespoons butter or margarine
2 tablespoons all-purpose flour
1 cup chicken broth
1 cup half-and-half
1 egg yolk
½ cup shredded natural Swiss cheese
¼ cup grated Parmesan cheese

1 In 2-quart saucepan over medium heat, melt butter; stir flour into butter until smooth.

2 Gradually stir in broth and half-and-half and cook, stirring, until sauce is thickened; remove pan from heat.

3 In small bowl with wire whisk or fork, beat egg yolk slightly; then into egg yolk beat small amount of hot sauce.

4 Slowly pour egg mixture back into hot sauce, stirring vigorously to prevent the sauce from lumping.

5 Add cheeses and cook over low heat, stirring constantly, just until thickened (do not boil). Serve hot on cooked vegetables, fish, baked chicken or poached eggs.

Peppery Blue-Cheese Sauce

Begin 15 mins ahead

1 cup

1 tablespoon butter or margarine
1 tablespoon all-purpose flour
¾ cup milk

½ cup crumbled blue cheese
½ teaspoon salt
¼ teaspoon coarsely ground pepper

1. In 1-quart saucepan over medium heat, into hot butter or margarine, stir flour until blended. Gradually stir in milk and cook, stirring constantly, until mixture is thickened.

2. Remove mixture from heat; stir in cheese and remaining ingredients. Serve hot over grilled steak, lamb or beef patties or lamb chops.

461

Accompaniment sauces

Bordelaise Sauce

Begin 25 mins ahead

1⅓ cups

2 tablespoons butter or margarine
2 tablespoons all-purpose flour
1 tablespoon minced onion
1 tablespoon minced parsley
1 bay leaf
¼ teaspoon thyme leaves

¼ teaspoon salt
⅛ teaspoon coarsely ground or cracked black pepper
1 10½-ounce can condensed beef broth (bouillon), undiluted
¼ cup dry red wine

1 In heavy, 1-quart saucepan over low heat, in hot butter or margarine, cook the flour until it is just lightly browned, stirring often.

2 Stir in minced onion, parsley, bay leaf, thyme leaves, salt and coarsely ground pepper.

3 Slowly add undiluted beef broth and red wine. Stir the mixture to blend together well. Increase the heat to medium-high.

4 Cook, stirring constantly, until the mixture thickens. Discard bay leaf. Serve Bordelaise Sauce hot over roast or broiled beef.

Mushroom Sauce

Begin 20 mins ahead

2 cups

¼ cup butter or margarine
½ pound mushrooms, sliced
¾ cup beef broth

1 teaspoon salt
1 tablespoon cornstarch
¼ cup sauterne

1. In 9-inch skillet over medium heat, in hot butter or margarine, cook the sliced mushrooms until tender, about 5 minutes, stirring occasionally. Stir in beef broth and salt and heat the mixture to boiling.
2. Meanwhile, in cup, blend cornstarch and sauterne until smooth.
3. Gradually stir sauterne mixture into mushroom mixture and cook, stirring constantly, until thickened. Serve Mushroom Sauce hot over broiled beef steaks or hamburgers, chicken croquettes, hot cooked green beans or peas.

Mayonnaise

Begin 30 mins or up to 1 wk ahead

2 cups

3 egg yolks
½ teaspoon salt
½ teaspoon sugar
¼ teaspoon dry mustard
1½ cups salad oil
3 tablespoons cider vinegar
1 tablespoon lemon juice

1 In small bowl with mixer at medium speed, beat egg yolks, salt, sugar and mustard 2 minutes.

2 Continue beating and gradually add ½ cup salad oil, ½ teaspoon at a time, until mixture is smooth and thick.

3 Still beating, gradually add cider vinegar and lemon juice to mixture.

4 Beat in remaining salad oil, 1 tablespoon at a time, until all the oil is absorbed and mixture is smooth and creamy.

5 Cover and refrigerate mayonnaise. Use as ingredient in salads. Serve with cold poultry and sliced meats.

MAYONNAISE VARIATIONS: To 1 cup of mayonnaise add 1 teaspoon each *tarragon* and *minced parsley;* or *¼ cup chopped chutney;* or *1 teaspoon curry powder*.

Sauce Rémoulade

Begin 10 mins ahead

1¼ cups

2 tablespoons chopped sour pickles
1 tablespoon chopped capers
1 cup mayonnaise

1 tablespoon chopped parsley
1 teaspoon prepared mustard
¼ teaspoon tarragon

Drain well any liquid from chopped pickles and capers. In small bowl, stir mayonnaise, pickles, capers, parsley, mustard and tarragon until well mixed. Serve over chilled cooked vegetables, shrimp, scallops or lobster.

Hollandaise Sauce

Begin 15 mins
ahead

2/3 cup

3 egg yolks
2 tablespoons lemon juice
1/2 cup butter or
margarine
1/4 teaspoon salt

1 Add egg yolks and lemon juice to double-boiler top; with wire whisk or slotted spoon, beat until well mixed.

2 Place double-boiler top over bottom containing hot, *not boiling*, water.

3 Add one third of the butter or margarine to the egg yolk mixture and cook, beating constantly, until the butter is completely melted.

4 Add another third of butter, beating constantly; repeat with remaining third, beating until mixture thickens and is heated through.

5 Remove from heat; stir in salt. Keep warm. Serve hot on hot cooked artichoke hearts, asparagus, broccoli, seafood or poached eggs.

Lemon Butter

Begin 5 mins
ahead

1/3 cup

1/4 cup butter or
margarine
1 tablespoon lemon juice
1 tablespoon chopped
parsley

1/2 teaspoon salt
1/8 teaspoon cayenne or
dash hot pepper
sauce

In 1-quart saucepan over medium heat, melt butter or margarine; stir in lemon juice, chopped parsley, salt and cayenne. (Or, in small bowl with spoon, stir butter or margarine until creamy. Slowly stir in remaining ingredients.) Serve Lemon Butter hot on hot boiled or steamed vegetables, broiled, fried or poached fish or shellfish.

Béarnaise Sauce

Begin 20 mins
ahead

1 cup

2 tablespoons red wine
vinegar
1 1/2 teaspoons chopped
green onion
1 1/2 teaspoons tarragon
1/8 teaspoon cracked
black pepper

4 egg yolks
3/4 cup butter or
margarine, softened
1 tablespoon chopped
parsley

1. In double-boiler top, combine first 4 ingredients. Over high heat, heat to boiling. Boil until vinegar is reduced to about 1 tablespoon.
2. Place double-boiler top over double-boiler bottom containing hot, *not boiling*, water. Add egg yolks and cook, beating constantly with wire whisk until slightly thickened.
3. Add butter, about 2 tablespoons at a time, beating constantly with whisk, until butter is melted and mixture is thickened. Stir in parsley. Serve about 1 tablespoon hot or cold sauce over broiled beef steak or fried, poached or baked fish.

Horseradish Sauce

Begin 10 mins
ahead

1 cup

1/4 cup horseradish,
drained
1 tablespoon white
vinegar
1 teaspoon sugar
1/2 teaspoon salt

1/4 teaspoon prepared
mustard
1/2 cup heavy or
whipping cream,
whipped

In small bowl, mix well first 5 ingredients. Fold into whipped cream. Serve with roast or broiled beef, hot beef tongue, baked ham, corned beef; baked, fried or poached fish.

Parmesan-Cheese Sauce

Begin 15 mins
ahead

3 1/2 cups

1/4 cup butter
1/4 cup all-purpose flour
1 1/2 cups half-and-half
1 1/2 cups water

2 chicken-flavor bouillon
cubes
1/2 cup grated Parmesan
cheese

1. In 2-quart saucepan over medium heat, into hot butter, stir flour until well blended.
2. Gradually stir in half-and-half, water and chicken bouillon cubes. Cook, stirring constantly, until sauce is thickened. Stir in the grated Parmesan cheese and heat just until melted. Serve with baked or poached fish or pasta.

Spicy Country Barbecue Sauce

Begin 15 mins
ahead

1 2/3 cups

2 tablespoons salad oil
1 medium onion, diced
1 8-ounce can tomato
sauce
1/2 cup packed brown
sugar
1/4 cup white vinegar

1 tablespoon
Worcestershire
4 teaspoons chili
powder
2 teaspoons salt
1/4 teaspoon dry mustard

1. In 1-quart saucepan over medium heat, in hot salad oil, cook onion until tender, about 5 minutes, stirring occasionally.
2. Add remaining ingredients; heat to boiling, stirring constantly. Use to baste spareribs, beef or lamb during grilling. Serve remainder with meat.

Dessert sauces

Caramel Sauce

Begin 20 mins
ahead or
early in day

2½ cups

2 tablespoons butter or
  margarine
2 tablespoons all-purpose
  flour
1½ cups half-and-half
¾ cup packed light
  brown sugar
¾ cup sugar
¼ teaspoon salt

1 In 2-quart saucepan
over medium heat, into
hot butter or margarine,
stir flour until blended.

2 Gradually stir in
half-and-half; cook,
stirring constantly, until
the mixture is thickened
and smooth.

3 Add brown sugar,
sugar and salt; stir until
well mixed. Serve warm or
cover and refrigerate to
serve cold.

Hot Butterscotch Sauce

Begin 10 mins
ahead

1 cup

1 cup packed light brown
  sugar
¼ cup half-and-half
2 tablespoons butter or
  margarine

2 tablespoons light corn
  syrup

In 1-quart saucepan over medium heat, heat brown
sugar, half-and-half, butter or margarine and corn
syrup to boiling, stirring occasionally. Serve Hot
Butterscotch Sauce warm over vanilla or chocolate
ripple ice cream, pound cake slices, peach or apple
pie, tapioca pudding, baked custard.

Hot Fudge Sauce

Begin 20 mins
ahead

1⅔ cups

1½ cups sugar
½ cup milk
⅓ cup light corn syrup
2 squares unsweetened
  chocolate

1 tablespoon butter or
  margarine
1 teaspoon vanilla
  extract
⅛ teaspoon salt

1. In 2-quart saucepan over medium heat, heat first 4
ingredients to boiling, stirring constantly. Set candy
thermometer in place and continue cooking, stirring
occasionally, until temperature reaches 228°F. or
until a small amount of mixture dropped from tip of
spoon back into mixture spins a ¼-inch thread.
2. Remove from heat; immediately stir in butter,
vanilla and salt. Serve sauce hot over vanilla ice
cream, vanilla or butterscotch pudding, poached
pears or toasted pound cake slices.

Chocolate-Marshmallow Sauce

Begin 15 mins
ahead

1½ cups

2 cups miniature
  marshmallows
⅓ cup heavy or whipping
  cream

⅓ cup honey
1½ squares unsweetened
  chocolate
⅛ teaspoon salt

In 2-quart saucepan over low heat, cook marshmallows, cream, honey, chocolate and salt, stirring
constantly, until marshmallows and chocolate are
melted. Serve hot over gingerbread, unfrosted
yellow or chocolate cake.

Chocolate Sauce

Begin 15 mins
ahead

1⅓ cups

1 6-ounce package
  semisweet-chocolate
  pieces (1 cup)
½ cup light corn syrup

¼ cup half-and-half
1 tablespoon butter
1 teaspoon vanilla
  extract

1. In 1-quart saucepan over low heat, melt chocolate
with corn syrup, stirring constantly.
2. Remove from heat; stir in remaining ingredients
until mixed. Serve warm over Bavarian cream,
cream pies, éclairs, cream puffs or ice cream.

Mint Sauce

Begin 15 mins
ahead or
early in day

⅔ cup

½ cup light corn syrup
½ cup packed mint leaves

2 tablespoons lemon juice
⅛ teaspoon salt

In covered blender container at high speed, mix all
ingredients until well blended. If prepared early in
day, stir before serving. Spoon over cut-up fruit for
salad or dessert.

Cherry Sauce

Begin 15 mins
ahead

2 cups

⅔ cup boiling water
1 pound sweet cherries,
  pitted

¼ cup sugar

In 2-quart saucepan over medium heat, in boiling
water, heat cherries to boiling. Reduce heat to low;
cover and simmer 5 minutes or until tender. During
last minute of cooking, add sugar. Serve over Cheese
Blintzes (page 368), waffles, pancakes.

Peach Sauce

Begin 10 mins
ahead

1 cup

1 10-ounce package
  frozen peaches, thawed
¼ teaspoon almond
  extract

⅛ teaspoon ground
  nutmeg

In covered blender container at low speed, blend
together all ingredients until smooth.

Hot Fruit Sauce

Begin 45 mins
ahead

4 cups

3 large nectarines
3 large plums
½ cup orange juice

½ cup sugar
2 tablespoons brandy
  (optional)

Cut fruit into wedges. In 2-quart saucepan over low
heat, cook fruit and juice 10 minutes or until tender,
stirring occasionally. Remove from heat. Stir in
sugar and brandy until sugar is dissolved. Serve Hot
Fruit Sauce over vanilla ice cream.

Orange-Fluff Sauce

Begin early
in day

2½ to 2⅔ cups

½ cup sugar
½ cup frozen orange-
juice concentrate,
thawed

⅛ teaspoon salt
2 egg yolks
1 cup heavy or whipping
cream, whipped

1 In 1-quart saucepan over low heat, cook sugar, undiluted juice concentrate and salt, stirring constantly, until sugar dissolves; set aside.

2 In small bowl with mixer at high speed, beat egg yolks until light and fluffy; at medium speed, gradually beat in orange-juice mixture.

3 Return mixture to saucepan; over low heat, cook, stirring constantly, until the mixture is slightly thickened.

4 Cool, then fold in whipped cream. Refrigerate until well chilled. Serve over cut-up fruit, dessert fruit salads.

Fluffy Sherry Sauce

Begin 15 mins
ahead

1⅔ cups

2 egg yolks
¼ cup sugar
1 tablespoon medium
sherry

⅛ teaspoon salt
½ cup heavy or whipping
cream, whipped

1. In small bowl with mixer at low speed, beat egg yolks, sugar, sherry and salt until well mixed. Increase speed to high and continue beating for 4 minutes or until light and fluffy.
2. With wire whisk, fold in cream until well blended. Spoon over cut-up mixed fruit.

Melba Sauce

Begin early
in day

2 cups

¼ cup red currant jelly
1½ 10-ounce packages
frozen raspberries

2 tablespoons cornstarch
1 tablespoon cold water
red food color

1. In 2-quart saucepan over low heat, melt jelly, stirring constantly; add frozen berries and heat.
2. In measuring cup, mix cornstarch with cold water until smooth; stir into berries. Over medium heat, cook mixture, stirring occasionally until slightly thickened. Stir in a few drops red food color. Cover and refrigerate until serving time.

Eggnog Sauce

Begin 15 mins
ahead

1¾ cups

½ cup heavy or whipping
cream
2 egg yolks

¾ cup confectioners'
sugar
3 tablespoons brandy

1 In small bowl with mixer at medium speed, beat cream until stiff peaks form; set aside.

2 In another small bowl with mixer at high speed, beat egg yolks until fluffy.

3 To egg yolks, add confectioners' sugar and brandy; at high speed, beat the mixture together to blend well.

4 Add whipped cream; with rubber spatula, gently fold together. Serve over warm fruitcake slices, steamed pudding.

Brandied Strawberry Sauce

Begin 20 mins
ahead or
early in day

2½ cups

3 10-ounce packages
frozen sliced
strawberries, thawed
½ cup red currant jelly

1 tablespoon cornstarch
few drops red food color
¼ cup brandy

1. Drain strawberries, reserving ½ cup juice.
2. In 2-quart saucepan over low heat, melt currant jelly, stirring constantly.
3. In small bowl, mix reserved juice and cornstarch until smooth. Gradually stir cornstarch mixture into melted jelly, stirring constantly; increase heat to medium and cook until thickened, stirring.
4. Add food color; stir in berries and brandy. Serve hot over rolled crêpes, waffles; or cover and refrigerate to serve cold over ice cream, vanilla or tapioca pudding.

Date-Nut Sauce

Begin 10 mins
ahead

2 cups

1 7¼- or 8-ounce package
pitted dates, chopped
⅛ teaspoon salt
¾ cup water

½ cup light or dark corn
syrup
½ cup chopped
California walnuts

In 2-quart saucepan over medium heat, heat dates, salt and water to boiling; remove from heat. Stir in corn syrup and chopped walnuts. Serve warm over apple, pear or pumpkin pie or ice cream.

BEVERAGES

A beverage can be anything from a glass of ice-cold milk to a highly complicated blend of flavors and textures. In general, winter is the time for warming hot drinks and summertime for refreshing cold ones. Some beverages, such as coffee and tea, are drunk all year round; both can be enjoyed hot or cold, plain or enhanced with other flavors. Then there are fruit-ades and milk-based drinks of all kinds; and, the alcohol-based drinks, ranging from cocktails to party punches; and, of course, wines.

However simple the beverage you make, an attractive container will do a great deal to enhance it. Rather than serving hot drinks in regular cups, use mugs, steins and demitasse cups. As well as looking more attractive in these, the drinks do stay hot. Cold drinks look better and seem to taste better if served in special glassware, such as brandy snifters or champagne glasses.

BUYING COFFEE
Most coffee sold in the United States is regular or American roast, which is light and fairly mild. Viennese or French roast is darker and stronger. Italian roast is darkest and is used for espresso.

If you grind your own coffee, try beans from supermarkets which often have quality beans priced lower than specialty-house beans or vacuum-packed coffee. Check that whole coffee beans are of uniform size and color with good coffee aroma and no trace of mustiness.

Select the grind that's right for your type of coffee maker. A percolator uses regular (coarse) grind; a drip pot generally uses drip (medium) grind; an automatic-electric drip coffee maker uses drip or the specially labeled grind; espresso pots also use specially labeled coffee grinds.

STORING COFFEE
Only fresh coffee gives good flavor. Unopened vacuum-packed ground coffee will stay fresh at room temperature for over a year. Once the can is opened, the flavor begins to dissipate immediately, so plan to use it within about a week. Replace lid quickly after using. Keep partially used cans, covered, in the refrigerator. If the vacuum-packed can contains more than a week's supply, immediately after opening it, portion weekly amounts of coffee into airtight containers and freeze them until they are needed.

Coffee beans begin to lose flavor and aroma as soon as they are roasted so plan to use them within about 3 weeks. If you don't brew a lot of coffee or can't shop often, buy beans as soon as possible after roasting and freeze in airtight containers. They will then keep fresh at least 12 months; do not refreeze them.

Unopened instant coffee will stay fresh over a year at room temperature. Once opened, use it within 2 or 3 weeks. Store opened jars at room temperature.

MAKING COFFEE
Coffee-oil residue can become rancid and give an off flavor to coffee so be sure coffee-making equipment is kept scrupulously clean. (Use a packaged coffee-pot cleaner, according to directions, to remove coffee oils and stains when necessary.) Always start with *fresh*, cold water and fresh coffee. For the best flavor, make at least three-quarters capacity of the coffee maker. Buy a smaller pot if yours is too big for daily use. Don't skimp on coffee or re-use grounds.

Coffee tastes best when freshly brewed, so try to make only what you'll serve within an hour or so. Remove wet coffee grounds as soon as brewing is completed. If you prefer to keep it hot and handy all day long, use paper coffee filters with your percolator or drip pot. Flavor keeps better when there's no sediment. If you reheat coffee, always remember to do so over low heat. Never let it boil or it will turn bitter.

When using a new coffee maker, first use the proportions of coffee to water recommended in the directions. Subsequently, if you wish to change the strength of the coffee, use more or less ground coffee. If no directions are included, use 2 level tablespoons of ground coffee to each 6 ounces (¾ cup) of cold water. (The rated capacity of most coffee makers is based on a 5-ounce cup of brewed coffee.)

COFFEE MAKERS
There are three basic ways to make coffee. All produce a good brew, but each has a distinctive taste.
Percolator: Available in automatic-electric and range-top models ranging in size from about 2 to 100 cups. Be sure water level is below the bottom of the basket. With electric model, start with cold water; with range-top, start with almost boiling water.

Drip: Drip coffee makers are available in automatic-electric and range-top models ranging in size from 2 to 12 cups. Ground coffee is placed in a filter cone or section through which almost boiling water is poured. This method of making coffee produces an exceptionally residue-free brew.

Instant coffee: This is the least expensive and quickest way to make small amounts of coffee. For best results, add boiling water to instant coffee in a cup or serving pot; stir. Use 1 teaspoon instant coffee for each ¾ cup boiling water.

BUYING TEA

There are innumerable blends of tea ranging from strong-flavored and smoky to delicate and flowery. They fall into three main types, according to how the leaves have been processed: black, green and oolong. The terms "orange pekoe" and "pekoe" do not refer to a particular variety or flavor but to the size of the leaf.

Black tea: Most of the tea sold in the United States is of this type. It is made by fermenting (oxidizing) the leaves so they turn black, producing a rich-flavored, amber brew. Well-known blends include *Assam*, a full-bodied high-quality tea; *Ceylon*, a delicate, fragrant blend; *Darjeeling*, the finest black tea from India, flavorful and aromatic; *Earl Grey*, an aromatic blend from India and Ceylon; *English Breakfast Tea*, a fragrant, mellow blend; *Keemun*, a mild yet robust Chinese tea; and *Lapsang Souchong*, a pungent tea from Taiwan, with a unique, smoky flavor.

Green tea: The leaves are not oxidized so that they retain their original green color. The resulting brew is light and greenish-yellow, with a mild, distinctive flavor. Green teas include *Basket-fired Tea*, a Japanese tea with a light flavor; *Gunpowder Tea*, which produces a delicate, pale brew; and *Hyson*, another fine Chinese tea.

Oolong tea: The leaves are only partially fermented with the result that they retain a greenish-brown color. The brew is light, with a subtle bouquet. Popular blends include *Canton Oolong*; *Formosa Oolong*, faintly wine-like in flavor; and *Jasmine Tea*, which is delicately flavored with white jasmine blossoms.

Store loose tea and tea bags in air-tight containers at room temperature and use within 6 months.

MAKING TEA

Use a teapot for brewing, and preheat it by rinsing out with hot water. Heat fresh, cold tap water to a rapid boil. Water that has been standing or reheated gives a flat taste. Also, only boiling water can extract the full flavor from the leaves. Allow ¾ measuring cup water per serving. Use 1 teaspoon loose tea or 1 tea bag per serving and pour boiling water over tea. Brew 3 to 5 minutes. Stir to make sure flavor is uniform and serve.

Coffee drinks

Café au Lait

hot coffee   *sugar*
hot milk

Color index page 110

Begin 15 mins ahead

Holding a pot of hot coffee in one hand and a pot of hot milk in the other, pour simultaneously into large cups. Serve sugar separately.

Pouring the coffee: Pour the coffee and milk from separate pots into the cup at the same time.

Caffè Espresso

8 tablespoons Italian-   *sugar*
roast coffee   *lemon twist*
1½ cups water

Color index page 110

Begin 15 mins ahead

4 servings

Brew coffee in drip pot or *macchinetta*. Serve in demitasse cups with sugar and lemon twist. Never serve Caffè Espresso with cream.

Iced Coffee

hot double-strength   *cream (optional)*
coffee   *sugar (optional)*
ice cubes

Color index page 110

Begin 15 mins ahead

Brew double-strength coffee. Fill tall glasses with ice cubes and slowly pour in hot coffee. Serve with cream and sugar, if desired.

Café Brûlot

1 cup brandy   *2 small cinnamon sticks*
peel of 1 medium orange   *3 tablespoons sugar*
6 whole cloves   *3 cups hot double-*
4 whole allspice   *strength coffee*

Color index page 110

Begin 15 mins ahead

4 cups or eight ½-cup servings

1. In 1-quart saucepan over medium heat, heat first 6 ingredients until brandy is hot.
2. Pour into warmed heatsafe serving bowl. Carefully ignite brandy; flame for 1 to 2 minutes.
3. Slowly pour coffee into flaming brandy. Ladle into demitasse cups.

Irish Coffee

1½ teaspoons sugar   *hot strong black coffee*
1 jigger Irish whisky   *whipped cream*

Color index page 110

Begin 15 mins ahead

1 serving

1. Into 6- or 8-ounce stemmed glass or coffee cup, measure sugar and Irish whisky. Add hot coffee to fill glass to within ½-inch of top; stir to dissolve sugar completely.
2. Top with a spoonful of whipped cream; do not stir. Sip coffee through cream.

Iced tea

Hot chocolate drinks

Iced Tea, Family Style

fresh cold water
⅓ cup loose tea or 15 tea
bags

ice cubes
sugar
lemon slices

Color index
page 111

Begin 15 mins
or several hrs
ahead

8 cups or
eight 1-cup
servings

1. In 3-quart saucepan over high heat, heat 4 cups fresh cold water to boiling. Remove from heat; stir in tea. Stir, cover and leave 5 minutes. Stir again and strain into a pitcher containing an additional 4 cups fresh cold water.
2. Cover and let stand until ready to serve. Serve over ice cubes with sugar and lemon slices.

Straining the mixture: Strain concentrated tea into pitcher containing fresh cold water.

Serving iced tea: Pour tea over ice cubes in 12-ounce glasses. Serve with sugar and lemon slices.

ICED TEA, COLD WATER METHOD: *About 6 hours or day ahead:* Into pitcher, measure **4 cups cold tap water**. Add **8 to 10 tea bags** (remove tags); cover; let stand at room temperature 6 hours or overnight; remove tea bags and stir. Serve as above. (Makes 4 cups or four 1-cup servings.)

GARNISHES FOR DRINKS

"Frost" the glass by dipping the rim first in beaten egg white and then quickly in sugar.

Serve cool drinks garnished with fruit slices, wedges or chunks; small scoops of sherbet or ice cream; mint sprigs; twists of cucumber peel.

Add flavor and color to hot milky drinks with cinnamon sticks, whipped cream or marshmallow cream; to clear drinks, add candy canes or clove-studded lime or lemon slices.

Hearty Hot Cocoa

½ cup plus 1 tablespoon
cocoa
½ cup sugar
⅛ teaspoon salt
6 cups milk

½ teaspoon vanilla
extract
whipped cream or 6
regular marshmallows
(optional)

Color index
page 111

Begin 15 mins
ahead

6 cups or
six 1-cup
servings

1 In 3-quart saucepan, stir cocoa with sugar and salt until mixed.

2 Stir in a small amount of milk to make a smooth paste; stir in remainder. Over medium-low heat, heat, stirring occasionally, until tiny bubbles form around edge.

3 Remove from heat; add vanilla; beat with hand beater until smooth and foamy, then pour cocoa into 6 mugs.

4 Top each serving with some whipped cream or a marshmallow, if you like, then serve hot cocoa immediately.

French Hot Chocolate

4 squares semisweet
chocolate
¼ cup light corn syrup
½ teaspoon vanilla
extract

4 cups milk
1 cup heavy or whipping
cream

Color index
page 111

Begin 50 mins
ahead

6 cups or
8 servings

1. In heavy 1-quart saucepan over low heat, or double boiler over hot, not boiling, water, heat chocolate and corn syrup until chocolate is melted and mixture is smooth, stirring occasionally with rubber spatula.
2. Cover and refrigerate 30 minutes or until mixture is cool. Stir in vanilla.
3. In 2-quart saucepan over medium-low heat, heat milk until very hot and small bubbles form around edge (do not boil).
4. Meanwhile, in small bowl with mixer at medium-low speed, beat heavy or whipping cream and chocolate mixture until soft peaks form.
5. To serve, pour milk into warm coffeepot. Carefully spoon whipped-cream mixture equally into 8 warmed, decorative coffee cups; gently pour hot milk mixture in cups.

Sodas and shakes

Ice Cream Soda

Color index page 110

Begin just before serving

1 serving

2 to 3 tablespoons chocolate syrup; fruit-flavored pancake syrup; light molasses; or cherry or pineapple sundae topping
¼ cup milk
scoop of ice cream
club soda, chilled
whipped cream and maraschino cherry (optional)

1 Place your choice of syrup in a tall glass. Add milk and stir.

2 Add ice cream and pour in club soda until glass is almost filled; stir.

3 Garnish with cream and cherry. Serve with iced-tea spoon and straws.

Strawberry Sodas

Color index page 110

Begin just before serving

Five 1½-cup servings

1½ cups milk
1 10-ounce package frozen sliced strawberries, partially thawed
1 pint strawberry ice cream
1 16-ounce bottle club soda or strawberry soft drink, chilled

1. In covered blender container at high speed, blend milk and strawberries 15 seconds; pour into five 12-ounce glasses.
2. Add scoop of strawberry ice cream to each; slowly add soda or soft drink to fill almost to top.

Chocolate-Orange Sodas

Color index page 110

Begin just before serving

Eight 1½-cup servings

1 6-ounce can frozen orange-juice concentrate, thawed
1½ cups quick chocolate-flavor-milk mix
1 juice-can water
2 pints vanilla ice cream
1 28-ounce bottle club soda, chilled

1. In medium bowl, stir orange-juice concentrate with chocolate-milk mix till smooth; stir in water.
2. Pour ¼ cup chocolate-orange mixture into each of eight 12-ounce glasses. Add 1 large scoop ice cream to each. Add soda to fill almost to top.

Egg Cream

Color index page 110

Begin just before serving

1 serving

2 tablespoons chocolate syrup
¼ cup milk
club soda

1. In 10-ounce glass, stir the chocolate syrup and milk to mix thoroughly.
2. Slowly stir in enough soda to fill glass. Serve Egg Cream with straws, if you like.

Mocha Float

Color index page 111

Begin just before serving

1 serving

¾ teaspoon quick chocolate-flavor-milk mix
¾ teaspoon instant coffee powder
½ teaspoon sugar
club soda, chilled
2 small scoops chocolate-ripple ice cream

1. Into an 8-ounce glass, measure first 3 ingredients. Gradually add enough club soda to fill glass ¾ full; stir until sugar is dissolved.
2. Add ice cream; stir. Serve with spoon and straw.

Chocolate Milk Shakes

Color index page 111

Begin 10 mins ahead

3 cups or two 1½-cup servings

¾ cup milk
3 tablespoons chocolate syrup
1 pint chocolate ice cream

1. In covered blender container at high speed, blend all ingredients until smooth.
2. Pour mixture into chilled 12-ounce glasses; serve milk shakes with large straws.

BANANA MILK SHAKES: Prepare as above but substitute *1 large ripe banana* for chocolate syrup and *1 pint vanilla ice cream* for chocolate.

Black Cow

Color index page 111

Begin just before serving

1 serving

½ 12-ounce can root beer, chilled
scoop of vanilla ice cream

1. Into a chilled, tall 10-ounce glass, pour the chilled root beer.
2. Top with a generous scoop of slightly softened vanilla ice cream. Serve Black Cow immediately with long straw and iced-tea spoon.

Strawberry Shakes

Color index page 111

Begin just before serving

4 cups or four 8-ounce servings

¾ cup water
1 10-ounce package frozen strawberries, thawed
1 cup instant nonfat dry milk powder
3 tablespoons sugar
1 teaspoon lemon juice
⅛ teaspoon salt
2 cups ice cubes

In blender container, place all ingredients except ice cubes; cover and blend at medium speed a few seconds until smooth. Increase speed to high; add ice cubes, one at a time, until all are finely crushed.

Party Orange Soda

Color index page 110

Begin 15 mins ahead

8 cups or sixteen ½-cup servings

4 egg whites
sugar
4 cups orange juice
1 cup milk
1 10-ounce bottle lemon-lime soda
¼ teaspoon ground nutmeg

1. In small bowl with mixer at high speed, beat egg whites until soft peaks form; beating at high speed, gradually sprinkle in ¼ cup sugar; beat until sugar is dissolved. Whites should stand in stiff peaks. Set beaten whites aside.
2. In chilled punch bowl, carefully stir orange juice, milk, lemon-lime soda, ¼ cup sugar and ground nutmeg until well mixed; stir in beaten egg whites. Serve immediately in punch cups or small glasses.

Lemonade

Cold punches

Color index
page 112

Begin 2 hrs
or up to
1 wk ahead

16 cups or
sixteen 1-cup
servings

Lemonade

1½ cups sugar
1 tablespoon finely grated
lemon peel
water
1½ cups lemon juice
(8 to 10 lemons)
ice cubes
club soda (optional)

1 Into 1-quart jar with
tight-fitting lid, put
sugar and lemon peel; add
1½ cups very hot water.

2 With lid fitted firmly,
shake jar until sugar is
dissolved. Add lemon
juice. Refrigerate.

3 *To serve:* Into each
12-ounce glass, over ice
cubes, pour ¼ cup of the
lemon syrup.

4 Add ¾ cup cold water
or, if you prefer, club
soda. Stir well to mix.

FOR 8 SERVINGS: In 2½-quart pitcher or container, combine half of the lemon syrup with 6 cups
cold water. Pour over ice cubes. Refrigerate remaining lemon syrup.

LIMEADE: Prepare Lemonade (above) but substitute *grated lime peel* for lemon peel and *lime juice*
for the lemon juice (you will need about 10 limes).
Reconstitute with water only.

Easy-Way Lemonade

2 lemons, thinly sliced   *4 cups boiling water*
½ cup sugar   *ice cubes*

Color index
page 112

Begin early
in day

4 cups or
five ¾-cup
servings

1. Into large heatsafe bowl or pitcher, place the
sliced lemons and the sugar.
2. Pour in boiling water; stir until sugar is dissolved.
Refrigerate until chilled.
3. *To serve:* Pour mixture over ice cubes in chilled 8-
ounce glasses. Serve immediately.

470

Color index
page 110

Begin 2 hrs
ahead or
early in day

19 cups or
thirty-eight
½-cup
servings

Eggnog

12 eggs, separated
1 cup sugar
1½ cups bourbon
½ cup brandy
6 cups milk
ground nutmeg
1 cup heavy or whipping
cream

1 In large bowl with
mixer at low speed,
beat egg yolks with sugar.
At high speed, beat until
thick and lemon-colored,
about 15 minutes, fre-
quently scraping bowl.

2 Carefully beat in
bourbon and brandy,
one tablespoon at a time
to prevent curdling
mixture. Cover and chill.

3 *About 20 minutes before
serving:* In chilled 5- to
6-quart punch bowl, stir
yolk mixture, milk and 1¼
teaspoons nutmeg.

4 In large bowl with
mixer at high speed,
beat egg whites until soft
peaks form.

5 In small bowl, using
same beaters, with
mixer at medium speed,
beat cream until stiff
peaks form.

6 With wire whisk,
gently fold egg whites
and cream into yolk
mixture until just blended.

7 To serve, sprinkle some
nutmeg over top of
eggnog; ladle into 6-ounce
punch cups.

Hot punches

Golden Punch

**2 20-ounce cans crushed
pineapple in pineapple
juice**
**2 6-ounce cans frozen
lemonade concentrate**
1/4 cup sugar
**1 28-ounce bottle club
soda, chilled**
1 tray ice cubes

1. In covered blender container at high speed, blend crushed pineapple with its liquid, one can at a time, 15 to 20 seconds until thick.
2. In chilled punch bowl, stir blended pineapple, undiluted lemonade concentrate and sugar; stir in soda. Add ice and serve at once.

GOLDEN CHAMPAGNE PUNCH: Prepare as above but add *one 4/5-quart bottle champagne*, chilled, with club soda. (Makes 13 cups.)

Sangria

1/2 cup lemon juice
1/2 cup orange juice
1/2 cup sugar
**1 4/5-quart bottle dry red
wine (3 1/4 cups)**
1/4 cup brandy
**1 7-ounce bottle club
soda, chilled**
**1 cup fruit (sliced orange,
lemon, apple, peach,
banana)**
1 tray ice cubes

Into large pitcher, pour lemon juice, orange juice and sugar; stir to dissolve sugar. Stir in remaining ingredients. To serve: Pour into glasses making sure each person gets some fruit.

Whiskey-Sour Punch

1 small orange
**3 6-ounce cans frozen
lemonade concentrate,
thawed**
3 cups orange juice
**1 4/5-quart bottle rye,
bourbon or Scotch**
**1 32-ounce bottle club
soda, chilled**
2 trays ice cubes

1. Prepare garnish: Thinly slice orange; discard ends. With small sharp knife, flute edges of the orange slices; set aside.
2. In punch bowl, combine undiluted lemonade concentrate and remaining ingredients; mix well. Garnish with orange slices.

Sparkling Strawberry Punch

**2 10-ounce packages
frozen sweetened
strawberries, slightly
thawed**
**1 6-ounce can frozen
lemonade concentrate,
slightly thawed**
**1 4/5-quart bottle rosé
wine, chilled**
**2 28-ounce bottles ginger
ale, chilled**
**1 28-ounce bottle club
soda, chilled**
2 trays ice cubes
1/4 cup sugar
**orange slices for
garnish**

1. In covered blender container at high speed, blend strawberries and undiluted lemonade concentrate until they are thoroughly blended.
2. Pour strawberry mixture into a chilled large punch bowl. Add wine and remaining ingredients except orange slices; stir punch until sugar is completely dissolved.
3. To serve: Garnish punch with orange slices.

Hot Mulled Wine

4 cups sugar
**1 tablespoon ground
cinnamon or 6 medium
cinnamon sticks**
**1 teaspoon ground cloves
or whole cloves**
2 cups boiling water
**3 medium oranges, thinly
sliced**
**1 medium lemon, thinly
sliced**
1 gallon dry red wine

1. In 8-quart saucepot, combine sugar, cinnamon, cloves and water.

2. Add orange and lemon slices to saucepot. Over high heat, heat to boiling; boil 5 minutes, stirring occasionally.

3. Reduce heat to medium; add wine; heat till piping hot but not boiling, stirring occasionally.

4. Carefully ladle individual servings of hot wine into punch cups or heatsafe glasses.

Glögg

**2 teaspoons dried orange
peel**
1 teaspoon whole cloves
**4 whole cardamom,
cracked**
**3 short cinnamon sticks
cheesecloth**
**1 cup dark seedless
raisins**
**1 8-ounce package dried
apricots**
**2 4/5-quart bottles
Burgundy
(6 1/2 cups)**
**1 4/5-quart bottle vodka,
gin or aquavit
(3 1/4 cups)**
3/4 cup sugar
**1 cup whole blanched
almonds**

1. Place orange peel and spices on a piece of cheesecloth; tie with string to form a bag.
2. In covered, 4-quart saucepan over medium-low heat, simmer raisins, apricots, spice bag and 1 bottle Burgundy 30 minutes.
3. Remove from heat and discard spice bag; stir in vodka, sugar and remaining Burgundy; cover mixture and let stand overnight at room temperature.
4. *To serve:* Over high heat, heat mixture until piping hot, but not boiling, stirring occasionally. Ignite mixture with long match; let burn a few seconds, then cover pan to extinguish flame. Add almonds; pour into heated punch bowl. Serve hot.

Hot punches

Wassail Bowl with Baked Apples

Color index page 112

Begin 45 mins ahead

18 cups or thirty-six ½-cup servings

3 large cooking apples, cored
1 gallon apple cider (16 cups)
6 whole cloves
6 whole allspice
2 teaspoons ground nutmeg
1 6-ounce can frozen lemonade concentrate
1 6-ounce can frozen orange-juice concentrate
1 cup packed brown sugar
sugar
short cinnamon sticks

1 Preheat oven to 350°F. Cut apples in half crosswise and place, cut side down, in 13″ by 9″ baking dish. Bake 25 minutes or until the apple halves are fork-tender.

2 Meanwhile, in covered, 6-quart saucepot over low heat, simmer 2 cups apple cider, cloves, allspice and nutmeg 10 minutes.

3 Add remaining apple cider, undiluted lemonade and orange-juice concentrates and brown sugar; heat until hot, but not boiling, stirring occasionally.

4 Pour hot cider mixture from saucepot into heated large punch bowl.

5 Float apples, skin side up, in punch; sprinkle tops with a little sugar.

6 To serve, ladle about ½ cup of the hot punch into each punch cup; add a short cinnamon stick to each serving.

Cocktails

Cocktails are best served icy cold. If possible chill liquors, mixers and glasses. Use fresh ice for every drink and put it in the glass before other ingredients.

Serve cocktails in the appropriate glass filled ⅔ full. Glasses most often used are: jigger, 1½ ounces; cocktail, 4 ounces; old-fashioned, 6 to 12 ounces; cordial, 1 ounce; whiskey sour, 6 ounces; highball, 8 to 12 ounces. For easy mixing, have on hand: ice bucket and tongs, mixing glass and long-handled spoon, shaker, muddler, strainer, knife and cutting board, lemon squeezer and jigger, which is the basic measure.

Frozen Daiquiris

Color index page 112

Begin day ahead

5 cups or thirteen 3-ounce servings

1 6-ounce can frozen limeade concentrate, undiluted
2½ cans light rum (use limeade can to measure)
3 cans water

1 In 1½-quart freezer-safe bowl, combine limeade, rum and water; cover and freeze. (Mixture does not freeze solid.)

2 *Just before serving:* Place half mixture in blender; cover and blend until slushy. Repeat.

3 Pour mixture into cocktail glasses. Serve Frozen Daiquiris with 2 short straws.

FROZEN WHISKEY SOURS: Prepare as above but substitute *one 6-ounce can frozen lemonade concentrate* for limeade and *blended whiskey* for rum. Use only 2 cans water and add *1 can orange juice*. Just before serving, garnish each drink with *maraschino cherry* and *half an orange slice*.

Margarita

Color index page 112

Begin just before serving

1 serving

lime or lemon peel
salt
1 cup crushed ice
1 jigger tequila

½ jigger triple sec
½ jigger lime or lemon juice

Rub rim of cocktail glass with lime peel; dip rim in salt; set aside. Over ice in cocktail shaker or large glass, pour remaining ingredients; stir; carefully pour into the prepared cocktail glass.

Company Bloody Mary

Color index
page 112

Begin just
before serving
or early in day

5½ cups or
8 servings

2 18-ounce cans tomato
juice (4½ cups)
1 cup vodka
2 teaspoons
Worcestershire
½ teaspoon salt
¼ teaspoon coarsely
ground pepper
few dashes hot pepper
sauce
ice cubes
2 limes, quartered
lengthwise

1 In large pitcher, combine first 6 ingredients. Cover and refrigerate mixture if made ahead.

2 To serve: Stir mixture, then pour over ice cubes in eight 10-ounce highball glasses.

3 Squeeze a lime wedge into each highball glass; stir Bloody Mary and serve immediately.

Bloody Mary

Color index
page 112

Begin just
before serving

1 serving

ice cubes
⅔ cup tomato juice
1 jigger vodka
dash Worcestershire

⅛ teaspoon salt
⅛ teaspoon pepper
dash hot pepper sauce
1 large lime wedge

Over ice cubes in 10-ounce highball glass, measure all ingredients except lime wedge; squeeze lime wedge into mixture and stir well.

Alexander

Color index
page 112

Begin just
before serving

1 serving

1 cup crushed ice
1 jigger brandy or gin
½ jigger crème de
cacao

½ jigger heavy or
whipping cream

Over crushed ice in cocktail shaker, pour remaining ingredients; shake together well. Strain mixture into a cocktail glass.

Old-fashioned

Color index
page 112

Begin just
before serving

1 serving

1 sugar cube
dash aromatic bitters
1 tablespoon water
cracked ice
1½ jiggers liquor
(bourbon, brandy, gin,
rum, rye or vodka)

stemmed maraschino
cherry and slice of
orange or lemon twist
for garnish

In old-fashioned glass with muddler, stir sugar with bitters and water until dissolved. Add cracked ice to fill glass; pour in liquor. Garnish with maraschino cherry and orange twist; serve with muddler.

Manhattan

Color index
page 112

Begin just
before serving

2 servings

1½ cups cracked ice
2 jiggers bourbon,
blended or Canadian
whisky

1 jigger sweet vermouth
2 dashes aromatic bitters
2 maraschino cherries

Over ice in cocktail shaker or large glass, pour next 3 ingredients; stir. Strain mixture into 2 cocktail glasses. Garnish each with cherry.

DRY MANHATTAN: Prepare as above but substitute *dry vermouth* for sweet vermouth.

PERFECT MANHATTAN: Prepare as above but substitute ½ *jigger each sweet and dry vermouth* for sweet vermouth.

Mint Julep

Color index
page 112

Begin up to
30 mins ahead

1 serving

4 sprigs mint
1 teaspoon sugar

finely crushed ice
1½ jiggers bourbon

1. In 12-ounce highball glass or tankard (preferably silver or aluminum), place 3 sprigs mint and sugar. Crush mint with muddler or handle of wooden spoon until sugar is dissolved, about 5 minutes.
2. Fill glass to brim with ice; pour in bourbon; don't stir. Add more ice to fill glass. Set in freezer.
3. *Just before serving:* Garnish with mint sprig. Serve with long straw.

Tom Collins

Color index
page 112

Begin just
before serving

1 serving

2 tablespoons lemon
juice
2 teaspoons sugar
1 cup cracked ice
1 jigger gin
ice cubes

club soda
maraschino cherry and
orange slice or lime
twist for garnish

In covered cocktail shaker, shake lemon juice and sugar until sugar is dissolved. Add cracked ice and gin; shake well. Strain mixture over ice cubes in highball glass. Add club soda to fill glass; stir. Garnish with fruit and serve.

Martini

Color index
page 112

Begin just
before serving

2 servings

1½ cups cracked ice
2 jiggers gin or vodka
1 teaspoon dry
vermouth

2 small stuffed green
olives or lemon twists
for garnish

1. Over cracked ice in cocktail shaker, pour gin and vermouth; stir.
2. Strain mixture into 2 chilled cocktail glasses. Garnish each glass with an olive or a lemon twist.

Stinger

Color index
page 112

Begin just
before serving

1 serving

1 cup cracked ice
1 jigger brandy

½ jigger white crème de
menthe

Over cracked ice in cocktail shaker, pour brandy and white crème de menthe; shake well. Strain mixture into chilled cocktail glass.

CALVADOS STINGER: Prepare as above but substitute *1 jigger Calvados* for brandy.

473

Wines

American wines

Wine can be divided into five basic classes: appetizer wines, white table wines, red table wines, sweet dessert wines and sparkling wines. For details of characteristics of these wines, see table, opposite

SERVING WINE
Serve appetizer wines well chilled, either straight (undiluted) or over ice. All white wines should be served chilled. Depending on the type, red wines are served either cool or chilled or at room temperature. Most dessert wines may be served cool or chilled. Sparkling wines, often served for special occasions, are always served chilled and go well with any food at any occasion.

The best way to learn about wine is to experiment until you find the one you like best. Try a few of the wines in each of the five classes, and for first-time testing, buy wine in small bottles. Some wines complement certain foods more than others.

WINE WITH FOOD
Traditionally, white wines are served with white meats such as poultry, fish and seafood; red wines accompany red meats and dishes with red or brown sauces; rosé and sparkling wines are served with any food. Sweet dessert wines are served with dessert, after dinner and as a between-meal refreshment.

However, let your own taste and personal preference be your guide. Just remember to serve light wines with light foods and heavier, full-bodied wines with fuller-flavored, richer foods. That way food and wine will complement, not over-power, each other.

COOKING WITH WINE
Easy to use, and inexpensive, wine will enhance your favorite recipes for soups, broiled fish and meat, roasts and stews. Special cooking wines are lightly salted, so that you cannot drink them. Make sure to use the type of cooking wine called for in the recipe, and adjust the seasoning if necessary. Experts recommend cooking with wine of a quality you would like to drink – use some in the recipe and serve more to enjoy as a beverage with the food. Here are a few suggestions about how to cook with wine.

To flavor soups, add a tablespoon of wine for each cup of liquid; try adding sherry to consommé, chicken or vegetable soups; Burgundy or claret go well in minestrone. Add a light Rhine wine to melted butter and pour over fish before baking or broiling, or poach seafood in cooking liquid laced with sherry. A dash of sauterne will improve the flavor of gravy for roast poultry, while a dash of Burgundy or Chianti adds depth to a rich gravy for duckling or goose. Red wines add that extra flavor to beef dishes, too. Stir in Chianti or Zinfandel to gravy for roast beef, or add Chianti or Burgundy to barbecue sauce for serving with broiled beef steaks and hamburgers.

RED TABLE OR DINNER WINES	
Baco Noir	Dry, medium- to heavy-bodied, deep red wine made from French-hybrid Baco Noir grapes.
Barbera	Dry, full-bodied, heavy, deep red wine made from Barbera grapes.
Burgundy	Dry, medium- to heavy-bodied, deep ruby-red wine with pronounced flavor and bouquet, usually made from several grape varieties.
Cabernet Sauvignon	Dry, aromatic, ruby-red wine with distinctive flavor, made from Cabernet Sauvignon grapes, which are used in the production of French Bordeaux wines; one of the best Californian red-wine grapes.
Chianti (red)	Dry, fruity and slightly tart, ruby-red wine with strong flavor.
Chelois	Dry, light- to medium-bodied, light red wine made from French-hybrid Chelois grapes.
Claret	The name applied to any dry, tart, light- to medium-bodied ruby-red wine, made from one or more red grape varieties.
Concord	Medium-sweet to sweet, fruity wine, pale gold to deep red in color with a characteristic grapey flavor.
Gamay	Burgundy-type dry wine made from Gamay grapes; light-bodied; often a rosé wine.
Grignolino	Dry, claret-type wine with decided orange-red color, and distinct flavor and aroma of Grignolino grapes.
Petite Sirah	Burgundy-type dry, full-bodied wine.
Pinot Noir	Burgundy-type wine. Body and flavor vary greatly with amount of Pinot Noir grapes present (by law, as of 1983, at least 75%). Finest are velvety to taste, beautiful red color.
Rosé	Dry to slightly sweet, pink wine; lightest of red table wines.
Ruby Cabernet	Fruity, medium-bodied wine made from Ruby Cabernet grapes.
Vino Rosso	Term applied to slightly sweet to semisweet, medium- to heavy-bodied, ruby-red wines. Sometimes called "mellow red wines," they are softer in flavor than Chianti or other red dinner wines.
Zinfandel	Claret-type wine with fruity taste and aroma, made from Zinfandel grapes, produced only in California.

WHITE TABLE OR DINNER WINES

Blanc de Blancs	White wine made from white grapes.
Catawba	Dry or semisweet wine made in Eastern and Midwestern U.S.A. from Catawba grapes that give it flavor and aroma reminiscent of roses.
Chablis	Dry, fruity, pale gold wine, made from several grape varieties.
Chardonnay	Dry varietal wine with distinctive flavor and aroma of Chardonnay grapes. Sometimes called Pinot Chardonnay.
Chenin Blanc	Dry to semisweet, light-bodied, fragrant Chablis-type wine.
Chianti (white)	Dry, medium-bodied, slightly fruity and tart white wine.
Delaware	Dry to semisweet wine with flowery aroma, made from Delaware grapes grown in Eastern U.S.A.
Folle Blanche	Dry, Chablis-type wine made from Folle Blanche grapes.
Light Muscat	Dry to very sweet, light wine with characteristic Muscat grape flavor and aroma.
Niagara	Semisweet, light-bodied wine with distinctive aroma of Niagara grapes.
Pinot Blanc	Dry, tart, Chablis-type wine made from Pinot Blanc grapes.
Rhine Wine	Dry, tart, light-bodied, often flowery or fruity pale gold to green-gold white wine.
Riesling	Rhine wine made from one or a blend of Riesling grapes. Wines include Johannisberg Riesling; Grey Riesling; Franken Riesling; Emerald Riesling.
Sauterne	Dry to sweet, full-bodied, fragrant, golden wine. Three sauterne-type wines are sold in U.S.A.: Dry Sauterne, Sauterne, and Haut Sauterne.
Sauvignon Blanc	Sauterne-type wine with flavor and aroma of Sauvignon Blanc grapes. Usually dry; sometimes semisweet.
Semillon	Dry or semisweet sauterne-type wine made from Semillon grapes.
Sylvaner	Dry, sometimes tart, fruity and fragrant Rhine wine made from Sylvaner (Franken Riesling) grapes.
Traminer	Dry or slightly sweet, medium-bodied Rhine wine made from Traminer grapes. *Gewurztraminer* is a "spicy" wine from grapes of the same name.

APPETIZER WINES

Sherry	Pale to dark amber wine with characteristic nutty flavor that ranges from dry to sweet. Dry and medium sherries are preferred as appetizer and cocktail wines; they are labeled *cocktail, dry,* or *medium* sherry.
Vermouth	Wine flavored with herbs or other aromatic substances. Two main types: French-type vermouth, dry and nearly colorless; Italian-type vermouth, sweet and dark amber.
Flavored wines	Wines to which natural flavors, such as herbs and fruit, are added. *May wine* is flavored with sweet, scented woodruff; *Retsina* is white wine treated with pine resin.

DESSERT WINES

Angelica	Sweet, mild, fruity, straw-colored or amber wine resembling white Port.
Cream Sherry	Sweet, heavy, rich golden in color.
Madeira	Semisweet, deep amber wine resembling sherry but sweeter and darker. (Imported from Portugal.)
Marsala	Medium-bodied, deep amber wine resembling sherry but sweeter and darker. (Imported from Italy.)
Muscatel	Rich, robust sweet wine with typical Muscat grape flavor and aroma.
Port	Sweet, heavy-bodied, rich, deep-red to tawny wine. (Some white Port is produced.)
Tokay	Sweet, amber-colored wine with slightly nutty or sherry-like flavor, usually made by blending Angelica, Port and Sherry.

SPARKLING WINES

Champagne	Sparkling dry to sweet wine, made from one or more grape varieties. Very dry Champagne is usually labeled *nature*; dry, usually labeled *brut*; semidry, labeled *sec* or *dry*; sweet, labeled *doux*. Wine is pale gold in color. Pink champagnes are also made.
Sparkling Burgundy	Semisweet or sweet red wine made by methods used for Champagne.
Sparkling Muscat	Sweet Champagne-like wine with flavor of Muscat grapes.
Sparkling Rosé	Similar to pink Champagne. Dry to semisweet; made from grapes used for rosé dinner wine.

USEFUL INFORMATION

Menu planning and entertaining

Whether you are planning a menu for everyday or elaborate entertaining, choose dishes from the Basic Four Food Groups: *Meat and protein-rich foods*, which include meats, fish, poultry, shellfish, eggs or cheese, dry or canned beans, dry peas and lentils, nuts and peanut butter; *Fruits and vegetables*; *Breads, cereals and pasta* and *Milk and milk products*, which include cheese and yogurt. By choosing from these groups, you will be able to supply the foods needed for good health in a variety of food flavors, colors and textures.

When planning a menu there are four important points to bear in mind: You should consider family nutritional needs, especially in everyday meals, the food preferences of family or guests, your budget and the available preparation time.

Another factor to consider in menu planning is the season of the year: for example, Chilled Cucumber Soup is better suited for summer rather than winter menus, while New England "Boiled" Dinner would be far more suitable for a cold winter's evening meal.

BALANCING THE MENU
The Basic Four Food Groups should be used as your guide. In everyday meal planning, work out a day's three menus all at one time so that the right number of servings from all groups are included.

Include two servings a day from the Meat group, four a day from Fruits and vegetables. Try to include one serving of citrus fruit or tomatoes and a serving of dark-green leafy or orange vegetable and fruit every other day.

Provide four servings from Bread, cereal or pasta. A serving equals either 1 slice bread, 1 medium potato, 1/2 cup starchy vegetable such as corn or 1/2 cup pasta or rice, or 1/2 cup cooked cereal.

From the Milk group, plan on two servings for adults, three to four for children. One serving equals either an 8-ounce glass of milk, 1 ounce of cheese, 1/2 cup cottage cheese or 1 cup plain yogurt.

CHOOSING THE DISHES
Select the main dish first. It should provide a serving from the Meat and protein-rich food group. Next choose the vegetables. Most menus include one starchy vegetable or one from the Breads, cereals and pasta group and at least one non-starchy vegetable chosen from Fruits and vegetables.

Plan vegetables that are varied in color. For example, serve a green or yellow vegetable with white potatoes or rice. You can also vary vegetable shapes to add interest to the plate.

Choose a salad that will add any needed fruits or vegetables for the day. Select a crunchy vegetable to add texture to an otherwise soft menu. A creamy fruit or molded salad can be served when the main dish is broiled or fried and eaten without sauce or gravy.

Select the dessert to balance the main dish. If the main dish is hearty such as beef stew, serve a light dessert such as sherbet or fruit and cookies. If the main dish is light, a salad or soup, top off the meal with a hearty sweet such as apple pie or chocolate cake.

While bread is not an essential part of any menu, it can supply a contrast to other dishes and provides additional interest when other foods are plain. It can provide a serving from the Breads, cereals and pasta group. If the meal is cold, serve a hot bread; if the meal is soft textured, serve a crisp and crunchy bread. Use bread to supply starch in a menu that does not include such food.

Pickles, olives, butter, jam, relishes and garnishes are little touches that add interest to a meal. Use beverages to round out a menu. Include milk if that has been omitted from the day's meal.

The last step to menu planning is to go over the entire menu once again to be sure that flavors are harmonious, colors are varied and attractive and textures and shapes offer agreeable variety.

PLANNING AHEAD
Occasional spur-of-the-moment entertaining can be fun but things will be easier on the hostess if parties are planned ahead. Make a guest list and send out invitations a week or two in advance for an informal function, two or three weeks ahead for a more formal party.

After you decide on the menu, check that you have all the equipment you need to prepare and serve the foods.

Make out a detailed work order so that as much preparation as possible can be done in advance. If you are going to need help, ask the family or close friends or for the day itself, hire outside help – a maid for serving or a bartender. It is important for the host and hostess to be relaxed – so make sure you have enough help.

Make a detailed shopping list, including items needed for a centerpiece and any decorations. Buy staple foods well ahead, perishables a day or two in advance.

ARRANGING AND SERVING FOOD
If the host and hostess jointly serve the main course, the main dish should be brought in from the kitchen after the appetizer dishes are removed. If there's no appetizer, then the main dish should be on the table covered and ready to serve.

The vegetables should be placed in front of the hostess. If the host is carving, he places a serving on a plate and passes it to his left and it is passed on to the hostess. She serves the vegetables and passes the plate left to be passed on up the table to the person to the right of the host.

After serving all guests and the host, the hostess' own plate is last. She should take a bite of food first to signal that it is time to begin eating. If the party is large, however, she may ask guests to begin ahead. Breads, sauces, condiments may be passed around the table.

If a maid is serving the meal, the hostess is served first then the person to her right and so on around the table. If the host is carving, the maid at his left receives the plate, takes it to the hostess; then the person to the hostess' right is served and on up the table to the host, then the person to the hostess' left and up to the host.

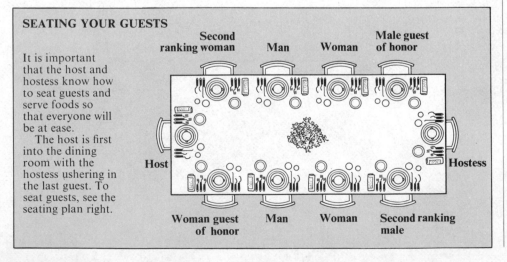

SEATING YOUR GUESTS

It is important that the host and hostess know how to seat guests and serve foods so that everyone will be at ease.

The host is first into the dining room with the hostess ushering in the last guest. To seat guests, see the seating plan right.

Brunch

Conveniently timed for late morning, yet early enough to allow for an afternoon of activity, brunch unites the good qualities of lunch and breakfast – it's the ideal way of casually entertaining weekend guests or merely anticipating a quiet day with the Sunday paper. A selection of fresh fruit or a fruit beverage might precede the main dish, while dessert is usually omitted.

Holiday Brunch Buffet
for 12 servings

Mimosa (orange juice with champagne)
Quiche Lorraine *page 156*
Crab Quiche *page 156*
Colonel's Lady's Salad Bowl *page 318*
Kolacky *page 443*
Coffee served with Crème de Cacao or
Brandy or Whipped Cream

Weekend Brunch
for 4 servings

Chilled Peach Nectar
Eggs Mornay *page 143*
Brown-and-Serve Sausage Links
Pan-fried Apple Wedges *page 301*
Toasted English Muffins
Coffee or Hot Tea

International Brunch
for 8 servings

Company Bloody Mary *page 473*
Orange-Apple Cup with Mint Garnish
Beignets *page 425*
Pan-fried Canadian Bacon
French Hot Chocolate *page 468*

Brunch Before Bridge
for 4 servings

Grapefruit Ambrosia *page 307*
Scrambled Eggs Archduchess *page 144*
Café au Lait *page 467*

Family Gathering
for 8 servings

Gingered Melon Wedges *page 310*
Chicken à la King *page 269*
Buttered Broccoli Spears
Sour-Cream Coffeecake *page 430*
Tea   Milk   Coffee

Country Brunch
for 8 servings

Pineapple Juice
Buttermilk Waffles *page 427*
(double recipe)
Homemade Sausages *page 243*
Hearty Hot Cocoa *page 468* or Coffee

Quick and Easy
for 6 servings

Cocktail Vegetable Juice
Welsh Rabbit *page 154*
Waldorf Salad *page 322*
Coffee   Hot Tea

Luncheon

A luncheon neither has to be large nor elaborate to be considered a party. A light soup or fruit, optional for first course, could be followed by any of these combinations: a cold salad with hot bread and a rich dessert, or a hot casserole or omelet, plus bread and a light dessert; or a hot main dish with a crisp salad and either a light or a rich dessert.

A. *Napkin;* B. *Luncheon plate;* C. *First-course bowl and liner plate;* D. *Bread-and-butter plate;* E. *Water goblet;* F. *Wine glass;* G. *Luncheon fork;* H. *Dessert fork;* I. *Luncheon knife;* J. *Teaspoon;* K. *Soup spoon;* L. *Bread-and-butter knife*

Soup Deluxe
for 10 servings

Bouillabaisse, American Style *page 136*
Sourdough Bread, sliced *page 441*
Tossed Salad with Lemony-Mustard
Dressing *page 318*
Deep-Dish Peach Pie *page 348*
Coffee   Hot Tea

Pre-Game Buffet
for 8 servings

Sacramento Fruit Bowl *page 322*
Chicken Tetrazzini *page 268*
Green Beans Amandine
Crusty Hard Rolls   Butter
Perfection Salad *page 323*
Devil's Food Cake *page 384*
Beer   Coffee

Business Lunch
for 4 servings

Vichyssoise *page 129*
Roast Rack of Lamb *page 227*
Baked Herbed Tomatoes *page 297*
Caesar Salad *page 318*
Strawberries Romanoff *page 304*
Caffè Espresso *page 467*

Summer Pre-Theater
for 4 servings

Crab Louis *page 325*
Bran Muffins *page 424*
Cinnamon Apricots in Cream *page 302*
Sugar Cookies *page 412*
Coffee

Tea

Tea parties range from an afternoon get together with just a few friends to a formal gathering. Four o'clock is the usual hour for serving tea, but any time between two and six is acceptable. Select foods which are suitable for eating in the hand.

Server

Server

A. *Tea service (teapot and tray);* B. *Lemon fork;* C. *Plate of lemon slices;* D. *Sugar spoon;* E. *Sugar bowl;* F. *Creamer;* G. *Teaspoons;* H. *Napkins;* I. *Tray of cookies, tea sandwiches;* J. *Bowl of mints;* K. *Bowl of nuts;* L. *Cups and saucers;* M. *Coffee service (coffee pot and tray);* N. *Centerpiece*

Come-for-Tea Party
for 12 servings

Swans *page 367*
Chinese Fried Walnuts *page 114*
Candied Fruit Tray: Orange Slices,
Figs, Apricots, Dates, Pineapple
Hot Tea   Coffee

Welcoming Tea
for 20 servings

Deviled Ham Pinwheels *page 459*
Pimento-Cheese Finger Sandwiches
Lemon Loaf, sliced *page 428*
Neapolitan Cookies *page 411*
Madeleines *page 409*
Chocolate-dipped Fruit *page 420*
Salted Almonds
Butter Mints
Herbal Tea   Coffee

Spring Reception Tea
for 25 servings

Ribbon Sandwiches *page 459*
Cream Cheese on Raisin-Bread Squares
Citrus Pinwheels *page 411*
Toffee Bars *page 404*
Marzipan Fruits *page 419*
Candied Orange Peel *page 311*
Diced Crystallized Ginger
Hot Tea   Coffee

Dinner

A family dinner is an informal occasion for entertaining visiting relatives or friends, while a party dinner is formal, usually given for very special occasions – for anniversaries, in honor of a community leader, when the boss is invited or for visits of very special friends. For a memorable party dinner, try basing your menu on a theme, and decorating and selecting appropriate dishes.

A. *Napkin;* B. *Dinner or service plate;*
C. *First-course bowl and liner plate;* D. *Salad plate;* E. *Water goblet;* F. *Wine glass;*
G. *Salad fork;* H. *Dinner fork;* I. *Dessert fork;* J. *Dinner knife;* K. *Teaspoon;*
L. *Soup spoon*

Candlelit Dinner
for 8 servings

Smithfield Ham on Honeydew Wedges
Chicken Périgord-style *page 257*
Oven-Dinner Rice *page 338*
(double recipe)
Carrots and Celery *page 298*
California Salad *page 318*
Giant Popovers *page 427*
Chocolate Chiffon Pie *page 353*
Dry Sauterne   Coffee

Gala Retirement Party
for 10 servings

Eggs en Gelée *page 141*
Individual Beef Wellingtons *page 192*
Cabernet Sauvignon
Peas with Lettuce
Cauliflower Polonaise *page 283*
(double recipe)
Tomatoes Vinaigrette *page 319*
(double recipe)
Ice-Cream Bombe Les Dames
d'Escoffier *page 379*
Coffee   Hot Tea

Elegant Dinner
for 6 servings

Jellied Madrilène Suprême *page 129*
Veal Forestier *page 237*
Mashed Potatoes *page 292*
Summer Squash Medley *page 295*
Danish Cucumber Salad *page 319*
Vienna Rolls *page 439*
Butter Curls *page 424*
Apricot-Cream Flan *page 360*
Demitasse   Cordials

Mostly Do-Ahead Dinner
for 8 servings

Celery Hearts Vinaigrette *page 321*
Fillets of Sole Thermidor *page 178*
Homemade Spinach Noodles *page 330*
Glazed Carrots *page 283 (double recipe)*
Tomato Aspic *page 323*
Dinner Rolls *page 439*
Very-Berry Compote *page 304*
Coffee   Hot Tea

All-American Christmas
for 12 to 14 servings

Roast Turkey
with Moist Bread Stuffing *page 249*
Spiced Carrots *page 283*
Creamed Onions *page 290*
Brussels Sprouts with Chestnuts
Perfection Salad *page 323*
(double recipe)
Cranberry Relish *page 306*
Corn Sticks *page 428*
Butter Balls *page 424*
Strawberry Shortcake *page 369* or
Apple Pie *page 346*
Coffee   Milk   Hot Tea

Mexican Fiesta
for 6 servings

Guacamole *page 124*
Margarita *page 472 (6 times recipe)*
Sour Cream Chicken Enchiladas
page 270
Mixed Fruit Salad
Caramel Flan
Hot Chocolate with Cinnamon

Festive Fall Meal
for 12 servings

Appetizer Avocados *page 303*
(double recipe)
Prune-stuffed Roast Pork *page 212*
Pan-roasted Potatoes *page 292*
(double recipe)
Confetti Vegetables *page 298*
Colonel's Lady's Salad Bowl *page 318*
Chocolate-Cherry Soufflé *page 361*
Coffee   Hot Tea

Mother's Favorite
for 6 servings

Teriyaki Beef Kabobs *page 198*
Rice Ring *page 341*
Stir-fried Asparagus *page 278*
Avocado and Radish Romaine Salad
Thousand Island Dressing *page 326*
Meringue Shells *page 364*
with Pistachio Ice Cream *page 377*
Hot Green Tea

In Ye Olde English Manner
for 16 servings

Cream of Leek Soup
Standing Rib Roast
with Yorkshire Pudding *page 191*
Potatoes au Gratin *page 293*
(triple recipe)
Sliced Parsnips and Carrots
Cucumber-Watercress Salad
Sherry Trifle *page 372 (double recipe)*
Earl Grey Tea

Far Eastern Dinner
for 6 servings

Mushroom-Snow Pea Soup
Striped Bass with Pungent Sauce
page 175
Hot Fluffy Rice *page 338*
(double recipe)
Stir-fried Broccoli *page 281*
Gingered Kiwifruit *page 307*
(double recipe)
Oolong or Jasmine Tea

Italian Repast
for 8 servings

Tortellini in Cream Sauce *page 335*
Veal Piccata *page 236*
Risotto alla Milanese *page 339*
(double recipe)
Pepper-and-Tomato Sauté *page 299*
Braised Fennel *page 286 (double recipe)*
Crisp Italian Toast
Strawberry-Orange Ice *page 381*
Caffè Espresso *page 467*
(double recipe)

SETTING UP A BUFFET

A buffet enables you to serve a large crowd in a small dining area and any meal, even dessert and coffee, can be served this way. Arrange plates and food in menu order for smooth service.

A. *Plates;* B. *Serving fork;* C. *Main dish;* D. *Gravy ladle;*
E. *Gravy boat on liner plate;* F. *Serving spoon;* G. *Vegetable dish;* H. *Salad fork and spoon;* I. *Salad bowl;* J. *Relish tray;*
K. *Basket of rolls;* L. *Napkins with knives, forks and spoons;*
M. *Salt and pepper;* N. *Centerpiece and candles*

French Provincial
for 4 servings

Artichokes Béarnaise *page 277*
Coq au Vin *page 267*
Potatoes Anna *page 293*
Sorrel Salad
Crusty French Bread
Camembert with Pears
Burgundy Wine   Coffee

Valencia Olé
for 8 servings

Tapas: stuffed green olives, Curried Almonds *page 114*, Marinated Mushrooms, Pickled Shrimp
Sherry
Paella *page 165*
Sliced Orange and Red Onion on Lettuce
Crème Caramel *page 359*
Sangria *page 471*

Aegean Feast
for 8 servings

Spanakopitas *page 121*
Retsina (wine)
Chicken Avgolemono *page 259*
Greek Salad *page 320*
Baklava *page 371*
Hot Tea with Mint   Espresso

Father's Day
for 6 servings

Shrimp Cocktail with Tangy Dip *page 164*
Filets Mignon with Mustard-Caper Sauce *page 195*
Baked Potatoes *page 292*
Green Beans with Zucchini *page 299*
Poached Pears in Sauterne *page 313*
Irish Coffee *page 467* (6 times recipe)

Anniversary Dinner Buffet
for 16 servings

Tiny Ham-stuffed Tomatoes *page 126*
Pumpernickel-Muenster Triangles *page 117*
Cocktails   Appetizer Wines
Châteaubriand *page 195*
Crab Imperial *page 167*
Rice Pilaf with Peas *page 339* (double recipe)
Salad Bar: choice of green pepper strips, cherry tomatoes, croutons, spinach, lettuce, salad dressings
Chocolate-Cinnamon Torte *page 373*
Minted Sherbet Ring with Berries *page 380*
Champagne   Coffee

Saturday Night Special
for 6 servings

Chilled Cucumber Soup *page 129*
Turkey in Champagne Sauce with Toast Flowers *page 260*
Zesty Tangelo Salad *page 315*
Walnut Tarts *page 357*
Hot or Iced Tea

Graduation Celebration
for 16 servings

Green Onion Dip *page 124*
Cheese Spreads *page 124* with assorted crackers
Golden Punch *page 471*
Turkey Breast with Glazes *page 250*
Spiced Nectarine Slices *page 311*
Ratatouille *page 298* (double recipe)
Deluxe Coleslaw *page 319* (double recipe)
Walnut-Fudge Cake *page 388*
Iced or Hot Tea

Friday Family Dinner
for 6 servings

Broiled Sesame Trout *page 174*
Brown Rice *page 338*
Whole Green and Wax Beans with Parsley Sauce *page 279*
Greens with Russian Dressing *page 326*
Lemon Meringue Pie *page 351*
Coffee   Hot Tea

Welcome Neighbor
for 8 servings

Marinated Artichoke Hearts and Mushrooms *page 319*
Hearty Manicotti *page 334*
Baked Creamed Spinach *page 294*
Chianti
Braided Herb Bread *page 437*
Cantaloupe Ice *page 310*
Caffè Espresso with Hot Milk and Cinnamon Stick

Coffee and dessert

Having family or friends over for coffee or some other hot beverage and a fancy dessert is a pleasant way to entertain, particularly on the weekends, after the theater or movies, or during the holidays.

Après-Ski
for 12 servings

Six-Layer Eggnog Cake *page 394*
Café Brûlot *page 467* (double recipe)

Summer Delight
for 8 servings

Raspberry Ribbon Pie *page 354*
Demitasse   Cordials

Spring Dessert Party
for 12 servings

Strawberry Soufflé *page 361*
Chocolate-dipped Butter Cookies *page 410*
Coffee   Hot Tea with Mint

A Special Occasion
for 16 servings

Chocolate Fancy *page 374*
Champagne   Coffee

Cocktail party

A cocktail party lets you entertain a few or a lot of friends with a minimum of space and money. Have hot and cold food selections and an assortment of liquors, mixers and garnishes for popular drinks.

Cocktails at Six
for 6 servings

Blue Cheese Dip (*page 124*)
Tray of Vegetables for Dipping: carrot sticks, broccoli flowerets, cucumber wedges
Bacon-broiled Scallops *page 163*
Caviar-Egg Rounds *page 115*
Salted Nuts and Pretzels
Cocktails   Wine

Cocktails for a Crowd
for 20 to 25 servings

Crisp Cheese Twists *page 114*
Chili Dip with Fresh Vegetables *page 125*
Pissaladière *page 117*
Chicken Liver Pâté *page 122* with Melba Toast *page 133*
Homemade Pepper-Herb Cheese *page 123*
Rye Crisps or Flat Breads
Tuna-Dill Rounds *page 115*
Steak Bites *page 119*
Cocktails   Appetizer Wines

OPENING A CHAMPAGNE BOTTLE

Hold bottle in one hand and with the other, remove wire muzzle.

Slightly tilt bottle and hold cork firmly while rotating bottle.

Pull bottle down gently and slowly to reduce internal pressure. Cork will come out with a soft "pop." Wipe rim before serving.

Menu planning and entertaining

Bridal or baby shower

Bridal showers may be given at brunch, luncheon, tea, dinner or in the evening, while baby showers are usually afternoon or evening functions.

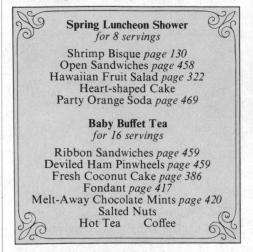

Spring Luncheon Shower
for 8 servings

Shrimp Bisque *page 130*
Open Sandwiches *page 458*
Hawaiian Fruit Salad *page 322*
Heart-shaped Cake
Party Orange Soda *page 469*

Baby Buffet Tea
for 16 servings

Ribbon Sandwiches *page 459*
Deviled Ham Pinwheels *page 459*
Fresh Coconut Cake *page 386*
Fondant *page 417*
Melt-Away Chocolate Mints *page 420*
Salted Nuts
Hot Tea   Coffee

Wedding reception

The reception after a wedding can be an intimate dinner for the wedding party and immediate family alone, or a large-scale event for all the invited guests. For a simple reception, just serve the Party Cake with nuts, candies and the punch. For the buffet below, set the table as shown on page 480, but place the cake, punch bowl, candies and nuts on another table.

**Luncheon or
Late Afternoon Buffet**
for 50 to 60 servings

Pickled Shrimp *(double recipe)* and
Crystalline Ice Bowl *page 120*
Blue Cheese Dip *page 124 (triple recipe)*
Basket of Vegetables for Dipping:
cauliflowerets, cucumber sticks,
radish roses, blanched asparagus or
green beans
Hot Mushroom Turnovers *page 118*
(double recipe)
Dilled Meatballs *page 208*
(triple recipe)
Golden Punch *page 471*   Champagne
Turkey Breast Glacé with Sherry Aspic,
sliced *page 250 (double recipe)*
Whole Smithfield Ham, sliced *page 221*
Roast Beef, thinly sliced
Horseradish Sauce *page 463*
(double recipe)
Sliced Breads: Marbled Loaf, Round
Rye Bread *page 435*, Potato Bread
page 438
Sweet Butter   Prepared Mustard
Party Cake *page 396*
Jordan Almonds   Bonbons *page 418*
Peppermint Patties *page 419*
Golden Champagne Punch *page 471*
Coffee   Hot Tea

NAPKIN FOLDING

Add a final decorative touch to your dinner table by folding napkins into any of the shapes below. Napkins may also be placed on the dinner plates.

SILVER BUFFET

Fold the napkin over twice to form a square. Hold the square in a diamond shape.

Take the top 2 flaps and roll them halfway down the napkin.

Fold under the right and left points at the sides. There is now a pocket into which you can place the knife, fork and spoon.

BUTTERFLY

Form a triangle from an open napkin. Fold the right corner to the center.

Take the left corner up to center, making a diamond. Keeping the loose points at the top, turn the napkin over, then fold upward, to form a triangle.

Tuck the left corner into the right. Stand up napkin; turn it round, then turn the petals down; it's now a butterfly.

WATER LILY

Place all 4 points to the center of an opened napkin.

Fold the 4 points to the center of the napkin once more.

Repeat a third time; turn napkin over and fold points to the center once more.

Holding finger firmly at center, unfold 1 petal first from underneath each corner.

Pull out 4 more from between the petals. Then pull out the next 4 under the petals.

The water lily now has 12 points.

Eating outdoors

Cooking outdoors on a grill can be a fun way of entertaining; however, it can be a disaster unless you think of safety first. Since many factors affect the amount of heat from a grill, cooking directions are very general. Follow our tips for successful barbecuing.

BARBECUE TOOLS
Brush
Skewers
Barbecue tongs   Oven gloves   Foil

LIGHTING THE FIRE
Be sure there is adequate ventilation to remove deadly carbon monoxide formed by the fire. Never grill in a closed camper, porch, garage, trailer or tent.

Place grill away from dry grass, bushes, the house. Never leave it unattended once coals are ignited.

Line the grill with heavy-duty foil. It reflects heat and so speeds cooking, makes cleaning a snap. If bottom of grill has vents, puncture foil so air can circulate.

To get the fire started quickly, push the briquettes into a pyramid.

Use a charcoal lighter to start the fire, choosing from liquid, solid and jelly types; or use a UL-listed electric starter. Follow manufacturer's directions to the letter. NEVER, NEVER use gasoline, alcohol or other highly volatile fluids.

Let briquettes burn until they are covered with a layer of gray ash in daylight or are glowing red at night. This will take 20 to 40 minutes. On a cold day, use more briquettes to offset lower outside temperatures.

If you're grilling fatty meats like hamburger, use fewer briquettes to keep the fire cool, reduce flare-ups. Use more briquettes when grilling lean meats.

Experiment with different brands of briquettes, some are easier to light.

BARBECUING TIPS
Spread hot briquettes in a single layer before placing food on rack.

To judge the temperature of the coals, hold your hand, palm down, at cooking height. If you can hold it there only 2 to 3 seconds, temperature is hot, above 375°F.; for 4 seconds, it's medium, above 300°F.; for 5 to 6 seconds, it's low, above 200°F.

To change the temperature when needed, raise the cooking rack and/or spread out coals to lower the heat. To raise the heat, push coals together.

To minimize flare-ups when grilling fatty meats, try tipping the rack slightly so that hot fat runs down the wires and drips off at the cool edge of the fire.

To put out flare-ups caused by dripping fat, raise the rack and spread out coals or remove the food and douse the flames with water in a plastic pump-spray bottle.

Bon Voyage Party
for 8 servings

Bluefish with Buttery Lemon Sauce
page 174
Potatoes Baked in Coals
Grilled Zucchini Halves
Three-Bean Salad *page 321*
Speedy Biscuits *page 423*
Cold Watermelon
Iced Coffee   Sparkling Wine

Graduation Barbecue
for 8 servings

Yogurt-Cheese Dip *page 125*
Potato Chips   Breadsticks   Corn Chips
Savory Chicken *page 261*
Corn-on-the-cob with Chive Butter
page 284
Sliced Tomato-Green Bean Salad
Chocolate Chiffon Cake *page 389*
Lemonade *page 470*   Iced Tea

Fourth of July
for 8 servings

Lamb Kabobs *page 228*
Spinach Mushroom Salad
Poori *page 431*
Peach Meringue Tarts *page 357*
Beer   Ice Tea, Family Style *page 468*

Mountain Park Barbecue
for 4 servings

Barbecued Spareribs *page 216*
Vegetable Trio *page 298 (foil-wrapped)*
Zesty Lima Beans *page 280*
Whole Wheat Rolls
Pears with Raspberry Sauce
Soft Drinks   Iced Coffee

Steak Grill
for 8 to 10 servings

Stuffed Eggs *page 141*
Deviled Round Steak *page 197*
Stir-fried Cabbage and Zucchini
page 299
Turkish Bean Salad *page 321*
Cherry Cream Tart *page 355*
Hearty Burgundy   Limeade

Picnics
Whether you're planning a light lunch in the park or a feast at the beach, proper food preparation and packing is important. If food is left standing too long at warm temperatures, bacteria such as salmonella can grow to dangerous levels leading to food poisoning. To ensure that food will be fresh when served, follow our suggestions and precautions below.

WHAT AND HOW TO PACK
The best picnic foods are those that keep well. Some favorites: cold fried chicken, marinated vegetable salads, breads.

Keep cooked foods refrigerated in shallow containers so they chill quickly until ready to pack.

Store hot and cold foods in vacuum containers. Line cold food carriers with ice cubes in plastic bags, ice bars made by freezing water in clean milk cartons, or frozen gel-filled containers.

Set out food in portions that will be eaten quickly; replenish only as needed.

For a Day in the Country
for 8 servings

Hot-Pepper Pecans *page 114*
Country Meat Loaf *page 207*
Pickled Onions *page 126*
Macaroni Salad
Olives
Cheese Crackers
Pineapple-Upside-Down Cake *page 384*
Soft Drinks   Dry Red Wine

Concert on the Mall
for 8 servings

Pea Soup *page 130*
Pâté de Campagne *page 122*
Herbed Mushrooms *page 126*
Salade Niçoise *page 324 (double recipe)*
Onion Thins *page 431*
Brie with Seedless Grapes
Iced Tea   Rosé Wine

Lunch in the Park
for 6 servings

Gazpacho *page 129 (double recipe)*
Chicken or Turkey Salad *page 269*
with Alfalfa Sprouts
Pita (pocket bread) *page 447*
Cucumber and Carrot Sticks
Backpacking Bars *page 404*
Apple Juice   Milk

Beach Party
for 10 servings

Tuna Dip *page 125*
Italian Cheese-and-Ham Pie *page 157*
Caponata *page 300*
Bananas or Nectarines
German Gold Poundcake *page 386*
Beer   Soft Drinks

Herbs and spices

Store all herbs and spices in tightly closed containers in a cool place, away from the heat of the stove. Red spices (paprika, chili powder, cayenne and crushed red pepper) will hold their color and keep their flavor longer if refrigerated. The flavor of ground herbs and spices doesn't hold up well during lengthy cooking, so add them toward the end of cooking time; if you have added them at the beginning, refresh the flavor with an extra pinch or two just before the dish finishes cooking. For an extra flavorful curry sauce, sauté the spices in part of the butter or margarine before adding the other ingredients.

NAME	CHARACTERISTICS	USE
Allspice	Whole berries, smoother and slightly larger than peppercorns, or ground, with flavor like a blend of cloves, cinnamon, nutmeg.	In meat and poultry dishes, pickles and relishes, cakes, cookies and pastries.
Anise Seed	Whole or ground seeds, with strong licorice flavor and aroma.	In braised chicken or steak dishes prepared with soy sauce; with fruits; in breads, cookies and candies.
Basil	Fresh or dried, broken or ground leaves with faintly anise-like flavor and sweet aroma.	Use in raw or cooked tomato dishes and sauces; in soups, stuffings, salad dressings; as garnish for egg, cheese, poultry dishes.
Bay Leaves	Whole dried leaves or ground, with strong flavor (especially if whole leaves are torn or crushed); ingredient in bouquet garni.	In meat and poultry dishes, particularly soups, pot roasts and stews; in fish and vegetable dishes; in pickles and in stuffings for poultry and meat.
Caraway Seed	Whole seeds with warm, sweet, slightly sharp taste.	In breads; in cheese spreads and dips, sauerkraut, sweet pickles; as garnish for breads, cheese, coleslaw.
Cardamom Seed	Whole pods with seeds, ground (seeds and pod) or decorticated (seeds only) and ground, with sweet, highly aromatic flavor.	Whole seeds in demitasse, pickles; ground in cookies and coffeecakes and with fruit.
Celery Seed	Whole or ground seeds with slightly bitter, fresh-celery flavor; combined with salt to make celery salt.	In meat, cheese, egg and fish dishes; in barbecue sauces, pickles, soups and salad dressings.
Chervil	Fresh or dried leaves similar to parsley but with subtler, faintly sweet flavor reminiscent of tarragon.	In fish and egg dishes, with vegetables, in soups, salads, meat sauces and stews.
Chili Powder	Red to very dark red powder with varying degrees of heat. Store in refrigerator.	In meat dishes, especially Spanish or Mexican style; in pickles, barbecue sauces, cocktail dips and salad dressings, snack foods and cheese, egg and seafood dishes.

NAME	CHARACTERISTICS	USE
Chives	Long, spiky, green leaves, fresh or freeze-dried and chopped.	Use wherever delicate onion flavor is desired: in egg, cheese, fish and poultry dishes; with vegetables; as garnish for salads, soups and cooked vegetables.
Cinnamon	Reddish brown sticks of rolled bark, or ground, with sweet, pungent aroma.	With sweet vegetables (baked beans, sweet potatoes); in fruit dishes, pickles, breads, cakes, cookies and in desserts.
Cloves	Whole nail-shaped buds, or ground, with pungent, warm, sweet aroma.	In meat and poultry dishes and in barbecue sauces; with sweet vegetables; in pickles and relishes; with fruits; in breads, cookies, desserts and candies; as garnish for relishes, ham and spiced fruits.
Coriander Seed	Whole or ground seeds with slightly lemony flavor and aroma.	In pickles, breads, cookies and cakes.
Cumin Seed	Whole or ground seeds with strong, slightly bitter flavor.	In Spanish- and Mexican-style meat and rice dishes; in cheese spreads and in egg and fish dishes.
Curry Powder	A blend of many spices which gives characteristic Indian flavor to cooking.	In meat, poultry, seafood, egg and cheese dishes and in soups, sauces and salad dressings.
Dill	Fresh or dried dill (weed) has distinctive yet mild, caraway-like flavor. Seeds are sharper, slightly bitter.	In pickles, cheese dishes, salad dressings, cocktail dips, fish and shellfish dishes; with vegetables. Use dillweed as garnish for salads, fish and seafood dishes and in casseroles.
Fennel Seed	Whole or ground seeds with sweet anise-like flavor.	In breads, pizza and spaghetti sauces, fish sauces and pickles; as garnish for baked goods.

NAME	CHARACTERISTICS	USE
Ginger	Whole roots, fresh or dried, ground or cracked (in small pieces), with pungent, sweet aroma and hot flavor.	In Oriental-style meat, poultry, seafood and vegetable dishes, pickles, salad dressings, breads, cookies, pies, cakes and desserts; with fruit.
Mace	Dried, net-like casing around nutmeg, available whole or ground. Flavor and aroma similar to nutmeg but stronger, less delicate.	In soups, salad dressings, meat and poultry spreads; egg, cheese and vegetable dishes, in breads, cookies, cakes, fruit pies; particularly good with chocolate.
Marjoram	Fresh or dried leaves or flakes, with strong, sweet aroma and cool aftertaste.	In meat, poultry, fish, cheese, egg, vegetable and Italian-style dishes.
Mint	Fresh, dried or ground leaves; similar to oregano, with spicy, slightly bitter flavor.	With vegetables, fruits, desserts; in jelly, sauces, relishes, in tea; as garnish for beverages, desserts.
Mustard Seed	Tiny yellow or brown seeds, whole or powdered. Yellow seeds are odorless; brown seeds have sharp, irritating odor and both have pungent taste when moistened.	In pickles and relishes, salad dressings, egg and cheese dishes, cocktail dips, sandwich spreads.
Nutmeg	Whole seed, or ground, with warm, sweet, aromatic flavor.	In beverages, vegetable dishes, breads, cookies, cakes, desserts; as garnish for beverages, sauces and desserts.
Oregano	Dried leaves or ground. Flavor and aroma similar to marjoram but stronger.	In Italian-, Greek- and Mexican-style cooking, in beef, poultry, seafood, cheese and vegetable dishes.
Paprika	Powder varying in color from bright to brick red, with sweetish aroma and flavor which may have slight "bite" Chill.	In meat, poultry, cheese dishes, salad dressings, snack foods, cocktail dips; as garnish for soups, dips and salads.
Parsley	Fresh leaves and stems (which contain much flavor), or dried flakes; mild in flavor.	To flavor and garnish almost any non-sweet dish, raw or cooked.
Pepper	*Black pepper* is available as whole peppercorns and cracked or ground. *White pepper* (the core of the pepperberry) comes whole or ground and is the mildest.	In most main dishes and main-dish sauces and gravies, salads, salad dressings, snacks, appetizers and pickles.

NAME	CHARACTERISTICS	USE
Pepper, Red	Whole or crushed pods, or ground; varies from mild to intense, *cayenne* is hottest of all. Store red and cayenne peppers in refrigerator.	In most main dishes and main-dish sauces and gravies, salads, salad dressings, snacks, appetizers and pickles.
Poppy Seed	Tiny whole blue-gray seeds with sweet, mild, nutty flavor and aroma.	Use in noodle dishes, salad dressings; as fillings for breads, pastries and cakes; as garnish for cheese, snack foods and rolls and breads.
Rosemary	Fresh or dried needle-shaped leaves with pungent tea-like aroma and bittersweet flavor.	In meat, poultry and fish dishes; in stuffings and breads; with vegetables; in salads; as garnish for salads and breads.
Saffron	Dried stamens of a crocus, available as strands or ground. Deep orange in color, with strong aroma and pleasant, slightly bitter taste.	In poultry, fish and shellfish dishes; in rice, breads.
Sage	Fresh or dried leaves, rubbed or ground, with pungent, slightly bitter aroma.	In meat, poultry and cheese dishes; in stuffings for meat and poultry.
Savory	Leaves or ground, with pine-like, almost peppery aroma.	In meat, egg, rice, vegetable dishes; in stuffings for meat and poultry.
Sesame Seed	Whole, small white flattish seeds with slightly nut-like aroma and flavor.	In breads, snacks and candy; as garnish for vegetables, breads and snack foods.
Tarragon	Fresh or dried leaves, or rubbed, with a sweet, aromatic flavor and piquant, anise-like tang.	Use in poultry, seafood, cheese and egg dishes; with vegetables; in salad dressings.
Thyme	Fresh or dried leaves or ground; pungent and aromatic in flavor.	Use in meat, poultry, seafood, egg, cheese and vegetable dishes; in soups, stuffings and salad dressings.
Turmeric	Ground root of plant related to ginger, brilliant yellow in color, with fragrant, pepper-like aroma and slightly bitter flavor.	An essential ingredient of curry powder and often used in prepared mustard. Use also in pickles and relishes, salad dressings, cheese, chicken, egg and fish dishes.

485

Storage guide

CUPBOARD STORAGE

Store foods in your coolest kitchen cabinets – not over the range or near the refrigerator's exhaust. Dry foods do best in airtight containers, which also keep out insects. Choose fresh-looking packages; avoid cans with swollen ends or dents and keep all foods in their original package or in a tightly closed container in a dry spot, unless indicated otherwise. With longer storage than the times recommended here, the flavors will gradually fade and nutrients are eventually lost.

Food	Time	Special Handling
Baking powder, soda	18 months	
Barbecue sauce, catchup, chili sauce	1 month	
Bouillon cubes, powder	1 year	
Cake mixes	1 year	
Canned foods fish fruits, vegetables gravies, sauces meat, poultry milk (both kinds) soups	1 year 1 year 1 year 1 year 1 year 1 year	Refrigerate after opening. See Refrigerator Storage.
Casserole mixes	18 months	
Cereals ready-to-eat ready-to-cook	check date on package 6 months	
Chocolate, cooking	1 year	
Coconut	1 year	Refrigerate after opening.
Coffee, vacuum pack	1 year	Refrigerate after opening vacuum pack.
Coffee, instant	6 months	Keep 2 weeks after opening.
Flour all-purpose, cake rye, whole-wheat	1 year	Keep refrigerated.
Frosting, cans, mixes	8 months	
Fruit, dried	6 months	
Gelatin (both kinds)	18 months	
Herbs, spices whole ground	1 year 6 months	Keep in cool spot. Replace if aroma fades. Refrigerate red spices.
Honey	1 year	
Jam, jelly	1 year	
Macaroni, spaghetti, pasta	1 year	After opening, transfer to airtight container.

Food	Time	Special Handling
Molasses	2 years	
Nonfat dry milk	6 months	
Olive oil	1 month	For longer storage, refrigerate.
Olives, pickles	1 year	Refrigerate after opening.
Pancake mixes	6 months	
Peanut butter	6 months	Keeps 2 months once open
Piecrust mixes	6 months	
Potato mixes, instant	18 months	
Pudding mixes	1 year	
Rice brown, wild white	1 year 2 years	
Salad dressings	6 months	Refrigerate after opening.
Salad Oil	3 months	Refrigerate after opening.
Sauce, gravy, soup mixes	6 months	
Shortening, solid	8 months	
Sugar brown, confectioners granulated	4 months 2 years	
Syrups, corn, maple-flavor, maple	1 year	Refrigerate after opening. Keep maple syrup 1 month after opening.
Tea, bags, loose	6 months	
Tea, instant	1 year	
Vegetables onions, potatoes, rutabagas, squash (hard-shelled), sweet potatoes	1 week at room temperature	For longer storage, keep at 50–60°F. but not refrigerated. Keep dry, out of sun, loosely wrapped.
Yeast, active dry	check date on pack	

PREPARED FOODS

Food	Time	Special Handling
Bread, rolls	3 days	
Bread crumbs	6 months	
Cakes	2 days	If butter-cream, whipped-cream or custard fillings, refrigerate.
Cookies, packaged	4 months	
Crackers	3 months	
Pies, pastries	3 days	Refrigerate cream, custard, chiffon fillings.

REFRIGERATOR STORAGE

Keep your refrigerator temperature between 34° and 40°F; above 40°F. food spoilage happens fast. Except as noted, wrap foods in foil, plastic wrap or bags, or place in airtight containers. This keeps food from drying out and odors from transferring from one food to another. Always keep uncooked meat, fish and poultry in the coldest part of the refrigerator. Fresh fruits and vegetables should be kept in the crisper or loosely closed in moisture-resistant bag or wrap. Except for greens, do not wash before storing. All packaged and prepared foods, all leftovers and dairy products should be kept tightly covered or wrapped in moisture resistant wrap or foil.

FRESH FRUITS AND VEGETABLES

Food	Time	Special Handling
Fruit apples	1 month	May also store at 60-70°F.
apricots, avocados, bananas, melons, nectarines, peaches, pears	5 days	If necessary, allow to ripen at room temperature before refrigerating.
berries, cherries	3 days	
citrus fruit	2 weeks	May also store at 60-70°F.
grapes, plums	5 days	Let ripen at room temperature; then refrigerate.
pineapples	2 days	
Vegetables asparagus	3 days	
beets, carrots, parsnips, radishes, turnips	2 weeks	Remove any leafy tops before refrigerating.
broccoli, Brussels sprouts, green onions, soft-skinned squash	5 days	
cabbage, cauliflower, celery, cucumber, eggplant, green beans, peppers,	1 week	
tomatoes		If necessary, ripen tomatoes at room temperature, away from light, before refrigerating.
corn	1 day	Leave in husk.
lettuce, spinach, all leafy greens	5 days	Rinse, drain before refrigerating.
limas, peas	5 days	Leave in shell.

DAIRY PRODUCTS

Food	Time	Special Handling
Butter	2 weeks	
Buttermilk, sour cream, yogurt	2 weeks	
Cheese cottage, ricotta	5 days	Cut off mold if it forms on surface of cheese.
cream, Neufchâtel	2 weeks	
sliced cheese	2 weeks	
whole pieces	2 months	
Cream	1 week	

Food	Time	Special Handling
Eggs, in shell	1 month	One week for best flavor.
whites, yolks	4 days	Cover yolks with water.
Margarine	1 month	
Milk whole, skimmed	1 week	Do not return unused milk to original container; this spreads bacteria to remaining milk.

MEAT, FISH, POULTRY BEFORE COOKING

Food	Time	Special Handling
Fresh meat beef, lamb, pork, veal		Leave in plastic wrap. Or if not prepackaged in plastic, wrap loosely in waxed paper so surface can dry slightly.
chops, steaks	5 days	
roasts	5 days	
ground, stew meat	2 days	
sausage, fresh	2 days	
variety meats	2 days	
Processed meats bacon, frankfurters	1 week	Times are for opened packages of sliced meat. Check date on unopened vacuum-packed meat.
ham canned (unopened)	6 months	
slices	3 days	
whole	1 week	
luncheon meats	5 days	
sausage, dry, semi-dry	3 weeks	
Fish, shellfish (all kinds)	1 day	Keep wrapped.
Poultry (all kinds) fresh, thawed frozen	2 days	If not in plastic wrap, wrap loosely.

PACKAGED AND PREPARED FOODS – LEFTOVERS OR AFTER OPENING

Food	Time	Special Handling
Cooked or canned foods broths, gravy, soup	2 days	
casseroles, stews	3 days	
fruit, vegetables	3 days	
juices, drinks	6 days	
meat, fish, poultry	2 days	
stuffings	2 days	Remove stuffings from poultry and refrigerate separately.
Cakes, pies: cream, custard	2 days	
Coffee, ground	1 week	After opening.
Flour: rye, whole-wheat	1 year	
Nuts (shelled)	6 months	
Pickles, olives	1 month	
Refrigerated biscuits, cookies, rolls		See expiration date on label.
Salad dressings	3 months	
Salads: potato, coleslaw	2 days	
Wine, table	3 days	
Wine, cooking	3 months	

Storage guide

FREEZER STORAGE

Keep freezer at 0°F. otherwise use food within a week or two. To wrap for storage for one month or more, use moisture-proof materials or specially coated or laminated papers. Properly wrapped and frozen, foods will hold full flavor and nutrients for times listed below; after that, flavors may fade but food is still safe to eat. It's safe to refreeze foods if they still contain ice crystals or have been thawed in the refrigerator and held no more than one or two days. Never refreeze, or eat, any food with off-odor or off-color. Do not freeze eggs in the shell, creamed cottage cheese or cream cheese, or custard pies.

COMMERCIALLY-FROZEN FOODS

Food	Time	Special Handling
Breads baked, dough	3 months	Pick up frozen foods immediately before going to check-out counter. Buy only foods frozen solid and with no dribbles on the package, odor or other signs of being thawed. Put all frozen foods together in one bag so they'll stay as cold as possible for trip home. Store in original wrapping. Place in home freezer as soon as possible. Cook or thaw as label directs.
Cakes angel-food layer cake, frosted pound, yellow cake	2 months 4 months 6 months	
Doughnuts, pastries	3 months	

Fish
"fatty" fish – mackerel,
  trout, etc.
"lean" fish – cod,
  flounder, etc.
	3 months
	
	6 months	

Fruit	1 year	
Ice cream, sherbet	1 month	
Juices, drinks	1 year	
Main dishes, pies fish, meat poultry	3 months 6 months	

Meat
beef
  roasts, steaks
  ground beef
lamb, veal
  roasts, steaks
pork
  chops
  roasts
	
	1 year
	4 months
	
	9 months
	
	4 months
	8 months	

Pancake, waffle batter	3 months	
Pies	8 months	
Poultry chicken, turkey parts chicken, turkey (whole) duckling goose turkey rolls, roasts	6 months 1 year 6 months 6 months 6 months	
Shellfish Alaska King crab breaded, cooked lobster, scallops shrimp (unbreaded)	10 months 3 months 3 months 1 year	
Vegetables	8 months	

HOME-FROZEN FOODS

Food	Time	Special Handling
Breads baked unbaked doughs	3 months 1 month	Use only special recipes.
Butter, margarine	9 months	
Cakes, baked	3 months	
Cheese dry-curd cottage cheese, ricotta natural, process	 2 weeks 3 months	Cut and wrap cheese in small pieces.
Cookies, baked, dough	3 months	
Cream, heavy whipped	2 months 1 month	Thawed cream may not whip.
Egg whites, yolks	1 year	To each cup yolks, add 1 teaspoon sugar for use in sweet, or 1 teaspoon salt for non-sweet, dishes.

Fish, shellfish
"fatty" fish – bluefish,
  trout, etc.
"lean" fish – cod,
  flounder, etc.
shellfish
	
	3 months
	
	6 months
	
	3 months
		All fish and shellfish. Wrap tightly in heavy-duty foil or freezer wrap.

Fruit pies	8 months	Freeze baked or unbaked.
Ice cream, sherbet	1 month	
Main dishes, cooked meat, fish poultry	 3 months 6 months	Freeze in freezer- and ovenproof baking dishes or freezer containers.

Meat
bacon
frankfurters
ground, stew meat
ham
leftover cooked roasts
  beef, lamb roasts
  pork, veal roasts
steaks, chops
  beef
  lamb, veal
  pork
variety meats
	
	1 month
	2 weeks
	3 months
	2 months
	
	1 year
	8 months
	
	1 year
	9 months
	4 months
	4 months
		Keep in vacuum packages. If meat is purchased fresh and wrapped in plastic wrap, check for holes. If none, freeze in this wrap up to 2 weeks. For longer storage overwrap tightly with freezer wrap or heavy-duty foil.

Nuts	3 months	

Poultry
cooked, with gravy
cooked, no gravy
uncooked (whole)
  chicken, turkey
  duckling, goose
uncooked (parts)
  chicken
  turkey
	
	6 months
	1 month
	
	1 year
	6 months
	
	9 months
	6 months
		Wrap in heavy-duty foil or freezer wrap as airtight as possible. Thaw uncooked poultry in refrigerator or under cool running water. Cook within two days of thawing.

Vegetables	1 year	

Calorie guide

Supplying nutrients and energy are the chief jobs of food. Energy, measured as calories, is supplied by the carbohydrates, proteins and fats in the food you eat. Of the three, fat is the most concentrated source – it supplies twice as many calories as a given weight of protein or carbohydrate. Foods with a high fat content will be the richest in calories, whereas foods such as vegetables and fruits, which contain an appreciable amount of water, are relatively low in calories, since water is calorie-free.

Alcohol also supplies energy and ranks next to fat as a source, providing approximately three-fourths as much as equal amounts of fat.

When you choose foods that supply more energy or calories than you need, the excess energy is stored in the body as fat. On a continuing basis, this can lead to an unwanted gain in weight. If you eat less than your body requires, stored fat serves as an energy source. Body weight is maintained when the energy from food matches the energy needs of your body.

Use the calorie chart below as a guide to your food selections. Calorie figures have been abstracted from *Composition of Foods – Raw, Process, Prepared* and *The Home and Gardens Bulletin, Number 72*, both prepared by the United States Department of Agriculture.

To reduce your calorie intake, you can follow some of these suggestions:

In future, use only a quarter of the butter or margarine you now put on your bread, vegetables, etc.

Cottage cheese, made smooth in a blender, is a tasty, low-calorie substitute for sour cream in dips and for toppings.

Use lean cuts of meat; trim off all the fat you can.

Avoid eating the skin of poultry as it contains most of the fat.

Keep your portion of meat down to 3 to 4 ounces per serving.

Substitute poultry and seafood for some of your meat meals. They're lower in calories.

Broil meats instead of frying them. This way fat drips into the broiling pan instead of adding unnecessary calories to the meal.

Use fruit to satisfy your sweet-tooth.

Use portion-control in your kitchen: it's automatic when you buy one-serving packets of food such as instant hot or ready-to-eat cereals.

More portion-controls: Cut cake into thin slices, wrap each separately and freeze for convenient desserts. Thaw at room temperature 15 minutes.

For instant low-calorie "creamed" soup, blend one can condensed chicken- or beef-noodle soup till smooth, then dilute and heat as directed. Just 65 calories a cup.

For fuller flavor, fewer calories, season vegetables with herbs or spices. Heat 2 teaspoons butter or margarine and ¼ teaspoon dried herbs or spices; stir in 2 cups cooked or drained canned vegetables and heat through. Experiment to find your favorites like carrots with cinnamon, green beans with oregano.

For spreading or in sandwiches, choose lower-calorie versions of cheeses – for instance, Neufchâtel or imitation cream cheese instead of the regular kind; reduced-calorie varieties of American or Cheddar.

Choose canned fruit packed in fruit juices or light syrup rather than the traditional heavy syrup – they save you 30 to 60 calories a serving.

Eat vegetables raw; they don't need buttering to give them taste appeal, and they fill you up. Try raw mushrooms, zucchini, cauliflower, spinach, green beans.

For a snack that will give you the most crunch for the calories, try lightly buttered popcorn instead of potato chips or pretzels. Only 40 calories per cup – the others are over 100 calories.

Use bouillon, thickened with a little cornstarch for a rich consistency, instead of regular gravy.

Cook scrambled eggs or omelets in a skillet with non-stick finish and no added fat. This way they have no more calories than poached or hard-cooked eggs.

For instant snacks, keep fresh fruit and low-calorie sodas in the refrigerator and put candy and other calorie-rich snack foods in a special off-limits spot.

Enjoy rye, whole-wheat, pumpernickel and other plain breads which have 60 to 70 calories a slice. But beware of muffins, biscuits and buns, which have extra fat.

Take advantage of low-calorie skimmed milk and reliquefied nonfat dry milk, 90 calories per 8-ounce glass compared with 115 to 140 for the modified skimmed (98 or 99 percent fat-free), 160 for whole milk.

Use Canadian bacon which has one-third fewer calories than regular crisp bacon.

FOOD	CAL
Alcoholic beverages:	
ale, *1 bottle (12 oz.)*	160
beer, *1 bottle (12 oz.)*	160
bourbon (86-proof), *1 jigger*	125
brandy, *1 jigger*	75
champagne, *1 glass (4 oz.)*	85
daiquiri, *1 average*	120
gin (90-proof), *1 jigger*	110
Manhattan, *1 average*	130
old-fashioned, *1 average*	130
rum (80-proof), *1 jigger*	100
rye (90-proof), *1 jigger*	110
Scotch (86-proof), *1 jigger*	105
vodka (86-proof), *1 jigger*	105
wine, dry, *1 glass (3½ oz.)*	85
sweet, *1 glass (3½ oz.)*	140
Almonds, *12 to 14*	85
Apple, *1 medium (2½″ diam.)*	70
Apple, baked, *1 medium*	130
Apple juice (cider), *½ cup*	60
Applesauce:	
sweetened, *½ cup*	115
unsweetened, *½ cup*	50
Apricots:	
canned in syrup, *4 medium halves, 2 tablespoons syrup*	110
dried, *5 halves*	50
fresh, *3 medium*	55
stewed, sweetened, *½ cup*	200
Asparagus, *4 medium stalks*	10
Avocado, *½ 10-oz. avocado*	185
Bacon:	
crisp, fried, *2 slices*	90
Canadian, cooked, *1 slice*	60
Banana, *1 medium (6″ long)*	100
Bagel, *(1¾ oz.)*	165
Bass, striped, raw, *3 oz.*	90
Beans:	
baked, with pork and tomato sauce, canned, *1 cup*	320
green, cooked, *1 cup (1″ pieces)*	30
kidney, canned, *1 cup*	230
limas, cooked, *½ cup*	95
wax, canned, *1 cup*	45
Beef, raw:	
chuck, lean meat only, *4 oz.*	180
as purchased, with bone, *1 lb.*	985
flank, lean meat only, *4 oz.*	165
as purchased, *1 lb.*	655
porterhouse, lean meat only, *4 oz.*	185
as purchased, *1 lb.*	1,605
rib roast, lean meat only, *4 oz.*	220
as purchased, no bone, *1 lb.*	1,820
round, lean meat only, *4 oz.*	150
as purchased, no bone, *1 lb.*	895
rump, lean meat only, *4 oz.*	180
as purchased, no bone, *1 lb.*	1,375
sirloin, lean meat only, *4 oz.*	160
as purchased, no bone, *1 lb.*	1,510
Beef, dried, *2 oz.*	115
Beef stew, canned, *1 serving (1 cup)*	210
Beets, cooked, *2 (½ cup, diced)*	25

Calorie guide

FOOD	CAL
Biscuits:	
baking powder, *1 (2" diam.)*	90
refrigerated, *1 biscuit*	60 to 80
Blackberries, *½ cup*	40
Blueberries, *½ cup*	40
Bluefish:	
cooked, baked, *4 oz.*	180
raw fillets, *1 lb.*	530
Bologna (all meat), *1 oz.*	80
Bouillon cubes, *1 cube*	5
Brazil nuts, *2 medium*	55
Breads, fresh or toasted:	
Boston brown, *1 slice*	100
cornbread, *1 slice*	190
cracked wheat, *1 slice*	65
French or Italian, *1 slice*	65
Melba toast, *1 slice*	15
rye, light, *1 slice*	60
white, *1 slice*	70
white, raisin, *1 slice*	65
whole wheat, *1 slice*	65
Bread crumbs:	
fresh, unbuttered *2 slices* *(1 cup)*	140
packaged dry, *¼ cup*	100
Broccoli, cooked, *½ cup*	20
Brussels sprouts, cooked, *1 cup*	55
Butter or margarine,	
1 tablespoon	100
1 cup	1,630
Buttermilk, *1 cup (8 oz.)*	90
Cabbage:	
cooked, *½ cup*	15
raw, *½ cup shredded*	10
1 lb.	100
Cakes:	
angel-food, *1/12 of 10" cake*	135
cheesecake (cream-cheese base) *1 slice (1/8 of cake)*	450
chiffon *1/16 of 10" cake*	215
chocolate cake, fudge frosting, *1/16 of 9" 2-layer cake*	235
cupcake, unfrosted, *1 medium*	90
poundcake, *½" slice*	140
spongecake, *1/12 of 10" cake*	195
yellow cake, chocolate frosting, *1/16 of 9" 2-layer cake*	275
Candy:	
caramel, plain, *1 small piece*	40
chocolate, milk, *1 oz.*	145
fudge, *1 oz.*	115
hard candy, *1 large sour ball*	35
Life Savers, *1*	10
peanut brittle, *1 oz.*	120
Cantaloupe, *½ (5" diam.)*	60
Carrots:	
cooked, *½ cup, diced*	20
raw, *1 lb. (tops trimmed)*	155
Catchup, chili sauce, *1 tablespoon*	15
Catfish, raw, *4 oz.*	115

FOOD	CAL
Cauliflower:	
cooked, *1 cup*	25
raw, *1 lb. (trimmed)*	50
Celery, raw, *1 cup, diced*	15
1 lb.	60
Cereals, cooked:	
cornmeal, grits, *1 cup*	120
farina, *1 cup*	105
oatmeal, *1 cup*	130
Cereals, ready-to-eat:	
bran flakes, *⅔ cup*	90
corn flakes, *1 cup*	110
oat cereal, *⅔ cup*	110
puffed rice, wheat, *1 cup*	60
crisp rice, *1 cup (1 oz.)*	110
raisin bran, *⅔ cup*	120
shredded wheat, *1 medium biscuit*	90
Cheese:	
American, *1 slice (1 oz.)*	105
Camembert, *1 oz.*	85
Cheddar, *1 slice (1 oz.)*	115
cheese spread, *1 oz.*	80
cottage, creamed, *⅓ cup*	85
uncreamed, *⅓ cup*	60
cream, *2 tablespoons (1 oz.)*	105
mozzarella, whole milk, *1 oz.*	90
Neufchâtel, *1 oz.*	70
Parmesan/Romano, grated, *2 tablespoons (⅓ oz.)*	50
ricotta, partially skimmed milk, *⅓ cup*	85
whole milk, *⅓ cup*	120
Roquefort or blue, *1 oz.*	105
Swiss, process or natural, *1 slice (1 oz.)*	105
Cherries:	
canned in syrup, *½ cup, 3 tablespoons syrup*	115
canned, tart, *1 cup*	105
sweet, fresh, *1 cup*	80
Chewing gum, *1 stick*	10
Chicken, fryers, raw:	
breast, whole, *1 small (¾ lb.)*	295
breast, skinned, *1 small (¾ lb.)*	265
leg and thigh, *1 small (½ lb.)*	190
roasted, no bone, *average serving (4 oz.)*	205
5 oz. (1 cup diced)	225
Chicken pot pie, *1 4" pie*	535
Chili con carne, canned, *1 cup*	335
Chocolate:	
milk, *1 oz.*	145
semisweet, *1 oz.*	145
unsweetened (baking), *1 oz.*	145
Chocolate milk drink:	
(skim milk), *1 glass (8 oz.)*	190
Chocolate syrup, *1 tablespoon*	50
Clams, uncooked, *6 (4 oz. meat)*	85
canned, *3 oz.*	45
Cocoa, *1 tablespoon*	20
Cocoa, prepared with milk, *1 cup*	245
Coconut, shredded, *½ cup*	225

FOOD	CAL
Cod, raw, *4 oz.*	90
Coffee, without sugar and cream, *1 cup*	0
Coffee lighteners, *1 tablespoon*	20 to 30
Cola drinks, *6 oz. bottles*	70
Cookies:	
chocolate chip, *1 (1" diam.)*	50
fig bar, *1 square*	50
gingersnap, *1 small (2" diam.)*	30
macaroon, *1 (2½" diam.)*	85
oatmeal, *1 large (3" diam.)*	65
sandwich-type, *1 cookie*	50
sugar, *1 medium (3" diam.)*	80
sugar wafer, *1 2½" × ¾"*	25
Corn:	
fresh, *1 ear (5" long)*	70
whole kernel canned, *½ cup*	85
creamed, canned, *½ cup*	100
Corned-beef hash, canned, *3 oz.*	155
Cornstarch, *1 tablespoon*	30
Cornstarch pudding, *½ cup*	140
Crab, cooked, *4 oz.*	105
Crackers:	
graham, *4 (2½" square)*	110
oyster, *10 crackers*	45
saltine, *4 squares*	50
soda, *2 (2½" square)*	50
whole rye, *1 double cracker*	20
Cranberries, fresh, *1 cup*	45
Cranberry juice, *½ cup*	80
Cream:	
half-and-half, *1 tablespoon*	20
heavy, *1 tablespoon*	55
1 cup	840
sour, *1 tablespoon*	25
Cucumbers, raw, *6 slices (⅛" thick)*	5
Custard, baked, *½ cup*	150
Dates, dried and pitted, *¼ cup*	125
Dessert topping, *1 tablespoon*	10 to 25
Doughnuts (cake type), *1 medium*	125
Duckling, raw, *1 average serving (4 oz.)*	185
Eggs:	
baked or poached, *1 large*	80
fresh, *1 large*	80
fried, *1 egg, 1 teaspoon butter*	110
omelet, *2 eggs, 2 teaspoons butter, milk*	215
white, *1 large*	15
yolk, *1 large*	60
Eggplant, raw, *1 slice (5" diam.)*	20
1 lb.	90
Figs, dried, *1 large*	60
Finnan haddie, *4 oz.*	120
Fish sticks, *1 breaded stick*	40
Flounder, raw fillets, *4 oz.*	90

FOOD	CAL
Flour:	
all-purpose, *1 cup*	455
cake, *1 cup, sifted*	415
whole wheat, *1 cup, stirred*	400
Frankfurters, *1 medium (8 per lb.)*	170
French toast, *1 slice (no syrup)*	140
Fruit cocktail, canned, *½ cup fruit and syrup*	95
Gelatin, flavored, *½ cup prepared*	70
Gelatin, unflavored, *1 envelope (1 scant tablespoon)*	25
Ginger ale, *1 glass (8 oz.)*	85
Gingerbread, *2″ square (unfrosted)*	175
Goose, cooked, *4 oz.*	260
Grapefruit, *½ medium*	45
Grapefruit juice:	
sweetened, canned, *½ cup*	65
unsweetened, *½ cup*	50
Grapefruit sections, *½ cup, 1 tablespoon syrup*	90
Grape juice, *½ cup*	85
Grapes, *1 cup*	65
Gravy:	
canned beef, *2 tablespoons*	15
homemade (from drippings), *2 tablespoons*	30
Haddock:	
pan-fried, *1 fillet (3 oz.)*	140
raw fillets, *1 lb.*	360
Halibut:	
broiled, *1 steak (4½ oz.)*	240
raw fillets, *1 lb.*	455
Herring:	
pickled, *3 oz.*	185
smoked kippered, *3 oz.*	180
Honey, *1 tablespoon*	65
Honeydew melon, *2″ wedge from 7″ × 6½″ melon*	50
Ice cream, vanilla, *1 cup (10 percent butterfat)*	255
1 cup (16 percent butterfat)	330
Ice-cream soda, *1 regular (vanilla)*	270
Ice milk, *1 cup*	200
Jam, *1 tablespoon*	55
Jelly, *1 tablespoon*	50
Kidneys, beef, raw, *3 oz.*	110
Lamb:	
chop, lean only, *4 oz. cooked*	140
leg, lean meat only, *1 lb. raw*	610
roast, lean only, *3 oz. cooked*	155
Lard, *1 tablespoon*	115
Lemon or lime juice, *4 tablespoons*	15
Lemonade, concentrated, frozen, *1 cup prepared as directed*	110

FOOD	CAL
Lettuce, *2 large leaves*	10
Liver:	
beef, raw, *4 oz.*	155
calf, raw, *4 oz.*	155
chicken, raw, *4 oz.*	145
Liverwurst, *2 oz.*	175
Lobster, cooked meat, *½ cup (3 oz.)*	80
Macaroni:	
cooked, *½ cup*	95
uncooked, *1 lb.*	1,675
Macaroni and cheese, *(1 cup)*	430
Mackerel, raw fillets, *4 oz.*	215
Mango, *1 medium*	85
Margarine, *1 tablespoon*	100
1 cup	1,630
Marmalade, *1 tablespoon*	55
Marshmallows, plain, *1 average*	25
Matzo:	
egg, *1 regular*	135
plain, *1 regular*	120
Meat loaf, *1 serving (1″ slice)*	370
Milk:	
buttermilk, *1 glass (8 oz.)*	90
condensed, sweetened, *½ cup*	490
evaporated, *½ cup, undiluted*	175
half-and-half, *½ cup*	165
liquid, skimmed, *1 glass (8 oz.)*	90
liquid, 98% fat-free, *1 glass (8 oz.)*	145
liquid, whole, *1 glass (8 oz.)*	160
malted, dry powder, *3 tablespoons (1 oz.)*	115
milk shake, *1 glass (8 oz.)*	400
nonfat dry milk, instant, *⅓ cup (dry powder)*	85
yogurt (made with partially skimmed milk):	
plain, *1 cup (8 oz.)*	120 to 150
coffee, vanilla, *1 cup (8 oz.)*	200 to 250
fruit flavored, *1 cup (8 oz.)*	230 to 290
Molasses, light, *1 tablespoon*	50
Muffins:	
blueberry, *1 (2½″ diam.)*	140
bran, *1 (2½″ diam.)*	100
corn, *1 (2⅜″ diam.)*	125
English, *1 (3½″ diam.)*	145
plain, *1 (3″ diam.)*	120
Mushrooms:	
canned, *1 cup*	40
fresh, *1 lb.*	125
fresh, *4 large*	10
Noodles:	
cooked, *½ cup*	100
uncooked, *½ lb.*	880
Oatmeal, cooked, *1 cup*	130
uncooked, *1 cup*	310
Oils:	
corn, cottonseed, olive, peanut, soybean, *1 tablespoon*	125
½ cup	975
Olives, green, pimento-stuffed, *4 medium*	15

FOOD	CAL
Onion, raw, *1 medium*	40
1 lb.	155
Orange, *1 medium (2⅝″ diam.)*	65
Orange juice, fresh, frozen or canned, *½ cup*	55
Orange sections, *½ cup*	45
Oysters, eastern, raw, *6 to 8 medium (4 oz. meat only)*	75
Pancakes, mix, *2 (4″ diam.)*	120
Parsley, *⅓ cup chopped*	5
Parsnips, cooked, *½ cup*	50
Peach nectar, *½ cup*	60
Peaches:	
canned, syrup pack, *½ cup*	100
16 oz. undrained	355
fresh, *1 medium*	35
1 lb.	150
frozen, sweetened, *½ cup*	100
Peanuts, roasted, *8 to 10*	55
½ lb. shelled	1,320
Peanut butter, *1 tablespoon*	95
Pears:	
canned, syrup pack, *½ cup*	100
16 oz. undrained	345
fresh, *1 medium*	100
1 lb.	250
Peas:	
frozen, cooked, *½ cup*	60
fresh, shelled, *1 lb. uncooked*	380
green, canned, *½ cup*	80
16 oz.	300
split, uncooked, *½ cup*	345
Pecans, *9 medium nuts*	70
1 cup, halves	740
Peppers, green, raw, *1 medium*	15
Pickles:	
dill, *1 medium*	10
sour, *1 large*	15
sweet, *1 small*	20
Piecrust:	
double crust, *1 9″ crust*	1,800
single crust, *1 9″ crust*	900
packaged mix, double crust, *1 8″ or 9″ crust*	1,480
Pies:	
apple, double crust, *⅙ of 9″ pie*	405
butterscotch, *⅙ of 9″ pie*	405
cherry, double crust, *⅙ of 9″ pie*	410
custard, *⅙ of 9″ pie*	330
lemon meringue, *⅙ of 9″ pie*	355
mince, *⅙ of 9″ pie*	430
pecan, *⅙ of 9″ pie*	580
pumpkin, *⅙ of 9″ pie*	320
Pineapple:	
crushed, canned, *½ cup*	100
16 oz.	335
juice, *½ cup*	65
sliced, canned, *1 large or 2 small slices*	90
sliced, fresh, *1 cup, chopped*	75
Pizza, cheese, *⅛ of 14″ pie*	185

Calorie guide

FOOD	CAL
Plums:	
canned, syrup pack, ½ cup with syrup	100
16 oz. (undrained)	360
fresh, 1 (2″ diam.)	25
Popcorn, popped, with oil, 1 cup	40
Popover, 1 medium	120
Pork:	
ham, boiled, 1 slice (1 oz.)	70
ham, cured, raw, 3 oz. (lean meat)	140
ham, fresh, raw, 3 oz. (lean meat)	130
loin chop, raw, 4 oz. (lean meat)	210
Potatoes:	
baked or boiled, 1 medium (1 cup, diced)	90
French-fried, 10 pieces (2″ long)	155
mashed, ½ cup, milk and butter added	95
scalloped, ½ cup	120
sweet, baked/boiled, 1 medium (5″ × 2″)	155
sweet, candied, 1 small (3½″ × 2¼″)	295
Potato chips, 10 medium (2″ diam.)	115
Poultry stuffing, 1 cup	195
Pretzels, 5 3⅛″-long sticks	10
Prune juice, canned, ½ cup	100
Pudding:	
chocolate, ½ cup	175
cornstarch, ½ cup	140
vanilla, ½ cup	140
Pumpkin, canned, ½ cup	40
Pumpkin seeds:	
shelled, 1 tablespoon	60
unshelled, ¼ cup	60
Radishes, raw, 4 small	5
Raisins, seedless, ¼ cup	120
Raspberries, ½ cup	35
Rhubarb:	
stewed/sweetened, ½ cup	190
uncooked, 1 lb.	55
Rice:	
brown, uncooked, ½ cup	300
cooked, 1½ cups	300
precooked, 1 cup cooked	180
regular long grain, ½ cup uncooked	325
cooked, ½ cup	90
wild, uncooked, ½ cup	295
Rice pudding, 1 serving (¾ cup)	225
Rolls, plain, 1 small (16 per lb.)	85
1 medium (12 per lb.)	115
1 large (8 per lb.)	175
Rye wafers, 2 wafers	45
Salad dressings:	
blue or Roquefort, 1 tablespoon	75
French, 1 tablespoon	65

FOOD	CAL
Italian, 1 tablespoon	80
mayonnaise, 1 tablespoon	100
Thousand Island, 1 tablespoon	80
Salmon:	
baked, 1 steak (4 oz.)	210
sockeye or red, canned, ½ cup, flaked (3 oz.)	120
Sardines, canned in oil, 4 medium (1½ oz.)	85
Sauces:	
barbecue, ¼ cup	80
chocolate syrup, 2 tablespoons	100
hard, 2 tablespoons	140
hollandaise, 2 tablespoons	175
spaghetti, canned meat sauce, ½ cup	100
tomato puree, ½ cup	45
white, medium, ½ cup	210
Sauerkraut, ½ cup	20
Sausage, cooked, 2 links (16 per lb.)	125
brown-and-serve, 4 oz. uncooked	445
Scallops, raw, 8 medium (4 oz.)	90
Sherbet, ½ cup	130
Shortening, solid, 1 tablespoon	110
1 cup	1,770
Shrimp:	
canned, 3 oz.	100
shelled, raw, 12 to 14 medium (3½ oz.)	90
unshelled, 1 lb.	285
Soups (canned soups are prepared according to label directions):	
beef broth, scant cup	20
beef-noodle, scant cup	60
chicken broth, scant cup	20
chicken, cream of (with milk), scant cup	135
chicken-gumbo, scant cup	50
chicken-noodle, scant cup	55
chicken with rice, scant cup	45
clam chowder: Manhattan, scant cup	65
New England, scant cup	145
consommé, scant cup	30
minestrone, scant cup	85
mushroom, cream of, scant cup	185
onion, scant cup	30
pea, green, scant cup	115
tomato, clear, scant cup	70
cream of, scant cup	140
vegetable, scant cup	60
Spaghetti, cooked, 1 cup	155
Spaghetti sauce:	
canned mushroom, 1 cup	155
canned with cheese, 1 cup	190
Spinach or other greens, cooked, ½ cup	20
Squash:	
soft-skin, cooked, ½ cup	15
hard-shell, cooked, ½ cup	65
Starch, (arrowroot, cornstarch, etc.), 1 tablespoon	30

FOOD	CAL
Strawberries, ½ cup	25
Sugar:	
brown, 1 tablespoon	50
1 cup	820
confectioners', 1 tablespoon	30
1 cup	460
granulated, 1 tablespoon	40
1 cup	770
Sundaes:	
chocolate ice cream with chocolate sauce and chopped pecans, ½ cup ice cream, 2 tablespoons sauce and 2 tablespoons pecans	355 to 405
vanilla ice cream with butterscotch sauce, ½ cup ice cream, 2 tablespoons sauce	250 to 300
Sunflower seeds, shelled, 1 tablespoon	45
Sweetbreads, calves, cooked, ¾ cup (3½ oz.)	170
Syrup:	
corn, 1 tablespoon	60
maple, 1 tablespoon	50
Tapioca, quick-cooking, 4 tablespoons	140
Tea without sugar or cream, 1 cup	0
Tomato juice, ½ cup (4 oz.)	25
Tomatoes:	
canned, ½ cup	25
16 oz.	95
fresh, 1 medium	40
Trout, raw, 4 oz. (fillets)	220
Tuna:	
canned in oil, ⅔ cup, drained	170
7 oz. (undrained)	576
canned, water pack, ⅔ cup (3 oz.)	110
Turkey, roasted (white and dark meat), 3 oz.	160
Veal, cooked:	
cutlet, no bone, 3 oz.	185
roast, no bone, 1 slice (3 oz.)	180
Vegetable juice, canned, ½ cup (4 oz.)	20
Vinegar, 1 cup	30
Waffle, 1 7″ waffle	205
Walnuts, chopped, 1 tablespoon	50
Watercress, 1 bunch 3″ long	20
Watermelon, 1 wedge, 8″ × 4″	115
Wheat germ, 1 tablespoon	15
Whipped toppings:	
aerosol, 1 tablespoon	10
frozen or mix, 1 tablespoon	10 to 25
Yeast:	
dried, 1 package active dry	25
cake, 1 cake, compressed	20
Yogurt, see Milk	
Zwieback, 1 cracker	30

Glossary of food and cooking terms

à la: In the manner of.

à la carte: A meal in which the diner selects individual items, paying for each, rather than taking a table d'hôte (complete) meal at a fixed price.

à la mode: In style. Desserts à la mode are served with ice cream; meats cooked à la mode are braised with vegetables and served with gravy.

Age: 1. To tenderize meat by allowing it to hang for a specified length of time in carefully controlled conditions.
2. To store cheese until it is mature and flavorful.
3. To store wine to improve flavor.

al dente: Italian term used to describe pasta that is cooked until it offers a slight resistance to the bite.

Amandine: Dishes made or garnished with almonds.

Antipasto: Italian term describing an assortment of appetizers.

Aperitif: A drink taken before a meal to stimulate the appetite.

Ascorbic-acid mixture for fruit: A crystalline or powdered mixture used to prevent darkening and loss of flavor of fruits low in ascorbic acid.

Aspic: Jellied meat, fish or poultry stock or vegetable liquid often used for molding meat, fish, poultry or vegetables.

au jus: A French term meaning served with unthickened natural juices that develop during roasting.

au lait: A French term meaning served with milk.

Bake: To cook food uncovered in an oven or oven-type appliance. When applied to meats and poultry, it is called roasting.

Baking powder: A leavening agent which makes foods rise when they are baked. It is a combination of baking soda, a dry acid or acid salt and starch or flour. The acid ingredient reacts with the baking soda to produce gas bubbles in the mixture. Double-acting baking powder (used in the recipes in this book) produces gas bubbles twice: first during mixing and second during baking.

Baking soda: An essential ingredient of baking powder, may be used alone as a leavening agent in mixtures containing an acid ingredient such as buttermilk or in combination with baking powder. Mixtures containing baking soda should be baked as soon as mixed, since the soda starts to react as soon as it comes in contact with the liquid.

Barbecue: To roast or broil food on a rack or spit over coals, or under a heat unit. The food is usually brushed with a highly seasoned sauce during the last of the cooking time.

Baste: To moisten food while it cooks, so that the surface doesn't dry out and flavor is added. Melted fat, drippings, sauce and fruit juice are the liquids generally used.

Basting steak

Batter: A mixture of fairly thin consistency, made of flour, liquid and other ingredients.

Bavarian: A molded cold dessert made with gelatin, eggs, cream and flavorings.

Beat: To make a mixture smooth with rapid, regular motion using a wire whisk, spoon, hand beater or mixer. When using a spoon, the mixture should be lifted up and over with each stroke.

Bisque: A thick, rich cream soup usually made with shellfish or pureed vegetables.

Blanch: To cook a few minutes in boiling water either to help loosen the skin from some foods, or as a step in preparing vegetables for freezing.

Blanquette: A white, creamy stew of veal, chicken or lamb with small onions and mushrooms.

Blend: To mix thoroughly two or more ingredients; or to prepare food in blender until pureed, chopped, etc., as desired.

Blintz: A thin pancake filled and rolled, usually with cottage cheese.

Boil: To cook food over high heat in liquid in which bubbles rise constantly to the surface and break.

Bombe: A dessert of frozen mixtures arranged and frozen in a mold.

Bone: To remove bones from meats, fish or poultry.

Bouillabaisse: A hearty stew made with several kinds of fish and shellfish.

Bouillon: A clear, seasoned broth usually made from beef or chicken; also obtained by dissolving a bouillon cube or envelope in boiling water.

Bouquet garni: A bundle of several herbs, usually including parsley, thyme and bay leaf, tied in cheesecloth. Added to stews, soups and sauces for flavoring, it is easy to remove when desired.

Making a bouquet garni

Braise: To cook food over low heat in a small amount of liquid in a covered pan. (Food may or may not be browned first in a small amount of fat.)

Bread: To coat with bread crumbs, cracker crumbs or cornmeal. Food may first be floured, then dipped in beaten egg or other liquid to help crumbs to adhere.

Breading a fish fillet

Brochette: A skewer. Food cooked "en brochette" is cooked on a skewer.

Broil: To cook food by direct heat on a rack or spit.

Broth: Liquid in which meat, poultry or vegetables have simmered. Same as stock.

Brush with: To use a pastry brush to spread food lightly with liquid such as salad oil, melted fat, milk, heavy cream or beaten egg.

Butter: 1. Made from sweet or sour cream, contains not less than 80 percent milk fat. It is available salted or unsalted.
2. To spread butter, margarine or other fat lightly over a dish or pan to prevent food sticking to it.

Canapé: Plain or toasted bread or crackers topped with a savory mixture, served as an appetizer or with cocktails.

Caramelize: To stir sugar in skillet over low heat until it melts and develops characteristic flavor and golden-brown color.

Carve: To cut meat or poultry in slices or pieces for serving.

Chill: To refrigerate food or let it stand in ice or iced water until cold.

Chocolate: Comes in several forms. Each reacts differently and gives a different flavor in recipes (see also page 363).

Chop: To cut food into small pieces with a knife, blender or food processor.

Chutney: A highly seasoned relish of fruits, herbs and spices.

Coat: To sprinkle food with, or dip it into, flour, sauce, etc., until covered.

Coating the back of a spoon

Glossary of food and cooking terms

Compote: 1. A dessert of fresh or dried fruits cooked in syrup.
2. A deep bowl, often stemmed, from which such desserts and other foods are usually served.

Condiment: 1. Sauces and relishes to add to food at the table, such as catchup or prepared mustard.
2. Seasoning, often pungent, used to bring out the flavor of foods.

Cool: To refrigerate food, or let it stand at room temperature, until no longer warm to the touch.

Corn syrup: Available as light and dark. Both can be used to glaze meats and vegetables and as ingredients in marinades, candies and desserts.

Court bouillon: Seasoned liquid in which fish can be poached (see also page 172).

Cream: 1. The fat portion of milk. Light cream contains at least 18 percent milk fat; light whipping cream, 30 to 36 percent; heavy or whipping cream, at least 36 percent. Half-and-half is a mixture of milk and cream containing not less than 10.5 but less than 18 percent milk fat. Sour cream usually has at least 18 percent and sour half-and-half 10.5 to 18 percent.
2. To cook food in, or serve it with, white or "cream" sauce.
3. To make soft, smooth and creamy by beating with spoon or with mixer (usually applied to blending sugar and a fat).

Crêpe: A thin, delicate pancake.

Croissant: A rich crescent-shaped roll.

Croquette: A mixture of chopped or minced food, usually shaped as a cone or ball, coated with egg and crumbs then deep-fried.

Crouton: A small cube of bread toasted or fried, most often used to garnish soups and salads (see also page 131).

Crustacean: Shellfish such as shrimp, lobster and crab with segmented body covered by crusty outer skeleton.

Cube: 1. To cut food into small cubes (about ½ inch).
2. To cut surface of meat in checkered pattern to increase tenderness by breaking tough meat fibers.

Cubing steak

Cut in: To distribute solid fat in flour or flour mixture by using pastry blender or two knives scissor-fashion until flour-coated fat particles are of desired size.

Deep-fry: To cook food in hot fat deep enough for food to float on it.

Demitasse: A small cup ("half cup") of black coffee, usually served after dinner.

Dice: To cut food into very small pieces (about ¼ inch).

Dijon mustard: A prepared mustard (originally made in Dijon, France) which can be mild or highly seasoned. Our recipes call for highly seasoned Dijon.

Dot: To scatter bits, as of butter or margarine, over surface of food.

**Dotting pastry
with butter**

Draw: To remove entrails from, and clean, poultry or game. Drawn fish are whole fish that have been cleaned (eviscerated) but not boned.

Dredge: To cover or coat food, as with flour, cornmeal, etc.

Dress: To mix salad or other food with dressing or sauce.

Dressed fish: Whole fish with scales and entrails removed. Usually head, tail and fins have also been cut off (see also page 172). Smaller fish are generally called pan-dressed.

Drippings: Fat and juice given off by meat or poultry as it cooks.

Durum: A wheat variety used in making high-quality spaghetti and other pastas.

Enchilada: A tortilla, stuffed, rolled and served with a highly seasoned sauce.

Enriched: Resupplied with vitamins and minerals lost during processing of food.

Entree: The main dish of the meal.

Escargot: An edible snail, usually a land snail imported from France and served in the shell.

Filet (or fillet): A piece of meat, fish or poultry which is boneless or has had all bones removed.

Fines herbes: A mixture of herbs used for seasoning. Traditionally includes parsley, chervil, chives and tarragon, though other herbs may also be used.

Flame: To ignite warmed alcoholic beverage poured over food. Also known as flambé.

Flaming crêpes

Flour: 1. *All-purpose.* Made from a variety of wheats, it produces good results for a wide variety of baked goods (most of our recipes call for it). *Whole-wheat flour* is milled from the entire wheat kernel while *rye flour* is milled from the rye kernel. *Cake flour* is milled especially for cakes and other light baked products. For best results always use the flour called for in the recipe. In recipes calling for all-purpose and whole wheat or rye, a certain proportion of all-purpose to the other flour is needed for best results; so don't substitute flour.
2. To coat lightly with flour.

Flute: To make decorative indentations.

Foie gras: Literally "fat liver", a term usually applied to goose liver.

Fold in: To combine delicate ingredients such as whipped cream or beaten egg whites with other foods by using a gentle, circular motion to cut down into the mixture, slide across the bottom of the bowl to bring some of the mixture up and over the surface (see also page 139).

Fondue: Most often a dish of hot melted cheese and wine, into which bread is dipped and then eaten. For meat fondues, at the table, cubes of meat are dipped in hot fat to cook, then into a choice of sauces. Dessert fondues include chocolate or other sauces for dipping chunks of poundcake or fruit. The term also denotes a baked main dish made with cheese, milk and bread.

Cheese fondue

Fortified: Supplied with more vitamins and minerals than were present in the natural state.

Freeze-dried: Term applied to food that has been dried by rapid freezing, then had most of its water content removed.

Fricassee: A stew made of chicken or veal cut into pieces and cooked in a gravy.

Fritter: A small quantity of a batter mixture, sometimes containing meat, vegetables or fruit, fried in deep fat until crisp.

Fruit pectin: A natural substance found in many fruits; also available in liquid or powdered forms. When pectin is used in the right proportion with sugar and acid liquid, it forms a jelly.

Fry: To cook food over high heat in a small amount of fat. See also Deep-fry, Pan-fry, Sauté.

Garnish: To add a decorative touch to food, as with parsley, croutons or prepared vegetables.

Gazpacho: A cold Spanish soup made with tomatoes and other fresh vegetables.

Gelatin: Available as unflavored and fruit-flavored. They are not interchangeable.

Glacé: 1. Glazed, as with a frosting. 2. Frozen.

Glaze: 1. To coat with a glossy mixture. 2. Concentrated stock used to add flavor.

Grate: To rub food on a grater (or chop in blender or food processor) to produce fine, medium or coarse particles.

Grating carrot

Gratin: A French term defining a brown crust formed by baking or broiling bread crumbs, cheese, butter or a mixture on top of a casserole or other dish.

Grease: To rub surface of dish or pan with fat, to keep food from sticking.

Greasing a cake pan

Grenadine: Pomegranate-flavored syrup used as flavoring and sauce.

Grill: To cook food on a rack by direct heat; also the appliance or utensil used for this type of cooking.

Grind: To reduce to particles in food grinder, blender or food processor.

Gumbo: A thick, Southern-style soup or stew made with meat, poultry, fish, shellfish or vegetables.

Hibachi: Small, portable charcoal grill.

Hoisin sauce: A thick sauce made of soy beans and seasonings used in Chinese cooking.

Homard: French word for lobster.

Homogenized: With fat broken down into such small particles that it stays suspended in liquid, rather than rising to the top.

Honey: Sometimes sold in the comb, but usually as the extracted liquid and in solid and granular forms. Our recipes always use liquid honey.

Hors d'oeuvres: Savory foods used as appetizers.

Jardinière: French term meaning garnished with vegetables.

Kabob: Cubes of meat or poultry and vegetables threaded on a skewer and grilled; also any food that is threaded on a skewer.

Threading meat kabobs

Knead: To work a food mixture (usually dough) with a press-fold motion (see also page 432).

Kosher: Ritually fit for eating in accordance with Jewish law.

Lard: The white fat of pork, rendered and sold in solid form; used in piecrusts, biscuits, other baked foods and for frying.

Liquor: 1. An alcoholic beverage, such as rum or vodka.
2. Liquid surrounding clams, oysters and other mollusks.
3. In recipe directions, sometimes a broth or juice.

Lukewarm: At a temperature of about 95°F. Lukewarm food feels neither warm nor cold when in contact with inside of the wrist.

Maple sugar: Made from the evaporation of maple sap. It is usually pressed into fancy shapes to serve as a confection.

Maple syrup: The pure variety comes from the evaporation of the sap of maple trees. Maple-flavor syrup is made from a blend of refined, corn and maple-sugar syrups.

Marbled: Term used to describe meat with visible fat running through the lean.

Margarine: Comes in several forms. Regular margarine with 80 percent fat is interchangeable with butter in our recipes.

Marinade: A seasoned liquid, in which food is soaked to enhance flavor.

Marinate: To soak in a marinade.

Marron: Chestnut. Marrons glacés are chestnuts preserved in syrup or candied.

Marzipan: Sweetened almond paste made into confections.

Matzo: Thin, unleavened, cracker-like bread made of flour and water.

Meat tenderizer: Papain from natural tenderizers such as papaya is used to soften meat tissue. It is usually sprinkled on the meat before meat is cooked.

Meringue: Mixture of stiffly beaten egg whites and sugar. Also the cooked soft mixture on desserts or the cooked "hard" mixture as a dessert shell.

Meunière: With sauce of butter, lemon juice and parsley.

Milk: Available fresh, canned and dried. Almost all milk and cream is pasteurized.

Mince: To cut into very small pieces, using knife, food grinder or blender, or food processor.

Mocha: Flavoring of coffee.

Mollusk: Shellfish such as clams and oysters, with soft unsegmented bodies protected by a hard shell.

Monosodium glutamate: White, crystalline salt that enhances natural flavor of foods without adding its own.

Mousse: A cold dessert made with whipped cream or beaten egg whites.

Nuts: May be purchased in the shell or shelled with the exception of cashews which are only available shelled. Shelled nuts are available chopped, ground, halved, blanched, slivered, plain, toasted or salted.

Macadamia nuts

Black walnuts

California walnuts

Chestnuts

Brazil nuts

Pecans

Peanuts

Cashews

Almonds

Filberts

Pistachio nuts

Oeuf: French word for egg.

Olives: Both varieties green and ripe (black) are processed to remove their natural bitterness. Green olives are packed in brine and may be unpitted, pitted or pitted and stuffed with pimento, almonds or anchovies, etc. Ripe olives are packed in light brine and may be pitted or unpitted.

Pan: To cook, covered, in very small amount of liquid.

Pan-broil: To cook food, uncovered, over high heat on ungreased or lightly greased hot surface, pouring off accumulating fat.

Pan-fry: To cook food over high heat in a small amount of fat.

Parboil: To boil until partially cooked, usually before completing cooking by another method.

Glossary of food and cooking terms

Parfait: A dessert made of layers of fruit, syrup, ice cream and whipped cream or beaten egg whites.

Pasta: Spaghetti, macaroni and similar products, usually of Italian origin.

Pasteurize: To destroy, by heating, certain undesirable bacteria in juices, dairy foods.

Pastrami: Highly spiced smoked beef, usually prepared from shoulder cuts.

Pâté: Spread or loaf of ground, seasoned meat, poultry or fish or vegetables.

Patty shell: A shell made from puff paste to hold creamed mixtures or fruit.

Filling patty shells

Peel: To remove outer covering of foods by trimming away with knife or vegetable peeler, or by pulling off.

Petit four: Small, decoratively iced cake.

Pilaf: Seasoned rice, often with meat or poultry added.

Pit: To remove seed from whole fruit.

Poach: To cook food over low heat in simmering liquid.

Polenta: A very thick mush usually made from cornmeal or farina, used in main dishes and as accompaniment.

Pot-roast: To cook large pieces of meat or poultry by braising; also certain meat cuts.

Potage: Soup.

Prawn: Term used primarily on the West Coast for larger shrimp.

Preheat: To heat oven to desired temperature before putting food in to bake.

Pressure-cook: To cook in steam under high pressure, using a special saucepan.

Profiterole: Tiny cream puff, filled with sweet or savory mixtures, served as dessert or hors d'oeuvre.

Prosciutto: Italian-style cured and spiced ham, served sliced paper thin.

Punch down: To deflate a risen yeast dough by pushing it down with the fist.

Purée: 1. A thick mixture made from a puréed vegetable base.

2. To press food through a fine sieve or food mill, or to blend in blender or food processor to a smooth, thick mixture.

Food mill

Quiche: Savory one-crust egg-and-cream main dish pie.

Reduce: To reduce volume of liquid by rapid boiling in an uncovered pan.

Roast: To cook meat or poultry uncovered in oven (see Bake).

Roulade: Rolled meat.

Salad oils: Consist of one or a combination of vegetable oils. They are used for salad dressings, in recipes and for cooking. They cannot be substituted for butter or other solid fats in recipes but can be used in place of melted fats in frying.

Scald: To heat liquid just to below the boiling point.

Scallopine: Small, thin pieces of meat.

Scampi: Shrimp or a dish of shrimp in garlic sauce.

Score: 1. To cut shallow slits in surface of food to increase tenderness or to prevent fat covering from curling.

2. To decorate.

Scoring ham

Shortening: Produced from bleached, refined, hydrogenated vegetable oil or animal fat, this solid fat is good for deep-fat- and pan-frying and as an ingredient in pastry. Can refer generally to fats.

Shred: To cut food into slivers or slender pieces, using a knife or shredder.

Shuck: To remove meat of oysters, clams, etc. from their shells (see also page 162).

Silver dragées: Tiny, ball-shaped silver-colored candies.

Simmer: To cook food over low heat in a liquid just below the boiling point in which bubbles form slowly and collapse just below the surface.

Skim: To remove fat or scum from surface of food.

Skimming fat from gravy

Steam: To cook food on a rack or in a colander in a covered pan over steaming hot water.

Stew: To cook food over low heat in a simmering liquid.

Stir-fry: To cook sliced food quickly Chinese-style in a skillet or wok.

Sugar: Available in several forms: Granulated white sugar is the kind used generally in cooking, for the table and in our recipes unless otherwise specified. Confectioners' or powdered sugar, used for frosting, is pulverized granulated sugar; brown sugars contain some molasses.

Table d'hôte: Set-price menu in a restaurant consisting of several courses.

Taco: Fried tortilla with filling rolled or folded inside.

Tamale: Corn mush, spread on corn husk filled with chili-seasoned mixture, rolled, tied and steamed.

Tempura: Japanese dish of batter-dipped, fried seafood or vegetables.

Toast points: Toast slices, cut in half diagonally.

Torte: Cake or meringue-type dessert, usually rich in eggs and nuts.

Tortilla: Very thin, Mexican bread made of cornmeal or flour.

Toss: To mix foods lightly with a lifting motion, using two forks or spoons.

Tostada: Tortilla fried until crisp, served flat topped with refried beans, other savory toppings.

Tournedos: Filet of beef steak.

Truffle: 1. Species of fungus that grows below the ground; used as garnish.

2. A very rich chocolate candy.

Truss: To secure poultry with string or skewers, to hold its shape while cooking (see also page 248).

Vinegar: An acid liquid used for flavoring and preserving. Among the types: Cider vinegar, made from apple juice, has a mellow fruit flavor; distilled white vinegar, usually made from grain alcohol; herb vinegars flavored with herbs; and red or white wine vinegars which also may be flavored with garlic.

Whip: To beat rapidly with mixer, wire whisk or hand beater, to incorporate air and increase volume.

Wok: Chinese cooking utensil with rounded bottom used as a skillet.

Wok and utensils

Yeast: Micro-organisms that produce carbon dioxide and alcohol from carbohydrates to cause baked goods to rise, fruits to ferment, etc. Our recipes call for active dry yeast.

Zabaglione: Delicate dessert made of beaten eggs and wine.

INDEX

Italic numbers indicate recipes with step-by-step illustrations